D1568344

Handbook of Military Institutions

SAGE SERIES ON ARMED FORCES AND SOCIETY

HANDBOOK OF

MILITARY

INSTITUTIONS

PREPARED BY INTER-UNIVERSITY SEMINAR ON ARMED FORCES AND SOCIETY

Roger W. Little, *Editor*

 SAGE PUBLICATIONS, Beverly Hills, California

For information address:
SAGE PUBLICATIONS, INC.
275 South Beverly Drive
Beverly Hills, California 90212

Printed in the United States of America

International Standard Book Number 0-8039-0078-3
Library of Congress Catalog Card No. 78-127989

First Printing

PREFACE

The *Handbook of Military Institutions* is a contribution to the ongoing research and publication program of the Inter-University Seminar on Armed Forces and Society. Since its inception in 1961, with the assistance of the Russell Sage Foundation, the Inter-University Seminar has sought to serve as a focal point for a group of thirty to forty university based social scientists concerned with research on the armed forces, peace keeping, and arms control.

A bibliography of the publications of the Inter-University Seminar is included at the end of this volume. We are pleased to add this latest effort which was undertaken in order to synthesize a wide range of scattered literature. Roger Little, who served as editor of this effort, encouraged the contributors to organize their findings in the format of a propositional inventory and to evaluate the adequacy of the available research and documentation.

The fifteen authors provide representation from the disciplines of political science, sociology, economics, social psychology, history, and social work. Whether they are members of a university faculty or a public agency, their views are necessarily their own and not those of the institution with which they are affiliated. The members of the Inter-University Seminar wish to express their thanks to Roger Little. The Seminar invites communications and contributions from scholars concerned with these and related research topics since we are obviously dealing with an area in which theory has outrun empirical research.

Morris Janowitz
Charles Moskos
Sam Sarkesian

CONTENTS

Contents

Part One

ORGANIZATIONAL STRUCTURE

Chapter 1

MILITARY ORGANIZATION

MORRIS JANOWITZ

Military organization is a reflection of the technology of war. Therefore, the history of military organization and the military professional is generally written from the point of view of changes in weapons systems. But from the perspective of the social scientist, and especially the sociologist, military organization is thought of in different terms and at a different level of abstraction. Although social scientists make similar assumptions about the central significance of technology and technological change, military organization is defined as a comprehensive social system and is analyzed by means of institutional and social-psychological categories.

*TECHNOLOGY AND
MILITARY ORGANIZATION*

In light of the overriding reality that military formations are organized on a national basis, social research into the military is faced with two sets of problems. First is the effort to highlight common patterns and uniformities in military institutions regardless of national or cultural settings. In this regard, the concept "organizational analysis" or "organization behavior" has gained widespread currency. Second, social scientists are aware that military organization reflects the social structure and political and cultural values of each particular environment. Because military formations are organized as national units, they reveal the consequences of historical and traditional values. These national differences influence not only organizational effectiveness, but also are basic elements in accounting for various patterns of civil-military relations. The notion of "armed forces and society" is an approach which focuses on this set of issues.

The purpose of this essay is to review some of the central concepts and available hypotheses about contemporary military institutions from the sociological perspectives both of organizational analysis and armed forces and society. This task also requires the additional perspective of the analysis of a profession. The essential elements of a professional group are (a) a system of training, (b) a body of expert knowledge and skill practices, (c) group cohesion and solidarity, (d) a body of ethics and a sense of responsibility, and (e) mechanisms of self-regulation. It is essential to apply the idea of responsibility to the military profession although it is a complex task. In fact, the military is a highly specialized profession because it is a profession that can only be practiced in modern times in governmental employment. Therefore, the notion of responsibility must always be evaluated in collective terms as well as individual terms.

In the contemporary period of rapid social and political change, that is, since the end of World War II, two basic assumptions about the nature of warfare seem essential.

First, the impact of technology and new mass destructive weapons has changed the pattern of international relations and altered the threat of general war. The major nuclear powers, while pursuing a policy of mutual deterrence, have had to face the severe limitation which mass destruction instruments place on the conduct of traditional diplomacy and international relations. For the military profession, the implication has been not merely that new weapons have had to be incorporated but that there has been a fundamental crisis in the profession itself. The military profession as it emerged in the nineteenth century had the overriding orientation that the outbreak of general war was inevitable. This inevitability, the profession assumed, was rooted in the nature of man, in the conduct of international relations, and in the consequences of each new arms race.

In the contemporary scene, the military profession must face the political imperative that the outbreak of general war is no longer defined as inevitable or in the national interest. General war continues to be a contingency and an undesirable one at that, and it is recognized as such by a significant proportion of the military profession. Therefore, the study of the military profession involves its reaction to the actual and proposed international schemes of arms control and disarmament. The sociology of the military must also encompass the consequences of multilateral arrangements and United

Nations peace-keeping activities which are designed to contain or reduce limited wars, especially those limited wars which might increase the possibility of general war.

Second, limited war is no longer "traditional." Since 1945, limited war has less often been a struggle between two legitimate governments, and more often a violent contest within a nation by some group against the existing regime. These wars are conflicts into which external national powers are drawn. These struggles involve use of nonprofessional forces and, therefore, the study of military organization shades off into the analysis of various forms of armed revolts, police systems, paramilitary formations, and other agencies of internal warfare.

"MORALE" VERSUS ORGANIZATION

During World War I, empirical research on American military institutions was first launched from a concern with the characteristics and motivations of recruits. A good deal of effort has been expended by social psychologists on this selected and specific aspect of military life. During World War I, a new approach to the use of military personnel was stimulated by social research, namely, the importance of considering a person's intelligence, skills, and aptitudes in assigning him to a military occupation. The experiences of military psychologists of this period provided a basis for the subsequent rapid development of personnel selection in civilian industry and business.

During World War II, an elaborate machinery was erected for matching men's skills to the jobs required. No large-scale organization as vast as the military establishment can operate without a standardized personnel selection system. But any personnel testing procedure runs the risk of developing overspecialization in both training procedures and personnel. It has even been argued that military personnel selection as administered during World War II resulted in draining off superior talent from essential but "unglamorous" assignments, such as the infantry. Moreover, no responsible personnel selector will claim that the dimensions of aggressive leadership in combat or strategic command have been satisfactorily conceptualized to the point where reliable personnel testing is possible.

Thus it was understandable that during World War II, social scientists broadened their interests beyond personnel selection and stressed the importance of research into motives and attitudes in military units. Research on "morale" was by no means a new approach to the analysis of complex and large-scale organizations. But the armed forces, that is, the ground and air forces, undertook morale studies on a most extensive scale. In the summary study of these efforts, *The American Soldier,* prepared under the guidance of Samuel A. Stouffer, et al. (1949), the potentialities and limitations of attitude and morale research were assessed. And again, as with the development of personnel selection during World War I, industry and business have continued morale and attitude studies which have been extended to a wide variety of civilian agencies and organizations, including welfare and educational settings.

Social research on attitudes and morale in the armed forces provides useful information for specific problems where it is assumed that the executive of a policy requires cooperation. The limitation of attitude research is not that the strategy and tactics of war cannot be based on the preferences of soldiers. This is obvious to all, including the social scientist. But, in fact, attitude research fails to describe the underlying social system—the realities of bureaucratic organization— of the armed forces. "Morale" is much too limited a concept to understand the coercive force of bureaucratic organization, especially of military formations as they operate in combat. The findings of *The American Soldier* studies serve to underline and reaffirm this sociological observation:

> Thus we are forced to the conclusion that personal motives and relationships are not uniquely determinate for organization in combat . . . officers and men must be motivated to make the organization work, but not *all* of them have to be so motivated, nor must they all agree on details of social philosophy or be bound by ties of personal friendship in order for a functioning organization to exist. To put it another way, the best single predictor of combat behavior is the simple fact of institutionalized role; knowing that a man is a soldier rather than a civilian. The soldier role is a vehicle for getting a man into the position in which he has to fight or take the institutionally sanctioned consequences [Stouffer, 1949: 101, vol. 2].

Therefore, in turn, the single concept of morale has been displaced by a theory of organizational and professional behavior in which an array of concepts are integrated: authority, communications, hierarchy, sanction, status, social role, and socialization (for early efforts, see Andreski, 1954; Williams, 1954; Office of the Secretary of Defense, 1951; van Doorn, 1956). Intellectual influences from historical writings, economic analysis, and social anthropology and sociological theory have emphasized the need for a comprehensive focus on the totality of the military, not merely on part of it. The line of analysis that has been developed has paralleled the institutional and organizational study of the factory, the mental hospital, the prison, and the school as a social system (March, 1965).

An additional intellectual element in the study of military institutions has derived from the early writings of such leading political scientists and political sociologists as Harold D. Lasswell (1951) and Hans Speier (1952) who have manifested a systematic concern with the implications of military organizations for social and political change.

Interestingly, the operational requirements of political warfare against the German and Japanese armed forces led to research efforts in which these forces were regarded as total social systems. During World War II, two social science units working independently recast operational and strategic intelligence into sociological models for explaining the strength and vulnerability of the Axis armed forces as they came under allied attack. One group, the Foreign Morale Analysis Division, Military Intelligence Service, was concerned with Japan, while the other worked on Germany and, in particular, on the Wehrmacht. This latter group, Intelligence Branch, Psychological Warfare Division, SHAEF, produced the research data on which the analysis by Edward A. Shils and Morris Janowitz (1948), "Cohesion and Disintegration in the Wehrmacht in World War II," was based (also see Leighton, 1949).

Their findings, as well as those reported in *The American Soldier*, showed high convergence in underscoring the central importance of primary group solidarity, een in totalitarian armies, as a crucial source of military effectiveness. Specifically, a social system perspective helped to focus attention on the important conclusion that it was not Nazi ideology which was at the root of German fanatical resistance, but rather the military and organizational practices which the Nazis permitted, encouraged, and required (for example, see Marshall, 1947).

Since the end of World War II, the United States military establishment has conducted a series of ongoing periodic attitude studies for administrative purposes. In particular, to the outside observer, it would appear that the effort of military agencies has been at times sporadic and without effective forethought. To be sure, the growth of social science in the military has been beset by organizational rivalries and difficulties. Such research has had to confront shortages of trained and committed personnel. At times, military agencies have undertaken projects in competition with civilian agencies so that important military topics were neglected.

But these efforts have produced a body of data relevant to the work of university-based specialists who are responsible for the major thrust.

The development of sociological research in the military is described by Raymond V. Bowers (1967) in the volume entitled *The Uses of Sociology* (see also Croker, 1969). The diffuse structure which has emerged for social science and sociological research in the armed forces articulates with the structure of the military establishment. At the level of the Department of Defense, there has been since 1947 a series of civilian-dominated groups charged with planning and coordinating social science research. The impact of these groups has been limited to fostering support for increased funds and identifying priority objectives. In each of the three major services, there is a centralized research office which grants funds, including funds for social science research, to civilian groups. In order to establish their position among civilian scientists, these agencies have strived to operate as general research-granting agencies and much of their work in the past has complemented civilian agencies of the government and even private foundation grants. These agencies have also operated to support strategic studies for which the Department of State could not mobilize funds. Military-sponsored research on social science aspects of military organization is undertaken to the extent that it is done by "in-house" agencies and laboratories and such efforts are stronger in data collection than in analysis.

Outside of the military establishment, work proceeds mainly by individuals. One of the major contributions to the analysis of military organization by an individual scholar since the end of World War II has been the volume by Samuel Huntington, *The Soldier and the State* (1957). Huntington is a political scientist who has sought to bridge political and organizational analysis. While his work has been subject to a variety of criticisms because of its implicit ideological overtones, his analysis highlights the effects of the political process on the historical development of American political institutions. A focal point for the work of university-based social scientists has been the efforts of the Inter-University Seminar on Armed Forces and Society. No single university has emerged as a center for research in this area, but through the efforts of this group independent research specialists are in communication. Through their efforts, including assembling existing sources of data, a limited body of research findings have developed. In *Sociology and the Military Establishment* by Morris Janowitz and Roger Little (1965; also see Lang, 1969), an overview of some of the essential materials are presented. The work of the Inter-University Seminar encompasses not only the internal organization of the American military, but is concerned both with comparative and cross-national analysis of armed forces and society.

ORGANIZATION: CIVILIAN VERSUS MILITARY

If an organizational perspective is applied to the armed forces, it then becomes necessary to contrast civilian and military organizations. Many features and characteristics of military organization, such as authoritarian and stratified hierarchical structures, are, in fact, to be found in varying degrees in civilian organizations. Moreover, transformations in technology and in military operations have brought about marked changes in the inner format of the military establishment. Speier (1952) points out that civilian social scientists tend to exaggerate and distort the differences between military and civilian organization and overlook what is common to large-scale organization in general.

The special characteristics of military organization derive from its goals, namely, the management of instruments of violence. However, the content of military goals has undergone tremendous changes under the impact of new technology and as the range of political considerations which impinge on military operations is altered. In general, the trend has been toward narrowing the differences between military organization and civilian organizations.

To analyze the contemporary military establishment in the United States as a social system, it is therefore necessary to assume that it has tended to display more and more of the characteristics typical of any large-scale, nonmilitary bureaucracy. The decreasing difference is a result of continuous technological change which vastly expands the size of the military establishment, increases its interdependence with civilian society, and alters its internal social structure. These technological developments in war-making require more and more professionalization of military personnel. At the same time, thy impact of military technology during the past half-century can be described in a series of propositions about social change. Each of the conditions symbolized by these propositions has had the effect of "civilianizing" military institutions and of blurring the distinction between the civilian and the military. Each of these trends has, of course, actual and potential built-in limitations:

(1) A larger percentage of the national income of a modern nation is spent for the preparation, execution, and repair of the

consequences of war. Thus there is a secular trend toward total popular involvement in the consequences of war and war policy, since the military establishment is responsible for the distribution of a progressively large share of available economic resources.

(2) Military technology both vastly increases the destructiveness of warfare and widens the scope of automation in new weapons. It is commonplace that both of these trends tend to weaken the distinction between military roles and civilian roles as the destructiveness of war has increased. Weapons of mass destruction socialize danger to the point of equalizing the risks of warfare for both soldier and civilian.

(3) The revolution in military technology means that the military mission of deterring violence becomes more and more central as compared with preparing to apply violence. This shift in mission tends to civilianize military thought and organization as military leaders concern themselves with broad ranges of political, social, and economic policies.

(4) The complexity of the machinery of warfare and the requirements for research, development, and technical maintenance tend to weaken the organizational boundary between the military and the nonmilitary, since the maintenance and manning of new weapons require a greater reliance on civilian-oriented technicians. The countertrend, or at least limitation, is the greater effort by the military establishment to develop and train military officers with scientific and engineering backgrounds.

(5) Given the "permanent" threat of war, it is well recognized that the tasks which military leaders perform tend to widen. Their technological knowledge, their direct and indirect power, andtheir heightened prestige result in their entrance, of necessity, into arenas that in the recent past have been reserved for civilians and professional politicians. The need that political and civilian leaders have for expert advice from professional soldiers about the strategic implications of technological change serves to mix the roles of the military and the civilian.

These propositions do not deny the crucial differences that persist between military and nonmilitary bureaucracies. The goals of an organization supply a meaningful basis for understanding differences in organizational behavior. The military establishment as a social system has unique characteristics because the possibility of hostilities is a permanent reality to its leadership. The fact that thermonuclear weapons alter the role of force in international relations does not deny this proposition. The consequences of preparation for future combat and the results of previous combat pervade the entire organization. The unique character of the military establishment derives from the requirement that its members are specialists in making use of violence and mass destruction.

Thus, the narrowing distinction between military and non-military bureaucracies can never result in the elimination of fundamental organizational differences. Two pervasive requirements for combat set limits to these civilizing tendencies.

First, while it is true that modern warfare exposes the civilian and the soldier to more equal risks, the distinction between military roles and civilian roles has not been eliminated. Traditional combat-ready military formations are maintained for limited warfare. The necessity for naval and air units to carry on the hazardous tasks of continuous and long-range reconnaissance and detection demand organizational forms that will bear the stamp of conventional formations. In the future, even with fully automated missile systems, conventional units must be maintained as auxiliary forces for the delivery of new types of weapons.

More important, no military system can rely on expectation of victory based on the initial exchange of firepower, whatever the form of the initial exchange may be. Subsequent exchanges will involve military personnel—again regardless of their armament—who are prepared to carry on the struggle as soldiers, that is, subject themselves to military authority and to continue to fight. The automation of war civilized wide sectors of the military establishment; yet the need to maintain combat readiness and to develop centers of resistance after initial hostilities ensures the continued importance of military organization and authority.

Second, what about the consequences of the increased importance of deterrence as a military mission? Should one not expect that such a shift would also result in civilizing the military establishment? If the military is forced to think about deterring wars rather than fighting them, the traditions of the "military mind" based on the inevitability of hostilities must change, and military authority must undergo transformation as well. There can be no doubt that this shift in mission is having important effects on military thought and organization. In fact, military pragmatism which questions the inevitability of total war is an important trend in modern society as the destructiveness of war forces military leaders to concern themselves with the political consequences of violence.

Again, there are limits to the consequences of this civilizing trend. The role of deterrence is not a uniquely new mission for the military establishment. Historically, the contribution of the military to the balance of power has not been made because of the civilian character of the military establishment. On the contrary, the balance of power formula operates, when it does, because the military establishment is prepared to fight.

With the increase in the importance of deterrence, military elites become more and more involved in diplomatic and political warfare, regardless of their preparation for such tasks. Yet the specific and unique contribution of the military to deterrence is the threat of violence which has currency, that is, it can be taken seriously because of the real possibility of violence. Old or new types of weapons do not alter this basic formula. In short, deterrence still requires organization prepared for combat. Moreover, the actuality and possibility of limited war permits the military to persist in maintaining conceptions of combat. These conceptions come to include a wide variety of functions with civilian and political components, but which are defined at least in part as military: guerrilla and counterguerrilla warfare, psychological warfare, military assistance and training, or even "nation-building."

These trends in self-concepts and roles are described and analyzed in *The Professional Soldier: A Social and Political Portrait* (Janowitz, 1960) as they have affected the officer corps during the past half-century in the United States. The military profession which has centered on the self-conception of the warrior types or the "heroic leader" requires the incorporation of new roles, namely, the "military manager" and the "military technologist." For the military establishment to accomplish its multiple goals, it must develop and maintain a balance between these different military types.

These basic changes in the military over the past fifty years can be summarized by a series of basic propositions (Janowitz, 1960: 7-16, 21-36) on the transformation of military organization in response both to the changing technology of war and to the transformation of the societal context in which the armed forces operate:

Changing organizational authority. There has been a change in the basis of authority and discipline in the military establishment, a shift from authoritarian domination to greater reliance on manipulation, persuasion, and group consensus. The organizational revolution which pervades contemporary society, and which implies management by means of persuasion, explanation, and expertise, is also to be found in the military.

Narrowing skill differential between military and civilian elites. The new tasks of the military require that the professional officer develop more and more skills and orientations common to civilian administrators and civilian leaders. The narrowing difference in skill between military and civilian society is an outgrowth of the increasing concentration of technical specialists in the military.

Shift in officer recruitment. The military elite has been undergoing a basic social transformation since the turn of the century. These elites have been shifting their recruitment from a narrow, relatively high social status base, to a broader base more representative of the population as a whole.

Significance of career patterns. Prescribed careers performed with high competence lead to entrance into the professional elite, the highest point in the military hierarchy at which technical and routinized functions are performed. By contrast, entrance into the smaller group, the elite nucleus—where innovative perspectives, discretionary responsibility, and political skills are required—is assigned to persons with unconventional and adaptive careers.

Trends in political indoctrination. The growth of the military establishment into a vast managerial enterprise with increased political responsibilities has produced a strain on traditional military self-images and concepts of honor. The officer is less and less prepared to think of himself as merely a military technician. As a result, the profession, especially within its strategic leadership, has developed a more explicit political ethos.

Thus, in partial summary, since the turn of the century, the military establishment has been fusing with civilian enterprise. There has been a weakening of organizational boundaries. This organizational trend has been encountered in many other sectors of modern society, for example, the increased fusion of industrial and governmental agencies or of higher educational and business organizations. But this process of fusion of the military and civilian sectors had reached its systemic limits by the early 1960s.

This is not to postulate that there is a trend toward a return to a distinct, separate, and isolated military establishment. The fusion of military and political goals alone makes this impossible. However, there is a trend in the military which seeks to strengthen its distinctive boundaries, jurisdictions, and competence while at the same time the military is deeply intertwined with the larger society. The increased political necessity for the military to act without unduly dislocating the civilian sector serves to make this a greater reality. Therefore, the notion of a completely voluntary military establishment becomes more and more a subject of popular discussion.

COMPARATIVE ANALYSIS:
HISTORICAL

Analysis of contemporary American military institutions can be clarified both by comparison with previous historical periods and by cross-national contrasts with existing institutions. One such approach is to reexamine the models of ideal types of the past, present, or the hypothetical future which have been presented by historians and social scientists. In order to highlight the linkage of military organization to social structure in Western industrialized societies, it is relevant to speak of the development of the aristocratic-feudal model into either the democratic or totalitarian, and the contingency model of the garrison state.

Aristocratic-Feudal Model

The aristocratic-feudal model is a relevant base only if seen as describing the conditions of Western Europe, and not fully applicable to the historical emergence of the military in other parts of the world. The aristocratic-feudal model is a composite estimate of the armed forces among Western European powers before industrialism had its full impact. Under the aristocratic-feudal model, civilian and military elites were socially and functionally integrated. A narrow base of recruitment for both elites and a relatively monolithic power structure provided the civilian elite with a comprehensive basis for political control of the military. There was a rigid hierarchy in the aristocratic model which delineated both the source of authority and the prestige of any member of the military elite. The low specialization of the military profession made it possible for the political elite to supply the bulk of necessary leadership for the armed forces. Birth, family connections, and common values insured that the military embodied the ideology of dominant groups in society. Political control was civilian control because there was a unity of interest between aristocratic and military groups. The system was rooted in concepts of authority and land tenure which produced a relatively stable ruling stratum. The military is responsible because it is part of the government. The officer fights because he feels that he is issuing orders.

Democratic Model

In contrast to the aristocratic-feudal model stands the democratic one. The democratic model is both a historical reality and an objective of political policy. Under the democratic model, the civilian and military elites are sharply differentiated. The civilian political elites exercise control over the military through a formal set of rules. These specify the functions of the military and the conditions under which the military may exercise its power. The military is professionals in the employment of the state. They are a small group and their careers are distinct from civilian careers. In fact, being a professional soldier is incompatible with any other significant social or political role. The military leaders obey the government because they believe it is their duty and their profession to fight. Professional ethics as well as democratic parliamentary institutions guarantee civilian political supremacy. The officer fights because of his career commitment.

Elements of the democratic model have been achieved only in certain Western industrialized countries, since it requires extremely viable parliamentary institutions and broad social consensus about the ends of government. The democratic model assumes that military leaders can be effectively motivated by professional codes of conduct and group loyalty. Paradoxically, certain types of officers with aristocratic backgrounds have made important contributions to the development of the democratic model.

Totalitarian Model

In the absence of a historical development toward the democratic model, the totalitarian model emerges in industrial societies as a replacement for the aristocratic-feudal one. The totalitarian model appearing in Germany and in Russia and, to a lesser degree, in Italy, did not arise from any natural or social unity of the existing political and military elites. On the contrary, a revolutionary political elite status, or a relatively low (middle-class) status based on a mass authoritarian political party, fashions a new type of control of the military elite. It may be forced into temporary alliance with the traditional military profession, but the revolutionary elites, bedecked with paramilitary symbols, are dedicated to reconstituting the military elites. Political control of the totalitarian variety is enforced by the secret police, by infiltrating party members into the military hierarchy, and by controlling the system of officer selection. Most important, the party develops and arms its own military units. Under party control of the totalitarian variety, the independence of the professional military is destroyed. The officer fights because he has no alternative.

Garrison State Model

The garrison state model, as offered by Harold D. Lasswell (1941), results from the weakening of civil supremacy which can arise even in societies which have had an effective democratic political structure (also see Mills, 1956, for an alternative formulation). While the end result of the garrison state produces some patterns similar to the totalitarian model, the garrison state has a different natural history. It Is, however, not the direct domination of politics by the military. Since modern industrial nations cannot be ruled merely by the political domination of a single small leadership bloc, the garrison state is not a throwback to a military dictatorship. It is the end result of the ascent to power of the military elite under conditions of prolonged international tensions. Internal freedom is hampered and the preparation for war becomes overriding. The garrison state is a new pattern of coalition in which military groups directly and indirectly wield unprecedented amounts of political and administrative power. The military retains its organizational independence, provided that it makes appropriate alliances with civil political factions. The officer fights for national survival and for glory.

The Military as a Modern Institution

In actual fact, and in a world perspective, the origins of the military in Western Europe and the United States derivatively represent one particular pattern of emergence and historical continuity. It was a pattern which generally linked the military to feudal institutions and to conservative traditions. The military emerged as a modern institution, in fact, as one of the first modern institutions in Western Europe, but it was a modern institution in a Western context.

From a historical point of view, the emergence of modern military institutions in Western Europe required that feudal military patterns be transformed, either by reformers from within or by the incorporation of new middle-class elements, so that complex technology could be made part of the apparatus of war-making. In Western Europe the concept of armed forces and society began to have fuller meaning as the military developed a separate bureaucratic organization. In this long-term development, which became intensified in the first half of the nineteenth century, a relatively common form of military profession and military organization was produced.

Because of the experiences of Western Europe, when scholars analyze the development of modern military institutions, it has been conventional to focus on the social origins of the officer corps. The historical emergence of the military establishment in Western Europe has been carefully documented by a decline in the concentration of officers from aristocratic and landed gentry background and growth in the infusion of middle-class patterns of recruitment (Demeter, 1965). The patterns and rates of change have varied from nation to nation, but there has been an overall uniformity in the long-term direction. But for Western Europe and for the United States, patterns of social recruitment are at best a partial indicator of patterns of civil-military relations. Even during the period of aristocratic dominance in the early nineteenth century the military profession was compatible with parliamentary institutions in Great Britain and with a nationalistic oligarchy in Prussia.

Middle-class elements entered a Prussian military which was predominantly recruited from landed higher and lower aristocratic groups, while the elite elements of the British armed forces were only slightly more distinct from their aristocratic counterparts. By contrast, the German system of education for its officer recruits served to differentiate them more from civilian institutions than did military education in Great Britain. What was important was that a political system emerged under the Prussian system in which the civilian political elites did not exercise control over the military through a set of formal rules. Instead, the policy was controlled by an oligarchy in which the military was an active and key element.

In the contemporary period, social recruitment supplies an even more partial index to patterns of armed forces and society in industrialized societies. Thus, for a variety of nations in Western Europe for which data are available—Great Britain, Germany, France, Norway, Sweden, and the Netherlands—the officer corps, and its elite members as well, continue to shift their recruitment from a narrow, relatively high social status to a broader base more representative of the population as a whole.

But this is not to say that the broadening of the base has taken place at a uniform rate in the countries under investigation. Nor is it to imply that the consequences of this transformation have been similar in all of these countries. Thus, for example, there is reason to believe that the long-term shift toward a "middle-class" profession has taken place at a slower rate in England than in other countries. The top elite in the military has a greater concentration of upper-middle-class sons than in some other industrialized nations, as a result of the system of education and formal requirements for entrance. But this pattern of recruitment has not weakened civilian parliamentary controls.

In the current period, one sociological issue in Western Europe is the extent to which the military profession, that is, the officer class, is accessible to the sons of the working class. In England and in the Netherlands, the amount of such mobility from the lower classes into the officer corps is negligible, while in France it is more pronounced. In Norway, the figure reached 18.7% of the cadets for the period 1950-1960, while for the United States in 1960 the percentage was over 30. The opening of the military to the working class represents general patterns of "democratization" and reflects the low prestige of the profession in industrial society. But the national differences derive in part from specific variations. In France this is the result of self-recruitment, especially recruitment of the sons of enlisted personnel into the officer ranks, and expresses a self-segregation trend in the military. To the contrary, in Norway it represents the desire for social mobility among working-class sons who are unable to enter a university career, and thereby serves to integrate the military with the civilian population.

Military Versus Civilian Control

In Western Europe or elsewhere, there is, of course, no guarantee that democratization of social origins (the broadening of the bases of recruitment) produces democratization of professional attitudes and a strengthening of the willingness to submit to civilian controls. In fact, there are clear-cut cases where the reverse may occur. Of significance are the process and content of professional socialization and the nature of the sociopolitical institutions for administering and controlling the military establishment and the organizational tasks of the military. In Western industrialized societies, as the military has become a bureaucratized and professionalized institution, the significance of social origins in fashioning military orientation declines.

In the evolution of professional military forms throughout the world, Western concepts and practices had a profound effect. But because of different historical settings and because often the military experienced sharp discontinuities, the pattern of development was one that produced a more independent type of establishment with fewer and weaker linkages to the landed interest groups. Elements of European feudalism were developed in South America so that the linkages between landed interests and the military emerge. But even in Latin America, the military rapidly developed a more independent political base. Under the Ottoman Empire, the practices of recruitment and administration pushed early to a "separate" establishment and place it under centralized control. In this case also, the land tenure system did serve to strengthen relations between the military and traditional landed groups.

In parts of Asia and Africa, the military evolved as one governmental bureaucratic service, among others, but a most crucial one. This was in part the result of the colonial practices of the European powers, which destroyed traditional military forces linked to feudal-type ruling groups and which in turn created civil-service-type establishments under their control. As a result, in the new nations of Africa and Asia the military establishment is recruited from the middle and lower-middle classes, drawn mainly from rural areas of hinterlands. In comparison with Western European professional armies, there is a marked absence of a history of feudal domination. As a result, the military profession does not have strong allegiance to an integrated upper class which it accepts as its political leader, nor does it have a pervasive conservative outlook.

Militarism in the new nations of Africa and Asia is often reactive or unanticipated because of the weakness of civilian institutions and the breakdown of parliamentary forms of government. Military officers in these countries develop a sense of public service and national guardianship as a result of their military training and experience. Their politics are "supra-political" because they are suspicious of professional politicians and the bargaining process. A range of typologies of civil-military relations which help explain the process of social change and political development has been offered (Janowitz, 1964). These typologies are designed to clarify the conditions under which militarism is restrained or developed in developing countries.

The power of the military in domestic politics and, derivatively, in international relations can be limited by an authoritarian regime based on personal and traditional power or it may be based on a newly developed personal autocracy. This is the (1) *authoritarian-personal* system of civil-military control and it is likely to be found in nations just beginning the process of modernization. The military can be excluded from domestic political influence by the power of a civilian single mass political party. When political power is lodged in a one-party state, under strong personal leadership without parliamentary institutions, it is possible to reduce old-fashioned militarism. This form of civil-military relations can be labeled (2) *a civilian mass party* system. In these states, both the civilian police and paramilitary institutions under the control of the mass party operate as counterweights to the military.

Militarism can be contained on the basis of (3) *a democratic competitive* system or a *semidemocratic* system. Competitive democratic systems have emerged mainly in industrialized societies where political power is exercised through a multiple-party and election system. Civilian political elites exclude the military from involvement in domestic partisan politics. Semicompetitive democratic patterns can be found in a few of the new nations because of powerful personal leadership of the chief executive and in part because colonial traditions have implanted a strong sense of self-restraint on the military. In these countries, there are competing civilian institutions and power groups, as well as a mass political party which dominates politics but permits a measure of political competition.

When the military expands its political activity and becomes a political bloc, the civilian leadership remains in power only because of the military passive assent or active assistance. The extent of political competition decreases, and it is appropriate to describe such a system as a (4) *civil military* coalition, because of the crucial role of the armed forces. Here the military serves as an active political bloc in its support of civilian parties and other bureaucratic power groups. The civilian group is in power because of the assistance of the military. The military may act as an informal, or even an explicit umpire between competing political parties and political groups. The military may, at this level, be forced to establish a caretaker government with a view to returning power to civilian political groups. Such alliances and caretaker governments can be unstable; they frequently lead to a wider level of involvement where the military sets itself up as the political ruling group. The result is a (5) *military oligarchy,* because, for a limited time at least, the political initiative passes to the military. When an actual takeover occurs and the military becomes the ruling group, civilian political activity is transformed, constricted, and repressed.

At each level of political intervention, and especially in the takeover of political power, the military operates as an incomplete agent of political change. In the new nations of Africa and Asia, military elites—because they are not linked to landed interest—are committed to an ideology of modernization. Lack of skills, both in economic management and in the arena of political negotiation, emerge as powerful barriers. In anticipating future developments, a variety of outcomes can be postulated in addition to the withdrawal of the military from the political arena under pressure because of administrative failure. One outcome is that the military seeks to transform itself into a quasi-political party undertaking for itself political functions or political activities. Another results when the military assumes leadership in the establishment of a political party in which its former personnel play a central role. A third development is the emergence of the army as an arbitrator between competing political groups. But the weight of evidence seems to indicate that the military per se is unable to supply essential political leadership, and effectiveness as a transitional government depends on its sensitivity and capacity to disengage itself or at least limit its involvement.

These forms of militarism must be distinguished from the intervention by the military in many South American countries where, in the past, it was much more designed and premeditated. Often coups represented power struggles between limited elite groups, and, in general, the military was not concerned with social and political change but rather with the maintenance of existing sociopolitical arrangements. More recently, military intervention in Latin American nations has been developing a posture of concern with social and political change, in the face of popular demands for such change.

COMPARATIVE ANALYSIS: STATISTICAL

The comparative study of military institutions also requires data and statistics on the form, size, and structure of military establishments throughout the world. The problems of assembling such information are immense because of the unreliability of the sources and problems of access to information, as well as difficulties of standardization terminology. What shall be included under the term "armed forces" and "military expenditures?" The general practice is to focus on the central government's formations of the army, the navy, and the air force of the respective country. Only those personnel on full-time active duty are included. The figures usually do not include reserve units, civilian defense forces, or special frontier guards and national police formations, which are very large in some countries and may, in selected cases, be as large as or larger than the central military establishment.

In examining these data, it should be pointed out that, among the leaders of the new nations which have attained political independence since 1945, only Prime Minister Julius Nyerere of Tanganyika has discussed the possibility of relying on an armed police force instead of a conventional army. Among the rest of the nations of the world, only in Costa Rica are there no central armed forces, but this country has a full-time national police force. National armed forces appear to be universal institutions and, in fact, in the present world are defined as essential marks of national sovereignty.

Despite the problems involved, it is possible to point to a growing body of fundamental data organized on a worldwide basis which throw some light on comparative military institutions and make possible the first steps in comparing trends in military expenditures. Arrays of such data have been presented by Morris Janowitz (1968) and Bruce M. Russett et al. (1964). However, the most comprehensive series has been collected by the United States Arms Control and Disarmament Agency, Economics Bureau (1968). In Table 1, data are presented on gross national military expenditures, population, and size of the armed forces for more than 120 countries during the year 1966. These data underline (a) the wide variation in the mobilization of personnal among nations, and (b) the markedly different overall patterns in specific regions of the world. Comparing the industrialized nations with the so-called less developed nations reveals that the "old nations" mobilized a larger percentage of their manpower for the arme; forces than did the "new nations." The same pattern held true for percentage expenditures of the gross national product on military operations, although the differences narrowed, and there were many specific exceptions in this measure. Among industrialized nations, the United States and the Soviet Union had a relatively equal and distinctively high level for both manpower and expenditures. For the United States, 1.5% of the population was in the armed forces, and military expenditures totaled 8.1% of the gross national product. For the Soviet Union, the figures were 1.4% of the population in the armed forces and an estimated 8% to 9% of the gross national product expended. For Mainland China, the figures reported by this source were 0.3% of the population and an estimated 8.1% of the gross national product expended.

On a region by region basis, NATO European countries had an overall 1.0% of the population in the armed forces and expenditures were 4.6% of the gross national product. Variation between individual European NATO countries was not marked. By contrast, the overall Warsaw pact nations were reported as 1.3%, and in military expenditure no single East European country reached the estimated 8.8% of the Soviet Union.

Among the less developed nations, the Near East stood highest with 0.8% of the population mobilized into the armed forces and 7.5% of its gross national product expended. The Far East was next with 0.5% and 4.3% respectively, while South Asia has 0.2% and 3.5%. It is interesting to note that the politically active armed forces of Latin America make use of 0.3% of the population and only 2.1% of the gross national product. Africa had very low figures of 0.1% of population and 2.5% of the gross national product, reflecting the newness and small size of many military establishments, although there are some notable exceptions in the region.

Trends in military expenditures from 1964 to 1967 are presented in Table 2. From these data it can be seen that there has been a rise in the amount spent on the military during these years. As expected, the bulk of the increase was in the industrialized nations of the world. In fact in the less developed nations, on a per capita basis, military expenditures did not increase.

These data make possible gross analysis based on aggregate statistics. An analysis based on a worldwide array of data must be extremely crude because of the difficulties of developing an adequate set of concepts to handle the wide heterogeneity of the nations and of military establishments. For example, in the case of new nations, the Libyan army of 4,500, composed exclusively of infantry troops, is hardly the same type of administrative organization as the Indian armed forces of more than 500,000 with first-line jet planes and naval units. Again, in Western Europe, despite the similarities in societal setting and technology, there are important differences between the military professions in Switzerland and Sweden, which were neutral during the last two wars, and the military formations of Holland and Belgium, which have been deeply influenced by their wartime experiences.

One effort at gross statistical analysis has been presented by Bruce Russett et al. (1964) which deals with a comparison of military expenditures and the size of military manpower in a selection of heterogeneous countries. Military expenditures are standardized in terms of expenditures on defense as a percentage of GNP, while military personnel is treated as a percentage of working-age population. The conclusion of the analysis seems hardly profound, in that the authors report "that the two ratios generally vary together: (they correlated with a fairly high $r = 0.68$ around the regression lines); that is, the size of the armed forces and military expenditures are linked. Deviations from the regression line are not errors in reporting, since some countries have large but poorly equipped military establishments."

A somewhat more rewarding approach is developed when a narrower and more homogeneous group of military establishments are examined in terms of a specific issue. Janowitz (1964) explored whether there is any relationship between economic development or

Table 1. Military Expenditures and Related Data, By Country, 1966

(Amounts in U.S. Dollars at current prices and exchange rates[a])

Region and Country	Gross National Product (GNP)		Military Expenditures		Population (Mid-Year)	Armed Forces	
	Mil $	$ Per Capita	Mil $	% of GNP	Thousands	Thousands	% of Pop.
World Total	$2,311,077	$ 687	$158,976	6.9%	3,363,414	20,305	.6%
North America	800,900	3,696	64,883	8.1	216,970	3,201	1.5
United States	747,600	3,796	63,283	8.5	196,920	3,094	1.6
Canada	53,300	2,658	1,600	3.0	20,050	107	.5
Europe	1,037,324	1,455	76,479	7.4	712,904	7,836	1.1
NATO, European	466,621	1,570	21,335	4.6	297,075	2,853	1.0
Belgium	18,130	1,903	530	2.9	9,528	107	1.1
Denmark	11,140	2,322	310	2.8	4,797	45	.9
France	101,380	2,052	5,300	5.2	49,400	523	1.1
Germany, West	119,580	1,990	4,950	4.1	60,076	450	.7
Greece	6,579	764	240	3.6	8,614	159	1.8

Iceland	556	2,837	0	0	196	0	0
Italy	61,440	1,182	2,125	3.5	51,962	376	.7
Luxembourg	676	2,018	10	1.5	335	3	.9
Netherlands	20,750	1,666	775	3.7	12,455	130	1.0
Norway	7,590	2,022	260	3.4	3,753	34	.9
Portugal	4,070	436	240	5.9	9,335	162	1.8
Turkey	9,420	295	445	4.7	31,880	440	1.4
United Kingdom	105,310	1,924	6,150	5.8	54,744	424	.8
NATO Total	1,267,521	2,466	86,218	6.8	514,045	6,054	1.2
Warsaw Pact	478,500	1,434	52,290	NA^b	333,689	4,253	1.3
Bulgaria	7,600	918	210E	2.8	8,257	156	1.9
Czechoslovakia	23,800	1,671	1,400	5.9	14,240	220	1.5
Germany, East	28,300	1,658	1,100	3.9	17,067	122	.7
Hungary	12,000	1,179	300	2.5	10,179	109	1.1
Poland	33,200	1,047	1,750	5.3	31,698	280	.9
Romania	16,600	867	530	3.2	19,143	201	1.0
Soviet Union	357,000	1,531	47,000	NA^b	233,105	3,165	1.4
Other European	92,203	1,123	2,854	3.1	82,140	780	1.0
Albania	700E	366E	70E	10.0^c	1,914	38	2.0
Austria	10,020	1,374	135	1.3	7,290	40	.5

Table 1 (Continued)

Region and Country	Gross National Product (GNP)		Military Expenditures		Population (Mid-Year)	Armed Forces	
	Mil $	$ Per Capita	Mil $	% of GNP	Thousands	Thousands	% of Pop.
Other European							
Finland	8,620	1,858	141	1.6	4,639	43	.9
Ireland	2,943	1,020	37	1.3	2,884	9	.3
Spain	24,570	771	753	3.1	31,871	291	.9
Sweden	21,340	2,733	924	4.3	7,808	70	.9
Switzerland	14,990	2,499	388	2.6	5,999	25	.4
Yugoslavia	9,020	457	406	4.5	19,735	264	1.3
Latin America	102,411	415	2,135	2.1	246,909	814	.3
Argentina	16,240	716	279	1.7	22,691	118	.5
Bolivia	661	156	17		4,235	15	.4
Brazil	25,790	310	798	3.1	83,175	220	.3
Chile	4,867	556	113[d]	2.3	8,750	46	.5
Colombia	5,457	293	92[d]	1.7	18,650	48	.3

Costa Rica	631	405	3	.5	1,558	0	0
Cuba	5,000E	638E	250E	5.0[c]	7,833	121	1.5
Dominican Republic	996	266	34	3.3	3,750	19	.5
Ecuador	1,245	237	25	2.0	5,250	19	.4
El Salvador	845	284	10	1.2	2,978	6	.2
Guatemala	1,388	292	15	1.1	4,761	9	.2
Guyana	220	328	1	.5	670	1	*
Haiti	334	74	8E	2.4[c]	4,485	5	.1
Honduras	536	227	7	1.3	2,363	5	.2
Jamaica	946	516	5	.5	1,833	2	.1
Mexico	21,770	493	166	.8	44,145	62	.1
Nicaragua	600	350	9	1.5	1,715	7	.4
Panama	698	542	1	.1	1,287	3	.2
Paraguay	493	221	8[d]	1.7	2,094	11	.5
Peru	3,547	295	83[d]	2.3	12,012	50	.4
Trinidad and Tobago	672	669	3	.4	1,004	1	*
Uruguay	1,565	569	26[d]	1.6	2,749	17	.6
Venezuela	7,940	890	182	2.3	8,921	30	.3
Far East	218,734	185	9,454	4.3	1,180,638	5,929	.5
Burma	1,700E	67E	113	6.6	25,246	110	.4
Cambodia	875E	139E	54	6.2	6,277	30	.5

Table 1 (Continued)

Region and Country	Gross National Product (GNP)		Military Expenditures		Population (Mid-Year)	Armed Forces	
	Mil $	$ Per Capita	Mil $	% of GNP	Thousands	Thousands	% of Pop.
Far East							
China, Mainland	80,000E	104E	6,500E	8.1^c	772,000E	2,500	.3
China, Republic of	3,138	235	350	11.2	13,326	544	4.1
Indonesia	10,740E	100E	165	1.5	107,431	350	.3
Japan	97,480	986	933	1.0	98,865	246	.2
Korea, North	2,900E	234E	225E	7.8^c	12,400	368	3.0
Korea, Republic of	3,822	131	150	3.9	29,086	572	2.0
Laos	189E	70	35	18.5	2,700	60	2.2
Malaysia	3,022	311	121	4.0	9,725	30	.3
Mongolia	500E	439E	25E	5.0^c	1,140	30	2.6
Philippines	5,728	171	84	1.5	33,477	42	.1
Thailand	4,654	141	97	2.1	32,922	132	.4
Vietnam, North	1,500E	77E	300E	20.0^c	19,500	350	1.8
Vietnam, Republic of	2,086E	126E	302	14.5	16,543	565	3.4

South Asia	54,160	83	1,919	3.5	655,782	1,399	.2
Afghanistan	1,355	88	15	1.1	15,397	90	.6
Ceylon	1,688	147	14	.8	11,491	10	.1
India^e	36,895	74	1,400	3.8	501,600	1,000	.2
Nepal	772	75	7	1.0	10,294	20	.2
Pakistan	13,450	115	483	3.6	117,000	279	.2
Near East	24,751	284	1,868	7.5	87,165	668	.8
Cyprus	440	730	8	1.8	603	1	.2
Iran	6,423	252	328	5.1	25,500	180	.7
Iraq	2,235	268	207	9.3	8,338	79	.9
Israel	3,822	1,454	400	10.5	2,629	71	2.7
Jordan	520	266	61	11.7	1,954	40	2.0
Kuwait	1,700	3,462	55	3.2	491	3	.1
Lebanon	1,250	476	38	3.0	2,624	12	.5
Saudi Arabia	1,670	380	202	12.1	4,399	30	.7
Syrian Arab Republic	1,101	201	97	8.8	5,480	60	1.1
Yemen	515	103	NA	NA	5,000	2	*
United Arab Republic	5,075	168	461	9.1	30,147	190	.6

Table 1 (Continued)

Region and Country	Gross National Product (GNP)		Military Expenditures		Population (Mid-Year)	Armed Forces	
	Mil $	$ Per Capita	Mil $	% of GNP	Thousands	Thousands	% of Pop.
Africa	42,532	171	1,053	2.5	249,129	326	.1
Algeria	2,662	219	99E	3.7	12,150	60	.5
Cameroon	720	135	16	2.2	5,350	3	.1
Central African Republic	183	127	3E	1.6c	1,437	1	.1
Chad	252	75	5E	2.0c	3,361	*	*
Congo, Brazzaville	123	145	7E	5.7	850	2	.2
Congo, Kinshasa	1,800	111	106	5.9	16,273	30	.2
Dahomey	170	71	4	2.4	2,410	1	*
Ethiopia	1,484	65	34	2.3	23,000	35	.1
Gabon	174	372	3	1.7	468	1	.2
Ghana	1,743	219	25	1.4	7,945	12	.2
Guinea	290	80	13	4.5	3,629	5	.1
Ivory Coast	1,020	260	13	1.3	3,920	4	.1
Kenya	1,114	116	12	1.1	9,643	3	*

Africa							
Liberia	226	207	3	1.3	1,090	4	.4
Libya	1,361	812	27	2.0	1,677	8	.5
Malagasy Republic	665	110	11	1.7	6,055	3	*
Malawi	207E	51E	1	.5	4,035	1	*
Mali	325	70	5	1.5	4,668	3	.1
Mauritania	148	138	4	2.7	1,070	1	.1
Morocco	2,503	182	103	4.1	13,725	45	.3
Niger	257	75	3	1.2	3,433	1	*
Nigeria	5,450	125	66	1.2	43,600	9	*
Rhodesia, Southern	997	227	15E	1.5c	4,400	5	.1
Senegal	716	200	15	2.1	3,580	4	.1
Sierra Leone	378	157	3	.8	2,403	2	.1
Somali Republic	155	60	7	4.5	2,570	8	.3
South Africa, Republic of	11,960	654	331	2.8	18,298	27	.1
Sudan	1,457	105	47	3.2	13,940	18	.1
Tanzania	860	75	8d	1.0	11,487	2	*
Togo	190	113	3	1.6	1,680	1	.1
Tunisia	931	209	17	1.8	4,460	21	.5
Uganda	714	92	20	2.8	7,740	3	*
Upper Volta	275	55	4	1.5	4,955	1	*
Zambia	1,022	267	20	2.0	3,827	3	.1

Table 1 (Continued)

Region and Country	Gross National Product (GNP)		Military Expenditures		Population (Mid-Year)	Armed Forces	
	Mil $	$ Per Capita	Mil $	% of GNP	Thousands	Thousands	% of Pop.
Oceania	30,605	2,153	1,185	3.9	14,217	82	.6
Australia	25,130	2,178	1,065	4.2	11,541	69	.6
New Zealand	5,475	2,046	120	2.2	2,676	13	.5

NA=Not available.   E=Rough ACDA estimate.   *=Less than one-half unit.

a. For most countries conversion into U.S. dollars is at official par value exchange rates as employed with rounding by AID. For Argentina, Brazil, Chile, Colombia, and Uruguay, "effective" rates estimated by AID are used. Approximate purchasing power equivalent rates are used for communist countries. See Appendix for further details.

b. The relationships between GNP and other dollar amounts shown or implied here may not be valid due to use of differentiated conversion rates for particular sectors. If measured in national currencies and at factor cost rather than at market prices, for example, Soviet military expenditures would be in the vicinity of eight to nine percent of GNP.

c. Because either or both GNP and military expenditure estimates are approximations, the resulting ratio should be used with particular caution.

d. Due to changes in the treatment of nonmilitary expenditures of regular defense agencies, which are excluded, data for 1966 are not fully comparable to data previously published in the ACDA report for 1965.

e. Value data are for fiscal year beginning April 1, and are converted at the new rate of Rs7.50, instead of Rs4.762, per U.S. dollar, established in mid-1966.

Source: United States Arms Control and Disarmament Agency, Research Report 68-52

Table 2. Summary Table: Trends in Military Expenditures and GNP, 1964-1967

MILITARY EXPENDITURES	TOTAL (Billions of Dollars)				PER CAPITA (Dollars)			
	1964	1965	1966	1967	1964	1965	1966	1967
In Current Dollars								
Worldwide	132	138	159	182	41	42	47	53
Developed	116	120	142	162	125	128	149	170
Less Developed	16	18	17	20	7	8	7	8
GNP								
Worldwide	1,920	2,120	2,311	2,500	597	642	687	729
Developed	1,589	1,743	1,916	2,040	1,715	1,847	2,020	2,141
Less Developed	331	377	395	460	145	160	1.64	186
In Constant 1967 Dollars								
Worldwide	147	148	164	182	46	45	49	53
Developed	128	128	145	162	138	135	153	170
Less Developed	19	20	19	20	9	8	8	8
GNP								
Worldwide	2,159	2,264	2,403	2,500	671	688	715	729
Developed	1,761	1,847	1,966	2,040	1,901	1,958	2,073	2,141
Less Developed	398	417	437	460	174	177	181	186

Source: United States Arms Control and Disarmament Agency, Research Report 68-52

absence thereof and the political role of the military in a sample of fifty developing nations. The results are mainly negative.

Students of comparative politics have offered the proposition that there is a positive association between economic development and democratic political competitiveness. By inference, the more economically developed a new nation is, the less likely it is that the military could hinder the competitive process in domestic politics. S. M. Lipset made use of selected indices of economic development to compare Western European and Latin American democracies as a basis for testing this hypothesis concerning the positive association between economic development and political competitiveness. Statistical support for this proposition is hardly impressive, and this type tical support for this proposition is hardly impressive, and this type of analysis appears to have limited relevance for understanding, on a comparative basis, the dynamic relationship between economic development and political forms. Since there are only a limited number of cases in the analysis, even a minor redefinition of the universe markedly alters the statistical conclusions. More important, in order to avoid a mechanical test of the proposition, one would expect that the changes in political competitiveness since the original analysis should at least be congruent with the basic proposition. This means that those nations high on the economic development index should have moved toward more competitiveness. For Latin America, the trend has been toward less competitiveness, and this trend cannot be directly related to the level of economic development; in some cases, it is inversely related. The same lack of support of this hypothesis is presented by an examination of the countries of Africa and Asia.

Some difficulties of this type of analysis rest in the crude nature of the political categories. Even when more refined categories of military involvement in politics are employed among the fifty-one new nations studied, there is no basis for asserting that, with higher levels of economic development, thery is a movement toward restriction of the military's involvement with the domestic political system. In fact, among those new nations with the highest levels of economic development, the absence of democratic competitive systems is more noteworthy than their presence, since competitive systems are concentrated in the middle level of economic development. On the other hand, there is an apparent but not profoundly explanatory relation between the length of time that a new nation has been independent and the increased political role of the military. The expansion of political involvement increases year by year after independence, while contraction of the military's political role remains a highly problematic issue, although a real alternative.

REDEFINITION OF MILITARY ORGANIZATION

The distinction offered by Alfred Vagts (1937: 13), the historian, between "militarism" and "the military way" is a useful approach for the study of military organization undergoing change.

> The Military way is marked by a primary concentration of men and materials on winning specific objectives of power with the utmost efficiency, that is, with the least expenditure of blood and treasure. . . .

Militarism, on the other hand, presents a vast array of customs, interests, prestige, actions, and thought associated with armies and wars and yet transcending true military purposes. Indeed militarism is so constituted that it may hamper and defeat the purposes of the military way.

This distinction is a specific application to military organization of the classic problem of rationality in large-scale organization, that is, the conditions promoting or hampering the effective adjustment of means to ends. Internally, militarism implies the development and persistence of practices which block scientific and administrative procedures designed to produce greater professionalism. Externally, militarism encompasses the social, economic, and political power that the military generates and its consequences on domestic social structure and international politics.

To the extent that the military officer is a professional, to that extent he must relate himself to the profound uncertainties in planning for and conducting military hostilities. Therefore, the ideal model of the military professional is not that of the scientist or the engineer or the business administrator. There is an irreducible component of a heroic posture in his professional self-image, for he must be prepared to face danger.

The development of the military profession has been a continuous struggle to be rational and scientific in the context of military requirements. Thus, it is possible to describe the history of the modern military establishment as a struggle between the previously identified military types—heroic leaders who embody traditionalism and glory—and military managers who are concerned with the scientific and rational conduct of war. Internal militarism in the sense that the military blocks technical progress has waned in most military establishments. As the military establishment becomes progressively dependent on more complex technology, the importance of the military manager increases. He does not displace the heroic leader, but he undermines the long-standing traditionalism of the military. As a result, there is a crisis in the strain between military managers and heroic leaders. However, this is a professional crisis that can be controlled by organizational resources, by compromise, and because the military manager acknowledges the worth and instrumental value of the heroic leaders in the military profession.

The proposition can be offered that the crisis in the professional self-image of the military man derives not primarily from internal organizational problems but from the crisis in military goals. At the upper end of the violence continuum, the development of nuclear weapons and strategic conceptions of deterrence means that the military officer—both the military manager and the heroic leader—is transformed into a teacher, that is, an instructor of men who will man and maintain a machine designed not to be employed. The past supplies little basis for organizing and maintaining a professional self-image under such conditions. At the lower end of the violence continuum, the scope of conventional warfare narrows. The tactics and techniques of limited war and internal warfare limit the authority of the military professional at the expense of civilian experts and civilian political leadership. It is almost possible to speak of civilian militarism as each aspect of military operations comes under the elaborate control of civilian leaders—democratic and authoritarian—and as the mechanics of warfare must be integrated with political strategy in the absence of an opportunity for traditional-type military victory.

The Constabulary Force

The notion of the constabulary force is one conception designed to contribute to the issues of restructuring military institutions to emerging technological, political, and moral considerations. In *The Professional Soldier: A Social and Political Portrait*, the constabulary concept is defined in the following way: the military establishment becomes a constabulary force when it is continuously prepared to act, committed to the minimum use of force, and seeks viable international relations rather than victory because it has incorporated a protective military posture (Janowitz, 1960: 418). For industrialized nations, the constabulary force concept encompasses the entire range of military power and organization, including the military contribution to arms control and disarmament. For developing nations, the constabulary concept involves reasoned and careful use of the military for social and national development, including civic action. The military is viewed moving in the direction of becoming a police-type operation in the sense that "victory" against a specific enemy is no longer its major goal, but creating stable conditions for social and political change is its major goal instead.

The constabulary concept is not tied to a specific strategic outlook; it is a concept designed to relate institutional analysis to enlightened self-interest. It is designed to facilitate creative innovation in military organization and doctrine to permit modification in national policy in order to reduce the risk of war.

The peacekeeping operations of the United Nations can be viewed as an application of the constabulary concept at the level of the world community. In the early evolution of the United Nations, there was considerable discussion of the possibility of a world military force to enforce the political and legal decisions of the United Nations. This would be a force recruited and staffed directly under United Nations jurisdiction, as a step toward "world government." The pressure of international relations plus the organizational defects of this approach rendered the concept inoperative from the very beginning.

The actual pattern of military operations of the United Nations has in effect conformed to a constabulary pattern. Peacekeeping operations have been undertaken by conventional national forces which have been welded into ad hoc organizations, and given political and administrative direction by United Nations organs. It is striking to note that, while there have been factual and operational reports of the United Nations peacekeeping operations, they have not been studied in depth from a sociological perspective.

Equally significant is the analysis of the impact of United Nations military experiences on member nations and their constituent forces. A large number of nations have sent forces to participate in United Nations operations with discernible impact on the participants and, in turn, on the internal processes of the particular member nation involved. Only one such study is available on the Irish Army, where the impact of United Nations peacekeeping activity has been of considerable importance for political integration of the country and for broadening and deepening ots international commitments. Participation in United Nations peacekeeping activities is not certain to have such consequences, since all experience has not been successful in this respect. In part, the outcome of the particular operation and the conduct of the troops are of some significance. Victory in the traditional military sense is not relevant, but success in the constabulary sense of making a contribution to the world community is relevant. (This was precisely the case for the Irish troops, which were hardly "victorious" in the field operations but succeeded in their operational mission.)

In recent years planning for United Nations military operations has, as a result of experience, undergone a radical change, and the notion of a permanent United Nations force has receded. Obviously, this is a result of international politics and the burden of existing United Nations military operations. It is also the result of creative thinking which is seeking to develop professional military forms appropriate to the political and administrative tasks of the United Nations. As a result, thinking and planning have progressed in the constabulary direction, namely, to create that kind of force which would satisfy the needs of the United Nations and which, in its organization format, would contribute to the reduction of tensions per se rather than create new imbalances. The evolving format is that of national standby forces which are designated in advance as potential United Nations units. These units are housed in member nations and are part of their national defense forces but are available on a constabulary basis for United Nations emergencies. It is noteworthy that some small nations, namely, Norway, Sweden, and Denmark, have designated specific units for such activities. It is, of course, such small nations that will be called on for United Nations constabulary duty. Canada has taken the lead and organized an international conference on these problems. As a result, the United Nations has the rudiments of a military force at its disposal without the political instabilities and administrative difficulties that would be generated if it had a force in being.

Arms Control and Disarmament

Beyond peacekeeping operations is the arena of arms control and disarmament. It is possible to develop sociological models of the world community under conditions of radical disarmament. Walter Millis and James Real in *The Abolition of War* (1963) are concerned with eliminating war as an instrument of national policy. Yet they conclude with an organizational concept which they label "national police forces." National police forces—not a world police—are seen as elements to enforce the domestic conditions required for a world community. The idea of the national police force converges with the concept of a constabulary force. Not only are specialists in violence seen to operate in a protective military posture, but by whatever name, they are seen to have a positive role in arms control and disarmament.

In the long run, successful systems of accommodation and arms control would reduce the size of the military, but in the very short run, such schemes are likely to require a shift in the pattern of military activity. From this point of view, each step and each type of international accommodation requires new involvements and adaptations by the military if the accommodations of arms control are to be stable, relatively enduring, and expanding in scope.

On the level more specifically related to the mechanics of arms control is the formulation of Thomas C. Schelling (1962) of a special surveillance force. The special surveillance force is seen as an instrument for implementing an arms control arrangement. It is an organizational device for making treaties and formal arrangements enforceable, effective, and expanding. The special surveillance force is an example of institution-building which would function "to observe the enemy's behavior, at the enemy's invitation, and to report home instantly through authentic channels. The purpose is to help tranquilize crises that threaten to erupt into general war, particularly crises aggravated by the instability of strategic deterrence." Thus, it is striking to note that Schelling sees arms control in part as a crash program in which new arrangements—formal and informal, unilateral and bilateral—can emerge in response to a sudden crisis. It is even more striking to note that the organizational characteristics he describes for his special surveillance force are military characteristics in part, and more specifically converge with the constabulary concept, namely, "the attributes of the forces should be readiness, speed and reliability, self-sufficiency, versatility and ability to improvise."

It is necessary to examine the full range of the nonmilitary activities of constabulary forces. At a minimum, national disasters are likely to persist whose consequences can be coped with in part by military forces. In addition to these national disasters, there are the continuous rescue missions and responses to the failure and breakdown of man-made systems of transportation, power, navigation, and the like. All of these adjunct roles can enhance military effectiveness to cope with its central function in a rational and adaptive fashion.

REFERENCES

American Journal of Sociology (1946) Human Behavior in Military Society. Special Issue 51 (March).

ANDRESKI, S. (1954) Military Organization and Society. London: Routledge & Kegan Paul.

BOWERS, R. (1967) "The military establishment," pp. 234-274 in P. F. Lazarsfeld et al. (eds.) The Uses of Sociology. New York: Basic Books.

CROKER, G. W. (1969) "Some principles regarding the utilization of social science research within the military," pp. 185-194 in E. T. Crawford and A. Biderman (eds.) Social Scientists and International Affairs. New York: John Wiley.

DAVIS, A. K. (1948) "Bureaucratic patterns in the Navy officer corps." Social Forces 27 (December): 143-153.

DEMETER, K. (1965) The German Officer-Corps in Society and State. New York: Frederick A. Praeger.

HUNTINGTON, S. (1957) The Soldier and the State. Cambridge: Harvard University Press.

JANOWITZ, M. [ed.] (1969) The New Military: Changing Patterns of Organization. New York: W. W. Norton.

———(1968) "Armed Forces and society: a world perspective," pp. 15-38 in J. A. A. van Doorn (ed.) Armed Forces and Society: Sociological Essays. The Hague: Mouton.

———(1964) The Role of the Military in Political Development of New Nations. Chicago: University of Chicago Press.

———(1960) The Professional Soldier: A Social and Political Portrait. New York: Free Press.

———(1959) "Changing patterns of organizational authority: the military establishment." Administrative Science Q. 3 (March): 473-493.

———(1957) "Military elites and the study of war." Journal of Conflict Resolution 1 (March): 9-18.

———and R. LITTLE (1965) Sociology and the Military Establishment. New York: Russell Sage Foundation.

LANG, K. (1969) The Sociology of War: A Selected and Annotated Bibliography. Inter-University Seminar on Armed Forces and Society. Chicago: University of Chicago.

———(1965) "Military organizations," pp. 838-878 in J. G. March (ed.) Handbook of Organizations. Chicago: Rand McNally.

LASSWELL, H. (1951) Politics: Who Gets What, When, How. New York: Free Press.

———(1941) "The garrison state." American Journal of Sociology 46 (January): 455-468.

LEIGHTON, A. (1949) Human Relations in a Changing World. New York: E. P. Dutton.

LEWIS, M. A. (1939) England's Sea-Officers: The Story of the Naval Profession. London: Allen & Unwin.

MARCH, J. G. [ed.] (1965) Handbook of Organizations. Chicago: Rand McNally.

MARSHALL, S. L. A. (1947) Men Against Fire. New York: William Morrow.

MERTON, R. K. and P. F. LAZARSFELD [eds.] (1950) Studies in the Scope and Method of "The American Soldier." New York: Free Press.

MILLIS, W. and J. REAL (1963) The Abolition of War. New York: Macmillan.

MILLS, C. W. (1956) The Power Elite. New York: Oxford Univ. Press.

PAGE, C. H. (1946) "Bureaucracy's other face." Social Forces 25 (October): 88-94.

POOL, I. et al. (1955) The Satellite Generals: A Study of Military Elites in the Soviet Sphere. Stanford: Stanford University Press.

RUSSETT, B. M. et al. (1964) World Handbook of Political and Social Indicators. New Haven: Yale University Press.

SCHELLING, T. C. (1962) "A special surveillance force," pp. 87-105 in I. Wright, W. M. Evan, and D. Morton (eds.) Preventing World War III. New York: Simon & Schuster.

SHILS, E. A. and M. M. JANOWITZ (1948) "Cohesion and disintegration in The Wehrmacht in World War II." Public Opinion Q. 12 (Summer): 280-315.

SPEIER, H. (1952) Social Order and the Risks of War. New York: George W. Stewart.

STOUFFER, S. A. et al. (1949) The American Soldier. 4 vols. Princeton: Princeton University Press.

THOMPSON, J. D. (1956) "Authority and power in 'identical' organizations." American Journal of Sociology 62 (November): 290-301.

TURNER, R. H. (1947) "The naval disbursing officer as a bureaucrat." American Sociological Rev. 12 (June): 342-348.

U.S. Arms Control and Disarmament Agency, Economics Bureau (1968) World Military Expenditures and Related Data. Research Report 68-52. Washington, D.C.: Government Printing Office.

U.S. Department of Defense, Office of the Secretary of Defense (1951) Report of the Working Group on Human Behavior Under Conditions of Military Service. A Joint Project of the Research and Development Board and the Personnel Policy Board, Washington, D.C.

VAGTS, A. (1937) A History of Militarism. New York: W. W. Norton.

VAN DOORN, J. A. A. (1969) Military Professionalism and Military Regimes. The Hague: Mouton.

——— [ed.] (1968) Armed Forces and Society: Sociological Essays. The Hague: Mouton.

———(1956) Sociologie van de organisatie: beschouwingen over organiseren in het bijzonder gebaseerd op een onderzoek van het militaire system. Leiden: H. E. Stenfert Kroese.

WILLIAMS, R. H. (1954) Human Factors in Military Operations: Some Applications of the Social Sciences to Operations Research. Technical Memorandum ORO-T-259. Chevy Chase, Md.: Operations Research Office.

Chapter 2

MILITARY MANPOWER PROCUREMENT AND SUPPLY

HAROLD WOOL

Since the early 1940s the armed services have constituted one of the nation's major claimants for manpower resources. In contrast to a maximum peacetime strength of about 300,000 prior to World War II, military strengths have averaged two and one-half million or higher in each year since 1951 and reached peaks of three and one-half million or more during the so-called "limited wars" in Korea and Vietnam, respectively. In order to maintain these strengths, it has been necessary to procure between one-half million and one million entrants from civilian life per year through voluntary programs or the draft (see Table 1).

The full dimensions of recent military manpower procurement programs are only partially suggested by aggregate numbers alone. The increased complexity of modern military technology and organization has generated a growing requirement for specialized personnel in a wide variety of professional, technical, and skilled occupations. The qualitative characteristics of military manpower resources, as measured by such criteria as educational background, aptitudes, skills, and experience level, have therefore received major emphasis in military manpower procurement programs in recent years.

In this chapter we shall first review the ways in which the military services have attempted to meet these large and diversified manpower needs, the broad framework of recent military manpower policies, and the major manpower procurement programs and

Table 1. Active Duty Military Strengths, Accessions, and Separations,
Fiscal Year 1951-68

(in thousands)

Fiscal Year	Active Duty Strength (30 June)	Accessions[b]					Total Separations
		Total	Draftees	Enlistees[c]	Involuntary Reserve Recalls	Officers[d]	
1951[a]	3,250	2,030	590	780	610	50	240
1952	3,640	1,090	380	560	80	70	700
1953	3,560	1,060	560	440	–	60	1,140
1954	3,300	750	270	430	–	50	1,010
1955	2,940	790	220	520	–	50	1,150
1956	2,810	670	140	490	–	40	800
1957	2,800	670	180	450	–	40	680
1958	2,600	540	130	370	–	40	740
1959	2,500	520	110	380	–	30	620
1960	2,480	500	90	380	–	30	520
1961	2,480	510	60	420	–	30	510
1962	2,810	800	160	450	150	40	470
1963	2,700	510	70	400	–	40	620
1964	2,690	600	150	410	–	40	610
1965	2,660	510	100	370	–	40	540
1966	3,090	990	340	610	–	40	560
1967	3,380	890	300	530	–	60	600
1968	3,550	990	340	570	30	50	820

a. Active duty strength as of June 30, 1950 was 1,460,000.
b. Entrants from civilian life; excludes immediate reenlistments.
c. Includes regular enlistments and reservists voluntarily entering active duty for tours of duty of two years or more.
d. Partially estimated.
Source: U.S. Department of Defense.

strategies. We shall then analyze the major sources of military
manpower supply as reflected in historical enlistment and retention
experience and in studies of the characteristics and motivations of
military service entrants. In the concluding section of the chapter we
shall relate these findings to an assessment of alternative manpower
procurement strategies in the post-Vietnam era.

MILITARY MANPOWER
PROCUREMENT POLICIES

The Role of the Peacetime Draft

The systems of procuring military manpower in most modern nations have tended to fall into two broad categories: those relying upon conscription for all, or nearly all, of their new manpower, and those relying entirely upon voluntary recruitment. The United States military manpower system which took shape about two decades ago falls into neither of these categories. Although a draft law has remained continuously on the statute books since mid-1948, the draft has in most years directly provided only a modest fraction of all new entrants into service; the balance have entered through voluntary programs. With limited exceptions, three of the armed services—the Navy, the Marine Corps, and the Air Force—have relied entirely upon voluntary programs. The Army, in most recent years, since 1948 has also obtained a majority of its new entrants through recruitment programs. Thus, the United States military system can best be characterized as a "mixed" system—partly compulsory, partly voluntary.

The origins of our present military manpower system are deeply rooted in American history and tradition. For the first one hundred fifty years of our existence as an independent nation, the strategic facts of our geographic insularity had permitted us to meet national defense needs in peacetime with relatively small standing military forces. Until the 1940s our regular peacetime forces had never constituted more than a modest fraction of one percent of our total labor force. Traditionally, the Armed Services had relied entirely upon voluntary recruitment to man these small regular forces— competing for manpower as best they could in the civilian labor market. In wartime, these sources were augmented by call-ups of militiamen or reserves, by massive patriotic appeals for volunteers, and by conscription.

As the armed services emerged from the immediate post-World War II demobilization, they were faced, in many ways, with a manpower procurement task without precedent in earlier experience. We were no longer at war; therefore, it seemed logical and inevitable that they should rely again upon volunteer sources of manpower. In March 1947, the World War II Selective Service Act expired, and no request was initiated by the administration for its extension. A large network of recruitment stations was established by the military services geared to maintenance of a peacetime regular military establishment.

It soon became evident, however, that our needs for standing military forces would be considerably greater than had been anticipated in the early demobilization period. Upon a reevaluation of national defense needs, President Truman submitted a special message to the Congress in early 1948 requesting enactment of a new peacetime draft law. In support of the need for the new draft law, testimony was offered indicating that, although the Navy and the Air Force had been generally able to meet their strength goals, the Army, in spite of extensive recruitment efforts, was already considerably short of its authorized strength. The Navy, as well as the Army, could not attain the higher strengths then requested through voluntary programs. In this context, Congress enacted, in July 1948, a new Selective Service Act establishing a twenty-month active duty obligation for men aged nineteen to twenty-five years, inclusive, who met minimum standards of qualification for service and who were not eligible for exemption or deferment.

Since 1948 a draft law has remained continuously on the statute books. Actual inductions into the Army under the 1948 draft law were limited initially to a few months in late 1948 and early 1949, totaling only 35,000. Thereafter, with an apparent abatement in international tensions and reduction in military strengths, the armed services did not require inductions until after the outbreak of Korean hostilities in June 1950. In June 1951, the draft law was basically revised and retitled the Universal Military Training and Service Act.

Between 1951 and 1967 the induction authority was regularly extended by Congress at four-year intervals. Thus, following the late 1940s, the existence of a military service obligation became an accepted (if not welcome) fact of life for young American males approaching adulthood.

Although the draft law was supported as necessary for maintenance of military strengths, it was never regarded, either by Congress or the Department of Defense, as a preferred means of military manpower procurement during peacetime.

In enacting the 1948 draft act, Congress made it clear that priority should be given to voluntary enlistments. Department of Defense officials have also reiterated this policy which is both consistent with American tradition and in the best interest of the military services. The draft, it has been emphasized, has served as a residual source of manpower for the armed services which is resorted to only to the extent that voluntary sources are inadequate.

The fluctuations in draft calls since enactment of the 1948 draft law illustrate this residual role of the draft as a source of military manpower. Between January 1949 and July 1951, during a period when military strengths averaged about one and one-half million, no draft calls were requested by any of thy military services. Since 1951 annual draft calls have ranged from totals of more than 500,000 per year, during the Korean war period, and over 300,000 per year, during the years 1966-1969, to a low of only 60,000 in fiscal year 1961 when our military strength dropped slightly below two and one-half million. In the latter case, inductions accounted for only fourteen percent of all new enlisted entrants into service, the remainder having been procured under enlistment programs.

Enlistment Programs

The emphasis placed by the military services upon voluntary recruitment as the preferred means of meeting their manpower needs is illustrated by the fact that, as of fiscal year 1968, they maintained a total of more than three thousand separate recruitment stations throughout the United States manned by some 8,600 recruiters at an annual cost of more than $100 million. The military services offer a variety of enlistment options to qualified applicants, including choices of entry into particular training courses, occupational fields, or branches of service. Extensive use is made of mass advertising media, direct mail campaigns, orientation programs for high school seniors, and direct solicitation of prospects.

The effectiveness of these programs is partially suggested by the level of annual enlistments achieved by the services in recent years. During the twelve-year period fiscal years 1954-1965, inclusive, initial enlistments into the regular forces averaged 340,000 per year. About two out of three men who entered military service during these years as enlisted men chose to enter upon regular enlistment of three or more years' duration rather than through induction.

Although the extensive efforts of the military recruitment organizations have undoubtedly contributed to this impressive record, military recruiters have long recognized that the existence of a military service obligation under the draft law has caused many young men to enlist who might not otherwise have done so. For example, the most important single source of enlistment prospects for recruiters consists of the lists of young men who have recently passed their preinduction examinations. Attitudinal survey results, summarized later in this chapter, also clearly confirm the major role played by the draft in motivating enlistments, particularly among some segments of the military-age population.

The draft also had an indirect influence upon other military manpower procurement policies, including those affecting standards of qualification for service. The relatively large manpower pool made available under the draft facilitated establishment of progressively higher qualification standards for service in the late 1950s and early 1960s. At the same time, reliance upon the draft imposed certain constraints upon the military services in their selection policies. These key policies are reviewed in more detail below.

Mental Standards of Qualification

Since World War II, all military services have established certain minimum passing scores on a psychological test, or tests, as necessary conditions for enlistment or induction. The reliance placed upon these psychological tests stems from the operational need of the services for an objective and rapid method of mass screening of young men to predict their future usefulness in the military.

The standard screening test used since 1950 has been the Armed Forces Qualification Test (AFQT). This test includes one hundred questions equally divided among four subtest areas: vocabulary, arithmetic, spatial relations, and mechanical ability (i.e., ability to interrelate tools and equipment). The scores on the AFQT are normally expressed as "percentile scores." A percentile score of ten represents the score which would be attained or exceeded by ninety percent of the "standard" population—as established originally by World War II testing experience. For purposes of qualitative allocation of new entrants, certain broad mental groups have been established based on the scores of this or equivalent tests as indicated below:

Mental Group	Percentile Score
I	93-100
II	65-92
III	31-64
IV	10-30
V	9 and below

Mental group III corresponds to a range of about one standard deviation of the population mean, and may be construed as the "average" group in terms of mental ability. Mental groups I and II correspond to the "above average" groups; mental groups IV and V, to those with "below average" scores.

In addition to the AFQT, the military services have made increased use of aptitude test batteries in initial selection, as well as classification of personnel. These aptitude test batteries are designed to predict the success of individuals in various occupational areas such as mechanical, technical, clerical, or combat. Individuals applying for enlistment under certain enlistment options providing for assignment to a particular school or occupational area must receive minimum qualifying scores in the corresponding aptitude areas. In addition, the aptitude tests have been used as a supplementary screening device in the case of applicants or draft registrants receiving marginal passing scores under the AFQT, i.e., mental group IVs.

The actual passing scores set on the tests have fluctuated widely since the end of World War II as the combined result of changing qualitative manpower needs and supply conditions, of legislative constraints, and of other policy considerations, as outlined below.

During the closing years of World War II, initial entry standards had been reduced to a level which permitted large numbers of functionally illiterate individuals to qualify for service—partly as a result of congressional pressures. In the years immediately following the end of World War II qualification standards were raised by all of the services as they adapted to the needs of a much smaller regular force.

In 1948, in enacting the Selective Service Act of 1948, Congress prescribed for the first time a statutory mental standard for induction, equivalent to a percentile score of thirteen on the AFQT. In June 1951, in the face of a shrinking manpower pool during the Korean war, this standard was lowered to a percentile score of ten. This standard applied only to draftees; however, under a Department of Defense policy, the same minimum score was set for enlistees as well, as part of a "qualitative distribution" policy to assure a proportionate qualitative allocation of new enlisted entrants into all services.

With a reduction in requirements for new personnel and a growing manpower pool of draft availables following the end of the Korean war, the Department of Defense requested—and obtained authority from Congress in 1958–to modify the standard of qualification for service, except in periods of declared war or national emergency. Under this authority, the mental test standard for draftees was raised by requiring those scoring in mental group IV on the AFQT to pass certain supplemental aptitude test batteries. Concurrently, enlistment standards were raised in all services to at least the twenty-first percentile on the AFQT with supplementary aptitude tests or educational requirements imposed by most services for those in the marginal group IV category.

The raising of mental test standards in the late 1950s and early 1960s was justified by military officials on two main grounds: the increasing requirements for higher aptitude personnel capable of training and assignment in the more technical specialties, and evidence that, irrespective of occupational specialty, individuals with low test scores, i.e., mental group IVs, accounted for a disproportionate share of disciplinary problems. Under conditions of a growing total pool of draft-available men, an increase in mental test standards had therefore seemed both feasible and desirable from a military personnel management standpoint.

These relatively high qualification standards were, however, subject to criticism for several reasons. They were inevitably accompanied by a sharp increase in rejection rates from an estimated "overall" rejection rate of about twenty-four percent, during the Korean war period, to thirty-five percent in 1963. (These rates are based on Defense Department estimate of rejections among all young men examined for service, including both volunteers and draft registrants. The rejection rates at preinduction examination, for draft registrants alone, were considerably higher, averaging forty-eight percent during the period August 1958 through December 1965.) In turn, the high rejection rates were subject to intermittent criticism on the ground that they were incompatible with the principle that the military service obligation should be shared as widely as possible among youth of military age.

The mental test standards were challenged on other grounds as well. The fact that the psychological tests are written tests, whose results depend substantially upon verbal skills and acquired knowledge, led some critics to question the inherent validity of these tests when applied to youth from deprived backgrounds. The tests, it was alleged, were geared primarily to measuring success in a formal classroom situation rather than to measuring other qualities such as motivation, courage, manual dexterity, and innate practical intelligence—qualities which are, perhaps, even more important in the actual performance of enlisted personnel, particularly in combat and other nontechnical duties. The contention that low test scores were necessarily predictive of high disciplinary problems was also found to be questionable as a result of more recent research which indicated, for example, that the fact of high school graduation was a much more reliable predictor of future adjustment to military life than mental test scores as such.

Another consideration influencing a major policy reassessment of the mental standards was the increased recognition of the role of the armed services as a training institution. Beginning with the enactment of the Manpower Development and Training Act in 1962, the federal government had undertaken a direct and substantial commitment for the training or retraining of workers as a major aspect of its national manpower policy. Other succeeding measures, including laws establishing the Job Corps and the Youth Conservation Corps, place prime emphasis on the development of needed skills for underprivileged youth in order to help them compete more effectively in the civilian job market. It appeared to top officials that the armed services, as the nation's largest employer of youth, and the nation's largest single training institution, could also contribute to such efforts and that this could be done as a "by-product" of its primary mission of training men for occupational duties in military service.

Based on these considerations, a phased reduction in mental qualification standards for draftees and Army enlistees was initiated in November 1965. In August 1966, this effort was further extended under a program identified by the code name, "Project One Hundred Thousand." Under this program Secretary McNamara announced a plan to accept for service forty thousand men in a twelve-month period beginning in October 1966, and 100,000 per year in succeeding years, who would not previously have qualified for service. To accomplish this, the supplementary aptitude test standards were completely waived for draft registrants in mental group IV who were high school graduates, as well as for nonhigh school graduates with AFQT scores of twenty-one or higher. Enlistment standards were correspondingly reduced. Provision was also made under the program for enlistment or voluntary induction of individuals with certain remedial medical conditions that could be corrected in relatively short periods after their entry into service. The effect of these revised standards was to lower the overall rejection rate for draft-age men from an estimated level of thirty-five percent in 1964 to about twenty-eight percent in 1967—the lowest rate since the mid-1950s.

Initial reports indicated that satisfactory progress had been made in achieving the goals of the program. During the first two years of the program—October 1966 through September 1968—a total of over 140,000 men were inducted or enlisted under the reduced standards, of whom about one-half were volunteers. Nearly ninety-six percent of those enrolled in the program had satisfactorily completed basic training, mainly without any remedial or special assistance. These men had been assigned to a wide range of occupational training courses and duties, about sixty-two percent in noncombat-type skills. Attrition rates from these courses, although higher than for other men, were generally in an acceptable range, averaging about ten percent.

From the standpoint of military manpower supply, the experience under the program served to highlight the potentials for expanding the supply of volunteers, as well as draftees, for military service, both during a period of active hostilities and in more normal peacetime periods. About one-half of all entrants into this program in the first two years of its operation were volunteers; plans called for increasing the ratio of volunteers to about two-thirds in fiscal year 1969.

Officer Procurement Programs

Commissioned officers have constituted about twelve percent of total active duty military personnel in most years since the mid-1950s. Their strengths have fluctuated, during the fiscal years 1955 to 1968, from a low of 315,000 in June 1961 to a high of 415,000 in June 1968. To maintain these strengths, the military services have procured an average of more than forty thousand new officer entrants per year during this period.

The military services offer a variety of programs for training and commissioning their officer personnel, designed to meet their requirements for both "line" officers and for various specialized professional categories. These programs include the Reserve Officer Training Corps (ROTC), Officer Candidate School enlistments, the service academies, direct appointment programs for physicians, dentists, nurses, and certain other specialists, and a variety of other special programs. The number of officers commissioned from these various sources is shown in Table 2, for selected years between fiscal year 1957 and 1967.

Table 2. Commissioned Officer Accessions By Source, Selected Years

Source	Fiscal Year 1957		Fiscal Year 1960		Fiscal Year 1964		Fiscal Year 1967	
	No.	%	No.	%	No.	%	No.	%
Academies	1,600	3.8	1,600	5.2	2,000	4.8	2,000	2.8
ROTC and other college student training programs	17,100	40.4	13,100	42.5	17,000	41.2	18,100	25.1
Officer candidate schools	6,700	15.9	4,900	15.9	11,100	26.9	34,800	48.1
Direct appointments of physicians, dentists, and veterinarians	6,900	16.3	4,600	14.9	6,100	14.8	5,800	8.0
Reserves to active duty	1,700	4.0	700	2.3	1,200	2.9	2,200	3.0
Aviation cadet programs	3,400	8.0	2,300	7.5	900	2.2	700	1.0
All others[a]	4,900	11.6	3,600	11.7	3,000	7.2	8,600	12.0
Total	42,300	100.0	30,800	100.0	41,300	100.0	72,200	100.0

a. Includes other direct appointments such as chaplains, legal staff, Medical Service Corps, and other specialists; female officers and nurses; direct commissions from ranks; temporary officers and interservice transfers.

ROTC and related programs. ROTC programs are offered by the Army, Air Force, and Navy at several hundred colleges and universities throughout the country. They provide officer training to college students concurrent with their college studies. ROTC courses consist of military science courses combined with summer training which may extend—at various institutions—for either a full four-year program or for the two final years of college study. A limited proportion of enrollees receive full scholarships while enrolled in the program. The Marine Platoon Leaders Class and the Naval Reserve Officers Candidate Program similarly offer reserve officer training to students enrolled in colleges without Navy ROTC programs during one or two summer periods rather than during the school year. These reserve officer training courses have been the largest single source of new officer entrants in recent peacetime years. Thus, in 1964, a total of seventeen thousand officers, or forty-one percent of all newly commissioned officers, were procured from these programs (see Table 2).

Officer candidate programs. A second major source of officer entrants consists of graduates of Officer Candidate School. All services offer opportunities for qualified college graduates to enlist for officer candidate training. In addition, some services also have permitted limited numbers of noncollege graduate enlisted personnel to enter Officer Candidate School. This program has the advantages of providing a more flexible source of officer recruitment than ROTC. In fiscal year 1964 about eleven thousand or twenty-seven percent, of all newly commissioned officers were obtained from this source. With the Vietnam force build-up, the number of officer candidates was sharply expanded, resulting in an output of 30,400, or forty-seven percent, of all newly commissioned officers in fiscal year 1968.

Direct appointments. A third major category of officer entrants consists of physicians, dentists, nurses, chaplains, lawyers, and certain other professionally trained personnel who receive direct appointments into the appropriate professional corps of the services. Nearly one-fifth of all new officer entrants in the 1957 to 1964 period came from this source, with physicians and dentists accounting for the largest share. Physicians, dentists, and certain allied specialists are also subject to induction by special call under the "doctors' draft" provision of the draft law. Draft calls have been placed for physicians by the Department of Defense in most recent years, and less frequently, for dentists and certain other specialists in the health professions. Since all such personnel have the option of volunteering for direct appointments until the time of induction, almost all have actually entered through acceptance of commissions rather than through the draft. The military services also provide subsidies for professional training of a limited proportion of their officers in health profession fields in exchange for longer service commitments. These include programs for senior medical students and interns, as well as nurses and certain other allied medical specialists.

Service academies. The service academies have traditionally represented the "elite" source of career regular officers. However, due to statutory limitation on enrollments, the academies have accounted for only a small percentage of new officers since World War II. The number of academy graduates receiving commissions averaged 1,800 per year between 1960 and 1964, or about five percent of total new officer entrants. Under legislation enacted in 1964 authorizing an increase in enrollments in the Army and Air Force academies, the number of academy graduates increased to about 2,100 by fiscal year 1968. In addition, several hundred officers have been trained each year by the Coast Guard and Merchant Marine academies.

Other programs. Most of the programs described above normally require a college degree or first professional degree as a condition for entry into the commissioned officer ranks. Channels have, however, been opened to limited numbers of personnel in each service through which noncollege graduates may also enter commissioned officer status. One of the most important of these programs, during World War II and the early postwar period, was the aviation cadet program under which qualified high school graduates were eligible for training as pilots and navigators or in related aeronautical specialties. About 3,400 officers were commissioned upon graduation from these programs in fiscal year 1957. However, the subsequent decline in Air Force pilot training requirements, combined with the sharp expansion in supply of college graduates, enabled the Air Force to meet its requirements for pilot training from ROTC, OCS, and similar college graduate programs and to phase out its aviation cadet program. Relatively small aviation cadet programs were continued by the Navy and Marine Corps.

Comparatively small numbers of noncollege graduate enlisted, and warrant officer personnel have also been advanced to commissioned officer status through direct appointments as "temporary" commissioned officers (in the Navy and Marine Corps) or through special scholarship programs, which have enabled small numbers of enlisted personnel to complete their college education and to enter officer training in exchange for a long-term service commitment.

As in the case of enlisted personnel procurement, the existence of the draft has generally assured the military services of an adequate supply of volunteers for the various officer programs. Selectivity has been high for preferred programs such as the service academies and the ROTC scholarship programs. The sharp expansion in college graduations during the post-World War II period has, moreover, enabled the military services to procure all but a modest fraction of their newly commissioned officers during peacetime years from the ranks of college and professional school graduates. This contrasts sharply with World War II experience when a majority of those commissioned were noncollege graduates. As a consequence of these policies, as well as of continued support of educational programs for active duty officer personnel, the percentage of commissioned officers with college diplomas has increased sharply since the mid-1950s, from 55.5% in 1956 to 72.3% in 1965.

Another indication of the generally favorable officer procurement climate in the late 1950s and early 1960s was a trend toward longer periods of obligated service for new officer entrants. The period of obligated service for service academy graduates was increased from four to five years; tours of duty for ROTC graduates were increased from three to four years in the Air Force and Navy, and corresponding adjustments were made in certain other officer programs.

The military services have, however, been faced with some short-term difficulties in meeting specific officer procurement objectives. These have resulted, at times, from relatively sharp increases in officer procurement quotas, notably during the early phases of the Vietnam force build-up. Thus, between fiscal year 1965 and fiscal year 1967, officer procurement increased from 38,000 to 72,000, a ninety percent expansion over a two-year period. Certain sources of officer procurement, such as ROTC and similar reserve officer training programs for college men, could not readily be expanded to meet this sharp increase in requirements. The number of newly commissioned officers from these programs is largely determined by the number who enrolled either two or four years earlier, either as college freshmen or juniors. Primary reliance was therefore placed upon other programs such as Officer Candidate School and in

the case of the Marine Corps and Navy—upon temporary appointment of senior enlisted men or warrant officers. An additional source
of officer entrants during the period consisted of reserve officers who
were solicited to apply for return to extended active duty.

Among the more specialized officer programs, the procurement
of women nurses has posed recurring difficulties; professional nurses
have been in chronically short supply in the civilian economy and,
since only a very small percentage of nurses are male, the military
services have been obliged to compete directly with civilian
employers in recruitment for their nurse corps. Significantly, nursing
is one of the very few professional fields in which the military
services offer programs providing a complete subsidy for professional
training—in contrast to professional fields such as medicine, where
only a modest proportion of medical officers receive financial
support in their senior medical year or internship—in exchange for an
extended service obligation.

Retention Policies

While the continued existence of the draft has generally assured
an adequate supply of both enlisted and officer entrants into service,
the armed services have reported chronic difficulties during the
post-World War II period in retaining a sufficient proportion of these
entrants in service beyond their initial tours of duty. Low military
personnel retention emerged as a military personnel problem of
major dimensions shortly after the end of the Korean conflict. The
overall reenlistment rate for regular enlistees, which had averaged
fifty-nine percent in fiscal years 1951 to 1953, dropped to
twenty-four percent in fiscal year 1954 and twenty-seven percent in
fiscal year 1955 (see Table 3). In the last case, nearly 400,000 regular
enlisted personnel, of about 550,000 completing tours of duty and
eligible to reenlist, had separated from service.

It became evident, at the outset, that the sharp reduction in the
overall reenlistment rates resulted primarily from the very heavy
losses sustained among the "first-term regulars"—those completing
their initial terms of enlistment in the immediate post-Korea period.
In the second half of fiscal year 1954, when separate Department of
Defense reports on first-term reenlistment rates were first established, the reenlistment rate for first termers was reported at 11%; it
increased only moderately to 15.8% in fiscal year 1955. Moreover,
these first-term enlistees accounted for more than 80% of all regular

Table 3. Reenlistment Rates by Category of Personnel, DOD, Fiscal Years 1950-1968

Fiscal Year		Regular Enlistees			Inductees (Army)
		Total	First Term[a]	Career[b]	
Unadjusted:[c]	1950	59.3	n.a	n.a	n.a
	1951-53 av.	54.6	n.a	n.a	n.a
	1954	23.7	*	n.a	n.a
	1955	27.2	15.8	73.6	3.0
	1956	43.6	22.8	89.7	3.5
Adjusted:[d]	1957	44.0	21.4	85.6	3.6
	1958	51.9	29.2	86.3	2.7
	1959	46.9	30.1	86.6	3.5
	1960	44.4	26.2	85.3	5.9
	1961	51.9	24.4	88.1	9.2
	1962	57.3	25.8	88.8	15.4
	1963	53.1	24.0	88.4	15.0
	1964	50.0	23.4	87.4	12.9
	1965	50.0	22.8	87.3	10.1
	1966-67 av.	46.2	21.6	84.6	3.6
	1968	43.6	21.5	80.6	9.7

* The first-term reenlistment rate for the second half of fiscal year 1954 was about eleven percent, according to unpublished records in the files of OASD (Manpower).

a. First-term regulars: personnel serving on initial terms of enlistment in regular component.

b. Career regulars: personnel serving on second or subsequent term of service as a regular.

c. Reenlistment rate, unadjusted: reenlistments of enlisted personnel separated in a given period, stated as a percentage of the total separated in that period eligible to reenlist.

d. Reenlistment rate, adjusted: since fiscal year 1957, a modified "adjusted" reenlistment rate has been computed, in addition to the "unadjusted" rate. This rate is designed to measure the net reenlistment yield from a group of separatees based upon normal date of completion of tour of duty rather than actual date of reenlistment action, and thus provides a more valid index of retention trends.

Source: U.S. Department of Defense.

enlisted personnel separations during this period. In contrast, the reenlistment rate for the much smaller group of "career regulars" averaged 74% in fiscal year 1955 and 80% or higher in each subsequent year.

The ten-year period following 1955 witnessed some improvement in reenlistment rates and in the size of the career force. As compared to a rate of 15.8% in fiscal year 1955, the first-term reenlistment rate rose to 30.1% in fiscal year 1959 and ranged between 22% and 26% in the following six-year period. Concurrently, the proportion of career personnel in the enlisted force increased from only 25% in 1954 to about 65% in 1965 as a combined result of improved retention, of a reduction in total military personnel strengths, and of a gradual "maturing" of the force. Officer retention rates and career manning ratios exhibited a general parallel trend.

Despite this improvement, military officials have continued to express concern about inadequate overall retention of military personnel. For example, a major review of the military pay system, completed in 1967, found "substantial and continuing shortages" of career officers and enlisted personnel with four to fourteen years of service and concluded that "re-enlistment and retention rates continue at levels substantially below those required to fill this gap" (U.S. Department of Defense, 1967: XIX).

The emphasis placed by military manpower officials upon personnel retention has conditioned a wide range of military manpower policies and programs. The need to increase the general career attractiveness of military service was advanced as a justification for a series of major legislative measures, including provision for increased reenlistment bonuses in 1954; military pay increases in 1955, 1958, 1963, and succeeding years; and improvement in various military "fringe" benefits, including dependents' medical care, survivors' benefits, group life insurance, and extension of certain veterans' benefits to active duty military personnel, among others. Administrative actions taken by the services to improve reenlistment rates included increased choices of base and duty assignments to reenlistees, opportunities for training or retraining upon reenlistment, and establishment of "recruitment from within" procedures, designed to acquaint all servicemen with the benefits to them of continuing in service on a career basis.

In addition to a continuing interest in improving overall retention of qualified personnel, military officials have been particularly concerned about inadequate retention in their most technical specialties. During the 1950s and early 1960s, first-term reenlistment rates had been generally lowest in the most technical occupational groups and highest in nontechnical occupations. Specialties with chronically low reenlistment rates included electronics equipment repairmen and operators, surveyors and draftsmen, intelligence analysts, musicians, and disbursing and finance specialists. Conversely, food service personnel, motor transport operators, and certain other less skilled occupations consistently reenlisted at much higher than average rates. The full range of difference in these rates is suggested by the fact that-with some exceptions—the reenlistment rate for food service personnel exceeded that for electronic maintenance technicians by ratios of between two to one, and four to one in all services.

As evidence accumulated on the extent of imbalance in career manning among various occupational categories, increased policy emphasis was placed upon selective reenlistment incentives for individuals with particular skills or special qualifications. In 1958, based on a recommendation of the Cordiner Committee, Congress enacted authority for a "proficiency pay" system under which monthly pay rates could be increased by amounts up to $150 to specialists in critical skills or possessing special qualifications. In 1964 a further specialist pay incentive was authorized in the form of variable reenlistment bonuses under which bonuses as much as four times the standard amount could be awarded to critically needed specialists.

THE SUPPLY OF
MILITARY MANPOWER

The preceding sections have described the scope of military manpower needs and the major programs and policies designed to meet these needs in recent decades. In this section we shall examine the supply of manpower for military service: the size of the manpower pool available for service, the number and characteristics of new entrants, and the key factors influencing their decisions to enter or continue in service.

If the military services were competing for voluntary entrants in a free labor market, the factors influencing the supply of manpower for military service would, in principle, be similar to those governing the supply of workers for civilian industries and occupations. They would include, for example, considerations of relative wage levels, working conditions, and individual likes or dislikes for particular kinds of work. However, in recent decades the initial supply of manpower for military service has not been governed by individual preferences and market forces alone, but has been determined to a significant extent by the existence of a military service obligation under the law. As a result it is necessary to distinguish between the de jure supply of manpower for service, i.e., the pool of militarily liable and qualified men who are available for induction under the existing draft law and regulations, and the voluntary supply of manpower for service, i.e., the number of men (and women) who would be available for voluntary military service in the absence of any military service obligation.

The former measure of manpower supply is capable of estimation with reasonable accuracy, based on the operating experience of the Selective Service System and collateral data. The latter measure is far more difficult to estimate since many individuals who volunteer for service, under conditions of a draft, do so only in preference to being drafted and would not volunteer for service in a completely free labor market. Both of these supply concepts have, however, played a significant role in influencing military manpower policies in the past two decades. We shall therefore separately examine the meaning and derivation of each of these supply measures and some of their policy implications.

The Selective Service Manpower Pool

Under the draft law all young men residing in the United States and its territories, except those already in service, must register with their local draft boards at their eighteenth birthday and are subject to classification as to their availability for service shortly after they register. If they are found available for service and pass the military qualifying examination, they become liable for induction under the law, beginning at age eighteen and one-half, and continue to be liable until their twenty-sixth birthday. If they have received a deferment—for example, because of college enrollment—this liability is extended until their thirty-fifth birthday.

Among those classified as available for service, the draft law regulations also prescribe the sequence under which they will be ordered for service. The first two "orders of call" consist of (1) registrants who have been found delinquent in fulfilling their obligations under the draft law, and (2) volunteers for induction. Following these two relatively small categories, the next order of call consisted, until January 1970, of men aged nineteen to twenty-five years. Inductees were selected from this group by each local draft board in inverse order of age, i.e., oldest first. This age group was the only age group required to meet regular Selective Service calls since original enactment of the current draft law in 1948.[1] However, the law does authorize the drafting of previously deferred Class I-A registrants, ages twenty-six to thirty-five, as well as men age eighteen and one-half to nineteen, if the latter groups should be needed.

The official Selective Service classification statistics provide a logical point of departure in analyzing the status of draft-liable men. To illustrate, as of July 1964, a total of 15.7 million registrants were reported in the ages of military service liability, that is, including men eighteen and one-half to twenty-six years, as well as those twenty-six to thirty-five years of age without service, if previously deferred. Of this total, 5.1 million were classified as either in military service or as having already fulfilled their military service obligation, and nearly two million additional were classified as "available for service." These two groups, in combination, constituted the "gross" supply of manpower which had been made potentially available under the existing Selective Service law. Of the remainder, nearly four million had been found disqualified for service for physical, mental, or moral reasons; an additional 1.3 million were deferred as students; 2.9 million had been deferred as fathers or because of other dependency grounds, and about 260,000 had received occupational deferments or other deferments or exemptions under the law. Nearly 200,000 had not yet been classified by their local boards.

These summary classification statistics are of limited value, however, in analyzing the actual participation of given age groups of men in military service. Since the draft system has enabled young men to fulfill their obligations at varying ages, within the draft-liable age span, the full extent of military service participation by particular age classes, or "cohorts," can best be measured by analyzing the experience of age groups which have already completed their normal span of military service liability, i.e., at age twenty-six. There was a sharp drop in military service experience for men in this age group—from seventy percent in June 1958 to only forty-six percent in 1966, mainly as a result of the reduction in military manpower needs following the mid-1950s. To accommodate this reduced military requirement, draft deferment rules had been liberalized in many ways; dependency deferments had been broadened to include all fathers, and, for a two-year period between September 1963 and August 1965, to effectively defer married men who were nonfathers, as well. Student deferments were liberally extended to nearly all full-time undergraduate and graduate students. Military qualification standards were increased, mainly through the revision of the mental test standards. Occupational deferments were also granted more liberally, particularly to college graduates engaged in defense-related research or in teaching activities.

These policies had the effect of limiting the growth of the de jure supply of qualified men in the prime Selective Service pool in Class I-A, but they inevitably resulted in increased public criticism of the fairness of the draft selection system itself. From a manpower policy standpoint, particular criticism was directed at the highly uneven incidence of military service among young men with different educational backgrounds. Studies initiated by the Department of Defense indicated that, among men aged twenty-seven to thirty-four years in 1964, only twenty-seven percent of those with one or more years of graduate study had even entered military service, as contrasted with more than seventy percent of high school graduates and thirty percent of those with only a grade school education. Among the latter group, the low incidence of military service resulted mainly from the fact that a large proportion, including many would-be volunteers, had failed to pass the mental qualification tests. In the case of the graduate students, the population group most qualified to serve in terms of educational level, low rates of military service participation were due to a combination of factors; many young men in this category had been able to "pyramid" successive deferments, moving from undergraduate student deferments to deferments for postgraduate study for dependency or occupation, and thus reaching age twenty-six without becoming vulnerable to induction. These findings were highlighted in the course of reviews of the operation of the draft law conducted both by the Executive Branch and the Congress in 1966-1967. They prompted certain initial changes in draft deferment policies affecting college students, including discontinuation of most graduate student deferments (effective in mid-1968) as well as a provision barring automatic fatherhood deferments in the future to registrants who had previously requested and received student deferments.[2]

From the standpoint of military manpower supply, the survey results on military service participation also provided valuable insights as to the modes of entry into service of those with some military experience (see Table 5). Among all military service entrants surveyed, aged twenty-six to thirty-four years in 1964, about eighty-four percent had entered active duty as enlisted men (either as enlistees or draftees); 5.5% had directly entered officer training or received direct appointments; and an additional 9.4% had originally entered into reserve training programs. The proportion of entrants who had directly entered active duty as enlisted men (either as enlistees or draftees) varied inversely with educational level, from

Table 4. Classification of Selective Service Registrants, 18½-26½ Years of Age, By Single Year of Age, July 1964

Classification	Total 18½-26½	18½-19½	19½-20½	20½-21½	21½-22½	22½-23½	23½-24½	24½-25½	25½-26½
Total Registrants (000)[a]	10,568	1,360	1,386	1,454	1,444	1,311	1,234	1,207	1,172
Percentage Distribution:									
Total Registrants	100.0	100.0	100.0	100.0	100.0	100.0	100.0	100.0	100.0
Unclassified	4.1	20.8	7.1	1.2	0.9	0.6	0.5	0.3	0.3
Classified (total)	95.9	79.2	92.9	98.8	99.1	99.4	99.5	99.7	99.7
Available for Service (I-A)	15.7	37.8	33.5	20.3	13.9	8.2	3.1	1.8	1.1
Deferred:	48.2	30.1	41.0	50.6	51.7	52.5	55.6	53.5	52.3
Disqualified (I-Y, IV-F)	19.0	7.0	12.4	20.3	21.2	21.9	24.1	23.8	22.9
Students (I-S, II-S)	11.2	20.2	20.9	18.5	13.0	6.6	3.5	2.1	1.0
Dependency (III-A)	16.0	2.4	6.5	10.5	15.5	21.0	25.0	24.9	26.2
Occupational Deferments (II-A, II-C)	1.3	0.2	0.6	0.8	1.3	2.1	2.2	2.0	1.7
Other Deferred Groups	0.7	0.3	0.6	0.5	0.7	0.9	0.8	0.7	0.5
In Service or Completed Service[a]	32.0	11.3	18.4	27.9	33.5	38.7	40.8	44.4	46.3
In Active Service	12.1	7.9	12.4	15.2	15.3	12.8	12.9	9.8	6.8
In Reserve Service	7.9	3.2	4.7	8.4	9.0	9.0	10.0	10.5	9.2
Completed Service	12.0	0.2	1.3	4.3	9.2	13.9	17.9	24.1	30.3

a. Excludes individuals who enlisted at age seventeen, prior to age of Selective Service registration, and who were still on active duty as of July 1964.
Source: U.S. Department of Defense. Adapted from sample inventory of Selective Service registrants.

ninety-four percent of all nonhigh school graduates to only 33.5% of the college graduates. Among the latter, nearly half had entered officer training programs or received direct appointments—options restricted mainly to college graduates during the past two decades. Reserve programs, including both reserve officer training and reserve enlistment programs, which often involved limited active duty training periods, were also relatively popular among college graduates. Over seventeen percent of college graduates with service had entered into these programs as compared to only five percent of those without high school degrees and ten percent of the high school graduates.

Table 5. Military Service Participation Rates and Mode of Entry Into Service, By Educational Level, Men Aged 26-34, 1964

	Total Ages 26-34	Less Than High School Graduate	High School Graduate No College	Some College	College Graduate
Total population (000)	9,830	3,877	3,306	1,408	1,212
Percentage distribution by military service status					
With military service	63.3	57.9	73.3	66.1	51.0
No military service	36.7	42.1	26.7	33.9	49.0
Total	100.0	100.0	100.0	100.0	100.0
Percentage distribution by military service entrants by mode of entry					
Enlistment	50.3	61.0	53.8	43.2	8.7
Induction	34.1	32.8	35.7	39.8	24.8
Officer programs	5.5	*	.2	2.7	48.9
Reserves	9.4	5.4	9.8	13.0	17.3
Other and unknown	.6	.9	.5	.3	.2
Total	100.0	100.0	100.0	100.0	100.0

* Less than .05%

Source: U.S. Department of Defense. Based on Census Bureau Survey of the Civilian Male Population, Ages 16-34, and Department of Defense Survey of Military Personnel, October 1964.

Among those men who initially entered active duty in the enlisted ranks, the contrast in the proportion of those enlisting—rather than waiting to be drafted—is equally sharp, by educational level. Nearly two-thirds of the nonhigh school graduates and sixty percent of the high school graduates with no college entered as enlistees. However, among college graduates who entered as enlisted men, only one-fourth had volunteered, the remainder entering as draftees.

One clear generalization is suggested by these statistics: under conditions of a military service obligation, men with the greatest educational attainment, i.e., the greatest investment in future civilian careers, have, when faced with the necessity of enlisted service, in large part elected to serve in those programs involving the shortest interruption in their personal career, such as reserve service or induction. Those with the least education have had the greatest propensity to enter regular enlistment programs.

These comparisons alone, however, do not provide a basis for estimating the number and characteristics of truly voluntary enlistees, i.e., those who would have enlisted even in the absence of the draft, nor do they provide other needed insights as to the motivating factors influencing enlistment and continuation in military service. Relevant research findings on these factors are discussed in the following section.

The Supply of Volunteers for Military Service

Considerable research has been conducted in recent years designed to measure the influence of both economic and noneconomic factors upon the supply of volunteers for military service. Such information has been required by manpower officials responsible for military personnel recruitment and retention programs. This research has been stimulated, too, by increased public interest in the issue of an all-volunteer force. In the latter context, President Johnson directed the Department of Defense to undertake a comprehensive study of military manpower procurement policies in 1964, and specified that, as one major objective, this study should evaluate the feasibility of ending the draft during the following ten-year period. (Results of this study were included in testimony by Assistant Secretary of Defense Thomas D. Morris; see U.S. Congress, House Committee on Armed Services, 1966.)

As part of this study, a comprehensive sample survey of military service experience, plans, and attitudes was conducted in the fall of

1964, including both civilian men, aged sixteen to thirty-four years, and those in military service. In order to obtain firsthand information on the influence of the draft and of other factors upon decisions to volunteer for service, military personnel on active duty were asked two pertinent questions. The first question solicited the most important reason for entry into active duty, listing twelve possible answers of which three were designed to identify those primarily motivated by the draft. The second, more direct question asked, "If there had been no draft and you had not had any military obligation at the time you first entered active military service, do you think you would have entered the Service?"

Analysis of the responses to each of these questions indicated a high overall degree of consistency. Among first-term enlistees, nearly four out of ten indicated that the draft was a primary factor in their enlistment decision and that they probably would not have enlisted in the absence of the draft (see Table 6). Of junior officers on their first tour of active duty, the proportion who stated they would not have entered if there had been no draft, was slightly higher: forty-one percent. The proportion of junior officers who were draft motivated varied, understandably, with the type of program under which they had entered. Draft motivation was lowest among the service academy graduates (eleven percent) and highest among professionally trained officers, such as physicians, dentists, and lawyers, who had entered through direct appointment after completing their civilian professional education (fifty-eight percent).

Based on these survey results and related data, the Department of Defense study estimated that if the draft were terminated and no additional recruitment incentives were offered, the number of enlistments would decline to about 235,000 by 1970 as compared to an actual average of about 480,000 new enlisted personnel entries in the five years prior to Vietnam, and that officer accessions would also decline substantially. These projections also indicated that the maximum military force which could be maintained in the early 1970s under these conditions would be about 2.0 million—a strength level about one-half million lower than the lowest required since 1951. These estimates assumed relatively favorable civilian employment conditions, i.e., an unemployment rate of about four percent.

The same study also provided significant insights as to the characteristics of "true" volunteers for service as compared to those who were draft motivated. Younger enlistees—those under twenty

Table 6. Estimated Percentage of Draft-Motivated Enlistees By
Selected Characteristics, 1964[a]

Characteristics	Percentage Draft-Motivated
Total	38.0
Service	
Army	43.2
Navy	32.6
Air Force	42.9
Marine Corps	30.4
Age at Enlistment	
17 to 19 years	31.4
20 to 25 years	57.9
Education	
Less than high school graduate	23.0
High school graduate	40.2
Some college or more	58.0
Mental Group	
Group I and II	44.0
Group III	33.2
Group IV	29.2

a. Based on responses of first-term regular enlisted personnel to question, "If there had been no draft and you had not had any military obligation at the time you first entered Active Military Service do you think you would have entered the service?" Percentage draft-motivated based on percentage responding "No, probably" and "No, definitely." In computing percentages, those responding "no idea" were excluded from the base.

Source: Department of Defense Survey of Active Duty Military Personnel as of October 1964.

years at the time of enlistment—were much less likely to be draft motivated than older enlistees, many of whom had volunteered for service only when their induction appeared imminent. Similarly, the proportion of draft-motivated volunteers was lowest among men who had not completed high school or with relatively low mental test scores; it was highest among those with one or more years of college and with high mental test scores.

In response to a question as to the "single most important reason" for enlistment into service, the motives cited most frequently by the nondraft motivated volunteer were related to the training or educational opportunities afforded by military service. Over twenty-two percent of all first-term enlisted men surveyed—and more than one-third of the nondraft motivated enlistees—gave these as primary reasons. Other enlistees also saw military service as a path to personal development and as a way to broaden their horizons, as evidenced by the large proportions who indicated that they had enlisted "to become more mature and self-reliant," or "for the travel, excitement and new experiences." Only 5.5% of all first-term enlisted men surveyed offered patriotism—the "desire to serve my country"—as their primary motive for peacetime enlistment and a similar percentage (forty-nine percent) indicated that they had enlisted because "career opportunities looked better than in civilian life."

The results of this survey, as well as of earlier attitude surveys, indicated that pay, as such, was not as important a factor in initial enlistment decisions as might be expected. Less than nine percent of all sixteen- to nineteen-year-old civilian youth surveyed indicated that pay was "the most important factor in choosing a job or career." Among those who said they would not enlist if there were no draft, less than four percent indicated that they would consider volunteering if military pay were equal to that which they could earn in civilian life, and only seventeen percent would consider volunteering even if military pay were raised to a level "considerably higher" than civilian wages.

Official estimates of the hypothetical cost of an all-volunteer force—at a pre-Vietnam force level—have been expressed in a relatively broad cost range, from a low of $4 billion to a high of about $17 billion.[3] A continuing program of research, utilizing a variety of analytical methods, has been sponsored by the Department of Defense in order to develop a more thorough understanding of the complex of factors influencing the rate of initial enlistment and to

develop more reliable estimates of the possible effect of increased
pay or other recruitment incentives.

Studies of Military Personnel Retention

Thus far, we have considered only the factors affecting the supply
of initial entrants into military service. The total number of men
available at any time to meet military manpower needs is
determined, however, by two key variables: the number of new
entrants and their average period of total service. The latter function
is critically influenced by first-term reenlistment or retention rates,
i.e., the proportion of entrants eligible to reenlist, who elect to
continue on active duty beyond an initial tour of service.

As in the case of enlistment experience, a variety of analytical
approaches are available in studying reenlistment behavior. These
include attempts to analyze fluctuations in reenlistment rates over a
period of years (time-series analysis); analysis of the differential
characteristics of reenlistees as compared to nonreenlistees during a
particular period (cross-sectional analysis); and, finally, insights
afforded by attitudinal surveys, which have attempted to identify
key motivational factors influencing reenlistment decisions.

Time-series analysis. Attempts to analyze the significance of
fluctuations in reenlistment rates, as officially reported, have been
seriously handicapped by certain inherent limitations in the basic
statistical data. Two methods of computation of reenlistment rates
have been used. The first, the "unadjusted" rate. is simply a crude
ratio (expressed as a percentage) of the number of personnel
reenlisting in a given period. This method suffers from obvious
limitations; under reenlistment procedures in most services,
individuals desiring to reenlist can generally do so before completion
of their tours of duty. This rate, thus, compares reenlistments drawn
from one entry population to nonreenlistees drawn from a different
and earlier entry group. As a result, this "unadjusted" rate has
tended to fluctuate erratically in relation to the size of successive
entering groups and to changing policies affecting "early" discharges
for reenlistment.

In an attempt to develop a more reliable reenlistment index,
"adjusted" reenlistment rates have been published since 1957 which
measure the relationship between reenlistments and total separatees,
eligible to reenlist, based on the date of normal expiration of tour of
duty for both reenlistees and separatees. In principle, this ratio for

first-termers should, therefore, provide a valid measure of the trend in reenlistment yields from successive entry classes or cohorts. In practice, however, a variety of administrative and accounting factors have continued to limit the validity of the "adjusted" rates as indexes of trends in career attractiveness—particularly over short-term periods.

From collateral information it is possible, however, to explain certain of the broad movements in reenlistment rate trends shown in Table 4. It will be noted that the reenlistment rates for first-term enlistees dropped particularly sharply in the fiscal years 1954-1955, following the Korean War period, and then were maintained at a significantly higher level in the following decade, albeit with considerably year-to-year fluctuation. A major factor contributing to the sharp initial drop in reenlistment rates following Korea, and to the subsequent recovery, was the fact that enlistments into some services during the Korean war period, notably the Air Force and Navy, had increased very sharply as a result of the step-up in draft calls. Relatively few of these draft motivated enlistees reenlisted following the completion of their tours of duty, mainly in fiscal years 1954 and 1955—hence, the sharp reduction in the rates. Direct confirmation of this interpretation is provided by the Air Force sample attitude surveys of enlistees during this period. These surveys indicated that among a group of Air Force enlistees who had entered during fiscal year 1952, 38.7% stated that the primary reason for enlistment was "to avoid being drafted," whereas among the smaller group of airmen who had enlisted in fiscal year 1957, only 7.2% indicated this as their primary reason. Based on statements of reenlistment plans, only small percentages (less than ten percent) of these draft-motivated enlistees reenlisted. In contrast, the number of enlistees who indicated an original interest in an Air Force career had remained fairly stable in these two years. In turn, the estimated reenlistment yield was much higher from this group, averaging more than thirty percent.

This evidence that the proportion of young men oriented to a military career has tended to be fairly stable in recent years is further supported by an analysis of military service participation rates of men aged twenty-seven to twenty-nine years during the ten-year period 1953-1963. This age group was selected because over ninety percent of the men in active military service in these ages are "career" men who have continued in service beyond an obligated tour of duty. When the number in this age group in active service is expressed as a percentage of men who had ever been in military service, a rising trend is indicated over the decade—from 6.5% in 1953 to 11.9% in 1963. However, when expressed as a percentage of the total population, the percentage of military service participants is found to be quite stable: it rose from a level of about five percent in the years 1953-1955 to about six percent by 1957 and fluctuated in a narrow range of slightly above six percent in the six succeeding years (see Table 7).

One of the corollaries of this analysis is that those groups in the population most prone to enlist in service voluntarily in the absence of a draft are also likely to have the highest reenlistment rates and thus to contribute disproportionately to the supply of career military personnel. For this purpose, we shall next examine available data on reenlistment rate differentials by socioeconomic characteristics.

Cross-section analysis. A variety of reenlistment rate studies are available in which reenlistment rates have been compared for personnel with differing socioeconomic characteristics, as measured by such variables as educational level, race, economic status of

Table 7. U.S. Male Population Aged 27-29 Years By Active Military Service Status, 1953-1963

(numbers in thousands)

Year Attained Age 27-29	Total Males 27-29	Ever in Service		In Active Service at Ages 27-29		
		Number	% of Total	Number	% of total males	% of ever served
1953	3,736	2,975	79.6	194	5.2	6.5
1954	3,703	2,827	76.3	181	4.9	6.4
1955	3,681	2,580	70.1	195	5.3	7.6
1956	3,663	2,448	66.8	210	5.7	8.6
1957	3,628	2,386	65.8	222	6.1	9.3
1958	3,568	2,344	65.7	228	6.4	9.7
1959	3,506	2,306	65.8	228	6.5	9.9
1960	3,486	2,207	63.3	218	6.3	10.0
1961	3,348	2,093	62.5	209	6.2	10.1
1962	3,354	1,936	57.7	209	6.2	11.0
1963	3,324	1,766	53.1	211	6.3	11.9

Source: Harold Wool (1968: 129).

parents, and geographical origin. Representative findings are summarized below:

(1) *Educational level.* Generally, the inverse relationship between educational level and propensity to enlist, previously noted, applies to reenlistment rates as well. For example, an Air Force study of reenlistment experience of airmen originally enlisted in the years 1956-1958 indicated that reenlistment rates of first-term airmen with less than high school education averaged thirty-one percent as compared to twenty-two percent for high school graduates and eighteen percent for those with some college. Scattered data on reenlistment rates by education for other services have revealed a generally similar pattern. An obvious interpretation is that the better educated enlisted men, as a group, were much more likely to have been influenced by "draft pressure" in their original enlistment decision, hence, much less likely to continue in service voluntarily beyond an initial tour.

(2) *Race.* One of the most consistent findings of recent studies of differential reenlistment behavior has been the tendency of Negro enlisted personnel to reenlist at much higher rates than their white counterparts. Reports compiled by the Department of Defense for the years 1964-1967 show that in each of these years the first-term reenlistment rates for Negroes were more than twice as great as for white personnel.
The explanation for this pattern lies mainly in the fact that the armed services—to a far greater degree than in civilian society—have afforded Negro personnel an opportunity to work and to live in a nonsegregated and nondiscriminatory environment. This applies both to occupational and advancement opportunities within service for the Negro as compared to civilian alternatives, and to the general absence of racial discrimination in the on-base military community.

(3) *Regional origin.* A variety of sociological studies indicate that a greater-than-proportionate share of career military personnel have come from the South. Janowitz in his study of elite military officers, as of 1950, found that a disproportionate number of Army and Navy officers had either been born in the South or had a southern affiliation. This pattern was also evident in more recent survey data on geographical origins of career enlisted personnel as of 1964.

(4) *Socioeconomic background of parents.* An unpublished longitudinal study of the differential characteristics of Air Force reenlistees and separatees, indicates significantly higher reenlistment rates among first-term airmen drawn from lower-economic-status families as measured by family income, rental value of home, and father's occupation. In the same study, airmen coming from rural areas and small towns had a higher reenlistment rate than those from large cities. Similar patterns have also been observed in Navy and Army surveys of reenlistment attitudes.

The above findings—although still not definitive in all respects—reinforce the inferences we have drawn, based upon analysis of factors affecting the supply of initial entrants into military service. The social and economic background characteristics of military service entrants, such as educational level, race, geographical origin, and family status, which seem best correlated with propensity to reenlist in military service, also have a direct bearing upon the perceptions of servicemen of their attainable income and occupational goals in civilian life. These perceptions, in turn, serve as standards of comparison of "yardsticks" against which the individual serviceman can assess the relative benefits of a military service career.

Attitudinal survey findings. We would, however, be guilty of seriously oversimplifying the complex of forces affecting individual career decisons if we conclude our analysis here. Individual preferences for particular types of work clearly play an important role in occupational decisions. These preferences may be influenced by many psychological and sociological factors: the individual's own aptitudes and skills, the working and living conditions associated with different pursuits, the social status or "image" of the occupation, the various personal associations involved, and the values he assigns to certain noneconomic rewards or costs associated with different occupational careers.

In order to identify and rank the relative importance of various influences upon reenlistment decisions, the military services have sponsored a large number of surveys of their personnel in the past two decades. Despite differences in coverage, timing, and methodology of the survey materials, certain generalizations suggest themselves.

First, it is clear that considerations other than strictly economic or financial factors have influenced a large proportion of first-term personnel against remaining in military service on a career basis. These have included such considerations as limitations of personal freedom; unsatisfactory living, working, and disciplinary conditions; dissatisfaction with assignment policies and skill utilization; and enforced absences from home and family.

Second, such factors as security and retirement benefits, training, and travel opportunities rank high among the positive aspects of military service for men who have elected to continue in military service on a career basis.

Finally, in most of the surveys we have reviewed, "pay" as such does not appear at the head of the list of stated reasons for either reenlisting or separating from service—although increased pay ranks high as a needed improvement. However, in those surveys directed at measuring the potential effectiveness of pay increases as a reenlistment inducement, significant proportions of personnel have responded that such incentives—if sufficiently great—would in fact induce them to continue in service.

Thy apparent contradiction in survey findings as to the relative role played by pay factors in reenlistment decisions illustrates one of the serious limitations of attitudinal surveys for this purpose. Most of the attitudinal surveys conducted among military personnel have been based on structured questionnaires in which the respondent is forced to select among a number of predetermined factors, or incentives, influencing his plans or attitudes. This method fails to allow for the fact that career decisions are often the result of a complex series of influences—some operating upon individuals for a period of years—and often not clearly perceived or identified by the individual himself. Under these conditions, the precise wording or form of the question asked can be decisive and can produce seemingly contradictory results.

Further progress in our understanding of this aspect of human behavior will, therefore, continue to require a combination of research strategies. It is clear that socioeconomic background factors, such as educational level, and race, have played important roles in both enlistment and reenlistment decisions. The capability afforded by modern computers to manipulate large numbers of variables permits the development of sophisticated multivariate regression models in which the influence of changing "mixes" of personnel, based on these background factors, can be separately measured, and enlistment or reenlistment trends for each of these groups can be analyzed in relation to other key variables, such as changes in relative pay, unemployment conditions, "draft pressure," or conditions of service life. Further insight as to the processes of occupational choice could also probably be obtained by use of more intensive motivational surveys in which greater reliance is placed upon depth interview techniques (with open-end responses) rather than upon the more limited structured questionnaires.

SOME TENTATIVE
CONCLUSIONS

Although there are, thus, clear limitations to our current knowledge of the relative importance of various factors in influencing enlistment and reenlistment decisions, our summary of available research does permit us to reach certain broad conclusions concerning the supply of volunteers for military service.

(1) In recent years thy existence of the draft has been the most important single factor motivating young men to volunteer for service either as enlistees or officers. In the absence of a draft obligation the loss of volunteers would be particularly great among those men with above average educational backgrounds or with specialized professional or technical skills.

(2) Indirectly, the existence of a large number of "draft motivated" volunteers has also significantly affected personnel retention rates. These rates have been lowest for categories of personnel predominantly motivated to volunteer because of the draft; they have also been lowest among groups of separatees who originally entered service during periods of high "draft pressure" such as the Korean war period. Hence, although the number of initial entrants to service would be sharply reduced by discontinuation of the draft (in the absence of other incentives) this effect would be partially offset by reduced turnover among those motivated to enlist on a completely voluntary basis.

(3) Apart from the influence of the draft itself, it is evident that—as in choice among civilian careers—economic factors have significantly affected the number and characteristics of volunteers for military service. Analysis of the socioeconomic background of volunteers consistently indicates that the appeal of military service careers has been greatest for youth with less favorable alternative civilian opportunities—either because of limited education, race, geographic origin, or other personal factors.

(4) However, results of attitudinal surveys suggest that the economic advantages of military service are perceived by such youth as a complex of potential benefits rather than in narrow terms of "pay" alone. Particular importance is attached by youth coming from deprived civilian backgrounds to the training and educational opportunities of military service and to considerations of economic security. Attempts have been made to isolate and measure the specific influence of pay alone, as a factor in enlistments or

reenlistments. In the judgment of this author, these attempts to date have been subject to serious methodological pitfalls.

(5) Finally, it is evident that many factors—other than strictly economic considerations—have influenced young men in their decisions concerning military service careers. These include both job-related factors and those factors related more generally to the style of military life. In the former category are included attitudes to specific military assignments or duty locations, hours and conditions of work, the degree of risk or hardship entailed, the quality of supervision and similar factors. In the latter category are included housing and family living conditions at or near military bases, extent of separation from family and frequency of transfers, and many other personal or sociological factors conditioning attitudes of servicemen and their families to military life. The fact that choice of a military career—unlike a choice among alternative civilian occupations or jobs—does involve acceptance of many constraints not normally entailed in civilian careers is likely, in our judgment, to limit the responsiveness of manpower supply to strictly economic inducements, such as increased pay or advancement opportunities.

The above generalizations are not intended to suggest that the supply of volunteers for military service is rigidly inelastic. They do suggest that any concerted effort designed to substantially increase military manpower supply—in the absence of the draft—should not be limited to pay incentives alone but must encompass the whole range of living and working conditions which shape the image of military service. Certain of these conditions are, of course, inherent in military service, such as limitations of personal freedom, enforced separations from family and home, and the physical risks and discomforts of many military duties. However, other conditions of service are more amenable to management control, including policies to assure more effective utilization of individual skills and abilities, improved housing and family living conditions at military bases, and increased emphasis generally on measures designed to enhance the status of military service as a career.

NOTES

1. Under authority of an amendment to the draft law, enacted in November 1969, this procedure was changed to provide for establishment of a prime-age class system, under which the top priority group for induction (after delinquents

and volunteers) will consist of men who had attained age nineteen at the beginning of a calendar year and of men nineteen to twenty-five years reclassified into class I-A from a deferred status during the year. The order of selection within this prime group is determined by a lottery of birthdates. Those whose birthdates have not been reached for selection by the end of the year will be placed in a progressively lower priority in each succeeding year.

2. In early 1970, following enactment of legislation authorizing a prime-age class system based upon lottery selection, active consideration was being given by the Nixon Administration to additional major revisions in draft deferment policies.

3. This range of cost estimates was, however, subjected to criticism on the part of some economists as being too high, and because it failed to allow for the offsetting reduction in social costs to the nation which were associated with a system of involuntary military service. In March 1969, President Nixon—reflecting his own conviction that a volunteer armed force was a tenable and feasible goal—appointed an Advisory Commission on an All-Volunteer Armed Force, chaired by former Secretary of Defense Thomas Gates, Jr. The commission report estimated the net additional budgetary costs of an all-volunteer force (mainly for increasing first-term pay) at $1.47 billion for a 2.0 million force, $2.12 billion for a 2.5 million force, and $4.55 billion for a 3.0 million force.

REFERENCES

ALTMAN, S. H. and A. E. FECHTER (1967) "The supply of military personnel without a draft," in Papers and Proceedings of the Seventy-Ninth Annual Meeting of the American Economic Association. American Economic Review 57 (May): 19-31.

Civilian Advisory Panel on Military Manpower Procurement (1967) "Report to the House Committee on Armed Services." Washington, D.C.: U.S. Government Printing Office.

Director of Selective Service (1951-1964) "Annual Reports." Washington, D.C.: U.S. Government Printing Office.

FECHTER, A. E. (1967) The Supply of First Term Military Officers. Arlington, Va.: Institute for Defense Analyses.

FRIEDMAN, R. P. and C. LEISTNER [eds.] (1968a) "Compulsory service systems—how can the United States best maintain manpower for an effective defense system." The Forensic Quarterly 42 (May).

———(1968b) "Compulsory service systems—how can the United States best maintain manpower for an effective defense system" The Forensic Quarterly 42 (August).

GINZBERG, E. and D. W. BRAY (1953) The Uneducated. New York: Columbia University Press.

KLASSEN, A. D., Jr. (1966) Military Service in American Life since World War II: An Overview. Chicago: National Opinion Research Center, University of Chicago.

Library of Congress, Legislative Reference Service (1968) "How can the United States best maintain manpower for an effective defense system?—a collection of excerpts and a bibliography relating to the National High School Debate Topic, 1968-1969." Washington, D.C.: U.S. Government Printing Office.

LITTLE, R. (1968) Selective Service and American Society. New York: Russell Sage Foundation.

OI, W. Y. (1967) "The economic cost of the draft," in Papers and Proceedings of the Seventy-Ninth Annual Meeting of the American Economic Association. American Economic Review 57 (May): 19-31.

President's Commission on an All-Volunteer Armed Force (1970) Report. Washington, D.C.: U.S. Government Printing Office.

TAX, S. [ed.] (1967) The Draft—A Handbook of Facts and Alternatives. Chicago: University of Chicago Press.

U.S. Congress, House Committee on Armed Services (1966) Hearings: "Administration and operation of the Selective Service System." Washington, D.C.: U.S. Government Printing Office.

U.S. Congress, House Joint Economic Committee (1967) "Economic effects of Vietnam spending." Washington, D.C.: U.S. Government Printing Office.

U.S. Department of Defense (1967) Modernizing Military Pay, Report of the First Quadrennial Review of Military Compensation 1 (November).

U.S. Department of the Army (1965) Marginal Man and Military Service—A Review. Washington, D.C.

U.S. National Advisory Commission on Selective Service (1967) In Pursuit of Equity: Who Serves When Not All Serve? Washington, D.C.: U.S. Government Printing Office.

WOOL, H. (1968) The Military Specialist: Skilled Manpower for the Armed Forces. Baltimore: Johns Hopkins Press.

Chapter 3

PERSONNEL PERFORMANCE PREDICTION

PAUL D. NELSON

In its review of the military manpower problems of World War I, the Committee on Classification of Personnel in the Army wrote in 1919:

> The American Army was a small one and accepted only physically fit men who could read and write. . . . With the Selective Service Draft system in full swing, it began to be realized that our physical standards were too high and we were falling short in numbers. Again the highly technical character of modern warfare was not realized. . . . Plans based on the experience of previous wars fought by infantry and a limited artillery of small calibre no longer held [U.S. Department of the Army, 1965: 53].

Thus, as early as fifty years ago the armed forces realized the need for something more than simple standards of physical and mental fitness if their technological requirements were to be met by personnel inducted into military service. The necessity for mass mobilization and for selection and training programs to meet the new requirements of the military system of that time, not to mention the historical absence of any systematic body of industrial personnel research, made the military manpower problems of World War I somewhat acute. And though such problems were to be solved with expertise available in those years, their importance lay as much in providing awareness of a need for continuous personnel research in the armed forces as in the specific solutions provided to problems at hand.

The industrialization and scientific progress of those interim fifty years have rendered the armed forces, as Lang (1964) puts it, one of the most technologically advanced sectors of American society in terms of occupational structure. But the complexity of contemporary military systems within our society is more than technological in nature. Janowitz (1964) addresses the modified mission of the armed forces, a mission responsive to increasingly complex and volatile international political relationships as well as to the development of warfare capabilities. The emphasis on the role of the armed forces as a deterrent system in international relations and in national defense, in addition to its combatant role in response to international aggression, has increased the need for scientific management, has made mandatory a prevalent atmosphere of skill, intelligence, and calm among its members, and has required those members of its organization to effectively cope with the unusual contingencies of most every type of environment known to man.

A final element in the character of the military organization within our society, in addition to those technological, strategic, and environmental elements, is its membership structure. Allowing for some variations during the past five decades, the armed forces are basically youthful in age structure, a trend of course which is neither unparalleled in present day civilian organizations nor in the national population itself. Comparative to large business and industrial organization, however, the armed forces remain composed of predominantly young men and, furthermore, are characterized by a relatively high degree of personnel turnover. Lang, for example, in a summary of military rank structure trends, presents data indicating that more than fifty percent of the officer and enlisted personnel fall within the first three and four grades of rank, respectively; grades are for the most part reflective of the first three or four years of military service representing an age range of approximately seventeen through twenty-five years (Lang, 1964).

One major impact of these several characteristics of the military organization upon its management has been a search for systems of efficient personnel performance predictions. The engineer employs prediction techniques in the development of life-expectancy forecasts of material technologies; strategies and tactics employed in military operations are based upon predictions of political-economic-military events; and long-range plans for manpower resources available for the armed forces are based upon population forecasts or predictions. So, too, the maintenance of reliably manned military systems and operations, under circumstances of complex technology, mission, environment, and relatively high personnel turnover, is dependent increasingly upon the capability to predict human behavior. Personnel decisions and interventions exercised by military management under the traditional labels of screening, selection, classification, training, assignment, maintenance, and retention are all in theory, if not always in practice, premised upon personnel performance prediction capability.

PERSONNEL PERFORMANCE RESEARCH

The volumes of personnel performance research on the military environment conducted during the past fifty years—most of which has been accomplished during the last twenty-five years—are probably not surpassed by any other major work organization within our society. Selected bibliographies covering the past two decades of research on selection, classification, training, and performance evaluation provide a sample of the efforts of the Army (HumRRO, 1968), Navy (Bureau of Naval Personnel, 1963), and Air Force (Elson, 1965). More substantive accounts of major issues confronted in military personnel research during the past two decades are provided in the published proceedings of a tri-service conference on selection research sponsored by the Office of Naval Research (1961) and, more recently, by a somewhat broader review of psychological research in the military today (Uhlaner, 1967).

In any review of the behavioral problems studied in the armed forces, one must keep in mind the cultural context in which such developments have occurred. The history of national and international affairs during the past fifty years, new technologies, the role of the behavioral scientist in industrial and public institutions, and the *zeitgeist* of psychological and sociological research in academic communities cannot be overlooked as partially influential factors in determining the course of personnel research within the armed forces. A recent review by Uhlaner (1968) of the role research psychologists have fulfilled in the Army from 1917 to 1967 provides a rather unique example of the historical approach so often required to better appreciate industrial research developments.

What then have been the major problems and orientations in military personnel research having to do with performance prediction over the past fifty years? It is the thesis of this chapter that the past fifty years of personnel performance prediction research in the armed forces can be represented by five major criterion orientations: *task proficiency, emotional adjustment, motivational effectiveness, interpersonal effectiveness,* and *systems effectiveness.* Each of those criterion orientations must be considered only analytically differentiable from the others and all are considered vital.

Task Proficiency

The genesis of personnel research in the armed forces, and perhaps the most developed area of performance prediction to date, is in the assessment of cognitive aptitudes required for proficient task performance in military occupations. The fact that psychologists, among all behavioral scientists, have been frequently identified with military research and by profession concerned with individual differences in mental functioning has undoubtedly influenced the preponderance of research in this area. Still, when one considers the high military personnel turnover, the hundreds of thousands of young men who each year must be acculturated and technically prepared for a vast array of military assignments, and the relatively little transfer of civilian skills to military jobs among the young men entering military life, it seems logical that major efforts would be made to develop means for estimating which men would do best in which jobs and means for training them to do so.

A major concern during the earliest stages of mobilization for World War I was the literacy level of conscriptees, a factor of utmost importance for training and on-the-job performance in a technical military world. Mass psychological testing, utilizing the Army Alpha and Beta tests developed by Yerkes and his associates (1921) during World War I, marked the beginning of formal mental testing in the armed forces, the primary goal of which was to differentiate individuals on their potential to profit from training. During that first world war, approximately 1,700,000 men were examined psychologically. Within the initial six months of 1918 alone, nearly 230,000 men were assigned to newly established "Development Battalions" for the special training of those considered physically, mentally, or morally "marginal" for military service. Only slightly more than half of these men were eventually retained for duty. Of approximately eighteen million men psychologically examined during the second world war, nearly five million were rejected from service—forty percent for illiteracy. Even by 1951, during the first eighteen months of the Korean conflict, nearly one-third of some two million Selective Service registrants examined were rejected from service; over half of these were considered relatively untrainable by standards of the Army General Classification Test (AGCT), a general cognitive aptitude screening test employed in various forms since World War II (U.S. Department of the Army, 1965).

The effect of such events over the years has led to an increasing awareness within the armed forces that individual differences of great magnitude exist among those men entering military service. Many men who seemingly adjust and perform adequately in civilian pursuits of life are marginal in aptitude for effective performance in the military where mass training programs must be executed over short periods of time and where duty assignments present different stresses from those encountered in civilian life. King and his colleagues (Department of the Army, 1965) present a comprehensive review of marginal man research in the military over the past fifty years, concluding somewhat philosophically that "Every man is marginal. Most of us are marginal for some things and for most things some of us are marginal."

One of the major problems encountered in developing selection and aptitude classification tests is that time is required for their validation. Such a requirement is frequently incompatible with demands to immediately implement a new selection program. Then, too, even with properly validated tests one is frequently faced in the military with a less than desirable selection ratio, a situation in which there are scarcely enough men available to fill the jobs required, let alone selecting the more promising candidates from among the total manpower pool available. The latter dilemma, of course, can benefit the long-range development of valid selection procedures in a new program by allowing men of a relatively wide range of aptitudes to fill the jobs.

By and large, however, substantial progress has been made in aptitude testing over the years. Flanagan and others (1948) review the development of standardized tests for selection of aviators in World War II; that work has been extended successfully to the point that aviator performance prediction systems have been developed sequentially from procurement through various stages of training, thus providing a system for performance quality control (Shoenberger et al., 1963). Fuchs (1967) and Fields (1967) discuss aptitude screening and occupational classification testing for enlisted personnel of the armed forces, developments which have resulted in the

standardized Armed Forces Qualification Test batteries and an array
of occupationally oriented classification test batteries calling forth
verbal, arithmetic, mechanical, clerical, electronic, and spatial apper-
ception aptitudes, among others. Within the past ten years, too, with
accelerated utilization of high speed computers, the armed forces
have begun to develop more efficient methods of optimizing the
allocation of personnel (from among any given distribution of
aptitude profiles) to various occupational fields and assignments.
Certainly, as exemplified by Cronbach and Gleser (1965), the
problems of selection and classification of personnel, and the
development of psychological tests for such purposes, have been
increasingly viewed within the context of decision theory.

The predictive validity of cognitive aptitude tests has rested
primarily with performance in training, as should be expected since
training performance criteria have been by far most frequently used.
Information on success in completion of training programs, as well as
training grades, are accessible in relatively short periods of time; they
are rather standardized as achievement indices and represent, of
course, necessary, if not sufficient, steps in getting men to the
technical jobs which await fulfillment. One assumption often made is
that training requirements simulate task requirements to be encountered on the job. While such an assumption is only partially valid,
there has certainly been a realization that elements of on-the-job
performance should be identified more adequately both for the
improvement of classification tests and training programs. Christal's
discussion (Department of Navy, 1961a) of military occupational
analysis and Morsh's fifty-year bibliography (1962) of industrial and
military job analysis denote the importance attributed to the
development of improved task dimensionalization and on-the-job
work criteria as a basis from which to improve selection and training
procedures.

Attempts to validate tests beyond the criterion level of training
performance have characteristically relied upon rating evaluations of
job supervisors, a natural inclination in most work organizations in
which supervisor judgments constitute a routine part of the
organization's appraisal of a man. Such has been the case in
evaluating both officer and enlisted personnel, although the vast
majority of research efforts have been devoted to noncommissioned
enlisted personnel who, over several decades, have represented
approximately ninety percent of the military active duty population
(Lang, 1964). Some of the technical problems encountered in using

supervisor ratings as criteria are discussed by Glickman and Kipnis (U.S. Department of Navy, 1961b). In keeping with that review, Groppe et al., (1967) provide statistical analyses of supervisor rating trends over a ten-year period within the Air Force. Such problems as halo effect in rating, greater variance between them within rank levels, and a relative paucity of critical incident or standardized work sample criteria for evaluation are certainly among the problems encountered. But overall, cognitive aptitude tests validated against training performance also have modest validity in predicting supervisor ratings. As Wallace (1965) puts it, in his critique of performance prediction and industrial job performance criteria in general, "while we cannot actually predict what a man does, we can predict what other people say about what he does."

Emotional Adjustment

The individual's capacity to adjust to the psychological stresses of the military environment must be considered as relevant to his effective functioning on the job. Noted as early as the first world war is the fact that cognitive aptitude is not necessarily paralleled by corresponding emotional assets to face the stresses of military life, as evidenced by the numbers of men hospitalized for reasons of neuropsychiatric disorders between 1917 and 1919 (U.S. Department of the Army, 1965). Thus, with the manpower mobilization of World War II, and on the basis of experiences gained two decades earlier, psychiatric screening was implemented in the armed forces during the early 1940s to filter out the patently unfit as well as to identify those conscriptees and enlistees sufficiently "marginal" in emotional stature to warrant more intensive follow-up evaluation during the early phases of military training. Hunt and his colleagues describe the psychiatric screening process as it was conceptualized (Hunt et al., 1944; Raines et al., 1954; Hunt, 1955).

That the psychiatric interview has been useful as a screening technique in the armed forces over the years cannot be denied; but despite its utility there remain substantial numbers of men, though small in percentage, who after screening fail to adjust to military life (Arthur, 1965, 1966; Ginzberg, 1959). On the other hand, too, as characteristic of any screening program, one seldom knows the validity of the decision to reject a man, except on the face value of situational standards. Such is particularly true of the young man who perhaps, through the developmental stages of late adolescence, appears emotionally immature though neither neurotic nor certainly psychotic. Plag and Arthur (1965) duscuss that problem in an account of a study of Navy recruits in which young men, characterized by psychiatric screening procedures in recruit training as marginal, were retained in the service for follow-up assessment. A good proportion of those sailors completed their four-year adjustment and were recommended for reenlistment.

The dimensionals of clinical psychiatric predictions in military settings has been studied within the context of both mass screening and special assessment programs, providing information about the relevance of psychiatric judgment for particular screening objectives (Glass et al., 1956; Gunderson and Nelson, 1962; Gunderson and Kapfer, 1966; Hunt et al., 1957; Plag, 1964; Sells and Mace, 1963). One apparent dilemma is that psychiatrists have often been imposed upon to predict behavior for a virtually unknown environment. To the extent that the service environment for which a man is being considered can be characterized, the assets and liabilities of an individual's personality of life style can be more validly weighed. Such, of course, is scarcely possible when psychiatric screening is conducted with a momentary interview of a new conscriptee who could be assigned to almost any environmental context imaginable. Another characteristic of psychiatric predictions is that they often tend to reflect a relative summation of major successes and failures in the individual's life history to date, data which, except for clinical interpretation, can be more economically obtained and analyzed for predictive value without the expense of the professional interview.

It has been chiefly within the domain of biographical data that the armed forces have achieved modest success in predicting emotional adjustment to military service—adjustment most globally characterized by the individual's having sufficient maturity to complete an obligated period of military service with a relative absence of disciplinary and psychiatric entries upon his records of performance and health. Primary among the life history variables, in importance of relationship to military adjustment, are those biographical data related to preservice schooling, as reported, among others, by Ginzberg (1959) after World War II and by many investigators again within the past ten years (Berry and Nelson, 1966; Flyer, 1963; Gordon and Bottenberg, 1962; Plag and Goffman, 1966a). Such studies have focused predominantly upon noncommissioned enlisted personnel, as has characterized so much of the development of cognitive aptitude tests. The enlisted population is generally more heterogeneous in educational background than the predominantly college-educated officer population, and probably more heterogeneous in a general cultural sense, though the officer corps of the armed forces today must certainly be considered more heterogeneous in cultural make-up than it was in the earlier years of our nation's military system (Janowitz, 1964).

In one of the more recent and systematic research efforts on the adjustment of military enlisted personnel, Plag conducted a longitudinal study of a cohort of eleven thousand Navy recruits entering the service in 1960 and 1961 (Plag and Goffman, 1966b). With a broad array of per-service biographical information; aptitude test scores; psychiatric interview judgments; early training performance evaluations; and extensive job performance, adjustment, and health record criterion information over a four-year enlistment period, his findings unequivocally demonstrate the predictive validity of school, community, and family life history data in relation to military adjustment. Since the major institutional demands made of the adolescent prior to his entry into military life are those of the community at large, and the educational system in particular, the young man's adjustment to those environs constitutes the most relevant index of his likelihood to adjust to military life, at least at the time of his entry into the armed forces.

While many studies have shown a relationship between biographical data and military performance, in the same sense many studies have shown validity of cognitive mental tests in relation to adjustment in military service (Helme and Anderson, 1964; Klieger et al., 1961; Plag and Goffman, 1967a). Plag's analyses emphasize the unique criterion variance accounted for by biographical data over and above that accounted for by information obtained from the AFQT, General Classification Test batteries, and the clinical prediction rendered from a brief psychiatric interview. Similar uniqueness in predictive validity of biographical data is noted in Air Force studies by Fisher and colleagues (1960) of the individual discharged for military unsuitability as well as in studies of the effectiveness of rehabilitated airmen by Smith et al. (1967). Thus, to predict broadly both job proficiency and emotional adjustment in military service, some combination of cognitive aptitude test data and biographical information are likely to provide the most relevant information at the early stages of a young man's affiliation with the armed forces.

The utility of biographical information for predicting adjustment in the military extends beyond cohort studies of the satisfactory completion of first enlistments. Life history information has similarly been noted to be among the more valid types of data in differentiating "aces" from other pilots (Torrance, 1954) and "fighters" from "nonfighters" (Egbert et al., 1957) in combat studies during the Korean conflict, in identifying those best able to adjust to the stresses of long-term isolation and confinement experienced in remote Arctic and Antarctic stations (Eilbert and Glaser, 1959; Gunderson and Nelson, 1965a), and in relation to overall adjustment and performance among highly select aquanauts in special underseas diving programs (Radloff and Helmreich, 1968). Then, too, taking a lead from the theory of psychosomatic medicine, several investigators have found social life history information, organized conceptually to reflect "life crises" related to subsequent health change among military personnel, a criterion of adjustment frequently overlooked (Rahe et al., 1967; Plag and Goffman, 1967b).

The particular aspects of life history which seem relevant for performance prediction can be expected to vary according to the population being evaluated, and similarly according to the environmental context and type of duty situation within which adjustment and performance are to occur. The predictive validity of such data also seems best when the performance or adjustment criteria reflect general dimension of behavior for which there are theoretical counterparts in the preservice life of the individual. Biographical data which reflect patterns of preservice adjustment, in contrast to situational incidents, thus suggesting basic developmental dimensions of behavior, would also be considered more important for predictive purposes. Finally, the relevance of any particular aspect of life history in relation to later behavior seems to be in part a function of the temporal proximity of the life event pattern used as a predictor to the subsequent behavior to be predicted. The individual continuously "updates" his life history, a fact which should not be overlooked in prediction of human behavior. Plag's analyses of the eleven thousand Navy recruits illustrate the way in which different bits of information, as they are chronologically accumulated through service experience, modify the prediction equation.

In any discussion of psychiatric adjustment or general performance effectiveness, the point should be made that standard personality tests have been relatively unsuccessful as predictors of such adjustment to military life. Varieties of personality test data have over the years been obtained on many military samples, particularly in the course of developing selection programs for special duty assignments or for subgroups which through the exercise of highly select achievement standards are relatively homogeneous on cognitive aptitudes and educational history. This is not to say that any given personality scale may not for a particular situation be correlated with certain types of behavior, but rather that in broadly assessing performance and adjustment on the job, such appraisals have infrequently, or unsystematically, accounted for much of the criterion variance beyond that accounted for by cognitive aptitude measures and life history information. Brokaw (1967) briefly reviews a variety of noncognitive measures in officer selection programs for the three services and concludes that relatively little success has been achieved in relating paper-and-pencil personality tests to operational criteria of officer effectiveness. On a more general but psychometrically technical critique of the state of the art in personality measurement, Fiske (1963) discusses reasons for which personality test data have been limited in predictive utility as well as ways in which future developments of such tests might be improved.

Sophisticated use of biographical information, as well as attitude and value assessment, may well be profitable in personality measurement. Biographical data can be used to develop constructs reflective of the dynamic manner in which the individual copes with and modifies his environment. Such an approach requires both an adequate sampling of life history items as well as analytic procedures for assessing their interactions. The conceptualization of biographical item analyses offered by DuBois et al., (1952) and in the more recent factor analytic study of biographical data by Baehr and Williams (1967) represent approaches in that direction. Other approaches to the development of constructs from life history data are represented in the insightful analyses conducted by Stouffer and his colleagues of the American soldier in World War II (1949) and in selected sociological studies more recently edited by Lazarsfeld and Rosenberg (1965). All too often, as it is, life history items are assessed as single discrete bits of information, the result being about the same as if cognitive test theorists were to study single test items, one per mental domain, in relation to complex behavior.

To summarize, Wilkins (1969) expresses it as "the prediction of effective performance in military life, as in so many other occupational areas, is most reliably made when the predictors emphasize significant items from the life history (of the individual) and good measures of aptitudes in the cognitive areas;" but, he adds,

While allowing selection at better than chance levels, and while very useful indeed for large scale selection programs, (the predictive validity coefficients thus obtained) leave most of the variance unaccounted for; . . . the improvement in identification of who *will* be effective, as distinguished from who *can* be effective, must come in the areas of values held, motivations, and attitudes.

Motivational Effectiveness

The fact that men often fail to perform at a level congruent with their capability needs no documentation. It is this very problem which can jeopardize the functioning of a military unit, a situation in which men are depended upon according to their ability and they fail to fulfill those expectations through lack of dedication, drive, or enthusiasm, or perhaps through inappropriate motivation. There is, at times, a fine line even differentiating the emotionally maladjusted from the inadequately or inappropriately motivated individual. The individual's life record of achievements, activities, past relationships with family and community, and the very circumstances under which he enters military service all reflect to some extent elements of that individual's motivational system. But other than the use of such personal history information, relatively little progress has been made in developing valid measures of motivation useful for predicting behavior in military service.

This is not to say that attempts to measure motivation and to conceptualize its relation to military performance and adjustment have not been made. The emergent awareness during the 1930s among psychologists and sociologists of the importance of motivational factors in job performance was illustrated in part through the well known Hawthorne studies wherein both personal motivation and interpersonal relations on the job were observed quite by accident to be of significance in work productivity (Roethlisberger and Dickson, 1939). Then, too, that decade witnessed a growing interest among social scientists in assessing community attitudes and public opinion, serving as a precedent for increasing research on attitudes among military personnel, which has survived to this day. The monumental efforts of Stouffer and his colleagues during World War II, an effort encompassing more than half a million men in some three hundred opinion surveys, was described by the *American Sociological Review* in 1949 as one of the most significant contributions to the social sciences during the last twenty years. And, as it pertains to attitude assessment within the armed forces, that statement remains reasonably descriptive of the work even today, another twenty years later. The insightful ways in which Stouffer's data were analyzed, and the meaningful theoretical constructs developed, perhaps were more important than the raw data on opinions and attitudes collected. And, it has been the relative absence of such conceptualization in subsequent studies of attitudes among military personnel that has signified a lack of progress made since that time toward improved measurement of motivation for more effective prediction of behavior among military personnel.

Bem (1967) takes the position that attitudes are a function of the enacted behaviors which precede them, a rationale, so to speak, for behavior already taken. Such a point of view is not inconsistent with general theories of attitude formation predicated upon the significance of past experience, but it serves as a precaution to those who would like to predict behavior from current attitudes without knowledge of past behavior, a situation which more often than not has characterized motivation research in the military. This is not to negate such findings as those of Stouffer in the *American Soldier* volumes, relating group attitudes about combat to subsequent group effectiveness in combat. For even there, troop attitudes were chosen to reflect in part the similarities and differences of previous war experience. In addition, Stouffer's concept of "relative deprivation" allowed interpretation of soldier attitudes to be made through a social comparison of past experiences. The point to be made is that life history events and their meaning to the individual might well be given greater consideration as a contextual basis from which to better understand those elements of motivation assessed by attitude questionnaires.

So much of the literature on military attitude research, and for that matter much industrial research, consists of descriptive studies of opinions an; affect regarding the organization; the job in its entirety; the living and working conditions; and the benefits of promotion, salary, and similar items. While this information is of face value to any organization's management for the information thus revealed, the typical "job satisfaction," "company satisfaction," and "employee morale survey" approaches to motivation have been unproductive in predicting performance effectiveness. They do not capture the essence of motivation, namely, those dynamic properties of aspiration, will, and striving; subjective estimates of success or failure; and perhaps what many simply refer to as "guts," tenacity under the most adverse of circumstances.

The individual's perception of his own progress in the attainment of personal goals has received some attention. Dunnette et al. (1967), in reviewing a series of studies directed in test of Herzberg et al.'s (1959) theory of the motivation to work, cite the three factors of perceived achievement, recognition, and responsibility as consistently salient in attitudes toward one's job. Vroom (1964), on work motivation, postulates the interaction between a value orientation (goal) and the perceived probability of achieving such a goal as the determinant of behavior, with the perceived outcome of that behavior providing, in turn, feedback for the modification of the two antecedent conditions. Among military research efforts, Tupes (1969) reviews twenty-five years of attitude research in the Air Force, much of which is focused upon career motivation. He notes among a history of relatively unsuccessful attempts to predict career decisions from attitudes, that the recent development of scales which assess both perceived value and probability of goal attainment within military life seems likely to improve predictive validities of attitude data.

The Air Force studies of career motivation introduce another consideration in attitude motivational research, namely, the cultural variations among military personnel with concomitant variations in personal value systems. Such variables as source of officer commission, type of college education, family occupational and socioeconomic history, and the individual's own employment history are suggested by Tupes as having a significant relationship to career decisions. Berkshire (1967), in a recent attempt to improve prediction of successful completion of training in naval aviation, obtained results also suggesting the importance of cultural value orientations. Prediction of flight training success, a good portion of which can be attributed to motivation to remain voluntarily in aviation, was improved, over and above cognitive aptitude predictors, by scales derived from trainees' evaluation of naval aviation in contrast to each of twenty alternative occupations on the dimensions of prestige and security. The relevance of cultural variations lies in the observation that for officer student aviators the perceived prestige of naval aviation was a significant predictor while for cadet student aviators, a group lower in educational attainment and perhaps more heterogeneous on family socioeconomic background, the perceived security of a naval aviation career was significant in relation to training success.

Relatively little research has been conducted on values among military enlisted personnel. Among Navy enlisted populations,

Gunderson (1965b), in a "blue-collar/white-collar" type analysis, finds that enlistees tend to serve in military occupations of similar nature to those civilian occupations in which their fathers work, possibly denoting the importance of value and socioeconomic status considered by Vroom (1964) and Hyman (1953) as determinants of occupational choice in addition to the importance attributed to vocational interests and personal traits described by others (Roe, 1956; Strong, 1955; Thorndike and Hagen, 1959). Further studies by Gunderson and Nelson (1966a) demonstrate interest and value differences among Navy occupational groups, although little of this has as yet been shown to have much predictive validity against behavior in the military service. That such differences do exist, however, would suggest that better understanding of social-cultural factors in the life history and status of military personnel might well lead to improved understanding of their motivation in relation to performance.

The military setting provides ample opportunity to explore more fully the nature of motivation—motivation to work, to serve and sacrifice, and to achieve. Studies of reenlistment and career decisions afford opportunity to better understand the role of values, life style, and personal influence in life decisions of some consequence. It is also well known, at least anecdotally, that the military is replete with circumstances calling forth the volunteer, circumstances often characterized at one extreme by virtual absence of excitement or challenge and at the other extreme of potential threat to one's life. Despite studies of characteristics of "the volunteer," our understanding of the dynamics of volunteering is limited. (Ambler, Berkshire, and O'Connor, 1961; Bair and Gallagher, 1958; Flyer and Potter, 1959; and Gunderson, 1964) To understand motivation requires not only a better assessment of basic value orientation among individuals, but also an assessment of situational context in which behaviors, reflective of motivation, occur. Not to be overlooked within such situational contexts is the cultural and personal influence exerted upon the individual through the membership and reference groups with which he is affiliated at points in time.

The history of military tradition, pride in the organization, the legendary "esprit de corps" of military units, the emphasis on leadership and teamwork, and the forces of primary group solidarity under the stresses of military duty must all be given greater attention in analyses of motivation among military personnel. Furthermore, the individual's interpersonal reliability, his loyalty to the goals, traditions, and policies of his military organizational unit, and his general ability to serve effectively as a team member constitute performance criteria of importance in military service, criteria worthy of prediction in their own right.

Interpersonal Effectiveness

World War II studies by Shils and Janowitz (1954) of primary group solidarity within military units, later analyses by Little (1964) of the role of "buddy systems" in combat, and the writings of Stouffer et al. (1949) and Marshall (1947) illustrate well the importance of interpersonal dependability among military unit members in contributing to performance effectiveness. With the development of sociometric methods encouraged by the work of Jennings (1950) and Moreno (1956), empirical studies of individual differences in interpersonal effectiveness gained momentum in military personnel appraisal programs. Notable were the peer evaluation studies conducted by Jenkins and others (1950; Jenkins, 1948) among aviator squadrons during World War II, followed by similar studies during the Korean conflict by Bair (1952). Both sets of studies, employing peer ratings and descriptive assessment of characteristics desired in aviators with whom one would want to fly during combat, attested to the value of teamwork and individual characteristics which contributed to the same.

During the past two decades, the peer rating, used in a variety of forms but essentially reflective of qualities important in interpersonal effectiveness, has been demonstrated to have predictive validity, among both officer and enlisted personnel in all three branches of military service, and over periods of time ranging from several months to as long as four years (Berkshire and Nelson, 1958; French, 1951; Goodacre, 1951; Hollander, 1964; Katz and Burke, 1955; Nelson and Berry, 1966a; Wherry et al., 1957; Hopkins, 1959; Wilkins et al., 1952; Wilkins, 1954). In not every instance have peer ratings accounted for performance variance over and above that accounted for by biographical and cognitive aptitude measures, but for interpersonal aspects of behavior the peer rating has been a powerful technique in identifying consistent individual differences in effectiveness, even across different membership groups with which the individual serves in the course of military service (Bell and French, 1950; Fiske et al., 1959; Medland and Olans, 1964; Nelson and Berry, 1965; Tupes and Christal, 1968).

Military environments place men in continuously close proximity to one another, under a variety of stresses, and in such a condition of interdependence that the behavior of one man is likely to affect the fate, even the lives of others. From even the first weeks of military training, interpersonal ties are so intense that peer evaluations rendered during such early acquaintance periods are sufficiently reliable as to be predictive of performance over months and years. Probably of critical value in behavior reflected in the military peer rating is the individual's ability to respond to stress in a way not only effective for that individual but equally effective in regard to other men about him. As in the combat aviator studies previously cited, the peer rating constitutes in many instances one of the most appropriate criterion measures, in addition to its utility in other instances as a valid predictor. As in combat, the unique stresses of remote isolated duty or novel physical environments, potentially threatening to life, provide settings in which peer ratings have been highly useful in assessing characteristics of interpersonal effectiveness (Gunderson, 1966; Gunderson and Nelson, 1966b; Radloff and Helmreich, 1968; Sells, 1961).

An area of interpersonal behavior of historical significance in the military, by fact and anecdote alike, is that of leadership. Attention given by the military organization to the selection and training of its potential leaders attests to that fact. As a general rule, selection programs tend to focus upon traits required of leaders while the training programs, though geared toward functioning as secondary screening programs themselves, tend to approach the situational aspects of leadership by providing guidelines of appropriate leadership tactics under various situations. Among leadership training programs which serve also as selection programs were those conducted by the O.S.S. Assessment Staff (1948) during World War II. Varieties of situational tests were designed to assess multiple combinations of skills and personal qualities considered essential in effective leaders; there was, however, a virtual absence of post training performance criterion measures. Further development of situational tests of leadership were conducted by the Army during the Korean conflict (Havron et al., 1952; Mathews, 1951; Greer et al., 1957).

After early emphasis on selection of leaders by general traits of intelligence and aggressiveness, there has emerged rather clearly over the years a position that leadership must be regarded as an interpersonal process such that effectiveness is as much a function of roles, situational demands, and group character as it is of the particular traits of the leaders. The Ohio State studies in naval leadership (Hemphill, 1949, 1950; Shartle and Stogdill, 1952) and general reviews of leadership theory and studies by Gibb (1954), Guetzkow (1951), and Bass (1960) provide background for such philosophy. In specific studies of military groups under a variety of environmental conditions, the importance of crew roles, past group experience, and type of decisions to be made by leaders in determining appropriate styles of leadership are discussed in writings of Campbell (1956), Hollander (1958), Nelson (1965), and Torrance (1957). Such studies do not negate the importance of traits for effective leaders, but rather suggest the necessity for assessing personal qualities of leaders in terms of the situational task and interpersonal process requirements inherent in the process of leadership. Hence, such characteristics as sensitivity to group climate and to the assets and liabilities of group members in various task settings, a capacity for flexibility in interpersonal style, and a proper sense of "timing" might be given attention at least equal to that given in the past to other types of cognitive and noncognitive traits.

Of recent theoretical formulations, tested on military groups as on industrial work groups, it is perhaps Fiedler's (1967) contingency theory of leadership which best assimilates the personal and situational aspects of the problem. Fiedler accounts for the predominant interpersonal style of individuals in formal leadership positions, and further acknowledges the roles and sentiments among group members, the type of task to which the group is oriented, and a sense of leader-group history from previous task situations. By giving proper weight to each of those parameters, the contingency model yields an optimal leadership style for various task situations which might confront the designated formal leader.

Fiedler's work has particular utility in military settings where, more often than not, formally designated leaders maintain responsibility for their groups over varieties of situations. While informal secondary leaders play vital roles in such groups, they are not likely to assume formal responsibility for the behavior of the group. A problem, however, for any model theoretically predictive of leadership effectiveness is the extent to which meaningful, reliably measured, criteria of group performance can be determined. When the group's attention is focused upon solution of a concrete problem, certainly speed and accuracy of solution can be measured. For most groups, cohesiveness and attitudes reflective of morale can be assessed, but the relationship between such sentiments and effective task performance are equivocal at best (Lott and Lott, 1965; Nelson and Berry, 1966b).

With a somewhat better than normal ability to define meaningful and measurable group performance criteria in infantry rifle squads, tank crews, and air crews, the Army and Air Force conducted large numbers of small group studies during the 1950s, paralleling an increased academic interest in small group behavior during that period (Cartwright and Zander, 1953; Hare et al., 1955). Havron and colleagues (1952) in a review of Army squad studies, and George (1962), in a general comprehensive analysis of the literature on small groups as relevant to military groups, discuss relationship among group member attitudes, traits, skills, interpersonal perceptions, and both individual and group performance. Among Air Force studies of air crews, Adams' (1953) study of congruency of personal and organizational status attributes, Rosenberg's (1956) analysis of the differential relevance of various personal attributes when forming crews from different population subgroups, Roby's discussion (1954) of the appropriateness of forming crews on the basis of self-selection peer ratings, and Haythorn's (1957) review of various small crew assembly procedures represent contributions to the understanding of interpersonal effectiveness in the context of group performance.

Nonetheless, the state of the art does not yet allow for a generalized method for assessing performance for groups per se across widely different types of groups and group task situations. Rather, each group situation tends to be evaluated in its own right, making it difficult to compare different types of groups by any standardized metric system. Bray (1962), citing a literature review conducted in 1957, notes that of approximately sixteen hundred studies of team performance, no more than ten percent were focused directly upon the problem of group performance criterion development. More recently, Altman (1966) discusses the critical need for improved conceptualization of small group performance if appropriate criteria are to be developed. More attention needs to be given to the dynamic processes of group function. When groups do not operate as autonomous or quasi-autonomous entities with a mission criterion definable independent of other groups, there must be greater attention given to the group as an element of a larger organizational system such that any one group's performance must in part be measured in terms of the greater system's effectiveness.

It seems appropriate to anticipate future developments in performance prediction capability from concepts and analytical techniques employed in the assessment of systems effectiveness. Uhlaner (1968) expresses the sentiments of the past decade of military personnel research as being "in reaction to compartmental-ism, by recognition that it is impossible to conduct sound studies within designated problem areas such as selection, classification, training, and human engineering without due regard for factors operating in other areas." Thus, Uhlaner continues, "human factors scientists in research organizations found themselves compelled, in the interest of valid products, to pursue their investigations beyond the confines of separate fractionated missions and to look at a problem in its totality."

Systems Effectiveness

With the post-World War II era came an accelerated growth in the development of complex technological systems. To the extent that man is an integral part of the operation of those systems, it was no longer possible to evaluate man and machine performance separately.

Building upon theory and experimental analysis of human learning, decision-making, perception, and psychomotor coordina-tion, increased emphasis during the 1950s was given to the technology of human engineering. On the basis of predictions made of man's performance within the context of alternative "hardware" system configurations, greater effort was made to design and develop those hardware systems in which man could perform optimally (see Christensen et al., 1967; Morgan et al., 1963). Further conceptual development in systems evaluation during this era led to the inclusion of human selection and training considerations in the planning of man-machine system design and evaluation. And finally, considerations of life-support and operational schedules, along with hardware maintenance, had to be included in overall system performance evaluation.

Melton, in his preface to Gagne's (1962) edited text on the principles of system development, summarizes thy conceptual developments as follows:

> As a theory of the psychotechnology of man-machine systems, it (this book) achieves integration of what has heretofore been variously called "human engineering," "human factors engineering," or "engineering psychology" on the one hand and "personal psychology" or "personnel and training" research on the other hand. This union comes easily and naturally once the concept of *system* is examined and once the full

implication of the concept of the human being as a *component* of a man-machine system are recognized. For it immediately becomes clear that the available properties or functions of man must be considered in planning the mating of man and machine components to achieve the desired system function; that the desired properties and functions of man must be exactly specified—as system development progresses; that the desired characteristics of man must be achieved through selection and/or training techniques of high precision and efficiency; and that the functional efficiency of the human component must be maintained and tested within the system context not only on installation but also continuously or at least periodically thereafter.

Once a system's mission or objective can be operationally defined by a measurable criterion of performance, prediction of system effectiveness can only be achieved through assessment of the multiple contingent relationships between human and hardware attributes over time and with the context of operational environments. Performance quality control can furthermore be achieved through comparison, at any point in time of a system's life cycle, of the actual and/or projected status or performance of a system with the optimal status or performance intended for the system at different points in time by virtue of its total design from the selection and training of its operators to the intended operational conditions for its use. Such quality control capability offers management a basis for decision-making in regard to improving system effectiveness. When actual or projected system performance critically deviates from optimal levels of performance expected, modifications can be made through either the system input characteristics (i.e., selection and training of men or design configuration of "hardware") or operational characteristics (i.e., life-support, work schedules, or hardware maintenance).

The general logic of systems evaluation is, in itself, a particularly important element of the past decade of research on performance prediction and assessment. Certainly, it is in theory as applicable to analyses of military organizations, and even broader man-environmental adaptation, as it is to the specific problems of man-machine technology (Buckley, 1968). Analogous to the developments achieved in relating man and machine attributes within a systems context, greater effort is required to identify attributes and measure functional relationships over time between man and his social-organizational environment and between man and his physical/biological environment if more efficient predictions of performance effectiveness are to be achieved.

We are not, of course, without data on such matters. Studies and theories of organizational structure and function have been pursued, largely through the interests of sociologists and social psychologists (Scott, 1964). Small groups have been studied as systems, with analyses of interactions over time among personality composition, task roles, and physical life-space characteristics of the group (Altman and Haythorn, 1967; and Haythorn, 1968). And, studies have been made of individual differences in, and normative effects upon, performance on various types of tasks as a function of physical and psychological stress induced through such varied parameters as climate, atmospheric pressure, gravitational force, sleep deprivation, work-rest cycles, sensory reduction or deprivation, isolation and confinement, and perceived threat (Appley and Trumbull, 1967; Solomon et al., 1965; Johnson, 1967; Wherry and Curran, 1966).

More often than not, however, less attention has been given to the dynamics of behavioral process, adaptation, and performance change over time, than is essential if improvement in human performance prediction is to be realized. Transactional and ecological analyses must be increased in studying man and his environment, be it social or physical. Improved classification methods for measuring environmental parameters, human characteristics sensitive to those parameters, and dimensions of transaction reflective of both reactive and proactive efforts of human coping with environment are needed (Sells, 1963). Then, too, analytical techniques for prediction must be capable of accounting for contingencies over time, requiring greater use of stochastic models of behavioral analysis (Borgatta, 1969). Making the problem even more complex, general concepts and analytical methods must be developed appropriate for various behavioral units of analysis ranging from the individual to the small group, to the larger organization, both within and outside of the context of man-machine systems.

We have focused predominantly on "inputs" during the past fifty years. We have most frequently interpreted selection as an initial procedure applied to men entering the service or entering special programs, rather than as a continuous decision-making process exercised by management for a large variety of purposes. We have most frequently interpreted training as an initial procedure calculated more often than not to provide development of task skills, rather than as a continuous management-directed process of developing skills and motivation appropriate for effectiveness in varied military environments. Management must make "predictions" of human potential throughout an individual's service career, throughout the design and operation of a man-machine system, and throughout the life of an organization. To do so, it requires continuous quality control procedures and updated information concerning the adaptation and performance efficiency of the behavioral unit of concern within a systems or environmental context. As Melton concluded, "the human component must be maintained and tested within the system context not only on installation but also continuously or at least periodically thereafter."

We must be alert to those heretofore relatively unmeasurable, but very real and important human qualities of ingenuity, tenacity, flexibility, sacrifice, and loyalty which contribute to man's environmental adaptation and his capacity to, at times, modify his environment. The focus of such endeavors, however, must be upon man's transactions with his environment over time, an ecological orientation for which the principles of systems evaluation, in a broad sense, are applicable to the prediction of personnel performance and human effectiveness in general.

REFERENCES

ADAMS, S. (1953) "Status congruency as a variable in small group performance." Social Forces 32: 16-22.

ALTMAN, I. (1966) "Aspects of the criterion problem in small groups research." Acta Psychologica 25: 101-131.

———and W. W. HAYTHORN (1967) "The ecology of isolated groups." Behavioral Science 12: 169-182.

AMBLER, R. K., J. A. BERKSHIRE, and W. F. O'CONNOR (1961) "The identification of potential astronauts." Research Report 33. Pensacola, Fla.: Naval School of Aviation Medicine.

APPLEY, M. H. and R. TRUMBULL [eds.] (1967) Psychological Stress. New York: Appleton-Century-Crofts.

ARTHUR, R. A. (1966) "Psychiatric disorders in Naval personnel." Military Medicine (April): 354-361.

———(1965) "Stability in psychosis admission rates: three decades of Navy experience." Public Health Reports 80: 512-514.

BAEHR, M. E. and G. B. WILLIAMS (1967) "Underlying dimensions of personal background data and their relationship to occupational classification." Journal of Applied Psychology 51: 481-490.

BAIR, J. T. (1952) "The characteristics of the wanted and unwanted pilot in training and in combat." Pensacola, Fla.: Naval School of Aviation Medicine.

———and T. J. GALLAGHER (1958) "Volunteering for extra-hazardous duty." Naval Research Review (November): 12-19.

BASS, B. M. (1960) Leadership, Psychology, and Organizational Behavior. New York: Harper Brothers.

BELL, G. B. and R. L. FRENCH (1950) "Consistency of individual leadership position in small groups of varying membership." Journal of Abnormal and Social Psychology 45: 764-767.

BEM, D. F. (1967) "Self-perception: the dependent variable of human performance." Journal of Organizational Behavior and Human Performance 2: 105-121.

BERKSHIRE, J. R. (1967) "Evaluation of several experimental aviator selection tests." Pensacola, Fla.: Naval Aerospace Medical Institute.

———and P. D. NELSON (1958) "Leadership peer ratings related to subsequent proficiency in the fleet." Pensacola, Fla.: Naval School of Aviation Medicine.

BERRY, N. H. and P. D. NELSON (1966) "The fate of school drop-outs in the Marine Corps." Personnel and Guidance Journal 45: 20-23.

BORGATTA, E. F. [ed.] (1969) Sociological Methodology. San Francisco: Jossey-Bass.

BRAY, C. W. (1962) "Towards a technology of human behavior for defense use." American Psychologist 17: 527-541.

BROKAW, L. D. (1967) "Non-cognitive measures in selection of officers," pp. 35-47 in J. E. Uhalner (ed.) Psychological Research in National Defense Today. Washington, D.C.: U.S. Army Behavioral Sciences Research Laboratory.

BUCKLEY, W. [ed.] (1968) Modern Systems Research for the Behavioral Scientist. Chicago: Aldine.

CAMPBELL, D. T. (1956) "Leadership and its effect upon the group." Columbus: Ohio State University, Bureau of Business Research.

CARTWRIGHT, D. and A. ZANDER [eds.] (1953) Group Dynamics. Evanston, Ill.: Row, Peterson.

CHRISTENSEN, J. M. et al. (1967) "Contributions of engineering psychology to military systems," pp. 208-227 in J. E. Uhlaner (ed.) Psychological Research in National Defense Today. Washington, D.C.: U.S. Army Behavioral Sciences Research Laboratory.

CRONBACH, L. J. and G. C. GLESER (1965) Psychological Tests and Personnel Decisions. Urbana: University of Illinois Press.

DuBOIS, P. H., J. LOEVINGER, and G. C. GLESER (1952) "The construction of homogeneous keys for a biographical inventory." Lackland AFB, Tex.: Human Resources Research Center, Air Training Command.

DUNNETTE, M. D., J. P. CAMPBELL, and M. D. HAKEL (1967) "Factors contributing to job satisfaction and job dissatisfaction in six occupational groups." Journal of Organizational Behavior and Human Performance 2: 143-174.

EGBERT, R. L. et al. (1957) "Fighter I: an analysis of combat fighters and non-fighters." Alexandria, Va.: Human Resources Research Office, George Washington University.

EILBERT, L. R. and R. GLASER (1959) "Differences between well and poorly adjusted groups in an isolated environment." Journal of Applied Psychology 43: 271-274.

ELSON, J. [ed.] (1965) Abstracts of Personnel Research Reports: VI. 1954-1965. Lackland AFB, Tex.: Personnel Research Laboratory, Aerospace Medical Division, Air Force Systems Command.

FIEDLER, F. E. (1967) A Theory of Leadership Effectiveness. New York: McGraw-Hill.

FIELDS, V. (1967) "Differential classification and optimal allocation of personnel in the military services," pp. 19-34 in J. E. Uhlaner (ed.) Psychological Research in National Defense Today. Washington, D.C.: U.S. Army Behavioral Sciences Research Laboratory.

FISKE, D. W. (1963) "Homogeneity and variation in measuring personality." American Psychologist 18: 643-652.

––––, J. A. COX, Jr., and F. VAN DER VEEN (1959) "Consistency and variability in peer ratings." Lackland AFB, Tex.: Personnel Laboratory, Wright Air Development Center, Air Research and Development Command.

FISHER, W. E., J. E. WARD, F. E. HOLDREDGE, and H. G. LAURENCE (1960) "Prediction of unsuitability discharges." Lackland AFB, Tex.: Personnel Laboratory, Wright Air Development Division, Air Research and Development Command.

FLANAGAN, J. C. [ed.] (1948) The Aviation Psychology Program in the Army Air Forces. Washington, D.C.: U.S. Government Printing Office.

FLYER, E. S. (1963) "Prediction of unsuitability among first-term airmen from aptitude indexes, high school reference data, and basic training evaluations." Lackland, AFB, Tex.: Personnel Research Laboratory, Aerospace Medical Division, Air Force Systems Command.

––––and N. R. POTTER (1959) "Characteristics of basic airmen willing to volunteer for a six-year tour in missile squadrons." Lackland AFB, Tex.: Personnel Laboratory, Wright Air Development Division, Air Research and Development Command.

FRENCH, R. L. (1951) "Sociometric status and individual adjustment among Naval recruits." Journal of Abnormal and Social Psychology 46: 64-72.

FUCHS, E. F. (1967) "Screening potential enlisted men," pp. 10-18 in J. E. Uhlaner (ed.) Psychological Research in National Defense Today. Washington, D.C.: U.S. Army Behavioral Sciences Research Laboratory.

GAGNE, R. W. [ed.] (1962) Psychological Principles in Systems Development. New York: Holt, Rinehart & Winston.

GEORGE, C. E. (1962) "Some determinants of small group effectiveness." Fort Benning, Ga.: U.S. Army Infantry Human Research Unit.

GIBB, C. A. (1954) "Leadership," pp. 877-920 in C. Lindzey (ed.) Handbook of Social Psychology. Cambridge: Addison-Wesley.

GINZBERG, D. (1959) The Ineffective Soldier: The Lost Divisions. New York: Columbia University Press.

GLASS, A. J. et al., (1956) "Psychiatric prediction and military effectiveness." U.S. Armed Forces Medical Journal 12: 1427-1443.

GOODACRE, D. M. (1951) "The use of sociometric tests as a predictor of combat effectiveness." Sociometry 14: 148-153.

GORDON, M. A. and R. A. BOTTENBERG (1962) "Prediction of unfavorable discharge by separate educational levels." Lackland AFB, Tex.: Personnel Research Laboratory, Aerospace Medical Division, Air Force Systems Command.

GREER, F. C., W. O. PEARSON, and M. D. HAVRON (1957) "Evasion and survival problems and the prediction of crew performance." Lackland AFB, Tex.: Air Force Personnel and Training Research Center, Air Research and Development Command.

GRINKER, R. R. and J. P. SPIEGEL (1945) Men Under Stress. Philadelphia: Blakiston.

GROPPE, L. B., R. W. ALVORD, and J. V. POLAND (1967) "Air Force officer performance evaluation: rating trends and relationships from 1954 through 1965." Lackland AFB, Tex.: Personnel Research Laboratory, Aerospace Medical Division, Air Force Systems Command.

GUETZKOW, H. S. [ed.] (1951) Groups, Leadership, and Men. Pittsburgh: Carnegie Press.

GUNDERSON, E. K. E. (1966) "Adaptation to extreme environments." San Diego, Calif.: Navy Medical Neuropsychiatric Research Unit.

———(1964) "Performance evaluations of Antarctic volunteers." San Diego, Calif.: Navy Medical Neuropsychiatric Research Unit.

———and E. C. KAPFER (1966) "The predictive validity of clinical ratings for an extreme environment." British Journal of Psychiatry 112: 405-412.

GUNDERSON, E. K. E. and P. D. NELSON (1966a) "Personality differences among Navy occupational groups." Personnel Guidance Journal 45: 956-961.

———(1966b) "Criterion measures for extremely isolated groups." Personnel Psychology 19: 67-80.

———(1965a) "Biographical predictors of performance in an extreme environment." Journal of Psychology 61: 59-67.

———(1965b) "Socioeconomic status and Navy occupations." Personnel Guidance Journal 44: 263-266.

———(1962) "Clinical agreement in assessment for an unknown environment." San Diego, Calif.: Navy Medical Neuropsychiatric Research Unit.

HARE, A. P., E. F. BORGATTA, and R. F. BALES [eds.] (1955) Small Groups. New York: Aflred A. Knopf.

HAVRON, M. D., R. J. FAY and J. E. McGRATH (1952) "The effectiveness of small military units." Washington, D.C.: Personnel Research Section, AGO, Department of the Army.

HAVRON, M. D., F. C. GREER, and E. H. GALANTER (1952) "An interview study of human relationships in an effective infantry rifle squad." Washington, D.C.: Personnel Research Section, AGO, Department of the Army.

HAYTHORN, W. W. (1968) "The composition of groups: a review of the literature Acta Psychologica 28: 97-128.

———(1957) "A review of research on group assembly." Lackland AFB, Tex.: Air Force Personnel and Training Research Center, Air Research and Development Command.

HELME, W. H. and A. A. ANDERSON (1964) "Job performance of EM scoring low on AFQT." Washington, D.C.: U.S. Army Personnel Research Office.

HEMPHILL, J. K. (1949, 1950) Situational Factors in Leadership. Columbus: Ohio State Personnel Research Board.

HERZBERG, F., B. MAUSNER, and B. SYNDERMAN (1959) The Motivation to Work. New York: John Wiley.

HOLLANDER, E. P. (1964) Leaders, Groups, and Influence. New York: Oxford University Press.

———(1958) "Conformity, status, and idiosyncrasy credit." Psychological Review 65: 117-127.

HOPKINS, J. J. (1959) "Behavior trait ratings by peers and references." Lackland AFB, Tex.: Personnel Laboratory, Wright Air Development Center, Air Force Research and Development Command.

HumRRO (1968) Bibliography of Publications as of 30 June 1968. Alexandria, Va.: Human Resources Research Office, George Washington University.

HUNT, W. A. (1955) "A rationale for psychiatric selection." American Psychologist 10: 199-204.

———, R. S. HERRMANN, and H. NOBLE (1957) "The specificity of the psychiatric interview." Journal of Clinical Psychology 13: 49-53.

HUNT, W. A., C. L. WITTSON, and H. I. HARRIS (1944) "The screen test in military selection." Psychological Review 11: 37-46.

HYMAN, H. H. (1953) "The value systems of different classes: a social psychological contribution to the analysis of stratification," in R. Bendix and S. Lipset (eds.) Class, Status, and Power. New York: Free Press.

JANOWITZ, M. [ed.] (1964) The New Military: Changing Patterns of Organization. New York: Russell Sage Foundation.

JENKINS, J. G. (1948) "Nominating technique as a method of evaluating air groups morale." Journal of Aviation Medicine 19: 12-19.

———, E. S. EWART, and J. B. CARROLL (1950) "The combat criterion in Naval aviation." Washington, D.C.: National Research Council Committee on Aviation Psychology.

JENNINGS, H. H. (1950) Leadership and Isolation. New York: Longmans, Green.

JOHNSON, L. C. (1967) "Sleep and sleep loss—their effect on performance." Naval Research Review 20: 16-22.

KATZ, A. and L. K. BURKE (1955) "Prediction of combat effectiveness of officer candidate school graduates." Washington, D.C.: Personnel Research Branch, AGO, Department of the Army.

KLIEGER, W. A., A. V. DUBUISSON, and J. E. DeJUNG (1961) "Predictions of unacceptable performance in the Army." Washington, D.C.: Human Factors Research Branch, TAG, Research and Development Command.

LANG, K. (1964) "Technology and career management in the military establishment," pp. 39-82 in M. Janowitz (ed.) The New Military: Changing Patterns of Organization. New York: Russell Sage Foundation.

LAZARSFELD, P. F. and M. ROSENBERG [eds.] (1965) The Language of Social Research. New York: Free Press.

LITTLE, R. W. (1964) "Buddy relations and combat performance," pp. 195-224 in M. Janowitz (ed.) The New Military: Changing Patterns of Organization. New York: Russell Sage Foundation.

LOTT, A. J. and B. E. LOTT (1965) "Group cohesiveness as interpersonal attraction: a review of relationships with antecedent and consequent variables." Psychological Bulletin 64: 259-309.

MARSHALL, S. L. A. (1947) Men Against Fire. New York: William Morrow.

MATHEWS, J. (1951) "Research on the development of valid situational tests of leadership." Washington, D.C.: Personnel Research Section, AGO, Department of the Army.

MEDLAND, F. F. and J. L. OLANS (1964) "Peer rating stability in changing groups." Washington, D.C.: U.S. Army Personnel Research Office.

MORENO, J. L. [ed.] (1956) Sociometry and the Science of Man. New York: Beacon House.

MORGAN, C. T., J. S. COOK, III, A. CHAPANIS, and M. W. LUND [eds.] (1963) Human Engineering Guide to Equipment Design. New York: McGraw-Hill.

MORSH, J. R. (1962) Job Analysis Bibliography. Lackland AFB, Tex.: Personnel Research Laboratory, Aerospace Medical Division, Air Force Systems Command.

NELSON, P. D. (1965) "Psychological aspects of Antarctic living." Military Medicine 130: 485-489.

———and N. H. BERRY (1966a) "Dimensions of peer and supervisor ratings in a military setting." San Diego, Calif.: Navy Medical Neuropsychiatric Research Unit.

———(1966b) "Cohesion in Marine recruit platoons." Journal of Psychology 68: 63-71.

———(1965) "The relationship between an individual's sociometric status in different groups over a two-year period." Journal of Psychology 60: 31-37.

O.S.S. Assessment Staff (1948) Assessment of Men New York: Rinehart.

PLAG, J. A. (1964) "The practical value of a psychiatric screening interview in predicting military effectiveness." San Diego, Calif.: Navy Medical Neuropsychiatric Research Unit.

———and R. J. ARTHUR (1965) "Psychiatric re-examination of unsuitable Naval recruits: a two-year follow-up." American Journal of Psychiatry 122: 534-541.

PLAG, J. A. and J. M. GOFFMAN (1967a) "The armed forces qualification test: its validity in predicting military effectiveness." Personnel Psychology 20: 323-340.

———(1967b) "Dimensions of psychiatric illness among first-term Naval enlistees." San Diego, Calif.: Navy Medical Neuropsychiatric Research Unit.

———(1966a) "A formula for predicting effectiveness in the Navy from characteristics of high school students." Psychology in the Schools 3: 216-221.

———(1966b) "The prediction of four-year effectiveness among Naval recruits." Military Medicine 131: 729-735.

RADLOFF, R. and R. HELMREICH (1968) Groups Under Stress. New York: Appleton-Century-Crofts.

RAHE, R. H., J. D. McKEAN, and R. J. ARTHUR (1967) "A longitudinal study of life-change and illness patterns." San Diego, Calif.: Navy Medical Neuropsychiatric Research Unit.

RAINES, G. N. et al. (1954) "Psychiatric selection for military service." Journal of the American Medical Association 156: 817-821.

ROBY, T. B. (1954) "An empirical evaluation of work partner choices after limited contact." Lackland AFB, Tex.: Air Force Personnel and Training Research Center, Air Research and Development Command.

ROE, A. (1956) The Psychology of Occupations. New York: John Wiley.

ROETHLISBERGER, F. and W. J. DICKSON (1939) Management and the Worker. Cambridge: Harvard University Press.

ROSENBERG, S. (1956) "Similarity of interest and attitude measures as a predictor of interpersonal relationships in a medium-bomber crew." Lackland AFB, Tex.: Air Force Personnel and Training Research Center, Air Research and Development Command.

SCOTT, W. R. (1964) "Theory of organizations," pp. 485-529 in R. E. L. Faris (ed.) Handbook of Modern Sociology. Chicago: Rand McNally.

SELLS, S. B. [ed.] (1963) Stimulus Determinants of Behavior. New York: Ronald Press.

———(ed.) (1961) Proceedings: Tri-Service Conference on Research Relevant to Problems of Small Military Groups Under Isolation and Stress. Fort Worth: Texas Christian University.

———and D. J. MACE (1963) "Prediction of Air Force adaptability of basic airmen referred for psychiatric evaluation." Lackland AFB, Tex.: Personnel Research Laboratory, Aerospace Medical Division, Air Force Systems Command.

SHARTLE, C. L. and R. M. STOGDILL (1952) Studies in Naval Leadership. Columbus: Ohio State University Research Foundation.

SHILS, E. A. and M. JANOWITZ (1954) "Cohesion and disintegration in the Wehrmacht in World War II," pp. 501-516 in W. Schramm (ed.) The Process and Effects of Mass Communication. Urbana: University of Illinois Press.

SHOENBERGER, R. W., R. J. WHERRY, Jr., and J. R. BERKSHIRE (1963) "Predicting success in aviation training." Pensacola, Fla.: Naval School of Aviation Medicine, Naval Aviation Medical Center.

SMITH, T. H., C. D. GOTT, and R. A. BOTTENBERG (1967) "Predicting the potential for active duty success of rehabilitated Air Force prisoners." Lackland AFB, Tex.: Personnel Research Laboratory, Aerospace Medical Division, Air Force Systems Command.

SOLOMON, P. et al. [eds.] (1965) Sensory Deprivation. Cambridge: Harvard University Press.

STOUFFER, S. A. et al. (1949) The American Soldier. 4 vols. Princeton: Princeton University Press.

STRONG, E. K. (1955) Vocation Interests 18 Years After College. Minneapolis: University of Minnesota Press.

THORNDIKE, R. L. and E. HAGEN (1959) Ten Thousand Careers. New York: John Wiley.

TORRANCE, E. P. (1957) "What happens to the sociometric structure of small groups in emergencies and extreme conditions?" Group Psychotherapy 10 (September): 212-220.

———(1954) "The development of a preliminary life experience inventory for the study of fighter interceptor pilot combat effectiveness." Lackland AFB, Tex.: Air Force Personnel and Training Research Center, Air Research and Development Command.

TUPES, E. C. (1969) "Attitude research in the U.S. Air Force," in Manpower Research in the Defense Context (NATO Conference Proceedings). London: English Universities Press.

———and R. C. CHRISTAL (1968) "Stability of personality trait rating factors obtained under diverse conditions." Lackland AFB, Tex.: Personnel Laboratory, Wright Air Development Center, Air Research and Development Command.

U.S. Department of the Army, Office of the Chief of Research and Development (1965) Marginal Man and Military Service. Washington, D.C.: U.S. Government Printing Office.

U.S. Department of the Navy, Bureau of Naval Personnel (1963) BUPERS Abstracts of Research Reports. Washington, D.C.: Department of the Navy.

U.S. Department of the Navy, Office of Naval Research (1961) Proceedings: Tri-Service Conference on Selection Research. Washington, D.C.: Department of the Navy.

———Office of Naval Research (1961a) "Occupational analysis: one route to improved selection procedures and better utilization of available talent" (by R. E. Christal), in Proceedings: Tri-Service Conference on Selection Research. Washington, D.C.

———(1961b) "Theoretical considerations in the development and use of a noncognitive battery" (by A. S. Glickman and D. Kipnis), in Proceedings: Tri-Service Conference on Selection Research. Washington, D.C.

UHLANER, J. E. [ed.] (1968) "The research psychologist in the Army—1917-1967." Pensacola, Fla.: Naval School of Aviation Medicine, Naval Aviation

———(1967) Psychological Research in National Defense Today. Washington, D.C.: U.S. Army Behavioral Sciences Research Laboratory. Medical Center.

VROOM, V. H. (1964) Work and Motivation. New York: John Wiley.

WALLACE, S. R. (1965) "Criteria for what?" American Psychologist 20: 411-417.

WHERRY, R. J., Jr. and P. M. CURRAN (1966) "A model for the study of some dimensions of psychological stress." Organizational Behavior and Human Performance 1: 226-251.

WHERRY, R. J., Jr., N. E. STANDU, and E. C. TPES (1957) "Relationship between behavior trait ratings by peers and later officer performance of USAF OCS graduates." Lackland AFB, Tex.: Air Force Personnel and Training Research Center, Air Research and Development Command.

WILKINS, W. F. (1969) "Attitudes and values as predictors of military performance," in Manpower Research in the Defense Context (NATO Conference Proceedings). London: English Universities Press.

———(1954) "The selection of Marine Corps platoon leaders." United States Armed Forces Medical Journal 5: 1184-1191.

———, O. F. ANDEHALTER, and M. RIGBY (1952) "Peer ratings." St. Louis: St. Louis University.

YERKES, R. M. [ed.] (1921) Psychological Examining in the United States Army, Vol. XV. (Memoires of the National Academy of Sciences). Washington, D.C.: U.S. Government Printing Office.

Chapter 4

THE RETIRED MILITARY

ALBERT D. BIDERMAN

For the first time in its history, the United States has a significant class of former professional military men pursuing careers in the civilian society. We will examine here their characteristics and their adjustments to and impact on American society.[1]

GENERAL
SOCIAL PROBLEM

The way in which a society has handled the problem of superannuated or supernumerary soldiers has been in large measure related to (1) the salience of institutionalized violence in its value structure; (2) the relations between the social and technological organization of military forces and that of the civilian society; and (3) the extent, frequency, and duration of its mobilization for warfare (Biderman, 1966). Also of particular importance has been the extent to which the warrior role was a primary or exclusive role of some members of the society, on the one hand, or one shared by most males as a part-time secondary role, on the other.

All of the major nations that were involved in the World War II alliance have had to deal in recent years with problems of retiring from the career service the large numbers of men who entered during the war. The problem is a continuing one since most nations have sustained military forces at a high level in recent decades. The United States has abandoned militia and reserve forces as the mainstay of its defense and has been moving toward continually greater reliance on a professional military.

INTERNAL
NEEDS

The military calling has always been associated with physical prowess. This provides a fundamental rationale for the retirement of the large majority of a military force at much earlier ages than is the usual case in other employments. But the unsuitability for warfare of those whose vigor has been sapped by age, wounds, or disease is a relatively minor factor underlying the present retirement system, although it is still an important one in its mystique. Currently, only about one-sixth of the retired military in the United States were retired with any degree of disability (Glenn, n.d.) The elaboration of military organization and technology has rendered large proportions of all military jobs no more physically demanding than many sedate and sedentary civilian occupations. Yet these developments have been accompanied by a general lowering, rather than raising, of the average age at which military careerists are required or encouraged to retire. (See U.S. Congress, Senate, 1967.) Nondisability retirements were first provided for in the United States after the Civil War: retirement for Army officers after thirty years of service became permissible by an Act of 1870; this privilege was extended to Army enlisted men in 1885 and to Navy enlisted men in 1899, provided that they were at least fifty years of age. The 1899 law permitted Navy officers to apply for voluntary retirement without limit as to service or age. The impetus for this provision was to relieve stagnation in the promotion system. The principle that was applied in accepting applications for retirement under the old voluntary systems was the contribution which retirements could make to the age-rank structure of the service, rather than a view of those past fifty years as superannuated warriors. Promotion opportunities and conceptions of ideal age-rank structure have provided the actual rationale for all subsequent modifications of the military retirement systems, although the need for youthful vigor of the combatant increasingly is given higher status in its rhetorical justification. (See U.S. Department of Defense, 1969: vol. 5.)

The lowering of the usual period of active service at retirement from thirty years to twenty years evolved first from custom. It was not until 1949 that the twenty-year eligibility received its uniform statutory basis.

The dimensions and character of military retirement derive primarily from the needs of adapting conceptions of the ideal form and size of military organization to the facts of demography. The conventionally desired military rank structure consists of two pyramids: one of enlisted ranks and the other officer. Movement into these pyramids takes place almost exclusively at their base. Intake is from a very narrow range of the postadolescent and earliest adult ages. Screening out the obviously unfit and voluntary attrition are usually at least enough to cut numbers back sufficiently to produce the ideal first step-backs of the pyramid. Most of those who complete more than the initial "hitch" in the service usually can be counted upon to have a lasting commitment to it.

Since progression to higher ranks is strongly governed by seniority, mandatory or incentive retirement systems are needed to provide accelerated staggered attrition. The following is a succinct description of the American system:

> For officers, the retirement system is closely integrated with an up-or-out selective promotion system. Each officer is periodically considered for promotion and those not selected for advancement are eliminated from the active duty force. Those who have 20 years or more of service are forced to retire upon completion of a specified career length (30 years or less, dependent upon the grade attained before promotion failure). Those with less than 20 years' service are discharged with a separation payment. Generally speaking, only officers selected for flag rank (admiral/general) can expect to be able to serve more than 30 years. Enlisted personnel are not subject to the up-or-out selection principle, but few (less than 4 percent of the total enlisted population) serve beyond 20 years, most availing themselves of the voluntary retirement option soon after completing a minimum-length career [U.S. Department of Defense, 1969: iii-4, vol. 5].

"Thirty-year-man" is thus as much a misnomer for the career soldier as is the more current G.I. slang term, "lifer."

Enlisted retirees make up a large and progressively increasing majority of the total retired population. The retired officer also rarely has been on active duty long enough to become a General Bullmoose or even a Colonel Blimp. He more typically retires as a lieutenant colonel or major, or a commander, or lieutanant commander in the naval service (see Table 1).

Another change in the composition of the retiree population in recent years is the increasing proportion of nondisability to disability retirees. Since the time in the middle 1950s when persons retired for disability accounted for almost half the total, the disability retirements have remained at an almost constant level, while the

Table 1. Retirements From Active Duty By Rank in Fiscal Year 1966

Rank	Officers (N=11,852)	Percentage
O-7 to O-10	Brigadier General-Rear Admiral to General-Admiral	1.4
O-6	Colonel-Captain	14.4
O-5	Lieutenant Colonel-Commander	36.2
O-4	Major-Lieutenant Commander	28.1
O-1 to O-3	Second Lieutenant-Ensign to Captain-Lieutenant	8.2
W-1 to W-4	Warrant Officers	11.7
	TOTAL	100.0

Rank	Enlisted Men (N=42,180)	Percentage
E-9	Sergeant Major-Master Chief Petty Officer	3.9
E-8	Master Sergeant-Senior Chief Petty Officer	8.9
E-7	Sergeant First Class-Chief Petty Officer	26.5
E-6	Staff Sergeant-Petty Officer	30.2
E-5	Sergeant-Petty Officer-1	20.3
E-4	Corporal-Petty Officer-2	5.9
E-1 to E-3	Recruit-Seaman Recruit to PFC-Seaman	4.3
	TOTAL	100.0

Source: Based on data from Glenn (n.d.) OASD.

nondisability retirements have grown rapidly. Thus, forty-three percent of those who retired in 1958 were retired for disability, but in 1967 only twenty-four percent were disability retirees.

A "second career" pattern is in large measure a response to the high cost of either full pensioning or prolongations of the period of service. Even with limited pensions, the direct cost of retired pay to governments is large—in the United States it is approaching $2.5 billion annually and will continue to mount.

SECOND
CAREER PROGRAMS

In the period since World War II, the major nations have had to develop elaborate specialized programs to accommodate in civilian careers large numbers of men whose vocational experience was largely or exclusively limited to the military. These special programs have been instituted at various times in several nations; for example, Britain in 1968 (Abrams, 1962), the Soviet Union in 1960, and the United States in 1960. "Humps" of personnel, representing the carry-over of war-period inflated rank structures have complicated their military retirement systems.

SOCIAL
CHANGES

The need for deliberate programs to provide for status-maintaining employment of men who complete military careers with many years of work-life still before them reflects (1) the changing social base of recruitment, (2) changes in the social and economic structure of areas from which current retirees were originally recruited, (3) the elaboration of technical specialization within the military, and (4) the unprofitability of warfare. These points have been discussed by Biderman (1966).

Those leaving the service, for instance, cannot, as in the past, return to their farms, manors, or towns to initiate or resume careers resting heavily on ascriptive status and simple managerial and technical skills.

The unprofitability of modern warfare—for the state in general, and for the military class in particular—has been another fundamental development complicating the problem of military retirement. Modern times are distinctive in that the immediate spoils of war are less prominent among the objectives for which wars are fought. Even when economic goals are among the motives for war, costs tend to outweigh gains because of the nature of modern weaponry. In earlier history, obsolete military men (among the victors, at any rate) could be rewarded with lands or administrative positions in conquered dominions. Where cash pensions were paid, the costs to the public treasury could be reconciled against the gains to it from plunder or the revenues of the imperial dominions gained. Contemporary warfare affords only a few parallels, although this presumably would not have been the case had the vanquished states of World War II been the victors. The closest current parallels are where a revolutionary military becomes the state apparatus and military men assume positions in (or as) the civil bureaucracy.

After two world wars, military occupation of the vanquished nations, as well as the postwar military operations arising from the war-caused disruptions of the political status quo in various regions of the world, provided some degree of time-elasticity for deferring the career problems of military careerists. The military occupations of defeated nations, the foreign aid programs, overseas base systems, and trust territory administration for a time provided a counterpart to the imperium of earlier epochs. The sustained active-duty strength of military forces through the postwar era, however, has contributed to swelling the retirement problem of the present day. The dissolution of empires has made for particularly acute retirement and second-career problems in Britain, France, and the Low Countries. The present trend toward American disinvolvement from overseas bases and client states can have analogous consequences.

GROWTH OF THE
RETIRED MILITARY POPULATION

The historical growth of the number of persons drawing military retired pay reflects the nation's wars and the tendency for its standing military forces to be stabilized at a new, elevated plateau after each war emergency. The levels of active duty forces before and after each war-emergency period are shown in Table 2. From the turn of the century until 1961, there was a slow and fairly steady increase in the military retired population, with spurts during war years, presumably from disabilities incurred by regulars during hostilities, and then again after the twentieth anniversary of the war mobilization. With the exception of the gap between the War of 1812 and the Mexican War, wars tended to be fairly conveniently spaced in time through World War II so that the augmented regular ranks of one war tended to be ripe for retirement after serving as senior figures in the next. As noted below, it was not until the post-Civil War period that there was any provision for involuntary nondisability retirements, however. Each postwar period shown in Table 2, therefore, also has a retirement bulge.

Table 2. Pre- and Postwar Active Duty Military Forces in the United States—1794-1968

	Year	Active Duty Military Personnel
Post-Revolutionary	1794	5,700
Before War of 1812	1811	11,500
After War of 1812	1817	14,600
Before Mexican War	1845	20,700
After Mexican War	1850	21,000
Before Civil War	1860	28,000
After Civil War	1871	42,000
Before Spanish-American War	1897	43,000
After Spanish-American War	1901	112,000
Before World War I	1916	179,000
After World War I	1923	247,000
Before World War II	1939	334,500
After World War II	1947	1,583,000
Before Korean War	1950	1,460,000
After Korean War	1955	2,935,000
Before Vietnam War	1965	2,653,000
Current	1968	3,489,520

Sources: U.S. Bureau of the Census (1960, 1968: 257).

Since World War II

Since World War II and for far into the future, the curves of growth of the retired military population show the escalation and acceleration of these patterns to much higher orders of magnitude than in the past. First of all, the cutback of military personnel after World War II never achieved the proportions of that after previous conflicts. Furthermore, two successive conflicts—Korea and

Vietnam—have come hard on the heels of one another. The number of retirements per year turned sharply upward with the twentieth anniversary of World War II. They climbed from about 21,000 retirements per year in fiscal years 1958 and 1959 to 42,000 in 1961, and reached 65,000 in 1968 (Glenn, n.d.). The number of persons retiring each month in recent years is greater than the total retired population in the period immediately before World War I. The current yearly additions to military retired rolls are greater than the entire military retired population at the close of World War II. To give one other perspective on the changed order of magnitude of the retired military population, it is now more than twice as large as the active duty force at the onset of World War II—the largest standing armed force in our peacetime history until that point.

Prior to the Vietnam war, the Defense Department projected a fairly steady growth of the retired military population through 1980. This assumed a relatively stable-sized peacekeeping force. In 1962, the expectation was that the total would reach one million men in 1980. In 1968, the number projected for 1980 became 1,235,000.

Effect of the Vietnam War

The Vietnam War has slightly retarded the current rate of retirements from the armed forces. It has also had complicated and unknowable consequences for the commitments to the armed forces of those whose period of service has been lengthened by war service. On thy one hand, many members of the armed forces who might otherwise have extended their period of service voluntarily have chosen to leave. Reenlistment rates have been declining as hostilities have become livelier. On the other hand, overall force levels have been higher than those projected earlier. The investment of time in active military duty may have become consequential for many men who have voluntarily or involuntarily stayed in the armed forces during what has begun to be called the longest war in our history.

The "Longest War"

The Cold War, rather than the Vietnam conflict, might more properly be called the longest war in our history, however. It is this "war" that has been most responsible for the maintenance of large active duty military forces and the creation within the society of a substantial military retired population. Despite the development of concepts of a "normal" career force during this period, with its associated implications for an expanded retiree population, projections of the size and composition of the retired population through the future ultimately involve assumptions such as those of the recent past that have had a habit of being contradicted by history. Radical escalations and deescalations of world tensions have repeatedly altered forecasts. The accuracy of projections also are markedly affected by changes in military policy, doctrine, and technology.

To a limited extent, however, the number of retired military personnel who will pass into the civilian society at various points in the future has been rendered predictable by previous, legislatively mandated policy. Although even in a fairly short-range future, this can be altered by changes of mind on the part of Congress; the implied moral commitment to the men involved and that which they take to be such a commitment sets some likely limits. As of 1969, more than 440,000 men have completed fifteen years or more of active military service (Glenn, n.d.). One may confidently expect that, with only small losses to the mortality tables and other premature removals from the ranks of those serving, most of these men will be added to the retired military list during the next five years.

COST TO
TAXPAYER

The predictable was anticipated. From a national political point of view, an unattractive aspect of the growing military retired population is the swiftly mounting slice of the annual budget required for their pay and the prospect that these sums have nowhere to go but rapidly upward. The magical figure of one billion dollars per year was a milestone reached in the early nineteen-sixties which led to a reexamination of the entire military retired system by Congress and the Defense Department.

But so far, no easy answers have been found to the staggering military retirement costs. In 1961, projected costs for 1970 were $1.74 billion and for 1980, $3.04 billion. These projections by the Defense Department repeatedly have had to be revised upward, however. The department now expects retired pay costs to have approached $2.5 billion in fiscal year 1969. The current estimate for 1970 is $2.7 billion, and for 1980, $6.2 billion (see Table 3).

Table 3. Projected Annual Nondisability and Disability Retirement Pay
Disbursements

Fiscal Year	Total Annual Retired Pay (000,000)	Percentage Increase Over Fiscal Year 1969 Retired Pay
1969	$ 2,450	
1970	2,735	11.6
1975	4,344	77.3
1980	6,164	151.6
1985	8,174	233.6
1990	10,536	330.0
1995	13,521	451.9
2000	17,350	608.2

Source: U.S. Department of Defense (1969: 2-30, vol. 5).

Political Significance

In terms of a purely political calculus, the unattractiveness of the
retired pay appropriation can be seen by contrasting it with other
items of the federal budget. Retired pay in fiscal year 1968 was
about one-tenth the amount needed to pay everyone in uniform. It
would have been even higher, relatively, had not the Vietnam War
swelled the active duty ranks.

Furthermore, the cost of retired pay is increasing disproportionately so that by 1980, expenditures for retired pay are expected
to be as much as one-fifth the total budget for military personnel,
and by the year 2020, almost thirty percent (U.S. Department of
Defense, 1969: vol. 4).

In pay alone, the retired military required greater expenditures
than the total expenditures of each of nine of the fifteen federal
departments. The costs of retired pay constitute a special thorn in
the side of those who worry about the federal budget because the
amount needed for retired pay must be appropriated anew each year.
Unlike most other modern pension plans, the uniformed services
system is noncontributory, nonfunded, and uninvested. Unlike

funded plans, the annual appropriation character of retired pay gives it special and painful visibility. Had a fund continually been put aside which, actually or theoretically, accrued interest during the entire period of the active duty of these men from which payments could be made upon their retirement, the bite on the public treasury would not have the vexing appearance it has now.

Pension or Pay?

Although the noncontributory and nonfunded features of the retirement system have thus far survived, there is a continual movement in the direction of defining the benefits more on the order of the "pension" than the "pay" model (Sharp and Biderman, 1966).

One casualty of this trend has been the principle of "recomputation," that is, recomputing retired pay to reflect any changes in active duty pay, as opposed to the alternative principle of readjusting retired pay to reflect changes in the cost of living (U.S. Congress, Senate, 1961).

This issue had been debated heatedly in Congress for a number of years. In 1958 compromise legislation created a situation in which persons retired after the 1958 military pay bill received retired pay based on the new higher rates for active duty personnel, while those retired earlier were granted a cost-of-living increase. The principle of recomputation has been the most prominent legislative cause of retired officers ever since. The complaints of their organization representatives regarding the inequities of the abandonment of recomputation of retired pay continue with undiminished vigor, even though Congress has explicitly rejected their appeal in each change that has been made in military pay during the 1960s. Communiques on the running battle over recomputation appear regularly in the Retired Officer Association's magazine, *Retired Officer.*

With each successive military pay increase, greater disparities are created between the retired pay of those who retired at a given rank and period of service in earlier years and the pay of more recently retired personnel, since military pay has been going up considerably more rapidly than the Bureau of Labor Statistics consumer price index to which retired pay is tied. The increases have been especially great at the higher ranks. From a military point of view, there is a peculiar offensiveness to the system of rates based on rise in the cost-of-living in that seniors (those of a given rank who retired earlier) receive less pay than their juniors (those who achieved the same or even a lower rank later and retired later). The retirement pay of a brigadier general who retired with thirty years of service in 1958, for instance, would be computed on basic pay of $1,175 per month, whereas the pay of a colonel retiring with thirty years of service on 1968 would be computed on basic pay of $1,373. The differences can be substantial—as much as twenty-five percent.

Recomputation has been a strong rallying cry for the military retired. Its abandonment as the basis of calculating retired pay has been regarded as not merely creating an anomaly but as "a breach of contract with the men who led our forces in two great wars."

Two-Step Annuity Plan

As a result of the comprehensive reevaluation of the military retired pay system which was begun in 1966, the Defense Department has now proposed a plan for giving more weight to the realities of the second career pattern. The Hubbell Committee (U.S. Department of Defense, 1969) has recommended a two-step annuity plan under which the retiree would receive small payments during the initial years of his retirement when his second-career income presumably would be substantial. He would become eligible for greater amounts beginning at age fifty-five.

Second-Career Assistance Programs

With its entire personnel structure dependent upon the effective operation of the partial-pension, second-career retirement system, the Defense Department had a vital stake for many years in encouraging the placement of retirees in civilian jobs. For a number of reasons, however, it has had to tread gingerly. Since 1958, the Labor Department rather than the Defense Department has been the locus of most attention to the second-career problem, as is the case in Great Britain. Paradoxically, Defense and the services were constrained both by the fact that the retired serviceman became a civilian and that a military identity clung to him after retirement. The appearance of the military meddling with the civilian society had to be avoided and the military also had to be wary of accusations of looking after its own men too aggressively (Biderman, 1959; 1960). Preparing men for the transition to civilian careers was not only outside the mission of the armed forces, but fears were also raised that it conflicts with it. The serviceman might be distracted from concentration on the business at hand and he might be encouraged to leave for a high paying job in industry. Retention was a higher priority concern than retirement. These conflicting concerns were focused by results of early studies of the second-career problem. These showed that very few men did anything specific to prepare themselves for a second career earlier than a few weeks before their date of retirement (U.S. Congress, Senate Committee on Armed Services, 1961; Sharp and Biderman, 1966). Many retired with no specific plans, no counseling, little applicable training. It had also been observed that the earlier a serviceman undertook to plan for his retirement, the more successful was his second-career placement (Sharp and Biderman, 1966). As retiree employment problems achieved more prominence in the sixties and as threats to even the existing levels of retired pay grew with their mounting cost to the taxpayer, proposals were pressed more vigorously for retirement counseling programs beginning at mid-career (U.S. Department of Labor and Air Force Association, 1963).

With considerable initiative from military alumni associations, notably the Air Force Association and the Retired Officers Association, an early preretirement counseling program was begun in 1964 on military bases, involving the cooperation of the Labor Department, state employment services, and Defense Department (Mailler, 1968).

Concentration of Settlement

One special area of concern has been the high concentration of retirees in just a few areas of the country. It was feared that the attractions of facilities in large military bases which retirees are eligible to use were leading to a situation in which retirees were competing with one another for the same jobs in the favored communities (U.S. Department of Defense, 1964; Biderman, 1960; U.S. Congress, Senate Committee on Armed Services, 1961). Just commissary and post exchange privileges can be worth between $600 and $700 per year for a family of four with an income in the $6,000 to $7,000 range, according to unpublished estimates provided us by the Hubbell Committee. Military medical and recreational facilities can be even more important considerations to a retiree in choosing his postretirement home.

Half of all current retirees live in ten states, states which between them have only about a quarter of the total population of the country. Just four states account for one-third of all the retirees: California, Florida, Virginia, and Washington. In each of these states, as well as in the District of Columbia, there are more than twice as many retirees as expected on a population basis. However, military retirees do not constitute a very significant part of the population of any state. In Florida, where they are most numerous in relation to total population, they comprise only seventy-six percent of the population of the state.

Although career military personnel tend to be recruited disproportionately from smaller communities, upon retirement they have a much greater concentration in large urban areas than is true of the population as a whole. Especially favored are the large metropolitan areas of the South Atlantic, Southwest, and Pacific states, and the national capital region.

In areas where the concentrations are the greatest, retirees can constitute a very important part of the work force. We estimate that military retirees made up about nine percent of the work force of the Pensacola area in 1967 and about ten percent of all civilian workers in San Diego County. For Tacoma, the figure was about eight percent and for Seattle about two percent. (These estimates are based on Zip Code tabulations. They assume that labor force participation by retirees in each area is about ninety percent as it is for the total retiree population. Only civilian workers covered by Social Security are considered in the total labor force estimates for these areas.)

More recent studies of retiree concentration, including some as yet unpublished, should at least partially allay anxieties about the effects of retiree concentration. If anything, retirees in the most favored localities and those who live close enough to bases to make moderate, regular use of military facilities have much more satisfactory adjustment to retirement (Watson, 1963), lower unemployment, and higher incomes (Sharp and Biderman, 1966). This is accounted for by the fact that the popular retirement areas are all ones of recent and rapid population growth. The bases of this growth—good climate and a growing economy stimulated by military spending—are the same as those which provide the attractions for retiree settlement.

Since the communities in which retirees concentrate are ones of high military activity, the pattern of settlement presumably does not at present justify concerns about retirees exerting a militarizing influence on these communities. For example, in the San Diego and

Pensacola SMSAs, which we estimate to be those with the highest ratios of military retired to total population, there are three times as many active duty military men as retirees.

In the event of sharp cutbacks in the size of the armed forces and military spending, however, all of the types of concern with retiree concentrations which we have discussed would be matched by real problems.

INCOME
MAINTENANCE

Although the sum of all retired pay appears substantial to congressmen as an item of the national budget, the monthly check received by most of the beneficiaries is far from sufficient to enable them to live according to their former standard, and is usually inadequate to meet their basic needs. Few could afford to live on retired pay alone.

Income Gap

The size of the gap between retired pay and the average money equivalent of pay and benefits received on active duty is shown for several selected ranks in Table 4. The average lieutenant colonel who retires after twenty years of service would have to earn in the neighborhood of $10,600 as a civilian to maintain his plane of living; a master sergeant would have to earn about $6,200. For the much smaller numbers who retire after thirty years of service, higher retired pay makes the gap smaller.

The need to work is heightened by the fact that most of those retiring in recent years have dependents. The Hubbell Survey showed about seventy percent of nondisability retirees as having two or more dependents at the time of retirement. Second-career employment, therefore, is almost universal. Only nine percent of all retirees dropped out of the labor force completely upon retirement and only four percent of the enlisted men (U.S. Department of Defense, 1969).

Second-Career Earnings

Despite the large number of studies that have been conducted, however, it is not possible to give a satisfactory answer to the question most often asked about the retired serviceman. "How well

Table 4. Active Duty Pay as Compared to Retired Pay

Pay Grade[a]	Average Active Duty Emolument (Adjusted) October 1, 1967[b]	Retired Pay 20 Years Service 1967 Pay Scale	Retired Pay 30 Years Service 1967 Pay Scale
O-8	$ 27,151	$ 9,698.40	$ 15,133.56
O-6	19,724	6,715.80	11,561.40
O-5	16,670	6,073.20	9,431.16
O-4	13,736	5,257.80	7,886.76
E-9	10,633	3,607.20	6,247.80
E-8	9,301	3,162.60	5,580.96
E-7	8,191	2,790.00	5,024.76

a. For relationship between "pay grade" designations (O-1, E-9, etc.), and military rank titles (Lieutenant, Sergeant Major, etc.), see Table 1, p. 126.

b. Estimated by adding to basic pay, average amounts for quarters and subsistence allowances, tax advantage, and retirement benefit. For many active duty servicemen there are also special pays such as those for flight, hazardous duty, parachuting, medical and dental needs, and so on.

Sources: Data on retired pay from Glenn (n.d.). Data on active duty pay from Louis Stockstill and James Hessman (1968: 36).

off is he compared to his situation in the service?" The reason for this is not a paucity of apparently reliable information on second-career earnings, but rather the inability of the retirees themselves or anybody else to assign a definite value to their preretirement, active-duty earnings. There is, first of all, the extremely difficult problem of attaching specific monetary values to various fringe benefits and government-provided services which active-duty military personnel receive, and the further complication that some retirees continue to receive some of these services. Beyond this, the relative economic well-being of the retiree in civilian life involves the broader problem of the need of retirees to adopt different patterns and styles of life which present different needs for monetary outlays than is the case during active duty. For example, when one is able to plan ahead on the basis of taking one's place of residence for granted, expenses are likely to be less. On the other hand, living totally in the civilian community may require greater cash outlays to achieve various satisfactions of life than living within the military society.

On the average, using Hubell Committee data, it appears that retiree postretirement income, including retired pay, is at least roughly equal to the total emoluments of active duty. But this means that many experience a decline in their plane of living while others end up better off. If very substantial numbers experience severe economic hardship after retirement, even though they are a minority of all retired personnel, news of this would have seriously adverse effects on the ability of the armed forces to recruit and retain career servicemen. Apart from the rhetoric about "doing the right thing by our fighting men," there is this very pragmatic consideration to the level of retirement benefits and the successful placement of retirees in second careers.

Future Hazards

The postretirement incomes revealed by surveys of the retired military suggest that the present level of benefits just barely does the job of keeping grounds for such negative feedback within tolerable bounds. It is quite possible that it may not do the job in the future. First of all, the second-career system of the post-World War II period has received its test under the most favorable circumstances of continual full employment. It is quite possible that the second-career jobs of military personnel might be particularly vulnerable ones in a period of "labor surplus."

In 1965, 6.7% of both officer and enlisted nondisability retirees were not employed and looking for work. An additional two percent of these retirees were employed only part-time and were looking for full-time work. Either retirees take a considerable period of time to reach full earning potential or more recent retirees have less civilian job potential, since each of the last half-dozen yearly retirement cohorts has progressively lower average second-career incomes and higher rates of unemployment.

Nonetheless, while there are appreciable problems among a minority of retirees, by and large the assumptions underlying the second-career retirement systems have worked out satisfactorily. Only a small minority fail to get jobs and most of the jobs they do get provide at least adequate income maintenance when supplemented by present rates of retired pay. Retired pay is indeed substantial enough to allow older retirees to drop out of the labor force altogether more frequently than civilians (Fechter and Mahoney, 1967).

SECOND-CAREER
EMPLOYMENT

Equitable Compensation

A career of military service can mean a great variety of occupational experiences. Some career patterns can actually add up quite useful credentials for remunerative and rewarding civilian employment. Other career lines are presumably of scant value in qualifying one for a civilian job. The most distinctively military specialities—the combat roles esteemed by the soldier—would be those expected to involve the greatest sacrifices. From this stand-point, an equitable military retirement system would compensate individuals in differential proportion to the degree to which their particular service careers affect their second-career earning potential.

Skill Utilization

The actual degree to which retirees use their military-acquired skills in their civilian jobs is difficult to assess, given the necessarily broad job categories, military and civilian, to which complex job descriptions have to be reduced. Judging from job titles alone, close relationships between military and second-career occupational specialities apparently occur only in a minority of the cases surveyed by Sharp and Biderman (1966). Such relationships obtain more often for enlisted men than for officers, since the former more often have a narrow specialty which they pursued consistently in their active duty career. But, even among enlisted men, close correspondence between military specialty and civilian job is far from universal. Even in the military specialities, where transfer appears most likely (such as medical and dental specialties; electronic, electrical, and mechanical repairmen; and craftsmen), judgments on the basis of broad job categories indicate that no more than one-third to one-half moved into directly comparable civilian jobs (Sharp and Biderman, 1966). There are, however, a minority of retirees with specialized technical training in such sought-after skills as engineering or electronics. It is these people who usually find civilian placement the easiest. This is not true for all specialties, however. Relationships between specialty and job-placement are not so automatic and clear-cut as one might expect.

Among officers—considering only those military specialty groups represented by sizable numbers of men in the BSSR study—those who had been in budgeting and in research had exceptionally high employment rates (over eighty-five percent employed full time within six months), while those with ordnance and signal specialties, as well as aircraft pilots, least often (sixty-five to seventy percent) worked full-time (Sharp and Biderman, 1966).

Importance of Formal Education

Educational attainment is consistently found to be the single most important correlate of all measures of second-career success— ease of job finding, earnings, skill-utilization, and satisfaction. One consequence of this is that those officers who were able to make the grade in the service on the basis of demonstrated abilities, rather than formal education, are frequently unable to match their military status in civilian jobs.

Military Specialties and Earnings

Data from the Hubbell Committee's survey on 43,000 of its respondents who had been fully employed during the entire year reaffirmed previous observations that second-career earnings were strongly correlated with education, age, and rank. To examine thy importance of military specialties while holding these factors constant, we determined how big a percentage each retiree's earnings deviated from the average for all other retirees who had approximately the same education, age, and rank as the given respondent. If we compare the means of these income deviation scores for general classes of military specialties, we find the differences generally of rather modest proportions. Among officers, only those in medicine stand out, with nurses earning on the average of about twenty-five percent less than other retirees of equivalent age, education, and rank, while other professional medical officers earn about thirty-five percent more than their peers. Those whose principal military specialty was one of the more "military" ones—that is, tactical operations, general or executive officers—averaged slightly greater incomes than other retirees of equivalent education, age, and rank. Administrative and supply officers deviated quite markedly in the negative direction. Engineers had a pronounced favorable earnings position in second careers and other nonmedical scientific, technical, or professional specialists also did well.

It is among enlisted men that the combat specialist is greatly disadvantaged in a second career. Infantrymen are at the bottom of the heap in second-career earnings. At the top are technicians and craftsmen of various kinds, particularly those in electronics specialties. The exceptions are medical technicians. Their earnings average appreciably under those of their education, rank, and age peers. Enlisted men whose primary jobs were administrative or service also have poor earnings. With the three variables controlled, however, the differences between the various classes of specialists are not as marked as in raw comparisons. Infantry specialists, for example, average about ten percent less in earnings than other retirees with whom they are matched in education, age, and rank.

Military Skill Utilization

The BSSR study reached the conclusion that highly specific skills of retired military men are not the dominant element in their successful transition to a civilian career (Sharp and Biderman, 1966; 1968). In analyzing the considerations that entered into employer's and job counselor's evaluations of retirees' job qualifications, it was concluded that various civilian, common-denominator criteria, such as education, articulation, personality characteristics, and status (for which rank achieved was an indicator), were given uppermost consideration. In both hiring and assigning men, the study found, employers usually did not attempt specific matching of jobs and specific military-acquired skills.

Although the career soldier (as well as the veteran) generally attaches high value to his experience in the service, many retirees feel that their skills were not utilized in their civilian jobs to the extent that they had been in the military.

Among officers, only those in the professional specialties and those who had specialized in communications, electronics, and research and development reported more skill utilization in their civilian job than in the military. Even among enlisted technicians, mechanics, and craftsmen, who most often found their military specialties helped them get jobs, many say their civilian employers made less, rather than more use of their skills than had the military.

These feelings that their skills are not being utilized does not involve a reassessment on contact with the civilian work world. For the most part, both before and after retirement, BSSR's respondents put a high rating on their work qualifications when asked to compare themselves with civilians doing identical jobs. In fact, the proportion of those who consider themselves better qualified than civilians most often increased after experience in civilian jobs (Biderman and Sharp, 1968). Those who were most successful in the military tend to be most successful in second careers. Studies of the second career jobs held by retired military personnel show very high correlations between civilian income and job satisfaction on the one hand and success in the military career. This is the case if success is measured by service in the more highly regarded military specialties, rank achieved, or subjective satisfaction with one's military career (Biderman and Sharp, 1968).

General Skills and Credentials

With the exception of the retirees who work for the Defense Department or in defense industry, few find jobs which use their distinctive military experience. By and large, the success of these men in getting jobs rests not so much on how different they are from other members of the labor force as on how similar they are to civilians competing for the same jobs. This is true even with regard to employment in defense roles in a society which for three decades has engaged a large part of its civilian labor force in the defense economy.

Recognition of this fact has precipitated rhetoric from military sources asserting the nonpeculiarity of the experience, skills, and outlook of the military man. In discussing Department of Defense policy on the military retired at the Conference on Military Retirement sponsored by the Air Force Association and the Department of Labor, Assistant Secretary of Defense Norman S. Paul stated,

> To properly understand this aspect we should *not* think of today's career military service as a separate and distinct profession, per se. Rather it is the bringing together of many professions as well as technical skills in an organized and coordinated effort toward a common goal. It is this broad diversity of capabilities within the overall military profession which is often overlooked by large segments of American Business.
>
> The fact is, there are probably few military skills which do not have some transference value for civilian occupations. The main difficulty appears to be in translating skills and experience gained in a military setting into specific civilian terms so that they can be "matched up" with employer needs [U.S. Department of Labor and Air Force Association, 1963: 5-6].

All of the various sources of vocational assistance urge and coach the military man to reformulate his experience using terms of the civilian work world in his resumes and job-seeking interviews. It is likely that he will continually experience less strain in doing so because of convergences of the military and civilian occupational structures (Biderman and Sharp, 1968).

Much contemporary American writing on the U.S. military, stresses not only how remarkably like civilian institutions the military is becoming but also, the degree of influence of military-originated forms and ways upon the conduct of civilian enterprises. Lang (1964: 45-47), for example, writes,

> First, in terms of enlisted men's occupational distribution, the military establishment stands out as one of the more technologically advanced sectors of American society. The military employs higher proportions of technical and scientific, administrative-clerical personnel, mechanics and repairmen, and service workers than are found in the male labor force. Likewise it employs significantly lower proportions of men in the categories "craftsmen" and "operatives and laborers." To these statistics, covering only enlisted personnel, must be added the scientific, technical, and administrative skills which are found in even greater concentration among officers. . . .
>
> . . . the civilian occupational structure reveals a decline in the number of self-employed managers and officials and of gainfully employed persons in the agricultural sector, . . . the decline of occupations with no civilian-military counterparts both in the armed forces and in the labor force suggests increasing overlap between skills required in the two sectors. As a result, experience acquired during military service has increasing transfer value in a civilian career.

The ease with which the large majority of retirees have found civilian jobs is itself an indication of the degree to which there is not vast disjunction between the civilian and military occupational worlds. True, large numbers of retirees remain in the "military-industrial complex"—our estimates from the data presented here are that perhaps as many as forty percent of those working are in DOD or other defense-related agencies, or in defense industry, or in a variety of jobs which have military personnel as their predominant market or clientele. This leaves a majority in exclusively or predominantly civil pursuits, however.

Table 5 showing occupations of men retired between 1960 and 1963 illustrates the broad range of skills which retirees can bring to their second careers. The general categories of this table suggest, although they do not convey as fully as does a more lengthy and detailed breakdown, the predominance of general administrative, managerial, sales, and educational work among the officer retirees.

Table 5. Occupation in 1963 of Service Personnel Retired Between
1960 and 1963

Occupation	Officers		Enlisted Men	
	N	%	N	%
Salesman	116	14	136	7
Personnel	32	4	33	2
Financial	36	4	21	1
Business executive	95	12	31	2
Other business occupation	104	13	125	7
Skilled craftsman	23	3	302	16
Semiskilled or skilled factory work	1	*	107	6
Engineering	74	9	42	2
College teaching	11	1		
High school or elementary school teaching	40	5	10	1
Physician	3	*		
Other professional occupation	52	6	38	2
Clerical	30	4	126	7
Electronic technician	14	2	78	4
X-ray technician	3	*	25	1
Other technician	10	1	42	2
Other technical occupation	37	4	97	5
Service occupation	50	6	358	18
All others	101	12	340	17
TOTAL	832	100	1911	100

*Less than one percent.
Source: Biderman and Sharp (1967).

Among enlisted personnel, skilled craftsmen, clerks, and service workers (this category includes guards, policemen, firemen)
predominated.

Typically then, these are nontechnical occupations—only sixteen
percent of the officers and fourteen percent of the enlisted men who
retired between 1960 and 1963 reported that they were working in
engineering and technical jobs. Among the most recent retirees, the
proportion of enlisted men in technical work was even lower.

Although elaborate hardware is a dominant aspect of the image
of the armed forces, most of those who stay in the service until

retirement have progressively more indirect relationships to equipment. People- and paper-manipulating experience tends to predominate among the retirees. In examining the actual credentials of those
who have retired in recent years, we find that the career management
systems of the armed forces, with rotation of assignments and
elaborate overhead organization, have tended to produce officers
with primarily managerial skills rather than technical ones. The
senior enlisted man, too, is as often in middle management as in a
technical job, but he has greater difficulty in finding comparable
employment in civilian institutions (see Biderman and Sharp, 1968).

Employers

This may account for the pronounced preference retirees voiced
in the BSSR survey for employment in large, bureaucratic organizations—big business and government. It is in such institutions that
they are most likely to be able to replicate the roles they had in the
biggest employing institution of all.

Among employed men who retired between 1960 and 1963,
fifty-one percent were employed in these types of institutions: about
one-fifth in business organizations with more than 2,500 employees,
about one-fourth in the federal government, and eight percent in
state and local government. An additional fifteen percent worked in
medium-sized businesses, i.e., those employing between fifty and
2,500 workers (Sharp and Biderman, 1966).

The concentration of retirees in larger enterprises is evident by
contrast with the picture for privately employed persons in the labor
force as a whole. Almost half of all business employees in the labor
force work in enterprises with under fifty employees (U.S. Bureau of
the Census, 1968: 476) while only about thirty percent of the
retirees who are employed in business work in these small
enterprises.

Even more noteworthy is the exceptionally high number of
retirees working outside of the business sector. Over forty percent
were employed in governmental, educational, medical, or other
nonprofit institutions.

Somewhat more detailed information on types of employers was
developed in the BSSR survey of May 1964 retirees. This survey, as
seen in Table 6, shows the wide variety of businesses in which
retirees are employed—financial and manufacturing organizations,
engineering and construction firms, transportation and communica-

tions facilities, or other types of industries as well as retail stores. Only seventeen percent of the officers were engaged in manufacturing industries. Many more were in financial institutions, principally those concerned with the sale of insurance or real estate. (Twenty percent of the enlisted men were in various kinds of retail establishments, another twenty percent in manufacturing.)

Only eleven percent of the employed officers were in the aerospace and electronics industries—those which figure most prominently in allegations of conflict of interest and complaints about the excessive power of the military-industrial complex. These data do not reveal a remarkable concentration of retirees in war industries. To the extent that there is a military-industrial complex, it does not appear to be taking care of its own as well as it might.

These gross figures, however, tend to understate the significance of retiree participation in big business, since the greater education and the rank of the retiree, the more likely he is to have big business employment. Further, as retirees gain experience in the labor force, there is some drift toward bigger enterprises.

Government as Employer

Goverment is the largest employer category. In 1966, the Hubbell Committee determined that one-third of all retired enlisted men and reserve officers as well as eighteen percent of all regular officers had held civil service jobs since retirement.

The lower rate for regular officers is due to the fact that until 1964 they were almost completely barred from taking civil service jobs by the Dual Office Act. Reserve officers also were impeded from taking government jobs by the "dual compensations" provisions of the 1932 Economy Act. It set $10,000 per year as the maximum a retired officer could receive from civil service and retired pay, combined (U.S. Department of the Air Force, 1957). This ceiling, which was a handsome sum in the thirties, continued in effect until 1964 because of the strong opposition of civil servants to federal hiring of ex-military men (Biderman, 1964). Liberalizations of the statutes enacted in 1964 now permit regular officers to take civil service jobs, but subject them as well as reserve officers to a forfeiture of one-half of all of their retired pay above $2,000 when they take a civil service job (U.S. Department of the Army, 1965). Despite the limitation, from data assembled by the U.S. Civil Service Commission (1965, 1966) we have calculated that there have been

Table 6. Type of Employer—Detail (BSSR Sample)

(in percentages)

Type of Employer	Job Holders		Total (N=1595)[a]
	Officers (N=399)	Enlisted Men (N=1196)	
Government	18	20	21
Department of Defense	8	8	8
Post Office Department	2	5	5
Other federal government	2	2	2
State government	4	2	3
Local government	2	3	3
Institutional	13	11	12
Educational	10	4	6
Medical	2	5	4
Other (including nonprofit)	1	2	2
Financial	23	8	11
Insurance—real estate	19	6	9
Banking and other financial	4	2	2
Manufacturing	17	20	20
Aerospace, electronic	11	7	8
All other manufacturing	6	13	12
Retail Stores	12	20	17
Retail (durable goods)	4	6	5
Repair and service	3	3	3
Food and liquor	1	3	2
Restaurant	1	2	2
Auto agency, garage, service	3	6	5
Transportation and communication	4	6	6
Engineering and construction	4	6	6
Detective agencies	1	3	2
All others	8	6	6
TOTAL	100	100	100

[a]Excludes (32) unknown.
Source: Sharp and Biderman (1966).

great increases in the rate of federal hirings of retirees since the 1964 change, particularly in the higher civil service grades.

Previously, the restrictions against regulars and the $10,000 dual compensation ceiling operated to make officer retirees in the federal establishment disproportionately low in both civil service and retired military rank. Colonels and generals were particularly underrepresented. Only eight percent of men in these ranks were in the civil service as compared with sixteen percent of all retired officers.

Among enlisted men, who have been unaffected by dual-office and dual-compensation provisions, the relationship between rank and civil service employment is quite the reverse of that among officers. The proportions of enlisted retirees in federal service is highest in the upper grades—E-6 to E-9. This presumably is related to the fact that enlisted retirees in the civil service have a somewhat higher distribution of skill levels than that for all employed enlisted men.

Government employment presents particularly attractive opportunities for applying skills and experience developed in the service. The Department of Defense is by far the largest employer of retired military personnel—over sixty percent of the retirees in the competitive federal service work for defense agencies (U.S. Civil Service Commission, 1966). But it has been suggested that there is a more fundamental appeal of governmental service to the military professional even where direct translation of skill to civil service role does not apply. Janowitz (1960) has contended that a public service orientation is an important basis for the choice of a military career, that military professionals tend to be recruited in the United States from subcultures with strong traditions encouraging the choice of public service occupations, and that the military career experience reinforces these motivations.

The major significance of the civil service for the second-career problem is that of a large and expanding employment market for the lower-level, and even more particularly, middle-ranking retired military personnel. In addition to the special features which make government jobs more congenial to people with military backgrounds, the civil service is relatively open to lateral entry. It is relatively free from such barriers to entry as rigid seniority systems, closed unions, and nepotistic hiring.

After the Defense Department, according to U.S. Civil Service Commission reports (1965, 1966) the second largest government employer of retired military is the Post Office Department which employs twelve percent of the federally employed officers and twenty-one percent of those who retired as enlisted men. If we add together the retirees reported working in the postal field service, those in the lower-level general service, white-collar categories, GS-1 to 7, and those holding blue-collar, wage-board positions, the bulk of all retiree civil service employment (seventy percent) is accounted for. Even considering retired officers, alone, almost forty percent are in these categories.

Retirees in the federal service, however, tend to have more important positions than those in the private sector. For example, about thirty-one percent of the retired officers working for the federal government held professional or technical jobs, as compared with only nineteen percent of all employed retired officers. The professional level appointments, however, were mostly in defense agencies.

State and Local Government Employment

Unlike the federal civil service, only a small percentage of retirees are working in state and local government. Excluding teachers, about six percent of the working retirees are found in such jobs in each of the surveys that have been made. This is less than one-third as many as in the federal civil service, yet the total state and local government work force was three times the size of the federal and growing more rapidly. Many functions similar to those in which retirees are engaged in the federal establishment are also carried out at these levels.

The seniority system and the difficulty the older person has in moving into an established bureaucracy may largely explain the fact that so few retirees are found in such jobs. Police systems, which superficially at least, would appear especially suitable employers, usually have particularly impenetrable barriers to lateral entry. Important also is the low degree to which military personnel are integrated into local communities. This restricts their access to the job information, recommendations, and preferment that flow in informal social channels and that are extremely important even where formal merit hiring procedures are in force. For the higher ranking retirees, of course, the bars against political activity during their active-duty career restricts their selection for policy level jobs in local government.

A number of exceptions exist, notably in the case of men who had duty as commanders, provost marshalls, public information officers, exchange officers, and other jobs in the administrations of military installations which involved close relations with local civilian officials and businessmen. Retirees in local offices presumably will establish greater links between the military and civil communities in the future which will, in turn, draw more retirees into political and bureaucratic roles at the state and local level. The pattern exists already in some southern cities with large military installations. Governor George Wallace's choice of General LeMay as his running-mate owed much to associations growing out of the location of the Air University in the Alabama state capital.

The integration of American military leaders with civilian elites contrasts sharply with that of many other countries. The American case, for example, is quite different from that of the retired British officer, discussed by Abrams (1962), who has far more extensive affinities with "the establishment" through family ties, common educational background, and intimate patterns of social intercourse.

In addition to the traditional apolitical position of the professional soldier, the largely local basis of political organization in the American federal system also helps account for the relatively low prominence of retired officers in national politics. This may change as mass media and population mobility make moving up from the grass-roots less typically the path of political advancement.

Teaching

Of all aspects of the second career placement of military personnel, by far the greatest amount of attention has been given to utilization as teachers. The congruity of this career with the public service image may account in part for this special emphasis. The first impetus came in 1957 from a report of the President's Committee on Education Beyond the High School. Attention to the shortage of teachers of science and mathematics in the post-Sputnik context was also important and the utilization of retired personnel in education has subsequently been studied by a number of federal and private educational organizations and a number of student theses (Biderman, 1960; Boegel, 1961; U.S. Department of Defense, 1961). The public service definition of education has also allowed the Defense Department and military men to be more vigorous in pursuing programs for placing retirees in teaching than where there were worries about sentiments toward the military taking care of its own.

Informational campaigns have been conducted to acquaint military personnel with opportunities in education and with the varied criteria determining eligibility for teaching posts. Programs were also instituted that helped some interested officers surmount the hurdles of certification for secondary school and junior college teaching. These included NSF-assisted programs at a few universities, specifically for preparing retired military personnel to teach science and mathematics. Many other schools have solicited students from among the retired group, as well. The 1963 Omnibus Education Bill had a specific provision for assisting universities in establishing graduate programs for training military retirees and others for second careers in elementary and secondary teaching.

Such efforts appear to have had a considerable measure of success. Officer retirees employed in educational institutions increased from about three percent of all retirees surveyed in 1960 (U.S. Congress, Senate Committee on Armed Services, 1961) to about 5.8 percent in the 1966 survey. On the basis of the latter survey, there were an estimated 13,700 military retirees in teaching and educational administration in 1966. About two-thirds of those working in education were employed in the secondary schools, and somewhat under a third at the college and university level. Nationally, the retirees, therefore, are a tiny drop in the educational manpower bucket—somewhat under one percent of the staffs of higher educational institutions, and a similar ratio in the secondary schools.

There will almost certainly be greater proportions of retired military personnel going into teaching in future years. Among recently retired officers, according to the BSSR Survey, about ten percent of the officers were employed by educational institutions—a much higher proportion than among the entire retired officer population (Sharp and Biderman, 1966). Future retirement cohorts will reflect the raised educational standards for officers employed by the armed forces.

Other Public Service Occupations

Some special efforts have also been made to recruit retired military for other public service occupations, including a great variety of positions in the many enterprises operated by churches and church-related institutions, in overseas assistance and development work, and in a number of antipoverty programs, particularly the Job Corps and VISTA. Success has been mixed. VISTA reports (personal communication) excellent response to a recruiting campaign it conducted recently among the military. In poverty programs, the participation probably was originally limited more by the desire of agencies to play down military participation so as to allay opposition to the idea of a new Civilian Conservation Corps, rather than by a reluctance of retirees to take jobs in the program. Many other programs, particularly those which involve low pay, travel, or undesirable locales, have met scant success.

That military personnel accept the low pay that soldiers traditionally have received, that they adjust to frequent moves to locations not of their own choosing, that they frequently are separated from their families and immediate friends does not mean that these are conditions they will find acceptable in their second careers. The more typical attitude, the BSSR survey (Sharp and Biderman, 1966) found, is for men on active duty to look forward to a situation after retirement which will compensate them in precisely these ways in which they were disadvantaged during their active duty. For example, although a somewhat greater proportion of military retirees would find traveling or overseas jobs attractive than would a random sample of workers, they are usually not as likely candidates for such jobs as might be imagined. About four out of five officers say that avoiding being away from home is an important consideration to them in choosing a second-career job. The large majority also have decided preferences regarding the place or kind of place in which they will settle.

Since most officers also put the respect accorded a job and the social importance it has among the top considerations they apply in second-career job-seeking, there undoubtedly is some special appeal to them of work that offers a sense of vocation. But most retirees prefer to follow such vocations on a nine-to-five basis in a comfortable climate near a military installation which has a good club, hospital, and golf course.

CONFLICT OF INTEREST

There has been vast erosion of the lines between what is military and what civilian. Many defense functions are performed inter-changeably by uninformed or civilian personnel, and others can be. Much of the knowledge and skill needed in the armed forces as buyer, user, and maintainer of hardware or software provided by private contractors is identical to that needed by suppliers and middlemen in the private sector.

There are two inherently inconsistent aspects of second-career employment in defense functions from the standpoint of the public interest. For keeping the costs of military pensions within bounds and having the economy benefit from the special skills and training of these men—in which the nation has made a considerable investment—the public interest is served by maximum utilization of their special skills and knowledge in civilian jobs. These objectives, however, are in direct opposition to the doctrine that public servants or former public servants should avoid situations involving conflict of interest.

An exceptionally broad and blunt statement of the latter principle was made by the report of Representative Hebert's subcommittee of the House Armed Services Committee which investigated the employment of retired officers by defense contractors: "We think it unethical and unconscionable for a person to have anything to do in private life with a subject with which he was directly concerned while in public employment" (U.S. Congress, House Subcommittee for Special Investigation of the Committee on Armed Services, 1960: 20).

The most comprehensive study of the conflict-of-interest question to date presented a more balanced view:

> The problem of most employment restrictions must be weighed in the context of the interpenetration of the private and governmental segments of the economy. In the earlier days, the government and the private company were regarded as opposed or at least completely separate, and no need was recognized for having a man outside the government with the experience gained inside the government.

> With the growth of government and the technological explosion of the twentieth century such a view has been becoming unthinkable. Today, we definitely need a maximum flow of information between the government and the outside and most employment restrictions tend to build a wall between them.

> It is a source of comfort to no one in this country, if an experienced military scientist or technical expert is forced by conflict-of-interest rules to take up truck farming or to sell life insurance when he leaves the government service [Association of the Bar of the City of New York, 1960].

Conflict of Interest Laws

Again, in the case of conflict of interest, there is a complex array of statutes and administrative regulations restricting the retired military officer in work in the world of government contracts (Califano, 1957; Clinard and Foltz, 1959). "Selling" war material to the government and to one's own service receives emphasis in both law and attitude. The statutes prohibiting selling have rarely been pressed, however. There has been no successful criminal prosecution for selling to one's service and the law prescribing denial of retired pay for selling war material was successfully invoked only against two individuals (they eventually recovered their lost pay). The material in question was beer for local bases, not a weapon system, and the officers were low-ranking ones (Taussig, 1967,a,b).

Congress, the public, and social scientists have fixed their attention on interest conflicts of the high ranking officer. (See, for example, Riessman, 1956.) The matter first was brought to prominence in 1958 by an inquiry conducted by Senator Paul H. Douglas of the employment of retired officers by the one hundred largest defense contractors. A result was a proposed amendment to bar completely the hiring of retired officers by defense contractors. Only the pledge of a further investigation kept the measure from passing (it lost by only one vote). (See U.S. Congress, House, 1959; U.S. Congress, House Subcommittee for Special Investigation of the Committee on Armed Services, 1960.)

The Douglas exposé and the resulting inquiry by Congressman F. Edward Hebert's House Subcommittee for Special Investigations are credited by the major author of President Eisenhower's farewell warning in 1961 against the military-industrial complex as being the initial stimulus to the speech and the genesis of the phrase itself.

The issue was revived ten years after Douglas' original inquiry by Senator William Proxmire (1969). He reported that the number of high ranking officers (O-6 or above) employed by the 100 largest defense contractors had tripled in the decade. The ten companies most prone to hiring retired brass accounted for more than half of the 2,072 officers on his list. Proxmire made several additional comparisons between the 1958 and 1968 lists: the 43 companies which were among the top 100 both in 1959 and 1969; the ten companies at each point employing the greatest numbers of retirees; and the ten largest contractors on each list. For all of these comparisons the result was an approximate tripling during the decade.

"This is a most dangerous and shocking condition," Proxmire concluded. "It indicates the increasing influence of the big contractors with the military and the military with the big contractors."

Although this represented a faster rate of increase than that in the population of retirees, the greater affinity of giant defense contractors for retired military employees is probably accounted for by the changed character of high-ranking retirees during the decade. In 1958, the high ranking retired officers were largely "black-shoe" Navy and Army ground force officers. Air Force and Naval Aviation officers in the high ranks did not begin to retire in great numbers until the years immediately following the 1958 exposé. Since the major employers of retirees are all aerospace firms, it was only then that the most valuable recruits for these companies—particularly officers with experience in the advanced systems of the missile era—became available.

The report that two thousand officers were working for big defense contractors had considerable dramatic impact in the campaign in 1969 to control defense expenditures and reduce the influence of the military-industrial complex by more restrictive legislation on retiree hiring. The number represented only a small fraction (8.8 percent) of all the 23,500 regulars on the retired list in these grades—with no allowance for reservists erroneously included and some directors and consultants employed by more than one firm. Even extrapolating the figure to the entire prime contractor complex, using the assumption that smaller contractors employ high ranking retirees in the same proportion to their dollar volume of defense business as the 100 largest, the total would be under twelve percent of all retired regulars in rank above colonel or roughly fifteen percent of those in the labor force.

To be sure, not all of the retirees working in these giant firms are engaged exclusively in defense-ralated work although the majority certainly are. Communications, autumbile, and petroleum companies are prominent on the list of the largest defense contractors, as well as a few conglomerates.

The familiar association of the names of prominent military leaders such as Clay, Groves, Doolittle, and MacArthur with big defense firms in the post-World War II period cannot be generalized to the conclusion that all or most of the 2,000-odd officers listed by Senator Proxmire have become captains of industry. And, despite instances which were adduced in the 1959 inquiry by the Hebert Committee (U.S. Congress, House Subcommittee for Special Investigations of the Committee on Armed Services, 1960), it cannot be concluded that such position and influence as these retirees exercise in industry is due as a rule to the influence they can exert with their colleagues still on active duty. There is no systematic evidence on the extent to which the latter allegation has substance. The most relevant indirect evidence on these matters comes from data on the earnings of retired high ranking officers.

The Hebert Committee gave figures for the pay received by officers retired in grades of lieutenant colonel or above who work for the large defense contractors. For firms, the medians of pay received by these retirees ranged from $500 to $1,650 per month, with $900 being the approximate median of the medians among all the major firms tabulated. For retired three- and four-star officers employed by the one-hundred largest defense contractors, almost half were payed $15,000 or less per year and more than one-fourth $10,000 or less. Five of these retired generals and admirals earned over $40,000 per year, but an equal number earned under $6,000.

The 1966 Hubbell Committee survey provides confirmation of these patterns with data from a more inclusive and recent sample. Responses from 603 retired general and flag officers were included in this sample survey. More than half (fifty-seven percent) of these retired generals and admirals reported that they were fully retired. (Almost sixty percent were sixty-five years of age or over at the time of the survey.) For the 258 who worked during 1965, the average income from work reported was $10,260. Only thirty percent of the retired generals and admirals worked a full year, however. For those who did, the mean reported income from work was about $18,000 (all but five of these officers had full-time jobs or were self-employed).

An indication that the high-ranking officers are selling more than their titles and contacts to business is that there is as pronounced a relationship between the educational qualifications of retired general officers and their civilian earnings as for other officers. For generals, the association between education and civilian income is more pronounced and linear than that between rank and civilian income, as is shown in Table 7.

Interpretation of these data must remain ambiguous as among the following possible alternatives: (a) a large proportion of the retired officers employed by industries work for relatively low pay in comparison with industrial executives; (b) retired senior officers generally have little influence to sell, or they are not generally selling such influence as they have, or they usually are selling the influence they have very cheaply; (c) the data are faulty, in not reflecting emoluments other than pay and income other than from work.

Table 7. Relations Between the Rank and Education of Retired
Generals and Admirals and Their Civilian Incomes

	Rank at Retirement		
	O-7	O-8	O-9 or O-10
Median Income	$15,013	$22,867	$11,850
	(n=52)	(n=58)	(n=18)

	Education		
	Less than Fours Years of College	Four Years of College	More than Four Years of College
Median Income	$13,539	$18,339	$19,871
	(n=28)	(n=30)	(n=70)

Source: Unpublished Hubbell Survey data for officers who worked fifty to fifty-two
weeks in 1965 and had no disability.

The concern regarding the employment of military retired
personnel by defense contractors of the late 1950s represented in the
Hebert inquiry had a different focus from that of Proxmire ten years
later. In the former period, the central issues were ethical ones—were
officers reaping ill-deserved personal gains by peddling their
influence? Were they securing undeserved preferment for their
employers? Were government dollars being wasted in
less-than-optimum defense procurement as a result?

In 1969, the implications were rather fears of the perpetuation of
the military-minded view of the world and of overinflated concepts
of the nation's defense needs that rested upon these concepts. As
Senator Proxmire (1969: S 3074) put it:

> This danger does not come from corruption. Except in rare circumstances
> this is no more prevalent among military officers than among those with
> comparable civilian responsibilities.
>
> The danger to the public interest is that these firms and the former officers
> they employ have a community of interest with the military itself. They
> hold a narrow view of public priorities based on self-interest. They have a
> large uncritical view of defense spending. . . .

In too many cases they may see only military answers to exceedingly complex diplomatic and political problems. A military response or the ability to make one, may seem to them the most appropriate answer to every international threat.

Civilianizing and Militarizing Influences

The pressure on military men to deemphasize the distinctively military aspects of their skill is occurring precisely at the time that the military is defending itself against progressively greater encroachments of civilian expertise into its domain. As the civilian scientist, political expert and administrator have taken on increasingly larger functions in the defense realm, the military has been faced with an increasing burden of asserting the claims of a specific military expertise and mystique. But, to assert their claim for postretirement, second-career jobs, the press is to emphasize how nondistinctive military experience is from that in the civilian world.

While the most commonly voiced concern about the retired military is that they will militarize civilian institutions, the major consequence of the second-career pattern seems to be preponderantly in the other direction.

NOTES

Author's Note: In addition to reflecting the present and past auspices of the Inter-University Seminar on Armed Forces and Society, the present paper draws on research performed by the writer under other sponsorships including that of the Office of Manpower Policy, Evaluation and Research, U.S. Department of Labor (Contracts 81-08-26 and MDTA 16-63 and Grant 91-09-69-31), the Twentieth Century Fund, and the Bureau of Social Science Research. I have drawn freely from work done in collaboration with Laure M. Sharp. Jean Ruffin assisted in the preparation of the present paper.

1. We are favored with a great deal of information because the military retired have been the subject of several major questionnaire surveys.

Among these was the "Michigan Survey" in 1961 conducted by the University of Michigan as part of the Senate Armed Forces Committee reexamination of the retired pay system (U.S. Congress, Senate, 1961). There were 3,168 respondents in this survey.

The second major survey of all persons on the retired lists, which is commonly called the "Medicare Survey," centered on the issue of medical care for retired military (U.S. Department of Defense, 1964). It was carried out by the Defense Department in 1964 with a sample of 11,985 retirees. As part of the same survey, a number of questions were asked regarding the second-career employment patterns of the military retirees to accommodate an interest shared by the Defense and Labor Departments in the problem of employment assistance for the retirees.

The questions in this national survey matched several which were employed in an intensive study carried out by the present author and Laure M. Sharp at the Bureau of Social Science Research which we will refer to as the "BSSR Study" in the same period with questionnaires going to 3,350 military personnel, all retirees who left the service during the month of May 1964. In the present paper, use is made of unpublished data from both the Medicare and BSSR Survey, as well as results contained in Sharp and Biderman (1966) and Biderman and Sharp (1968).

A third major survey of a sample of all military retired was carried out as a part of a general reexamination of the military pay structure by the Defense Department, the "Hubbell Committee Survey" in 1966. Responses of 98,629 retired officers and enlisted men were analyzed in this survey.

In connection with a study being conducted by the present author for the Twentieth Century Fund, data from this survey were made available to the present author, and special tabulations were prepared under the direction of Captain Michael O'Connell, USAF. We hae drawn extensively on these as yet unpublished materials as well as on data that have been presented in the report of the Committee (U.S. Department of Defense, 1969).

The present paper, as well as each of the surveys mentioned above, relies greatly on basic data prepared by the Defense Department actuary, Joseph B. Glenn. A number of tabulations provided by Mr. Glenn in unpublished form are referred to in the text as Glenn (n.d.).

In addition, a few of the very large number of military retirees who have gone into graduate education have done studies of the problems of their colleagues for their dissertations. Some of these studies have been elaborately executed and are of major informational value. There have also been a number of special studies directed toward particular kinds of retirees, for example, those interested in teaching and those of a particular branch of service or in a particular locality (see References).

REFERENCES

ABRAMS, P. (1962) "Democracy, technology and the retired British officer," pp. 150-189 in S. P. Huntington (ed.) Changing Patterns of Military Policies. New York: Free Press.

ANDERSON, E. P. (1965) "An economic analysis of retired military officers in metropolitan Phoenix." M.A. thesis. College of Business Administration, Arizona State University, Tempe.

Association of the Bar of the City of New York (1960) Conflict of Interest and Federal Service. Cambridge: Harvard University Press.

BIDERMAN, A. D. (1966) "Civilianizing and militarizing influences of military retirement systems." Presented at Sixth World Congress of Sociology, Bureau of Social Science Research, Washington, D.C., July.

―――(1964) "Sequels to a military career," pp. 287-336 in M. Janowitz (ed.) The New Military: Changing Patterns of Organization. New York: Russell Sage Foundation.

―――(1960) Needs for Knowledge Regarding the Military Retirement Problem: Summary Report of a Conference Held in Washington, D.C. Washington, D.C.: Bureau of Social Science Research, Inc.

―――(1959) "The prospective impact of large scale military retirement." Social Problems 7 (Summer): 84-90.

―――and L. M. SHARP (1968) "The convergence of military and civilian occupational structures: evidence from studies of military retired employment." American Journal of Sociology 73 (July): 381-399.

―――(1967) "Out of uniform: the employment experience of retired servicemen who seek a second career." Monthly Labor Review (January-February): 15-47.

BINDER, E. M. (1964) "The utilization of military retirees in teaching, administrative and service positions in education, 1965-1975." M.A. thesis. Ohio State University.

BOEGEL, T. J. (1961) "The potential resource for teachers from the ranks of retiring military personnel." Ph.D. dissertation. St. John's University, Jamaica, New York.

CALIFANO, J. A. (1957) "Limitations on the employment of retired Naval officers." JAG Journal (November): 2.

CLINARD, D. M. and J. A. FOLTZ (1959) "Retirement and the law." JAG Journal (June-July): 3.

COLLINGS, K. T. (1965) "Should a retiree stay for thirty? A financial appraisal." Retired Officer 21 (January-February): 25-26.

―――(1963) "Employment of retired military officers in the West Coast area: a pilot study." M.A. thesis. University of Washington.

Committee of Retired Army, Navy and Air Force Officers (1958) Retirement from the Armed Forces. 2nd ed. Harrisburg, Penn.: Military Service Publishing.

FECHTER, A. E. and B. S. MAHONEY (1967) "The economics of military retirement." Arlington, Va.: Institute for Defense Analyses.

GARRETT, D. G. (1961) "Retirement experiences and employment status of United States Air Force retired enlisted personnel." M.A. thesis. University of New Mexico.

GLENN, J. B. (n.d.) Unpublished data prepared for the Office of the Assistant Secretary of Defense, Manpower and Reserve Affairs.

HASSELL, G. E. (1965) "Employment of retired Army officers in the Atlantic Seaboard area." M.A. thesis. Ohio State University.

HUBBELL COMMITTEE, See U.S. Department of Defense, 1969.

JANOWITZ, M. (1960) The Professional Soldier: A Social and Political Portrait. New York: Free Press.

———(1959) Sociology and the Military Establishment. New York: Russell Sage Foundation.

LAMPOS, Lt. Col. N. T. (1962) "The retired military executive: his problems in making the transition from a military to a civilian career." M.A. thesis. Boston University College of Business Administration.

LANG, K. (1964) "Technology and career management in the military establishment," pp. 39-81 in M. Janowitz (ed.) The New Military: Changing Patterns of Organization. New York: Russell Sage Foundation.

LASSWELL, H. D. (1941) "The garrison state." American Journal of Sociology 46 (January): 445-468.

LENZ, A. J. (1967) "Military retirement and income maximization: an examination of the economic incentives to extended military service." Ph.D. dissertation. Stanford University.

McNEIL, Maj. J. S. and Col. M. B. GIFFEN (1967) "Military retirement: the retirement syndrome." American Journal of Psychiatry 123 (January): 848-854.

MAILLER, Lt. Col. J. R. (1968) "Pre-retirement counseling." Retired Officer Magazine 24 (October): 24-26.

MASSEY, R. J. (1963a) "Operation second career." Armed Forces Management 10 (December): 22-24.

———(1963b) "A survey study of the integration of retired Naval Academy graduates into the national economy." Unpublished report. Armed Forces Management Association.

PROXMIRE, W. B. (1969) "Over, 2,000 retired high ranking military officers now employed by 100 largest military contractors." Congressional Record S3072-3081 (March 24).

Printer's Ink. (1959) "Do our military leaders make good executives in industry?" (December 6): 29-32.

RIESSMAN, L. (1956) "Life careers, power, and the professions: the retired army general." American Sociological Review 21 (April): 215-221.

SHARP, L. M. and A. D. BIDERMAN (1966) The Employment of Retired Military Personnel. Washington, D.C.: Bureau of Social Science Research, Inc.

STOCKSTILL, L. and J. HESSMAN (1968) "Modernizing military pay." Journal of the Armed Forces 105 (May): 2 ff.

TAUSSIG, J. K. (1967a) "Post retirement selling restrictions." Retired Officer Magazine 23 (October): 9-12.

———(1967b) "Post retirement selling restrictions—conclusion." Retired Officer Magazine (November-December): 9-11.

U.S. Bureau of the Census (1968) Statistical Abstract of the United States: 1968. Washington, D.C.: U.S. Government Printing Office.

———(1960) Historical Statistics of the United States, Colonial Times to 1957. Washington, D.C.: U.S. Government Printing Office.

U.S. Civil Service Commission (1966) "Report on the survey of retired members of uniformed services, June-July, 1966." United States Senate Committee on Post Office and Civil Service.

————(1965) Report on the Operations of the Executive Branch Under Title II of the Dual Compensation Act.

U.S. Congress, House (1959) Hearings before the Subcommittee for Special investigations of the Committee on Armed Services, Retired Military and Civilian Personnel by Defense Industries. 86th Congress, 1st Session. Washington, D.C.: U.S. Government Printing Office.

————(1960) Subcommittee for Special Investigations of the Committee on Armed Services Employment of Retired Commissioned Officers by Defense Department Contractors. 86th Congress, 1st Session. Washington, D.C.: U.S. Government Printing Office.

U.S. Congress, Senate (1967) Federal Staff Retirement Systems. 90th Congress, 1st Session. Washington, D.C.: U.S. Government Printing Office.

————(1961) Hearings before the Subcommittee of the Committee on Appropriations, H.R. 7851, Making Appropriations for the Department of Defense for the Fiscal Year Ending June 30, 1962. 87th Congress, 1st Session. Washington, D.C.: U.S. Government Printing Office.

————(1961) Committee on Armed Services, A Study of the Military Retired Pay System and Certain Related Subjects. 87th Congress, 1st Session. Washington, D.C.: U.S. Government Printing Office.

U.S. Department of the Air Force (1957) Air Force Guide for Retirement. AFP 34-4-3 (January 31).

U.S. Department of the Army (1965) Retired Army Personnel Handbook. Washington, D.C.: Headquarters, Department of the Army.

U.S. Department of Defense (1961) Teaching as a Second Career. Washington, D.C.: Office of Armed Forces Information and Education.

U.S. Department of Defense, Office of the Assistant Secretary of Defense, Manpower and Reserve Affairs (1969) "Modernizing military pay." Report prepared by the Retirement Study Group, Compensation and Career Development Directorate.

————(1964) "Medical care for retired military personnel and their dependents." Unpublished report to the Secretary of Defense by the Defense Study Group on Health Care for Retired Personnel and Their Dependents.

U.S. Department of Labor and the Air Force Association (1963) Proceedings: The First National Conference on the Utilization of Retired Military Personnel. Washington, D.C.: Air Force Association.

WATSON, J. H. (1963) "A study of social and occupational adjustment in relation to civilian and military identification of United States Air Force retired officers." Ph.D. dissertation. State College, Mississippi.

Part Two

OCCUPATIONAL SOCIALIZATION

Chapter 5

BASIC EDUCATION AND YOUTH
SOCIALIZATION IN THE ARMED FORCES

MORRIS JANOWITZ

This chapter seeks to assess the available empirical evidence on
the effectiveness of the military services as agencies of basic
education and youth socialization. The scope of the analysis
focuses initially on the socioeconomic characteristics of those who
serve in the armed forces, and explores the impact of military
service on their social and economic status. Available data and the
emphasis of this effort is mainly on enlisted personnel and basic
education (the equivalent of high school). However, it is also
possible to examine aspects of professional education in the armed
services and the consequences of military service for college
graduates. This chapter includes an overview of the consequences
of military service on personal controls and social values, to the
limited extent that systematic data is available. Finally, it seeks to
identify those organizational characteristics of the military which
account for its impact as an agency of basic education and
socialization.

The armed forces have long been thought of as offering a
"second chance" to youngsters from lower-class backgrounds, and
even to middle-class youths. A second chance means an opportunity for education and personal development for those who did
not have access to appropriate schools and for those who had
access but failed. Since its revolutionary origins, the United States
has continuously maintained military and naval forces which have
provided these second chances. However, it has only been since

the end of World War II that the size of the military establishment has been large enough to supply a significant number of
such opportunities.

DEFINITION OF
BASIC EDUCATION

By basic education in the United States we arbitrarily mean the
academic or vocational equivalent of a high school education. This
includes fundamental literacy and related skills, plus basic vocational
training or work experience. The accompanying socialization involves
a complex of motives and values, plus personal controls, which
permit the youngster to function in the larger society on the basis of
a sense of dignity and self-esteem.

It requires a number of years after service before the consequence of that military service on a person's civilian occupational
status fully emerges. However, given the magnitude of the number of
young men who have served for a period of two years in the armed
forces, there is strikingly little information available on the impact of
military service. Since 1965, research interest has increased because
of policy questions connected with the renewal of Selective Service
and the war against poverty.[1]

Since 1940, in order to support its military missions, the armed
forces have operated as a vast training, engineering, and logistical
enterprise. They have functioned as a specialized large-scale training
organization which has produced a veteran population of well over
thirty million persons. The skills that these men have accumulated
have produced changes in the occupational and professional structure
of the nation. The experiences that these men had, produced some
impact on their social perspective, although changes in skill have
apparently been greater than changes in social and political perspectives as a result of military experience.

As of September 1968, there were 26,300,000 veterans living in
the United States. The Spanish American veterans had all but
disappeared since there were only nine thousand left. The veteran
population from World War I was two million; from World War II,
fifteen million; and from the Korean conflict, six million. The
military operations in South Vietnam have already produced
2,500,000 veterans. The overwhelming bulk of these veterans served
short terms of duty from two to four years and more often closer to
two years.

It would be important to estimate the proportion that had been exposed to prolonged or even intensive combat. Adequate data are not available and the definition of such exposure is difficult to standardize. But it is estimated that during periods of combat, the distribution is combat, ten percent; combat support, fifteen percent; and seventy-five percent noncombat, for the ground forces. The military establishment consists of vast numbers of men who serve for a short period of time and of whom only a limited proportion are directly involved in combat functions. However, there is a small stable core of professionals—officers and enlisted men—who typically serve for twenty years or more, many of whom have been involved in combat and who rise to be the essential managers of the system. By 1963 there were already 350,000 men who were receiving retired pay after having spent more than twenty years of active service as officers or enlisted men. The number is projected to rise to over one million by the early 1980s. Obviously the impact of military experience is very different on these two groups.

The methodological problems in assessing the impact of military experience on basic education or on professional skills represents a most complex research problem. Until recently, it was only possible to make inferences based on data about the characteristics and behavior of those who had actually served in the armed forces. More recent surveys involve comparisons between those who served and those who did not. These limited bodies of data supply a more adequate basis for making judgments about the impact of military experience, but even for these surveys, selective factors among those who served are of unknown magnitude and thereby, it is difficult to speak of the comparability of veteran and nonveteran groups. The argument can be raised that, regardless of changes in the criteria for selection, since the military have tended over the past three decades since the outbreak of World War II to reject the most unfit, those who served are better endowed—constitutionally, emotionally, and intellectually—than those who were rejected. If this assumption is made, then the differences—especially in resulting higher occupational attainment—are not mainly the result of military experience, but of the selective characteristics of those who served, especially in the enlisted ranks.

In interpreting the available data, it does not appear that this assumption is overriding or correct. At any given socioeconomic level, there is no reason to suppose that selective factors have been operating to get the most effective person. Particularly among the lower socioeconomic groups, this does not appear to be the case since there is a strong element of chance as to who gets inducted and who does not. In fact, it might be the case that the standards of selection produce a systematic bias which tends to screen out many who would benefit the most.

It needs to be emphasized again that the analysis of the impact of military service is a very complex task, and given the present state of empirical data, different inferences can be drawn. The materials presented in this analysis seek to deal both with economic and social aspects. By contrast, some economists argue that the consequences of military service are negligible and this point of view is represented in the thinking of the staff of the President's Commission on an All Volunteer Armed Force. Clearly comparable consequences could be achieved if military expenditures were diverted to effective civilian institutions; there is no basis for public policy which would justify military expenditures because of the educational consequences.

However, in assessing the outlook of economists, two issues need to be kept in mind. First, most of the studies on which strictly economic benefits are based are sample surveys which greatly underenumerate the number of economic positions of unemployed young men, especially unemployed blacks, and therefore introduce a strong bias in their results and underemphasize the positive consequences of military service. Second, economists overlook the possibility, and the data underline, that for some, military service at least reduces the possibility of a decline in social position.

In assessing the impact of military service, it can be argued that the consequences of service derive not only from the specific and specialized training that is offered, but even more importantly, from essential features of the milieu of the military as a social organization. For young men who spend a limited number of years—between two and four—the military can serve as a kind of "residential institution" in which their prior social and personal backgrounds, their ascriptive traits and achieved disabilities are deemphasized or even denied. Instead, the manpower practices and the organizational life create opportunities for the development of self-esteem and material rewards which are not linked to success based on particular and narrow vocational or academic criteria. In fact, it can be argued that where the armed forces succeed in basic education, it is because relative acceptance and involvement in the larger organization comes before or at least at the same time as skill training.

An initial hypothesis in evaluating the existing documentation was that the lower the socioeconomic background of the recruit, the more likely he would benefit from basic education and socialization experiences offered by the armed services. This was an obvious point of departure, although we were aware of the fact that recruitment and Selective Service practices since the end of World War II tended to eliminate young men from the very lowest socioeconomic groups–those who, by our reasoning, could most benefit from military service. Nevertheless, our hypothesis was seen as applying to those who were admitted into the enlisted ranks either by volunteering or by Selective Service.

In the popular image, the military offers a second chance because as an agency of basic education, it operates a vast number of technical and vocational schools. There can be no doubt that the military establishment is the largest vocational training institution in the United States. Despite the scope of its vocational training program, it is important to keep in mind that only a minority of enlisted personnel receive advanced and complex technical training, some of which is not directly applicable to the civilian economy. But it is not the sheer existence of these technical schools that accounts for the relevance of the military as an institution of basic education. Equivalent technical schools could be established by civilian authorities.

Moreover, in actual fact the wide range of skills taught in the armed forces often requires adequate educational background and specialized aptitudes. Such educational backgrounds are to be found among young men entering the service with high school education, who are already integrated into the educational-occupation structure since they come from the middle majority of the civilian social structure–stable working class or lower middle class–and less often from the more depressed groups.

The popular image of the strong emphasis of vocational and technical training is augmented by a widespread recognition that over the last hundred years, there has been an increase in the transferability of military skills and specialties to civilian industrial needs. The convergence of the civilian and military occupational structure has been carefully documented (Biderman and Sharp, 1968). Moreover, since the end of World War II, military manpower policy has tended to emphasize and highlight the continuation of this trend. It does appear that the limits of this trend have been reached.

However, analysis is not based on the assumption that the transferability of skills per se accounts for the contributions of the military as an agency of basic education. This transferability is an expression of an environment which is concerned with training and which does provide a wide range of opportunities for training. To the contrary, emphasis on skill transfer leads the military to screen and select civilians for particular tasks and for presumed aptitudes. Each effort at more refined recruitment and selection, aside from lack of validity, weakens or limits the military's ability to serve as an agency of basic education. In this sense, the military becomes more like civilian industry and more competitive for that portion of the young labor force which has already been effectively educated and socialized.

Thus to the contrary, the military serves as an agency of basic education and youth socialization precisely because it is a user of unskilled manpower. There are many important tasks that can be accomplished with limited educational background, and with limited on-the-job training. The military serves as an agency of basic education or youth socialization because each year it must recruit and allocate vast numbers of personnel and, therefore, it must proceed on the basis of minimum standards and assume the maximum potential in its personnel. The result is a system of manpower allocation training which is the reverse of civilian industrial enterprise. A task is found for each person rather than a person for each task. In this sense it is a "total" institution. Once admitted, all men have a place in the institution. For some individuals, especially those with college degrees, this results in an underutilization of skills and aptitudes, but for persons from the lowest social strata, there is a built-in process of upgrading. What sort of an impact from military experience is expected among persons who in civilian life were not effectively integrated into the educational-occupational structure because they were at the very lowest strata? At best, for such persons a positive impact would be a definite but modest increment: completion of high school while in the service, acquiring some basic vocational skill, or even a satisfactory personal experience which would lead to lower rates of deviant behavior and a stronger desire for stable employment upon return to civilian life.

However, social mobility in the United States also involves movement from low socioeconimic ranks into a position of responsi- bility and authority that represents the social equivalent of the upper middle class and on occasion into the very top strata of contempo- rary society. There is an extensive lore, and there is some documentation in autobiographies and biographies which portrays the process by which the military serves as a school for mobility from the very lowest ranks into such positions. In this country the military operates as the equivalent of the night law school. Therefore, our definition of basic education must include those experiences which lead a young man to seek advanced training or develop the motivation that leads to marked advancement and the belief that social mobility is possible for him. The services are fully aware of the personal importance of this opportunity as well as the relevance of such opportunities for organizational effectiveness. For these reasons, all of the services have programs in which enlisted men, after a number of years of service, can apply for training as officers and receive the equivalent of college training. Again, while adequate data is not available, there is reason to believe that promotion from the ranks is as great in the military as in industrial organizations where entrance with a college degree has emerged as a prerequisite for advancement into the managerial rank.

SOCIOECONOMIC PATTERNS
OF MILITARY SERVICE

The first step in assessing the impact of military service is an examination of the socioeconomic background of those who served as enlisted personnel. The basic hypothesis, as mentioned above, that the lower the socioeconomic background of the serviceman the greater the positive consequences of basic education and youth socialization, is limited by the pattern of selective recruitment which reduces the proportion of the very lowest socioeconomic groups serving.

The data on socioeconomic backgrounds of those who have served show, on the basis of a large-scale survey conducted in 1964, that the extremes in socioeconomic background are especially significant (Klassen, 1966: 20).[2] Sons of fathers with less than eighth grade education and with graduate study are less likely to serve (sixty-one percent and fifty-five percent respectively) than sons of fathers with intervening levels of education (from ninth grade through college graduate), who average sixty-nine percent. Those with highly educated fathers were most likely to be deferred (twenty-nine percent), while those with fathers of less than eight years of school were most likely to be rejected for service (twenty-three percent). When occupation is considered the criterion of socioeconomic status, the same effect is apparent. The lowest participation rates are among

Table 1. Education Before Service of Enlisted Men by Father's Occupation. All Branches of Armed Forces 1964.

Highest grade of regular school attained by respondent before entering active service	Father's Occupation (Respondent at Age Fifteen)[a]									
	PT&K	MOPS	Sales	Clerical	Crafts-men	Opera-tives	Service workers	Laborers	Farm-ing	Son's Education Distribution
Eighth grade or less	2.0%	3.4%	2.9%	2.9%	6.2%	7.9%	5.8%	10.8%	15.3%	7.5%
Ninth to eleventh grade	22.2	23.0	26.3	25.7	33.4	34.7	30.5	33.9	30.5	30.9
High school graduate	39.6	42.9	46.2	50.0	47.0	47.7	49.7	45.8	43.2	45.8
Less than two years of college	20.0	17.2	15.4	12.3	9.1	6.6	9.5	6.0	6.8	9.8
Two or more years of college, without bachelor's degree	10.9	9.3	6.3	6.2	3.2	2.5	3.3	2.6	3.1	4.3
Bachelor's degree or graduate study	5.2	4.2	2.8	2.8	1.1	0.7	1.2	0.9	1.1	1.7
Total percentages	100%	100%	99.9%	99.9%	100%	100%	100%	100%	100%	
Number of cases	2,420	4,173	1,216	1,150	10,532	9,461	1,979	2,439	6,008	Total number of cases 39,378[b]
Distribution of father's occupation	6.1%	10.6%	3.1%	2.9%	26.7%	24.0%	5.0%	6.2%	15.3%	

a. Occupation groups used in the table are the major categories defined by the Bureau of the Census. "Private household workers" are excluded and the "farming" group used in the table combines the Census titles "Farmers and Farm Managers," and "Farm Laborers and Foremen" since this distinction was not present in the data.

b. Excluded from the table are 10,539 individuals who did not respond to one of the questions, or whose response was inapplicable for miscellaneous reasons. Total enlisted men in this subsample are 39,378 + 10,539 = 49,917.

Source: The 1964-1965 Department of Defense Study of the Draft prepared by the National Opinion Research Center. The determination of this subsample is described in Albert D. Klassen, Jr. (1966) "Subsampling the Survey Data of the Military Manpower Policy Study." Military Manpower Survey Working Paper 7. National Opinion Research Center, University of Chicago (October).

sons whose fathers would be classified as "professional, technical, managerial, and official" (sixty-three percent). Sons of white-collar and blue-collar employees had participation rates of sixty-nine percent and sixty-eight percent respectively.

The socioeconomic background of the enlisted personnel in the armed forces is also clearly reported by the data in Table 1, which presents father's occupation and the enlisted man's education before entering active service. These data are for a sample of some forty thousand enlisted men serving in the armed forces in 1964 and combine all types of recruitment. By examining the bottom row it is possible to see the distribution of the occupation of fathers of enlisted men—they are mainly recruited from "craftsmen" and "operatives" categories. An underrepresentation is revealed for the white-collar managerial and professional groups, and a greater underrepresentation from "service workers" and "laborers." The military serves as a device for integrating sons of the farming population, since they continue to be overrepresented in the armed forces. By examining the education of the recruit at the time of his entrance into the armed forces, it is also possible to demonstrate the same pattern of underrepresentation of the social extremes. Only 7.5 percent of active duty enlisted personnel in 1964 had eighth grade or less education. The better educated are also markedly screened out of the enlisted ranks. One and seven-tenths percent of enlisted personnel had a bachelor degree or more. With the increased manpower requiremens of the South Vietnam war, this pattern undoubtedly changed and inequalities in the social basis of military service were reduced. First, criteria of selection were lowered, thereby increasing the rates of participation among lower socieco-nomic groups. Second, in 1968, graduate school deferments were restricted, thereby increasing the rates of participation of higher socioeconomic groups.

IMPACT ON
SOCIOECONOMIC STATUS

Education and income are direct measures of a person's position in the social structure. Therefore, the second step in assessing the available data on the armed services as an agency of basic education is to examine the extent to which service in the military changes a person's educational level. A crude and gross measure can be seen in the sheer rise in the educational attainment of samples of military personnel as a result of their term of service. These data reflect the extensive educational effort in the armed forces, and especially the emphasis to supply an opportunity to complete high school. The opportunity to complete high school for the lower socioeconomic groups is demonstrated particularly in Table 2, which indicates that twenty-seven percent of the enlisted personnel in the army as of 1961 completed their high school education while on active duty. Even five percent of the field grade officers in the army completed their high school work while on active duty. These data also highlight the wide extent to which higher ranking personnel were also able to complete varying degrees of advanced education.

It is difficult to hold that such advancement is the result of selective recruitment alone. Thus, in a study of a small but carefully selected sample of civilian men in the Newburgh area contrasted with those who served in the army, Katenbrink (1969) found that military samples had higher levels of educational attainment because of the high rate of completion of high school which could be attributed to the work done while in the armed forces. This sample is of particular relevance because the civilian 4-Fs were eliminated in the matching, thereby making the two samples more comparable than most studies. Or, in other words, there is less reason to assume that the higher levels of educational attainment, especially completion of high school, reflect greater selectivity of the military sample as opposed to the civilian sample.

The armed forces' ability to stimulate young men to complete their high school education is an expression of the educational strategy which seeks to integrate general schooling with occupational responsibility. One of the basic instruments is the United States Armed Forces Institute which operates both on the basis of correspondence courses and by offering remedial and regular courses on military installations. These offerings are available both on and off duty, and it is military policy to permit time off from duty to enroll. The soldier has a continuous opportunity throughout his service to join in such an educational effort.

Often enlisted men become involved in these educational programs after basic training, that is, after they have achieved some status and recognition in the military community. Such educational involvement also reflects the emphasis of military authorities. A significant percentage of the active duty enlisted personnel have not completed high school; as of February 1965, twenty-eight percent of the enlisted strength of the Army had not completed twelve years of

Table 2. Education Acquired by Personnel on Active Duty During Their Military Service[a]

Educational Level	Army, August 31, 1961			
	Field Grade Officers	Company Grade Officers	Warrant Officers	Enlisted Men
	Percentages			
Some graduate work	21	8	1	b
Earned college degree	19	11	2	b
Attended college for first time (no degree)	30	23	51	5
Completed high school	5	7	39	27

	Air Force, May 31, 1960					
	Colonel	Captain	Warrant Officers	Master Sergeant	Technical Sergeant	Staff Sergeant
	Percentages					
Some graduate work	21	12	1	b	b	b
Earned college degree	18	18	3	1	1	b
Attended college for first time (no degree)	7	29	35	18	16	10
Completed high school	1	4	21	7	11	4

a. Based on difference in percentage who had completed given amount education at present and at time of entry into military service.

b. Less than .5%.

Source: Sample survey prepared by Systems Development Branch Adjutant General's Office, Department of the Army; Personnel Statistics Division, Comptroller of the Air Force, Headquarters, U.S. Air Force.

education (U.S. Department of the Army, n.d.). Thus, to be actively involved in finishing high school while in the armed forces is not a rare or deviant concern, but a normal and relatively widespread practice.

While education is an important measure of social stratification, the third step in the analysis is to examine actual changes in occupational and economic positions that have resulted from military service. The analysis problem hinges on the ability of isolated comparable groups of men who have served in the military and those who have not.

The effect of military service on occupational mobility was studied by Otis Dudley Duncan and Robert W. Hodge (1964) by means of an analysis of the Chicago portion of the Six City Survey of Labor Mobility which included the job experiences of some 1,105 males who were 25-64 years old in 1951 when the survey was taken. On the basis of regression analysis, they found that 30-39-year-old male veterans in 1950 held occupations somewhat higher in socioeconomic status than did nonveterans. There was, of course, some selectivity among the veterans in terms of higher socioeconomic background. Yet the occupational position as determined by the survey was higher than would be expected on the basis of their backgrounds, indicating that the "veterans had come to enjoy some advantages in the competition with nonveterans." The results for the group aged 40-44 revealed no difference between veterans and nonveterans, which led Duncan and Hodge to emphasize the importance of selectivity. This finding appears to us to underline the fact that the impact of military service is more discernible on men who are younger at the time of their military experience.

Although Katenbrink's study of men from the Newburgh area is limited in the size of the sample, it is revealing because of the careful design and because he was able to relate educational experiences in the military to occupational status after service (Katenbrink, 1969). These data give support to our general hypothesis that it is not the specific vocational training that is crucial in assisting men from the lowest socioeconomic strata, but rather the more general organizational milieu and opportunity structure of military life.

Katenbrink found that there was a slightly greater amount of occupational mobility for the military sample as compared with the civilian group sample (+12.6 for the military sample and +9.4 for the civilian sample). Occupational mobility was measured by comparing the father's occupation with that of the son's by means of the Duncan socioeconomic index.

Mobility was concentrated among those who had completed less formal education at the time of their entrance into military service and who were from lower socioeconomic backgrounds. Moreover the impact of military education is most revealing. For this sample, occupational mobility was not primarily linked to attendance at technical military service schools. Occupational mobility was concentrated among those draftees who entered the Army without high school education and who completed high school education by means of the United States Armed Forces Institute programs. For these men, it was not the specific skills that the military provided but basic education and socialization as social maturity took place. The high school degree is an important symbol in civilian society, and it appears that the increased self-respect and increased sense of achievement derived from military service led these men to complete their education.

Likewise, in a study based on Social Security and Selective Service records, the relationship between military service and civilian earnings among 556 Maryland Selective Service registrants is examined (Cutright, 1964). Men with low AFQT scores (and correspondingly low levels of education) who had served in the armed forces were earning up to $500 more a year ten years later than were men who did not serve. This relationship held even for men whose AFQT scores were so low that they should have been rejected (score of ten or less), but were inducted by accident.[3] The advantage of military experience appears to be greatest for men with AFQT scores between ten and twenty. Above a score of twenty, there appears to be little difference in later earnings between men with and without military service.

The most adequate investigation and amplification of the impact of military service on socioeconomic status is presented in the materials from a comprehensive 1964 survey based on data collected by the Current Population Survey and the National Opinion Research Center. On the basis of these data, in Table 3, a comparison of veterans and nonveterans aged 18-34 is presented, classified by census occupational groupings. The relevance of these data rests on the large size of the sample in contrast to other studies; in this instance over six thousand cases are involved. On an overall comparison, the clearly higher position of the veterans can be seen. Moreover, it is striking to note the categories of difference which give a clue to the impact of military service. Laborers are lower in concentration among the veterans than the nonveterans (4.5% versus

Table 3. Full-Time Occupation of Male National Sample Nonveterans and Veterans, Aged 18-34, Autumn 1964

Occupational Group[a]	Nonveterans	All Veterans
Professional, technical, and kindred workers	13.7%	14.5%
Farmers and farm managers	2.0	1.2
Managers, officials and proprietors, except farm	6.2	11.0
Clerical and kindred workers	7.6	8.4
Sales workers	6.3	6.6
Craftsmen, foremen, and kindred workers	16.2	22.4
Operatives and kindred workers	26.1	24.6
Service workers, except private household	7.5	5.8
Farm laborers and foremen	4.0	1.1
Laborers, except farm and mine	10.3	4.5
Total Percentage	99.9%	100.1%
Number of cases	(3,970)	(2,651)

a. Occupation groups are those listed as major groupings in the 1960 *Alphabetical Index of Occupations and Industries* (Bureau of Census, Washington, 1960). Private household workers are excluded from the table.

Source: Special survey conducted by the Current Population Survey in November 1964 for the Department of Defense Study of the Draft.

10.3%) and service workers are also lower among veterans (5.8% and 7.5%). In turn craftsmen, foremen, and kindred workers are higher among veterans (16.2% versus 22.4%). It is at this middle level that the greatest amount of mobility appears to take place. There is also some increase in clerical and kindred workers and managers, officials, and proprietors but of a much more limited amount. These data point to the process of upgrading through education and military experience; it is a process of assisting individuals from the very bottom to move upward into the more middle-level occupations.

This body of data becomes more revealing if the pattern of social mobility of each man is traced, that is, if a comparison is made between his father's occupation and his own occupation. In Table 4, a summary of the mobility experiences is presented in a highly condensed fashion, which nevertheless indicates limited but discernible consequences which are linked to military service since it seems difficult to attribute them only to selective recruitment. A comparison between white veterans and nonveterans under 26 reveals a difference of five percent in upward mobility (36.1% and 31.2%) and a corresponding difference in downward mobility. Among older age groups of whites, the difference is less but the veteran still displayed more upward social mobility. (It should be kept in mind that these nonveterans included those who received higher education and therefore should have experienced more upward mobility, but this was not the case.)

Among nonwhites, similar consequences of military service are seen by the striking lower concentration of downward social mobility among veterans as compared with nonveterans. Although the number of cases involved is limited, the percentage of downward mobility among nonveterans was 27.2%, while that for veterans was 17.8%.

In addition, Table 5 presents the patterns of mobility in greater detail, that is, occupational category by occupational category. From these data, it can be more clearly seen that the military experience serves to a limited extent as a device for assisting both some whites and blacks who are at the very bottom of the social structure in attaining a modest level of upward mobility and also in inhibiting those near the bottom from some additional downward mobility. Moreover, military service is linked to the reverse process of downward social mobility for some sons of professional and managerial fathers. Service in the armed forces becomes one factor along with a series of other experiences which facilitate the social process of upward and downward movement.

Table 4. Summary of Intergenerational Mobility, National Sample. Males Age 18-34, Veterans and Nonveterans, White and Nonwhite, Autumn, 1964

	White								Nonwhite			
	Nonveteran Under 26		Veteran Under 26		Nonveteran 26-34		Veteran 26-34		Nonveteran 26-34		Veteran 26-34	
	No.	%	No.	%	No.	%	No.	%	No.	%	No.	%
Upward mobility	381	31.2	171	36.1	318	40.9	645	42.1	36	51.4	38	52.1
Stable	379	31.1	145	30.6	281	36.2	526	34.3	15	21.4	22	30.1
Downward mobility	460	37.7	158	33.3	178	22.9	361	23.6	19	27.2	13	17.8
	(1,220)	100.0	(474)	100.0	(777)	100.0	(1,532)	100.0	(70)	100.0	(73)	100.0

In Table 5, detailed patterns of social mobility for specific occupational categories are presented. By comparing the occupational position of sons of service workers and laborers, as well as operatives, for veterans and nonveterans in each age category, the pattern of social mobility emerges.

Thus, among the nonveterans under 26, the concentration of sons of service workers and laborers who remained in this lowest occupational category was 22.9 while for the comparable group with military experience, the percentage was only 10.5. Correspondingly, the proportion of sons of service workers who achieved the status of craftsman was greater for those who were veterans as compared with nonveterans. These relations hold true for the older age category twenty-six to thirty-four but not as sharply. Likewise, for the sons of operatives and even for those of craftsmen, military service tended to produce lower concentrations at the bottom of the occupational scale. The same overall patterns were encountered for the nonwhite samples, but the small number of cases limited the adequacy of the documentation.

However, examination of the impact for sons of clerical and sales personnel has less clear-cut consequences. For these groups the opportunity of college and postcollege education already serves as the equivalent, or even superior basis for additional mobility. Among the sons of professionals and managerials, the reverse process can be seen, namely, those with military service have a somewhat greater degree of downward social mobility. For them, military service during a period of liberal educational deferments represents the fact that they are not getting the amount of higher education required to maintain their father's social status. The same overall patterns were encountered for nonwhite samples, but the small number of cases limits the support of this observation.

All of these data deal with the overall impact of short-term military experience and one cannot expect change of greater magnitude. They make possible the conclusion that the lower the social position, the more positive the impact of short-term military service. For the converse, for men from high civilian social status, short-term service has less effect and even some negative effect. There is another body of data which helps to clarify this more complicated social process.

The consequences of short-term military service on civilian college graduates can be inferred from a cohort survey of a large sample (over fifteen thousand) who received their B.A. in 1958 and

Table 5. Intergenerational Mobility National Sample. Males Age 18-34, Veterans—Nonveterans, Autumn 1964 By Specific Occupational Category

Veteran White Under 26

Son's Occupation	Father's Occupation											Total	Percentage
	Professional* Managerial		Clerical Sales		Crafts		Operatives		Service Laborers				
	No.	%	No.	%	No.	%	No.	%	No.	%		No.	%
Professional; Managerial	25	28.4	15	29.4	20	13.3	18	12.3	5	13.2		83	17.5
Clerical; Sales	16	18.2	12	23.6	32	21.2	27	18.5	6	15.8		93	19.6
Crafts	16	18.2	11	21.6	46	30.5	25	17.1	10	26.4		108	22.8
Operatives	25	28.4	6	16.8	41	27.2	58	39.8	13	34.2		143	30.2
Service; Laborers	6	6.8	7	13.7	12	7.9	18	12.3	4	10.5		47	9.9
Total	88		51		151		146		38			474	100.0

Nonveteran White Under 26

	N	%	N	%	N	%	N	%	N	%	N	%
Professional; Managerial	90	35.0	23	20.0	58	14.4	44	14.5	14	9.9	229	18.8
Clerical; Sales	47	18.3	36	31.3	61	15.2	34	11.2	19	13.5	197	16.2
Crafts	39	15.2	23	20.0	103	25.6	52	19.1	23	16.3	240	19.7
Operatives	48	18.7	19	16.5	117	29.0	118	38.8	53	37.6	355	29.1
Service; Laborers	33	12.8	14	12.2	64	15.9	56	18.4	32	22.7	199	16.2
Total	257		115		403		304		141		1,220	100.0

Veteran White 26-34

	N	%	N	%	N	%	N	%	N	%	N	%
Professional; Managerial	176	51.6	60	46.1	142	29.9	91	22.2	40	22.8	509	33.1
Clerical; Sales	63	18.5	41	31.5	63	13.3	67	16.3	21	12.0	255	16.6
Crafts	40	11.7	11	8.5	143	30.1	83	20.2	44	25.2	321	21.0

Veteran White 26-34 (Continued)

Father's Occupation

Son's Occupation	Professional* Managerial		Clerical Sales		Crafts		Operatives		Service Laborers		Total	Percentage
	No.	%	No.	%	No.	%	No.	%	No.	%	No.	%
Operatives	41	12.0	12	9.2	89	18.7	130	31.6	34	19.4	306	20.0
Service; Laborers	21	6.2	6	4.6	38	8.0	40	9.7	36	20.6	141	9.2
Total	341		130		475		411		175		1,532	
Nonveteran White 26-34												
Professional; Managerial	127	61.6	37	58.7	68	30.8	27	14.8	19	18.4	278	36.8
Clerical; Sales	27	13.2	11	17.5	28	12.7	23	12.6	7	6.7	96	12.4
Crafts	27	13.2	7	11.1	62	28.0	49	26.8	18	17.3	163	21.0
Operatives	18	8.8	2	3.2	37	16.7	63	34.4	42	40.4	152	19.6

	n	%	n	%	n	%	n	%	n	%	n	%
Service; Laborers	7	3.4	6	9.6	26	11.8	21	11.4	18	17.3	78	10.0
Total	206		63		221		183		104		777	
Veteran Negro 26-34												
Professional; Managerial	2	50.0	3	60.0	6	27.2	5	18.5	6	40.0	22	30.2
Clerical; Sales	0	0.0	2	40.0	5	22.7	6	22.2	3	20.0	16	21.9
Crafts	0	0.0	0	0.0	6	27.2	1	3.7	2	13.3	99	12.3
Operatives	0	0.0	0	0.0	2	9.1	9	33.3	1	6.7	12	16.4
Service; Laborers	2	50.0	0	0.0	3	13.7	6	22.2	3	20.0	14	19.2
Total	4		5		22		27		15		73	
Nonveteran Negro 26-34												
Professional; Managerial	2	100.0	1	33.3	6	46.2	5	16.6	1	4.6	15	21.5

Nonveteran Negro 26-34 (Continued)

Father's Occupation

Son's Occupation	Professional* Managerial		Clerical Sales		Crafts		Operatives		Service Laborers		Total	Percentage
	No.	%	No.	%	No.	%	No.	%	No.	%	No.	%
Clerical; Sales	0	0.0	0	0.0	2	15.4	2	6.7	3	13.6	7	10.0
Crafts	0	0.0	0	0.0	0	0.0	5	16.6	2	9.1	7	10.0
Operatives	0	0.0	0	0.0	4	30.8	6	20.0	9	40.9	19	27.2
Service; Laborers	0	0.0	2	66.6	1	7.7	12	40.0	7	31.8	22	31.3
Total	2		3		13		30		22		70	

*Professional Technical and Kindred Workers—Managerial, Officials and Proprietors.

whose careers were followed up in 1963 (Sharp, 1967). This study reports economic earnings which is a more refined measure than occupational mobility. Since these were men who had completed their service before 1963, if they were to serve, they had participated in the armed forces before the build up of South Vietnam, and therefore their service was in a period of relative "peacetime."

The sample divided itself into three roughly equal groups. One-third did not serve in the armed forces; another third served before 1958, that is, before they were graduated from college (early military service); the final third served after 1958, that is, after they were graduated from college (late military service). If a comparison is made between those who served early and those who served late, the economic earnings of the early servers are somewhat superior to the late servers. In short, it appears as if the time spent in the military is less important than the number of years on the job. From this line of reason, it may well be the case that in ten or fifteen years after military service, the differences in income between the late and the early servers will disappear.

But it is important to examine the economic earnings of those college graduates who had military service with those who did not serve. Many of those who did not serve in the armed forces continued in graduate and professional schools and thereby increased their potentials for income. Moreover, since the data on the difference between the early and the late servers indicates that number of years in the labor market is crucial in accounting for increased economic income, military service might be viewed as a handicap to subsequent earnings. Nevertheless, those with service in the armed forces did not uniformly have lower incomes than those without. To the contrary, in specific professional categories, their earnings were as good or better than those who did not serve.

In order to assess this impact, it is necessary to note that in varying proportions the early servers (those who served before college graduation) and the late servers (those who served after college graduation) did their military tour of duty as officers or as enlisted personnel. Of the 36.2% who were early servers, the overwhelming majority were enlisted men (33.4% enlisted to 2.8% officers). On the other hand, the 29.8% late servers were equally divided between officers and enlisted men (14.5% enlisted to 15.3% officers). In short, to serve before college graduation meant duty as enlisted personnel and often reflected lack of clarity about educational plans and career goals, while to serve after graduation increased the opportunity for officer assignment either because of a particular officer procurement program in which the man was involved or because his chances of selection as an officer were increased.

Thus, it is necessary to distinguish between officers and enlisted men when making comparisons about incomes in 1963. Both the early- and late-serving officers had an annual income higher than the men who never served (never in service, $7,130; pre-1958 officers, $9,490; post-1958 officers, $8,020). Even the pre-1958 enlisted man's annual salary ($7,805) was higher than that of men who never served. Only the post-1958 enlisted men (those who had their college degrees before service) had a lower annual income ($7,140) and this particular difference was very small indeed, the smallest of all the differences. When individual occupations are compared, the results are mixed. In particular, for example, natural scientists and engineers did better if they did not serve, but health and "humanistic" professionals did better with service, while others were mixed or inconsistent. A large percentage—twenty-seven percent—in contrast to seventeen percent for the entire cohort, was still unmarried five years after graduation. "It is not surprising that we found among them a higher proportion of salesmen and clerical workers than in any other group." These findings link to the previously reported data on downward social mobility among some of the recruits. "It becomes evident that for these men, military service was one more input into a gradual deprofessionalization process, which seems to characterize this small group of marginal unsuccessful college graduates" (Sharp, 1967: 154). These men, as reported above in the National Opinion Research Study, came from high status families and were experiencing some downward mobility.

Insight into the dynamics of mobility in general can be drawn from the attitudes of these officers and enlisted men to their military experiences, Officers, both early- and late-serving men, viewed their military service in positive terms. Nearly three-fourths of the officers felt their service made an important contribution to their careers, while fewer than half of the enlisted men were of this opinion. In particular, those who served as enlisted personnel after graduation (that is after 1958) were the most negative. They disagreed that the time spent in the service gave them new ideas for careers (seventy-eight percent), new skills (fifty-nine percent), time to think about a career (sixty-eight percent), achievement of work-related experience (eighty-two percent), or made important contributions to their careers (eighty percent) (Sharp, 1967: 154). Their negative response was grounded in the belief that their skills were being underutilized, and that in part they were competing with noncollege personnel on the basis of their real skills rather than on their social position.

CONSEQUENCES OF
PROFESSIONAL TRAINING

Another aspect of military service is the opportunity available for young men, including many with limited educational background and from low socioeconomic status, to be given professional education while on active duty and therefore gain access to high status positions within the military or in civilian life as a result of their experience in the military. Therefore, the fifth step in this analysis is to probe the consequences of the professional level of training offered by the military.

One measure of the consequences of professional training on mobility is the social origin of the top military leadership group, brigadier general and above. From Table 6 it can be noted that the concentration of sons of white-collar and working-class fathers in the top military leadership of the United States has been increasing since 1910. In part this represents the expansion in size of the military establishment but it also represents a system of recruitment which seeks to emphasize achievement criteria. The fact that collegiate level education is supplied by the profession itself serves to broaden the base of recruitment. Thus, it is most striking that as of 1960, nineteen percent of the West Point class of 1960 were from working-class origin. This makes the military as open a professional group as any in the United States, although there is no reason to assume that such recruitment produces men more prone to accept realistic military policies.

There are, of course, important limiting conditions in this trend toward broader recruitment. For example, a college degree is increasingly required for entrance to Officer Candidate School (OCS) or is given priority value among applicants, which suggests that armed forces' personnel agencies *do not* fully recognize the significance of opportunities for occupational mobility as incentives for service. For example, the Air Force controls the input to such schools by increasing amounts of formal education as a prerequisite, despite evidence that such criteria are of negative value in career retention. Army policies give priority to direct college enlistments

Table 6. Military Leadership, 1910-1950

Father's Occupation

	Army 1910-20 %	Army 1935 %	Army 1950 %	Navy 1950 %	Air Force 1950 %	West Point Class 1960 %
Business	24	16	29	32	26	15
Professional and managerial	46	60	45	38	38	50
Farmer	30	16	10	7	15	–
White collar	–	6	11	8	16	13
Worker	–	2	5	5	5	19
Other	–	–	–	–	–	3
Total	100	100	100	100	100	100
Number	(37)	(49)	(140)	(162)	(60)	(765)

Source: Morris Janowitz (1960: 91).

for OCS over enlisted applicants. These policies tend to diminish the opportunities for mobility, and reflect the sensitivity of the armed forces to their "professional" image in the larger society.

In addition, the armed forces extend college and professional education to their officers and enlisted personnel while on active duty. The core of this effort is resident study at civilian colleges and universities for career officers to obtain advanced degrees, numbering annually in the many hundreds. The armed forces also operate two technical institutes authorized to grant master's degrees. The impact of these efforts can be seen by the fact that more than one-quarter of all career officers have advanced civilian degrees and the percentage continues to increase. This schooling is distinct from the attendance at the various levels of military professional schools conducted by the armed forces. The services also assist enlisted men in completing college education as a channel for entrance into the officer corps.

Moreover, civilian universities conduct educational programs on or near military bases which enable enlisted. men and officers to pursue college and advanced degrees on a part-time basis. Wide exposure to college level education is offered through correspondence courses, which during the early 1960s reached 900,000 service personnel annually. To these efforts must be added hundreds of specialized technical and professional courses. The result is that the armed forces operate as a vast educational institution not only in supplying basic (high school) level education, but even more resources are committed to college and professional level education. In this connection, it should be pointed out that the three-level hierarchy of military professional school, through which a large proportion of career officers pass, supplies instruction in administrative and management skills with high transferability to civilian life. The impact of the military on the distribution of occupational and professional skills flows not only from the educational enterprise but from on-the-job experience and internships that military life affords. Because of the constant inflow of new personnel, the armed forces must extend education and training to men who are destined only to spend a few years on active duty. Each year before the South Vietnam buildup, approximately 500,000 personnel left the service for civilian life, of whom an estimated fifty percent had received some relevant posthigh school occupational and professional education and training.

As in the case of basic education, the bulk of military personnel who receive posthigh school technical and professional training are relatively short term personnel; that is, they have tours of duty which lead them to leave the military after two to six years. The professional affiliations which they had before or which they developed during and after military service become overriding in their career orientations. In civilian life, they constitute only a limited proportion of their profession and they become scattered throughout the United States. It is rare indeed when the military serves as the major supplier of a specialty, as for example air line pilots, of whom about eighty percent receive their basic pilot training in the armed forces. For some professions, as for example doctors and lawyers, military experience is a period of intensive internship. In the case of psychiatry, the consequences of military service have been to speed up the development of community and preventive psychiatry in civilian life with dramatic results.

The consequences of technical and professional training for the career officer with a commitment to a twenty- to thirty-year tour of duty are much deeper and become apparent on retirement. These are men who received their professional training in the military environment and who must make a transition to civilian society. The issues of the retired military officer have focused in the past on the selected number of high ranking officers who received government posts during World War II (Janowitz, 1960).

Since the number of nationally prominent officers retiring has sharply declined, the role of the military in government policy-making posts has receded. Instead, the public focus of attention has been on the role of the military in defense-related industries and especially in the aerospace complex. There can be no doubt that these industries continuously recruit technical personnel and individuals knowledgeable in the procedures of defense procurement. Congressional investigations have documented their number and salaries, and a survey such as one of 399 retired officers in 1964 revealed that eleven percent of the group were hired by aerospace and electronic concerns (Sharp and Biderman, 1966).

But the implications of the enlarging group of retired career military personnel—both officers and enlisted men—present a broader and more pervasive impact as the number increases. The employability of retired professional soldiers has been enhanced by the increased convergence of military and civilian skill hierarchies. Even the troop commander and the military staff officer think of themselves as administrative specialists. However, clearly there is an inverted hierarchy of transferability in that those with the most valued military skills often encounter the greatest difficulty in transfer. Therefore, it has become an aspiration of the military establishment to give each officer a second skill to improve his prospects for retirement employment.

The problem of the retired career personnel looms greater than for the short-term veteran. Despite the number of studies that have been done on the retired military of 1968, their economic position is not fully clear (Sharp and Biderman, 1966). It is estimated that about twenty percent of them suffer some decline in income. Economic adjustment thus far constitutes a more important or at least more visible problem than their social adjustment. The range of retirement employment is wide with a strong movement toward employment in various levels of government. The equal concentration in "financial" areas, that is, as salesmen, or involvement in insurance and real estate, is not necessarily an appropriate or rewarding type of employment given their previous activities and interests. There is also considerable interest in teaching. As many as ten percent of the retired military enter teaching, but existing barriers operate to keep out many more.

The development of a distinct social grouping of retired military, especially retired officer personnel, depends not only on their economic adjustment, but on the growing tendency to concentrate in certain localties. The desire to be with former colleagues and the advantage of close residence to military installations, plus previous experience and geographical preference, has led to concentration in certain localities: California, Texas, and Florida.

CONSEQUENCES ON PERSONAL
CONTROLS AND SOCIAL VALUES

The sixth step is to probe the consequences of military service on personal controls and social values. Analysis of personal controls and social values leads to an examination of a variety of topics such as deviance, social maturity, and personality responses. For this purpose, two different types of evidence are required since differential effects are possible. On the one hand, it would be necessary to demonstrate some positive effect, such as the growth of effective personal controls, or the decline of deviant behavior. But it is also necessary to establish the absence of negative effects among other recruits, especially in the area of social values. If military service brought about personal growth at the expense of inculcating a set of "undemocratic" or "absolutist" military values, the overall consequences could hardly be viewed as desirable.

For example, if military service increased a person's authoritarian responses or developed rigid absolutist military perspective, it would be precisely among long term career enlisted officers that one would expect such changes. These men must accommodate the internal pressures of a role that stands between the rank and file of enlisted personnel and the officer corps. If the commissioned officer has an educational background and a set of job requirements that continue to relate him to the larger society and its values, the noncommissioned officer is much less integrated in these respects. Unpublished reports indicate that even in an armed force with the traditions and outlook of the Israeli, military leaders are alert to such vulnerability among noncommissioned officers.

Likewise, the impact of prolonged exposure to combat, especially intense combat, has observable consequences on recruits which are very different from those presumed to be associated with basic education in the armed forces. There is a body of literature which deals with the immediate disruptive impact of combat on human personality and human values (Grinker and Spiegel, 1945). Data on long-term consequences are less adequate. Likewise, the formation of a veteran's ideology depends on the organization of ex-combat soldiers into intimate social and fraternal groups. The bulk of the peacetime recruits do not join veterans' groups.

It is again necessary to emphasize that our focus is on those men who are not career personnel. One approach to the analysis of the impact of military service on personal controls and social values is to examine the success or failure of delinquents in the armed forces. The military as an agency of basic education includes the notion of the armed forces as a second chance for young men in trouble to "grow up." Near delinquents are often encouraged to join or are informally "paroled" into the armed forces. The armed forces are prepared to disregard a young man's previous record once he is admitted into service. The same young man can instead earn an honorable discharge which will supersede his past police record. The military are reluctant to induct such personnel because it is seen as lowering the prestige of the profession, but during periods of military hostilities, recruitment policies encourage the admission of personnel with minor criminal records. Research by Hans Mattick (1960) has produced precise evidence that felons who were paroled into the armed forces during World War II had a much lower recidivism rate than those paroled to civilian life (see also Lejins, 1957). This often cited study was limited to a wartime situation and it might be argued that these particular circumstances contributed to the success of this program.

The study of the impact of military service on personal controls and self-esteem requires panel data on a group of recruits as they pass through basic training and military service. For the United States, no such data exists, although there is one study on selective aspects of the impact of basic training. It is, of course, in basic training that the most profound changes take place because of the intensity of the experience, the contrast with civilian life, and the high sense of social solidarity that is engendered (Uyeki, 1966). More specifically, in his study of forty-eight squads involved in the basic infantry training cycle at Fort Dix during the summer of 1952, Richard Christie (1954) found that among the recruits there was an improvement in personal adjustment—as measured by the individual recruit's perception of himself as being in good physical and psychological condition—and improvement in his positive relations with his peers. Thus, under these conditions, basic training did succeed in developing self-esteem and a sense of social solidarity among recruits. In delineating the factors which assisted in adjustment to basic training, the study revealed that recruits who remained in contact with their homes and families made the poorest adjustment to military training. (Contact with home depended on whether the recruit's residence was close to the military base.) Furthermore, by 1953, this study already revealed that the practice of involving the trainees in the leadership hierarchy on a rotation basis produced a strikingly more positive adjustment than for those who had no such opportunity.

But such changes may have been brought about at the cost of altered social values including the possibility of the oft-repeated charge of increased authoritarian response. The Christie research supplies some suggestive but hardly definitive data. It was found that there was only a slight and statistically insignificant increase in authoritarianism (California F scale) during the basic training cycle of six weeks (Christie, 1962). However, at the same time, he reported that basic training produced some attitude changes toward the institutional aspects of military life and authority figures in the army. Opinions about officers and noncommissioned officers became more negative.

Other research underlines that as training becomes more complex and more advanced, authoritarianism actually decreases, as measured by the California F scale. Thus, Campbell and McCormack (1957) in "Military Experience and Attitudes Toward Authority," set out to prove that air cadet training would increase authoritarian predispositions among officer candidates. Since characteristics of a military organization include authoritarian procedures, the consequences of participation in its training program would necessarily heighten authoritarian personality tendencies among those who successfully pass through such training. Authoritarian personality tendencies imply both the predisposition to arbitrarily dominate others of lower status and to simultaneously submit to arbitrary higher authority. When the results of the research as measured by the "F" scale showed a decrease in authoritarian traits among cadets after one year of training, the authors were tempted to conclude that perhaps their research tools were inadequate.

Direct examination of combat flight training would indicate an emphasis on group interdependence and on a team concept of coordination to ensure survival that should have cautioned these researchers not to make the predictions they did. Of course, the military environment has features of any large scale bureaucracy— arbitrary exercise of authority—and the special characteristics of preparation for combat. But a modern managerialism and keen sense of the limits of authority have come to pervade wide sectors of its structure.

Perhaps a more precise explication of the authoritarian issue is that within the military establishment there exists a range of patterns in the exercise of authority—from arbitrary to the more group—process approach. Different styles produce different consequences. During basic training, research indicates the negative consequences of an arbitrary exercise of authority. A suggestive study by Hanan Selvin (1960) demonstrates how leadership style influences the outcome of basic training and indicates the potentials for creating a social climate appropriate for assimilating civilian recruits. Using categories similar to the original Lewin-Lippitt-White group dynamics experiment, the investigator was able to identify three types of leadership at work in an infantry basic training installation, which reflect the changes in military discipline. First, there was the arbitrary climate in which leadership operated by fear and with no admiration; second, there was the climate of the team concept—the persuasive climate—based on admiration for the leaders and without fear; and finally, there was what was called a weak climate—the leaders were merely organizers and were neither arbitrary nor persuasive.

In partial summary, these fragmentary studies, taken together with the findings of educational achievement and occupational mobility, indicate some systematic evidence to support the notion that basic training and noncombat service for limited periods have positive effects on a portion of the recruits, particularly in developing self-esteem and social maturity. For these groups there is some evidence that negative effects as measured by the authoritarian syndrome were not particularly present.

None of the available sources of data adequately confronts the issue of whether for a very small minority, military service could be disruptive by causing increased antisocial behavior at a later date. It may well be the case that for persons with pathological predispositions or character weaknesses, the pressure and tension of military service serve to exacerbate personality defects and to produce disruptive personal and social consequences after release. Although there is no body of evidence in disproof, the hypothesis cannot be dismissed. Moreover, none of the available data, including the Mattick study on parolees in the armed forces, leads to the inference that military service does not produce some deviant behavior—of longer or shorter duration—among particular recruits. Young men, as they pass from adolescence to adulthood, must learn to cope with the complexities of the larger world, in educational institutions or in work settings. In this process, personal failure or the inability of the institution to meet their needs is apt to increase the likelihood of deviant behavior, and this is also the case for service in the military.

In particular, at least passing speculation on the impact of weapons training on aggressive behavior of the recruits is required. We are dealing with at least two different levels of analysis. On the one hand, participation in the armed forces teaches an individual the mechanics of warfare and the use of force which can find organized application in conscious criminal behavior or in paramilitary activities in civilian life. On the other hand, there is the question of what the handling of firearms and particularly the use of the bayonet do to a person's conscious and unconscious impulses. We are dealing not only with aggressive impulses which are directed outwardly but also with those directed inwardly.

While the evidence presented above included data on stronger personal controls as a result of military experience, there are no simple answers to these questions. Again the possibility exists that for particular individuals, military training experience strengthens aggressive impulses. We offer the hypothesis, and it is no more than a hypothesis, that the type of firearms instruction that a typical recruit receives in military training contributes to the control of his aggressive impulses by sublimation and by socialization in a regulated context. At least it would appear to be the case that such training is more desirable than experiences with weapons obtained in a semicriminal gang. This is not to assert that the present system of training is fully satisfactory from this point of view; there is still needless exposure to bayonet training.

Beyond the direct handling of firearms, there is the larger question of the impact of limited and prolonged involvement with complex weapons systems, including nuclear weapons. Social research has overlooked this awesome and significant question, but it is part of the larger question of the impact of complex technology on personal controls.

But what of the issue of the impact of military service on social and political values? The amount of explicit indoctrination of social and political issues in the United States armed forces is indeed limited. But changes in attitudes could well develop from involvement in the total situation of the armed forces.

American society operates in a relatively pragmatic framework, although there are clear ideological themes in the political system.

The armed forces reflect this absence of ideology. The professional ethos of the military resists the introduction of political indoctrination as a basis of military morale. While some civilian political groups have sought to increase the amount of attention paid to troop indoctrination in political themes, the military profession has received support in its resistance to such measures from social research findings which emphasized primary group solidarity and adequate leadership as the basis of organizational effectiveness (Shils and Janowitz, 1948; Stouffer et al., 1949). Even the dramatic events of the Korean conflict have served to reinforce the nonideological posture of the American military profession. Careful research by Albert Biderman (1963) and others has revealed that contrary to the claims of psychologists and psychiatrists, the American troops behaved in captivity as well as could be expected given the pressures applied to them. The weaknesses they displayed were weaknesses in effective training and not in ideological indoctrination. Charles Moskos' (1968) field study of enlisted men found that even in the special conditions in Vietnam, at most, only the term "latent ideology" could be applied to their attitudes and motivation. None of this is to deny the importance of nationalism as a factor, but it is difficult to equate political ideology with nationalism.

Realistically, in the armed forces, the typical American recruit is exposed to a set of communications similar to those he would encounter in civilian life. Especially through the radio, which each soldier personally owns and regulates, he is linked to the mass communication of the civilian world. The response to the limited troop information and education programs conducted officially for enlisted personnel shows a tremendous suspicion of manipulation and a powerful resistance to any official "line." Even the military's efforts to indoctrinate and socialize its officer personnel is subject to powerful built-in limitations. John P. Lovell (1967) has completed a study of the impact of West Point training on officer attitudes, West Point being a central institution of officer professionalization. While acknowledging the limitation of his data, he is able to conclude that "socialization at West Point produces only slight impact upon professional orientation and strategic perspectives of the cadet." By contrast, important changes occur in the preferences that cadets express for the branch of service in which they hope to serve and for the extracurricular activities that provide them the most satisfaction. It would appear that self-selection into the officer corps is more important in determining attitudes than the impact of life in the military academies.

Officers are particularly prone to avoid political and ideological discussions with noncommissioned personnel. The culture of the military is carried by the noncommissioned officers whose ideological orientation is a vague and diffuse anticommunism and an undifferentiated feeling of a national mission.

In the fashioning of political orientations and politicomilitary perspectives, it does appear that both the processes of self-selection and selection for promotion as well as the impact of professional experiences are more important than conscious indoctrination. At each point in the promotion process, officers have the opportunity to continue to select themselves out. In turn, officers who fit in with the official doctrine of their service or particular weapons system are most likely to rise, although the presence of the deviant is institutionalized to a considerable extent (Janowitz, 1960). Moreover, the perspectives of a particular segment of the military are profoundly influenced by the lessons presumably learned from prior military engagements.

CHARACTERISTICS OF THE MILITARY ENVIRONMENT

The final step in our analysis is to seek a clearer and more precise identification of those particular attributes in the military environment which help to explain its impact on basic education and socialization. First, as mentioned above, is the skill structure of the armed forces. By skill structure, we do not mean merely the particular technical and professional requirements which are essential for the military service. We mean the logic of the organization including the rules by which it operates in the allocation of its manpower. The military is an organization through which each year new cohorts of young men enter. Once a person is admitted into the institution, there is no question but that the organization must incorporate him into a functioning role. In this sense, despite its complex skill structure, the military is a primitive organization or a noneconomic organization. In this sense, all of its members are equal; all of its members are soldiers in a basic sense.

There is no need for the new recruit to have any doubt as to whether there is a place for him in the institution. This is not to assume that all new members adjust to the system or that the institution does not seek to reject some persons. But by comparison with most civilian institutions, and particularly by comparison with the public education system, it is an organization based on the complete availability of opportunity plus a basic standard of acceptance of each member.

This logic of full incorporation works precisely because there is a pervasive element of reality involved. The military is a highly centralized organization in terms of strategic decision-making, and it is a highly complex organization. But in his day-to-day assignments, each soldier quickly recognizes that he has real work to perform and that he has a real capacity to assist or retard the function of his immediate group. There is a diffusion of operational responsibility throughout the institution. Even the rifleman, who is located at the bottom of a vast organization, has a sense of competence—not only because of the power of his weapon, but because in the modern military, concepts of team and group authority make him rapidly aware of his individuality. Regardless of the hierarchical features of the system, to be effective requires not military compliance with orders, but positive participation.

Second, the military operates with a set of training procedures which assume maximum potentials for personal growth. The very notion of basic training implies that there are a set of skills which all members of the institution can and must know. Basic training is required of all members as a mechanism of assimilation. As indicated above, prior social characteristics are deemphasized during this period, and this includes in particular social disabilities accumulated during civilian life, such as delinquency records and academic grades.

But even more pointedly, the training procedures operate on the assumption that each person has the potentiality of mastering the contents of basic training, or that it is up to the system to teach each young man the essentials for success in basic training. This does not mean that there are no failures in basic training, but rather that those who manage the training develop the perspective that they can teach almost anyone.

Without the benefit of the educational psychologists, the basic training systems of the armed services incorporate many so-called "advanced" procedures. There is no ability grouping and all recruits are mixed together, so that the heterogeneous character of the group will create the optimum conditions for learning and group support. The training cycle is based on the equivalent of the nongraded or continuous educational development scheme. The recruit is not graded at the end of the course with a pass or fail, but at the end of each subsection he is evaluated, given remedial help or recycled through the specific phase of his training in which he is deficient. There is extensive emphasis on instruction by the equivalent of the apprentice system in which instruction is given during the actual exercise or task.

The operation of Project 100,000 is a striking example of the operation of basic training in the military establishment. In August 1966, it was decided that an experimental program would induct 100,000 men who, according to the then existing standards, ordinarily would be screened out. Included in this group were young men with limited educational background or low educational achievement (Category Four). Project 100,000 meant that a group of "deprived" young men would be taken into the armed forces both because of the pressure of military manpower needs and as an experiment in basic education. If the task were assigned to a civilian educational system they would have most likely segregated these men, devised a special curriculum, and engendered in them the feeling that they are clearly inferior manpower resources. However, the armed forces merely included them in its regular training cycle.

As of 1967, under Project 100,000, more than 49,000 men had entered the armed forces under "new standards" which permitted the acceptance of men who had previously been rejected for induction or enlistment. Previously, only a small proportion of men who scored between ten and thirty on the AFQT were accepted, and then only after they had scored above ninety on two or more aptitude tests. The revised standards permitted the acceptance of all high school graduates in Category Four, without additional testing. Nonhigh school graduates with AFQT scores between sixteen and thirty were accepted if they scored ninety or higher on at least one test; those with scores between ten and fifteen were required to pass two aptitude tests. More than a third of those who entered in this program were voluntary enlistments. Their average age was twenty-one years. They had completed an average ten-and-one-half grades of school. About thirty-two percent had failed at least one grade of school, and seventeen percent had failed two grades. More than twenty-nine percent were unemployed and an additional twenty-seven percent earned less than $50.00 a week.

After one year, there was sufficient evidence to demonstrate the wastage of human resources that had previously occurred because of rigid entry requirements. More than ninety-six percent successfully completed basic training, although the discharge rate ranged from a low of three percent in the Army to 9.5% in the Air Force. (The

Defense-wide discharge rate for all other men is about two percent. These rates also include medical discharges for conditions other than lack of aptitude.) Equally noteworthy was their achievement in advanced training, where the attrition rate was 12.3% compared to the average Army attrition rate for all men of eight percent. Their success in some highly complex fields was as follows: seventy-three percent in communications and intelligence, and medical and dental specialists; eighty-seven percent in administration and clerical schools; seventy-eight percent in electrical and mechanical equipment repair; and eighty-eight percent in crafts. Over half of those in training for electronic equipment repair successfully completed their courses (fifty-five percent). It should be noted that these success rates were not achieved in special courses designed for the "intellectually disadvantaged," but were made under the same requirements as those established for men with higher entry attributes.

After training, these men were assigned not only to "infantry, gun crews, and allied specialties" (thirty-three percent), but their success in advanced training had increased their versatility so that relatively more are ultimately assigned to tasks which will provide useful civilian skills: electrical and mechanical equipment repair, twenty percent; service and supply handlers, eighteen percent; and administration and clerical, ten percent.

After twenty-two months of Project One Hundred Thousand, 125,152 men had been accepted under the new standards for recruitment, of whom about half were volunteers and the remainder were draftees. A progress report issued by the Department of Defense in September 1968 pointed out that ninety-five percent of the new-standards men were accepted by lowering the mental test standards, while five percent were accepted for remedial medical treatment after induction (Office of the Secretary of Defense, 1968).

A comparison of these new-standards men with a control group revealed them to be of the same average age (20.4 years for the new-standards men and 20.2 for the control group). They were by no means predominantly black; not even a majority were black, confirming the well-known observation that deprived groups in our society are heterogeneous. In the control group 9.1% were nonwhite, while among the new-standards men the concentration of nonwhite was 39.6% (and nonwhite is a broader category than Negro). The outstanding difference was in their reading ability. The control group had a median reading ability of grade 10.9, with 1.1% reading below the fourth grade; the new-standards men displayed a median reading ability of grade 6.1 and 14.4% were reading below fourth grade.

Almost two years after the program had been launched, the preliminary results were highly successful. Nearly ninety-four percent of the new-standards men successfully completed basic training as compared with ninety-eight percent for all other men. Strong efforts were made to expose these men to skill training in a formal course. In the Army and Marine Corps, nearly all new-standards men received such training while in the Air Force, about forty percent were given on-the-job training, and in the Navy most men also received on-the-job training. In formal skill courses the attrition rate varies from service to service, but the overall rate for these men was about ten percent, as compared to about four percent for other men attending similar courses. Men who are dropped from training are not discharged from service, but usually reassigned to other courses or on-the-job training more suited to their aptitudes.

As a result of such training, the new-standards men could be given a wide range of assignments, and their allocation to combat and noncombat tasks was similar to the overall intake of recruits. About sixty-two percent of the new-standards men were assigned to noncombat-type skills, while seventy percent of the control group were assigned to noncombat-type skills.

Perhaps the most sensitive measure both of the progress of new-standards men and the response of the various services to these men is their rate of promotion. Of the first group of new-standards men who entered the Army during October-December 1966, 84.4% were E-3s and above after an average of 16.5 months of service, while for the control group the percentage was 92.6%. At the E-4 level and above, a wider difference emerges with 47.0% of the new-standards men reaching that level while the percentage was 64.3% for the control group.

Disciplinary records revealed that only 2.8% of the Army men of the new standards had court martial convictions after 16.5 months of service. Finally, of the first group of new-standards men, 90.4% were still in service on March 31, 1967. This attrition from active service includes battle deaths and wounds and discharges due to physical disabilities as well as separations for unsuitability, unfitness, misconduct, hardship, and other causes.

Success in basic training, which involves an opportunity for developing a sense of self-esteem and a feeling of group participation, becomes the basis in part for further education and advanced training. Of special importance are the experiences of Project Transition as representing the emerging approach of the military to technical training. As a response to the task of preparing its recruits for transition back to civilian life and as a contribution to larger societal goals, the armed forces have instituted a program of technical training for enlisted personnel who are completing their term of service and who did not have an opportunity for such technical training. Such training is of special importance for recruits from lower socioeconomic backgrounds, who have entered combat units and who have developed skills which are not transferable to civilian employment.

It is important to emphasize that the skill training in Project Transition comes after the recruit develops some involvement and acceptance in the military. This is just the reverse of the civilian society where educational success is first demanded as a criteria for institutional involvement. The Israeli Army, of course, is an example of the military force which strongly emphasizes its basic education function. In the Israeli armed forces, all citizens are eligible to serve, except a tiny group of very handicapped personnel. There are no social or educational barriers. After mastering basic training and the rudiments of soldiering and not before, the recruits are given basic literacy education. This is also the assumption of Project Transition.

Third, the organizational climate of the military supplies an appropriate context for its basic education and socialization function, especially for recruits from the lower socioeconomic background. One does not have to offer any romantic notions to point to actual realities. In contrast to the material conditions of the slum, life in the military is organized and relatively satisfactory from a material point of view.

Of particular importance are the large amounts of available food. The uniform is of special significance both because of its intrinsic quality and the fascination that develops around being conspicuously dressed. The physical activity and athletic-like character of basic training also need to be mentioned. Of equal or greater importance is the fact that the culture of the enlisted man is a direct outgrowth of civilian working-class existence. The standards of personal language and physical contact, and the style of indulgence such as "beer drinking" do not require the recruit to suddenly denounce earlier patterns of gratification.

Fourth, the basic social context is strikingly important. The recruit soon discovers that it is operated under a juridical system which, despite its particular features, offers the person from lower socioeconomic and minority groups a greater sense of protection than he had in civilian life. His medical needs, his welfare and insurance, his personal protection are directly available and not as the result of exchange relations in which he feels he is being exploited. This is not to underestimate the resentment that develops toward authority that is always potentially present, but to emphasize the importance for the recruit of being in a stable environment. The fact that the environment is socially integrated is important both for Negroes and for the white population.

The information and control systems of the military serve to enhance the position of the recruit who enters the military from a deprived and disorganized background. The military accepts responsibility for his well-being. This implies that specific personnel are responsible for observing and monitoring the recruit's experiences and the results. The machinery is elaborate, cumbersome, and at times inefficient. But there is a peculiar sensitivity to the needs of a particular individual, especially of those who are in need of assistance. In part, this derives from the professional ethic that the officer—both commissioned and noncommissioned—has prestige among other officers to the extent that he takes care of his men. In part, it is the result of the information system which makes it possible to follow up on a particular recommendation or a particular action. The recruit is living in a residential setting and it is therefore more difficult to avoid confrontation with a human problem or to push aside personal needs. If a recruit has a medical problem, or is in need of some remedial educational assistance, the circumstances are different from civilian life where intervention often means referral to a particular agency without follow-up. In the military, a report will be generated as to the final outcome.

The recruit comes to deal with, to work with, and to become the comrade of men with diverse styles and aspirations. He comes to recognize the existence of a larger world. In contrast to a social agency, or the community settlement house, the military is not based on the notion that the young man must accept himself. The military is a school for fashioning new self-conceptions, and it is a system in which informal communications serve to explore and test out these alternatives. The special character of the military means that lower-class youths can assimilate new values because during the time of military service they are on a somewhat more equal footing with the more privileged members of the larger society. It is the "underutilization" of the more middle-class groups that supplies an important ingredient for change.

The bulk of the data and observations of this chapter are drawn from the period between 1945 and the build-up of the armed forces in South Vietnam. The armed forces during this period have mainly served as a large-scale training and logistical enterprise. The specific impact of combat, in terms of the social, psychological, and psychiatric consequences are explored elsewhere. Moreover, limits are placed on the observations and hypotheses that are offered by the changing military environment. In particular, military operations in South Vietnam have been without popular support among specific youth and college groups, and have been strongly opposed. The result has been a negativism toward military service which—if it has had its counterpart in other historic periods, particularly the Civil War—may well produce new consequences for both those who have and who have not served. Finally, if the armed forces come to operate without reliance on the Selective Service system, there will again be profound changes in the military environment which will influence their role in basic education and socialization.

NOTES

Author's Note: I am indebted to William M. Mason, Graduate School of Business, University of Chicago, for the preparation of special tables on the socioeconomic characteristics of personnel who have served in the armed forces.

1. In September 1968, Secretary of Defense Clark M. Clifford delivered a public address in which he stated that in his view "the Department of Defense is not doing enough to promote in a positive way those aspects of our national life which are so essential to preservation of our fundamental institutions." His objective was to make greater use of the resources of the military establishment in improving education, housing, employment opportunities, and health and hospital care for deprived groups in the United States. In particular, as a result of the directives that were issued after his address, there was a greater effort to make available facilities and personnel of the armed forces to adjoining communities for educational programs. Included in these efforts were tutorial programs, vocational training, and demonstrations for youngsters in local schools.

2. "The data were gathered on self-administered questionnaires by Armed Forces from 102,000 men in uniform, and by the Bureau of the Census, from some three thousand veterans and six thousand nonveterans, during the months of November and December, 1964."

3. All of the low AFQT men with military service earned more than $3,000 and most were beyond the $4,000 level, but only three of the thirteen men without military service were in this wage range.

REFERENCES

BIDERMAN, A. D. (1963) March to Calumny. New York: Macmillan.

―――and L. M. SHARP (1968) "The convergence of military and civilian occupational structures: evidence from studies of military retired employment." American Journal of Sociology 73 (July): 381-399.

―――CAMPBELL, D. T. and T. H. McCORMACK (1957) "Military experiences and attitudes toward authority." American Journal of Sociology 62 (March): 482-490.

CHRISTIE, R. (1962) "Changes in authoritarianism as related to situational factors." American Psychologist 7: 307-308.

―――(1954) Transition from Civilian to Army Life. HumRRO Technical Report 13. Washington, D.C. (October).

CUTRIGHT, P. (1964) A Pilot Study of Factors in Economic Success or Failure: Based on Selective Service and Social Security Records. Washington, D.C.: U.S. Department of Health, Education and Welfare, Social Security Administration, Division of Research and Statistics (June).

DUNCAN, O. D. and R. W. HODGE (1964) "Education and occupational mobility: a regression analysis." American Journal of Sociology (May): 642.

GRINKER, R. E. and J. SPIEGEL (1945) Men Under Stress. Philadelphia: Blakiston.

JANOWITZ, M. (1960) The Professional Soldier: A Social and Political Portrait. New York: Free Press.

KATENBRINK, I. G., Jr. (1969) "Military service and occupational mobility," in R. W. Little (ed.) Selective Service and American Society. New York: Russell Sage Foundation.

KLASSEN, A. D., Jr. (1966) Military Service in American Life since World War II: An Overview. Chicago: National Opinion Research Center, University of Chicago.

LEJINS, P. B. (1957) "Juvenile delinquency and the armed forces," in Juvenile Delinquency, Report 130, U.S. Senate, 85th Congress, 1st Session.

LOVELL, J. P. (1967) "The professional socialization of West Point cadets," in M. Janowitz (ed.) The New Military. New York: John Wiley.

MATTICK, H. W. (1960) "Parolees in the army during World War II." Federal Probation (September).

MOSKOS, C. (1968) "Latent ideology and American combat behavior in South Vietnam." Center for Social Organization Studies, Working Paper 98. Chicago: University of Chicago (January).

SELVIN, H. (1960) The Effects of Leadership. New York: Free Press.

SHARP, L. M. (1967) Five Years After the College Degree, Part IV: "Military Service." Washington, D.C.: Bureau of Social Science Research (July).

―――and A. D. BIDERMAN (1966) The Employment of Retired Military Personnel. Washington, D.C.: Bureau of Social Science Research, Inc. (July).

SHILS, E. and M. JANOWITZ (1948) "Cohesion and disintegration in the Wehrmacht in World War II." Public Opinion Quarterly 12 (Summer): 281-315.

STOUFFER, S. A. et al., (1949) The American Soldier. 4 vols. Princeton: Princeton University Press.

U.S. Department of Defense, Office of the Assistant Secretary of Defense, Manpower and Reserve Affairs (1968) "Project one hundred thousand: characteristics of performance of new standards men" (September).

U.S. Department of the Army (n.d.) "Survey estimate of educational level of male enlisted personnel by grade and component," 550 Report 52-65-E. Washington, D.C.

UYEKI, E. (1966) "Sociology of the cold war army." Delivered at the American Sociological Association Convention.

Chapter 6

OFFICER EDUCATION

AMOS A. JORDAN, JR.

Education for a profession can be sensibly discussed only in terms of its function in preparing those being educated for roles in that profession. Accordingly, any analysis of military education should begin with a description—if only in the sketchiest terms—of the profession of arms and the duties and skills essential to its practitioners.

THE MILITARY PROFESSION

The military has the same general characteristics as the other professions, namely, a specialized body of knowledge acquired through advanced training and experience, a mutually defined and sustained set of standards, and a sense of group identity and corporateness (Janowitz, 1960). In addition, the military profession has several characteristics not shared by such other professions as law, education, or medicine; it is, for example, bureaucratized, with a hierarchy of offices and a legally defined structure (Huntington, 1957), and it is a uniquely public profession marked by its members' commitment to unlimited service, extending to the risk of life itself. These characteristics have important implications for military education, as we shall later see.

The peculiar expertise of the military profession has been defined in various ways. Beside Harold Lasswell's familiar formulation of it as the "management of violence," is Lieutenant General Sir John W.

Hackett's (1962) similarly narrow but precise definition: "The ordered application of force in the resolution of a social problem." Colonel G. A. Lincoln has observed that General Hackett's term "force" should be interpreted broadly as "military resources," to include their deterrent and peacekeeping roles (Lincoln, 1964). Blending these various formulations and interpreting them in the context of the likely national security environment of the 1970s and beyond, we can arrive at a working definition of the expertise which today's and tomorrow's military education system should be principally devoted to developing, namely, "the management and application of military resources in deterrent, peacekeeping, and combat roles in the context of rapid technological, social, and political change."

This definition of military expertise necessarily implies a broader set of roles for the military officer than has traditionally been expected of him. This set includes (a) helping to define the nature of the nation's security tasks, especially their politicomilitary dimension; (b) applying scientific and technological knowledge to military matters; and (c) training, supplying, deploying, and—if necessary—employing the fighting capability of military units in the changing politicomilitary and technological environments. Rather than focusing exclusively on the narrow aspects of this third and traditional role, the model of a modern major general (or major, for that matter) must not only master the broader dimensions of the third task but also develop a competence in one or both of the other roles. He must do so that is, if he expects to rise in his profession, for the politicomilitary and scientific-technological dimensions of security problems interact with the narrowly tactical-technical ones in such a complex and continuing way that, if the military man masters only the traditional role, he cannot deal with the modern profession's problems—except at the simplest level.

The distinctive expertise of the military profession is, of course, generated and transmitted by means other than the military's educational system. In particular, the more narrow aspects of military tasks are generally taught in on-the-job or technical school training. While "training" and "education" are not always sharply differentiated activities, it is generally useful to separate them. Thus, "training programs are those which develop specific skills and are nonoriented, while education programs tend to be more complex and their learning outcomes to be more general in nature" (Shelburne and Groves, 1965). Masland and Radway (1957) expand this basic distinction by noting that training emphasizes form, procedure, uniformity, and immediate utility, whereas education is directed to developing the students' judgment and intellectual growth and to preparing them for the long-range future. Though the military school system—and in most cases a single school within it—contains training activities, this discussion is primarily focused on educational programs.

In addition to developing professional expertise, the military educational system contributes to building the other characteristics already noted as defining the profession, namely, a common set of standards, a sense of group identity, and a special commitment. These indoctrination and socialization functions are, again, not exclusively the province of the educational system, nor even of the school system. Depending on the particular pattern of his assignments, the young officer may well learn more in military units than in school about the professional code; in particular, his identification with service values and with his colleagues may grow more out of his experience in a battalion, squadron, ship, or staff unit than from his attendance at schools.

EVOLUTION OF THE
MILITARY SCHOOLING SYSTEM

Although the origins and timing of the transformation of "military officership" from a trade to a profession are obscure, it is clear that by the latter part of the nineteenth century, military professionalism was well advanced both in Europe and America. During the half century between the Civil War and World War I, a comprehensive system of military education was built in the United States which not only reflected but further developed and reinforced this burgeoning professionalism. In this period, both the Army and the Navy constructed a comprehensive system of military schools, with two or three professional levels as well as a precommissioning level—a system which was augmented for a few officers by education in civilian institutions, mainly in scientific and technical subjects. Thus, the basic outlines of both the Army's and the Navy's school systems were largely set by the start of World War I (Huntington, 1957). Since then—under the impact of science, technology, and the broadened character of American security problems—there has been evolution of the services' school systems, and an outright revolution within the individual schools and courses.

Though largely isolated from outside political and pedagogical currents, the military schools apparently served the profession and the nation in the years between the world wars. In commenting on the small, prewar American Army's "mysterious" ability to raise, move, and utilize its very large forces in World War II, Winston Churchill pinpointed the role of the military education: "Professional attainment, based upon prolonged study and collective study at colleges, rank by rank, age by age—those are the title needs of the commands of the future armies and the secret of future victories" (Churchill, 1967).

Convinced, along with Churchill, that military schooling contributed to the World War II victory and recognizing the rapid pace of change in the technological and strategic environment confronting the United States after the war, the profession's leaders moved, in the late 1940s—as they have periodically thereafter—to strengthen further the services' educational systems. For instance, the Army, probably the most "education-minded" of the services, undertook a series of reforms based on major, systemwide studies of military schooling, ranging from the Gerow Board in 1946 (which recommended reshaping the Army's schooling pattern and creation of joint military schools), to the Haines Board of 1966 (which analyzed the Army's entire officer training and education effort in comparison with other services, foreign armies, and industry). The newly independent Air Force, building upon the base of the flying schools of the old Army Air Corps, created an entire educational and training complex of its own. Alone among the services, it centralized its professional schools and colleges into a "university" organization, complete with its own institute of technology. Though their actions were not so spectacular as the Air Force's innovation, both the Navy and Marine Corps also expanded and strengthened their educational systems (Shelburne et al., 1968).

By the late 1960s the armed forces had become, in Secretary of Defense Clifford's words, "the world's largest educators." The Army alone was operating thirty-seven schools with five hundred separate curricula (Jordan, 1968). Another gauge of the scope of the services' educational efforts is the Department of Defense estimate that about forty thousand resident officer students were enrolled in service and joint school educational courses in fiscal year 1967. In addition there were about ten thousand cadets in the three service academies and nearly four thousand military officers enrolled in postgraduate programs, either in civilian institutions or in the Navy's and Air

Force's own equivalent, postgraduate schools (see U.S. Department of Defense, OSD/Manpower, 1966). Tens of thousands of other officers were enrolled in off-duty programs and nonresident courses at the various military schools and colleges or through correspondence school centers throughout the world which offer hundreds of college and postgraduate courses (Clark and Sloan, 1964).

Structurally, the services' educational systems, as they had evolved by the mid-1960s, could be described as a combination of generalist and specialist subsystems, the former category comprising three types—preprofessional, entry, and professional levels—and the latter category consisting of courses offered in both military and civilian educational institutions in managerial, politicomilitary, scientific and technological fields, as well as in more narrowly military subjects such as procurement and intelligence. The entire system is shown diagrammatically in Figure 1.

PRECOMMISSIONING EDUCATION

The first or precommissioning rung of the military education ladder is occupied by essentially two educational programs: the service academies and the Reserve Officer Training Corps (ROTC). Each service leans on various officer candidate school or officer training program sources for commissioned recruits, but these other sources—which tend to be significant when wartime needs necessitate a large-scale, rapid force buildup—focus essentially on short-term training and indoctrination and are not basically educational in character. Although officers from these latter sources tend to be highly committed to the services, they tend to have considerably lower educational qualifications (Zald and Simon, 1964).

The Service Academies

Though numerically far from the dominant source of newly commissioned officers, the Military, Naval and Air Force Academies are generally viewed as key sources of career officers, because of the relatively high degree of career commitment by their graduates and the distinctive ethos inculcated by them. (The Marines, who do not have a separate academy, draw on the Naval Academy which provides graduates to both the Navy and the Marine Corps; in exceptional cases such as a family tie, graduates from one service's academy may be commissioned in another service.) In 1968 the three

Figure 1

OFFICER EDUCATION SYSTEMS*

A. *GENERAL EDUCATION*	B. *SPECIALIZED EDUCATION*

3rd PROFESSIONAL LEVEL
National War College
Industrial College of the Armed Forces
Service War Colleges
Selected Foreign War Colleges

Specialized Courses in Management, Logistics, Intelligence, and so forth, and Postgraduate Civilian Courses

0-20 years service

16-23 years service

2nd PROFESSIONAL LEVEL
Armed Forces Staff College
Service Command and Staff Colleges

9-15 years service

1st PROFESSIONAL LEVEL
Army Branch Schools
Air Force Squadron Officer School
Marine Amphibious Warfare School

3-8 years service

ENTRY LEVEL
Basic and Indoctrination Courses

0-1 years service

PREPROFESSIONAL
Service Academies
Reserve Officer Training Corps
Officer Candidate and Training Schools

---

*Adapted from "Officer Education Study," 1966.

academies furnished only about one-third (2,500 or 7,500) of the new regulars, which comprised in turn only about fifteen percent of all new officers (about forty thousand total regulars and reservists). When both the Military and Air Force Academies complete expanding their student bodies in the early 1970s to the 4,417 strength figure long authorized for the Naval Academy, the annual output of all three will still only be about three thousand, roughly one-half of the anticipated regular officer intake.

The service academies bear a distinct family relationship to each other for they have a common mission, namely, to develop the qualities of character and intellect essential to their graduates' progressive and continued development as career officers of the regular forces. Each is an undergraduate, four-year college with a largely prescribed general education curriculum which emphasizes breadth of preparation across the fields of mathematics-science-engineering, social sciences, and humanities. Despite relatively high prescription of courses, each academy offers a cadet or midshipman some latitude to follow his intellectual interests, the Air Force going somewhat further in the direction of electives and majors than its two sister academies. (The respective academy catalogs show the 1969 ratios of prescribed to elective courses as USMA 84/16, USNA 85/15, USAFA 71/29.)

Although the academies resemble each other more than they resemble any civilian institution, each has its own character. Variations among them stem from differing patterns of evolution and from the different missions of the services which, in turn, have led to distinctive personnel systems and traditions. As one example, the Naval Academy faculty is roughly fifty percent civilian, whereas both the Military and Air Force Academies' faculties are almost one hundred percent military. The argument for a military faculty is the same in all three institutions, namely, that outstanding professional officer instructors stimulate student career motivation and professional socialization. The Navy's deviation from this logic and from the Army-Air Force pattern apparently had its origin in the fact that the Navy's leadership held (and still holds) that its officers must not be away from the sea more than two or three years at a time, thus making it extraordinarily difficult for a Naval officer to carve out a sufficient bloc of time in his career to permit a combination of the needed graduate schooling and teaching at the academy (U.S. Congress, House Committee on Armed Services, Special Subcommittee on Service Academies, 1967). As a further example of variation, the Air Force Academy planners, who were unencumbered by the tradition of civil and Naval engineering primacy found at the Military and Naval Academies, prescribed a fifty-fifty balance in the new academy's core curriculum between mathematics, science, and engineering on the one hand, and social sciences and humanities on the other. The ratios at West Point and Annapolis are roughly fifty-five/forty-five and seventy/thirty respectively, weighted toward mathematics, science, and engineering. This relatively greater emphasis on the liberal arts at Colorado Springs is especially noteworthy since the Air Force is generally acknowledged to be more scientifically and technologically oriented than the other services.

The academies have been criticized occasionally for too much of a lock-step approach to education, with too little attention to individual cadet's interests and abilities and too great an emphasis on conformity and uniformity (Boroff, 1962, 1963a, 1963b).

It is certainly true that by retaining the view that they are responsible for character development as well as for intellectual growth, the academies maintain a controlled environment more akin to the nineteenth-century college than the modern university. It is true, also, that this climate has extended to curriculum, for it was not until after World War II that cadets and midshipmen were offered any real choice of subjects—except among several foreign languages. Perhaps it is natural that institutions which prepare men explicitly to defend society should not leave the form of preparation purely or even mainly to chance or individual choice (Masland and Radway, 1957).

But, as the previously cited proportions of electives in the academies' curricula indicate, the lock-step charges of the past were far from true by the late 1960s. Moreover, the rapid evolution of the profession, stemming from scientific advances and the deepening complexity of the politicomilitary environment, assures that the curricular trend toward diversity and adaptation to student abilities and interests will continue (Simons, 1965). Even so, the academies will not likely become typically liberal arts or engineering colleges— nor is it clear that, in view of their mission, they should so become. Their educational climate will undoubtedly remain too "directed" for many tastes, though their products measure up well when compared with other college graduates—not only in performance in the profession, but by such educational yardsticks as graduate record examination scores, scholarship and fellowship competition, and achievement in postgraduate studies (U.S. Congress, House Committee on Armed Services, Special Subcommittee on Service Academies, 1967).

John Hannah (recently President of Michigan State University), while serving as President Eisenhower's assistant secretary of defense for manpower and personnel, stated his strong support for the acedemies on grounds other than academic quality. Before he became intimately aware of what the academies were like, he told Congressional inquirers, he judged them too narrowly. He went on to explain, "While there are some things they may not do as well as our good civilian institutions . . . they do one thing much better, and that is they do instill in their students . . . a loyalty to the service, a loyalty to the government, an appreciation for ethics and integrity to a degree beyond what we do at our civilian institutions" (Masland and Radway, 1957).

Professional standards are inculcated at the academies in large part by the demanding military environment in which the students live. To the surprise of many critics, formal military instruction per se takes relatively little student time at any of the academies, perhaps two or three hours of class attendance a week during the academic year. (The Naval Academy places more stress than the other academies on preparing its graduates to assume their duties as junior officers upon graduation, perhaps because the Navy has no initial postcommissioning orientation for new line officers.) In all three academies, the curricular emphasis is overwhelmingly that of general education from September to June, though each does offer some academic year courses of a distinctively professional character, such as military history or weapons engineering. By far the greatest part of the military instruction occurs in the summer when cadets and midshipmen spend approximately two months each year in learning the skills and techniques of their profession.

The military environment of the academies, their summer training and professional courses, and their emphasis on tradition combine to set standards of "duty, honor, country" but they do not produce a monolithic value system among graduates (Lovell, 1964). What the experience of an academy education does do is to give graduates a strong sense of corporateness and identification with the service. Comparing the British, French, and American military academies, one observer (Barnett, 1967) commented on this latter point:

Although in each of these three armies the national military school trains only a portion of the entrants to the Officer Corps, nevertheless its personality deeply marks the Officer Corps because its graduates remain a cohesive body. . . . Leaving aside the detail of curriculum and method, the essential and constant factor common to all three national academies is the indoctrination with tradition: potent emotional conditioning in military myth, habits, and attitudes.

In sum, the service academy rung plays a key role in the professional education ladder, perhaps less in generating distinctly military expertise—which is largely the purpose of subsequent rungs—and more in providing a *general education* and in indoctrinating and socializing a particularly significant portion of the officer-corps-to-be.

Reserve Officer Training Corps (ROTC)

Military training of college students to prepare them to lead the militia originated in a few "military colleges" such as Norwich in the early nineteenth century. The concept was extended nationwide in 1862 by the Morrill Act, which provided that the land-grant colleges established under its provisions should include military tactics in their curricula. The ROTC in its present form began with the National Defense Act of 1916 which specified it as a source of officers to man the reserve structure created by the act (Lyons and Masland, 1959). Up to World War II the Army, Air Corps, and Navy ROTC programs had together produced over one hundred thousand officers who, with relatively few exceptions, went directly into the reserves upon commissioning and did not serve in the active forces until the outbreak of war. General Marshall summed up this "mobilization base" as follows: "Without these officers the successful rapid expansion of our Army . . . would have been impossible" (see Lyons and Masland, 1959).

After World War II, when the Army and newly independent Air Force reinstituted their ROTC programs along essentially prewar lines, the Navy turned, instead, to the idea of using the NROTC to develop career officers. It began, in 1946, to pay its midshipmen a living allowance, tuition, costs of textbooks and uniforms, and other fees in exchange for an active duty commitment. At the same time, it continued a small-scale "contract" NROTC program, with less rigorous demands, specifically to produce reserve officers (and paid therefore only a living allowance and the cost of Naval science texts and uniforms). As the United States shifted in the 1950s from a "mobilization" philosophy of defense, which relied on small regular forces and large reserves, to a "preparedness" posture entailing relatively large standing forces, the Army and Air Force, too, were increasingly forced to treat the ROTC as a source of active duty officers.

But attracting a fair share of the nation's talent into a military career, particularly in a climate of economic boom and youthful disestablishmentarianism, has proven difficult. The ROTC Vitalization Act of 1964 has helped, for it enabled the Army and Air Force to match the Navy's attractive program with 5,500 competitive, full-tuition, fees, books, and allowance scholarships. Partly as a consequence of the Vitalization Act's stimulus, and even more because they furnished college students an alternative to the Vietnam draft, the service ROTC programs were apparently flourishing by the late 1960s. The Navy had some ten thousand NROTC midshipmen enrolled at fifty-three colleges; the Air Force figures were sixty thousand at 175 institutions; the Army had about 160,000 on 247 campuses. (The Marine Corps has no separate ROTC program of its own but draws upon the NROTC's and its own "Platoon Leaders" course for college-trained officers.)

Despite these evidences of apparent health, the ROTC programs have been the subject of increasingly sharp questioning as to their necessity, curricula, faculty, and relationship to the college and university community. To some degree this questioning stems from critics' failure to realize how important the programs are to national defense. Yet the facts are clear; since the military academies provide but a minor part of the needed new officer intake each year and since the short-term officer candidate schools generally produce few college-educated officers, even in "normal times" the bulk of second lieutenants—including half or more of the regulars—must come from the ROTC or something like it. (The abnormally large number of college graduates in OCS in the late 1930s is a wartime phenomenon and will undoubtedly disappear along with the Vietnam conflict.)

The managerial, scientific, technical, and politicomilitary tasks marking the modern profession virtually necessitate a new officer's starting out with a college degree. And practically all new officers now have a bachelor's degree, as have nearly three-quarters of the entire officer corps. (Table 1 includes historical data, inasmuch as the characteristics of the officer corps have been changed somewhat by the force buildup accompanying the Vietnam conflict; it might therefore be useful to look at the figures for 1956 to 1963, before the major force increases, as well as for 1967.)

A second major reason why the new officer should have a college degree emerges from an examination of the data on the educational level of the enlisted men he is expected to lead; by the late 1960s about eighty percent of them had graduated from high school and over twenty percent had completed some college.

All three service ROTC programs have two common purposes, first to provide cadets or midshipmen with a general military background and basic military skills and, second, to motivate them for a military career—this latter objective involving both the indoctrination and socialization objectives of the military education. ROTC curricula have changed considerably over time as the services have experimented with various ways to achieve these purposes. At various times all three services have insisted that the military skills

Table 1. Educational Level of Active Duty Officers*

(cumulative percentage)

By Service, on December 31, 1967	Total DOD	Army	Navy	Marine Corps	Air Force
Graduated from college	72.9%	67.5%	78.1%	62.5%	77.3%
Completed two or more years college	84.1	81.3	86.6	71.3	87.6
Completed some college	91.0	91.1	92.9	80.4	91.5
Graduated from high school	99.9	100.0	99.6	99.3	100.0
Total Commissioned Officers	100.0	100.0	100.0	100.0	100.0

All Services, Selected Dates	May 1956	Dec. 1958	Feb. 1960	Dec. 1962	Dec. 1963	Dec. 1965	Dec. 1967
Commissioned Officers							
Graduated from college	55.5%	56.1%	57.2%	64.6%	69.4%	72.3%	72.9%
Completed two or more years of college	n.a.	n.a.	78.0	n.a.	n.a.	n.a.	84.1
Completed some college	84.5	88.2	90.0	92.7	93.1	90.9	91.0
Graduated from high school	98.3	98.6	99.4	99.6	99.7	99.7	99.9
Total Commissioned Officers	100.0	100.0	100.0	100.0	100.0	100.0	100.0

*DOD, Directorate of Statistical Services

taught should be fully sufficient to prepare the newly commissioned officer for his initial assignment. In recent years the Army and Air Force have receded somewhat from this view; but the Navy, in keeping with the relatively greater vocational emphasis which marks its schooling system, clings to the notion that the NROTC should produce an "immediately employable" ensign.

Each service ROTC has a four-year military science curriculum focused on such topics as the historic and current roles of military power, customs and courtesies of the service, drill and ceremonies, military organization, techniques of leadership and command, military administration and justice, and duties of a junior officer. The Army and Air Force generally divide their programs into a basic course, given two or three hours a week during the first two years, and an advanced course given five hours a week during the last two years, and a four- to six-week summer camp between the final two years; both services offer cadets the option of a summer camp in lieu of the initial, two-year basic program. Additionally, both Army and Air Force cadets can receive a limited amount of flight instruction. The NROTC provides a three-hour-a-week program for four years with summer cruises or shore duty each summer.

Although the services have sought to make the ROTC curricula challenging, they have had great difficulty in bringing many of the subjects to an intellectual level comparable with other college courses. Since the military background and skills needed by a new officer do not apparently have a high intellectual content, the services have been driven to develop courses with less immediate applicability to postcommissioning service but with more mental challenge, such as the Army's "American Military History" or the Air Force's "World Military Systems," or to permit substitution of related normal college courses for part of the ROTC program. Both broad approaches call into question the viability of the ROTC goal of fully preparing a new officer for active duty; the former also raises the subject of the competence of the military faculty to handle such courses.

In narrowly military courses the uniformed instructors typically assigned to ROTCs by the services are undoubtedly competent. But broader courses, such as military history or the "Role of the United States in World Affairs" require a background and sophistication often lacking in the ordinary military instructor, sometimes even in the senior officer on campus, the Professor of Military, Naval, or Air Science. The Army, for instance, while increasingly appointing only highly rated and experienced officers to the senior ROTC posts, has found that it can supply men with advanced degrees for only about forty percent of the PMS positions. The Army's problem is common to all the services: by the time higher priority needs have been met, there are not enough officers with the proper credentials for ROTC faculties. It may be that the customary priority given the ROTCs in a quieter era when their mission was to prepare reserve officers will have to be upgraded in light of their new situation and responsibilities.

There are two other related matters which have tended to generate problems between the armed services and the campuses, namely, indoctrination and the institutional control. Both have caused tensions since the early 1920s (Lyons and Masland, 1959). The military profession necessarily prizes such martial values as duty, courage, and devotion to country; one of the ROTC's implied missions is to strengthen such values in its neophytes. But the inculcation of values, of indoctrination per se, is apparently anathema to the spirit of the modern university, particularly so when the values involved bear on immediate issues such as a citizen's military service obligation or the role of force in international affairs. The military has lost much of the missionary zeal it often displayed toward the campus during the pacifist clamor of the 1920s and 1930s, but it cannot entirely forego efforts to impart its values to its new members without defaulting in its professional role.

Regarding themselves as self-governing and self-sufficient communities, the universities have sometimes viewed the ROTC units as "foreign embassies within otherwise sovereign territories." The universities cannot, of course, be entirely indifferent to the interests—including defense—of the larger community they serve; but their sensitivity about jurisdiction is understandable, particularly when it is grounded in legitimate concern about the educational level of ROTC courses, the competence of military faculty, or overambitious military indoctrination efforts (Lyons and Masland, 1959).

By the late 1960s, these concerns had led some colleges and universities to question whether *any* academic credit should be awarded for ROTC courses and whether ROTC instructors should be given faculty status (Muhlenfield, 1969). Believing that their position on campus and their ability to persuade able young men to choose a military career rest in considerable part on a favorable resolution of these issues, the armed forces have been reluctant to yield on either point. Some compromise seems inevitable, however, for the continuation of a ROTC-type program as a source of officer recruits is too important to the nation, and hence ultimately to the university, to permit its disappearance or sharp curtailment. An experimental Army program, underway in eleven colleges and universities in 1968-1969, suggests one way forward; the trial program shortens the course by twenty-five percent, all of the cut falling in the first two years—during which narrowly military subjects except a limited amount of drill are eliminated, with the remaining time used for "World Military History" and "Concepts of Military Force" courses to be taught jointly by civilian and specially educated military faculty (U.S. Department of the Army, 1968). Whether this approach, recourse to a variant of the Marines' Platoon Leaders School which eliminates all academic-year attendances, or some other compromise is the best answer, the services will likely have to realize that the primary role of the ROTCs should be to recruit and socialize to military life a fair share of the nation's talent. In view of the campus climate, most of the training needed by the new officer will have to be provided as he enters commissioned service.

ENTRY
LEVEL

Immediately after commissioning, virtually all new Air Force, Army, and Marine Corps officers—and, in a few cases, Navy officers—attend "basic" or "technical" schools. (It is noteworthy that, though part of the Navy Department, the Marine Corps' schooling pattern for officers is generally closer to the Army's than the Navy's.) The emphasis in the relatively brief, generally two to four month, courses taught at the basic schools is on training, but they also contribute importantly to the indoctrination and socialization functions of military education. Apart from the significant but too-brief association with his ROTC instructors and the glimpse of military life afforded by summer camp, the typical new officer, other than the academy graduate, gets his first sustained exposure to the profession and fellow officers at the basic schools.

With one or two exceptions, each of the Army's nineteen branches (for example, infantry, engineer, and quartermaster) conducts a basic course, as well as more advanced general and specialist courses (U.S. Department of the Army, 1966). The Marine's basic course is similar to the Army's in purpose and scope, i.e., an initiatory, practical experience aimed at preparing the officer for his immediate assignment. Instruction is chopped into small blocks and given at rapid-fire tempo in lectures and demonstrations; there is little time or inclination for students to philosophize about "why," for attention is centered on their engaging in practical exercises devoted to "what" and how."

The Air Force generally sends all its new officers except prospective pilots and navigators, on the one hand, and scientific and developmental developmental engineering officers, on the other, to technical courses keyed directly to their first assignments. Would-be pilots and navigators go to flight school, and the scientific and engineering officers go either directly to graduate school or to a regular assignment.

Navy line officers (i.e., nonspecialists) do not attend a basic course, for the Navy has believed that the new ensign's precommissioning experience should suffice to launch him, and that on-the-job training aboard ship is the best way for him to learn whatever else he needs early in a career.

PROFESSIONAL
EDUCATION

Each of the services has a multitiered system of "general military professional" education. The Army and Marine Corps professional schools are sequential; that is, an officer must study at the first level before he is eligible for the second, and so on, whereas the Air Force and Navy take a less structured approach; their officers may be chosen, for example, to attend a third-level school without any prior professional schooling. Most of the professional schools offer correspondence or "nonresident," as well as resident, instruction.

At all levels, professional courses are a mixture of training and education, with the former tending to predominate at the lower levels. Even the higher professional schools devote some attention to developing skills and techniques and to imparting doctrine, but the higher up the ladder, the more dominant the educational content of the courses.

The skills and techniques taught at each level are those appropriate to the officer's likely assignments for the next few years ahead. As a consequence of this explicit keying of schooling to hierarchically defined duties, the military officer's advanced professional education is necessarily incremental, rather than concentrated as is largely the case in the other professions. Periodic return to school has the advantage that the officer can stay abreast of scientific, technological, and strategic changes. In noting this point, some (see Clark and Sloan, 1964) have observed,

> Whereas the civilian—if he can afford to so do—may elect to forego such continuous learning, and may stand aside while the world passes him by, the commissioned officer of the United States armed forces has no such option. For him, continuous education is practically mandatory. If he stands aside while the world passes him by, the result could be disastrous for the nation.

First Professional Level

After three to eight years of variegated line and staff duties, career officers in three of the four services (the Navy again excepted) return to school for "advanced" or "career" courses. These courses are designed to prepare their students for duties at the intermediate level in the military hierarchy, e.g., command of a battalion or squadron and staff work at the next two or three higher headquarters. They seek to deepen the officer's competence in his own career field, to bring him up-to-date in developments in it, to widen his understanding of his own service, its roles, missions, and doctrines, and to introduce him to subjects that transcend his own service. Although instruction of this last type is limited, explicit attention is often paid, generally for the first time in a typical officer's schooling, to the other services and to the functions of the armed forces as a whole. As an example, the Army's advanced courses, which virtually all career officers attend, devote a portion of their nine-month-long instruction to such extra service subjects as joint Army-Air Force operations, Department of Defense organization, and orientation on foreign armies.

The Marine's school at this level, the five-month-long Amphibious Warfare School which roughly one-half the Corps' eligible officers attend, necessarily gives attention to the Navy's role; it also includes materials on the defense establishment as a whole and on related national security and international affairs topics. The fourteen-week-long Squadron Officers School, which roughly two-thirds of the eligible Air Force officers normally attend, is much shorter than the other services schools at this level, but it too aspires to provide both a service-wide and interservice orientation.

While the contribution of these first professional level courses to developing military expertise is important, their focus tends to be narrowly vocational, more one of training than of education. Instruction tends, as in the basic courses, to be rapid-fire and the subjects numerous and compressed. The emphasis at this level is again clearly on imparting techniques and military doctrine rather than on generating independent thinking and analyses. The Army is a partial exception, for, in the wake of the Haines Board criticism that career (advanced) course students were not being sufficiently challenged, a limited number of elective courses have been introduced into the curricula at this level in such fields as systems analysis, logistics management, and international relations.

The greater length of career courses in contrast to the entry level courses and their emphasis on inculcating service doctrine make the indoctrination and socialization functions of these schools important. (The dual meaning of the word "indoctrination" as used here should be noted; it carries both the connotation of inculcation of professional values and of impartation of military doctrine on such subjects as the principles of warfare, blending of fire and maneuver, completed staff action, and so on. In both senses indoctrination is important in developing the professional solidarity and the dependable response of the officer corps.)

Second Professional Level

All the services conduct "Command and Staff" courses for selected mid-career officers. This is also the level at which, for the first time, there is a "joint school"—namely, the Armed Forces Staff College (joint schools are those conducted under the supervision of the Joint Chiefs of Staff, rather than of an individual service; both faculty and student body in such schools come from all the services and, further, the curricula emphasize subjects of interest to all).

The oldest and best known of the courses at this level is at the Army's Command and General Staff College. In Masland and Radway's (1957) appraisal,

> In terms of the primary job of the Army to fight and short of that to be prepared to fight, the regular course at the Command and General Staff College at Leavenworth is the most important single educational experience open to the career Army officer. . . . It is the senior Army tactical school and the only school of *combined arms and services,* that is, it is the only school concerned with the employment of all the branches of the Army as an integrated fighting team. As such, it is the common training ground of officers from all the different sources utilized by the

Army—West Point, the colleges and universities, the ranks, and civilian life—and from all branches, combat and technical and administrative.

Sometime between their ninth and fifteenth year of service, about one-half of all eligible Army officers are selected for the Command and General Staff College (or the Armed Forces Staff College or one of the other service's schools at the same level). Since this will be the final general military educational experience for the vast bulk of these officers, the college focuses its attention on bringing all of them to a uniform, high level of staff competence and to a common understanding of the principles of military leadership and command of forces in the field. This leveling objective necessitates the college's aiming instruction below the potential of the ablest students; it also necessitates a great deal of curricular attention to drill in doctrine and techniques and stress on the "approved solution."

Electives in such fields as financial management, foreign languages, and systems analysis are available to exploit student interests and backgrounds, but there is only time for one such course, a semester in length, unless the officer "overloads." With more than two hundred prescribed subjects to study, often for as little as three class hours per subject, and with frequent examinations and accompanying pressure for high grades, the C&GSC students have little time to follow their interests or to reflect on what they are doing.

The important role that the college played in an earlier era, in doctrinal development and in thinking through the profession's problems, has largely disappeared. The college still publishes *Military Review,* but research by the faculty is no longer a major activity; the college's once important responsibility for developing Army doctrine has been transferred to the "Combat Development Command," which has a branch collocated at Fort Leavenworth (and with the Army War College as well) in order to draw on and augment faculty expertise.

The Marine Corps Command and Staff College course is similar to the Army's in duration and objectives. As in the Army's case, too, roughly the top half of the eligible officers are selected for the course. The Navy's Command and Staff course is also ten months in length and also devoted to "emphasis upon the operational functions of command including operational planning . . . (and upon) the organization, functions, and procedures of operational staffs." It differs somewhat from the Army and Marine Staff colleges in devoting considerable time to military history and Naval and global strategy, probably because it is collocated with the Naval War College and shares some of the latter's lecturers. Only about fifteen percent of eligible Naval officers attend the course, but nonattendance does not bar later selection for the war college.

The Air Command and Staff College is again roughly equivalent to the other service colleges at this level in terms of objective and duration. As in the Navy's case, the Air Force C&GSC is a bit more selective (about one-quarter of the eligible officers attend) and—collocated with the Air War College—spends more time on national and global problems than is the case with the Army and Marines.

The Armed Forces Staff College is directly supervised by the Joint Chiefs of Staff. Even though the students from the four services who attend the five-month AFSC course are not exposed to the same amount of indoctrination in service viewpoints and of drill in staff techniques as those who go to their own Command and Staff Colleges, they are given the same credit for second professional level schooling. The AFSC course naturally stresses joint and combined operational planning and attendant command and staff problems—roughly one-half the total course is spent on these subjects. (As Table 2 shows, "jointness" is also introduced at this level by each service's sending some of its officers as students to the other services' command and staff courses; also a few officers attend foreign staff colleges, just as foreign officers attend the American staff colleges.)

Looking at graduates from all five colleges, an observer cannot help being impressed with the professional competence which marks them. Carefully selected to begin with, they have been through a rigorous course of study focused squarely on the kinds of problems that will be theirs over the next few years. Perhaps their minds have not been stretched enough in view of the pace of technological advance and the changing politicomilitary environment, nor have they been sufficiently encouraged in innovative and creative thinking, but these are difficult objectives for a single year's schooling—especially when the students are already fairly mature professionals. In any case, the more promising of them will have further opportunity to cope with such problems at the next, final level of general military education—the war colleges.

Third Professional Level

At the pinnacle of the military education system stand five coequal institutions: two joint colleges—the National War College

Table 2. Second Professional Level College Enrollment

Schools			Service		
U.S. Military	USA	USN	USAF	USMC	Total
AFSC[a]	169	125	163	36	493
Army C&GSC[b]	1,288	3	14	10	1,315
Navy CSC	14	155	6	14	189
Air Force CSC	14	7	506	8	535
Marine CSC	6	6	2	106	120
Total U.S. Military	1,491	296	691	174	2,652
Foreign Staff Colleges	14	6	10	2	32
Total Staff College Equivalents	1,505	302[c]	701	176	2,684

a. The figures represent two classes per year of about two hundred and fifty each.

b. Figures are for both the regular course and its shorter associate version. After 1966 only the regular course was given with the overall number of students increasing somewhat.

c. Programmed increase for the Naval School of Command and Staff will bring the total to approximately 365 beginning with fiscal year 1970.

Source: U.S. Department of Defense, OSD/Manpower (1966).

and the Industrial College of the Armed Forces—and the Army, Navy, and Air War colleges. The goal of each institution is roughly the same: to prepare selected officers to man the highest level command and staff positions within their own services and with national and international forces and headquarters. The Industrial College of the Armed Forces (ICAF) has a somewhat different mission and curricular emphasis from the others, for it focuses on the "economic and industrial aspects of national security and . . . the management of resources . . . giving due consideration to the interrelated military, political, and social factors affecting national security, and in the context of both national and world affairs" (U.S. Department of the Army, 1966). As Table 3 indicates, all five colleges have students from each service; in addition, civilian agencies with defense-related responsibilities, such as the Department of State and CIA, send students to these colleges.

All five colleges examine the military and international environment, the strategic threats to the nation, allied and U.S. capabilities

Table 3. Third Professional Level Approximate Yearly Input

(active duty only)

Schools			Service		
U.S. Military	USA	USN	USAF	USMC	Total
Army War College	161	10	16	6	193
School of Naval Warfare	16	92	16	16	140
Air War College	16	10	226	6	258
National War College	34	26	34	7	101
ICAF	49	40	49	9	147
Total U.S. Military	276	178	341	44	839
Other U.S. and Foreign[a]					
Canadian National Defense College	1	1	1	(1)[b]	
U.S. Foreign Service Institute		1			
French War College	1				
Inter-American Defense College	1	1	1	(1)	
NATO Defense College		1	1		
RAF War College			1		
Australian Air War College			2		
U.K. Imperial Defense College	1	1	1	(1)	
U.K. Joint Service Staff College		2			
Total Other U.S. and Foreign	4	7	7	1	19
Total Senior Service College Equivalents	280	185	348	45	858

a. Although a service may send officers to the other U.S. or foreign schools listed, if a number is not shown in the service column, then the school is not equated at senior service college level.

b. Rotating billet. Same officer attends all three schools.

Source: U.S. Department of Defense, OSD/Manpower, (1966). It should be noted that the size of the Army War College student body has expanded somewhat, and that of the Air War College has contracted, since the data depicted here were recorded.

to meet those threats, and optimal strategies and programs to use those capabilities. The special emphasis of ICAF has already been noted; differences in curricula among the other four colleges are principally traceable to the importance each service attaches to assuring that the graduates of its colleges are steeped in its own perspective and doctrine. Thus, nearly half of the Army War College course is devoted to "Army doctrine, higher tactics, and operations within the joint and international environment" (U.S. Army War College, 1968). Similarly the Air Force places "particular emphasis on aerospace power" and lists making its students "better informed as articulate advocates of aerospace power" as one of its objectives (Air War College, 1968-1969).

All five colleges offer their students a choice of several electives. (All except the Army War College also have a cooperative arrangement with a civilian university to permit their students to enroll in an associated graduate study program; at the three war colleges this leads to a master's degree in international affairs and at ICAF to a master's of business administration; the Army War College prefers that its students focus exclusively on the war college's own course.) A partial listing of the electives available at the Army War College is illustrative: economics of national security, international law and U.S. national security, analytical techniques of management, and political systems of developing nations. As at the staff college level, however, time for electives is scanty so that inadequate advantage is taken of the rich backgrounds which many students bring to various parts of the course. The officer with an M.A. or Ph.D. in international relations or management, for example, has to take virtually the same course as a man with no graduate study or experience in the field.

The colleges capitalize on diversity among their students in a different way, namely, by arranging matters so that the students learn, to a very large extent, from each other. Small student committees or seminars are normally appointed in each of the various courses for group study and staff projects and for discussions of lectures and reading materials. Since the college faculties generally give but limited guidance to these committees, their members rely essentially on each other's insights and backgrounds. A related, unusual feature of the war colleges' educational method is their heavy reliance on guest lecturers, each of whom generally gives a single lecture and then spends several hours in intensive discussion with the students (Crawford, 1965). Comparison of 1965-1966 syllabi show that the Naval War College had the fewest, 113, and the Air War College the most, 155, visiting lecturers in that academic year (U.S. Department of the Army, 1966).

Although there has been a recent trend in several of the colleges away from lectures, and especially from visiting lecturers, the colleges' freedom in this regard is limited by the fact that their own faculties are not always prepared to take up the normal lecturer-discussion leader and research counselor roles generally played by higher education faculty members in nonmilitary institutions. Some of the war colleges are better off in this regard than others; indeed, most generalizations about the five have at least one whole or partial exception to them.

Civilian educators who have appraised the war colleges have generally fastened upon the lack of preparation and tenure of their faculties as their weakest point and one reason for the colleges' undue stress on visiting lecturers and committee work. The typical war college faculty member is a highly qualified military professional, but he often lacks any formal preparation and sometimes even wide experience in the politicomilitary or resource management fields on which the college curricula center. In addition to trying to recruit better prepared military faculty members as a way to meet this problem, the colleges have also hired a few qualified civilians. Educators (Masland and Radway, 1957) agree that

> The civilians who have been associated with the colleges appear to have made substantial contributions. That they are being used at more of the colleges and on an expanding and continuing basis indicates that their services are well received. The colleges probably could make even more effective use of the civilian faculty members, however. Even at the National War College these individuals, in spite of their qualifications as teachers and scholars, are used primarily for planning and administrative duties.

It has been argued that "the war colleges should be the locus of development and analysis of doctrine" (Katzenbach, 1965). Whether one goes this far in assigning doctrinal responsibilities, it is clear that as the highest level of military education, these colleges should encourage the questioning of doctrine and the most rigorous analyses of it by both faculty and students. The traditional criteria of faculty selection—ready availability and professional attainment—which were appropriate to a less specialized and dynamic era, with the short tours of faculty duty, undue emphasis on visiting lecturers, and dependence on fellow students which were frequent concomitants, will probably have to change before the colleges can contribute to expanding military expertise and hold their own against the "defense intellectuals" with their "think tanks" and university research seminars.

That the colleges provide their students a broad, stimulating experience and a change of pace at an appropriate juncture in their high-pressure careers is clear. It may also be true, as one critic has charged, that the "high demand for war college graduates derives more from the professional qualifications that led to their initial selection than from the instruction they received (Katzenbach, 1965). Since roughly twenty years of experience and prior education have inevitably shaped an officer's basic abilities long before his war college experience, the point is not moot. Still, with increasingly sophisticated students and highly dynamic subject matter, the colleges cannot (and, as a matter-of-fact, for the most part do not) take for granted the continued relevance of past patterns.

SPECIALIST
EDUCATION

Technological progress, changes in the politicomilitary environment, and the strategic revolution which has flowed from these developments have combined to generate an increasing degree of specialization within the military profession. The trend toward increasing specialization is not unique to the military profession. As Huntington has pointed out, the medical and legal professions also share the problem, but in their cases increasing specialization and professional advancement are correlated for the individual professional (Huntington, 1963). Specialization provides the military with a distinctive problem. Bureaucratic hierarchical in structure, the military needs generalists at all levels; however, the requirements for specialists, who are increasingly vital to its functioning, are largely concentrated in the junior and intermediate ranks. The services have typically tried to meet their dual bureaucratic and specialization needs by two means: increased attention to formal education and training for specialists and, second, management of officers' careers so that they can develop and practice some specialization while in the lower and intermediate ranks without so narrowing their competence as generalists as to foreclose their rising as generalists to the top of the profession.

Specialist Military Education and Training

When confronted with a major development for the profession such as a scientific breakthrough or a significant shift in strategy, the services have tended both to orient all professionals about the new development through the general military education schooling system and to prepare a smaller number of officers to focus directly upon the development through more intensive and specialized schooling arrangements. Thus, the development of battlefield nuclear weapons necessitated the introduction of material on nuclear warfare throughout the basic, advanced, and professional schools of the Army in the late 1940s and, in addition, resulted in intensive courses on nuclear weapons and their application at certain of the specialist schools—these latter courses leading to "military occupational specialty" designations as "Nuclear Weapons Officer" for anyone completing them.

Similarly, by the late 1960s, the Army had concluded, largely from its experience in Vietnam, that it needed to improve its ability to deal with insurgency and "stability operations" in less developed areas. Consequently, it not only increased the amount of attention to such subjects throughout its general military education courses, but it also instituted a new career field, the "Military Assistance Officer Program," and designated over one thousand positions throughout the military structure to be filled by officers in the new field having appropriate politicomilitary specializations. Selected officers will prepare for the "MAOP" field by graduate schooling in one of the social science disciplines at a civilian university and by attending a sequential line of specialist courses in the Army's own schools on civil affairs, psychological operations, and similar topics (U.S. Army Regulation 614-134, 1969).

As an indicator of the scope of military specialist training and education, the Army operates ten specialist schools of its own and two for the Defense Department, in addition to specialist courses taught at the nineteen "branch" schools already mentioned as part of the pattern of generalist schools. In fiscal year 1965, over nine thousand Army officers attended these twelve specialist schools, pursuing such subjects as helicopter pilot training, resource management, and guided missiles (U.S. Department of the Army, 1966).

In addition to service-conducted specialist courses, there are also a number of joint or "defense" schools for specialist training and education; for example, the Defense Language Institute, the Defense

Information School, the Defense Computer Institute, and the Defense Intelligence School. Both the Office of the Secretary of Defense and the Joint Chiefs of Staff have responsibilities for joint training and education in areas of specialization which affect more than one service. But despite the expanding reach of OSD and the statutory responsibility of the JCS to "formulate policies for the joint training of the armed forces and . . . for coordinating the military education of members of the armed forces," the services retain the bulk of the responsibility for specialist as well as generalist education. In fact, the individual services usually operate the joint or defense specialist schools with only broad guidance from OSD or the JCS.

Civilian Higher Education

The practice of sending military officers to civilian institutions for postgraduate work, which was begun by the Army shortly after the Civil War, has greatly expanded and broadened since World War II. Impelled by the deepening complexity of the tasks facing the profession, the services steadily enlarged their programs until academic year 1965-1966 when there were nearly four thousand officers taking postgraduate courses, ranging in length from a few months to three or four years. Enrollments have dropped somewhat since 1966 as a consequence of the manpower needs of the Vietnam conflict; but, since requirements for various specializations have continued to increase, the numbers in civilian universities will probably surge ahead again with the conclusion of that war.

The military forces' graduate school programs began in the sciences with an 1868 law authorizing medical training at civilian institutions for Army officers. Engineer and ordnance officers were authorized equivalent privileges in 1871 and 1873, respectively, and as civilian schooling expanded up to World War II, the emphasis continued to be almost exclusively upon scientific and engineering studies (Shelburne and Groves, 1965). Experience in and since World War II convinced the services, however, of a need for a broader range of expertise. By the 1960s this awareness had led the services to prepare their officers in political science, economics, international relations, psychology, sociology, anthropology, journalism, business administration, political and economic geography, and so on.

The Army, in particular, turned increasingly to social science-type graduate specialization, as it became interested in "stability operations" in less-developed countries and as its resource management tasks grew more complex. The number of positions throughout the Army structure designated as requiring graduate preparation grew from 2,376 in 1963 to 5,353 in 1967, the physical and biological sciences and engineering positions growing by roughly seventy percent in the period, while the business figures more than tripled, and the social sciences positions nearly quadrupled (U.S. Department of the Army, 1963-1967). Creation of the new "MAOP" career field, mentioned above, and the additional schooling requirement stemming from the need for ROTC instructors to be graduate school trained indicate both tha overall number of Army officers pursuing graduate education will increase in the future and that the growth in the social sciences and business fields will likely continue to be disproportionately large.

Assignment to graduate school—probably sometime in the first decade of his service—is becoming part of the typical career officer's expectations. Projections are not available across the services, but the fact that about two-thirds of the Military Academy's graduates of the past two decades have gone to graduate school is one indication of the pattern (Stevens, 1968). The West Point figure will probably grow to three-quarters or five-sixths in the next few years.

The Navy and Air Force offer graduate-level academic programs in their own fully accredited institutions. The Naval Postgraduate School focuses primarily on scientific, engineering, and management fields but also offers limited work in such social science subjects as economics and political science. In constrast to the Navy, which leans heavily on its in-house postgraduate training facilities, the Air Force depends essentially on civilian institutions for the postgraduate education of its officers. But the Air Force Institute of Technology (AFIT) does conduct a limited postgraduate program (in addition to undergraduate and nondegree programs) in such subjects as engineering, systems management, and business administration. In addition to its own in-house instruction, AFIT manages the Air Force's entire postgraduate education program at scores of civilian institutions (U.S. Department of Defense, OSD/Manpower, 1966).

The Army does not have a postgraduate institution authorized to grant advanced degrees. In 1963 it instituted a master's degree program at the Command and General Staff College at Fort Leavenworth, which was duly endorsed by the necessary accrediting organizations, but failed to secure the authorizing legislation needed by federal institutions before they can grant degrees. By 1968 about

one hundred officers had completed the college's stringent requirements, but it was still awaiting authority to grant its first "Master of
Military Art and Sciences" (Armed Forces Journal, 1968).

Not counting the Army's pending program, the services' full-
time, on-duty postgraduate programs for a typical year are
summarized in Table 4.

The figures in Table 4 understate the amount of officer
postgraduate study actually occurring, for each service provides
tuition assistance for personnel pursuing higher education on an
off-duty basis. Any university near a military post will have dozens,
perhaps hundreds, of officers so enrolled on a part-time basis. And to
complete the description of higher education for members of the
armed forces, another form of off-duty study, namely, correspondence courses should be noted. Whether out of a desire for
self-improvement, hopes for quicker promotion, preparation for a
second career, or sheer boredom, thousands of officers are among the
hundreds of thousands of servicemen enrolled at any one time in
correspondence courses. The services have their own voluntary
programs in addition to those of the U.S. Armed Forces Institute, an
enterprise under the direction of the Assistant Secretary of Defense
for Manpower. "USAFI offers some 200 high school, college, and
technical-vocational correspondence and group-study courses, including courses in twenty-four spoken languages. Forty-three colleges and
universities now cooperate in offering correspondence courses
through USAFI" (Shelburne and Grove, 1965).

Judgments differ as to whether so much civilian higher education
is necessary or desirable. In addition to antimilitary critics who
would prefer to see professional military men fenced off from all
civilian contact in their own enclaves, there are military tradition-
alists who fear the contaminating effect of too much graduate
education, who are concerned that soldiers will be seduced thereby

Table 4. Officer Enrollments, Academic Programs, Spring 1966

	USA	USN	USAF	USMC	Total
Postgraduate					
In-House		994	204	91	1,289
Civilian Institutions	931	322	1,323	11	2,587

Source: U.S. Department of Defense, OSD/Manpower (1966).

to stray from the paths of duty. Is there any real danger that military men will become so "overeducated," particularly in nonscientific fields, that—in Hamlet's words—their "native hue of resolution is sicklied o'er with the pale cast of thought"? It is hard to take the question seriously. For one thing, military men are universally skeptical of the intellectual community with its characteristic antimilitary values. For another, military officers are fully aware of the perpetual tension between "thinkers" and "doers," between the academician's "why?" and the military man's need to make and act on decisions, even when judgments differ and all the facts are not available. Yet, despite this skepticism and awareness, as the trends described above show, the profession's leaders recognize the need for higher education; the deepening demands of the military specialist's tasks and widening complexity of the generalist's realm comprise an irresistible force which the profession cannot ignore.

Moreover, although widespread graduate schooling is only about two decades old, there is already substantial evidence that tradition- alist fears are simply unwarranted. Apparently the roles of "military executive," with attendant civilian graduate school preparation, and of "combat leader," with the usual generalist and specialist military schooling, are not generally antithetical; in terms of combat record, retention in the service, promotion to high rank, and selection for senior service schools, officers with higher education backgrounds are proving to be outstanding professionals. Thus, the Air Force has found a strong correlation between graduate schooling and combat performance in Vietnam among its academy graduates (U.S. Con- gress, House Committee on Armed Services, Special Subcommittee on Service Academies, 1967); the Navy has discovered that an astonishingly small fraction of the eight thousand Naval officers who have completed postgraduate training since 1948 have resigned before completing twenty years of service (U.S. Department of the Army, 1966); the Army has noted that a large share of its officers currently being selected for colonel's rank and roughly half of those being chosen to attend the Army War College have graduate degrees, in comparison with the servicewide proportion of eleven percent holding such degrees.

FUTURE
TRENDS

Judged by overall results, the military's educational and training system has, by and large, continued since World War II to serve the profession well. The leaders, managers, and specialists flowing from it have played a major role in deterring nuclear war and in safeguarding other national interests through the training, equipping, deploying, and—as needed—the utilization of fighting capability of military units of unprecedented complexity and power. As required, they have also served other national goals, been loaned to other government departments, trained foreign forces, administered military aid programs, and so on. It is not self-evident, of course, that the educational system has always contributed to these accomplishments as effectively and efficiently as it might have; indeed, it would be surprising if schooling patterns which have emerged through evolution and accretion, as well as by overall design, were ideally fitted to the needs of the past, let alone to those of the future.

Aware of concern within the profession on this point, President Johnson, in 1964, announced that he was "directing the Secretary of Defense to review the educational systems and major schools within the services—and the opportunities now offered for continued civilian education while in service—to broaden and strengthen these programs." That defensewide analysis, shoved aside by Vietnam's mounting demands on top officials' attention, has yet to be undertaken, although a partial, small-scale review of current programs was made in 1965 as a direct consequence of the President's initiative. The military profession still awaits its Flexner or Conant.

Any total "systems" study of professional schooling must inevitably ask whether, in the interest of service cooperation and efficiency, there should not be more common, joint, or interservice education—perhaps starting with the academies and ROTCs. The lack of enthusiasm within the services for this approach (or even for centrally directed studies of the question) is rooted in the virtually unanimous view among professionals that schooling should be keyed directly to service personnel systems, which are themselves based directly upon service tasks. Thus the question is not merely one of service or joint schools, but of the very existence of the services themselves.

Yet the increasing interdependence of the services, which necessitated the first joint school—the Army-Navy Staff School—in 1943 and which has gained impetus in the quarter-century since, shows no sign of lessening. In fact, the trend has picked up momentum in the last decade, especially in combat support activities as exemplified by the creation of the Defense Communications Agency, Defense Intelligence Agency, Defense Supply Agency, and so forth. In view of this trend, it may well prove impossible in the future, in contrast to the past and present, for an officer to rise to positions of high rank and responsibility without schooling or experience outside his own service.

Achieving the service integration needed in some functional fields may necessitate increasing the number of joint or defense schools. In many cases, however, a better approach may be "interservice" schools, i.e., schools in which one service provides facilities, faculty, and curriculum for students from all the services. The respective roles and responsibilities of the services, the Joint Chiefs, and the Office of the Secretary of Defense will undoubtedly need further sorting out and clearer delineation, if any of these approaches to the challenge of interdependence is to proceed further. (It might be noted here that the increasing requirement to consider grand strategy with other members of alliances has also led in the past decades to another form of "interservice" officer education. U.S. officers in very small numbers already attend the Imperial Defence College, the Ecole Superieure de Guerre, and a few selected others, and it has been advisable to establish an alliancewide NATO Defense College in Rome and an Inter-American Defense College in Washington. Service officers also attend the Foreign Service Institute and the National Interdepartmental Seminars, educational institutions of the Department of State. See Table 3.)

In addition to adapting to increasing service interdependence, future military schooling patterns will also have to cope with still more specialization. More schooling for more officers may be part of the answer, but part may also lie in strengthening the line between specialists and generalists so that the latter need not try to be part-time specialists and the former need not forego high rank and responsibility unless they also try to be part-time generalists. Whatever the personnel management approach to the specialization dilemma, the question of whether an increasingly complex profession necessitates officers' spending still more time in school must be faced. In 1963 Acting Secretary of State Ball, in noting that the Department of State's officers needed more schooling, told a Congressional committee that the average military officer spent twelve percent of his career in postgraduate professional training and education, in contrast to the Foreign Service Officer's five percent.

For the future, Secretary Ball's estimate of military schooling (which was probably based on Army, or perhaps Air Force, figures) is likely low. For the Army officer, for example, three extended courses of professional schooling, two years of civilian postgraduate work, and a year or more of cumulative military specialist schooling will represent about twenty percent of a thirty-year career. Such a ratio may be unacceptable in the future, even in the most education-minded of the services, as decreasing funding and manpower levels clash with increasing needs for sophisticated skills arising from growing complexity and specialization.

A related major issue will have to be dealt with in the future, namely, the already-noted general tendency of the service school systems to load their curricula with training-type materials at the expense of education. One critic has written of this tendency, "It is one thing to apply the 'kitting-out' approach to other ranks in particular trade skills; quite another to apply it to the higher education of officers, where judgment and understanding is the aim" (Barnett, 1967).

Distillation of past experience and/or straight-line projections from military doctrine will continue to form an important part of military schooling in the future, but the military educational system of the future must also take responsibility for creating the kind of environment which will generate innovative and creative thinking among its students. The future's military environment seems unlikely to be an extrapolation from the past. Less emphasis can, therefore, be put on "approved solutions"; more time be spent on thought and less on memorization; fewer subjects covered, but those more deeply investigated—these are some of the guidelines which at least the higher military schools need to press still further to meet the challenges of a changing profession.

REFERENCES

Air War College (1968-1969) "Bulletin."

Armed Forces Journal (1968) "Completion of Masters degree program." 20 (July).

BARNETT, C. (1967) "The education of military elites." Journal of Contemporary History 2 (July).

BOROFF, D. (1963a) "Annapolis: teaching young sea dogs old tricks." Harper's (January).

———(1963b) "Air Force Academy: a slight gain in altitude." Harper's (February).

———(1962) "West Point: ancient incubator for a new deal." Harper's (December).

CHURCHILL, W. (1967) Address to the U.S. Army General Staff, April 19, 1946. Cited in G. Pappas, Prudens Futuri: The Army War College, 1901-1967. Walsworth Publishing.

CLARK, H. and H. SLOAN (1964) Classrooms in the Military. New York: Bureau of Publications, Teachers College, Columbia University.

CRAWFORD, E. (1965) "Education for policy roles: an analysis of lecturers and reading materials at selected colleges." CFSTI document AD 669-840.

HACKETT, Lt. Gen. Sir J. W. "The 1962 Lees Knowles lectures." Trinity College, Cambridge, England.

HUNTINGTON, S. (1963) "Power expertise and the military profession." Daedalus 92 (Fall).

———(1957) The Soldier and the State. Cambridge: Harvard University Press.

JANOWITZ, M. (1960) The Professional Soldier: A Social and Political Portrait. New York: Free Press.

JOHNSON, L. B. (1964) Speech to the National War College and Industrial College of the Armed Forces, Ft. McNair, August 21.

JORDAN, A. (1968) "Army service schools." Encyclopedia Americana.

KATZENBACH, E. L. (1965) "The demotion of professionalism at the war colleges." Naval Institute Proceedings (March).

LINCOLN, Col. G. A. (1964) Hearings on Administration of National Security, U.S. Senate Committee on Government Operations, Subcommittee on National Security Staffing and Operations, 88th Congress, 2nd Session.

LOVELL, J. R. (1964) "The professional socialization of the West Point cadet," in M. Janowitz (ed.) The New Military. New York: Russell Sage Foundation.

LYONS, G. and J. MASLAND (1959) Education and Military Leadership. Princeton: Princeton University Press.

MASLAND, J. and L. RADWAY (1957) Soldiers and Scholars. Princeton: Princeton University Press.

MUHLENFELD, Maj. W. F. (1969) "Our embattled ROTC." Army (February).

SHELBURNE, J. and K. GROVES (1965) Education in the Armed Forces. New York: Center for Applied Research in Education.

———and L. BROKAW (1967) "Military education," in Encyclopedia of Educational Research.

SIMONS, W. E. (1965) Liberal Education in the Service Academies. New York: Bureau of Publications, Teachers College, Columbia University.

STEVENS, P. (1968) "West Point and graduate school." Assembly (Fall).

U.S. Army Regulation 614-134 (1969) "Military assistance officer program" (March 7).

U.S. Army War College (1969) "Curriculum Pamphlet."

U.S. Congress, House Committee on Armed Services (1967) Special Subcommittee on Service Academies, Report and Hearings, 90th Congress, 1st and 2nd Sessions.

U.S. Department of the Army (1968) "Briefing on the ROTC program" (July 28).

———(1963-1967) "Reports of the Army educational requirements boards."
———(1966) Report of the Department of the Army Board to Review Army Officer Schools, Vols. I, II, III (Haines Board).
U.S. Department of Defense (1968) "Estimated educational level of military personnel on active duty." Directorate for Statistical Services (November 6).
———(1966) Officer Education Study, Vols. I, II, III. OSD/Manpower.
ZALD, M. and W. SIMON (1964) "Career opportunities and commitments among officers," in M. Janowitz (ed.) The New Military. New York: Russell Sage Foundation.

Chapter 7

THE MILITARY FAMILY

ROGER W. LITTLE

Few subjects in the sociology of military organization have received as little attention as the military family. Janowitz (1960) was the first to point out its strategic significance in the perspectives of career officers. Although there are earlier references in the literature (Lindquist, 1952), they are problem-centered and primarily concerned with the adverse effects of military service on family life or marital adjustment as observed in psychiatric clinics. In part, this neglect of a central institution may be attributed to a tendency of military sociologists to study issues which have been defined as critical by members of military organization rather than selecting subjects of study from a sociological perspective. Consequently, the military family has been neglected because its significance within military organization has been traditionally denied or relegated to a secondary level of importance.

CHANGING STATUS OF THE MILITARY FAMILY

The contemporary significance of the military family may be attributed to changed conditions of recruitment and employment of military forces. Historically, no provision was made for family life within the military community (Ganoe, 1942). The recruitment base was typically young, unmarried men. No monetary allowances for family life were provided. The frontier post which was the dominant form of the military garrison made no provision for family quarters except for the senior officer. Even officers were barred from marriage until they had attained the rank of captain. Deviant forms of family life appeared early in the role of the laundress whose daily occupational role was augmented by providing sexual outlets for unmarried troops in primitive habitations immediately outside the garrison, thus providing a term, "shacking up," which survives to describe a temporary domiciliary arrangement. Even through World War I, no monetary allowances were provided for the families of men who enlisted or were conscripted.

During the years between the world wars, the military family was thought of predominantly as the officer's family, and community life was organized around patterns of gentlemanly conduct characteristic of the officer corps (Janowitz, 1960). The service academies (whose graduates dominated the officer corps during this period) provided intensive indoctrination in social customs typical of upper-class family life in the larger society. Social activities at the academies also tended to recruit daughters of upper-class East Coast families as officer wives, reinforcing an elitist culture of the family life.

The full-scale mobilization of World War II marked the emergence of a new conception of military service as related to family life. For the first time, the federal government assumed limited fiscal responsibility for the changed standard of living imposed by conscription for military service. Family allowances and limited medical care (for obstetrical services) were provided. After the war, the necessity of maintaining a volunteer force led to the more formal recognition of provisions for family life as recruitment and career incentives. A full range of community institutions providing services to the family were required for dependents: housing, primary and secondary schools, medical care, and social welfare agencies.

The explicit recognition of the significance of the military family in personnel policy came with the problems of career retention after the Korean conflict. Attitude surveys consistently indicated that disruption of family life was one of the major deterrents to career service, ranking third (after "uncertainty about the future" and "kind of housing available") among officers. Forty-seven percent of the enlisted men reported "interference of Army routine with family life" as a factor influencing separation from the Army (Cline, 1955).

Operation Gyroscope was initiated in 1954 and developed in an attempt to alleviate the problems of family life and thus reduce the steady loss of career personnel. Units in the United States exchanged places with others of the same size in Japan and Europe. A survey of attitudes toward Gyroscope in 1955 indicated that eighty-one percent of the officers, seventy percent of the regular Army senior noncommissioned officers (top three pay grades), and seventy-four percent of all other regular Army enlisted men believed that the program would be "some or a big improvement over the old system." Even among draftees, only four percent of whom intended to reenlist, eighty percent believed that Gyroscope would improve life in the Army (Cline, 1955).

Gyroscope was discontinued by the Army in 1960 because it was very expensive and had not significantly affected career retention rates. The success of the policy had been contingent upon the availability of overseas dependent housing and variable preferences for locations upon return to the United States. When these could not be fulfilled, interest in the program and retention rates declined. The program was more effective with Negro soldiers than white (sixty-four percent of the Negroes said that they would reenlist for Gyroscope, compared to fifty percent of the whites). A majority of the Gyroscope reenlistees had intended to reenlist anyway, and many had intended to remain until retirement (Cline, 1955).

Nevertheless, the experience with Gyroscope fostered the development of other agencies concerned with the military family. Military manpower policies and congressional attitudes toward the issue became crystallized. Increased attention was paid to such programs as on-post housing and medical care for dependents.

In 1965, the Army instituted the Army Community Service Program (ACS) modeled after the earlier Dependent's Aid Program of the Air Force. The objective of the ACS was to centralize and formalize the major "helping resources" for the military family, especially for newly arrived families and emergency situations. Such centers, staffed by volunteers from the military community, have now been established on most Army posts, and comparable agencies exist on Navy and Air Force bases.

THE PRESENT SITUATION

The military family has come to be considered an essential component in personnel policy and management. In September 1968, more than seventy-six percent of the officers and forty-two percent of the enlisted men of the armed forces were married. In aggregate numbers, family status added about 1.6 million wives and

Table 1. Marital Status of Military Personnel By Rank and Service

Officers				Enlisted			
Rank	Percentage Married[a]			Rank	Percentage Married		
(Army, Navy, Air Force)	Army	Navy	Air Force		Army	Navy	Air Force
Colonel/Captain	96.7	96.0	98.1	E-9, E-8	96.8	92.0	95.3
Lieutenant Colonel/Commander	95.8	96.0	96.1	E-7	92.0	92.0	93.8
Major/Lieutenant Commander	95.4	93.0	95.0	E-6	88.1	86.0	90.0
Captain/Lieutenant	85.7	87.0	88.3	E-5	53.2	67.0	67.6
1st. Lieutenant/Lieutenant J.G.	62.6	66.0	64.2	E-4	26.3	38.0	28.8
2nd. Lieutenant/Ensign	51.0	38.0	38.2	E-3	22.7	19.0	8.0
Warrant Officers	92.2	92.0	98.9	E-2, E-1	21.1	8.0	12.8
TOTAL (% Married)	78.7	82.0	81.7		36.1	47.0	59.7

a. Percentages for categories other than "married" and "single" are negligible except for Navy E-9s, eight percent of whom report themselves as "divorced, separated, widower, or other," and only eighty-six percent married. Averaging obscures the differential.

Sources: *Army*: SAMPLE SURVEY OF MILITARY PERSONNEL: "Survey Estimate of Marital Status and Dependents of Army Male Personnel." Washington: Department of the Army, 1967. Sample size: officers, 6,126; enlisted men, 31,860. *Navy*: NAVY PERSONNEL SURVEY 65-1, Basic Report. Washington: Department of the Navy, Bureau of Naval Personnel, April 1966. Sample size: officers, 3,605; enlisted men, 16,538. *Air Force*: U.S. AIR FORCE PERSONNEL REPORT: "Characteristics and Attitudes from Sample Surveys. Washington: Department of the Air Force, November 1966. Sample size: officers, 8%; enlisted men, 3.9%.

2.5 million children to the military community (see U.S. Department of Defense, 1967). Annual rates are affected by periodic procurement of relatively large numbers of new officers, either from officer candidate schools or the Reserve Officer Training Corps (ROTC) who are usually unmarried upon entry. The data in Table 1 is for normal nonwar conditions (1965), and the only period for which separate data is available for specific ranks and branch of service. These data indicate that marital status in all ranks except the lowest (2nd lieutenant/ensign) is about equal for all three services. Army 2nd lieutenants are significantly more frequently married (fifty-one percent) than comparable ranks in the Navy and Air Force (thirty-eight percent). Senior enlisted men in the upper two grades are married almost as frequently as senior officers. Air Force enlisted men are most frequently married (sixty percent), followed by Navy (forty-seven percent) and Army (thirty-six percent). (See Table 1.)

These data suggest the significance for the family of differing conditions of life among services, status groups (officers and enlisted men), and at varying points in the military member's career.

The services differ in the stability of duty tours and consequently in the amount of time that the member actually participates in family life. Navy and Marine Corps duty involves especially long absences from home on cruises or at foreign stations without provisions for families. Air Force personnel are most likely to lead stable family lives; relatively more remain at fixed bases, i.e., personnel to service craft and personnel who travel a high speeds on missions of brief duration. Army members occupy a median position: the larger size of the Army implies a correspondingly greater differentiation (some units are like the Navy and others like the Air Force), and a larger annual input of recruits who are unmarried (especially those who are conscripted). These differences might be expected to produce variations in the percentage of personnel who are married, and correspondingly, the fertility rate by service.

Status group affiliation also differentiates in family status. Officers are more likely to be heads of families than enlisted men. The marriage of an officer is elaborately ceremonialized by traditional customs, such as the arched swords' at the exit from the chapel. The prototype for such ceremonies is the academy wedding which follows the commissioning of cadets in "June Week." All formal social activities for officers require the participation of female companions, either wives or dates. In contrast, there is no corresponding traditional wedding for the enlisted men, and bisexual formal social activities are relatively rare. Since enlisted men tend to enter the service at an earlier age, most enlisted men are unmarried. Consequently, the officer family has a quality of legitimacy that is lacking in perceptions of the enlisted family.[1]

During the military career, family status is of variable significance. Initially, it is discouraged. Personnel policy often limits procurement of enlisted men to those who are married. Cadets are forbidden to marry while attending the academy as a matter of "honor" and are expelled if they breach the code. Basic training for either enlisted men or officer candidates is especially incompatible with family life. Absences from the post are rarely permitted; the training regimen is long and arduous; no government quarters are authorized for persons in such a status, and substitute lodgings in local civilian communities is too expensive and inadequate. Pay for junior enlisted men, even when supplemented by dependent allotments, is insufficient to maintain a family household.

As the career progresses, family status is increasingly prevalent and even requisite. For enlisted men, the point at which family status is authorized is usually after being promoted through the fifth pay grade. Usually this occurs after reenlistment for a second term which implies career intentions. At this stage family quarters are authorized, allowances are provided for transportation of household goods, and families are permitted to accompany sponsors to many overseas stations at government expense. Informal social activities at the noncommissioned or petty officers' clubs increasingly involve wives. Very senior enlisted men may be involved in formal social activities at which wives play as significant a role as among officers.

It is significant that at this career level, the status of the unmarried noncommissioned or petty officer becomes increasingly ambiguous. There are rarely facilities comparable to the Bachelor Officers' Quarters (BOQ), and only married personnel are permitted to live off-base and to draw the monetary allowance in lieu of government quarters. Consequently the unmarried non-commissioned officer is compelled to live in the barracks (usually in a private room) with the junior enlisted men with a correspondingly limited range of permissible activities.

Family status is significant at a much earlier point in the officer's career. The existence of such a facility as the Bachelor Officers' Quarters signifies the legitimacy of the unmarried status (although in contemporary usage it is as frequently utilized by transient—as by unmarried—officers). However, even at the earliest stages of his career, the officer is expected to be accompanied at social functions by a woman. The most significant stage is when he is assigned to attend a service school. Attendance at such schools involves a process of socialization and evaluation by peers in which the officer's wife is likely to be an important consideration. This is especially true of advanced service schools and the war colleges which function as screening echelons for senior command and staff positions in which the ceremonial role of the wife is an essential component of the occupational role of the military member.

THE FAMILY IN
THE MILITARY COMMUNITY

Collectively, military families comprise a community with relationship to a set of institutions comparable to those in the civilian community. Some important differentials in participation in community life are the status group affiliation of the father (officer or enlisted man), residence on- or off-base, residence in the United States or at a foreign station. Some common features are participation in an esoteric occupational culture, periodic disruptions of family relationships, residential instability, and socialization in a segment of the life cycle.

Status Groups

Several factors differentiate the families of officers and of enlisted men. First, there is a higher degree of normative regulation of marital choice among officers than enlisted men. Enlisted men are three times as likely to be married to foreign-born wives (20.2%) as compared to commissioned officers (6.2%). Warrant officers, who hold a marginal status between commissioned officers (and are usually promoted to that status from senior enlisted grades) are most frequently married to foreign-born wives (21.8%).

Second, officers' wives are less likely to be working to supplement the family income (16.2%) than enlisted men's wives (31.6%) (see Table 2). This fact is due partly to income differentials, but also because the role of the officer's wife is subject to more specific normative regulation. Officers' wives are generally dissuaded from outside employment, but no such norm affects the wife of the enlisted man. Much of the employment, of course, is on the military post: clerks and cashiers in the exchange and commissary, and the like. The integrity of the officer role is maintained by insulating his family from subordinate roles in relation to enlisted men. The one work role which is "acceptable" for officers' wives is teacher in the dependent schools, and this role is compatible with the officer role.

Third, officers' families tend to include more children than the families of enlisted men. More enlisted couples have no children, or only one, than officer couples at approximately comparable age levels (see Table 3). Although it is difficult to interpret these data because important demographic indicators are not included in the survey design, the highest three grades of officers and enlisted men may be considered approximately equal in age and duration of marriage. Data for the rank of colonel in both tables is biased because the definition of "dependent children" would exclude those who had left the household.

Assuming some degree of comparability among these ranks, lieutenant colonels and majors can be safely compared with E-7s, E-8s, and E-9s. Fifty-one percent of the Army lieutenant colonels' families and fifty-three percent of the majors' families include more than three children compared to thirty-seven percent of the families

Table 2. Working Wives of Married Army Personnel

Officers' Wives		Enlisted Men's Wives	
Rank of Officer	Percentage Working	Rank of Enlisted Man	Percentage Working
Colonel	8.2	E-9 and E-8	23.7
Lieutenant Colonel	13.1	E-7	30.8
Major	11.9	E-6	29.5
Captain	11.5	E-5	29.4
1st. Lieutenant	23.4	E-4	34.9
2nd. Lieutenant	32.0	E-3	39.2
Warrant Officers	18.5	E-2 and E-1	31.0
TOTAL OFFICERS	16.2	TOTAL ENLISTED	31.6

Source: SAMPLE SURVEY OF MILITARY PERSONNEL: "Survey Estimate of Attitudes and Opinions Related to Development of Family Service Centers." Washington: Department of the Army, 1965. Comparable data not available from the other services. Sample size: officers, 6,588; enlisted men, 13,000.

Table 3. Dependent Children of Army Personnel By Rank of Father

Rank	Percentage with this number of children						Average number of children for each rank
	Total	None	1	2	3	4 or more	
Officers							
Colonel	100%	13.0	24.2	27.4	19.9	15.5	2.0
Lieutenant Colonel	100	8.5	12.6	27.6	23.2	28.1	2.5
Major	100	8.7	9.6	28.4	28.2	25.1	2.5
Captain	100	19.7	25.1	29.6	15.8	9.8	1.7
1st. Lieutenant	100	50.6	29.5	15.5	3.7	0.7	0.7
2nd. Lieutenant	100	66.1	19.3	9.6	3.6	1.4	0.5
Warrant Officer	100	13.6	16.9	27.8	18.2	23.5	2.2
TOTAL OFFICERS		23.7	19.4	25.1	16.8	15.0	
Enlisted							
E-9 and E-8	100%	13.9	18.3	25.4	16.2	26.2	2.2
E-7	100	13.6	15.1	25.0	20.9	25.4	2.3
E-6	100	15.0	19.9	25.7	18.4	21.0	2.8
E-5	100	32.4	26.6	20.3	11.5	9.2	1.4
E-4	100	60.7	26.6	8.9	2.7	1.1	0.6
E-3	100	68.7	24.3	4.9	1.2	0.9	0.4
E-2 and E-1	100	78.1	14.6	3.7	3.2	0.3	0.3
TOTAL ENLISTED		43.9	21.4	15.2	9.7	9.8	

Source: SAMPLE SURVEY OF MILITARY PERSONNEL: "Survey Estimate of Marital Status and Dependents of Army Male Personnel." Washington: Department of the Army, 1967. Sample size: officers, 6,126; enlisted men, 31,860.

of E-8s and E-9s, and forty-six percent of the E-7s. If equivalent Air Force ranks are compared, the same differential does not occur: forty-four percent of the lieutenant colonels and forty-eight percent of the majors, and forty-five percent of the E-9s and E-8s, and forty-six percent of the E-7s have families of more than three children (see Table 4).

Fourth, there are significant variations in the kinds of community groups with whom officers and enlisted men and their

Table 4. Dependent Children of Air Force Personnel By Rank of Father

Rank	Percentage with this number of children						Average number of children for each rank
	Total	None	1	2	3	4 or more	
Officers							
Colonel	100%	12.3	20.5	27.9	19.9	19.3	2.1
Lieutenant Colonel	100	10.3	16.0	29.8	22.3	21.5	2.3
Major	100	11.4	12.9	27.6	23.9	24.2	2.4
Captain	100	20.4	15.4	28.6	20.6	15.0	1.9
1st. Lieutenant	100	61.8	22.6	10.6	3.8	1.3	0.6
2nd. Lieutenant	100	88.7	7.1	2.6	0.8	0.9	0.2
Warrant Officer	100	11.1	23.3	32.3	13.8	19.5	2.1
TOTAL OFFICERS		31.3	15.8	22.8	16.3	13.9	
Enlisted							
E-9 and E-8	100%	13.6	14.9	29.1	21.9	20.8	2.2
E-7	100	13.4	12.7	26.7	22.6	24.7	2.3
E-6	100	17.4	14.8	26.6	20.9	20.3	2.1
E-5	100	47.6	20.9	16.9	8.6	6.0	1.0
E-4	100	85.1	10.6	3.4	0.6	0.2	0.4
E-3	100	97.2	2.0	0.6	0.1	0.0	0.0
E-2 and E-1	100	91.3	3.2	3.2	1.6	0.0	0.1
TOTAL ENLISTED		50.8	13.1	15.5	10.7	10.0	

Source: U.S. AIR FORCE PERSONNEL REPORT: "Characteristics and Attitudes from Sample Surveys." Washington: Department of the Air Force, November 1966.

families are affiliated and the extent of their participation. Wives tend to be more active in the community than are the military officers. Officers' wives are generally more active than enlisted men's wives. Enlisted men's wives at senior levels are more active in education activities (E-9, forty-two percent; E-8, forty percent; E-7, forty-seven percent) than officers' wives (colonel, twenty-six percent; lieutenant colonel, twenty-nine percent; major, thirty-one percent). Enlisted men are five times as active in veteran organizations (ten percent) as officers (two percent). Senior officers are more active in youth groups than senior enlisted men, although their wives participate with about equal frequency.

These data suggest that participation is affected by the salience of rank in the activity. In educational activities (PTA, room mother, and the like), rank is less likely to be as significant as the achievement of the child. In youth groups (teen clubs and the like), the father's rank is likely to be an important variable in social activities; hence, enlisted men do not support them as actively as their wives do.

One major activity is participation in church groups. Among both officers and enlisted men, the church is the group most actively supported. Again, wives are more active than military members; wives of junior officers and enlisted men are more active than wives of senior officers and enlisted men; and wives of junior enlisted men are more active than wives of junior officers. These data indicate the critical significance of the church in the military community as an integrating mechanism with the larger society. Although a civilian institution, it has preserved its integrity in the military community and has been least influenced by military norms. The church provides opportunities for participation in which the significance of military rank is minimized, and substitute "rank" can be obtained as an usher, choir member, Sunday School teacher, and so on. Participation in church activities also provides a reputation for being a "good citizen" of the military community and, consequently, entry to other kinds of organizations.

Finally, there are also variations in the kinds of activities most actively supported by the children of military families. Children of colonels and lieutenant colonels are more active in youth clubs (twenty-nine percent and twenty-two percent) than E-9s (twenty percent) and E-8s (nineteen percent). On the other hand, children of senior enlisted men are more active in scouting (E-9s, thirty-nine percent; E-8s, forty-six percent) than children of colonels (thirty percent) and of lieutenant colonels (thirty-nine percent), and in Little League baseball. The strong support given to scouting by both officers and enlisted men indicates its unique compatibility with the military community. In discipline, uniforms, formations, and outdoor experiences it is remarkably similar to the military member's occupational role and thus may be especially effective as an agency of socialization. Scouting also provides periodic contacts with peer groups in the civilian community, thus reducing the isolation of youth in the military community.

Base Residence

Residence on the military base is dependent on the objective criteria of eligibility and availability, and also on personal choice. Although the Department of Defense owned or controlled 374,000 family housing units in 1966, this was sufficient for only one-third of all eligible personnel (see U.S. Department of Defense, 1967: 481). Consequently, a majority of military personnel are compelled to live in adjacent civilian communities during a substantial proportion of their careers. Generally, all married officers are eligible for family quarters, and enlisted men above pay grade 5. However, housing is more likely to be *available* to higher ranks than lower, and to officers more often than to enlisted men. In all cases, the service member is eligible only for housing on the post to which he is assigned for duties. When he is on a transient status between stations, or on an overseas tour without accompanying dependents, the family is not eligible for post housing.

Personal choice also influences base residence. Government quarters do not provide the same range of choice as housing in the civilian community and may even be inferior. If the sponsor is frequently absent on tours or cruises and returns to the same base, an owned house in the local community would entail less disruption of family life than the use of military family quarters when available. This is especially true of Navy personnel. The data in Table 5 suggests that Navy housing is one of the least preferred choices and that home ownership is more common. Naval bases are fewer in number, less likely to be closed and reopened, and more frequently located near metropolitan areas than are Army or Air Force bases. Home ownership is thus a more realistic choice for personnel of the Navy than of other services.

Base residence involves continued affiliation with the organization even in off-duty periods. However, the occupational and family roles are differentiated and insulated by the maintenance of segregated housing areas for officers and enlisted men. Base residents are in more continuous contact with military organization also through the services provided, such as utilities and maintenance of the family quarters; opportunities to use such facilities as the post exchange, commissary, and hospital; and attendance at the base dependents' school. They are more likely to discover old social relationships from previous assignments, or to view existing neighborhood relations as having a persisting significance in the expectation

Table 5. Type of Housing Occupied By Married Navy Personnel With
One or More Dependents, By Rank

| Rank | Percentage of each rank group occupying this housing type | | | | | |
	Navy Housing	Rented Civilian Apartment	Rented Civilian House	Owned Civilian House	Owned Trailer and Other	No Wife or Children
Officer:						
Captain, O-6	34	9	20	33	2	2
Commander, O-5	26	6	24	40	3	2
Lieutenant Commander, O-4	21	7	28	37	1	6
Lieutenant, O-3	23	12	26	26	2	11
Lieutenant J.G., O-2	15	25	17	8	3	32
Ensign, O-1	5	20	10	3	2	60
Warrant Officer	18	9	14	49	4	5
TOTALS	21	13	22	25	3	17
Enlisted:						
E-9	20	3	13	51	9	6
E-8	22	9	22	42	3	2
E-7	22	10	19	37	6	6
E-6	20	16	21	21	10	11
E-5	14	21	17	9	9	30
E-4	5	18	9	3	6	60
E-3	2	9	4	2	3	80
E-2	1	3	2	1	2	91
TOTALS	8	14	11	10	6	51

Source: NAVAL PERSONNEL SURVEY 65-1, Basic Report. Washington: Department of the Navy, April 1966. Sample Size: officers, 3,605; enlisted men, 16,538. Comparable data not available from other services.

that they may be renewed at some future time. There are also opportunities to identify with the father's occupation by observation of organizational activities.

Off-base residence requires the development of relationships with substitute institutions on a transitory basis. Neighborhood life is more likely to involve contacts with persons who have stereotyped misconceptions of military life, or who are overtly exploitative (Hunter, 1952). Military personnel are often viewed as transients with whom persisting relationships are futile. Distance from the base limits their opportunities to use support facilities. Children must attend local public schools of uncertain quality, with peers having no common experiences. Finally, there are more limited resources for mutual aid during emergencies.

However, in one respect, off-base residence is preferable. On-base organizational control extends to the family through neighbors and the military police. A family quarrel or the delinquency of a child may result in the intervention of the military police or the necessity for medical care. Reports are then made to the sponsor's organizational commander through "channels," often with an accompanying requirement for a reply as to what action was taken. Such "Delinquency Reports" may be of crucial significance if the sponsor is being considered for promotion, or if it reinforces derogatory information from other sources. Even gossip about family relationships or the deviant eccentricities of family members is more easily and rapidly communicated to status peers in the service community neighborhood and ultimately to the organization commander, than in the civilian community where such reports are aborted by the lack of a significant audience. These events are of particular significance to senior military personnel in sensitive positions requiring periodic "security" investigations since military police blotter entries are routinely checked and neighbors often interviewed (Little, 1969).

Such social control does not affect the family residing off-base in the civilian community. Police are less likely to be called, delinquency is recorded in civilian police records, and there is no routine report to the sponsor's commander. There are no corresponding channels in the civilian community for communicating such informal appraisals of the military member or his family to his organization. Occupational and family roles are thus more effectively insulated.

Foreign Station Residence

Assignment to a foreign station is usually considered highly desirable, especially in those few instances when the family is permitted to travel with the sponsor. This is also an aspect of military service that has had wide publicity in the larger society. The image of the service family overseas, living in lavish circumstances and attended by maids provided free by the service, is one based on experiences during the occupation after World War II rather than the more recent experience.

The desirability of the foreign station assignment is based on complex and varied motives. Certainly, travel to a strange land and culture is a prominent one. But there are important economic rewards in such an assignment. The assurance of furnished family quarters on a scale which could not be afforded in the United States, lower costs of commodities not available from service facilities but available "on the economy" (native market), and free dental care for dependents from service facilities are among other positive features of a foreign station. Commissaries and post exchanges are generally larger and more completely stocked than in the United States. Secondary schools are usually of more certain quality than the variability in schools in civilian communities adjoining bases in the United States.

There is also an element of increased solidarity among service families living abroad. There is increased reliance on the institutions of the military community because substitute native institutions (religious, economic, and educational) do not express the same values as those of the society from which they came. Family quarters are usually arranged more compactly in apartments rather than single family dwellings as in the United States, so there is more neighboring. Customs of mutual aid which at home are largely informal become institutional: sponsors are assigned to each arriving family to insure the availability of help during the arrival process and their integration into the social system of the community. There is more participation in the activities of the organization: families jointly experience the departure of fathers on maneuvers or cruises and await their return. There are also the "alerts" in which families must be prepared to rehearse procedures for mass evacuation in the event of active warfare in the area. Common experiences are also facilitated by the economical recreation facilities maintained by the services in foreign areas.

There are also negative features. The compact dwelling arrangement and intensive social interaction within organizational boundaries greatly intensifies social control. Attempts to avoid negative reports of family life often result in a more rigid, suppressive attitude toward the behavior of children. Presence in a foreign area also increases sensitivity to the native government. Delinquency which involves contact with native authorities is especially likely to result in more serious sanctions from American military commanders than would be true for corresponding behavior in the United States. These factors contribute to a feeling of spatial compression.

There is a corresponding feature of temporal compression which is an effect of the limited term of the overseas tour. The fact that the father may frequently be absent on maneuvers or cruises may result in interludes of intensive interaction and corresponding periods of "marking time" while awaiting his return. Families pass through a cycle of adjustment to the foreign area, the first stage characterized by an excited exploration of the experiences and products available, the second by a systematic use of a few found most desirable; finally, as the tour is about to end, there is an engorgement of all the experience possible and accumulation of products available more cheaply in the foreign area.

Children of the military family are especially dependent upon the military community in the foreign area. It is important to recognize the difference in cross-cultural experiences at various points in the life cycle. The adult family members are unlikely to lose their culture, but it is essential that children be socialized in the culture in which they will spend their lives as adults. The tour in the foreign area often occurs during the most formative years of their lives. Thus, a latent function of the varied substitute institutions provided by the services for the military family as a microcosm of American society is to ensure that this socialization does occur.

The institution most critical in the socialization process is, of course, the dependents' school. Such schools are maintained by each service in areas where their personnel predominate, although children of members of all services are eligible to attend. Teaching staffs are employed in the United States by the separate services, and locally at the foreign station. Both sources contribute to a high degree of staff instability. Teachers hired in the United States are often attracted by the opportunity for travel and adventure with a full-time position. Locally-hired teachers are usually wives of military members and thus remain only during their foreign area tours. Physical facilities are usually temporary or adapted to classroom use, and are rarely originally designed or constructed as schools. Elementary schools are usually located in the family housing area or within walking distance. However, high schools must draw from larger attendance areas for efficient operation. Consequently students at remote satellite stations often must travel long distances each day, or remain at the school during the week in dormitory facilities.

Military members are generally "satisfied" with the quality of education provided by overseas dependent schools. However, enlisted men (except grade E-5) are more "satisfied" than officers, and there are wider variations in the satisfaction of enlisted men as compared to officers (see Table 6). The most satisfied enlisted men are senior noncommissioned officers (E-9 and E-8, seventy-nine percent), while the least satisfied are grade E-5 (fifty-two percent). A possible explanation for these variations is the differential educational aspirations of officers and enlisted men. Officers, who are more frequently college graduates, would be expected to be more critical of the school curriculum and staff. Younger, lower-ranking enlisted men have higher levels of (and more recent experience in) education and are correspondingly less satisfied.

A Navy survey presents similar data but the design precludes direct comparison (see Table 7). If the opinions "Very adequate" and "Adequate" are equated with the Army item "Satisfied," it would appear that Navy personnel are less satisfied with their overseas schools than Army personnel (officers, fifty-seven percent; enlisted, sixty-two percent).

COMMON FEATURES OF FAMILIES IN THE MILITARY COMMUNITY

Esoteric Occupational Culture

All military families have in common, knowledge and experience in an occupational culture which is more distinct than that of other occupations in the larger society. The military family is continuously related to organizational activities—if only vicariously—but the civilian family is less likely to participate in the father's occupational life. This is especially evident in teaching materials used in dependents' schools. Such materials continuously press home to the military child—as civilian materials do to the lower-class child—the uniqueness of their fathers' occupation and the family's way of life.

Table 6. Opinions of The Quality of Education Provided By Department of Defense Overseas Schools By Army Officers and Enlisted Men

Rank	Percentage whose children have attended an overseas school	Percentage "satisfied" with quality of education
Officers		
Colonel	27.3	67
Lieutenant Colonel	30.4	66
Major	28	69
Captain	11	66
TOTAL (Colonel-Captain)	14	67
Warrant Officers	33	67
Enlisted		
E-9, E-8	41	79
E-7	35	71
E-6	26	70
E-5	8	52
TOTAL (E-9 − E-5)	28	63

Source: Adapted from SAMPLE SURVEY OF MILITARY PERSONNEL: "Survey Estimate of Satisfaction with the Education Provided by DOD Overseas Schools as Expressed by Male Army Personnel." Washington: Department of the Army, 1967. Sample size: officers, 1,071; enlisted men, 1,956. Officer ranks of first and second lieutenants, and enlisted ranks below E-5 omitted because percentages are negligible and of questionable reliability. Survey item limited responses to male Army personnel who have had children in a Department of Defense overseas school at any time since August 31, 1964.

Fathers who go to work in "fatigues" (work clothing); who are absent for long periods on unaccompanied tours, maneuvers, or cruises; or who are subject to complete organizational control, are less likely to be encountered than the familiar middle-class father of Dick and Jane who takes them to the office on a school holiday. The uniqueness of the occupational culture also limits interaction with civilians, especially when living off-post. It is one of the most important factors in the centrifugal tendencies of the military community to maintain relationships in a familiar universe of discourse.

Table 7. Opinions of The Quality of Education Provided By Department of Defense Overseas Schools By Navy Officers and Enlisted Men

Opinion of latest overseas dependent school their children attended	Percentage of each rank group expressing that opinion	
	Officers	Enlisted
Very adequate	27%	32%
Adequate	30	31
Fair	25	18
Completely inadequate	4	3
No opinion	1	6
TOTAL	100%	100%

Source: Adapted from NAVY PERSONNEL SURVEY 65-2, "Research Memorandum: Dependent Overseas Schooling." Washington: Department of the Navy, 1965. Sample size: officers, 6% (553); enlisted men, 3% (497).

Periodic Disruptions of Family Life

Such disruptions occur as a condition of life rather than by chance as in the civilian community. Although they occur so commonly that they are routine occurrences for military organization generally, for the individual family they have more singular significance. The uncertain presence of the father imposes exceptional stresses on the mother who must be prepared to assume periodically his role as well. Frequently such disruptions are accompanied by the requirement that the family move off-post, into the civilian community or to the homes of relatives, at precisely the time that the support of the military community is most urgently needed.

Such disruptions also introduce strains in the relations between spouses. Suspicions of infidelity are often activated or reinforced (Lindquist, 1952). On the other hand, such separations may have a temporizing effect on long-term marital conflicts by imposing a reprieve from the ultimate dissolution of the marriage. Issues and problems which appear to be critical at the time of the disruption subside in significance during the separation and provide opportunities for an abstract objective perspective, promising a change when reunion occurs. The same effect may occur in the relations between the father and his children: the heroic role is more easily fulfilled in fantasy than in reality (Lynn and Sawrey, 1962; McCord, 1962; Stolz, 1954).

Residential Instability

Transfers across the continent and between widely disparate regions every two to three years (and often more frequently) occur again as a condition of life rather than as a choice for occupational advancement as in other occupations. Between June 1965 and May 1966, about half of all married Army personnel made at least one transfer requiring the movement of the family and household goods. About half of these moves were in connection with transfers to or from an overseas assignment (see Table 8).

Such mobility has important implications for family life. Primary group ties can be maintained for such brief periods of time that they may be initially established with the expectation that they will not endure. Children especially feel the impact of a succession of schools, of varying quality, grade and admission policies, conditions of attendance, and peer group relationships. Long-term medical care for chronic conditions is repeatedly interrupted, and begun again at the new station only after the repetition of an exhaustive initial diagnostic process.

However, there are positive aspects to residential instability. As a minimum it enables the family to tolerate immediately unpleasant situations with the expectation that they will not have to be endured very long. A lack of family quarters on-post requiring off-post residence, unsatisfactory quarters on-post, the presence of noxious neighbors, or an unsuitable duty assignment for the father—all are terminated by transfer. There is also the institutionalized expectation that "the service is your family" which induces neighbors of the newly assigned family to facilitate their adjustment to the new station. Membership in voluntary associations with counterparts at the new station, such as Scouts, Gray Ladies (Red Cross hospital aides), and religious organizations also provide entrees to the social system (Grusky, 1964).

Segmental Socialization

The experiences of the military family are confined to a segment of this life cycle: the fertile years of the young family. The later years with chronic illnesses and death are missed. Partly as a result of residential instability, the military family is more tenuously related to the larger kinship group than the civilian family. Those purposes for which the nuclear family might turn to relatives in the civilian community (such as help during sickness) are usually fulfilled by

Table 8. Numbers and Purpose of Transfers of Married Army Personnel and Families During a One-year Period (June 1965 through May 1966)

Number of Transfers	Percentage transferred	
	Officers	Enlisted Men
None	45.0	43.0
One	49.2	46.6
Two	5.1	7.6
Three	0.5	2.1
Four or more	0.2	0.7
TOTAL	100.0	100.0

Purpose of first transfer during period	Percentage transferred for this purpose	
	Officers	Enlisted Men
Entered Army	18.4	17.2
Service School	6.7	3.3
Transferred within U.S.	17.1	22.0
Transferred to or from overseas	51.6	49.2
Transferred between overseas commands	6.2	8.3
TOTAL	100.0	100.0

Source: Sample Survey of Military Personnel: The Number and Purpose of Permanent Changes of Station (PCS) Made by Male Military Personnel During the Period 1 June 1965 through 31 May 1966 by Grade, Component, Command Areas, Marital Status and Control Branch (Officers Only). Washington: Department of the Army, May 1966. Sample size: officers, 5,939; enlisted men, 27,259.

neighbors in the military community. Spatial limitations in family quarters are such that older parents of the spouses can rarely be accommodated. By the time that children have reached marriage age, the father will often have retired. Even when the father's death occurs in earlier years as a result of war, it is probable that the family will be living off-post in a civilian community so that the experience is not vicariously experienced by those who continue to live in the military community. Consequently, the socialization process of the child in the military community is relatively incomplete.

PROSPECTS FOR
THE MILITARY FAMILY

We have emphasized the internal aspects of the relationship between the family and military organization. However, recent events suggest that the military family will become an increasingly significant element in the civilian community.

First, the military "Medicare" program, the Civilian Health and Medical Program, United States (CHAMPUS), established in 1966, enables dependents of active duty personnnel when separated from the military member, and retirees and their families, to obtain medical care from civilian facilities. Previously such care was available only from military medical facilities, primarily located on service bases. Although a certificate is required from dependents of active duty personnel that military medical facilities are not available, the program greatly enlarges the range of choices available only in the military community. More significantly, however, it reduces the dependence of the military family on service facilities and correspondingly extends its relationship to the civilian community.

Second, families of retired military personnel have become an increasingly significant element of the civilian community. As of June 1968, there were over 631,000 retired military personnel. All of these former military personnel reside and work in civilian communities but maintain some relationship to the military community, primarily through the availability of such facilities as the post exchange and commissary. The military medicare program has reduced the significance of the support facilities of military bases. Previously, military retirees (and their families) tended to settle in the vicinity of military bases, especially those with extensive medical facilities. Under present conditions, it is probable that retired military personnel will be less likely to settle in a concentrated pattern and instead, will be more widely distributed. Their effect on local communities will be correspondingly dispersed.

Third, since 1967 the Department of Defense has sought to enforce a program of "equal opportunity in housing" with the objective of assuring that Negro personnel are not discriminated against in obtaining housing in local communities adjacent to military posts. All military personnel must register with the post housing office upon arrival at a new station and certify that they will not engage lodgings from landlords who discriminate on the basis of race. A list of such landlords is maintained in the housing office. The effect of this program is also to extend the influence of the military family into the civilian community. The military family thus becomes an agent of social change in the local civilian community.

CONCLUDING PROPOSITIONS

In this chapter, the available data on the military family and its relationship to the military community have been discussed. The following propositions emerge:

First, the family has become an increasingly significant element in military personnel programs and management.

Second, family status increases in significance with each stage of the career of the military member as indicated by frequency of married status and community participation.

Third, families of officers and of enlisted men have significantly different characteristics with respect to social control of family roles, family size, and participation in community activities.

Finally, recent developments affecting the military family suggest that it will be an increasingly significant element of the civilian community.

NOTE

1. The many "guides to service customs" refer almost exclusively to the officer's family. The "Officers' Guide" for each of the services includes a chapter on etiquette and "social obligations"; the comparable guides for noncommissioned and petty officers scarcely refer to the existence of a wife or family. The following is a selection of such guides: Murphy and Parker (1966), Kinzer and Leach (1966), and Wier (1966a, 1966b). Also see the occasional articles in *Army* by Katherine Elder. For other sources see R. W. Little, "Field Research in Military Organization," in R. W. Habenstein, Ed., *Pathways To Data.* Chicago, Aldine, 1970.

REFERENCES

Army Times Publishing (1968) Handbook for the Military Family. Washington, D.C.

BEVILACQUA, J. J. (1967) "Civilianization and health-welfare resource participation on an Army post." Ph.D. dissertation. Ann Arbor: University Microfilms.

CLEVELAND, H. et al. (1960) The Overseas American. New York: McGraw-Hill.

CLINE, V. B. et al. (1955) "A survey of opinions regarding Operation Gyroscope in the First Division" Staff memorandum. Washington, D.C.: Human Resources Research Office, George Washington University.

GANOE, W. A. (1942) The History of the United States Army. New York: Appleton-Century.

GRUSKY, O. (1964) "The effects of succession: a comparative study of military and business organization," in M. Janowitz, (ed.) The New Military. New York: Russell Sage Foundation.

HUNTER, F. A. (1952) Host Community and Air Force Base. Chapel Hill: Institute for Research in Social Science, University of North Carolina.

JANOWITZ, M. (1960) The Professional Soldier: A Social and Political Portrait. New York: Free Press.

KINZER, B. and M. LEACH (1966) What Every Army Wife Should Know. Harrisburg, Pa.: Stackpole Press.

LINDQUIST, R. (1952) The Family Life of Officers and Airmen in a Bomb Wing. Chapel Hill: Institute for Research in Social Science, University of North Carolina.

LITTLE, R. W. (1969) "Dossiers in military organization," in S. Wheeler (ed.) On Record: Files and Dossiers in American Life. New York: Russell Sage Foundation.

———(1955) "Solidarity in the mass Army." Combat Forces Journal 5 (February): 26-31.

LYNN, D. B. and W. L. SAWREY (1962) "The effects of father-absence on Norwegian boys and girls." Journal of Abnormal and Social Psychology, vol. 64: 258-264.

McCORD, J. et al. (1962) "Some effects of paternal absence on male children," Journal of Abnormal and Social Psychology, 64 (May): 361-367.

MURPHY, M. K. and C. B. PARKER (1966) Fitting in as a New Service Wife. Harrisburg, Pa.: Stackpole Press.

STOLZ, L. M. (1954) et al. Father Relations of War-Born Children. Stanford: Stanford University Press.

U.S. Department of Defense (1969) Selected Manpower Statistics. Washington, D.C.

———(1967) Annual Report, Fiscal Year 1966, Department of Defense. Washington, D.C.: Government Printing Office.

WIER, E. (1966a) What Every Air Force Wife Should Know. Harrisburg, Pa.: Stackpole Press.

———(1966b) The Answer Book on Naval Social Customs. Harrisburg, Pa.: Stackpole Press.

Chapter 8

MINORITY GROUPS IN MILITARY ORGANIZATION

CHARLES C. MOSKOS, JR.

The study of race relations and minority groups has been a mainstay of much of sociological research. As is to be expected, some of this substantive interest is reflected in studies of military organization. From one viewpoint, research on minority groups in the armed forces is a valuable opportunity to further understanding of intergroup relations in other than military contexts. Indeed, in many ways research on minority groups in the military has engendered both methodological and conceptual breakthroughs having wide sociological applicability. It can also be argued that the situation of minority groups within the armed forces is an important topic in its own right. This is because literally millions of persons pass through the military system and because of that system's unique qualities. Although both of these perspectives are incorporated in the ensuing discussion, it is toward the latter—the findings especially relevant within the military context—that emphasis is placed.

Inasmuch as the bulk of this literature is based upon the American experience, the findings deal largely with the role of black servicemen, black-white relations, and the American military's overseas involvement with allied military forces. Initially, the major studies, official reports, and data sources dealing with this topic are reviewed. Second, and comprising the bulk of the chapter, an inventory of findings derived from this literature is summarized and given in propositional form. Next, there is a brief section covering the situation of racially and ethnically heterogeneous armed forces

271

other than those of the United States. Finally, some concluding remarks are made concerning those areas of study on minority groups in military organization where research needs are most pressing.

RESEARCH ON
MINORITY GROUPS

Major studies. The social science literature on racial relations in the armed forces is of two basic kinds. On the one hand, there are the military authorized studies which were explicitly conducted to answer immediate questions on the effective military utilization of manpower resources. On the other hand, there are the independent studies of social scientists who have used evidence based on participant observations and/or secondary analysis of military manpower records, Selective Service statistics, and various survey data. Both kinds of studies go back to the second world war and continue into the present. It was over this period that the American military was transformed from a segregated institution into one that is now in the forefront in its degree of racial integration. In fact, some of the credit for this remarkable achievement in directed social change must go to the social scientists who documented the deleterious consequences on black morale of segregation and the relatively unstressful acceptance of integration on the part of white servicemen.

Studies of racial relations and attitudes based on the experience of the armed forces during the second world war are of a varied sort. There are descriptive accounts of black servicemen (Mueller, 1945; Davenport, 1947; Hall, 1947; Weil, 1947); a detailed discussion of the black serviceman within the broader context of utilizing human resources (Ginzburg, 1956); a contrast of black combat behavior in segregated and integrated units (Rose, 1947); and analysis of psychoneurotic breakdown among black soldiers (Rose, 1956); and a comprehensive treatment of official U.S. Army policies toward black soldiers (Lee, 1966).

The major source of information pertaining to racial matters in the World War II military, however, is found in the multitude of surveys conducted by the Research Branch of the War Department's Information and Educational Division. These surveys—which dealt with issues of adjustment of enlisted men to military life and their motivation in combat—were subsequently reanalyzed and published in final form in the volumes of *The American Soldier.* The first volume of this series has a section, "Negro Soldiers," covering the topics of black-white comparisons on views toward the war, reactions to overseas and combat duty, adjustment to the Army, attitudes toward racial segregation, and a special note on black groups in combat (Stouffer, 1949).

During the Korean conflict, the Army authorized another set of large-scale surveys of enlisted men, this time dealing specifically with attitudes toward racial integration. The results of these surveys—called "Project Clear"—were declassified in 1965 and are now available for professional scrutiny (Operations Research Office, 1955). The bulk of the Project Clear data is conveniently presented in a recent volume which also includes a perceptive discussion of the planning and execution of the project (Bogart, 1969). However, like the World War II findings of the Army's Research Branch, the Korean conflict data of Project Clear are somewhat dated. Nevertheless, in both instances the empirical data is so rich as to allow for formulation of propositions having current relevance.

In addition to the survey findings of Project Clear, there are also several independent treatments of racial desegregation in the armed forces of the 1950s. These include descriptive and summary accounts of the early days of integration (Kenworthy, 1951; Nichols, 1954; Evans and Lane, 1956); contrasts between black performance in the segregated and integrated military (Mandelbaum, 1952; Ginzburg, 1956); a participant observation of troop reactions to racial integration (Moskos, 1957); and the consequences of desegregation for the military organization (Coates and Pellegrin, 1965).

With the escalation of the war in Vietnam, a renewed interest in racial relations in the military has developed. These include sociological analyses (Moskos, 1966, 1970); an historical overview focusing on the contemporary situation (Stillman, 1968); a survey of attitudes of black youth toward military service (National Analysts, 1968); and journalistic accounts by black participant-observers in Vietnam (Parks, 1968). Moreover, the general debate on the Selective Service system which began in the middle 1960s has also been reflected in attention given to the proportion of minority-group members in the armed forces and their manner of service entrance (Klassen, 1966; U.S. National Advisory Commission, 1967; Moskos, 1969).

The overseas involvements of United States forces has also focused some research attention on the relations between American military personnel and those from allied countries such as the Philippines (Duff and Arthur, 1967), Korea (McCrary, 1967),

Vietnam (Personal Response Project, 1967), and relations of American troops with foreign nationals (Caudill, 1955; Humphrey, n.d.). Although these studies do not deal with minority groups in the strictest sense, they do nevertheless have relevance for understanding interethnic-group relations in the military system.

Official reports. Another genre of literature dealing with minority groups in the American armed forces are the reports of official bodies which have been periodically constituted to assess racial relations in the military. After World War II, pressure from Negro and liberal groups coupled with an acknowledgment that black soldiers were being poorly utilized led the Army to reexamine its segregated racial policies. A 1945 report by an Army board of officers, while making recommendations to improve black opportunity in the service, concluded that practical considerations required a maintenance of segregation and adherence to a quota limit—ten percent—on black military membership (Gillem Board, 1945). The report further recommended that black personnel be exclusively assigned to support rather than combat units. Five years later, another Army board report came out with essentially the same conclusions (Chamberlin Board, 1950). Both of these reports placed heavy stress on the supervisory and disciplinary problems resulting from the disproportionate number of blacks, as established by Army examinations, found in the lower mental and aptitude classification levels.

The 1948 Executive Order of President Truman abolishing segregation in the armed forces, however, enjoined the military to adopt racially egalitarian policies. The President followed his edict by setting up a committee, chaired by Charles Fahy, to pursue the implementation of equal treatment and opportunity for armed forces personnel (U.S. President's Committee, 1950). Under the impetus of the Fahy Committee, rapid strides were made and by the middle 1950s racial integration was an accomplished fact at home and abroad. A 1963 Presidential Commission on Civil Rights, chaired by John A. Hannah, devoted special attention to black servicemen. The Hannah Committee, while finding a greater degree of racial equality in the armed forces than in other areas of American life, nevertheless pointed to the disproportionate number of blacks in nontechnical positions and the prevailing discrimination found in off-base housing and education (U.S. Commission, 1963). Another Presidential Committee, under the chairmanship of Gerhard A. Gesell, was established in 1964 to report on racial integration in the armed forces. The Gesell Committee, reflecting the generally satisfactory situation in the active-duty military forces, addressed itself primarily to off-base discrimination and to the racial exclusivism of many National Guard units (U.S. President's Committee, 1963, 1964).

Data sources. Racial data on the American military is quite extensive. Information is continually being collected for all four services on racial distributions by rank, time in service, aptitude scores, military occupational specialty, and initial and reenlistment rates. Additionally, casualty reports by race and service are also kept current. Most of this information is routinely available from the Civil Rights and Industrial Relations (CR&IR) officer of the Deputy Assistant Secretary of Defense for Manpower.

The complete results of examinations of youths for military service are annually reported in supplements to *Health of the Army* issued by the Medical Statistics Agency, Office of the Surgeon General, Department of the Army. These supplements describe, among other items, differential race rates on Selective Service mental and physical examinations (Karpinos, 1968).

Another source of data is that collected in 1964 by the National Opinion Research Center (NORC) of the University of Chicago. Now available for secondary analysis, the NORC survey was conducted during the course of an official review of Selective Service policies. The 1964 NORC data is based on a ten percent sample of all officers and a five percent sample of all enlisted men on active duty at that time. Over one hundred separate items were included on the questionnaires, covering the topics of personal background information (including race), military occupation and training, occupational values, future career plans, and attitudes toward military service and the draft.

A PROPOSITIONAL INVENTORY

Any effort to make meaningful generalization about human behavior is always formidable. Specification of contexts, availability of data, evaluation of evidence, all must enter into such an endeavor. Fortunately, as we have just reviewed, the literature on minority groups in military organization is not insubstantial—at least with regard to blacks in the armed forces of the United States. As a general rule, I have tried to include only the best supported findings in this area—findings which have a generally accepted high level of validity. Nevertheless, there are instances where propositions appear warranted but which do not have definitive empirical proof.

Six topics are covered: (1) recruitment, (2) assignment, (3) performance, (4) attitudes toward service life, (5) inter-group relations, and (6) armed forces and society. Within each of these broad topics, propositions are stated in italicized form. The supporting evidence, discussion, and qualifications are in regular print. All told, twenty-four such propositions are presented. They range from statistical statements (e.g., reenlistment rates), to empirically based concepts (e.g., attitudes toward service life), to interpretive propositions (e.g., the dynamics of intergroup accommodation).

Recruitment. A much higher proportion of blacks, compared to whites, fail to meet the entrance requirements for military service. The results of preinduction examinations given potential draftees over the past two decades show black disqualification rates to be about twice that of whites. For the time period 1950 through 1967, 62.7% of blacks were disqualified compared to 35.6% of whites. Most important, the primary factor in the higher disqualification ratio of blacks is due to failures on the mental tests. Since 1950, for virtually every year, blacks are four times more likely to be disqualified on mental grounds—a paramount indicator of socio-educational handicaps—than are whites. Indeed, with regard to failure for medical reasons only, white disqualification rates are slightly higher than that of blacks (Karpinos, 1968).

Although the proportion of blacks failing to meet the entrance standards required for military service is markedly higher than that of whites, blacks are still more likely to be drafted than whites. For the years 1961 through 1966, blacks averaged 14.8% of those drafted, a figure higher than the eleven to twelve percent of blacks in the eligible age groups. This discrepancy between the high black disqualification rate and the disproportionate number of blacks drafted is indirect but convincing evidence that blacks have a lower likelihood of obtaining draft deferments—deferments that are more available to whites and that often become de facto exemptions. It should also be noted, however, that the proportion of blacks inducted is highest during those years when draft calls are lowest. Put in another way, during times of high draft calls, with the resultant necessity of drawing deeper into the draft pool, the overproportionate induction of blacks tends to decline—but not disappear (Moskos, 1969).

A complete picture of black entrance rates into the military, however, requires more than an assessment of disqualification, induction, and deferment rates. For excepting times of war, voluntary enlistments account for approximately three-quarters of all incoming military personnel. An examination of the initial enlistments in each of the four armed services for the years 1961-1966 shows that it is the Army, besides its drawing upon the draft, that also has the highest black enlistment rate of any of the armed services. Over the six-year period, blacks constituted 10.9% of Army initial enlistments, followed by 9.8% for the Air Force, 7.2% for the Marine Corps, and 4.2% for the Navy. In 1967, blacks accounted for 9.0% of all active-duty personnel, a figure slightly lower than the black proportion in the total American population.

An insight into the causes underlying volunteer initial enlistments can be gained by looking at reasons mentioned for entering the armed forces. Based on the 1964 NORC survey, motivations of volunteers were grouped into four categories: (1) personal, e.g, get away from home, mature, travel, excitement; (2) patriotic, e.g., serve one's country; (3) draft-motivated, e.g., choose time of service entry or branch of service; and (4) self-advancement, e.g., learn a trade, receive an education, military as a career. There are only slight differences between whites and blacks with regard to personal and patriotic reasons for service entry. The variation between the races is found almost entirely in their differing mentions of draft-motivated versus self-advancement reasons. Among white volunteers, 39.1% gave draft-motivated reasons compared to 24.5% of the blacks. Conversely, only 20.7% of the white volunteers replied they entered the military for reasons of self-advancement compared with 37.2% of the blacks who gave that reason. These differences between the races diminish only slightly when educational level is held constant. In other words, the draft serves as a major inducement for whites to volunteer, while the belief that self-advancement will be furthered through military service is much more typical of black volunteers (Moskos, 1969).

Assignment. The larger the proportion of blacks in an armed service, the more equitable is the distribution of blacks throughout its ranks. This is also to say that the proportion and internal distribution of blacks differ markedly between the military services. In 1967, blacks made up 11.2% of the Army, 9.6% of the Air Force, 9.1% of the Marine Corps, and 4.3% of the Navy. That same year, the ratio of black to white officers was roughly one to twenty-five in the

Army, one to fifty in the Air Force, one to one hundred fifty in the Marine Corps, and one to three hundred in the Navy. Also for 1967, the ratio of black to white senior noncoms (pay grades E-7 through E-9) was approximately one to eight in the Army, one to twenty-one in the Air Force, one to twenty-two in the Marine Corps, and one to twenty-eight in the Navy. It is also the case that blacks are disproportionately concentrated in the lower noncom ranks (pay grades E-5 and E-6) in all of the armed services. This is especially so in the Army where twenty percent of all staff sergeants are black. In brief, it is the Army, followed in order by the Air Force, Marine Corps, and Navy, which has the largest proportion of blacks in its total personnel and the most equitable grade distribution of blacks.

On a service-wide basis, blacks have been assigned to all occupations, but are still overrepresented in combat and nontechnical positions. Thus, 36.7% of all black servicemen in 1967 were in combat positions or service work compared to 22.7% of all whites. Conversely, of all black servicemen 27.7% were found in technical occupations (e.g., electronics, communication, medical and dental, equipment repairmen) compared to 39.5% of all whites. As is to be expected, the overconcentration of blacks in combat units is all too obviously shown in the casualty reports from Vietnam. During the 1961-1966 period, blacks constituted 10.6% of American military personnel in Southeast Asia while accounting for 16.0% of those killed in action. In 1967 and the first six months of 1968, however, the proportion of black combat deaths dropped to between 13.0% and 14.0%. Yet even in these later figures, black combat deaths were still about three percentage points above the proportion of blacks stationed in Southeast Asia, and about five percentage points above the total black proportion in the American military (1968 DOD statistics).

The disproportionate number of blacks in combat units in the contemporary military contrasts directly with the Army's reluctance to use black soldiers in combat units in World War II. Indeed, the likelihood of a black serving in a combat arm is well over two times greater in the 1960s than it was during the earlier segregated period (Moskos, 1966). The current direction of assignment of black soldiers is testimony to the continuing consequences of differential racial opportunity that make blacks available for military service and cause them to be, at the same time, unavailable for many technical job opportunities in expanding skill areas within the military organization (Lang, 1964).

The above findings, however, must be placed within a broader context. While there are many pitfalls in comparing civilian and military occupations, the evidence shows that both black enlisted men and officers have attained higher occupational levels than have blacks in the civilian employment market. Black servicemen enjoy relatively better opportunities in the armed forces than in the civilian economy in every clerical, technical, and skilled field for which the data permit comparison (U.S. Commission, 1963). Nevertheless, it must be kept in mind that the social and educational deprivations suffered by the black in American society can be mitigated but not eliminated by the racially egalitarian policies of the armed forces.

Performance. The military performance of integrated black servicemen contrasts markedly and favorably with that of all-Negro units. Virtually all studies and observers of black servicemen are in agreement on this proposition (Rose, 1947; Stouffer, 1949: Mandelbaum, 1952; Ginzberg, 1956; Coates and Pellegrin, 1965; Moskos, 1966; Stillman, 1968; Bogart, 1969). This in no way denies the valor of individual black servicemen or of particular black units, but it does point to the generally deleterious effects of segregation on black performance. Thus, in World War I, the combat record of the all-Negro 92nd Infantry Division came under heavy criticism. During the second world war, the combat record of the 92nd was also blemished. Moreover, there was considerable apprehension within the Army's hierarchy of the fighting qualities of any all-Negro unit (Lee, 1966). In the Korean conflict, the performance of the all-Negro 25th Infantry Regiment was judged so poor that its divisional commander recommended the unit be dissolved as quickly as possible (Operations Research Office, 1955).

On the other hand, even during the first world war it was noted that black units operating under French command, in a more racially permissive situation, performed well (Lee, 1966; Stillman, 1968). In World War II, in an important exception to the segregated utilization of black troops, black volunteers fought in previously all-white units during the Ardennes battle. Both in terms of black combat performance and white soldiers' reactions, the Ardennes experiment was an unqualified success (Rose, 1947; Stouffer et. al., 1949). In the Korean conflict, manpower requirements in the field for combat soldiers resulted in many instances of ad hoc integration. As integration in Korea became more standard, observers consistently reported that the fighting qualities of blacks differed little from that of whites (Operations Research Office, 1955). With the advent of full integration, all significant differences between white and black combat performance have disappeared. In both Vietnam and the Dominican Republic, there was little discernible differences between the races concerning combat motivation or military performance (Moskos, 1966, 1970).

By itself, however, segregation of minority groups is not a sufficient explanation of ineffective combat performance. A unique military venture in World War II was the formation of three all-Negro—including officers—air combat units. Those units that saw combat received very favorable evaluation by impartial observers (Nichols, 1954; Lee, 1966). Another kind of segregation which resulted in a remarkable combat record was that of the 442nd Infantry Regiment composed of Nisei, Japanese-Americans. This famed "Go For Broke" regiment was one of the most highly decorated units in World War II. In both the black air squadrons and the Nisei units (as with the black volunteers in the Ardennes battle), the quality of men selected was far above the average white unit—as measured by mental test scores (Kenworthy, 1951). A less tangible but equally important factor was that for the men in these units segregation was perceived as a challenge which they could and did meet. A similar situation seems to have occurred among many black soldiers in the Civil War who saw the opportunity to fight on the Union side, even in segregated units, as a challenge to prove themselves (Higginson, 1962). On the other hand, segregation for the majority of black troops during the two world wars and the early part of the Korean conflict was seen not as an opportunity for achievement but as an assurance of personal defeat (Mandelbaum, 1952).

It is also relevant to note here the highly effective combat performances of segregated units which are drawn from particular ethnic groups where fighting prowess appears to be a strongly valued cultural feature. Notable in this regard are the Himalaya Gurkhas, who constitute a separate brigade in the British Army, and the Chinese Nungs, a mercenary group working closely with U.S. forces in Southeast Asia. In a somewhat analogous social situation are the Filipino nationals who have long been a major source of recruitment for the steward ratings in the U.S. Navy (Duff and Arthur, 1967). In these instances, occupational commitment to a military career *qua* career rather than ideological considerations seems to account for high performance standards.

Attitudes toward service life. Blacks, compared to whites, have a consistently more favorable attitude toward service life. This proposition is supported by several sorts of evidence. For one thing, the servicewide black reenlistment rate throughout the 1960s was approximately twice that of white servicemen. That black servicemen have a more favorable view of military life than whites is reflected not only in their higher reenlistment rates, but also by the 1964 NORC survey data. Whether broken down by branch of service, educational level, pay grade, or military occupational specialty, black servicemen compared to whites persistently have a less negative view of life in the armed forces (Moskos, 1970). Another survey found few black youths who perceived military life as having negative racial aspects. Rather, military life was seen as offering career advantages, foreign duty, and educational gain (National Analysts, 1968). The relatively benign terms in which black men regard military life, however, speaks not only of the racial egalitarianism of the armed forces, but more profoundly, of the existing state of affairs for blacks in American society at large.

Further, despite the demonstrable inequities for blacks in the existing draft system, the fact remains that Selective Service even as it was operating in the 1960s was seen in more favorable terms by blacks than by whites. This anomalous circumstance is illustrated by the following findings from the 1964 NORC survey: among blue-collar workers with no military experience, 41.3% of blacks, compared to 28.5% of whites, view the draft as very fair; among Army enlisted men, whether draftees, first-term, or career regulars, blacks are much more favorable in their views concerning the draft's equity; among civilians with military experience, only 3.0% of the black veterans who were drafted, compared to ten times that proportion among whites, said the Selective Service system was unfair (Moskos, 1969).

Intergroup relations. Commenting on the difficulties of social analysis, the authors of *The American Soldier* wrote that "few problems are more formidable than that of obtaining dependable records of attitudes toward racial separation in the Army" (Stouffer et al., 1949: 566). Without underestimating the continuing difficulty of this problem, an opportunity exists to compare attitudes toward racial integration held by American soldiers in two different periods. This is done by contrasting responses to equivalent items given in World War II (1943) as reported in *The American Soldier* with those reported in Project Clear during the Korean conflict (1951).

The trend is toward increasing acceptance of military racial integration on the part of both white and black servicemen.

However, black servicemen are much more supportive of racial integration than whites. Among white soldiers, opposition to integration goes from eighty-four percent in 1943 to forty-four percent in 1951. Among black soldiers, opposition goes from thirty-six to four percent over the same time period. It may be argued that recent developments—separatist tendencies within the black community in the late 1960s—have eclipsed the earlier findings. Nevertheless, the data is still convincing that on the eve of integration, black soldiers overwhelmingly rejected a segregated armed forces (Bogart, 1969).

One of the most celebrated findings of *The American Soldier* was the discovery that the more contact white soldiers have with black troops, the more favorable was their reaction toward racial integration. "The closer men approached to the mixed (racially) company organization, the less opposition there was to it. That is, the men actually in a company containing a Negro platoon were most favorable toward it, men in larger units in which there were no mixed companies were least favorable, while men in all-white companies within a regiment or division containing mixed companies held intermediate opinions" (Stouffer, et al., 1949: 594). This conclusion is consistently supported in the surveys conducted by Project Clear during the Korean conflict. Again and again, comparisons of white soldiers in integrated units with those in segregated units show the former to be more supportive of desegregation (Operations Research Office, 1955).

However, social contact is not enough to change racial attitudes. The social contact must take place under conditions of equal status and in which mutual interdependence is required for unit cohesion. These circumstances are not uniformly found in military social organization. Thus, the more military the environment, the more egalitarian are racial relations. On the whole, racial integration at informal as well as formal levels works best on-duty vis-á-vis off-duty, on-base vis-á-vis off-base, basic training and maneuvers vis-á-vis garrison, and sea vis-á-vis shore duty. This is especially demonstrable in the actual combat situation where close living, strict discipline, and common danger all serve to preclude racial conflict between whites and blacks. In other words, the behavior of servicemen resembles the racial (and class) separatism of the larger American society, the more they are removed from the military environment (Moskos, 1966).

Whatever the level of military organization, closest friendships normally develop within races among individuals of similar socio-educational background. This is to say that primary groups within the military organization tend to be racially exclusive (Mandelbaum, 1952; Moskos, 1957, 1966). Nevertheless, even at primary group levels, the integrated military system exhibits a much higher interracial intimacy than exists in the nonintegrated civilian society. Moreover, beyond an individual's hard core of reigns, there exists a larger number of friendly acquaintances. Here the pattern seems to be one of educational similarities overriding racial differences.

A different insight bearing on intergroup relations is gained by examining responses of servicemen asked to compare their personal views with what they perceive to be the attitudes of their fellow servicemen. Individuals are much more likely to hold favorable views of other racial or nationality groups than they ascribe to their fellow servicemen. This proposition—a kind of inverted cognitive dissonance—has been documented in a variety of attitudinal contexts: white soldiers *viz* black soldiers during the Korean conflict (Operations Research Office, 1955); Army personnel *viz* Japanese (Caudill, 1955); Marine Corps personnel *viz* Okinawans and Vietnamese (Personal Response Project, 1967). These findings can be interpreted as indicating a hidden reservoir of intergroup good will, or alternately, as a projection of personally held discriminatory attitudes unto others.

One of the consequences of America's global military posture has been to expose large numbers of servicemen to foreign cultures and societies—even if only in a peripheral manner. While the evidence is not entirely conclusive, it appears that service abroad is more likely to foster parochial American sentiments rather than engender a more appreciative understanding of foreign societies (Glaser, 1946; Moskos, 1970). Some of the factors bringing this about are the serviceman's invidious comparison of material standards of living in foreign countries, language barriers, and primary exposure to the exploitative ambience of the so-called "boomtowns" which ring American overseas bases. However, overseas duty offers the black serviceman an opportunity to witness societies where racial discrimination is usually less practiced than it is in his home country. Thus, black servicemen are more likely to be favorably disposed toward foreign societies than are whites (Stouffer, 1949; Moskos, 1966). Moreover, there is evidence that black soldiers are much more likely to learn local languages when stationed abroad than are whites (Caudill, 1955; Moskos, 1966).

Armed forces and society. The analogy between enlisted men vis-á-vis officers in the military and blacks vis-á-vis whites in the larger society has often been observed. "It is noteworthy that the phrases which white enlisted men used to express their dissatisfaction with the military system were in many instances exact duplicates of phrases which some of the more vocal Negro civilians have been using for years with reference to their treatment at the hands of white society" (Stouffer, et al., 1949: 503). It is also the case that the apparent lack of awareness on the part of whites of black attitudes has its counterpart among officers' assessment of enlisted attitudes. In both cases there is a tendency by the subordinate group to conceal its true attitudes, and the tendency on the part of the dominant group to avoid believing what is uncomfortable to believe. It has been less frequently observed, however, that enlisted men's behavior is often similar to many of the sterotypes associated with blacks, for example, laziness, boisterousness, emphasis on sexual prowess, consciously acting stupid, obsequiousness in front of superiors combined with ridicule of absent superiors, and so on. Placement of white adult males in a subordinate position within a rigidly stratified system appears to produce behavior not all that different from the so-called personality traits commonly held to be an outcome of cultural or psychological patterns unique to Afro-American life (Moskos, 1966).

Nevertheless, the fact remains that although the military was until modern times one of America's most segregated institutions, it has leaped into the forefront of racial equality in the past two decades. What features of the military establishment can account for this about face? For one thing, the generally successful racial integration of the armed forces is due to the military being an important degree discontinuous from others of society (Nichols, 1954; Moskos, 1966; Bogart, 1969). And this apartness served to allow—once the course has been decided—a rapid and complete racial integration. The path of desegregation was further made easier by characteristics peculiar or at least more pronounced in the military compared to other institutions. With its hierarchical power structure, predicated on stable and patterned relationships, decisions need take relatively little account of the personal desires of service personnel. Additionally, because roles and activities are more defined and specific in the military than in most other social arenas, conflicts that might have ensued within a more diffuse and ambiguous setting were largely absent. This is to say that the desegregation of the armed forces was facilitated by the pervasiveness in the military of a bureaucratic ethos, with its concomitant formality and high social distance, that mitigated tensions arising from individual or personal feelings.

At the same time it must also be remembered that the military establishment has means of coercion not readily available in most civilian pursuits. Violations of norms are both more visible and subject to quicker sanctions. The military is premised, moreover, on the accountability of its members for effective performance. This in turn means that satisfactory carrying out of stated policy advances one's own position. It is to each individual's personal interest, if he anticipates receiving the rewards of a military career, to ensure that decisions going through him are executed with minimum difficulty. Or put in another way, whatever the internal policy decided upon, racial integration being a paramount but only one example, the military establishment has unique sanctions to realize its implementation.

On this point, it is also probably true that racial integration of military life has not served to increase the acceptance or prestige of the armed forces. In fact, the reverse may be the case. Those sections of the civilian community which are egalitarian on racial matters are most often the least sympathetic to the military. Many of those who espouse militaristic values, on the other hand, are those who find the military's racial integration distasteful. Put in another way, the racial integration of the armed forces has probably cost the military support among some of its traditional defenders, while not gaining any increased support for the military among liberal-radical groups.

It is also probable, however, that the military establishment—at least into the foreseeable future—will no longer be immune to the racial conflicts occurring in the larger American society. Incidents with racial overtones will become more frequent. That the black soldier may find he owes higher fealty to the black community than to the U.S. Army is a possibility that haunts commanders. The likelihood of such an eventuality, however, will be serious only if the Army is regularly summoned into action in black ghettos. Sensitivity to broader civil rights issues coupled with racially egalitarian internal practices will most likely be sufficient—barring repeated military intervention in black ghettos—to preclude any widespread black disaffection within the armed forces.

The nature of black participation in the military organization has nevertheless become inextricable with broader criticisms of America's politicomilitary policies. Much attention has been given to the relationship between elements of the black militant movement with the antimilitary movement of the late 1960s. Yet the black movement as a whole has remained removed from those white radical groups vociferously attacking the military services. Although it would be premature to offer a final statement on any future interpenetrations between the black movement and antimilitary groups, a major turning away of blacks per se from military commitment is viewed as highly doubtful. Most likely, and somewhat paradoxically, there will be more vocal antimilitary sentiment with certain black militant groups at the same time that the armed forces continue to be a leading avenue of career opportunity for many black men (Moskos, 1966).

NEEDED
RESEARCH AREAS

A high priority must be given to collecting data and formulating propositions on minority groups in military organization which have generality extending beyond the particulars of a single national entity. Knowledge in this area is overbalanced by the research dealing with the American military, and within that context by the almost exclusive attention given to the situation of black servicemen. Even within the American military establishment, the situation of other than black minority groups is virtual *terra incognita.* There are large numbers of Puerto Ricans, Mexican-Americans, Oriental-Americans, American Indians, and Pacific Islanders serving in the armed forces of the United States. We need to know if their position is analogous or qualitatively different from that of blacks. Moreover, the position of women in military organization is almost completely unresearched. (However, see Coates and Pellegrin, 1965.)

Finally, and perhaps most important, the development of a valid analytic framework for understanding minority groups in military organization requires systematic comparative research. It is only in this way that observations of minority groups in military organization can be continually incorporated into the cumulative literature on minority groups in general and, beyond that, into the wider body of social scientific knowledge.

REFERENCES

BOGART, L. (1969) Social Research and the Desegregation of the U.S. Army. Chicago: Markham.

CAUDILL, W. (1955) "American soldiers in a Japanese community." Unpublished manuscript.

Chamberlin Board (1950) Report of Board of Officers on Utilization of Negro Manpower in the Army (February 9).

COATES, C. H. and R. J. PELLEGRIN (1965) "Minority groups in the military service," pp. 337-372 in C. H. Coates and R. J. Pellegrin (eds.) Military Sociology. University Park, Md.: Social Science Press.

DAVENPORT, R. K. (1947) "The Negro in the Army: a subject of research." Journal of Social Issues 3: 32-39.

DUFF, D. F. and R. J. ARTHUR (1967) "Between two worlds: Filipinos in the U.S. Navy." American Journal of Psychiatry 123, 7: 836-843.

EVANS, J. C. and D. A. LANE, Jr. (1956) "Integration in the armed services." Annals of the American Academy of Political and Social Science 304: 7-85.

Gillem Board (1945) Report of Board of Officers on the Utilization of Negro Manpower in the Postwar Army (November 17).

GINZBERG, E. (1956) "The Negro soldier," pp. 61-91 in E. Ginzberg (ed.) The Negro Potential. New York: Columbia University Press.

GLASER, D. (1946) "The sentiments of American soldiers abroad toward Europeans." American Journal of Sociology 51: 433-438.

HALL, E. T., Jr. (1947) "Race prejudice and Negro-white relations in the Army." American Journal of Sociology 52: 401-409.

HIGGINSON, T. W. (1962) Army Life in a Black Regiment. New York: Collier Books.

HUMPHREY, R. L. (n.d.) Fight the Cold War. Washington, D.C.: International Research Institute of the American Institute for Research.

KARPINOS, B. D. (1968) "Results of the examination of youths for military service, 1967," in Supplement to Health of the Army. Washington, D.C.: U.S. Department of the Army, Office of the Surgeon General (December).

———(1967) "Mental test failures," pp. 35-53 in S. Tax (ed.) The Draft. Chicago: University of Chicago Press.

KENWORTHY, E. G. (1951) "The case against Army segregation." Annals of the Academy of Political and Social Science 275: 27-33.

KLASSEN, A. D., Jr. (1966) Military Service in American Life since World War II: An Overview. Chicago: National Opinion Research Center, University of Chicago.

LANG, K. (1964) "Technology and career management in the military establishment," pp. 39-82 in M. Janowitz (ed.) The New Military. New York: Russell Sage Foundation.

LEE, U. G. (1966) The Employment of Negro Troops in World War II. Washington, D.C.: Office of the Chief of Military History, Department of the Army.

MANDELBAUM, D. G. (1952) "Negro grouping," pp. 89-132 in D. G. Mandelbaum (ed.) Soldier Groups and Negro Soldiers. Berkeley: University of California Press.

McCRARY, J. W. (1967) "Human factors in the operation of U.S. military units augmented with indigenous troops." Professional Paper 48-67. Alexandria, Va.: George Washington University, Human Resources Research Office (November).

MOSKOS, C. C., Jr. (1970) The American Enlisted Man. New York: Russell Sage Foundation.

———(1969) "The Negro and the draft" pp. 139-162 in R. W. Little (ed.) Selective Service and American Society. New York: Russell Sage Foundation.

———(1966) "Racial integration in the armed forces." American Journal of Sociology 72: 132-148.

———(1957) "Has the Army killed Jim Crow?" Negro History Bulletin (November): 27-29.

MUELLER, W. R. (1945) "The Negro in the Navy." Social Forces 24: 110-115.

National Analysts, Inc. (1968) "A study of military attitudes among Negro males—16 to 25 years of age, nationally and in Camden, New Jersey. Philadelphia (mimeo).

NELSON, D. D. (1956) The Integration of the Negro into the U.S. Navy. New York: Farrar, Straus, & Young.

NICHOLS, L. (1954) Breakthrough on the Color Front. New York: Random House.

Operations Research Office (1955) Project Clear: The Utilization of Negro Manpower in the Army. Chevy Chase, Md.: Johns Hopkins University.

PARKS, D. (1968) G.I. Diary. New York: Harper & Row.

Personal Response Project (1967) Assessment of Attitudes Between USMC Personnel and Civilian Workers Employed on U.S. Bases in Japan, Okinawa, and Vietnam. Fleet Marine Force, Pacific (mimeo).

ROSE, A. M. (1956) "Psychoneurotic breakdown among Negro soldiers." Phylon 17: 61-73.

———(1947) "Army policies toward Negro soldiers—a report on a success and a failure." Journal of Social Issues 3: 26-31.

STILLMAN, R. J., III (1968) Integration of the Negro in the U.S. Armed Forces. New York: Frederick A. Praeger.

STOUFFER, S. A. et al., (1949) The American Soldier, vol. 1. Princeton: Princeton University Press.

U.S. Commission on Civil Rights (1963) "The Negro in the armed forces," pp. 169-224 in Civil Rights '63. Washington, D.C.: U.S. Government Printing Office.

U.S. National Advisory Commission on Selective Service (1967) Who Serves When Not All Serve? Washington, D.C.: U.S. Government Printing Office.

U.S. President's Committee on Equality of Treatment and Opportunity in the Armed Forces (1950) Freedom to Serve: Equality of Treatment and Opportunity in the Armed Forces. Washington, D.C.: U.S. Government Printing Office.

U.S. President's Committee on Equal Opportunity in the Armed Forces (1964) Final Report: Military Personnel Stationed Overseas and Membership and Participation in the National Guard (mimeo).

———(1963) Initial Report: Equality of Treatment and Opportunity for Negro Personnel Stationed within the United States (mimeo).

WEIL, F. E. G. (1947) "The Negro in the armed forces." Social Forces 26: 95-98.

Part Three

ORGANIZATIONAL DYNAMICS

Chapter 9

PRIMARY GROUPS, ORGANIZATION, AND
MILITARY PERFORMANCE

ALEXANDER L. GEORGE

Soldiers come to accept the hardships of military service and the dangers of combat in different ways. They may come to believe that it is necessary to endure them, a feeling created when the military service is accepted as legitimate and its requirements are internalized, or they may anticipate even worse deprivations if they seek to avoid these demands. An Army fights best when discipline and the performance of military duties rest at least in part on genuinely voluntaristic motives and are not extracted solely through fear of punishment for disobedience. All modern armies recognize, therefore, the desirability of blending coercion with persuasion in some way in order to obtain discipline and obedience. While the methods they employ vary, all modern armies seek to minimize reliance on coercion by subjecting soldiers to indoctrination, by resocializing men taken from civilian life and attempting to assimilate them into the social organization of the Army, and by bringing to bear material inducements as well as symbolic rewards and deprivations.

PRIMARY GROUPS IN
MILITARY ORGANIZATIONS

Studies of military morale during and since World War II have underscored the central importance of comradely ties among individuals in small combat groups. This has been established for national armies of quite different social-political origins and for different service branches of the armed forces. Those who conducted these studies were by no means oblivious to the complexity and diversity of motivational structure among combat soldiers. They were cognizant, too, of the variety of factors and circumstances that can affect combat performance. Notwithstanding this, they were impressed with the evidence of the relative importance of comradely ties in small military groups. Thus, for example, two eminent psychiatrists, Roy R. Grinker and John P. Spiegel (1945), summarized their work with the U.S. Air Force in World War II with the following, often-quoted observation: "The men seem to be fighting more for someone than against somebody."

That cohesion in the small combat unit is to be understood in part as a collective response to an external threat is a common theme that runs through detailed studies of combat behavior by Samuel Stouffer and his associates, S. L. A. Marshall, Edward Shils and Morris Janowitz, Roger Little, Charles Moskos, and others. Investigators have called attention again and again to the fact that the most significant persons for the combat soldier are the men who fight by his side and share with him the ordeal of trying to survive. The point has been made authoritatively more than once by S. L. A. Marshall, a military historian and trained observer of combat in many different kinds of wars, perhaps most succinctly in his classic study, *Men Against Fire* (1947): "I hold it to be one of the simplest truths of war that the thing which enables an infantry soldier to keep going with his weapons is the near presence or the presumed presence of a comrade." It is indeed ancient wisdom that groups often become integrated more closely when faced by an external threat. And it is also true that over the ages military leaders have attempted to incorporate this theorem into military doctrine and practice, and to operationalize it in organizational and morale-building practices.

Modern weapons have only exacerbated a long-standing problem of warfare: the task of getting everyone to engage effectively in combat and the related task of maintaining the cohesion and performance of the combat unit under the shock, danger, and cumulative stress of battle. As early as 1880, Colonel Ardant du Picq, a French combat officer and military theorist, noted that the problem of troop morale had worsened with the increase in the destructuve power of weapons. As a result the courage to face these new weapons was becoming more rare. No longer could soldiers comprising the company mass their fire by standing shoulder to shoulder, firing volley after volley at the company commander's orders. In this classic formation they were now too vulnerable before the new infantry weapons and suffered high casualties. The shoulder-to-shoulder tactic clearly had to be extended, but when this was done new problems arose. Thus, in dispersed formations the company commander could no longer control his men's fire. Fire control was also lost if each man was allowed to act independently. There was need, clearly, for devolution of the company commander's leadership, direction, and control of combat to lower levels of authority. Thus was set into motion a long period of experimentation with combat tactics employing smaller groups: platoons, squads, and fire teams of three or four soldiers (Holmes, 1952).

Du Picq thought that the solution to problems created by more destructive weapons lay in "mutual aid," in strengthening the comradely ties and informal organization within combat units. His views in this respect foreshadowed in a remarkable way some of the sophisticated innovations in organizational doctrine that were to come many years later. Du Picq (1958) summarized his views in a pithy observation: "Four brave men who do not know each other will not dare to attack a lion. Four less brave men, but knowing each other well, sure of their reliability and consequences of mutual aid, will attack resolutely. There is the science of the organization of armies in a nutshell."

What is noteworthy here is the explicit recognition that individual bravery will not suffice, and that the morale and performance of the individual soldier depends on membership in a cohesive small group. Elsewhere in his *Battle Studies,* Du Picq (1958) noted that to base military discipline on formal sanctions alone was of limited effectiveness. Foreshadowing modern sociological research once again, Du Picq argued that a special system of social and organizational relationships would be needed to sustain the individual combat soldier under the changed conditions of modern warfare:

> But to order discipline is not enough. . . . Discipline itself depends on moral pressure which actuates men to advance from sentiments of fear or pride. But it depends also on surveillance, the mutual supervision of groups of men who know each other well.

> A wise organization insures that the personnel of combat groups changes as little as possible, so that comrades in peace time manoeuvres shall be comrades in war. From living together, and obeying the same chiefs, from commanding the same men, from sharing fatigue and rest, from coopera-

tion among men who quickly understand each other in the execution of war-like movements, may be bred brotherhood, professional knowledge, sentiment, above all unity. The duty of obedience, the right of imposing discipline and the impossibility of escaping from it, would naturally follow.

In the modern era Du Picq's view and similar ones advanced by Lieutenant C. B. Mayne of the Royal Engineers and Lieutenant D. H. Mahan, USN, were either forgotten or overlooked (Holmes, 1952). Perhaps Du Picq's stature as a military theorist suffered, too, because those strategists of World War I who, like Foch, had drawn upon Du Picq in developing their infantry tactics, fell into disrepute when their insistence upon *l'offensive a l'ottrance* led to calamitous casualties and occasional mutinies within the ranks.

Following World War II, empirical findings on matters of military morale and combat performance led to sharper formulation of some of the ideas Du Picq had advanced sixty years earlier. The sociological perspective on these matters has steadily broadened since World War II. Mature reflection on cumulative research findings has led investigators to conclude that the concept of "morale" is too limited and needs to be replaced by a more inclusive *theory of organizational behavior.* In a comprehensive review of trends in theory in this research area, Morris Janowitz (1964) has emphasized that morale can no longer be regarded as "a vague dimension or organizational behavior grounded in personal attitudes. Even in the smallest unit there is an 'iron framework' of organization which serves as a basis of social control." The single concept of military "morale" must give way, therefore, to "a theory of organizational behavior in which an array of sociological concepts is employed: authority, communications, hierarchy, sanctions, status, social role, allocation, and integration" (Janowitz and Little, 1965).

In World War II, two separate groups of social scientists independently recast operational and strategic intelligence into sociological models (Leighton, 1949; Shils and Janowitz, 1948). The social system perspective they applied to these problems helped focus attention on the fact that it was the ability of combat leaders to maintain primary group functions in small fighting units rather than adherence to Nazi ideology that lay at the root of the stubborn resistance put up by hard-pressed units of the Wehrmacht. Let us look more closely, therefore, at what sociologists mean by "primary group" and how it has been applied to the study of military organizations and, in particular, to combat behavior.

PRIMARY GROUP
AS A VARIABLE

By primary groups sociologists mean those small groups in which social behavior is governed by intimate face-to-face relations. The term was employed initially sixty years ago by Charles H. Cooley in his book, *Social Organization* (1909). Cooley defined primary groups in the following terms:

> By primary groups I mean those characterized by intimate face-to-face association and cooperation. They are primary in several senses, but chiefly in that they are fundamental in forming the social natures and ideals of the individual. The result of intimate association . . . is a certain fusion of individualities in a common whole, so that one's very self, for many purposes at least, is the common life and purpose of the group. Perhaps the simplest way of describing this wholeness is by saying it is a "we"; it involves the sort of sympathy and mutual identification for which "we" is the natural expression.

The most explicit and detailed application of the primary group concept to the study of small military groups appears in the study of the cohesion and disintegration of the Germay Army in World War II by Shils and Janowitz (1948). These investigators made ingenious use of a rich body of theory to illuminate some of the complexities and puzzles surrounding the combat performance of German soldiers, and to account for the ability of German units to stand up in the face of severe, prolonged stress. Shils and Janowitz (1948) saw the small military unit as maintaining itself insofar as it was able to fulfill a number of the essential needs of the individual soldier:

> For the ordinary German soldier the decisive fact was that he was a member of a squad or section which maintained its structural integrity and which coincided roughly with the social unit which satisfied some of his major primary needs. He was likely to go on fighting, provided he had the necessary weapons, as long as the group possessed leadership with which he could identify himself, and as long as he gave affection to and received affection from the other members of his squad and platoon. In other words, as long as he felt himself to be a member of his primary group and therefore bound by the expectations and demands of its other members, his soldierly achievement was likely to be good. . . . In the army, when isolated from civilian primary groups, the individual soldier comes to depend more and more on his military primary group. His spontaneous loyalties are to its immediate members whom he sees daily and with whom he develops a high degree of intimacy.

Subsequent investigators have clarified and more precisely delimited the *scope* and *quality* of primary group ties within small military units. Earlier studies based on World War II experiences in Western Europe (Stouffer, et al., 1949; Shils and Janowitz, 1948), postulated or seemed to imply the existence of a rather rich cluster of primary group ties shared by many members of units as large as squads or even platoons. In the more recent literature, however, a new conception of primary group ties under conditions of miltiary stress has emerged which reflect different military setting. They are now described as being more molecular or granular in structure, often taking the form of a series of two-person relationships rather than affiliations among larger numbers of men. Several investigations have noted a more elementary, less developed type of primary group structure (Marlowe, 1959; Little, 1964; Seaton, 1964).

This changed conception of primary group ties may be a result of more precise and more direct observation than was possible in the earlier studies. Or, as seems more likely, it may reflect the fact that *considerable variation in scope and content of primary group ties is to be expected, depending on the conditions and circumstances surrounding small military groups.* Thus, in Korea spatial dispersion and personnel rotation may have inhibited the development of more extensive interpersonal systems of a comradely character. The "buddy" relationship between two soldiers was built around mutual interest in minimization of risk; a buddy was a fellow soldier on whom one could rely in situations of danger. But the buddy relationship was maintained as private knowledge (Little, 1964; see also discussion in Janowitz and Little, 1965). Similar observations were made by Seaton (1964) in a study of military work groups under severe environmental stress in arctic Greenland. Support relations were developed by the individual with just one or two others; resources and opportunities for interaction with larger numbers in the unit were limited by circumstances. As a result, the form of social organization that emerged in these small groups was "primitive and immature, and unable to sustain extended or sustained friendships."

The instrumental aspect of "buddyship" and primary group ties is given particular emphasis by Marlowe (1959) and Moskos (1968). In a study of social adjustment during the course of basic training, Marlowe concluded that buddyship and friendship were not coterminous; rather, buddyship appears to be "an operational concept designed to take the place of friendship and serve as the initial stage in the foundation of a friendship." The instrumental importance of buddyship, he found, was at times expressed forthrightly and with vehemence: "Everybody has to have a buddy. Without a buddy you could never make it here." The use of a two-man buddy system has also been reported for the British commandos in World War II.

In his recent study of U.S. soldiers in Vietnam, Moskos, too, found it necessary to challenge the earlier hypothesis that primary group ties are based on deep identifications and solidarity with fellow squad and platoon members, and the related hypothesis that, as a result, individuals value the maintenance of the group and the group ties independently of selfish interests in physical survival. As against this, the data obtained in Vietnam pointed to the greater importance of "the instrumental and self-serving aspects of primary relations in combat units." Even the buddy relationship was at its core "a mutually pragmatic effort to minimize personal risk." Hence, rather than viewing primary group relations in combat units as "some kind of semi-mystical bond of comradeship," Moskos argues they can be better understood as essentially "pragmatic and situational responses" (Moskos, 1968).

It seems reasonable to conclude from available empirical studies, therefore, that the *scope* and *content* of primary group ties within small military units are both subject to variations. While the general character of primary group ties is suggested by the traditional definition of the concept and in sociological theory, care must be taken by the investigator not to reify the term or, a more likely danger, to utilize one or two indicators of the existence of primary group ties (such as evidence of buddyship) as a basis for inferring that a richer, more pervasive form of primary group relationships necessarily exists within the military groups that are being studied.

Thus, the scope and content of primary groups should be regarded as an open question to be settled in each case by empirical observation. We can now turn to a broader discussion of the emergence and significance of primary groups in different military organizations.

PRIMARY GROUPS IN DIFFERENT TYPES OF MILITARY ORGANIZATIONS

While the phenomenon of primary groups is ubiquitous, the context in which it occurs varies depending on the type of military organization in question and the attitude higher authorities take toward close informal relations within small military groups. Thus, the study of primary group ties takes on greater significance if it is an integral part of a broader study of any given army. A more comprehensive study of this kind should describe (a) *the kind of social organization that is officially fostered and/or tolerated within the army in question,* (b) *the major policies regulating service conditions, and* (c) *the practices employed to mold and shape civilian recruits* (or conscripts) into the kinds of soldiers and cadres wanted within the framework of the preferred disciplinary and social system.

The fact that armies differ in these three respects is sometimes passed over in calling attention to features common to all military organizations. Military sociology will be enriched, however, if the way in which armies differ from each other is also systematically examined. In this section we shall indicate some of the directions in which comparative military sociology might move by contrasting as best we can on the basis of available data the origins and nature of comradely relations in small units in several different armies. (A more detailed comparison is presented in George, 1967.)

In the U.S. armed forces the development of comradely ties is not officially sponsored as it is, for example, in the Chinese Communist Army. Rather, comradely ties in small U.S. units are a consequence of the men's recognition that they are working together on a common job, that each is dependent on the other, and that teamwork is to everyone's advantage. It is expected that most soldiers have the capacity, derived from earlier experiences in civilian society, to develop comradely ties within their units that will reinforce the workings of formal authority.

In contrast, Chinese Communist authorities make explicit provision for creating and maintaining small social groups. What is even more intriguing about the Chinese Peoples Liberation Army (PLA) is that its leaders insist that the social system within the Army should have the explicit political-ethical content of their revolutionary ideals. The purpose of basic training and indoctrination in the PLA is not simply to produce "good soldiers." Rather, Chinese Communist leaders have been engaged in an ambitious pedagogical enterprise which attempts to alter important aspects of the individual's personality, attitudes, and behavior in order to make a "good Communist soldier" out of him. It is not an exaggeration to say that PLA leaders attempt to socialize raw conscripts not only for service in the Army but also for their subsequent role as citizens of a revolutionary communist society. The PLA organizational model, that is to say, sprang from its revolutionary origins. The political-ethical goals of the Chinese Communist revolution have been infused into the social organization sponsored within the Army.

A comparison of the PLA and Soviet models for small group life reveals important differences. Many of the strikingly egalitarian features of social political organization that were still visible in the PLA at the time of the Korean War were either altogether lacking or much muted in the history of the Soviet Army, or have survived only in a much attenuated form. Bolshevik leaders recognized the importance of military professionalism at the outset of their successful revolution; and they gave professional values and forms priority over the revolutionary-egalitarian model in creating the Soviet Red Army. Moreover, professionalism has continued to grow in scope and emphasis within the Red Army and this is evident in many aspects of its social organization. For example, higher authority in the Red Army attempts to keep relations between officers and men on a formal, hierarchical basis while units are in training or in garrison. In contrast, within the framework of a revolutionary-egalitarian model, in which formal ranks were abolished, PLA authorities have actively encouraged friendly comradely relations between leaders and men in periods of indoctrination and training, and under garrison conditions.[1]

Though comradely ties between officers and men in the Soviet Red Army were officially discouraged during peacetime they developed spontaneously in combat during World War II. A detailed study of the basis of Soviet military morale, based on detailed interviews with defectors, reported as follows:

> Comradely solidarity in small informal groups plays an important part and enters significantly into the motivations of the Soviet soldiers in battle. . . . Under combat conditions the formalization of relationships among officers and men is greatly reduced. The genuinely personal qualities of the men becomes more apparent; the organization comes to rest more upon its informal bases, upon the spontaneously worked out human relations which have, in a sense, been held in check by the formal organization. . . . A change takes place in combat. The danger and the tremendous piling up of acute discomforts creates a sort of community and solidarity among the men which hardly existed in the garrison [Dicks et al., 1951].

These comradely ties, it is further reported, were often grounded in patriotism; but what the Russian soldier typically expressed thereby was a nationalism that was largely divorced from communist ideology. Early in World War II Soviet leaders realized that the large reserve of patriotism in the Russian people could be utilized for purposes of military as well as civilian morale. In contrast, the PLA system prior to and during the Korean conflict had very little tolerance for comradely ties that were not cemented, at least on the surface, by mutually shared communist convictions or orientation.

We noted earlier that PLA authorities (unlike both their Soviet and U.S. counterparts) took an active interest in developing and controlling the character of small group ties. Comradely ties were not permitted to have an autonomous basis, for evidently PLA authorities felt threatened by informal group ties and loyalties that were essentially apolitical in character. From the standpoint of the PLA political organization, interpersonal ties within combat units that rested largely on human considerations and to which the men gae priority over political values were potentially dangerous, being thought of as too vulnerable to subversion and transformation into oppositional activity.

In contrast, the informal ties that cement small groups within the U.S. Army are extraordinarily spontaneous, overtly apolitical or even antipolitical, and largely unregulated by higher authorities. Higher leadership does not feel its control threatened by these autonomous comradely ties. Rather, it regards the personal loyalties felt by the men toward each other as contributing to good military discipline, and it builds upon small group loyalties to create larger loyalties that reinforce the formal authority structure and its goals.

We note that in more systematic analyses of primary groups in military organizations, primary group can be employed either as a dependent variable and/or as an independent variable, depending upon what aspect of military organization is singled out for attention. Thus,

> "Primary group" is a *dependent* variable when the investigator seeks to ascertain the preconditions and variables that contribute to or impede the formation of social cohesion in small units.

> "Primary group" is an *independent* variable (one among many) when the investigator seeks to determine the conditions and variables that determine the level (a) of combat motivation and (b) of combat performance.

Let us consider, first, primary group cohesion as a dependent variable and ask what antecedent conditions and independent variables determine the formation and degree of social cohesion in small military units.

FACTORS AFFECTING FORMATION OF
PRIMARY GROUP TIES IN SMALL UNITS

Some dozen preconditions and variables have been identified as contributing to formation and maintenance of primary group ties in small military units. Since they have been discussed in some detail by a number of investigators (Janowitz and Little, 1965; Dicks et al., 1951; Lang, 1965; Mandlebaum, 1952; Coates and Pellegrin, 1965; George, 1967; Moskos, 1968), we need summarize them only very briefly here without attempting to order them or to consider their interrelationships:

Social background of unit members: A number of investigators have noted that a common social background assists soldiers in a unit to develop intimate interpersonal relations; similarities in previous social experience—such as social class, regional origin, or age—appear to contribute in this way. Conversely, heterogeneous ethnic and national origins among soldiers within a unit tend to inhibit formation of primary group relations (Janowitz and Little, 1965; Shils and Janowitz, 1948; George, 1967).

Personality of unit members: Among the characteristics mentioned as facilitating an individual's participation in the primary group life of his unit is the ability to offer and receive affection in an all-male society. Attention has been called also to the importance of family stability, especially satisfactory identification with one's father, as affecting the individual soldier's capacity to enter into informal group relationships (Shils, 1950; Janowitz and Little, 1965).

Protectiveness of immediate leaders: The individual soldier's need for a protective, exemplary authority whose qualities permit identification is well documented (Shils, 1950; Shils and Janowitz, 1948; George, 1967). In the U.S. Army in World War II, companies with high morale were characterized by a far higher frequency of belief that the officers were "interested" in their men, "understood" them, were "helpful," would "back them up"—all of which are qualities of primary group leaders (Stouffer et al., 1949: vol. 2).

Performance of immediate leaders: Tactical leadership based on example and demonstrated competence promotes social cohesion and reduces the need to rely on commands based on the threat of sanctions (Dollard, 1943; Shils and Janowitz, 1948; Homans, 1946; George, 1967; Stouffer et al., 1949).

Military discipline, professionalism, and role of soldierly hours: Apolitical motivation of the order of "getting the job done," being "a good soldier who does his duty," and not letting comrades down, were found to be dominant in several armies that have been studied (Shils and Janowitz, 1948; Stouffer et al., 1949; Moskos, 1968). Subjugation to military discipline supports those young soldiers who experience the need for asserting manliness and toughness, a need which regression to an adolescent condition in military life reactivates. Coincidence of these personal needs with group norms and military codes reinforces group cohesion.

Commitment to one's social-political system, ideology, and patriotism: There is substantial agreement among those who have studied different military organizations that a soldier's patriotism and attachment to related secondary symbols generally can provide at the very least, "the rudiments of one of the most important preconditions for the formation of primary groups which (in turn) have a more positive and immediate function in strengthening the soldier's will to exert himself under dangerous conditions." This formulation which Shils (1950) provided in his commentary, *The American Soldier*, did much to clarify seeming ambiguities of data and conflicting interpretations, and has generally been accepted as being of probable application to other armies as well (see also George, 1967; Moskos, 1968; Dicks et al., 1951).

Political ideals are of greater significance in strengthening solidarity in those armies in which the cadre structure is highly politicized. Thus, the Nazi "hard core" within the Wehrmacht played an important role in strengthening the stability and effectiveness of the military primary groups (Shils and Janowitz, 1948). A similar function is performed by communist adherents within the cadre structure of communist armies, particularly in the Chinese Communist Army at the time of the Korean War, in which politicization of the cadre structure extended to the squad and subequal level (George, 1967; Dicks, et al., 1951).

War indoctrination: This is related to the tacit patriotism and the attachment to other secondary symbols and plays a similar indirect role as a precondition for formation of primary groups. War indoctrination typically stresses two themes: (a) the legitimacy and/or justification of the war, which is based upon an account of the origin of the war, the nature of the enemy, and the character of the war aims, and (b) the wisdom and/or necessity for fighting it (which includes an estimate of expectations of success and a prediction of the probable consequences of defeat (Dollard, 1943; Speier, 1950; George, 1967).

Exigencies of military life and of the combat situation: These will often suffice in themselves to create a sense of elementary social cohesion, a mutually-shared recognition of the necessity for buddy-ship and cooperation, if not also comradeliness.

Technical aspects of weapons systems: It has been postulated that "weapons systems which maintain close physical proximity of team members and enhance the process of communication contribute most to primary group cohesion" (Janowitz and Little, 1965).

Replacement system and rotation policy: The replenishment of understrength units by *individual* replacements has been thought to exacerbate the problem of maintaining group cohesion. An alternative replacement practice of *packets of small groups* has also been tried, but this appears to bring with it a different set of problems (Janowitz and Little, 1965). In the Vietnam War there has been a rapid turnover of personnel in the U.S. Army units, occasioned by the unusually benign rotation policy followed in this conflict. As a result, the development of closer primary group ties appears to have been limited even while, paradoxically, the rotation policy has contributed to the usually high morale of the individual combat soldier (Moskos, 1968).

Social prestige of soldierly profession: There is some indication that raising the social prestige of the soldierly profession and improving civil-military relations in countries such as China where soldiers have been held in traditional disrepute by the civilian population helps to enhance the self-respect of soldiers and thereby contributes to the formation of social cohesion in small military units (George, 1967).

Egalitarian practices within the military organization: There is some indication, once again, that favorable results have been achieved with the introduction of egalitarian practices into the armies of countries such as China, in which military service has been traditionally associated with highly coercive, arbitrary, and discriminatory practices. There is evidence that practices within the PLA which served to "democratize" respect; equalize and rationalize service conditions; encourage mass participation in official ideology, rituals, and group decision-making have been successful in encouraging the individual soldier to identify with, and participate in the prescribed type of small group life (George, 1967).

PRIMARY GROUP COHESION AS AN INDEPENDENT VARIABLE AFFECTING COMBAT MOTIVATION AND COMBAT PERFORMANCE

Linkage of Primary Group Cohesion to Formal Military Organization

A number of investigators have emphasized that primary group solidarity in small military groups can work either to reinforce or to impede the goals of the formal military organization. As is the case in other kinds of organizations, peer group cohesion among soldiers in small units may take a direction that is positive or negative from the standpoint of higher military authority (Etzioni, 1961: ch. 8).

Clearly, therefore, social cohesion that is generated in small groups has to be extended to larger units and higher levels of the military organization. "Cohesive primary groups contribute to organizational effectiveness only when the standards of behavior they enforce are articulated with the requirements of formal authority" (Janowitz and Little, 1965).

How, then, is this linkage established? Two factors are of particular importance here. First, the leaders of small military groups are often the vehicle through which the formal demands and sanctions of higher military authority are linked with the norms and sanctions of the small group itself. The primary group member's identification with the leaders of his unit often results in commitment to the norms of the formal organization which these leaders represent. In this fashion "hierarchical cohesion" is established along with peer cohesion at the lowest working level.

In the Wehrmacht, Nazi soldiers and the apolitical but tough professionalized NCOs constituted the nucleus or "hard core" of the primary group.

> The presence of a few such men in the group, zealous, energetic, and unsparing of themselves, provided models for the weaker men, and facilitated the process of identification. For those for whom their charisma did not suffice and who were accordingly difficult to incorporate fully into the intimate primary group, frowns, harsh words, and threats served as a check on divisive tendencies [Shils and Janowitz, 1948].

An even more systematic application of the "hard core" organizational principle was evident in the Chinese Communist Army at the time of the Korean War. The PLA organizational model called for merging the entire military cadre structure, even down to the squad level, with membership in the Party; moreover, a separate political organization was created within the Army that straddled its military command structure from top to bottom. In addition to installing political co-commanders alongside military commanders at every organizational level, the PLA attempted to place communist personnel, insofar as possible, as leaders of platoons, squads, and subsquad groups of three. This was a particularly useful device for shaping group life along desired lines. By this means, PLA authorities tried to ensure that comradeliness and peer cohesion in the small units would take on a communist hue and be responsive to the demands and goals of the higher organization (George, 1967).

A political hard core type of organization has also been employed in the Soviet Army with some variations over the years; but it does not ever seem to have been extended to the squad level or applied as thoroughly as in the PLA (Dicks et al., 1951; Kolkowixa, 1967; George, 1967). On the other hand, this and other features of the PLA military model were evidently taken over by Vo Nguyen Giap in organizing the Viet Minh People's Army, which fought and finally defeated the French Army in Indochina (Roy, 1965). The Viet Cong in South Vietnam has also been using a military model closely patterned on that of the PLA (George, 1967; Zasloff, 1968).

A second means by which peer group cohesion is linked with the higher organization is the soldier's acceptance of the legitimacy of its demands. As noted earlier, a hypothesis along these lines has emerged from the work of several investigators and was stated most recently by Moskos (1968):

> Primary groups serve to maintain the soldier in his combat role only where there is an underlying commitment to the worthwhileness of the larger social system for which he is fighting. This commitment need not be formally articulated, nor even perhaps consciously recognized. But at some level there must be an acceptance, if not of the specific purposes of the war, then at least of the broader rectitude of the social system of which the soldier is a member.

This states, as it were, the "minimal" role of ideology and war indoctrination. But it is clear that these factors are also capable of playing a far more important role in combat motivation. Of three hundred veterans of the Abraham Lincoln Brigade who had fought in the Spanish Civil War, seventy-seven percent stated that "belief in war aims" had been among the most important things that had helped to overcome fear in battle. This factor was mentioned more frequently than other factors such as leadership (forty-nine percent), military training (forty-five percent), and material (forty-two percent) (Dollard, 1943).

Such is the ubiquity of primary groups in military organizations, however, that we must not be surprised to find that under special circumstances they can promote compliance with the goals of the organization even when members of the small group are highly dissatisfied with, and even alienated from formal military authorities. In a Chinese Nationalist Air Police company, studied by Wen-Lung Chang (1968), the dissatisfaction of ordinary soldiers with their military lives and with the rigid and harsh system of rule enforcement by military authorities was the most important basis for formation of primary group cohesion. The men needed each other's friendship for psychological support in order to be able to better meet the hardships of military service inflicted on them by higher authorities. The informal primary groups that sprang up in this oppressive milieu, though composed of dissidents, nonetheless promoted compliance by members with the organization's goals and demands. For primary group norms enjoined the individual member to "play it safe," to obey rather than subject himself to the likelihood of harsh punishment by higher authorities.

Finally, we should take note of the fact that primary group norms that support the goals of the organization under one set of circumstances may have the opposite effect when combat stress is intensified and prolonged. Thus Little (1964) noted that the longer a platoon was on the line in Korea, the more intensive the relationship of its members became,

> and the more their behavior deviated from the norms of the organization. Even the officers who lived with their platoons tended to think like their men. . . . Relations between the company commander and the platoon leaders became increasingly contentious. The probable response of the latter in executing orders in situations involving great risk was accordingly uncertain. When an organization reached this stage, it was described as having "low morale" and withdrawn into reserve for "retraining."

Other Independent Variables Affecting Level of Combat Motivation and Combat Performance

While the present chapter focuses on the nature and significance of primary group cohesion in military organizations, it would be grossly misleading to discuss as we have been doing its role in combat motivation and performance without some brief mention of the many other variables that are also relevant in this respect. For this purpose it is useful to separate "combat motivation" from "combat performance," since the latter depends on a variety of factors in addition to the level of motivation for combat within fighting units.

The complexity of factors affecting in turn combat motivation and combat performance are suggested in Chart 1.

Functions of Primary Group in Combat

It is widely recognized by military leaders that informal comradely ties that often develop in small groups can contribute greatly to morale and performance of combat duties. This is particularly true in guerrilla warfare and special warfare action which require highly motivated, closely knit small groups.

The special motivational impetus provided combat soldiers by their membership in primary groups is all the more critical insofar as the formal coercive powers at the disposal of military authorities tend to lose some of their efficacy and force in the battle situation and with increased duration of combat experience (Shils, 1950; Stouffer et al., 1949: vol. 2).

What then, do primary group ties contribute to combat motivation? The authors of *The American Soldier* (Volume 2) concluded that the primary or informal group "served two principle functions in combat motivation: it *set and emphasized group standards* of behavior and it *supported and sustained the individual* in stresses he would otherwise not have been able to withstand." Thus, a primary group generates norms of its own and joins or withholds its own informal sanctions to enforce organizational commands and expectations (see also Stouffer et al., 1949: vol. 1).

It is striking in this respect that even after the end of the war ninety percent of U.S. enlisted men interviewed by the Research Branch in one survey expressed the belief that soldiers are greatly concerned with the opinion in which they are held by other enlisted men in their units. Other surveys indicated that the desire to avoid "letting the other fellow down" was one of the most important reasons given by soldiers in their assessment of factors which caused them "to keep going" (Stouffer et al., 1949: vols. 1, 2). This consideration was given even broader recognition by the three hundred veterans of the Abraham Lincoln Brigade who had fought in Spain. Ninety-four percent stated that the wish not to let fellow soldiers down had made better soldiers of them. Moreover, some said

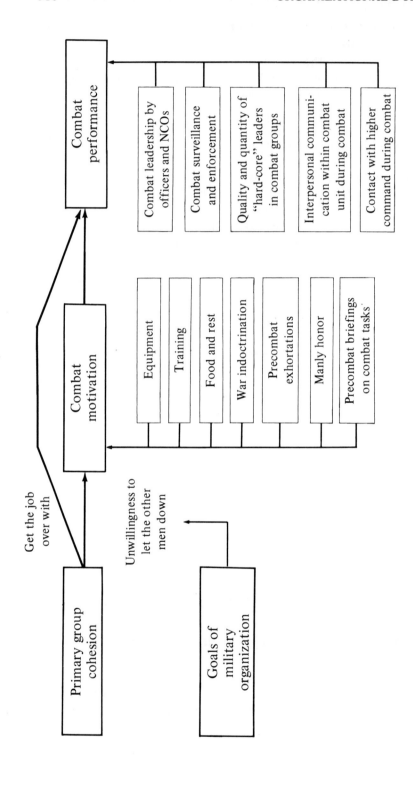

CHART 1. FACTORS AFFECTING COMBAT MOTIVATION AND PERFORMANCE

that the thought of their comrades and of the outfit as a whole had helped them to overcome fear in battle (Dollard, 1943).

In this connection, Janowitz and Little (1965) note that research efforts to establish the thresholds at which combat psychiatric breakdowns occur have shifted emphasis from efforts to ascertain individual tolerance for stress to an understanding of the positive sustaining effects of the primary group.

Organizational Controls as an Alternative to Primary Group Support for Combat

When primary group motivations wither or are nonexistent, military authorities must rely increasingly on combat surveillance and enforcement. The implied or immediate threat of official coercive sanctions must then assume the burden of motivation that concepts of duty and legitimacy no longer provide and that the informal norms and sanctions of the small group can no longer reinforce.

The efficacy of combat enforcement under these circumstances depends on the *numbers* and *quality* of combat leaders. The same hard-core cadres who in more favorable circumstances provide the models with which the men can identify, thus facilitating the critical linkage of primary groups with the goals of the formal organization we noted earlier, must now exact and enforce combat on the part of reluctant soldiers. The integrity of the combat unit now depends critically on the efficacy of the organizational control structure.

Such a trend was noted within the Chinese Communist Armies in Korea during the late winter and spring of 1950 (George, 1967). What is remarkable is not that morale within PLA combat units should sag under the adverse conditions encountered in Korea, but that the PLA's organizational controls should succeed as well as they did in preventing the disintegration of demoralized combat units and in extracting performance of combat duties. Increasingly strong emphasis was placed upon mutual supervision and surveillance during combat. Depending on the numbers and quality of personnel filling the cadre positions in fighting units, tendencies toward unit disintegration could be more or less effectively controlled. So long as reasonably well-motivated Party adherents straddled the cadre structure of a unit down to the squad and subsquad level, as was called for in PLA organizational doctrine, each group leader had only two or three non-Party, rank-and-file soldiers to watch over and control.

PLA prisoners taken during this period frequently noted that the surveillance and control system within their units had been quite effective in combat. Disaffected soldiers were afforded few opportunities to desert to the rear or to voluntarily surrender to the enemy. The effectiveness of the surveillance network in preventing desertion or surrender was indirectly conveyed by the answers eighty-six PLA prisoners (sixty-three privates, twenty-three cadres) gave to the question: "What made you follow the PLA to the last, undergoing so many hardships in this war?" Eighty-three percent of the privates and over forty percent of the cadres referred to the deterrent effect of the surveillance system in their units.

Moreover, so long as surveillance remained pervasive it operated to isolate the individual soldier and to prevent him from coming together with like-minded members of his unit to discuss and plan desertion or surrender. At this level of efficiency, it may be noted, surveillance effectively prevented the development of informal peer cohesion within small groups that would have been directed against the goals of the organization.

It is sobering to recognize the considerable extent to which the erosion of morale within PLA combat units and the disruption of the officially sponsored primary groups was compensated for by the strength of the PLA's organizational controls. In this respect, it may be noted, the experience of the PLA differed from that of the German Wehrmacht in World War II. Primary groups evidently survived longer under severe pressure in the Wehrmacht than in the PLA, and this enabled the German combat units to keep fighting without having to rely as much as the PLA on coercive sanctions applied by hard core cadres (Shils and Janowitz, 1948).

A more serious development from the standpoint of higher PLA leaders was the general demoralization and attrition of the all-important junior cadres who manned the control structure of their combat units. As the war dragged on during the spring of 1950, the caliber of combat leadership declined markedly as the PLA began to run out of skilled and well-motivated junior cadres. Party adherents who had formed the hard-core cadre in their units suffered heavy casualties, particularly at company and lower echelons, and many of them lost their ideological fervor and became demoralized. That the Achilles Heel of the PLA was not the erosion of morale in its combat units, but rather, the erosion of organizational controls became evident in late May when the Eighth Army's counter-offensive hit the Chinese Armies before they could carry out their usual practice of withdrawing after an offensive to rest, reorganize, resupply, and replenish the cadre structure. The Eighth Army's heavy blows on the ground and from the air imposed a severe strain on the ability of the already weakened and demoralized cadres to maintain control over their units. The remaining cadres were unable in many units to prevent the PLA withdrawal from taking on the character of a precipitous, disorderly flight. For the first time in the war surrender was no longer confined to single individuals or small groups; remnants of platoons, companies, and even battalions were now giving up.

SOME RESEARCH DIFFICULTIES

A number of practical difficulties arise in attempts to employ the primary group concept as a variable in rigorous research. In the first place, it is important but often difficult to develop a research model that employs the small group rather than the individual soldier as the *unit of analysis.* In the second place, it is far easier to obtain data on the *individual soldier's attitudes* than on the *behavior of the small group* to which he belongs or belonged.

These difficulties are accentuated when, as is often the case, the investigator obtains his data largely through interviews with individual soldiers (or prisoners of war) who have been selected through a sampling procedure, whether fortuitous or purposive, that cuts across the natural small units within the military organization. Insofar as few soldiers interviewed in a study of this kind belong to the same small military group, the information they provide tends to be sparse and highly fragmented when the investigator attempts to use it as data bearing on the behavior of small groups.

While interview data of this kind is useful at the level of micro-analysis and while it is also capable of being aggregated to study some general preconditions and effects of membership in primary groups, it has important limitations. Information about discrete individual soldiers who have no relationship to each other cannot be combined very well for studying the etiology and dynamic processes of primary group behavior. The problem of bridging the gap between micro- and macro-analysis is, therefore, particularly severe.

This problem was evident in *The American Soldier,* truly a monumental and pioneering study, but one based essentially on studies of attitudes of individuals with no direct observation of groups in action and only occasional indirect observations of group performance. In consequence, the actual operation of primary group life was not described in this study and indeed was seldom referred to. The result was that many important problems having to do with primary groups could not be studied at all (Stouffer et al., 1949 vol. 1; Shils, 1950). Extending this point to a discussion of the limitations of attitude research more generally for sociological study of military organizations, Janowitz and Little (1965) warn that "attitude research fails to describe the underlying social system—the realities of bureaucratic organization—of the armed forces."

Still another kind of research model, one employing sociometric techniques of analysis, was utilized in a recent study, "Cohesion in Marine Recruit Platoons" (Nelson and Berry, 1968). The investigators developed a "cohesiveness measure" for each of the twenty-four recruit training platoons by asking each soldier to nominate the five men in his platoon whom he liked best. The linkages established by reciprocal nominations were the basis for postulating, by definition, the existence of cliques. The study suffers, however, from the fact that findings regarding both cohesion and cliques are too much an artifact of the special mode of analysis. The operational definitions of cohesion and clique are at best only loosely relevant to the richer concepts and hypotheses of primary group theory. For what it is worth, cohesiveness as measured in this study did not correlate very significantly with other variables, nor was there much indication of change in cohesion over a two-month period.

The complex social organization and social processes within an army can be more advantageously studied by methods which rely at least in part on participant observation. Ideally, a group of investigators might be assigned the task of observing many small military units directly, employing a variety of data acquisition techniques. Longitudinal studies are needed, moreover, in which the same unit is observed over a period of time, in a variety of situations and circumstances. In this connection, Janowitz (1964) persuasively argues that the dynamics of small comradely groups can best be studied when the organization is under pressure. But prolonged and systematic participant observation of this kind is not easily arranged. One of the few examples thus far of research which employed this preferred approach is the study by Roger Little (1964) who directly observed a single U.S. Army combat unit in Korea from November 1952 through February 1953.

Also interesting from the standpoint of research methodology is a study of the socialization of two types of officer candidates in the Royal Netherlands Navy (Lammers, 1963). This study illustrates the value of combining several methods; the investigator employed intensive, prolonged participant observation initially for hypothesis formation and then undertook systematic surveys for more rigorous assessment of hypotheses.

When direct observation of individual military units is not possible and only individual soldiers or prisoners-of-war are available for interview, the investigator may nonetheless attempt to utilize the subjec s to provide an opportunity for *indirect* participant observation. Thus, each subject who is interviewed can be cast into the role of *informant* on matters affecting the character, development, and significance of small group ties within his old unit.[2]

The investigator attempts in this fashion to bridge as best he can analysis at the micro and macro levels. This kind of improvised research model was employed by George (1967) in his study of the Chinese Communist Army in Korea. It may be noted that while individuals are interviewed in this approach too, as in a Gallup Poll type survey, nonetheless the research model differs in important respects. It is not the individual soldier but rather the small military formation (company, platoon, squad, or subsquad—depending on the nature of the specific problem being investigated) which constitutes the *unit of analysis.* This research approach requires, typically, a more flexible mode of interviewing to take advantage of the varying utility of different respondents as informants about their units. When possible the investigator employs multiple informants on each unit; in principle, this could extend to the entire membership of the unit. Finally, if the investigator wishes to generalize about the state of affairs in the total order of battle, he must "sample" an appropriately broad and representative number of the individual military formations comprising the whole.

Still another approach for partly bridging the gap between micro-analysis of individual behavior and macro-analysis of groups based on variables common to political sociology has been suggested by Moskos (1968). He develops a concept of combat motivation that draws on the recent emphasis in social science writings on the nature of underlying aspects of a group's belief systems—such as political culture, basic value orientations, political ideology, and the like—which may set the context for political behavior. It is from this standpoint, Moskos argues, that one can best examine the dynamics of attitude formation on the part of American combat soldiers in the Vietnam War. He singles out several sets of attitudes or underlying value orientations that comprise the "latent ideology" of many American soldiers in the present conflict. These he calls anti-ideology, Americanism, materialism, and manly honor. The latent ideology of American soldiers in Vietnam, he argues further, is generally supportive and contributes indirectly to good combat performance.

NOTES

1. After the conclusion of the Korean War, Chinese Communist leaders attempted to graft important features of military professionalism on to their revolutionary-egalitarian type of army. Ranks and a professional officer class were introduced into the PLA for the first time in 1955. Following Soviet practice, PLA authorities tried to allow greater scope for military professionalism by permitting the role of the political apparatus within the Army to be curtailed, particularly at the all-important company level. But the consequences of this innovation frightened top-level Chinese leaders and this led to reimposition of political controls in 1959-1960 (Joffee, 1965; George, 1967). This abortive effort to introduce professionalism into the PLA may be contrasted with the successful experience of the leaders of the new Israel state in combining features of their egalitarian underground army with the model of a professional army such as the British Army in which many Israeli soldiers had earlier served (Etzioni, 1959, 1960).

2. Generally, research efforts of this kind place the respondent in the position of serving as a retrospective informant on events which occurred some time ago; but in principle at least it is possible to arrange for informants to report on more recent events.

REFERENCES

BIDERMAN, A. D. (1963) March to Calumny. New York: Macmillan.
CHANG, WEN-LUNG (1968) "A study of a Nationalist Chinese air police company: leadership and primary groups." M.A. thesis. Kansas State University.
COATES, C. H. and R. J. PELLEGRIN [eds.] (1965) Military Sociology. University Park, Md.: Social Science Press.
COOLEY, C. H. (1909) Social Organization. New York: Charles Scribner.
DICKS, Lt. Col. H. V. (1952) "Observations on contemporary Russian behavior." Human Relations 5.

———(1944) The Psychological Foundations of the Wehrmacht. London: Directorate of Army Psychiatry, War Office.

———, E. A. SHILS, and H. S. DINERSTEIN (1951) Service Conditions and Morale in the Soviet Armed Forces. Santa Monica, Calif.: RAND Corporation.

DOLLARD, J. (1943) Fear in Battle. New Haven: Institute of Human Relations, Yale University.

DU PICQ, Col. A. (1958) Battle Studies: Ancient and Modern (Col. J. N. Greeley and Maj. R. C. Cotton, translators). Harrisburg, Pa.: Military Service Publishing.

ETZIONI, A. (1961) A Comparative Analysis of Complex Organizations. New York: Free Press.

———(1959-1960) "The Israeli Army: the human factor." Jewish Frontier 26 (November) and 27 (January), two parts.

GEORGE, A. L. (1967) The Chinese Communist Army in Action: The Korean War and Its Aftermath. New York: Columbia University Press.

GINZBERG, E. et al. (1959) The Ineffective Soldier: The Lost Divisions. New York: Columbia University Press.

GRINKER, R. E. and J. P. SPIEGEL (1945) Men Under Stress. Philadelphia: Blakiston.

HOLMES, 2nd Lt. L. M. (1952) "Birth of the fire team." Marine Corps Gazette 36: 17-23.

HOMANS, G. C. (1946) "The small warship." American Sociological Review 11: 294-300.

JANOWITZ, M. [ed.] (1964) The New Military: Changing Patterns of Organization. New York: Russell Sage Foundation.

———and R. LITTLE (1965) Sociology and the Military Establishment. New York: Russell Sage Foundation.

JOFFEE, E. (1965) Party and Army: Professionalism and Political Control in the Chinese Officer Corps, 1949-1964. Cambridge: Harvard East Asian Monograph 19.

KOLKOWICZ, R. (1967) The Soviet Military and the Communist Party. Princeton: Princeton University Press.

LAMMERS, C. J. (1963) The Royal Institute of the Navy: A Sociological Analysis of the Socialization of Candidate Officer Groups in the Royal Netherlands Navy [in Dutch with English summary]. Amsterdam: Van Gorcum.

LANG, K. (1965) "Military organizations," pp. 838-878 in J. G. March (ed.) Handbook of Organizations. Chicago: Rand McNally.

LEIGHTON, A. (1949) Human Relations in a Changing World. New York: Dutton.

LITTLE, R. (1964) "Buddy relations and combat performance," pp. 195-224 in M. Janowitz (ed.) The New Military. New York: Russell Sage Foundation.

MANDELBAUM, D. G. (1952) Soldier Groups and Negro Soldiers. Berkeley: University of California Press.

MARLOWE, D. H. (1959) "The basic training process," pp. 75-98 in K. L. Artiss (ed.) The Symptom as Communication in Schizophrenia. New York: Grune & Stratton.

MARSHALL, S. L. A. (1947) Men Against Fire. New York: William Morrow.

MEYERS, S. M. and A. D. BIDERMAN [eds.] (1968) Mass Behavior in Battle and Captivity: The Communist Soldier in the Korean War. Chicago: University of Chicago Press.

MOSKOS, C. (1968) "Latent ideology and American combat behavior in South Vietnam." Chicago: Center for Social Organization Studies, University of Chicago.

NELSON, P. D. and N. H. BERRY (1968) "Cohesion in Marine recruit platoons." Journal of Psychology 68: 63-71.

PIKE, D. (1966) Viet Cong. Cambridge: MIT Press.

PIPPING, K. (1947) "The social life of a machine gun company." Acta Academiae Aboensis Humaniora 17. [English summary.]

PYE, L. W. (1956) Guerrilla Communism in Malaya. Princeton: Princeton University Press.

ROY, J. (1965) The Battle of Dienbienphu. New York: Harper & Row.

SEATON, R. W. (1964) "Deterioration of military work groups under deprivation stress," pp. 225-249 in M. Janowitz (ed.) The New Military. New York: Russell Sage Foundation.

SHILS, E. A. (1950) "Primary groups in the American Army," pp. 16-39 in R. K. Merton and P. F. Lazarsfeld (eds.) Studies in the Scope and Method of "The American Soldier." New York: Free Press.

———and M. JANOWITZ (1948) "Cohesion and disintegration in the Wehrmacht in World War II." Public Opinion Quarterly 12 (Summer): 280-315.

SPEIER, H. (1950) "The American soldier an; the sociology of military organization," in R. K. Merton and P. F. Lazarsfeld (eds.) Studies in the Scope and Method of "The American Soldier." New York: Free Press.

STOUFFER, S. A. et al. (1949) The American Soldier. 4 vols. Princeton: Princeton University Press.

ZASLOFF, J. J. (1968) Political Motivation of the Viet Cong: the Vietminh Regroupees. Santa Monica, Calif.: RAND Corporation.

Chapter 10

PSYCHIATRIC AND SOCIAL WORK SERVICES

BERNARD J. WIEST and DONALD A. DEVIS

The armed forces of the United States have evolved authoritarian, bureaucratic hierarchies existing within the context of a democratic, individualistic, humanitarian society. Since World War 1 for military psychiatry and since World War II for military social work, the armed forces have had both these human professional services as integral parts of the military organization, thereby successfully joining the seemingly contradictory ethics of the military with those of the larger society.

On the one hand, this arrangement was acceptable to the military, first because these professionals were made part of the ongoing military system, with rank and uniform—thereby making them hardly distinguishable from the rest of the traditional military organization. Second, the armed forces experienced rather severe losses of manpower due to mental illness at the entry level as well as at the organization level; these professional services were regarded as important elements in the conservation of manpower. As a further return to the military for its broadening welfare outlook, both psychiatric and social work services were personnel benefits of importance to the military careerist.

On the other hand, psychiatry and social work were confident enough in their identity to accept the conditions of the military organization. The psychiatrist found the military tolerable, if not acceptable, because of the precedence his medical brother had established in the long tradition of military medicine, the extra pay for being a doctor, and finally, the somewhat good probability of assignment within a traditional medical setting, such as a large military hospital. Mental illness evoked the traditional medical behavior in the military psychiatrists as other diseases and injuries evoked it in other military doctors. Although social attitudes toward mental illness placed it and the specialists connected with it in a special category of the social stratum, a good deal of the psychiatrist's formal and informal professional behavior was nondistinguishable from the normative behavior of other medical practitioners. The social worker's orientation was different from the psychiatrist's and the institutional acceptance and acclimation of social work was much more difficult in some respects. The professional, humanitarian ethic of social work first evoked in the military is best described by Maas (1951: 9):

> The military psychiatric social worker's dynamic formulation was: an individual who found himself having difficulty in carrying out his Army responsibilities was a person out of tune with his environment and, therefore, revealed increasing tension, dissatisfaction, and nonproductivity. To effect change in such a picture, it was necessary to bring the soldier into harmony with his military surrounding.

Modern military social work is not as categorical about social environment as one might be led to believe from the last sentence quoted above. Today, social service confines itself not just to stimulating coping skills for the individual soldier, but includes the soldier's family, group, and community under the operational umbrella of malleable social structure. Furthermore, the social worker was brought into the service under the sponsorship of a higher prestige profession, that of psychiatry, thereby experiencing a professional identity not heretofore existing and for which social work was struggling.

Since the inauguration of these human services during World War II, there has been little expansion of psychiatry and psychology in the military. In fact, recruitment to their ranks has been a chronic and sometimes quite severe problem since World War II and its immediate aftermath. In contrast, social work has flourished and developed to the point today where it is a considerable professional group in numbers, organization, hierarchical decision-making participation, and spread of service.

The institutionalization of psychiatric and social service in the military is the essence of this chapter. The manpower requirements of the military demanded heroic use of human resources; society-at-large demanded this conservation of individuals in a humanistic manner. The medical tradition as embodied by psychiatry as well as the residuals of social Darwinism demanded the individualistic mode of human services. But the special demands of the military made problems for the traditional dyadic medical model and led psychiatry to change its perspective, a prelude to the present day community mental health movement. Social work did not have the problems of psychiatry or psychology since it was based, however loosely and vaguely, on an environmental model and provided a most logical bridging service for psychiatry. Professional psychology ran into problems early for several reasons, primarily because of the cultural derivatives of academia: it had a power fight with psychiatry about freedom of activity and judgment; it had a normative conflict with the military in general about military-like behavior; it had a professional struggle about the relative rewards, including those of professional freedom and compensation, of the military versus civilian conditions.

Although this chapter is not a comparison of the various military services with each other, the developments of psychiatric and social services of the three major services—the Army, the Navy, and the Air Force—were and are different. Although the topic is that of the military forces, the basis of most of the material is the Army experience. The Army, particularly in the tradition of the infantry, in contrast to the Navy and Air Force, has been interested in human behavior. The Navy and Air Force seemed more interested in the mystique of their powerful machines and even perhaps avoided some of the Army's personnel problems because of human attraction and fascination with these machines. The Navy particularly was rather conservative about its personnel and personnel policies in comparison with the other services which began early using such items as psychological tests, thereby opening up the standards and systems to an outside profession.

Second, the Air Force was not a separate entity until 1947. Before that time, it was the Army Air Corps, and, therefore, medical care including that of psychiatric and social services was Army medical care. This remained so for several years after 1947 until the Air Force built and staffed some of its own facilities. Today, the federal departments—the Army, Navy, Air Force, Coast Guard, Public Health Service, and others—reciprocate their medical services. It is true that there are still meccas of medical care such as the Army Walter Reed Medical Center, the Navy Medical Center at Bethesda, and the Air Force Center at Maxwell Air Force Base. Nonetheless, a distinct trend has begun that obscures the distinctions of specific service-based medical care.

Several basic assumptions were used to organize much of the material presented in this chapter. The first of these was that the intrinsic professional role development of psychiatry and social work had progressed to the point where both professionals were confident enough to call themselves psychiatrists and social workers in the military. Second, as American society defined mental problems, these mental problems became serious manpower contingencies for the military commander and a solution was required in order to maintain a viable organization. Third, the state of knowledge about mental health and mental ill-health, and the services and treatments pertinent to them, progressed to the point of practicality for the military. Fourth, the military changed in viewing its resources only in terms of its primary mission—defending the country—and gradually developed a broader welfare outlook for its constituency.

THE DEVELOPMENT OF
COMBAT PSYCHIATRY

The first evidence of psychiatry as an agent of change in the military service is found in World War I. At that time, a discernible "awareness of mental disorder as a military medical problem" emerged and "medical officers of various countries noted an excessive prevalence of mental diseases in military personnel." Prior to that time, "insanity" and "nostalgia" were, of course, recognized and labeled by the military physicians of that day. Civil War medical records reported 2,410 cases of the former and 5,213 cases of the latter, but there was little effort to understand and treat these syndromes in the modern sense of psychiatric or social casework. Moreover, there was no effort to analyze them as derivatives of the limitations of the military service as a social system or to relate such disorders to concepts of individual or group behavior under stress (Glass, 1966: 3).

The special relief agent of the U.S. Sanitary Commission of Civil War days constitutes the analogue of modern military social service. That part of today's social work formula consisting of welfare needs and tangible services existed during the Civil War, but the professional equipment of the modern social worker did not (Torgerson, 1956). There was precious little psychiatry applied prior to World

War I and certainly nothing of social psychiatry or psychiatric social work.

During World War I, however, embryonic concepts of personality development and psychological stress led civil and military medical authorities to experiment with predictive and preventive measures through psychiatric screening of recruits. The impetus for this effort came not only from the growing state of knowledge about the etiology of mental disorders but also from the organization of the bearers of such knowledge into the National Committee for Mental Hygiene (NCMH). This vigorous new organization was dedicated to developing and improving both the prevention and treatment of mental illness. Under the leadership of its Medical Director, Dr. Thomas W. Salmon, NCMH strongly influenced the Army surgeon general to begin planning for the management of psychiatric disorders as early as 1915 (Glass, 1966: 6). This convergence of expressed professional confidence, of new knowledge of behavior and deviance, and of organizational structure, at a point in time, served as a model for subsequent efforts to analyze and manage mental illness in the military service. The simpler dichotomy of organism and environment was no longer an adequate perception of a person and his situation. Behavior had to be viewed as "a complicated cross-organization of body, self, and social environment" (Stainbrook, 1965: 217).

On the practical side, this meant the incorporation of psychiatrists, like Dr. Salmon, into the military medical system and the request to the American Red Cross (ARC) in 1918 to provide psychiatric social workers to aid in the diagnosis, treatment, and aftercare of soldiers with "functional neuroses" (O'Keefe, 1966: 605). The ARC clearly demonstrated the need for social workers at Camp Plattsburg, New York. The Plattsburg experience led to the assignment of Red Cross psychiatric and medical social workers to the large military hospitals and provided an important antecedent to the establishment of military social work in World War II (Starks, 1952).

Dr. Salmon was also detailed as senior consultant in Psychiatry to the surgeon in France where he gave immediate attention to the problem of "shell shock." He had earlier been exposed to the treatment of such casualties by the British and French and had noted significant differences in management and treatment results. The French "hard line" approach featured aggressive demands for continual performance, holding men near the front and administering punishment for failure to respond. The British, on the other hand, evacuated their combat neuroses to psychiatric hospitals in England. While the British approach was certainly considered more humane, the rate of return to duty was quite low and the incidence of chronicity was high in contrast to the French experience. Salmon, therefore, assigned a psychiatrist to each division with duties to

(1) Examine and sort all cases of exhaustion, shell shock or war neuroses in advance posts in order to *control* their evacuation.
(2) Treat light cases at divisional level to preserve greatest number for duty.
(3) Examine prisoners and men suspected of self-inflicting wounds.

This procedure established the basic concepts of combat psychiatry which underpin all modern efforts in the prevention and treatment of war neuroses—whether termed shell shock, combat exhaustion, or neuroses. Its principles are conceptualized by Hausman and Rioch (1967: 729) as "immediacy, proximity, and expectancy." The objective of combat psychiatry is to enable the casualty "to obtain the *concurrence* of the group and to *commit* himself to the group and its task" (Hausman and Rioch, 1967: 734). The efficacy of this approach was documented again in World War II and reached such dramatic success in the Korean conflict that it has become the prototype of social and preventive psychiatry in the United States. It is the conceptual and operational keystone of community psychiatry and crisis intervention.

There was little role for social work in these developments either in the screening of recruits or in the early efforts of combat psychiatry. ARC social services was focused primarily on aiding in the diagnostic process of hospitalized patients, on communicating with families and communities, and on planning and arranging aftercare for men separated from the service—primarily through the Veterans Administration. There were no social workers in uniform, none at least who functioned as medical or psychiatric social workers. It is important to recognize, however, that ARC social workers strongly influenced the military service toward a more humanitarian view of its citizen-soldiers. It was a significant early force along with religion in the form of a uniformed chaplaincy, in pushing military organizations to develop a broader welfare outlook for citizen-soldiers.

TOWARD SOCIAL PSYCHIATRY
AND MENTAL HYGIENE

In the early days of World War II, the behavior of medical authorities and the management of psychiatric problems proceeded as if World War I had never occurred and Dr. Salmon had never existed. Screening at the induction level and rapid evacuation of psychological casualties from the battlefields were the modes of the day and only their blatant failure at an early stage of the war led to new concern and new efforts at prevention and treatment. Menninger has rationalized this inept beginning: "We expected too much from induction center screening and fell in with the overselling of what psychiatry could accomplish at this level. Initially, we were blind to the needs and significance of the methods of preventive psychiatry" (Glass, 1966: 23).

Glass also contrasts the two wars (I and II) in terms of the attitudes of the total population, pointing up the lack of enthusiasm for World War II and the general attitude of pessimism about its pursuit and outcome. Certainly no organization of professionals or others presented the vigorous effective thrust into the military medical thinking as did the NCMH in World War I. The National Research Council formed a committee on neuropsychiatry to aid the surgeon general but while it was constituted in 1940, not one of its major recommendations about training of psychiatrists was acted on until 1944.

Meanwhile, with hardly time allowed to recover from the Great Depression and its proliferation of government offices and agencies, new organizational ties, and a new division between public and private social welfare, the foreboding of World War II considerably influenced professional social work. Social work sought out new areas of service delivery to alleviate the hardships of wartime; it began to formalize its structure more in congruence with the military posture of the nation. In these respects, on the one hand, social workers as employees and as volunteers assisted the Selective Service boards by ferreting out appropriate information on inductees for the boards to make better decisions about particular inductees. On the other hand, the American Association of Psychiatric Social Workers formed a Defense Committee, later reconstituted as the War Service Office (WSO), with Elizabeth N. Ross as its first executive secretary, to help the Army to understand the role and functions of psychiatric social workers. Further, the WSO had previously made important connections with the NCMH, the ARC, and professional social work associations—e.g., the American Association of Social Workers and the National Association of School Social Workers—and, therefore, served as an effective interlocking instrument for social work (Maas, 1951: 176).

Nonetheless, the strong influence of psychoanalysis on psychiatry and social work served to operate against a social psychiatric or preventive approach to combat breakdown. Psychiatric casualties were diagnosed as combat or traumatic war neuroses which at once invited the application of analytically oriented treatment intervention. Such treatment was designed to deal with manifest symptoms by assisting with the discharge of anxiety. The psychiatrist under these conditions tended to identify with the needs of the patient and was impelled to promise relief from combat duty (Janowitz and Little, 1965). The end result was the same as that observed by Salmon in the British plan of World War I: many casualties evacuated to rear hospitals, few returns to combat, and chronicity of symptomatology. The remedy ultimately arrived at was the application of the principles of immediacy, proximity, and expectancy, albeit in a new guise as "short term repressive treatment in the total therapeutic atmosphere of the group" (Mora, 1959: 41). The principles of primary groups and military effectiveness spelled out by Janowitz (1959) were recognized and implemented in treatment.

Paralleling this reawakening was the research of the sociologist Stouffer (1949: 101, vol. 2) and others resulting in the publication of *The American Soldier,* which concludes,

> The best single prediction of combat behavior is the simple fact of the institutionalized role; knowing that a man is a soldier rather than a civilian. The soldier role is a vehicle for getting a man into a position in which he has to fight or take the institutionally sanctioned consequences.

Explicit role expectation and performance coupled with group support and cohesion become the meaningful dynamics of adaptation in the war setting rather than the patient role and dyadic therapeutic interaction.

Since psychiatric breakdown is not only a concern of medicine but also of military command, the rapid acceleration of hospital admissions for neuropsychiatric disorders was a source of grave concern. By mid 1943, admissions had peaked at a rate of 67.6 per one thousand mean strength per year with sixty percent of these being made in the continental United States. More than half of the psychiatric diagnoses made in the United States were psychoneuroses and in overseas theaters this category reached seventy percent in 1943 and seventy-five percent in 1944. This situation led to major policy changes both at command level and in the practice of psychiatric intervention and management. Appel (1966: 378) reports "Both the rise and fall (in admission rates) reflected changes in policies and criteria for admitting patients to hospitals and, evidently, were in no way related to changes in actual incidence of neuropsychiatric disorders." The central principle in this policy change was that of conservation and utilization rather than the original reliance on screening and elimination. Men with psychiatric disorders were to be kept in the service if capable of performance at any reasonable level. Discharge was firmly prohibited.

This concept, relating to the utilization of manpower, shifted the entire focus of the psychiatric services in the military organization to a social psychiatry approach, involving mental hygiene services, consultation to command, and preventive psychiatry. It also made possible the significant entry of additional professionals into the programs—namely, psychiatric social workers and clinical psychologists. Their backgrounds, more broadly based in behavioral sciences and the social interaction of individuals and groups, added new dimensions to the understanding of the military establishment as a social system, the assimilation of military roles, and the contributions of primary groups to both military effectiveness and individual performance. They also made possible the development of additional mental health workers: the social work and psychology specialists. These latter were enlisted men whose contributions were not only significant to the military mental hygiene effort but also represent a prototype of "new career" specialists in present day public mental health programs.

Army social work, in contrast to that of the Air Force and Navy, essentially constitutes all of military social work services since social work's professional inception in the U.S. armed forces during World War II. One military social worker served in the Navy and the Coast Guard each during World War II; otherwise services were delivered by the ARC and civilian social workers. The Air Force presently has about forty commissioned officers who provide professional social work services and management in the Air Force hospitals. Today, the Army has about three hundred professionally trained social workers.

Army social work traces its establishment to the time when the ARC was unable to provide social workers for the newly established mental hygiene consultation service in the Army and looked to the

WSO for help (Maas, 1951: 179). The WSO, well aware of several highly motivated but scattered social workers in military service, negotiated with the chief of neuropsychiatry for the official recognition, classification, and use of these dispersed military psychiatric social workers. Likewise, the WSO contributed importantly to the newly formed Women's Army Corps, recognizing social work as a legitimate role for its personnel. Ironically, the WSO held a very special position concerning social workers vis-à-vis the military. The WSO was a communications center linking social workers in the Army with the Neuropsychiatry Consultant, Army Surgeon General's Office, two elements of the same organization who had trouble talking with each other.

SOCIAL SERVICE IS FORMALLY INSTITUTIONALIZED

In February 1942, six enlisted professional social workers were brought together by a psychiatrist at Ft. Monmouth, New Jersey, and thereby constituted the first social service of any dimension in the Army (Starks, 1952: 6). Although the immediate demand for social work was history-taking for purposes of psychiatric diagnosis and for immediate service requirements, the professional role soon expanded into other areas of competence, such as individual and group therapy and command contact.

World War II demonstrated the legitimation of social work in the military service. The legitimation also included the establishment of the first Chief, Psychiatric Social Work Branch, in the person of Major Daniel O'Keefe; the branch being incorporated in the Neuropsychiatry Consultant Division, Office of the Surgeon General, Department of the Army. This occurred in 1945.

BASIC ORGANIZATIONAL CHANGE

The introduction of new professionals and new personnel management policies and concepts in training areas ultimately led to the establishment of a Mental Hygiene Consultation Service in 1942. The recognition of the need for such programs arose spontaneously in widely separated training groups and while there was much variance in the operational approaches, there was a common concern about prevention and early intervention. It is significant to note that this was a "grass-roots" movement which flourished in a setting often described as a stifling, bureaucratic organization. By 1943, a coordinating and information exchange was organized at Army level and a year later a staff officer (psychiatrist) was assigned to the Office of the Surgeon General with "primary duty of supervising the 35 mental hygiene consultation services" (Hausman and Rioch, 1967: 732). In their early phases, these units tended to focus on evaluation and classification of personnel but very soon the emphasis shifted to providing psychiatric and social work services aimed at enhancing adaptation of individuals and groups and to consultation with leaders and commanders. Finally, the concepts and operational principles of this effort were articulated into the construct of preventive psychiatry with its concerns with authority, communication, status, and role allocation and integration.

There were two important pieces of social work history that began during World War II and carried over into the peacetime period. The first was the formal designation of social work as a legitimate military occupation. The second was the remarkable number of military social workers used during the war and their total exodus immediately after the war.

As early as 1941, the first efforts were made to classify social workers in the Army through military channels. Fred K. Hoehler, Director of the American Public Welfare Association and a member of the Joint Army and Navy Committee, tried, with the Army Personnel Section, to have social workers classified as student sociologists. In addition, the classifications of psychologists and athletic coaches were written in order to have some relationship to certain areas of social work practice. These early efforts proved fruitless until 1943, the year the Army first recognized, officially, social work as an enlisted-level military occupation and assigned it the Serial Specification number 263. This code number lasted until 1946 when social work was recognized as a profession, received officer status, and was recoded as 3605. Organizationally and formally then, two explicit designations were legitimized that considerably helped with the perpetuation of social work in the military: (1) the designation of military status not only at the enlisted but also at the officer rank level, and (2) the assigning of a military occupational specification number to the professionally trained social worker—3605. Military settings in which there were explicit personnel slots for social workers were general hospitals, station hospitals, training divisions, and disciplinary barracks. The official designation in combat divisions and mental hygiene services was not to come until later in spite of the fact that personnel actually had been assigned to these settings during the war.

As noted above, Major O'Keefe was the first Chief of social work and held that office from July 1945 to February 1946, when he returned to civilian life. The other 770 social workers of World War II also returned to civilian status. Their writings clearly show an enthusiasm about their learning while in the armed forces; yet, imponderably, every one of them left the Army. This was a very critical period in the life cycle of military social service since there was no chief and no Indians; all that remained were the organizational positions. A new chief was not appointed until fourteen months after Daniel O'Keefe had left. During this time, Elizabeth Ross, mentioned earlier, continued to serve as civilian consultant to the Army surgeon general and thus provided a vital link in the military social work program (Maas, 1951: 203), until the appointment of a second Chief, Elwood Camp.

A final note on World War II must recognize the major contributions of this kaleidoscopic period:

(1) The principles of combat psychiatry were reestablished, analyzed, refined, and made available for use in the ensuing Korean conflict.

(2) Social work, social and preventive psychiatry, and mental hygiene consultation were institutionalized in the military services, and led to the addition of new professional occupational roles, these being prototypical for later civilian community developments.

(3) The heavy reliance on screening based on the concept of predisposition to mental disorders was negated and concepts of stress and cumulative strain were developed to permit a fuller range of intervention.

(4) Understanding of group process received remarkable impetus both from a sociological and a therapeutic perspective. The studies of Stouffer, Shils (1950), and other sociologists, and the work of the group therapists, Bion (1961) and others, laid important groundwork for both diagnostic and restitutive efforts as well as for the development of concepts of group dynamics.

EXPANDING PROFESSIONAL ROLES AND SERVICES

The period between World War II and the Korean Conflict epitomized the ambivalence of the nation about both military readiness and mental health intervention. On one hand, there was a spate of professional papers and books on the "lessons of World War

II" all pointing to the need for planning, recruitment, and training and for vigorous exposition of the "promises of the field of prevention" in mental health. On the other hand, the Mental Hygiene Consultation Services (MHCS) and the division psychiatrists were demobilized and austerity became the watchword for all programs of the military including medical and psychiatric services. Thus, by 1950, only two consultation services remained operational in the military forces.

Two important developments during this period proved auspicious for successful management of mental health problems and psychiatric casualties during the Korean Conflict. The first was the continuing expansion of group dynamics and of social and preventive psychiatry. The second was that at least a limited number of combat-experienced psychiatrists were available to provide the timely transmission of the pragmatic approaches learned in World War II. Glass and Peterson provided the early structuring of the psychiatric management of casualties in Korea by immediately establishing psychiatric services in the combat divisions with neuropsychiatric treatment centers close by (Hausman and Rioch, 1967: 732). The impact of these developments is impressively documented in the data on evacuations and separation for psychiatric disorders. At the same time, mental hygiene units were reestablished in the training posts, and preventive programs were given early emphasis in the orientation of both medical and command personnel.

Glass presented persuasively the social context of individual adjustment to combat and other military stresses, and he led in the development of treatment and consultation procedures that pinpointed the interactional base of mental breakdown (Hausman and Rioch, 1967: 732). In the United States, the strongest effort of military psychiatry was made in basic training units where the greatest stress was deemed to exist for the individual soldier. All large bases with training missions soon had Mental Hygiene Services and both the mental health specialist and the command became vigorously involved in the application of preventive and social psychiatric principles. While theoretical constructs were nonexistent or at least rudimentary for modeling and testing, there was much in the way of experimentation and innovation during this period.

In general, three main operational principles seem to have evolved empirically in this effort. *First,* study and assessment of the military unit as an operational system was considered at least equally important to the evaluation of the individual on an intrapsychic and interpersonal level. Units were viewed as extensions of family and community with needs and dynamics which were capable of expression, scapegoating, and labeling and were as likely to be "pathological" as any one of its members. Both social workers (e.g., Little) and sociologists (e.g., Janowitz) influenced the mental hygienists to attend to group and interactional processes as importantly as they attended to individual personality problems. Fortunately, many commanders—at company level especially—were receptive to these community mental health approaches.

Second, group interviewing and group counseling and therapy were heavily relied on for both diagnostic and correctivy efforts. The research and theory of the social psychologists, the psychodrama of Moreno (1946), and the group therapy efforts of psychiatry and related disciplines all made a strong impact on psychiatry and social services in the military setting. An almost measurable ripple could be felt at the publication of *Group Dynamics* (Cartwright and Zander, 1953). Soon thereafter a spate of conference papers reported group work projects in mental hygiene centers, correctional institutions, psychiatric clinics, and within military units, for leaders, problems groups, and personnel advisors (Social Service Consultant, 1955-1956).

At the personnel management level this ultimately led to the use of sensitivity and T-groups in the development of middle managers and personnel executives. While not directly related to psychiatry and social services, this development reflected the pervasive influence of social psychological concepts and the effect of change in the total system which enabled mental health services to flourish and to expand their impact.

Third, the medical model of diagnosis and treatment for emotional disorders (less than psychotic) was modified drastically and Lewinian field theory constructs were used to elucidate the rigidly structured social system of the military services and its manipulable features. The mental hygiene offices were physically moved out of hospitals settings and were set up in barracks and administrative buildings in troop areas. Personnel wore the "uniform of the day," putting aside the whites of the medic and playing down the role of healer with all its mystical, often ·magical, assumptions. "Working in the field" became the method of operation. The military social system and the problems of assimilation of military roles engaged the attention of medical and behavioral science staff as intensely as had personality and physical aberrations of the individual. Intervention, of necessity, became focused on interpersonal and interactional transactions.

Conceptually and operationally, military social work was caught up in the same thrust as was psychiatry because psychiatry was the host profession. Although formally there was no break in the continuity of military level there was an important turnover in personnel. None of the 770 military social workers of World War II, who left the military service, returned. The social workers who entered the military subsequently had been in service during World War II but not as social workers. They were ex-flyers, ex-infantry-men, ex-seamen, and the like, who had left the service, completed civilian graduate professional education, and then reentered the service as professional social workers.

The permanent basis for social services became well-established in World War II. The logic of incorporating the new profession was sound. The results of World War II social work service had been good; psychiatry saw the need for continuance of the collaboration; social work was compatible with the military service of a democratic, humanitarian nation; and the size of the peacetime Army was expected to remain large, and welfare resources would, therefore, be required.

After the demobilization that followed World War II, and soon after the threads of continuity had been reconnected, military social work entered the Korean War period. As the war began, a number of new social workers brought into the program were much concerned with professional role identity and appropriate extensions of the social service program. These two concerns apparently led them to compartmentalize the Korean War, for it had remarkably little impact on the military social workers. The "police action" was looked upon as an incident meaningfully apart in almost every respect. Only one published account of combat social work came out of the war period (Morgan, 1953). One other publication, not having to do with combat social work, came out of Korea written by a military social worker (Little, 1955). The significance of this event was threefold: (1) it was and is the only published participant-observer research of a combat unit in action during the Korean War; (2) the research was published as a doctoral dissertation written by a military social worker; and (3) it was the first of a continuing series of doctoral dissertations completed by military social workers in advanced studies at civilian universities while on active duty.

The Korean War ended in 1953 and serious efforts to expand the social service role in the military began in earnest. In 1952, there were 165 military social workers who were commissioned officers in the U.S. Army. One hundred seven of these were psychiatric social workers and fifty-eight were medical social workers. There were sixty-five civilian social workers working in Army hospitals and there were 260 enlisted social work technicians—a grand total of 490 social workers in direct service or welfare management. Medical social work had become a military occupation the year before in 1951. This occurred at the behest of the ARC, which, because of straitened finances and personnel, asked to withdraw medical casework services from the military; the important communication and home service of the ARC was to remain as it has to this day. Medical social workers were designated MOS 3606; a few years later, in recognition of the generic base of social work and to economize on administration, psychiatric (3605) and medical (3606) were combined and social work became MOS 3606, a fortuitous piece of administration as it served as an important facilitating element in social work's expanding role in the Army.

The later expansion and diversification of the military social service role in the sixties had its early precursors in the fifties. This was particularly true in regard to a broad social welfare perspective. In 1952, Colonel Elwood Camp, the post World War II ex-chief, exhorted the social work officers clearly and precisely to broaden their roles and expand their services.

> Military social workers, through these other disciplines (group work, community organization, public welfare administration, social action, social research), can offer the Army a great deal of service in addition to the casework, patient-worker relationship and that the Army can very profitably utilize these additional services.

> I emphasize that our Army communities need a well-rounded social service program. Our Army communities deserve a well-rounded social service program. But they are going to get such a program only if we, the military social workers, perform as well-rounded social workers [Camp, 1952: 10, 24].

Later, in 1955, the most sweeping social welfare view yet was presented by Elizabeth Wickenden, as representative of the National Committee on Social Work in Defense Mobilization, in her analysis of the social problems concomitant to large-scale and continuing military programs. She pointed out areas requiring closer collaboration between government and military agencies and the social work profession. Although not specifically directed at them, the inferences were clear-cut for military social workers. In hindsight, the conjunction of the national trends of social work in general and the blueprint of wide scope articulated by Wickenden provide essential backdrop to the concerted efforts of military social workers in the sixties to break out of the narrow medical-psychiatric paradigm and to assume a more preventive or public health role.

This change was accelerated when the Army began to subsidize doctoral candidacies. Earlier, mention was made of the first doctorate attained by a military social worker; this was in 1955. Thereafter, until well into the sixties when the number was radically increased, a small but steady stream of officer social workers attended various social work doctorate programs throughout the country. The social work schools at this time were beginning to insist on a "social welfare" outlook rather than just "social work," and experimentation with the social sciences was going on apace. With the infiltration of these orientations by means of the doctorally trained social workers, the military was both increasing the social worker's professional-military status and storing up knowledge for social welfare implementation in the following decade.

BASIC INSTITUTIONAL
CHANGE

Today the military social worker has come full circle from his early days in 1942 and World War II. At that time, the civilians-turned-soldiers were formalized from amorphous bits into a going social service enterprise. Twenty-seven years later the same firmly integrated enterprise returns social work retirees to civilian practice at an increasing rate. Within this time span, several developments in military social service have occurred: social service methodology has increased its repertoire, the soldier-command social services have been intensified; social service consultation has been extended into more of the military structure; exchange with civilian social work has increased considerably; and perhaps more importantly, military social workers have assumed a new role in community and welfare planning. Concurrently, the changing role of the military in the national scheme affects the organization, the practice, and the knowledge requirements of military social workers.

From the early forties to the present, the highlights of the methodological development in the military program are quite clear and understandably similar to developments in civilian practice. At first, the military social work method and practice area was confined to casework in the psychiatric setting. It remained so for the greatest portion of military social work's existence. Casework, with added sophistication, continues to be an important method. There is little doubt that it will remain an institutionalized method primarily because casework, of all the methods, most nearly approaches the essence of individual lives and their primary group connections. The early years of military casework were characterized by an exploration of the professional role with psychiatry and psychology, and be the search for an identity as professional social workers. As knowledge and experience accumulated, extentions of practice were tested, with group work emerging as a major emphasis. Research and administration remained a peripheral interest. Functionally, activity in the area of community organization consisted largely of isolated, piecemeal activities, and managerial social policy issues were left as a future goal.

FAMILY AND COMMAND SYSTEMS: A DIVISION OF LABOR

Meanwhile, another evolutionary development occurred. The command consultative role at the clinical-post level emerged as distinctive, and is now a flourishing feature of military social service. This development stemmed partially from the uneasy constraints of the early caseworker's dyadic patient model and individual psychology. At the same time, the social worker's traditional ties with social history gathering and environmental assessment remained a part of his functions in the military. This led him rather logically and naturally into the military unit-command system. Then with the reinforcement of social science reawakening during and after World War II, the formerly mundane environmental, military facets came alive with new meaning and relevancy, and stimulated an understanding of community forces and primary prevention of social-emotional problems, not only of individual soldiers but also of group and community.

While these changes in operational perspective were taking place, military social workers thrived. Being a stable group in terms of career commitment, there came a gradual increase in rank and cumulative gain in professional and military sophistication. With the higher rank, movement within the military bureaucratic structure became easier, and the professional and military sophistication abetted the marriage of humanitarian values and authoritative situation. Consultative positions were the consequence. The consultative role became positioned both upwardly and laterally throughout the military hierarchy, thus adding another influential element to the growing social service role.

Formerly, research and model-building had not been a notable characteristic of military social workers. There are probably several reasons for this, one of which is the fact that military social workers frequently change jobs. Each new assignment faces him with a cluster of professional and personal pressures different from the last assignment, causing a reorientation and recommitment of personal investment. During the 1960s, there has been a decided increase in the quantity of professional journal and dissertation literature; and the growing public depository of current thinking in military social service has been effectively disseminated by the documentation of the annual military social welfare conference and the biennial short-training course held in Washington, D.C., and Denver. Conceptual and methodological explorations concerning the family and command-unit systems have made appreciable inroads into useful operational referents (Hiatt, 1963; Kisel, 1963; Lanier, 1963; Hill, 1964; Montalvo, 1964). The trends have been an increase in abstraction and generalization in contrast to the specifics of setting and technique; a surge in sociological and social-psychological construct application in contrast to individual, primarily psychoanalytic theory; a new-found vigor in placing the military social worker in a sociological-historical perspective; and an increased readiness to describe innovative research and clinical methodologies. The extent and diversity of the knowledge generates a presently serious need for synthesis and analysis in order that the knowledge becomes of practical use for social service at large.

LARGER SOCIAL SYSTEM
TIES AND INFLUENCES

Professional

As the stable group of military social workers became acculturated to the military system and found that they were able to survive, as the increase in rank and influence was reinforced positively, one is in a position to speculate on a totally different direction that military social services could have taken. Survival in a bureaucracy can also occur by increased use of the bureaucracy to encapsulate professional life style, by becoming ingrown and extremely parochial, by closing the system onto oneself, by creating a segmented, alienated minority system with little, if any, communication with other and larger systems. This did not happen to military social work. Early in its life, interchange with social work civilian counterparts was structured by the establishment of the now traditional annual military social service conference held in conjunction with the National Social Welfare Conference. This traditional meeting was later extended by the military group becoming formal members of the national association and by means of individual members actively participating in the National Welfare Conference. Another reason for the openness of the military social service system is the fact that recruitment input is and has been civilians from schools of social work. A further reason from the mid-fifties is the number of military social workers who entered doctoral training programs. In the mid-sixties, the number increased from about three to five a year to about twelve or thirteen. In 1965, of 155 professionally qualified social workers, twenty-two had doctoral training in various universities throughout the country—a proportion considerably higher than the present ratio nationally of doctoral versus masters degrees held by professional social workers in general. An additional civilian-professional link, lately coming into prominence, is the reorientation of senior military social workers toward a civilian professional career as their retirement from the services approaches. Thus, as the senior members fill teaching, supervisory, managerial, and clinical assignments in the civilian establishment, military social services is provided another important linkage with civilian social work. These professional and interpersonal ties with the profession have been and are significant in keeping military social service current and relevant. As of this writing, there are three retired military social workers who are deans of schools of social work, two who are assistant deans, and the majority of retirees occupy faculty positions in universities throughout the country.

Military

The military social system has also influenced changes in welfare services. From a demographic viewpoint, there is a radical change in the composition of the military population since World War II. For example, prior to World War II, single men constituted seventy to seventy-five percent of the military. Today, eighty-two percent of all officers and forty-seven percent of all enlisted men are married. There are about four million dependents of active duty servicemen. However, the demography of the military has substantially stabilized over the past few years. In fact, it has not changed significantly since the early fifties with an exception of the black-white ratio in overall number and in number of careerists. Another exception has been the sharp increase in the educational level of military personnel. This has been most striking in the enlisted men group where the percentage has gone from fifty percent high school graduates during the Korean War to seventy-five percent at present.

In November 1964, General Harold K. Johnson, the Chief of Staff, U.S. Army, published a policy statement in *Army* magazine. In writing about the change in the Army's mission in support of the nation's domestic and foreign policy, he said that never again can our Army regard itself as a double purpose tool of national military power, its weapons and doctrines being designed for use in nuclear and conventional warfare. Rather, our Army must continue to orient its creative energies and resources toward a multipurpose concept so that stability operations as well as other types of wartime land-power operations, are regarded as normal missions. He entitled this policy as "Land Power Missions Unlimited." He referred to the facts that American soldiers serve in ninety countries, that about forty percent of U.S. personnel are overseas, and that eight of sixteen combat divisions are in foreign lands (Johnson, 1964: 42). It has been reported by the *Army Times* (1965: 1) that a career soldier can expect to spend fifty percent of his career overseas, with or without his family.

Although the population remains roughly the same, demographically, the military ethos reflecting the national culture has developed new intricacies in the traditional structural-functional model of the military establishment. The reapportionment of labor within and between the armed forces, and the military's accommodation of the diffusion of its historical role in order to meet the demand of the nation's changing domestic and foreign policy, impose strains upon the organization that touch poignantly on individual lives, families, and special groups within the military. Furthermore, as the military community molds increasingly with the artifacts and life style of civilian society, both here and abroad, the health and welfare problems of the military assume an order of complexity comprising problems idiosyncratic to the military and our national and international state of social being.

The reverberations of these changes in the broader framework of the military and the nation are experienced by military social service at the clinical level as searing problems of soldiers, their families, and their communities. At the command-consultation level they are felt as urgent requirements for reorganization and increase of community welfare resources, and for bureaucratic decision-making facilitation.

What this has meant to military social service is indicated by three recent developments. It was pointed out earlier that the movement of military social workers into the command-unit system led to the emergence of the consultative role at the clinical-post level. This eventually evolved into what is now a pervasive military agency, the MHCS. In the attempt to service a broad spectrum of military community problems, dissatisfaction led to a reconsideration of the Consultation Service model and to a bifurcation of the agency function.

NEW COMMUNITY MODEL

The new consideration of the MHCS model eventuated in a concerted community organization method with emphasis upon primary prevention, and based upon organizational systems and managerial concepts for the delineation of programs at various levels in the soldier-command system. The new model permits the Consultation Service to approach the various organizational strata of social interrelationships, managerially and differentially. Simultaneously, it is a mental health *education* service, a case consultation approach, and a program consultation resource (Hiatt, 1963; Kisel, 1963; Lanier, 1963). It is a public change vehicle, a social system-individual intervention device, and a convergence of resource development and decision-making. This restructuring is a parallel to the civilianizing influences analyzed by Janowitz. This is particularly true as military social services accommodate the managerial leadership influx in the military and the growing technological complexities of the armed forces. The model allows military social service to develop a meaningful analysis and differential approach to variations within the military—from post to post, from highly technological units to traditional combat units, from straightforward combat missions to remote support role, from military interchange with civilian community to military interchange with foreign cultures.

NONMEDICAL STRUCTURE
VENTURE

The bifurcation mentioned above more specifically refers to the splitting off of the family-community system of the former MHCS. Prior to this reinstitutionalizing, family welfare care was piecemeal, fragmented, and bewildering to families in need. This basic social service restructuring is called the Army Community Service (ACS) and is a community organization and welfare planning method designed to meet the spectrum of social welfare needs in a military community. Institutionally, it places the decision-making at higher echelons of command, it acts as a catalyst for welfare information, and it formalizes a command-community sensitivity in the direction of current social problems and military tasks. Thus, the model of ACS is similar to that of the MHCS, the main difference being that ACS stands in a different direction to the military community than the MHCS does, to the family rather than to the soldier.

The ACS centers are designed to assist families on an emergency basis in catastrophies. Housing, civilian, and military health and welfare resources, youth employment, community orientation for the newly arrived, and assistance in establishing social-legal ties in the community are other aspects of the program. A spectrum of humanitarian and mental health approaches are structured to meet the human needs of a highly technical, highly mobile, multimission military population in a cultural transition crisis. The ACS center is a reinstitutionalization of military social services under new auspices providing for a broad range of welfare problems, explicated several years before by Elizabeth Wickenden (1955).

SOCIAL WELFARE
DECISION-MAKING

Until recently, military social services have not been actively involved in shaping social welfare as such. Instead, the process of becoming institutionalized, of finding professional identity, of developing a consultative role, and of exploring problems of clinical practice, absorbed most of its energies. It is only within the last six years that the military social worker has become involved in social welfare policy at a level to affect choices between alternatives and to affect the set of choices that are recognized and acknowledged (Bobrow, 1965: 66). It is not that this has not been in social work's cognizance for some time. References were made above to the exhortations of Colonel Camp in 1952 and of Elizabeth Wickenden in 1955 about moving out from the strictly clinical role. Others added their voices. In 1961, Colonel Morgan in his historical analysis of military social work points out the structural problems that inhibited social workers from expanding their operations into nonmedical areas (Morgan, 1961: 27). In 1962 General Westmoreland, while addressing a group of military surgeons, suggested that the servicing professions of the Army become involved with the personnel staff in the development of overall policies pertaining to mental health (Westmoreland, 1963: 212). Both in 1960 and in 1962, Colonel Torgerson, then the surgeon general's consultant in Social Services, encouraged military social workers to assume responsibility for the broader welfare needs of the military population (Torgerson, 1960: 5; 1962: 8).

Since 1965, military social work has had a substantial investment in the social welfare area. In 1965, a military social worker was assigned full-time, and then later part-time, in the Economic Opportunity Program in Washington, D.C. Officers are presently assigned at the Department of Army level to the Office of the Surgeon not only as social service consultants but also in the Directives and Policies and the PS & O Officers, the Medical Service Corps, and the Warrant Officer Career Planning Office. In the Army's Deputy Chief of Staff for Personnel Office, there is an officer responsible for the Army-wide ACS program and there is also an officer who has responsibilities in the Personnel Research Division. At the continental Army level, a social work officer is assigned to the Personnel Services Division. These are indicative of the social service impact on the military and its widening welfare outlook.

Thus, military social service is now giving back to the civilian profession the returns on its original investment of knowledge, skill, and experience during World War II. Military social service has also been reinstitutionalized in the military establishment, a change equal in magnitude to the original institutionalization during World War II. Social services in the military are in the same thrust as the nation in terms of its concern for the poor and minority groups. Perhaps it is this larger societal motivation that has helped carry military social service to its peak today. This is in contrast to military psychiatry and psychology which, with the exception of some forays into community mental health and ACS, have remained essentially the same in overall military structure and service since shortly after World War II.

REFERENCES

APPEL, J. W. (1966) "Preventive psychiatry," pp. 373-415 in Neuropsychiatry in World War II. Office of the Surgeon General, Department of the Army.

Army Times (1965) 25, 36 (April 21).

BION, W. R. (1961) Experiences in Groups. London: Tavistock.

BOBROW, D. B. (1965) "Soldiers and thy nation-state." Annals of the American Academy of Political and Social Service 358 (March).

CAMP, E. W. (1952) "A social work program," Symposium on Military Social Work. Washington, D.C.: Social Service Branch, Office of the Surgeon General, Department of the Army.

CARTWRIGHT, D. and A. ZANDER [eds.] (1953) Group Dynamics. Chicago: Row, Peterson.

GINZBERG, E., J. K. ANDERSON, S. GINZBERG, and J. L. HERMA (1959) The Ineffective Soldier: The Lost Divisions. New York: Columbia University Press.

GLASS, A. J. (1966) "Army psychiatry before World War II," pp. 3-23 in Neuropsychiatry in World War II. Office of the Surgeon General, Department of the Army.

———K. L. ARTISS, J. J. GIBBS, and V. C. SWEENEY (1961) "The current status of Army psychiatry." American Journal of Psychiatry 117 (February): 673-683.

GRINKER, R. and J. SPIEGEL (1945) Men Under Stress. Philadelphia: Blakiston.

Group for the Advancement of Psychiatry (1967) Clinical Psychiatry. New York: Science House.

———(1960) Preventive Psychiatry in the Armed Forces: With Some Implications for Civilian Use, Report 47. New York: Science House.

HAUSMAN, W. and D. M. RIOCH (1967) "Military psychiatry." Archives of General Psychiatry 16: 727-739.

HIATT, R. S. (1963) "Consultant or staff officer: a critical analysis of a mental hygiene consultation service innovation." Proceedings, Thirteenth Annual Army Social Work Conference (mimeo). Office of the Surgeon General, Department of the Army, May.

HILL, W. G. (1964) "An examination of two approaches for analyzing family group interaction." Proceedings, Fourteenth Annual Military Social Work Conference. Office of the Surgeon General, Department of the Army, May.

JANOWITZ, M. (1960) The Professional Soldier: A Social and Political Portrait. New York: Free Press.

———and R. W. LITTLE (1965) Sociology and the Military Establishment. New York: Russell Sage Foundation.

JOHNSON, Gen. H. K. (1964) "Landpower missions unlimited." Army 15 (November).

KARDINER, A. (1941) The Traumatic War Neuroses. Cambridge, Mass.: Paul B. Hoeber.

KISEL, J. G. (1963) "A conceptual framework for case consultation in the military systems." Proceedings, Thirteenth Annual Army Social Work Conference (mimeo). Office of the Surgeon General, Department of the Army.

LANIER, D., Jr. (1963) "Mental health education at an Army basic training center—concepts of an operation model." Proceedings, Thirteenth Annual Army Social Work Conference (mimeo). Office of the Surgeon General, Department of the Army.

LEWIS, N. and B. ENGLE (1954) Wartime Psychiatry. New York: Oxford University Press.

LITTLE, R. W. (1955) "A study of the relationship between collective solidarity and combat role performance." Ph.D. dissertation. Michigan State University.

MAAS, H. [ed.] (1951) Adventure in Mental Health. New York: Columbia University Press.

MARSHALL, S. L. A. (1947) Men Against Fire. New York: William Morrow.

MENNINGER, W. C. (1948) Psychiatry in a Troubled World. New York: Macmillan.

MILLER, E. (1942) The Neuroses in War. New York: Macmillan.

MIRA, E. (1943) Psychiatry in War. New York: W. W. Norton.

MONTALVO, F. F. (1964) "Homeostasis in functional and dysfunctional family systems." Proceedings, Fourteenth Annual Military Social Work Conference. Office of the Surgeon General, Department of the Army, May.

MORA, G. (1959) "Recent American psychiatric developments," pp. 18-57 in S. Arieti (ed.) American Handbook of Psychiatry. New York: Basic Books.

MORENO, J. L. (1946) Psychodrama. New York: Beacon House.

MORGAN, R. (1961) "Clinical social work in the U.S. Army, 1947-1959." Ph.D. dissertation. Washington, D.C.: Catholic University of America.

———(1953) "Psychiatric social work in a combat area." U.S. Armed Forces Medical Journal 4 (June): 847-856.

O'KEEFE, D. E. (1966) "Psychiatric social work," pp. 605-630 in Neuropsychiatry in World War II. Office of the Surgeon General, Department of the Army.

SHELLASE, L. (n.d.) "Bibliography of social work," in The First Twenty Years, 1942-1962. Office of the Surgeon General, Department of the Army.

SHILS, E. A. (1950) "The contribution of the American soldier to the study of primary groups," in R. Merton and P. F. Lazarsfeld (eds.) Studies in the Scope and Method of the American Soldier. New York: Free Press.

———and M. JANOWITZ (1948) "Cohesion and disintegration in the Wehrmacht in World War II." Public Opinion Quarterly 12 (Summer): 280-315.

SLADEN, F. S. [ed.] (1943) Psychiatry and the War. Springfield, Ill.: Charles C. Thomas.

Social Work Consultant (195-1960) Proceedings, Annual Military Social Work Conference. Department of the Army.

STAINBROOK, E. (1965) "Society and individual behavior," in Handbook of Clinical Psychology. New York: McGraw-Hill.

STARKS, L. E. (1952) "Development of the social service program," in Symposium on Military Social Work (mimeo). Social Services Branch, Office of the Surgeon General, Department of the Army, May.

STOUFFER, S. A. et al. (1949) The American Soldier. 4 vols. Princeton: Princeton University Press.

TORGERSON, F. G. (1962) "Annual report of the social service consultant." Proceedings, Twenty Years of Army Social Work (mimeo). Office of the Surgeon General, Department of the Army.

———(1960) Collected Papers from a Short Course on Current Trends in Army Social Work (mimeo). Washington, D.C.: Walter Reed Army Medical Center.

———(1956) "A historical study of the beginnings of individualized social services in the United States Army." Ph.D. dissertation. School of Social Work, University of Minnesota.

WESTMORELAND, Maj. Gen. W. C. (1963) "Mental health—an aspect of command." Military Medicine 128 (March).

WICKENDEN, E. (195) Military Defense and Social Welfare. New York: National Association of Social Workers.

Chapter 11

TROOP INFORMATION AND INDOCTRINATION

AMOS A. JORDAN, JR.

As a military organization becomes larger, more complex, and more highly differentiated, its usual sources of cohesion and control, such as authority, hierarchy, and normal internal communications, may need buttressing. "Troop information," the generic term for the orientation and indoctrination activities carried on within armed forces for the members of those forces, can be an important indirect means of such buttressing (Janowitz and Little, 1965).

Troop information has been a feature of American military life since the start of the Revolution. This tradition may have had its roots in the Continental Army's necessity to assimilate and impart a common purpose to soldiers of diverse origins, or it may simply have been that the typical independent Yankee farmer would not follow orders just because they were issued by someone ostensibly in authority. Baron Von Steuben, the Prussian drill master and tactician who trained the Americans at Valley Forge, focused on this latter explanation in a letter to a fellow European: "The genius of this nation is not in the least to be compared with that of the Prussians, Austrians or French. You say to your soldier, 'do this' and he doeth it; but I am obliged to say: 'This is the reason you ought to do that,' and he doeth it" (Palmer, 1937).

George Washington was alert to this characteristic of his countrymen. In July 1776, in the first instance of what would today be called a "command information directive," he ordered that the several brigades be assembled and the Declaration of Independence be read to them "in an audible voice. . . . The General hopes this important Event will serve as a fresh incentive to every officer, and soldier, to act with Fidelity and Courage, as knowing that now the peace and safety of his country depends (under God) solely on the success of our arms" (Washington, 1776). Similarly, Washington had Thomas Paine's pamphlet, *Crisis,* read to the Continental Army, squad by squad, before it crossed the Delaware to attack the Hessian forces at Trenton.

During the Civil War, less attention was paid to troop information and indoctrination, but various individual commanders stressed this approach to motivation. Brigadier General August Willish, Commander of the Indiana Regiment, believed that "men who see clearly why they are fighting will be the bravest soldiers" (U.S. President's Committee, 1949). He conducted a program or orientation lectures and discussions for his troops on the background and causes of the war. Unionwide, various pamphlets on the war (some 900,000 in all) were distributed to the troops, but there was no systematic effort to reach the rank and file throughout the Army. A Washington newspaper of the era decried the lack of a "regular system of public speaking in the Army to lift the morale of the soldier by teaching them why they were fighting."

Again, in World War I, troop orientation efforts were largely left to individual commanders. News was relatively plentiful; *Stars and Stripes,* which had started as a private publication during the Civil War, became a widely available official publication. Various civilian groups, such as the YMCA, banded together as the "Commission on Training Camp Activities," functioning in part as an unofficial information and education organization.

It was only during World War II, and immediately preceding it, that the American armed forces turned again to the Continental Army's stress on information. In 1940 the Army established a "Morale Branch" to stimulate orientation efforts. In 1941, to counter the strong sentiment against continued service by the conscripts who had been called up in 1940 and who were fearful that their term of active service would be extended as the war clouds gathered in Europe, General Marshall directed the Army's Bureau of Public Relations to prepare a course of lectures to orient soldiers about the perilous state of the world and the necessity for their service. The fifteen lectures, which were published as *The Background of our War,* and which were the basis for the "Why We Fight" films, traced developments from Munich and Mukden down to 1941;

they were supplemented by a program of day-to-day discussions of current developments by company commanders with their men, and by distribution of maps, pamphlets, and other materials to camp libraries and day rooms (U.S. War Department, 1942).

Despite being shuttled back and forth in the Army's organizational structure, and changing its name several times in the process (finally becoming the "Information and Education Division"), the Morale Branch managed a large and ambitious orientation program throughout the war. (The Information and Education Division also sponsored major studies, published after the war, such as *The American Soldier* by Stouffer et al., (1949); these were the first systematic attempts by an armed force to learn what soldiers thought about a war and the Army; these surveys continue to have their counterparts in the services today.) From the "Why We Fight" movies, from weekly *Army Talk* pamphlets, through the Armed Forces Radio Service, *Stars and Stripes,* and hundreds of camp and unit newspapers, the American soldier received an unprecedented flow of information. The programs of the Navy and Marines were less ambitious but also significant; those services as well as the Army Air Corps, used a large part of the Army-produced materials.

For a period after the war, the troop information program maintained the status it achieved during hostilities, the creation of the Air Force as a separate service in 1947 affecting the program in name only. However, during this early postwar period, more emphasis was placed on improving soldiers' educational levels than on informing them, using "inform" in the by-then traditional sense of the term. The Army supported the Army-Air Force Information and Education Program with regulations and materials and continued to require weekly Army Information Hours, while the Air Force, Navy, and Marines required participation in orientation activities on a less regular, often voluntary basis. Even where similar policies were determined by the three departmental secretaries, implementation varied widely from service to service; the total system was something less than unified (Bowles, 1956).

In 1949, the Secretary of Defense directed unification of all information activities; the functions of the Army-Air Force Information and Education (I & E) Division were transferred to his office, placed directly under the Chairman of the Secretary of Defense's Personnel Policy Board, and renamed the Armed Forces Information and Education Division (AFIE). In practice, this meant that DOD took over direction of the radio and news services and assumed the task of producing a major part of the films, pamphlets, and other information materials; the services retained responsibility for conducting the program, supporting it as necessary by their own materials. From 1949 to 1961, AFIE functioned solely as a "service and support" agency for the services, producing some fifty to sixty pamphlets and fifteen to twenty movies per year for them, the latter largely on topics in the general areas of democracy versus communism and area orientation.

In 1961 trouble signs appeared as troop information became embroiled in domestic politics. The Cold War's recurring crises in the 1950s, added to concern over the behavior of a few American prisoners of war during the Korean Conflict, had created a climate in which some political leaders were hunting for domestic culprits sabotaging American defense efforts, while others were berating America's defense leaders for trying to propagandize the public with their version of the communist menace (C. Phillips, 1961). In the midst of this furor Major General Edwin Walker, USA, burst into public view with such an overly zealous troop information program that the Army relieved him of command on charges of "controversial activities . . . contrary to long standing customs of the military service and beyond the prerogatives of a senior military commander" (Pentagon News Release, 1961).

The Walker incident precipitated a decision by the Secretary of Defense to strengthen DOD participation and supervision in the troop information field. The Directorate for Armed Forces Information and Education (formerly AFIE) was charged with developing a long-range information program and supporting materials for all the services in the areas of democracy and communism, world affairs, forces for freedom (U.S. and friendly forces), citizenship (including voting), orientation for overseas duty, and code of conduct. It was also directed to review, assess, and evaluate the effectiveness of the services' internal information programs and materials in the areas cited and to play a more active role in providing policy guidance and supervision in the press service, radio, and television fields (U.S. Department of Defense, 1961).

To make doubly sure that the sensitive subject of indoctrination was being properly handled throughout the armed forces the Secretary of Defense appointed a prestigious advisory committee in early 1962 to recommend "appropriate objectives and goals of this type of instruction, the appropriate subjects to be included, the practical mechanics and criteria for measuring its effectiveness and, finally, the changes, if any, which should be made in present assignments of responsibility within the Department of Defense" (U.S. Advisory Committee, 1962a). Despite the advisory committee's useful report, little change was made in the guidelines and allocations of responsibilities already made in 1961. And despite the services' concerns that they might lose control of DOD over this important aspect of training, the changes instituted in 1961 did not significantly centralize responsibilities. Through mid-1968, DOD continued to use sparingly its authority to provide guidance on the utilization of information and materials, the services continued to lean heavily upon DOD for the production of materials while also producing their own, and the individual services continued to adapt information activities to their own patterns of organization and training.

THE PURPOSES OF
TROOP INFORMATION (TI)

Despite this extended history of information activities and their institutionalization within the services and the Department of Defense, there has been less than full understanding among those concerned about the purposes such activities should serve.[1]

At a minimum, all would probably agree that the officers who take an oath "to support and defend the Constitution of the United States against all enemies, foreign and domestic," and the enlisted men who swear "true faith and allegiance to the United States" should be informed about the meanings of these oaths. But beyond some understanding of the Constitution, possible threats to the United States, and the meaning of "true faith and allegiance," what should the military man know and why?

During World War II, the mission of the Information and Education Division was defined as "assisting commanders in maintaining a high state of morale." The general objective was amplified to include acquainting soldiers with the causes of the war and the principles at stake, informing them about the progress of the war and the nature of the enemy, and fixing in their minds a sense of their "personal roles and responsibilities in the current struggle" (U.S. War Department, 1944). This series of objectives—comprehending "why we fight"—remained in effect throughout the war and provided the pattern for all subsequent orientation goals.

The dimensions of the information task have, of course, changed since World War II. For one thing, it appears easier to tell soldiers "why we fight" in wartime, than to explain "why we serve" in peacetime or during cold war. "When men are in combat the issues are usually much more clearly drawn than in time of peace. Simple survival is often an effective motivation for fighting. In peacetime, international relations and national issues become clouded and extremely difficult to evaluate" (U.S. President's Committee, 1949).

We might logically have expected that the difficulties of explaining "why" to the troops during the Korean Conflict and the Cold War of the 1950s, which had led in part to the Walker incident and the other problems cited, would have been intensified by the ambiguous character of the war in Vietnam during the latter 1960s. Yet there were few troop morale difficulties in spite of the national trauma over the United States' role in that conflict. This fact might be taken either as a testament to the effectiveness of service information programs, or contrarily, as an indicator that, by and large, soldiers are not as responsive to political issues and motivations as is commonly supposed. There is reason to believe that both explanations are partly correct. The services have been very thorough in keeping their men informed, and the troops have focused their attention on the military tasks at hand, fighting because they are there (Moskos, 1967).

Apart from improving the morale of the soldiers by increasing their information levels, what other purposes have been adduced for the information program? It has sometimes been argued that the armed forces have an obligation to the citizen-soldiers in their charge to see that they have as much information as would be available to them in civilian life. Theoretically, this "right" to be informed could be met simply by provision of newspapers and radio and television broadcasting and without the other activities associated with an orientation or information program. But there is considerable evidence to show that news is not enough, that the serviceman's morale is improved by formal orientation. Soldiers in the second world war felt "better" about the Army if they believed it was trying to keep them informed. Lectures and discussion sections were found to improve soldiers' attitudes by giving them both a means to express their views and a sense that the Army recognized their status as individuals, not as mere serial numbers (Stouffer et al., 1949).

More ambitiously, it can be argued that the information program should have as a major purpose the objective of developing "personnel who have a full understanding of the responsibilities of citizens in a democracy and who will assume those responsibilities after they leave the service" (Eurich, 1952). After examining this purpose, the Fund for the Advancement of Education (which undertook analyzing the information programs of the armed forces for Assistant Secretary of Defense Anna Rosenburg) concluded that it was "demonstrably unattainable" (Eurich, 1952).

Finally, it has been argued that troop information should be used to improve the services' public image. The Army, for example, has concluded from various opinion research studies which it has commissioned that the public's view of it stems in considerable part from its own members' views—which in turn are related to how well the Army has explained to its men the purpose of their service. The stream of letters and visits home by the serviceman, and the views of the ex-serviceman when he rejoins civil life, apparently create the basic public image of the service (U.S. Department of the Army, 1967b).

WHAT KIND AND HOW
MUCH INFORMATION IS NEEDED?

Although the chestnut that "the *informed* soldier is a good soldier" is widely accepted, its scientific basis is somewhat shaky. On the other hand, there is little doubt that a *committed* soldier is a good soldier. Stouffer and his colleagues confirmed scientifically in World War II what every troop commander has learned from experience: "Men with stronger convictions about the war not only tended to have a stronger sense than others of personal commitment, but also . . . were more favorable on other attitudes reflecting personal adjustment/ to the Army/ . . ." (Stouffer et al., 1949). Following this line of analysis, it was reasoned by those in the morale and information fields that if soldiers' attitudes toward the war could be improved, their sense of commitment would be heightened, or, phrased differently, if reservations about the conflict which tended to make the serviceman's commitment a limited one could be removed, his efficiency as a fighting man would be enhanced.

The foregoing reasoning—and the assumption that information can change attitudes—has underpinned a good share of the TI effort both during the latter stages of World War II and since. But translating accepted generalities into program specifics has produced continuing sharp differences of opinion—both among military men and civilians. Three rather distinct approaches have evolved in answer to the questions: "Precisely what should the soldier be informed about?" and "To what extent and intensity should the information program be carried?" These three approaches might be labeled the "military orientation," the "mild indoctrination," and the "militant ideologue" approaches.

Those who adhere to a military orientation point of view generally believe, with General S. L. A. Marshall (1962), that

> the strongest motivation that may be possessed by the citizen in military service is the feeling of confidence that he personally is achieving success and winning prestige and respect in a unit that he regards as a superior body well-qualified for its assigned mission . . . there is no substitute for the methodology and the relentless grind of technical instruction and exhausting exercise afield which gives the individual confidence in his role as a fighter and gives the unit a feeling of superiority in its military task. The unit, confident of its own fighting power and its mastery of tactics and weapons, but relatively ignorant of its cause, will outlast and outperform any company of zealots who lack the knack the field requires.

While focusing on more narrowly military information subjects (for example, the mission and role of the particular unit, the nature of the enemy forces, and the tradition and history of the particular U.S. service and unit), proponents of this view are generally prepared also to devote some time to such political subjects as the values of democracy, communist ideology, and world affairs. But, they maintain, soldiers do not need to know, are not much interested in, and will not absorb very much information of this latter type.

Those adhering to the mild indoctrination viewpoint admit, even underline, the worth of military information but go on to stress the value of political information as well. Typifying this perspective is the statement of John Broger, Director of Armed Forces Information and Education (Department of Defense) before the Special Preparedness Subcommittee of the (see U.S. Congress, 1962) Senate Committee on Armed Services:

> The problem is that America today is facing an enemy the like of which we have never before faced . . . what concepts of American life, attitudes, motivations and convictions must be refreshed, engendered, or sharpened to a new dimension if we are to keep the morale of the fighting forces prepared "at the ready" over a protracted period of time to engage in conflict from a small-scale limited war to worldwide conflict? Over this same period United States troops will continue to be stationed in many parts of the world. How are these troops to be trained and educated in the issues of why they are there, who is the enemy, what are the needs of literally day-to-day resistance against enemy propaganda and techniques of subversion?

The militant ideologue viewpoint of the TI holds that the types of information advocated by proponents of the other two points of view are needed, but that they do not go far enough to strengthen the American serviceman against communist "revolutionary antimilitarism," i.e., attempts to subvert, demoralize, and infiltrate the armed forces of noncommunist nations. To counter these communist tactics, the ideologue maintains, the serviceman must become well-versed in communist ideology and methods and must realize that the communists are totally and perpetually committed to destroying free societies. These arguments for intensive indoctrination, which are scattered through the Special Preparedness Subcommittee's Hearings in 1962 (see, for example U.S. Congress, 1962: 1990-2024, 2323-2345), lean on two propositions: first, it is necessary to put iron in the serviceman's backbone inasmuch as the typical soldier has been inadequately prepared at home and at school to comprehend his own heritage or the nature of the communist threat to it; second, the armed forces are a special target for communist propaganda and subversion and, hence, need special counter-preparation in a period of protracted cold war.

To some extent the difference between the mild indoctrination and military ideologue points of view is one of tone, not substance. Thus, General Edwin Walker's militant "Pro-Blue" Indoctrination Program for the 24th Division then serving in Germany, a program which ultimately resulted in his relief and chastisement, was essentially comprised of the standard ingredients, namely, "citizenship in service, discipline, morality, integrity, German-American relations, leadership, Americanism, and other aspects of the soldier's life. The Pro-Blue Program set forth (1) the methods of communism and how to combat them, (2) the value of the American heritage and how to preserve it, (3) our duties toward and benefits from the NATO shield" (U.S. Congress, 1962).

The militant ideologue approach has gained strength from the widely held conclusion that American POWs in Korea performed badly. In 1955, the Secretary of Defense's Advisory Committee on Prisoners of War lent credence to the idea that the American prisoners could have stood up to the communists better if they had been properly oriented: "The uninformed POWs were up against it. They couldn't answer arguments in favor of Americanism because they knew very little about America. The committee heard a number of ex-POWs who stated that a knowledge of Communism would have enabled them to expose its fallacies to their camp-mates" (U.S. Depart-

ment of Defense, 1955). Whether any feasible amount of troop indoctrination prior to capture would have made a real difference in POW
behavior is of course the point at issue. Albert Biderman's careful
studies of the point led him to the conclusion that there was little to
be gained, and perhaps something to be lost, by intensifying the
political indoctrination of troops (Biderman, 1963).[2]

Behind the clash among the three approaches to information
activities are sometimes differences of perception of the threat to
American security; more important, perhaps, are variations of view
about the nature of motivation among servicemen. Although the
evidence is inconclusive, a careful reading of both the record and the
findings of behavioral research suggests that nonideological factors
are primary in military motivation. For example, the results of the
low-key indoctrination efforts during World War II, even using such
excellent materials as the "Why We Fight" films, were generally
disappointing. Although studies showed that soldiers were better
informed as a consequence of the information effort, and although
their opinions about the war were frequently affected, the relevant
attitudes (those regarding personal commitment or willingness to
fight) remained obdurately unchanged. Analysts concluded that the
assumed information-opinion-attitudes linkage was either an invalid
or a very tenuous one, or perhaps that it really had no operational
significance because the relationships among the factors were such
that only a very "large change in opinion pursuant to a large change
in information" would have "any appreciable effect on personal
commitment" (Stouffer et al., 1949).

Stouffer and his colleagues showed that small group relations,
rather than ideology, were the key to the American soldiers' World
War II combat performance. Similarly, the Shils and Janowitz
analysis of the *Wehrmacht* substantiated the role of the small unit in
meeting the German soldier's basic needs for esteem and support
from both officers and comrades (Shils and Janowitz, 1948). Little's
Korean War findings tended to confirm the World War II studies; he
discovered that the platoon and company were the significant
primary groups for morale and that "buddy relations" between
individual soldiers were central to unit and individual effectiveness.

Little did not dismiss altogether the explanation that men fight
because of "abstract values or the symbols of the larger society, such
as patriotism, the flag, or 'our way of life'." He concluded, however,
that although these values have inspirational influence, when used by
themselves to motivate the combat soldier they are not major

factors—unless reinforced by other more intimate relationships (Little, 1964). It is interesting to note in this connection that, despite the stress the Russians place on the ideological training of their forces, a poll of Soviet servicemen reportedly also showed that military factors rank ahead of ideological ones in creating positive attitudes toward service; when asked which "elements of military service exerted a positive influence" on their attitude toward duty and combat training, forty percent placed "discipline, sound order, and organization" first, in comparison with thirty-three percent who ranked the "system of political and cultural education and physical training" first (Shelyag, 1967).

If the evidence supporting the case for even a mild indoctrination program is negative or inconclusive, that justifying the view that the average soldier can be converted into a militant ideologue—even if that were desirable—is totally lacking. For one thing, the American soldier balks at being indoctrinated. During World War II, when the average serviceman was not nearly so well educated as his counterpart twenty-five years later, a considerable part of his sleepy resistance to official orientation efforts was traceable to his suspicion that he was being propagandized. Responses to questionnaires submitted by commanders in the European Theatre at the end of 1945 focused on this suspicion as one of the "principal weaknesses" of the wartime program (J. Philips, 1948). The soldier's wariness of the "official" line has not lessened since.

A second factor limiting effective ideological indoctrination is the difficulty of changing adults' basic attitudes by a few hours of formal instruction per week or month. Educators are clear that a person's basic structure of values and concepts is slow to yield and largely impervious to classroom-type experience. The scope of the problem which confronts military indoctrinators is suggested by the fact that the bulk of the Chinese Communist prisoners of war refused repatriation to Mainland China after the Korean Conflict, apparently persisting in their prerevolutionary attitudes despite the Red Army's heavy emphasis on ideological conditioning; this fact should be placed beside the parallel fact that only twenty American POWs refused repatriation, despite little formal indoctrination.

Finally, it is questionable whether it is practical, let alone desirable, in an open, democratic society such as ours to inculcate in the serviceman a set of militant attitudes which are widely different from those of his civilian counterparts. In 1962, the U.S. Advisory Committee (1962a) to the Secretary of Defense on Non-Military Instruction[3] made an observation germane to this point:

We have found that the average serviceman shares the general attitudes and values of the American public of which he is a part. This is true of his devotion to his country and his opposition to Communism. There is little evidence to support the view expressed in some quarters that a serviceman lacks an awareness of the Communist threat. The fearful, the confused and the pessimistic do not populate the armed forces.

The implication is, of course, that the soldier's acquiring a new set of values would require his being set apart from the society of which he is a representative. The extensive interplay between soldier and civilian in contemporary American life indicates the improbability of such ideological compartmentation.

CURRENT PROGRAMS

The Army, which has traditionally been the most active in the information field, continued in the late 1960s to have the most comprehensive program of any of the services. In the Basic Combat Training period of eight weeks the new soldier is given at least three hours of troop information covering such topics as Army traditions and customs, the code of conduct of the soldier, and the responsibilities and privileges of the citizen-soldier. In the next eight-week phase of his training, Advanced Individual Training, he receives another five hours of "Command Information" (CI). The topics covered in this phase are national heritage, international communism, defense against enemy propaganda, and—again—the privileges and responsibilities of citizenship. A two-hour special orientation is given Army personnel bound for overseas theaters. This instruction includes a discussion of the particular situation requiring the soldier to go overseas, his legal rights as a U.S. soldier, a description of the area to which he is being sent, and the customs and standards of conduct he must observe there (U.S. Department of the Army, 1964).

The same topics covered in the three special programs sketched out above are included in the Army-wide weekly CI program, generally termed "Commander's Call," which is mandatory for all company-sized units. The entire CI program, but particularly Commander's Call, is viewed by the Army as a "tool of leadership," designed to contribute to the accomplishment of the command's mission.

The one-hour Commander's Call period normally includes a general "indoctrination" topic such as "American Heritage" and one or more subjects of a more narrowly military nature pertaining to the command and its mission. Commander's Call frequently includes a film and a "guided discussion" on its contents. Numerous pamphlets and other training aids are made available to the commander to support these lectures or discussions. As the formally appointed leader, the unit commander is expected to conduct the information hour; if the subject for the week entails expertise which the commander lacks, or if for some other reason he wishes to designate someone else to conduct the session, he can pass the task to a subordinate, but the Army insists that he be present during the class to lend his authority and prestige to the program (U.S. Department of the Army, 1964).

To assure the needed flexibility and responsiveness of the CI program to the various units' needs, a great deal of discretion as to precise scheduling and selection of topic and content is left to the unit commander. The Department of the Army prepares an annual plan for procuring and distributing materials which are designed to reinforce the individual's sense of responsibility, to increase his understanding of why he serves, and to inform him about the Army. The department prepares any materials which it needs to implement its plan beyond those being made available by the Department of Defense or other agencies. The Army produces about twenty percent of the movies it uses, depending on DOD for the remaining eighty percent; it also prepares roughly sixty percent of the pamphlets and fifty percent of the Fact Sheets and other miscellaneous materials (Boiler, 1968).

Army-wide, the CI program costs more than a million man-hours of instructor and soldier time each week, the full-time services of thousands of information officers from Department of the Army level down to company level, and an annual budget of about $4,000,000 not including salaries or materials provided from outside the service.

The Air Force program is similar to, but less intensive than, the Army program. The same themes and the same general division of responsibility between the Department of Defense and the service mark the Air Force as the Army. The program for beginning airmen approximates that for the apprentice soldier, as does the pre-overseas orientation program. The Air Force, however, requires only a monthly, rather than a weekly, Commander's Call. Consequently, it does not have as large a requirement for information materials and budget as does the Army.

The Navy program does not compare particularly closely with the Army and Air Force programs, for it is integrated into a servicewide leadership program which is highly decentralized in both planning and execution. Naval commanders are encouraged to hold frequent orientation periods, but there may be little attention in such periods to the broader themes of freedom versus communism, national heritage, and so on, which mark the Air Force and Army programs.

The Marines also decentralize, leaving it to the field commander to determine the amount and type of information which his unit requires. The Marine Corps has the least enthusiasm of any of the services for indoctrination subjects, being more inclined to stress the military aspects of information and to emphasize Marine tradition. Nevertheless, Marine commanders are held responsible for including the full range of TI subjects in their training schedules on as frequent a basis as necessary (U.S. Marine Corps, 1964).

The Department of Defense does not conduct information activities on its own; rather, through the Assistant Secretary of Defense for Manpower and Reserve Affairs, it provides visual, audio, and printed materials on various subjects for service use, and coordinates and evaluates portions of the service information programs. The Department of Defense is also responsible, again acting through its ASD (M and RA), for policy guidance for the Armed Forces Radio and Television Service (AFRTS) comprising over three hundred radio and fifty television stations. These stations, which the services actually operate, broadcast a variety of programs, of both local and stateside origin, which provide the serviceman with generally the same professional quality and quantity of news and commentary as is available to his civilian counterparts (U.S. Department of Defense, 1961).

CONTINUING PROBLEMS

Command views. Perhaps the most persistent problem in the history of the information program has been to obtain the enthusiastic implementation in the field of the plans conceived at headquarters. During World War II this problem was clearly discernible; despite enthusiastic endorsement from the top, unit commanders were frequently lukewarm or outright hostile to the program.

This weakness persisted in the early postwar era. The Weil Committee reported in 1949 that "the most important single factor in the effective conduct of the Information and Education program is command support. The success of any such program in the field is usually in direct relation to the amount of enthusiasm and interest shown by the commanding officers" (U.S. President's Committee, 1949). During the Korean War, many commanders remained dubious. Typical of the attitude of unit commanders, at least during the early stage of the conflict, was the view of Lieutenant Colonel (now Lieutenant General) John Michaelis: "We've put too much stress on Info and Education and not enough stress on rifle marksmanship and scouting and patrolling and the organization of a defense position. . . . They'd spent a lot of time listening to lectures on the difference between Communism and Americanism and not enough time crawling on their bellies on maneuvers with live ammunition singing over them" (Michaelis, 1950).

Post-Korea, the problem remained. In the mid-1950s an independent study group found that unit commanders were "apathetic or antagonistic towards information programs, partially because the programs offered were often unattractive but, in large part, because of the press of other duties and the shortage of time which is so chronic in any officer's day." From this finding and similar discouraging ones about general lack of command support, the group concluded, "the underlying concepts of officer education and training were the key to the success or failure of information programs" (Bowles, 1956).

The persistence of the problem is indicated by the finding of the U.S. Advisory Committee (1962a) that "despite Service efforts the degree of command interest and understanding of this training is still inadequate. Although there is agreement that this instruction, like other types of instruction, is a function of command, the Services have not effectively made it a duty of command, as it must be."

In spite of the Advisory Committee's identification of this continuing difficulty and various recommendations to cure it, the services were still wrestling with the problem five years later. In a 1967 pamphlet entitled "Theirs to Reason Why," the Army gave its commanders "A Word of caution: in a successful program, the most important single element is the unit commander. Commander's Call cannot accomplish its true purpose without participation by the unit commander" (U.S. Department of the Army, 1967a).

One is struck by the apparent inverse correlation between rank and enthusiasm for information activities. Generally, the closer to the ordinary soldier that a questioner gets, the more lukewarm the attitude toward troop information—or at least its indoctrination aspects. In November of 1961, the Air Force confirmed this widely observed phenomenon by conducting a survey of several hundred Air Force colonels and generals to obtain their views on the information program; it contrasted these senior commanders' opinions with those of a sampling of Air Force enlisted men and officers of all ranks. Roughly seventy percent of the senior commanders thought that further instruction about communism was needed in the Air Force; only thirty-six percent of the Air Force officers in general and thirty-nine percent of the enlisted men felt that they were not getting enough information on the subject (U.S. Advisory Committee, 1962b).

Personnel problems. From the first days of the program in World War II, information activities have been plagued by shortages in sufficiently qualified personnel (U.S. War Department, 1945). In 1949 the Committee on Information reported "There is a serious shortage of qualified trained personnel to administer and implement the program." In the 1950s another appraisal confirmed the theme, "the second most important factor hampering the I & E Program is the inadequacy of instructor skills on the part of the Officer Corps" (Bowles, 1956). A decade later, the U.S. Advisory Committee (1962a) reported that "second only to inadequate command support as an information weakness was a lack of adequate qualification in many of the commissioned and non-commissioned officers who conduct this instruction."

In some part, the problem of acquiring qualified instructors is being eroded by the rising educational level of the entire officer corps; in 1968, for example, seventy-three percent had college degrees in contrast to fifty-four percent in 1956. But even if the overall educational level of potential instructors is rising, able men may shun a career field which suffers from inadequate command support and relatively low prestige. An unofficial 1961 study of prestige of TI duty in the Army showed that eighty percent of the troop commanders and fifty-seven percent of TI personnel did not consider such duty a prestige assignment. In a related response, seventy percent of the commanders and sixty-two percent of those engaged in TI stated that they thought fellow officers looked upon a TI assignment as undesirable (they confirmed this low opinion by their response to the question of whether they would like a TI assignment in the future; only twelve-and-one-half percent of the commanders and thirty percent of TI personnel answered affirmatively (Haggis, 1961).

The Navy and the Marines have not encountered the prestige problem to the same degree as have the Army and the Air Force, probably because the latter two services have not carved the information programs out from other training and leadership activities. At one extreme, in the Air Force, "information" has been developed as a separate career field in which an officer might spend his entire service, either as a Public Information Officer or as an Internal Information Officer; at the other extreme, the Marines have viewed information activities as an integral part of the duties of normal training and operations officers. Marine information activities may be conducted by instructors with less expertise, but they carry the same psychological weight with the troops as other general training activities, and instructors to conduct them are not in short supply.

In an effort to meet the shortage of qualified personnel, the three military departments organized a Joint Information School in 1948, specifically designed to train officers and enlisted personnel in public information and troop information skills. By late 1953 the school (located at Ft. Slocum, New York) was foundering, largely because the Navy and Air Force had reduced their stated requirements for information trained personnel and hence were filling less than fifty percent of their allocated student quotas. The joint school was terminated in April 1954, and the Army conducted its own school on the same premises for a time until the joint school was reconstituted at Ft. Benjamin Harrison, Indiana. Although the reorganized Defense Information School is charged with both public and internal information training, the former receives more attention than the latter. In any case, the brief eight- and ten-week courses afford little opportunity to do more than improve the students' communication skills and give them a thin veneer of familiarity with the information field. The few hundreds of internal information officers and noncommissioned officers sketchily trained at Ft. Benjamin Harrison each year show little sign of solving the chronic shortage of skilled personnel.

A separate corps of "orientation officers" specifically and solely developed to conduct motivational instruction, has been suggested from time to time as one way to meet the shortage of qualified personnel. But the hostility toward information activities which the use of separately anointed orientation officers in World War II apparently engendered among commanders has lingered on (Marshall, 1962). One variant of this concept, the "orientation team," still enjoys some support. The director of AFIE, for example, expressed enthusiasm for such teams at the Stennis Committee Hearings, but residual skepticism by military commanders has so far kept this means of mitigating the shortage of skilled manpower from being employed (U.S. Congress, 1962).

Another approach which has sometimes been suggested for bolstering the quantity and quality of troop information specialists has been to use civilian specialists to supplement or supplant military personnel. This has generated even more fears among military commanders of a "political commissariat" than the proposal for orientation officers. Despite military opposition, the notion of turning the information program over to civilians continues to crop up. In his controversial, private memorandum, *"Propaganda Activities of Military Personnel Directed at the Public,"* Senator Fulbright suggested in 1961 the desirability of a civilian committee being "appointed to review troop education activities of military personnel from the standpoint of their necessity and, if found to be (necessary), to develop procedures for bringing the content of such programs and, if possible, their *actual operation,* under civilian control" [emphasis added] (U.S. Congress, 1961).

If the proposition of using civilians to inform troops is examined closely, however, it is usually rejected on the grounds that the information program is an intrinsic part of the military training program and must be accomplished through regular command and staff channels with military personnel. (Veterans of the World War II experiment suggest, too, that most civilians have difficulty in communicating with troops on such subjects.) The Bendetsen Committee came down clearly on the point that the program must be "supervised and administered by the same staff agencies charged with supervision over all other military training" (U.S. Advisory Committee, 1962a). Of course, these findings are not antithetical to Senator Fulbright's view that civilian control must continue to be exercised in the preparation of information materials and in the specification of general program content at the higher levels of the services and DOD.

Management issues. In addition to inadequate command support and personnel shortages, the information program has long confronted two other problems, largely managerial in substance, namely, how much to centralize planning and execution and how to evaluate results. The centralization issue arises from the tension between, on the one hand, the desirability of giving subordinate commanders flexibility in tailoring the total training effort, including the information program, to the particular situation they confront and, on the other, the necessity to retain a significant central check on the planning and execution of politically sensitive parts of the program. The commander needs to be able to focus on the motivational approaches appropriate to the situation of his unit and the status of training of his troops; yet, he cannot have free rein, for, as expressed by the spokesman for the American Veterans Committee in the Stennis Hearings, "The man in the ranks should be studying the meaning of America and not the personalized wisdom or ignorance, not the individual ideals or prejudices of his commander" (U.S. Congress, 1962).

As of the late 1960s a reasonably satisfactory solution to this dilemma had been achieved on the basis that (a) politically sensitive materials would generally be produced by the Department of Defense, which would consult fully with the services about their needs, and (b) the services would conduct the programs with maximum latitude left to lower unit commanders. In 1967 the Secretary of Defense formalized consultations about materials and programs through the appointment of the Armed Forces Information Program Advisory Council, thereby bringing together the concerned DOD officials at the Deputy Assistant Secretary level and the general or flag officers in the services charged with responsibility for internal information programs (U.S. Department of Defense, 1967). In rare cases materials may be prescribed by higher headquarters, but the current approach is essentially one of providing lower commanders with a pool of suitable items from which to develop their own programs, placing "back on the unit commander where it belongs, the responsibility for preparing the men under his command for the duties they have assigned," as recommended fifteen years earlier by the Fund for the Advancement of Education (Bowles, 1956). Though a reasonable compromise, this particular answer to the centralization issue will probably last only until there is another of the periodic upsurges in public interest about the adequacy of the services indoctrination efforts—the pendulum may then swing either way, but the long-term trend since World War II has been toward centralization.

The second management problem, namely, how to evaluate information programs, turns on whether such programs should be judged by the extent to which they contribute to unit effectiveness or by their efficacy in improving information levels, opinions, and attitudes. Those who view information activities as essentially geared to indoctrination and as primarily political in character, tend to judge information materials and programs by their effectiveness in generating appropriate opinions and attitudes, on the other hand, those who regard information programs as a leadership tool—as is usually the case within the services—generally insist that a unit's information activities can be evaluated only in the context of its overall performance. The obvious evaluation problem raised by this latter approach is that the information program is only one of many factors contributing to unit performance, and its influence cannot logically be separated from that of the other factors. Recognizing this, the services have generally limited their evaluation efforts to seeing whether programs are conducted as schedules, by qualified personnel, using quality materials—beyond those criteria there are only subjective judgments as to troop morale and esprit de corps. The Department of the Army, as an example, evaluates its information program by five methods: (a) normal staff surveillance of directives, correspondence, and reports; (b) staff liaison visits from higher to lower headquarters; (c) quarterly reports from the field on materials originating there and actions taken with respect to centrally provided materials; (d) annual inspections of records by an inspector general to verify performance; (e) a quarterly survey by the adjutant general conducted through a questionnaire of individuals to ascertain opinions on the value of the program (U.S. Department of the Army, 1964).

In addition to judgments by the services, the Department of Defense evaluates the materials it produces for accuracy, objectivity, relevance, technical quality, and consistency with national policy. From time to time, DOD has also attempted to measure—using its own resources through contracts—changes in soldier information levels, opinions, and attitudes resulting from exposure to its materials. This type of evaluation, which was performed extensively in World War II—with the rather negative results described above—has invariably turned out inconclusive. The consequence has been that information enthusiasts are driven back to faith in the adage that the informed soldier is a good soldier.

REFLECTIONS

When General George Marshall directed the Army to start the orientation program just before World War II, he indicated the two general paths which it might follow: one toward "making firmer the military character of a soldier," the second toward "educating him about the political objectives of the war" (Marshall, 1962). Information activities have since proceeded down both paths simultaneously, with those in charge not always focused on the fact that they were dealing with two quite different sets of objectives. After World War II and up to the early 1960s, during the height of the Cold War and partly as a consequence of the POW issue arising out of the Korean Conflict, top officials tended to emphasize the second path of doctrinal education of the soldier (though commanders at lower levels and troops generally continued in the same period to look down the other path). Similarly, major outside appraisals of the information effort in this era, notably the study by the Fund for the Advancement of Education (Bowles, 1956) and the Advisory Committee (1962a) survey, focused largely on doctrinal questions on whether or not troops were receiving the right amount and kind of political information and indoctrination. The answers at which they arrived were invariably ambiguous, for though they deemed political indoctrination desirable, or essential, they recognized that such indoctrination could neither extend very far nor have its results penetrate very deeply.

During this same period (the 1950s and into the early 1960s), questions about appropriate goals for military information gradually became entangled with issues concerning the role of the military in American life. The post-Korean War shift in American security strategy—from a mobilization-when-needed approach, such as had been followed between World Wars I and II, to a plateau-of-readiness approach—meant that the nation's armed forces would inevitably play a larger role in national life than before. The large "permanent" defense establishment comprising several million men and tens of billions of dollars of annual spending aroused anxiety in many quarters about the erosion of democracy and the evolution of a garrison state. Even President Eisenhower, the architect of the plateau-of-readiness policy, inveighed in his farewell address against "unwarranted influence" by the "military-industrial complex." Lending further weight to the fears of those concerned about undue military influence were the alliances into which a few military officers were drawn by right-wing groups.

The confluence of the concerns and problems described above impelled the defense establishment to reexamine its goals and programs in the information field in the early and mid-1960s to see if George Marshall's other path was receiving enough emphasis. By the latter 1960s this examination—together with some lessening of interest in indoctrination per se—had produced a situation in which some attention was being given to political indoctrination but in which information efforts were centered on the path of "making firmer the military character of the soldier." This emphasis is probably a "natural" one for the armed forces of a pragmatic society, or at least when that society is not locked in a life and death struggle with an ideological foe. The situation recently arrived at is probably also "natural" inasmuch as the armed forces are not the best forum for teaching about democracy; analysts of the World War II orientation effort found that the "ordinary enlisted man returned from his discussion hour (concerning the values of democracy and the integrity of the individual) to the depersonalized world of the Army in which he found little democracy and not much regard for him as an individual. Little wonder, then, if enlisted men accepted the larger part of their Army lives as reality and took orientation with a large grain of salt" (Stouffer et al., 1949).

It is noteworthy that the kind of information program emphasis which the American defense establishment was reaching in the late 1960s tended to resemble the emphasis which the information programs of its democratic allies had reached earlier. Both the British and Canadians, for example, had had formal information programs during World War II, and on into the 1950s, which approximated the American programs of those periods in content, if not intensity. Both nations taught their troops about citizenship, allied forces, and world affairs, as well as about more narrowly military topics. The British also included materials on communism; the Canadians did not. Canada cut down its "current affairs" program in 1954 due to doubt about its utility and because it was viewed as an unacceptable diversion of training time. The British, too, have greatly reduced the political content of their information programs since World War II and the Korean Conflict.

But the current balance in American troop information program emphasis is an inherently dynamic one. Our involvement in Vietnam, whatever its outcome, will probably result in demands for a fresh analysis of the information programs of the services as those institutions attempt to adjust to the post-Vietnam environment. It is likely, also, that periodic rethinking of troop information goals and programs will be necessitated by evolution of the armed forces themselves—from largely conscript to all-volunteer, professional forces, for example. And, finally, TI programs may increasingly have to deal with divergence between civilian and military value systems arising out of broader societal changes as well as from alterations in the armed forces or their missions.

Whatever the program changes wrought by competing factors and interests, there will be strong elements of continuity. The American soldier and his immediate superiors will undoubtedly remain profoundly concerned about the "military" part of the information task and just as profoundly skeptical of its indoctrination element. The troops will themselves set sleepy limits beyond which the information officer's skill and zeal will rarely carry, once he ventures into topics with little direct military application. The culturally set gyroscope which keeps the American political system aright, despite an occasional tendency to wobble, will in all likelihood prove equally capable of limiting the yawing of future information programs.

NOTES

1. The term "TI" includes such activities as (1) informing servicemen about the armed forces, about their missions and traditions, and about the roles of their subordinate units; (2) inculcating pride of unit and service among servicemen; (3) informing them of the values and goals of their nation and indoctrinating them with the ideal of service thereto; (4) teaching them the nature of the potential or actual enemy and particularly its armed forces; (5) orienting them about friendly or allied nations; (6) teaching them about world affairs and the possible threats arising therefrom; (7) acquainting them with citizenship responsibilities—including voting; (8) developing their resistance to enemy propaganda; and (9) indoctrinating them in the appropriate "code of conduct" should they become prisoners of war. A related "character guidance" program of moral and religious instruction, under the aegis of military chaplains, occasionally bears on some of these same topics, but is not within the scope of this essay. Whether or not political indoctrination should be considered a part of TI is discussed at length in the next section of this paper.

2. For an interesting example of the clash of views on lessons to be learned from the Korean POW experience, readers should contrast Kinkead (1959) with Biderman (1963).

3. The Advisory Committee, which had been asked by Secretary McNamara to look into the proper objectives, appropriate subjects, methods of evaluation,

and lines of responsibility for troop information, made a comprehensive assessment of the entire topic. During six months of intensive work, the thirteen committeemen visited over one hundred U.S. units in more than a dozen countries, were briefed by scores of experts, saw dozens of TI films, read hundreds of pamphlets and studies, and so on. The committee's report of July 20, 1962 continues to be an authoritative guide to those assessing troop information activities.

REFERENCES

BIDERMAN, A. (1963) March to Calumny. New York: Macmillan.

BOILER, Col. W. F. (1968) Letter to the Author (January 26).

BOWLES, F. (1956) "The information program of the armed forces." Report of a project sponsored by the Fund for the Advancement of Education.

EURICH, A. (1952) Letter to Mrs. Anna Rosenberg, Assistant Secretary of Defense, appended to Bowles Report (March 31).

HAGGIS, Maj. A. (1961) "An appraisal of the administration, scope, concept, and function of the U.S. Army troop information program." Ph.D. dissertation. Wayne State University.

JANOWITZ, M. and R. W. LITTLE (1965) Sociology and the Military Establishment. New York: Russell Sage Foundation.

KINKEAD, E. (1959) In Every War But One. New York: W. W. Norton.

LITTLE, R. (1964) "Buddy relations and combat performance," pp. 195-224 in M. Janowitz (ed.) The New Military. New York: Russell Sage Foundation.

MARSHALL, S. L. A. (1962) "Troop indoctrination: its history and principles." Statement to the Advisory Committee on Non-Military Instruction (March 31).

MICHAELIS, Lt. Col. J. (1950) "Interview by Harold Martive." Saturday Evening Post (September).

MOSKOS, C. (1967) "A sociologist appraises the G.I." New York Times Magazine (September 24).

PALMER, J. M. (1937) General Von Steuben. New Haven, Conn.: Yale University Press.

Pentagon News Release (1961) June 12.

PHILIPS, C. (1961) "Rightwing officers worrying Pentagon." New York Times (June 18): 1.

PHILIPS, J. D. F. (1948) "Considerations affecting a program for the political education of military personnel." Typewritten (January).

SHELYAG, V. (1967) "The Soviet serviceman." For the Inter-University Seminar on Armed Forces and Society, The International Sociological Association Conference, London.

SHILS, E. A. and M. JANOWITZ (1948) "Cohesion and disintegration in the Wehrmacht in World War II." Public Opinion Quarterly (Summer): 280-315.

STOUFFER, S. A. et al. (1949) The American Soldier: Adjustment During Army Life, vol. 1. Princeton: Princeton University Press.

U.S. Advisory Committee on Non-Military Instruction (1962a) Report. Washington, D.C.: Secretary of Defense.

———(1962b) Staff papers. Washington, D.C.: Secretary of Defense.

U.S. Congress, Senate Committee on Armed Services (1962) Cold War Education and Speech Review Policies. Hearings before the Special Preparedness Committee, 87th Congress, 2nd Session.

U.S. Congress, Senate (1961) Senator William Fulbright, Memorandum on "Propaganda activities of military personnel directed at the public." Congressional Record (August 2).

U.S. Department of the Army (1967a) "Theirs to reason why." Pamphlet 360-300.

———(1967b) "Military information—a hard skill of leadership." CINFO.

———(1964) "Command information program, general provisions." Army Regulation 360-81.

U.S. Department of Defense (1967) "Armed forces information program advisory council." Directive 5120-37.

———(1961) "Armed forces information and education program." Instruction 5120-32.

———Office of Secretary of Defense (1955) POW. . . The Fight Continues After the Battle. Washington, D.C.: Advisory Committee on Prisoners of War.

U.S. Marine Corps (1964) "General military training of enlisted men." Order 1510.2D (June 22).

U.S. President's Committee on Religion and Welfare in the Armed Forces (1949) Report of Committee on Information and Education in the Armed Forces. Washington, D.C. (December 1).

U.S. War Department (1945) "The information and education program in the European theater." General Board Study 76.

———(1944) "The information and education program." Circular 360 (September 5).

———(1942) The Background of Our War. New York: Farrar & Rinehart.

WASHINGTON, G. (1776) "General orders." New York: Headquarters (July 9).

Part Four

POLITICAL MILITARY

FUNCTIONS

Chapter 12

REVOLUTIONS

WILLIAM KORNHAUSER

*R*evolutions always involve armed forces, whether regular or irregular, unified or divided, friendly or hostile. The role of armed forces is as varied as revolutions: there is no clear distinction between "military" and "civil" revolution. However, the contemporary proliferation of military regimes is preceded by the burgeoning political participation of military officers in engineering the destruction of civil regimes.

This analysis identifies several dimensions of revolution, constructs a typology of revolutions, and describes the incidence of different types of revolution. These conceptual distinctions and applications may help provide a framework for the study of military roles in revolutions. The bibliography shows that scholarship is just beginning to grapple with this subject, notably in nations of the Third World. The coming years no doubt will witness the closer integration of military and political sociology, as military forces become increasingly politicized and as politics become increasingly militarized.

DIMENSIONS OF REVOLUTION

There are three principal concerns in the current literature on modern political revolutions. One is the *transformation* of whole societies, especially in the non-Western world, including the establishment of new nations and the modernization of social institutions. The second is the *polarization* of social forces within societies and "internal war." The third is the *mobilization* of large numbers of people under the banner of revolutionary ideology. Thus "revolutionary societies" are sometimes identified as societies undergoing radical change, as societies experiencing violent conflict, and as societies that are politically mobilized.

These three notions of revolution need to be distinguished because they may not vary together. Thus radical transformation may occur without much mobilization, as in the Meiji revolution. Moreover, a considerable amount of mobilization may take place without much transformation, as in Argentina under Peron. Then, too, governments may be overthrown with little polarization, mobilization, or transformation of society, as in so-called "palace revolutions."

The relations among revolutionary change, revolutionary conflict, and revolutionary movements provide a framework for the comparative analysis of variations in the character, conditions, and consequences of revolutions in different societies and historical periods.

Revolution as a Type of Social Change

Social change in many parts of the non-Western world is revolutionary in that (1) it is of very wide scope, involving the fundamental transformation of cultural values and social organization; (2) it occurs at a very rapid rate, especially when compared to the rate of change in the past; (3) it tends to be developmental, resulting in the formation of new institutional capacities in society; and (4) it generally is sponsored and directed by the state—it is purposive and deliberate change. Revolutionary change as described by these four criteria generally is what modern regimes calling themselves "revolutionary" claim to be seeking: the comprehensive and rapid development of society by the state.

(1) The scope of change is revolutionary when not only political arrangements but also the cultural and social foundations of political order are transformed. This means, first, that the principles of cultural legitimacy as well as the members of governing groups are changed, and second, that the bases of social stratification as well as of political authority are transformed. These two kinds of change are intimately related, for the new principles legitimizing authority presuppose new social groups to promulgate them.

(2) Change is revolutionary when there is a sharp break with the past; revolutionary change is sudden and *discontinuous* compared with social change in the preceding period. Revolutionary change also is *rapid*: usually change has been occurring in the prerevolutionary period, but now the *rate* of change sharply increases in the revolutionary period.

(3) The direction of change is revolutionary when there is institutional development as well as redistribution of power. Whether by transforming old institutions or by creating new ones, revolutions seek to enlarge institutional capacities for continuous development and the integration of change. Above all, they create *new social consciousness* of existing conditions and of potential alternatives.

(4) The agency of change is revolutionary when it is deliberately organized to initiate and consolidate radical and rapid social transformation. This generally means that the state is made over into the primary agency for the tranformation of society.

Revolution as a Type of Social Conflict

A central issue posed by revolution is whether and under what conditions great transformation can occur without massive conflict and the destruction of the institutional order. The principal function of revolutionary conflict is to destroy institutional constraints on social change. Hence the intensity of conflict generally depends on the strength of the resistance of the old order to social change.

In rare cases, revolutionary change is sponsored by duly constituted authority, or at least by duly reconstituted authority. Even in these cases, however, the rulers may find themselves in profound conflict with other parts of society. Revolutionary change characteristically is preceded or accompanied by revolutionary conflict. Revolutionary conflict possesses the following characteristics: (1) it tends to be violent, (2) it is illegitimate, and (3) it is highly polarized.

(1) Although revolutionary conflict tends to be violent, violence is not a distinguishing characteristic of revolution. In the first place, many other kinds of conflict may involve violence, such as racial conflict. Second, violence is a highly variable attribute of revolutions, and one that may not even be closely associated with the extent to which opposition to the government is based on fundamental differences. Thus the civil strife in Colombia beginning in 1948 cost some quarter of a million lives without issues of revolutionary change

centrally at stake, whereas the Cuban revolution of 1959 generated profound change at the cost of but few casualties.

(2) Revolutionary conflict is illegitimate in that it is not governed by valued modes of political life. Note, however, that it is the conflict itself which is illegitimate, not necessarily the revolutionaries. Legitimacy is not whatever is decreed by a ruling group, and it is not uncommon for those in power to flagrantly violate the principles upon which they claim the right to rule. The English and American revolutions, for example, generated considerable constitutional development. Thus illegitimacy is a highly variable attribute of attempts to overthrow governments, and some revolutions may advance the rule of law rather than subvert it.

(3) The most distinctive feature of revolutionary conflict is that it is highly polarized. Revolutionary conflict entails the extreme polarization of social and political forces, and of basic values as well as power, such that there tends to be sharply defined choices and an *unrestrained* struggle to determine the outcome. This is to be contrasted with the nonrevolutionary situation, where the institutional system blurs choices in order to dampen conflict, and places severe restraints on the means of pursuing conflict. Institutional leadership has already suffered a significant loss of authority when it has to confront sharply defined choices and unlimited means, even though it may prevail in the struggle for power.

Revolutionary conflict greatly increases the extent to which no compromise or exchange is possible between the opposing parties, but only a decision as to who will exercise governing power. A dramatic expression of this situation is that of dual government: the opposition constitutes an alternative government which actually governs part of the territory and population.

Revolutionary conflict, then, implies the weakness of the moderates (Brinton, 1957: 128-154). This will tend to be true among the forces supporting the government as well as among those opposing it: moderates generally are defeated in the conflict between extremes, or they are neutralized or mobilized by the extremes.

Levels of revolutionary conflict may be distinguished by the levels of society which are polarized. Polarization may be restricted largely to elements within the elite, as in Ataturk's revolution. Or it may generate polarization of elements within the society at large, as in the Chinese Communist revolution.

The general problem of revolutionary conflict and revolutionary change is the relationship between destructive and constructive aspects of revolutions. The fact that a large part of the current literature focuses primarily on conflict or primarily on change leads to a much too negative view of conflict or a much too sanguine view of change (compare Eckstein, 1964; Friedrich, 1966).

Revolution as a Type of Social Movement

Revolution may not involve social movements, as in revolutionary conspiracies and "spontaneous revolutions" where the old regime collapses in the face of an unorganized uprising. Revolutions which are more or less spontaneous place in power men who do not possess a revolutionary base or a revolutionary program. The presumption is that the lack of such a program and base makes revolutionary change less likely and also makes the new regime highly vulnerable to displacement by a party which is more radical and programmatic, thus the February Revolution in 1917. Revolutions that are primarily conspiracies by small groups also may be expected to have more difficulty in promoting revolutionary change than revolutions that are based on mass organization: mass organization provides revolutionary leadership with support and resources to attempt radical change.

Revolutionary movements are characterized by *mass mobilization* and *ideological organization.*

(1) An influential view makes popular involvement in efforts to found a new social order a criterion of revolutions. Popular involvement is not, of course, unique to revolutions. Other kinds of social movements, including reform movements, frequently command widespread support. Mass mobilization, rather than mere popular support, characterizes revolutionary movements. Mobilization provides mass energies for the achievement of political power, economic development, national integration, and ideological identity. Mobilization, then, is a *weapon* in the revolutionary struggle, a source of power rather than a mode of governance. Mobilization places a premium on organization and indoctrination, and in turn generates power for the capture and consolidation of the state. It should be noted, however, that revolutionary leaders often seek mass mobilization only *after* they acquire governing power, as in the case of Castro. Under certain circumstances, it may be easier to acquire power without mobilization, but *it may not be possible to consolidate power or to make radical alterations in the social order without mobilization.*

380 POLITICAL MILITARY FUNCTIONS

(2) Revolutionary mobilization, unlike military mobilization, rests on an ideological basis. It may not be too much to suggest that revolutionary groups are ideological groups, that the ideological bond is the fundamental basis of revolutionary integration. Of course, leaders are more ideological than followers, and some revolutions are more ideological than others. Even military regimes bent on radical change may try to develop revolutionary ideology and organization, as in Egypt. This is not to deny an "elective affinity" between ideology and interests, but it would seem rather wide of the mark to treat interests rather than ideology as the wellspring of revolutionary solidarity and action. The abstract, activist, and doctrinaire qualities of ideology have great consequences for the behavior of revolutionaries, notably the inclusiveness and intensity of their commitment. The ideology serves the critical function of providing commitment and direction to revolutionary efforts to change the existing order. (This is not to deny that ideology also may reduce the capacity of a revolutionary movement or regime to adapt to new conditions, thereby impairing its ability to bring about social change.)

Conclusion

This analysis is based on a view of revolution as fundamentally a process of change. This view is to be contrasted with notions of revolution as "internal war." To seek to assimilate the study of revolution to the study of war and violence is to fasten on a secondary feature of revolution at the expense of its central purposes. It also tends to prejudge the efficacy of specific revolutions, and to ignore the potential contributions of revolution. Conflict is better considered as a variable feature of attempts to achieve rapid and radical social transformation. Moreover, revolutionary conflict needs to be studied in the light of efforts to resist change as well as efforts to destroy resistance to change. Even where revolutions fail to build new institutions, they are likely to help tear down old institutions. Where preexisting institutions are more receptive to social change, revolutionary conflict is likely to be less severe. Therefore, the study of revolution properly includes the study of institutional regidities and resistances in the face of changing conditions.

Finally, revolutionary mobilization is also a variable feature of attempts to achieve revolutionary change. Under certain conditions, the mobilization of large numbers of people on an ideological basis may serve to further the process of change, but under other conditions, it may activate new sources of resistance to social transformation or serve as a basis for political and military adventures. Revolutionary rhetoric and organization may disguise the lack of purpose and program until such time as a new group rises to challenge what prove to be merely revolutionary pretensions. In short, the purposes of revolutionaries need to be taken seriously, but not assumed to be efficacious. Revolutionary movements and regimes, like all other social enterprises, may subvert their own purposes. Revolutionary purposes are precarious values, and revolutionary movements often achieve political power only to fail to realize social change.

TYPES OF REVOLUTION

A revolution may be said to have occurred whenever a national government is "overthrown"—that is, abruptly changed by extrainstitutional means. A government is to be understood as overthrown when it is excluded from a territory over which it has exercised jurisdiction, as well as when its rulers are removed. Thus the effort of the Southern states to secede from the United States is an instance of revolution.

In addition to cases in which the government is actually overthrown, "significant" attempts at overthrow which have not succeeded also will be considered here (significant attempts are those considered of sufficient importance to be reported in major historical works on a given nation). These "unsuccessful" cases are included, first, because they may result in greater transformations of central institutions than "successful" revolutions, and second, because they signify a major if not fatal failure to contain conflict within tolerable limits (e.g., they generally result in a continuation of severe conflict and new upheavals). In addition, they can be compared to successful cases to ascertain differences in modes of control. Initially, they will be grouped together in the following count of the incidence of revolution in all nations over one million population in Europe, Asia, the Middle East, and Latin America from 1917 to 1966. ("Nations" are to be understood as formally independent nation-states: there were fifty-one nations over one million in 1917, and this figure grew to seventy-eight in 1966.)

There were approximately 200 successful revolutions and 185 significant unsuccessful revolutions, for a total of 385 revolutions from 1917 to 1966. This averages out to about one revolution per nation every eight years (taking into account the changing number of nations during this period), or about one successful revolution per nation every sixteen years. The actual national incidence ranges from no revolutions in seven nations to one revolution every two years in five nations. In Europe, there is an average of one revolution per nation every fourteen years, in Asia one every seven years, in the Middle East one every seven years, and in Latin America one every six years.

A revolutionary upheaval on the average occurred in about one nation in six for each year between 1917 and 1966. Here again the range is very great: from one nation in twenty-five during 1939 to one in three in 1948. There were three major peaks of revolutionary upheaval in the world during the past fifty years: 1917-1921, 1930-1934, and 1945-1949. The first and second peaks are about equal, but the third is much higher and does not fall below the first and second peaks for some fourteen years (until 1963). These three periods were times of high revolutionary upheaval in Europe and Latin America, but the first period (1917-1921) did not hold in Asia and the second period (1930-1934) did not hold in the Middle East (moreover the third period started later in the Middle East, not until 1952).

These three peaks obviously correspond to periods of massive stress: World War I, the Great Depression, and World War II. In the case of the two world wars, the general picture is simple: revolutionary upheaval occurred within imperial territories, at the center in those empires that suffered defeat in World War I (Russian, German, Hapsburg, and Ottoman empires), and in outlying territories in those empires that were victorious in World War II (British, French, Dutch, and Belgian colonies). In addition, World War II paved the way for communist revolutions in Eastern Europe, China, North Vietnam, and North Korea.

The world wars created revolutionary conditions primarily because they speeded up the disintegration of central authority in places where it was already breaking down in the prewar period. However, in the absence of war and major military defeat, the system of authority and control in some cases might have undergone orderly rather than revolutionary transformation. The political destructiveness of military defeat above all consists in a loss of confidence on the part of a large number of people in the capacities of their rulers. (This is of only limited relevance to colonial territories, although even here military failure plays a part, as in the case of the European colonies in Asia conquered for a time by the Japanese during World War II.) The fact that there was a peaking of revolutionary upheavals in Latin America at the end of the two world wars cannot be accounted for in these terms, since Latin America was not deeply involved in these wars. This is particularly true of the Mexican Revolution, which began before World War I and reached its climax during that war for reasons mostly unrelated to the war.

The major source of massive stress between the two world wars was, of course, the Great Depression. In Europe, the general pattern appears to be this: the greater the amount of unemployment, the stronger the revolutionary forces of both the right (facism) and the left (communism). In fact, there were no successful communist revolutions during the depression. Fascist and quasi-fascist revolutionaries were successful in several nations, notably in Germany and Spain, to some extent in Japan, and to a small extent in Brazil (the out-and-out fascists were defeated there). Italy, of course, already had its fascist revolution, and Austria moved in a fascist direction before finally being occupied by Nazi Germany. There wery other predominantly unsuccessful fascist revolutionary attempts. Suffice it to say that fascism rather than communism was the chief beneficiary of the depression, in part because the depression fed the nationalist frustrations spawned by World War I. As in the case of war, depression appears to be politically destructive only where the structure of authority and control was already crumbling. Where, on the other hand, the system of authority and control was operating effectively, conflict was contained even though the depression was severe—as in the United States.

These general patterns mask the very great *variation* in the character of revolutions. The following discussion, therefore, considers different types of revolution, their incidence, and conditions that favor them.

A revolution may or may not be the work of a revolutionary movement, involve revolutionary conflict, or result in revolutionary change. Treating each of these dimensions as dichotomous attributes, eight patterns are discernible. At one extreme, an extraordinary transformation of government is the work of a revolutionary movement that emerges victorious in a highly polarized conflict, and subsequently produces radical change in the social order, as in the modern mass revolution.

Table 1. Revolution Types and Dimensions

Types of Revolution	Dimensions of Revolution		
	Polarization	Mobilization	Transformation
1. Palace revolution	−	−	−
2. Communal revolution	+	−	−
3. Coopted revolution	−	+	−
4. Nationalist revolution	+	+	−
5. Orderly revolution	−	−	+
6. Elite revolution	+	−	+
7. Imposed revolution	−	+	+
8. Mass revolution	+	+	+

Palace Revolution

In a palace revolution, one section of the ruling group overthrows another section without changing institutional arrangements. During the past fifty years, seventy percent of all revolutions have been palace revolutions. Of the 267 palace revolutions, 162, or sixty percent, occurred in Latin America, over half (fifty-four) took place in six nations: Portugal, Iraq, Syria, Thailand, Greece, and South Vietnam, in order of decreasing frequency. There has been a sharp increase in palace revolutions in Latin America, Asia, and the Middle East since World War II, and a sharp decrease in Europe.

Palace revolutions generally are engineered by military officers, with the ostensible purpose of restoring the integrity of government by removing rulers allegedly responsible for corruption, ineptness, or oppression. Most palace revolutions occur in societies where there have been numerous such revolutions (only three of the twenty Latin American republics had fewer than five palace revolutions between 1917 and 1966). This may be taken as an indication that palace revolutions generally fail to renew governing authority, but instead increase the likelihood of further palace revolutions. Moreover, recurring palace revolutions tend to be the work of military officers who generally prove to be incapable of establishing effective authority. Thus, palace revolutions demonstrate the weak legitimacy of constitutional arrangements for changing rulers; and they contribute to the further weakening of that legitimacy.

Palace revolutions occur under regimes that consider themselves "revolutionary" as well as under those that do not. Recent examples of palace revolutions in revolutionary regimes include Algeria, Iraq, Syria, Burma, and Bolivia. The result in all these cases has been to substitute military regimes for party or charismatic regimes. Communist regimes also are vulnerable to palace revolutions because they lack effective institutions for succession, although the result has not been the establishment of military rule.

Only advanced industrial societies by and large have avoided palace revolutions. (France and Germany experienced attempted palace revolutions, in both cases at a time when military action abroad was proving more or less unsuccessful.) This would appear to be the result of relatively strong political institutions rather than weak military organizations. Conversely, palace revolutions tend to occur where political institutions are weak, whether or not military organizations are strong; witness sub-Saharan Africa during the 1960s (see Zolberg, 1968). Moreover, palace revolutions generally further weaken political institutions.

Communal Revolution

Communal revolutions are attempts to reestablish the *responsiveness* of government to the customary expectations of a community, either by changing the government or by acquiring greater autonomy for the community. Communal revolutions, then, seek to renew community rather than to transform society. They are the work of communal groups rather than revolutionary movements, and generally are spontaneous uprisings with only rudimentary organization. In consequence, they usually are defeated—but only after considerable polarization and violence between the communal group and the governing group. Between 1917 and 1966, some twelve percent of all revolutions against the national government were communal.

Peasant jacqueries are one kind of communal revolution. Although they tend to be legitimist and restorationist, they also may be anarchist rebellions. Regional, provincial, and ethnic revolts for autonomy from the central government represent another kind of communal revolution with ancient roots. Since they are direct attacks on the unity and hegemony of the nation-state, these revolts generally are forms of resistance to modern political development.

Communal revolutions for autonomy tend to occur in societies where ethnic groups are territorially separated. Thus, they currently are frequent in Southeast Asia (notably in Burma, Indonesia, and India), and in the Middle East (notably in Iraq).

A third kind of communal revolution is the urban-based uprising, typically centering in the capital city, against repression or tyranny on the part of the central government. Such were the revolutionary strikes in Russia in 1905, and more recently the uprisings in East Germany and in Budapest. All these revolutions were defeated, in part, because they lacked effective organization.

Communal revolutions, then, are more or less unorganized attacks on the central government by subordinate communal groups seeking reinstatement of real or imagined past conditions.

Coopted Revolution

Coopted revolutions are attempts by elements of the regime to preserve the structure of continuity of authority by cooptation of leaders or members of a revolutionary movement into the government. A coopted revolution, therefore, does not significantly change the social order. It is revolutionary only in the sense that an extraordinary transformation of government occurs, but without much conflict or change. The cooptation may change the formal structure of government (e.g., from monarchy to republic) but not significantly the structure of power. The revolutionary opposition acquires some of the symbols of power with (at least initially) a minimum of its substance. Thus nationalist leaders may be coopted into a colonial regime preparatory to a transfer of power; the newly independent regime will therefore tend to remain close to the former colonial power in military and economic relations. Many former British and French colonies in Africa became independent through such coopted revolutions.

The German Revolution of 1918 was an instance of cooptation, since the Social Democratic leaders helped overthrow the Imperial State while also suppressing the mass movement when they entered the government. The military thereby was able to maintain its pivotal position of power and privilege in the Weimar Republic.

There are relatively few cases of coopted revolutions, but many attempted cooptations which failed to stem the tide of revolutionary change. When Hindenburg offered the chancellorship to Hitler in 1933, he and his associates thought that they were thereby not only reestablishing German unity but also blunting the revolutionary edge of the Nazi movement. The attempt to bring the Communists into a coalition government in Czechoslovakia to preserve the existing order is another example of cooptation that failed.

Another variant of coopted revolution is the attempt by a governing group to mobilize masses for the purpose of consolidating political power. Such a system of mobilization must be distinguished from the truly revolutionary aim of enlisting mass energies in order to sustain his rule rather than to transform the society. (That it has led to considerable polarization in Argentina after Peron's personal rule was terminated testifies to the general tendency for coopted leaders or masses to seek independent power. Thus, the Peronists may yet prove to be a force for revolutionary change.) Mass mobilization may give a regime the appearance of revolutionary purpose and achievement, when in fact masses have been coopted into the political process merely to shore up a regime.

Nationalist Revolution

Nationalist revolutions seek national independence and unity. They are to be distinguished from communal revolutions by virtue of their commitment to the foundation of a new political order. This aim gives rise to an organized movement that seeks to be comprehensive of the whole society. Communal revolutions generally precede nationalist revolutions, as local consciousness prevails over national consciousness. The struggle for independence creates as well as expresses national consciousness, and thereby facilitates the development of political integration.

The nationalist revolution in its pure form aims *only* at national independence and unity, and does not seek power for the additional purpose of transforming the society. The nationalist revolution leaves the social structure intact, except insofar as it creates and strengthens national ties. There have been only about twelve such revolutions between 1917 and 1966. The Latin American nationalist revolutions in the early nineteenth century sustained rather than transformed the social order. The Algerian revolution, on the other hand, sought a radically new social order along with national sovereignty. The central difference is whether the revolutionary movement is based on an ideology of nationalism or in addition on an ideology of comprehensive social change. But even when there is comprehensive ideology and organization, the winning of national independence may be followed by stagnation rather than development.

Orderly Revolution

Orderly revolutions seek a radical and comprehensive transformation of society without polarizing or mobilizing the population. In the minimum case, the commitment to orderly change is tactical, as in the instance of the Italian Communist party's avowal of an electoral revolution. In the maximum case, the commitment is normative: Gandhi's adherence to nonviolence represents such a maximum commitment to orderly revolution.

The conflict between order and change has been only rarely transcended in revolutions. Even Gandhi could not prevent the great polarization and violence of the partition. Since independence, the Indian Congress party has been more successful in developing constitutional order than in effectuating radical social transformation. The Congress party itself has ceased to be a revolutionary movement and instead has become a loose coalition of diversy and often contradictory tendencies. Both polarization and mobilization have been eschewed as strategies of social change. This leaves the regime with very little political leverage.

Orderly revolution, then, remains more in the realm of aspiration than achievement. Where the aspiration exists, political development is likely to be more impressive than social or economic development. If social and economic development is slow, however, the constitutional order may loose the support required for its own viability.

Elite Revolution

Elite revolutions are attempts to transform central institutions from above. They tend to occur when reform movements within the traditional elite are frustrated. The revolutionaries are themselves members of the traditional elite, or at least occupy high positions within ruling institutions, such as the bureaucracy and army. Considerable polarization between traditional and revolutionary forces takes place; but it generally is confined within the elite, while the bulk of the population remains quiescent. The revolutionaries do not seek to fashion a popular movement, and there is little political mobilization of society. There have been nineteen elite revolutions during the past fifty years, eleven of which have been at least partially successful.

The principal difference between elite revolutions and palace revolutions lies in their orientation toward social change rather than in their social composition: in both types, military officers generally play a key role. Palace revolutions accommodate existing elites, whereas elite revolutions seek to destroy elites that retard national development. Their elite character, however, makes these revolutions much less discontinuous with the traditional society than in the case of mass revolutions. Where mass revolutions seek to substitute comprehensive ideology for tradition, elite revolutions attempt to substitute national values for dynastic and feudal values. Correlatively, where mass revolutions tend to emphasize class interests and power, elite revolutions stress national interests and power. Thus, the Ataturk revolution was an elite effort to develop national institutions and power; it was not much concerned with effectuating major change in the class structure, other than eliminating the power of certain traditional groups opposed to national development.

Since elite revolutions presuppose fairly strong and coherent elite institutions, new nation-states are not hospitable to elite revolutions. The current model of elite revolution would be Nasser's revolution. Efforts to emulate it in Iraq and Syria show the difficulty of consolidating a revolutionary regime where elite instructions are very weak. The weakness of the prerevolutionary regime tends to be recapitulated in the revolutionary regime.

After seizing power, leaders of elite revolutions may seek to build mass organization as a source of power to effectuate radical social change, but they generally fail in this attempt. Nasser's efforts at mass mobilization show the limitations of elite revolutions, especially the difficulty of organizing masses when they have not been previously aroused.

Imposed Revolution

Imposed revolutions occur when a foreign state seeks to transform a society. Such "revolutions from without" are to be distinguished from simple foreign conquests and puppet governments by the commitment to extending revolutionary change into new areas rather than only political control. The decisive consideration, then, is the extent to which revolutionary change is sought and achieved by the imposed regime. War and conquest pave the way for imposed revolutions. Indigenous revolutionary movements may exist or arise in association with the foreign state, but decisive power, initially, at least, is exercised by the foreign state rather than the indigenous revolutionaries. If only feeble indigenous revolutionary forces exist prior to the revolution, the imposed regime generally will try to organize a revolutionary movement to consolidate power and transform social institutions.

The Napoleonic Wars in the nineteenth century and the world wars in the twentieth century led to numerous revolutions from without. Examples include the formation of communist regimes in Eastern Europe where the intervention of Soviet power proved decisive. The extent to which the communist revolution was imposed varied from country to country, being most fully imposed in East Germany, whereas in Yugoslavia local communists came to power without Soviet intervention.

Imposed revolutions have a much more profound impact on society than do simple foreign conquests. All revolutions imposed by the Soviet Union have led to political mobilization and comprehensive change. Where revolutions are imposed, however, the regime often has difficulty in harnessing the forces of nationalism to work for it. Moreover, the state that imposed the revolution may seek to exploit it for its national interests at the expense of the revolutionary goals.

Mass Revolution

Mass revolutions seek to create a mass order by means of the polarization, mobilization, and development of society. By polarization, the revolution isolates and then destroys traditional elites. By mobilization, the revolution uproots the masses from traditional commitments and indoctrinates them with ideological values. By development, the revolution creates the political, social, and economic bases for a mass order. There have been thirty-one mass revolutions during the past fifty years, thirteen of which have been successful. Communist revolutions in Russia and China are the major mass revolutions of our time. German Nazis and the Italian Fascists also made mass revolutions, albeit with the help of the old elites. The Nazi and Fascist regimes were not so revolutionary, however, because although they helped create considerable polarization and mobilization, they did not sponsor much development. Hence, they did not progress very far in laying the basis for a mass order before they were destroyed by their military adventures.

There is a fundamental tension in mass revolutions between polarization and mobilization, on the one hand, and institutional development on the other hand. The combination of polarization and mobilization constitutes a posture of combat and warfare, whether against class enemies or foreign enemies. Warfare can serve the purpose of destroying old institutions, but it is not so conducive to the development of new institutions. For warfare places a premium on single-mindedness of purpose, quickness of action, and discipline of mass organization, whereas institution-building requires the ordering of diverse purposes and values, adaptation to multiple centers of power, and governance of conduct by rules. Perpetual revolutionary warfare, then, tends to invite totalitarian controls (totalitarian ideology in turn encourages perpetual warfare whether against internal or foreign "enemies").

Only a few revolutions have generated mass integration without totalitarian controls. The Mexican Revolution may be the outstanding case. Although there were many years of violent conflict, once the revolution was consolidated, the emphasis shifted from mass mobilization to institutional development. The relatively simple and pragmatic ideology of the Mexican Revolution facilitated this change.

Mass revolutions are very unlikely unless great and cumulative *cleavages* exist in society. This may mean substantial class conflict, as existed in France in the late eighteenth century, in Russia in the late nineteenth and early twentieth centuries, and in China in the nineteenth and twentieth centuries. More fundamentally, mass revolutions require the disintegration of a ruling class and the social fragmentation and disorganization of the society as a whole.

Conclusion

The typology of revolutions is intended to facilitate inquiry into variations in the relation between revolution and national development. The eight types of revolution have been presented in an order of their increasingly revolutionary character. This does not mean, however, that mass revolution will always contribute more to development than palace revolution. The contributions of different kinds of revolution to development vary according to the specific context, including the character of the regime, strength of political unity, level of economic development, system of social classes, and many other factors.

The types of revolution vary in their causes as well as in their consequences. Causes cannot be adduced from consequences: a society may not get the kind of revolution it needs. But clearly, revolutions are not random mutations: they express real social needs even when they exacerbate rather than alleviate them. Further research is needed to determine the types of revolution which occur under different conditions of national development, as well as the kinds of national development which result from different types of revolution (see Kornhauser, 1964).

REFERENCES

This bibliography consists mainly of studies published since 1963. For studies published between 1945 and 1963, see Lissak, M. (1964) "Bibliographic guide: selected literature of revolutions and coups d'état in the developing nations," pp. 339-362 in M. Janowitz (ed.) The New Military. New York: Russell Sage Foundation.

AFRIFA, Col. A. A. (1966) The Ghana Coup, 24th February, 1966. New York: Humanities Press.

ANDRESKI, S. (1961) "Conservatism and radicalism of the military. Archives Europeennes de Sociologie 2 (Spring): 53-61.

BARBER, W. F. and C. N. RONNING (1968) Internal Security and Military Power: Counterinsurgency and Civic Action in Latin America.

BASHINE, M. O. (1968) The Southern Sudan: Background to Conflict. New York: Frederick A. Praeger.

BELL, M. J. V. (1968) "The military in the new states of Africa," pp. 259-273 in J. van Doorn (ed.) Armed Forces and Society. The Hague: Mouton.

BELTRAN, V. R. (1968) "The Army and structural changes in 20th century Argentina," pp. 317-341 in J. van Doorn (ed.) Armed Forces and Society. The Hague: Mouton.

BIENEN, H. (1968) Violence and Social Change. Chicago: University of Chicago Press.

———(1968) "Public order and the military in Africa: mutinies in Kenya, Uganda, and Tanganyika," pp. 35-70 in H. Bienen (ed.) The Military Intervenes. New York: Russell Sage Foundation.

BLASIER, C. (1967) "Studies of social revolutions: origins in Mexico, Bolivia, and Cuba." Latin American Research Review 2 (Summer): 28-64.

BOBROW, D. B. (1965) "Soldiers and the nation-state." Annals of the American Academy of Political and Social Science (March).

BRILL, W. H. (1967) Military Intervention in Bolivia: The Overthrow of Paz Estenssoro and the MNR. Washington, D.C.: Institute for the Study of Political Systems.

BRINTON, C. (1957) The Anatomy of Revolution. New York: Vintage.

CALVERT, P. A. R. (1967) "The 'typical Latin American revolution'." International Affairs 43 (January): 85-95.

———(1967) "Revolution: the politics of violence." Political Studies 15 (February): 1-11.

CHAPLIN, D. (1968) "Peru's postponed revolution." World Politics 10 (April): 393-420.

CLAPHAM, C. (1968) "The December 1960 Ethiopian coup d'état." Journal of Modern African Studies 6 (December): 495-507.

CLIFFORD-VAUGHAN, M. (1964) "Changing attitudes to the Army's role in French society." British Journal of Sociology 15 (December): 338-349.

CONDIT, D. M., B. H. COOPER, et al. Challenge and Response in Internal Conflict, vols. I, II, III. Washington, D.C.: American University, Center for Research in Social Systems.

DAVIES, J. C. (1967) "Circumstances and causes of revolutions: a review." Journal of Conflict Resolution 11 (June): 247-257.

DEBRAY, R. (1967) Revolution in the Revolution? New York: Grove Press.

DEUTSCH, K. W. (1964) "External involvement in internal war," pp. 100-110 in H. Eckstein (ed.) Internal War. New York: Macmillan.

DUDLEY, B. (1965) "Violence in Nigerian politics." Transition 5, 21: 21-24.

ECKSTEIN, H. (1965) "On the etiology of internal wars." History and Theory 4, 2: 150-151.

———[ed.] (1964) Internal War. New York: Macmillan.

———(1963) "Internal war: the problem of anticipation," pp. 102-132 in I. Pool et al. (eds.) Social Science Research and National Security. Washington, D.C.: Smithsonian Institute.

EDINGER, L. J. (1963) "Military leaders and foreign policy-making." American Political Science Review 57 (June): 392-405.

EVANS, R. D. (1968) "Brazilian revolution of 1964: political surgery without anaesthetics." International Affairs 44 (April): 267-281.

FEIT, E. (1968) "Military coups and political development: some lessons from Ghana and Nigeria." World Politics 20 (January): 179-193.

FELD, M. D. (1968) "Professionalism, nationalism, and the alienation of the military," in J. van Doorn (ed.) Armed Forces and Society. The Hague: Mouton.

FELDMAN, A. S. (1964) "Violence and volatility: the likelihood of revolution," pp. 111-129 in H. Eckstein (ed.) Internal War. New York: Macmillan.

FISHER, S. N. [ed.] (1963) The Military in the Middle East. Columbus: Ohio State University Press.

FOSSUM, E. (1967) "Factors influencing the occurrence of coups d'état in Latin America." Journal of Peace Research 4, 3: 228-251.

FRIEDRICH, C. J. [ed.] (1966) Revolution. New York: Atherton Press.

GESCHWENDER, J. A. (1968) "Explorations in the theory of social movements and revolution." Social Forces 47 (December): 127-135.

GILMORE, R. E. (1964) Caudillism and Militarism in Venzuela, 1810-1910. Columbus: Ohio State University Press.

GLUBB, Sir J. B. (1965) "Role of the Army in the traditional Arab state." Journal of International Affairs 19, 1: 8-15.

GOLDWERT, M. (1968) "Rise of modern militarism in Argentina." Hispanic American Historical Review 48 (May): 189-205.

———(1966) "Dichotomies of militarism in Argentina." Orbis 10 (Fall): 930-939.

GRAHAM, H. D. and T. R. GURR (1969) Violence in America: Historical and Comparative Perspectives. New York: Bantam Books.

GRUNDY, K. W. (1968) "Negative image of Africa's military." Review of Politics 30 (Spring): 28-35.

GURR, T. (1968) "A causal model of civil strife: a comparative analysis using new indices." American Political Science Review 32 (December): 1104-1124.

———with C. RUTTENBERG (1967) The Conditions of Civil Violence: First Tests of a Causal Model. Princeton: Center of International Studies.

GUTTERIDGE, W. F. (1967) "Political role of African armed forces: the impact of foreign military assistance." African Affairs 66 (April): 93-103.

———(1965) Military Institutions and Power in the New States. New York: Frederick A. Praeger.

HADDAD, G. M. (1965) Revolutions and Military Rule in the Middle East. New York: Robert Speller.

HAHNER, J. E. (1967) " 'Paulistas' rise to power: a civilian group ends military rule." Hispanic American History Review 47 (May): 149-165.

HARRIS, G. S. (1965) "Role of the military in Turkish politics." Middle East Journal 19 (Winter-Spring): 169-176.

HELGUERA, L. (1961) "The changing role of the military in Colombia." Journal of Inter-American Studies 3 (October): 351-358.

HINDLEY, D. (1967) "Political power and the October 1965 coup in Indonesia." Journal of Asian Studies 26 (February): 237-249.

HOPKINS, K. (1966) "Civil-military relations in developing countries." British Journal of Sociology 17 (June): 165-182.

HOROWITZ, I. L. (1967) "The military elites," pp. 146-189 in S. M. Lipset and A. Solari (eds.) Elites in Latin America. New York: Oxford University Press.

HOWE, R. W. (1967) "Togo: four years of military rule." Africa Report 12 (May): 6-12.

HUNTINGTON, S. P. (1968) Political Order in Changing Societies. New Haven, Conn.: Yale University Press.

HUREWITZ, J. C. (1969) Middle East Politics: The Military Dimension. New York: Frederick A. Praeger.

JANOS, A. C. (1964) The Seizure of Power. Princeton: Center of International Studies.

JANOWITZ, M. (1964) The Role of the Military in the Political Development of New Nations. Chicago: University of Chicago Press.

JOHNSON, C. (1967) Revolutionary Change. Boston: Little, Brown.

———(1964) Revolution and the Social System. Stanford, Calif.: Hoover Institute Studies.

JOHNSON, J. J. (1964) The Military and Society in Latin America. Stanford, Calif.: Stanford University Press.

KAUTSKY, J. H. (1964) "The military in underdeveloped countries." Economic Development and Cultural Change 12 (July): 436-443.

KELLY, G. A. (1965) Lost Soldiers: The French Army and Empire in Crisis, 1947-1963. Cambridge, Mass.: MIT Press.

———(1963) "Global civil-military dilemma." Review of Politics 25 (July): 291-308.

KIM, C. I. E. (1968) "The South Korean military coup of May, 1961," pp. 298-316 in J. van Doorn (ed.) Armed Forces and Society. The Hague: Mouton.

KLING, M. (1969) "Violence and politics in Latin America," pp. 191-206 in I. L. Horowitz, J. deCastro, and J. Gerassi (eds.) Latin American Radicalism. New York: Random House.

KOLKOWICZ, R. (1967) The Soviet Military and the Communist Party. Princeton: Princeton University Press.

KORNHAUSER, W. (1964) "Rebellion and political development," pp. 142-156 in H. Eckstein (ed.) Internal War. New York: Macmillan.

LAMBERT, J. (1968) Latin America: Social Structures and Political Institutions (H. Katel, trans.). Berkeley: University of California Press.

LANG, K. (1968) "The military putsch in a developed political culture," pp. 202-228 in J. van Doorn (ed.) Armed Forces and Society. The Hague: Mouton.

LEIDEN, C. and K. M. SCHMITT [eds.] (1968) The Politics of Violence: Revolution in the Modern World. Englewood Cliffs, N.J.: Prentice-Hall.

LEV, D. S. (1963-1964) "Political role of the army in Indonesia." Pacific Affairs 36 (Winter): 349-364.

LEVINE, D. N. (1968) "The military in Ethiopian politics: capabilities and constraints," pp. 5-34 in H. Bienen (ed.) The Military Intervenes. New York: Russell Sage Foundation.

LIEUWIN, E. (1968) Mexican Militarism: The Political Rise and Fall of the Revolutionary Army. Albuquerque: University of New Mexico Press.

———(1964) Generals vs. Presidents. New York: Frederick A. Praeger.

———(1961) "The changing role of the military in Latin America." Journal of Inter-American Studies 3 (October): 559-569.

LISSAK, M. (1964) "Modernization and role expansion of the military in developing countries: a comparative analysis." Comparative Studies in Society and History 9 (April) 233-255.

LOVELL, J. P. and C. I. E. KIM (1967) "The military and political change in Asia." Pacific Affairs 40 (Spring and Summer): 113-123.

McCOLL, R. W. (1967) "A political geography of revolution: China, Vietnam and Thailand." Journal of Conflict Resolution 11 (June): 153-167.

McWILLIAMS, W. C. [ed.] (1967) Garrisons and Governments. San Francisco: Chandler.

MAZRUI, A. A. (1968) "Anti-militarism and political militancy in Tanzania." Journal of Conflict Resolution 12 (September): 269-284.

————and D. S. ROTHCHILD (1967) "Soldier and the state in East Africa; some theoretical conclusions on the army mutinies of 1964." Western Political Quarterly 20 (March): 82-96.

MENARD, O. D. (1967) The Army and the Fifth Republic. Lincoln: University of Nebraska Press.

MIDLARSKY, M. and R. TANTER (1967) "Toward a theory of political instability in Latin America." Journal of Peace Research 4, 3: 209-227.

MITCHELL, E. (1968) "Inequality and insurgency: a statistical study of South Vietnam." World Politics 20 (April): 421-438.

MOORE, B. (1966) Social Origins of Dictatorship and Democracy. Boston: Beacon Press.

NEEDLER, M. C. (1968) "Political development and socioeconomic development: the case of Latin America." American Political Science Review 62 (September): 889-897.

————(1966) "Political development and military intervention in Latin America." American Political Science Review 60 (September): 616-626.

————(1963) Anatomy of a coup d'état: Ecuador.

NORTH, L. (1966) Civil-Military Relations in Argentina, Chile, and Peru. Berkeley: Institute of International Studies, University of California.

NUN, J. (1968) "A Latin American phenomenon: the middle class military coup," pp. 145-185 in J. F. Patras and M. Zeitlin (eds.) Latin America, Reform or Revolution? Greenwich, Conn.: Fawcett Publications.

NUNN, F. M. (1967) "Military rule in Chile: the revolutions of September 5, 1924 and January 23, 1925." Hispanic American Historical Review 47 (February): 1-21.

PAGET, R. K. (1967-1968) "Military in Indonesian politics: the burden of power." Pacific Affairs 40 (Fall and Winter): 294-314.

PARET, P. (1968) French Revolutionary Warfare from Indo-China To Algeria. New York: Frederick A. Praeger.

PAYNE, A. (n.d.) The Peruvian Coup d'Etat of 1962: Its Origin and Significance.

PAYNE, S. G. (1967) Politics and Military in Modern Spain. Stanford, Calif.: Stanford University Press.

POTASH, R. (1961) "The changing role of the military in Argentina." Journal of Inter-American Studies 3 (October): 571-578.

PUTNAM, R. D. (1967) "Toward explaining military intervention in Latin American politics." World Politics 20 (October): 83-110.

PYE, L. W. (1964) "The roots of insurgency and commencement of rebellions," in H. Eckstein (ed.) Internal War. New York: Macmillan.

RIPPY, J. F. (1965) "Latin America's postwar golpes de estado." Inter-American Economic Affairs 19 (Winter): 73-80.

RUSTOW, D. A. (1967) "Military regimes," pp. 170-206 in D. A. Rustow (ed.) A World of Nations. Washington, D.C.: Brookings Institute.

SAYEED, K. B. (1968) "The role of the military in Pakistan," pp. 274-297 in J. van Doorn (ed.) Armed Forces and Society. The Hague: Mouton.

SHARABI, H. (1966) Nationalism and Revolution in the Arab World. Princeton: Princeton University Press.

SOHN, J. S. (1968) "Political dominance and political failure: the role of the military in the Republic of Korea," pp. 103-126 in H. Bienen (ed.) The Military Intervenes. New York: Russell Sage Foundation.

SPRINGER, P. B. (1968) "Disunity and disorder: factional politics in the Argentine military," pp. 145-168 in H. Bienen (ed.) The Military Intervenes. New York: Russell Sage Foundation.

———(1965) "Social sources of political behavior of Venezuelan military officers: an exploratory analysis." Il Politico 30 (June): 348-355.

TANTER, R. (1966) "Dimensions of conflict behavior within and between nations, 1958-1960." Journal of Conflict Resolution 10 (March): 41-65.

TERRAINE, J. A. (1961) "The army in modern France." History Today 11 (November): 733-742.

THORNTON, T. P. (1964) "Terror as a weapon of political agitation," pp. 71-99 in H. Eckstein (ed.) Internal War. New York: Macmillan.

TILLEY, C. (1964) The Vendee. Cambridge: Harvard University Press.

———and J. RULE (1965) Measuring Political Upheaval. Princeton: Center of International Studies.

TORREY, G. H. (1964) Syrian Politics and the Military, 1945-1958. Columbus: Ohio State University Press.

TRAGER, F. N. (1963) "Failure of U Nu and the return of the armed forces in Burma." Review of Politics 25 (July): 309-328.

VAN DEN BERGHE, P. L. (1965) "Role of the army in contemporary Africa." Africa Report 10 (March): 12-17.

VAN DER MEHDEN, F. R. and C. W. ANDERSON (1961) "Political action by the military in the developing areas." Social Research 28 (Winter): 459-480.

VATIKIOTIS, P. J. (1967) Politics and the Military in Jordan: The Arab Legion, 1921-1957. New York: Frederick A. Praeger.

WERTHEIM, W. F. (1966) "Indonesia before and after the Untung coup." Pacific Affairs 39 (Spring and Summer): 115-127.

WILCOX, W. A. (1965) "The Pakistan coup d'état of 1958." Pacific Affairs 38 (Summer): 142-163.

WOLF, E. R. and E. C. HANSEN (1967) "Caudillo politics: a structural analysis." Comparative Studies in Society and History 9 (January): 168-179.

YALMAN, N. (1968) "Intervention and extrication: the officer corps in the Turkish Crisis," pp. 127-144 in H. Bienen (ed.) The Military Intervenes. New York: Russell Sage Foundation.

YOUNG, J. (1964) "Military aspect of the 1930 Brazilian revolution." Hispanic American Historical Review 44 (May): 180-196.

ZOLBERG, A. R. (1968) "The structure of political conflict in the new states of Tropical Africa." American Political Science Review 62 (March): 70-87.

———(1968) "Military intervention in the new states of Tropical Africa: elements of comparative analysis," pp. 71-98 in H. Bienen (ed.) The Military Intervenes. New York: Russell Sage Foundation.

Chapter 13

SOCIAL DYNAMICS OF
REVOLUTIONARY GUERRILLA WARFARE

FRANKLIN MARK OSANKA

*A*lthough some sociologists and other social scientists have concerned themselves with various aspects of revolution and guerrilla warfare, limited systematic knowledge exists on these critical aspects of societal conflict. The nature of revolutionary guerrilla conflict, with its inherent internal and external sociopolitical subtleties, seems to defy the systematic application of modern social scientific theory and methodology. In recent years elements of the various social sciences, particularly sociology and political science, have vigorously raised the issue of professional ethics in regard to government-sponsored research in the areas of counter-insurgency. The concern with professional ethics is real and widespread throughout the sociological profession, and at least two sociologists argued very eloquently for sober consideration for professional ethics and legitimacy in relation to counter-insurgency and United States-sponsored research in the so-called Third World (Horowitz, 1967; Moskos, 1968). Other sociologists, on the other hand, have determined that such research is generally legitimate and ethical, and they have advocated that more professional attention should be addressed to the question (Lowry, 1965; Tackaberry, 1968).

Most of the present controversy centers around the question of government-sponsored and funded research which relates to United States foreign policy rather than being a question of the appropriateness of the subject matter itself as a legitimate area of social scientific inquiry. Indeed, most sociologists recognized that in this age of potentially devastating nuclear weaponry, revolutionary, guerrilla, and other forms of internal war may become the most frequent forms of political violence. War has always been considered a social problem deserving of the attention of sociologists. The first step toward that goal is an acceptance by the international community of social scientists that the subject is worthy of scientific inquiry. The second step is the application of social scientific theory and research methodology to this laboratory of violence. The third step is to make the findings of research available, through open publications and university curriculum, to the academic community and to those who frame and implement policy.

This essay deals with a brief overview of the phenomenon of revolutionary guerrilla warfare but in the main will concentrate on the role that the civilian populace plays in such sociopolitical conflict. Specifically, it will concentrate on the social dynamics of revolutionary guerrilla recruitment and populace control in the early stage of the conflict.[1]

Guerrilla warfare is scarcely new. In fact, guerrilla tactics are the oldest form of armed conflict known to man. The term "guerrilla," which means literally "small war," was originally used to define the resistance activities of armed Spanish civilians who harried the French occupation army during the Peninsular War of 1808-1814.

Guerrilla activity has been an adjunct to battle operations in major wars as well as popular modus operandi of suppressed peoples in dealing with unpopular governments. It has been a favorite tactic of small and poorly armed societies against greater powers, and every country occupied by the Axis in World War II produced some type of guerrilla movement that contributed to the Allied victory (Osanka, 1962: xii).

In contemporary times, the objectives of guerrilla warfare have been more political than military. Since the end of World War II, there have been many revolutionary wars using guerrilla warfare as the principal means of violence. In some cases the revolutionary leaders have ascended to national power. Where the revolutionary wars were lost militarily, the conflict nevertheless often had the effect of influencing, if not directly initiating, critical political and social changes, and in several cases national independence ulitmately resulted. The principles of revolutionary war and guerrilla warfare have become so enmeshed in recent times that the two seem inseparable. The most adequate descriptive term would seem to be "revolutionary guerrilla warfare."

> It is revolutionary in that it is used as a means of acquiring national power for the purpose of altering or completely changing the social and political structure of a nation. It is guerrilla warfare in that its participating advocates of change are indigenous civilians waging a small war utilizing principles learned from guerrilla history.
>
> The strategic objectives of the guerrillas are to reduce the military and political strength of the ruling power while increasing their own until the guerrilla force can be organized and trained as a regular army capable of defeating the ruling-power army on the open battlefield or causing the ruling power to collapse or otherwise surrender to revolutionary guerrilla demands, thus producing guerrilla national victory by political default [Osanka, 1968: 503].

The main tactical strength of the guerrilla is his intimate knowledge of the local terrain and populace. Guerrilla tactics are adapted to the local social conditions, capabilities of the participating guerrillas, terrain, and strength of the ruling-power forces earmarked for attack. Guerrilla tactics consist of raids, ambushes, and sabotage. The primary targets of attack are isolated police and army outposts and units, national and military communications, transportation and supply, and sources of ruling power economic revenue.

Guerrillas usually attack only when numerically superior, hold the tactical advantage, and are otherwise assured of success. Guerrillas avoid pitched battles not of their own choosing, rapidly concentrate for an attack and rapidly disperse afterwards, and avoid concentrating on large numbers for long periods of time thereby depriving the enemy of a lucrative target for the utilization of power. Guerrillas attack at times and places where the enemy is most vulnerable, planning attacks so that many occur at the same time at widely different locations thereby creating the impression of numerical strength out of proportion to actual strength. The guerrilla seeks to engender within the ranks of the ruling power and the populace the psychological perception of seeming to be everywhere yet nowhere. "The modern army with its complex equipment is very dependent on its lines of communications and its supply bases which in turn provide guerrillas with an abundance of targets" (Doheny, 1966: 40).

Guerrilla attacks, particularly the destruction or disruption of national and military lines of communication, transportation and supply, and sources of economic revenue create a paralyzing effect in that they restrict the ruling-power forces' mobility, reduce the ruling-power forces' numerical superiority by forcing the expenditures of troops on status protection duties, and force the ruling-power forces to concentrate in large numbers. All of these tactics reduce considerably the ruling-power's political and economic administrative control, thereby demonstrating to the populace an inability to maintain law, order, and protection while providing the time, space, and conditions for the guerrillas to implant their own substitute political and economic administrative apparatus, or *political infrastructure,* which further insures guerrilla strength and population, and population and national resources control.

To be successful, the revolutionary guerrilla must establish an effective political mass base. "A political mass base is a sociopolitical condition resulting when the guerrillas successfully gain the support or neutralization of the majority of the populace in given areas" (Osanka, 1968: 504). While the modern guerrilla relies heavily on political and logistical support from the international foreign community, more importantly he relies, as did his historical predecessors, on the indigenous populace. Effective control of the local populace is the indispensable condition of success, and consequently, favorable control and support of the population is a major goal of the guerrillas. Guerrillas cannot operate or exist for long without the active support of an enthusiastic minority plus at least the passive political apathy of a significant portion of the remaining majority of the populace. Operationally, the guerrillas carry out overt and covert actions on the basis of timely intelligence information from its agents within the populace concerning the movements of the ruling-power's political and military forces. The populace further aids the guerrilla by providing food, shelter, medical supplies and care, guides, laborers, and recruits. Most significantly, the population under guerrilla control denies information to the ruling-power forces concerning the activities and locations of the guerrillas. Guerrilla operations are fought by few but dependent on many. Men, women, and children of all ages participate in a variety of roles such as couriers, intelligence agents, fighters, and food providers.

It is dangerous to generalize about geographic areas, but it is now commonly recognized that most rural areas of the less-developed nations manifest certain environmental characteristics which guerrillas can exploit in order to achieve their own ends. In many of these rural areas, living conditions are intolerable: illiteracy, disease, hunger, poverty, inadequate housing, a low crude-birth rate, a high early death rate, definite levels of social stratification, and tribal animosities are the rule rather than the exception. The peasants are usually a simple people, primarily farmers, who do not own the land they (as have probably their fathers before them) have worked all their lives and who are frequently exploited by the land owners. They are often mistreated by the representatives of the government that they encounter (e.g., security forces and tax collectors) and as a result are extremely suspicious of all strangers. Probably their greatest desire is to own their own land.

They are politically unsophisticated and their opinions and attitudes are formed on the basis of what they see and hear in their own immediate area rather than influenced by mass media. Communications from the ruling class (which is traditionally located in the urban areas) is usually poor at best. The ruling powers seldom view the peasants as an important or powerful political threat. Revolutionary guerrillas take the opposite view.

The following discussion of control measures employed at the village level to insure populace loyalty represents the first step in the establishment of a political mass base.[2] Prior to the sounds of the first guerrilla gun shot, revolutionary guerrilla organizers (hereafter mentioned as organizers) infiltrate the sparsely populated regions of the target country. These men are natives of the target country and very often were born in or near the area they have been assigned to control. They speak the local dialect, are of the same ethnic origin, and blend easily into the population.

The organizers have had at least three years of intensive revolutionary training in a communist country with heavy emphasis on the political-military doctrine as expressed in *Selected Works* by Mao Tse-tung (1954). Although the organizers are dogmatic in purpose, they are extremely practical and flexible operationally. They realize that each target area has its own social dynamics and that they must adapt their methods according to the norms, folkways, and mores of the region. They are hard-core communists who sincerely believe that their creed is just.

They believe, as do their Chinese Communist mentors, that thought determines action. Therefore, if one can control the thoughts of people, one can dictate the actions of the people. Their mission is to establish an effective underground apparatus. Their method of area penetration will follow three phases: *identification, propagation, organization.*

The populace control process begins when a team of two organizers enters a village and requests an audience with the village leader. The organizers are very polite and humble men. They say, "We have come to tell you of the things that we have seen. But first, as we can see that it is harvest time, we would like to help you gather in your life-sustaining crops. We shall have plenty of time to talk later." The organizers labor in the field and continually talk to the villagers. In the evening, the organizers entertain the villagers with folk songs and stories of the wonderful countries they have seen: countries where "everyone" owns land, all farmers have a good mule and fine house, where children wear fine clothes and go to fine schools and live a long life, where no one is ever hungry because the people work together for the benefit of all, and where the government's function is to serve the people.

The organizers never mention communism nor the pending insurgency. Political terminology is avoided; "plain talk" is the vogue. The organizers' songs, folk tales, and conversations are always designed to have some meaning to the immediate lives of the villagers. The objectives of the *identification* phase are to establish rapport by identifying with the lives of the villagers, determine the basic needs and aspirations of the villagers, discover the weaknesses of the social norms that dictate the accepted reaction to problems, and slowly plant the seeds of rebellion.

The *propagation* process is both destructive and constructive in nature. Destructively, the organizers must aggravate all the existing social ills and raise them to the surface, then transfer the cause of the ills to the existing government. Constructively, the organizers must convince the villagers that through cooperation, united action, and loyalty to each other, all social ills can be eliminated and individual aspirations can be realized. Sociologically, the process is one of inducing an awareness of definite in-group/out-group relationships, the in-group being the people and the out-group being the government. The organizers know that stories of the corruptness of the ruling group in the capital city will have little impression on the villagers. In many cases villagers do not realize there is a capital city, much less an established government. To establish credibility and meaning to their propaganda theme, that government is the source of all social ills, the organizers most often use the indirect approach.

The organizers' propaganda as transmitted in folk tales, songs, and conversations all has the same general theme: "the rich get richer while the poor get poorer." For example, a conversation with a tenant farmer might sound like this: "You have been working this same plot of land for twenty years. Before you, your father worked it and before him, his father worked it. And what, my friend, do you have to show for an accumulated seventy years of sweat and labor? Of the seven children you have created, four died at birth, two never lived to enjoy their second birthday, and one has survived to do what you, your father, and his father have done—sweat and labor so that the landlord can live in comfort in his fine house and watch his healthy children grow up to exploit your son. Is that right? Is that just? The answer, of course, is that it is not just. Did God create some men to live in comfort by the sweat of other men? The answer is no! How then has it occurred that a small minority of men can legally exploit the larger majority of men? The answer is organization. Many years ago, a small group of men discovered that by working together and cooperating with each other, they could enjoy the fruits of the people's labor. Using various devious methods, they acquired all of the land. They knew that in order to rule they would need a permanent police force and an army; otherwise the people would take back the land. So you see, my friend, your landlord is the grandson of one of these men who originally stole the land. He is able to exploit your labors because he has organized a police force and an army in order to suppress the people's ability to acquire what is justly theirs anyway.

"How then can the people attain what is legally and morally theirs? The answer, my friend, is organization. The minority can exploit the majority because they are organized. Does it not follow then that if the people who are the majority organize, they will be stronger than the minority landlords? All over this country, the people are beginning to organize. Men like yourself are preparing to acquire what is justly theirs. These men know that some will die but they say, 'Is it not better to die quickly and honorably for one's

POLITICAL MILITARY FUNCTIONS

rights than to suffer a living slow death at the hands of the exploiters?' "

Perhaps Roucek (1960: 164) best sums up the propagation phase when he writes, "At the core of their activities lies the argument that the . . . oppressor has no legal or moral right to exercise power . . . and that the members and leaders of the secret societies are the expression of the 'legal' will of the . . . people. The leaders must generate in their followers a readiness to die and a proclivity for united action."

Once three villagers have been won over, the organizers can establish the firs cell of the underground organization within the village. As more recruits join the organizers, they are sent off to previously established training camps. Here their training is seventy-five percent ideological and twenty-five percent military. Most of these individuals return to their village and form the nucleus of the underground apparatus, and can serve as a reserve force for the guerrillas. Others receive further military training and later form into small bands which will establish camps in rugged areas near the village. A few receive further ideological training and serve as assistant organizers to penetrate other villages in the area. One or two will be sent to a communist country for a year and undergo intensified ideological and military training.

The organizers encourage and direct the establishment of a village medical clinic as well as an elementary school. A variety of civic activities are performed by the underground organization. The organizers' purpose here is to enhance village solidarity behind the insurgents. Tactically, the village medical clinic will prove useful once the guerrilla stage of the insurgency is under way. Psychologically, the school provides the organizers an additional opportunity to propagandize the young. If the government troops, in an effort to weaken the insurgents' organization, requisition the medicines of the clinic and outlaw the school, the insurgents have won a psychological victory. The organizers can attribute the government's action to a desire to suppress the people by keeping them ignorant and weak with diseases. The organizers' propaganda theme will be, "the government knows that an educated and healthy people cannot be exploited!"

The successful completion of the indentification, propagation, and organization phases at the village level results in four principal conditions of control: in-group loyalty, insurgent terror tactics, personal commitment, and government terror tactics.

The in-group loyalty condition is the result of acceptance by the majority of the villagers of the idea that the insurgent activities are just and that the government is unjust. Insurgent terror tactics are directly related to the in-group loyalty condition. Those who aid the enemy are traitors and harmful to the people and, therefore, must be eliminated. The penalty for traitors, while not often quick, is final. Here, the in-group loyalty condition is reinforced by the underground's spy system which keeps the organizers informed of everything that is happening in the village.

Personal commitment is probably the most effective condition of control. The organizers make every effort to involve, in one way or another, a member of every family. Consequently, families are reluctant to betray the insurgency, thereby directly or indirectly increasing the possibility of prison, and most likely death, for a member of their family. The personal commitment condition is also operating in those individuals who have made large contributions to the insurgency and expect to be rewarded when the insurgents win.

Being unable to locate and annihilate the guerrilla forces, many governments have resorted to terroristic methods in an attempt to secure the support of the population. Government terror tactics such as burning villages, slaughtering innocent people, and generally mistreating the population are well-documented in the annals of guerrila warfare history. It is equally well-documented that such tactics tend to reinforce the solidarity of the people behind the insurgents. The communist insurgents are well aware of the population's reaction to such action and very often provoke the government into committing drastic actions. Indeed, one noted specialist maintains that, "the greatest contribution of guerrillas and saboteurs lies in catalyzing and intensifying counter-terror which further alienates the government from the local population" (Zawodny, 1962: 292).

The populace control measures that we have discussed generally occur during the previolence stage and the early phase of the combat action stage in a revolutionary guerrilla warfare environment. As the violence escalates into countrywide guerrilla fighting, and later even limited warfare, we are aware that additional populace control conditions are created. The identification and explanation of these conditions will have to await additional social scientific investigation.

We can make some generalizations, however, about various historical techniques of recruiting the civil populace into the revolutionary guerrilla organization. The remainder of this paper is devoted to that topic.[3] We do not propose to cover all of the factors involved nor will we confine ourselves to guerrilla recruitment techniques as evidence in any specific past or current revolutionary guerrilla war.

Recruiting personnel for the guerrilla force is probably one of the most critical missions of the guerrilla command apparatus. For in order to achieve the ultimate aim of overthrowing the ruling power, the guerrilla command apparatus must expand and swell the guerrilla force until it approaches the character of a regular army. This thought has been demonstrated in all of the guerrilla movements occurring after the end of the second world war. Historically, most guerrilla forces begin with a modest number of personnel. This initial force ranges anywhere from twenty to one hundred men and, in some cases, women.

Before discussing specific techniques of recruiting personnel for the guerrilla force, it will be beneficial to recognize and elaborate on certain conditions that are necessary to assure maximum success of the recruitment program. The first of these is *area assessment*. Before embarking on an ambitious recruiting program the guerrilla leadership must make a complete and exhaustive area assessment which will include information about the complete social strata in the guerrilla warfare operational area. This assessment will include the prevalent political motivations, an index of the social stratification of the area, existing occupational specialties, and many other factors. An example of the utility of such an assessment is as follows. Area "X" contains several mineral and rock mines. The guerrilla leaders know that very often mine workers make excellent demolitions specialists because of their utilization of dynamite. The guerrilla area assessment shows that Mr. "Y" does not entertain the same political belief as the government in power and the assessment also shows that Mr. Y is dissatisfied with his current class position and feels that the present ruling power restricts the degree of social prominence that miners can attain. Obviously, Mr. Y will be a ready and attentive audience for the guerrilla technique of persuasion (which will be discussed in detail later). The above example, while admittedly a simple one, does illustrate for the purpose of this short discussion the value of an accurate and up-to-date area assessment which must be conducted by the guerrilla leadership.

The second condition necessary to successful recruitment for the guerrilla force is *security*. The existence of an adequate guerrilla force security system is of paramount importance to the continual existence of the guerrilla force. One of the best methods for the ruling power to penetrate the guerrilla force is to utilize individual agents who, once in the guerrilla force, provide information to the ruling power regarding guerrilla movements and actions. Thus, it is extremely important that the guerrilla leadership be especially cautious in assessing the loyalty of guerrilla recruits. Lieutenant Colonel Willian C. Wilkinson, who served with the OSS in Burma in the Second World War, sums up the problems of security facing outside agents who are introduced to a strange area.

> In a new and underdeveloped guerrilla area, it is extremely difficult to check each man to determine where his loyalties really lie and this becomes still more difficult when a language barrier exists. Each man was screened, insofar as possible, to determine his loyalty and whether he was joining with an active desire to fight. A basic error was made in recruiting, in that the group leader, without an adequate knowledge of Kachin traits, personalties, and past history of the individuals, personally interviewed candidate. (sic) The errors which resulted from this selection showed up in the form of a revolt during training by five men desiring higher pay and later by the refusal of a few men to leave Ngumba for patrol or ambush. In retrospect, it would have been better to have selected one or two individuals about whose loyalty and desire to fight there was no question, and to have allowed them to examine applicants under the supervision of the group commander. Although this system is not perfect by any means, it did produce excellent results when finally adopted at Ngumba.

Wilkinson's "retrospect technique" while primitive, was expedient for the moment and might very well be applicable in some future operation. Other guerrilla leaders suggest that Wilkinson's techniques be taken several steps further to insure adequate security. These further steps include a questionnaire which would further establish the recruit's true loyalties and motives and also help the guerrilla leadership determine the most profitable means of utilizing the recruit. For example: if the recruit mentions on the questionnaire that he has had experience as a radio mechanic the guerrilla leadership would consider utilizing the individual in a communications position.

The length and the time permitted to complete this paper do not allow the writer to further develop this extremely important condition of a successful guerrilla recruiting program. Suffice to say that a guerrilla force cannot just accept any recruit into the ranks. All recruits must be thoroughly screened. The most stringent methods will not insure that no agents will successfully infiltrate the guerrilla movement, but it does insure that the majority of the agents will be detected before they have an opportunity to do any serious damage.

The third condition that deserves attention here is that the guerrilla leadership must establish an effective *psychological operations program*. The guerrilla force must propagate the thought that their fight is a just one and that they will eventually achieve victory. They must also widely propagate the thought that the guerrilla force is winning and shall continue to win. The enemy must be presented as an oppressor of basic human needs and rights. A continual objective of the guerrilla force must be to encourage the population to identify psychologically and physically with the guerrilla movement. The farmer who donates a bag of grain has taken the first step in physically identifying with the movement. The motive that stimulates the gift may have been purely a selfish one such as fear that the guerrillas might terrorize him if he did not make some overt show of approval of the guerrilla movement. Regardless of motive, if the guerrilla leadership is psychologically sophisticated, the farmer will soon be an ardent supporter of the movement. Upon receipt of the bag of grain, the guerrillas should praise the farmer as a true patriot. Perhaps Bayo (1963: 53) explains the process most appropriately when he asks and then answers the question in the following way:

> How must a guerrilla behave with farmers? No matter how much food may be obtained, it should be well paid for after having repeatedly thanked the proprietor and having reminded him that he is helping the revolution. Then the men should volunteer to repair things in the house; beds, closets, tables, etc. They will help the owner put fences up on the farm, to sow or to do any kind of manual work in order to demonstrate our affection and gratitude, and bring him over to our cause, so that those living in the house will be interested in our return.

Much of what Bayo advocates is what Dr. Virgil Ney (1961) labels "propaganda of the deed." Other examples of propaganda of the deed would be successes in combat against the enemy and material support from an outside power in the form of supplies parachuted into the given country. While propaganda of the deed is certainly effective, it must be reinforced by other psychological warfare operational techniques such as rumors, pamphlets, and informal lectures in order to insure that the maximum amount of people learn of the deeds.

We have thus far discussed certain operational conditions which should be realized by the guerrilla force before the guerrilla leadership can expect maximum response to their recruiting drive. The remainder of this paper will be devoted to specific techniques and/or procedures of recruitment which have been utilized in one form or another throughout the history of guerrilla warfare. The three major procedures which are to be listed and elaborated on in this paper are here labeled as *paid, forced,* and *persuaded.* They will be discussed in reverse order of historical frequency.

The *paid* procedure of guerrilla recruitment is the least practiced procedure of the three. Guerrilla leadership will usually resort to this method only in cases where a unique technical skill is needed and the individual possessing the unique skill cannot be persuaded to perform the needed task by ideological or moral argument. Professional people such as chemists, pharmacists, and doctors of medicine are the most common types that might be induced to serve the guerrillas by this means. There are actually very few cases of the utilization of this technique in the history of guerrilla warfare because of the many weaknesses inherent in the system. Guerrilla leaders have been traditionally reluctant to practice this procedure because financial incentive is always subject to outbidding by the enemy. Jacobs and de Rochefort (1962: 168) offer a particularly clear thought on this subject when they write:

> Material incentives alone are not sufficient to secure this cooperation to any sizeable extent because material incentives are not sufficient to overcome fears of betrayals, reprisals, etc. . . . Except for some entirely insignificant exceptions, no member of the French or Dutch resistance movement during the German occupation was tempted by material rewards into helping Allied agents. No possible profit was worth the risks of torture by the Gestapo or the death oven of Matthausen. Only ideological incentives can cause men to accept the dangers and fears involved in unconventional operations.

The *forced* procedure of guerrilla recruitment has become fairly common in the guerrilla movements of the last twenty years. Basically, it is what the term force implies. Individuals are forced against their will to serve the guerrilla cause. As in the case of the paid procedure above, professional people are often the individuals forced to serve the guerrillas. The guerrilla leadership will usually resort to this procedure rather than the paid procedure if the current local situation does not make it politically out of the question. In Greece, during the guerrilla war from 1946-1949, the Communists often practiced wholesale forced recruitment with seemingly mixed results. On this matter the late Field Marshal Alexander Papagos (1962: 231) wrote:

> Force was used both directly, by the compulsory enlistment of the population, and also indirectly. Under the latter method, individuals refusing to join the Communist ranks were dubbed collaborators of the enemy, a charge which involved the death penalty or at least the burning down of the delinquent's home. Peasants who saw this happen and feared similar treatment joined the Communist ranks.

Since the support of the population is needed for eventual success of the guerrilla forces it would seem that forced recruitment on a large scale would be ineffectual and out of the question since it would antagonize the population. And yet, "intensive forced recruiting inside Greece netted approximately 24,000 civilians" for the Communist ranks (Wainhouse, 1962: 224).

It is interesting to observe that students of the 1946-1949 guerrilla war in Greece list the lack of population support as one of the major factors contributing to the Communists' defeat in that guerrilla war.

The final procedure of guerrilla recruitment to be discussed here is the *persuaded* procedure. This is the most often used procedure and by far the soundest. The guerrilla leadership must persuade the people that the guerrilla fight is just and that the eventual victory of the guerrilla movement is inevitable. Appeals must be made to the national aspirations, popular causes, and the population's dissatisfactions with the power. Very often the guerrilla leadership tries to avoid "specific pronouncements at the inception of the organization. By remaining vague, they are able to accommodate individual aspirations and thus increase their ranks" (Zawodny, 1962: 390).

The leadership of the French resistance movement against the Nazi occupation forces in World War II seemed to have adhered to this policy of "accommodating individual aspirations" and thereby gained the support and talent of many different classes of the French social system. As Gordon Wright (1962: 339) points out, "the working class furnished most of the militants, and 'infantry,' of the underground, but it was the bourgeoisie that furnished most of the organizers and leaders."

Historically, the enemy of the guerrillas have been instrumental in aiding the guerrillas in achieving success using the persuasion procedure. The enemy does this by harshly mistreating the population. General Alexander Orlov (1963: 165-166), formerly a member of the Soviet NKVD, vividly describes how harsh treatment by the governing powers serves to escalate popular support for, and the number of recruits for, the guerrilla movement.

> Peaceful peasants and other groups of hard-working people do not take up arms lightly against superior forces of the government, unless they have been driven to it by unendurable hardships, onerous taxation, property confiscations, and naked violence. Before armed resistance succeeds in gaining land reforms and concessions from greedy landlords and corrupt government, peaceful life is disrupted, the rural economy is disorganized, trade is at a standstill, whole communities are devastated, and lives are destroyed. It is because the injustices and sufferings have reached the boiling point that the most desperate and determined men take whatever weapon they can lay their hands on—from fowling pieces to axes and clubs—and retire into the hills and woods, from where they stage fierce raids on the estates of their feudal overlords and local police outposts. The men become outlaws. The authority of the government is defied. Punitive detachments of rural police arrive to track them down. People suspected of aiding the rebels are persecuted. Many are arrested. Order is gradually restored. The authorities learn from the population that the outlaws have fled to another country. But when everything seems quiet and the detachments are getting ready to depart, the rebels come down from the hills in the middle of the night, overwhelm the sentries, destroy the police force, and make away with their rifles and ammunition. The population begins to regard the guerrilla band not only as a fighting unit, but also as a political entity united by the ideal of freeing the inhabitants from the arbitrary rule of the landlords and their feudalistic regime.

Often, the persuasion process simply amounts to the guerrilla force making it known that they are accepting recruits. Many youths will volunteer for excitement while other types will join the guerrillas in order to avoid police or government persecution. Obviously of the three procedures of guerrilla recruitment, the persuasion procedure is the most effective.

In summary, we have illustrated that there are three major historical techniques of guerrilla recruitment. These are the paid, forced, and persuaded procedures. In order for these procedures, and particularly the persuasion procedure, to be most effective, three distinct conditions must exist. These conditions were labeled in this paper as area assessment, security, and psychological operations programs.

Upon examination of past revolutionary guerrilla wars we can easily note that when the ruling powers react to the widespread guerrilla violence solely with traditional military and police repressive measures, they simply reinforce the validity of the insurgent propaganda and insure continual population support to the insurgents. When, on the other hand, the ruling powers incorporate into their pacification program at the village level, "psychological action," "civic action," and "population security" principles, they often destroy the very foundation on which the insurgency rests. For it is only when the ruling power demonstrates by attitude and action their desire and ability to eliminate the basic social ills and legitimate personal grievances, as well as to protect the people from the insurgents, will the population adhere its loyalty to the ruling power.

In conclusion, mass media coverage and world maps vividly indicate many areas in which sociopolitical and geopolitical conditions exist for the introduction of violence for political objectives. Indeed, "revolutionary guerrilla warfare, when induced or applied by revolution-inclined world powers, can become both the strategy and the tactics of political violence as a means of social and political change" (Osanka, 1968: 506). In modern times, guerrilla warfare (historically thought of as useful only as a tactical adjunct to regular warfare) has become an entity in itself. As the struggle in the Republic of Vietnam has demonstrated, limited warfare has become a by-product of revolutionary guerrilla warfare.

NOTES

1. In this connection the author has relied heavily on his earlier works: "Population Control Techniques of Communist Insurgents: A Sociological Analysis" and "Historical Procedures of Recruiting Guerrillas," which appeared in the *Australian Army Journal* in 1964. Indo-China War, the Cuban rebellion, the current struggle in the Republic documents and diaries captured during the Chinese Civil War, the French Indo-China War, the Cuban Rebellion, the current struggle in the Republic of Vietnam, and interviews with veterans of these conflicts.

3. This section is based on an analysis of the open literature and interviews with both guerrilla and counter-guerrilla warfare veterans.

REFERENCES

BAYO, A. (1963) 150 Questions for a Guerrilla. Boulder, Colo.: Panther.

DOHENY, W. F. (1966) "The evolution of guerrilla warfare." An Cosantoir (Ireland) 26: 37-45.

HOROWITZ, I. L. [ed.] (1967) The Rise and Fall of Project Camelot. Cambridge: Massachusetts Institute of Technology.

———(1966) Three Worlds of Development: The Theory and Practice of International Stratification. New York: Oxford University Press.

JACOBS, W. D. and N. DE ROCHEFORT (1962) "Ideological operations in unconventional warfare," pp. 164-172 in F. M. Osanka (ed.) Guerrilla Warfare Readings. Washington, D.C.: Human Resources Research Office, George Washington University Press.

LONG, W. F. (1963) "Counterinsurgency: some antecedents for success." Military Review 43: 90-97.

LOWRY, R. P. (1965) "Changing military roles: neglected challenge to rural sociologists." Rural Selected Works. New York: International Publishers.

MAO TSE-TUNG (1954) Selected Works. New York: International Publishers.

MOSKOS, C. C., Jr. (1968) "Personal remarks on sociological research in the third world." Behavioral Scientist 12: 26-30.

———(1967) The Sociology of Political Independence. Cambridge: Schenkman.

NEY, V. (1961) Notes on Guerrilla Warfare. Washington, D.C.: Command Publications.

ORLOV, A. (1963) Handbook of Intelligence and Guerrilla Warfare. Ann Arbor: University of Michigan Press.

OSANKA, F. M. (1968) "Internal warfare: guerrilla warfare." International Encyclopedia of the Social Sciences 7: 503-507.

———[ed.] (1962) Modern Guerrilla Warfare. New York: Free Press.

PAPAGOS, A. (1962) "Guerrilla warfare," pp. 228-241 in F. M. Osanka [ed.] Modern Guerrilla Warfare. New York: Free Press.

ROUCEK, J. S. (1962) "Sociological elements of a theory of terror and violence." American Journal of Economics and Sociology 21: 165-172.

———(1960) "Sociology of secret societies." American Journal of Economics and Sociology 19: 161-168.

TACKABERRY, T. H. (1968) "Social science research, aid to counter-insurgency." American Journal of Economics and Sociology 27: 1-8.

WAINHOUSE, E. R. (1962) "Guerrilla war in Greece, 1946-49: a case study," pp. 217-227 in F. M. Osanka (ed.) Modern Guerrilla Warfare. New York: Free Press.

WRIGHT, G. (1962) "Reflections on the French resistance." Political Science Quarterly 77: 336-349.

ZAWODNY, J. K. [ed.] (1962) "Unconventional warfare." Annals of the American Academy of Political and Social Sciences 341: 1-107.

———(1962) "Unconventional warfare." American Scholar 31: 384-394.

———(1960) "Unexplored realms of underground strife." American Behavioral Scientist 4: 3-5.

Chapter 14

PSYCHOLOGICAL WARFARE

KONRAD KELLEN

*T*he following essay is not "technical" in the strict sense of the word. Nor does it try to do justice or even discuss the existing literature in the field or the various ways in which different armed forces organize psychological warfare. Rather, the following discussion is based on the personal experiences of the author who has been active in "psywar," primarily on the psywar intelligence side, for an aggregate of almost twenty years in war and peace—for four years as a member of the Second Mobile Radio Broadcasting Company (2nd MRB) in World War II (European ETO), for 11 years as chief of Radio Free Europe's Information Department, and for three years as an analyst of interrogations with VC defectors and prisoners. The author believes that such a discussion of theory, with examples, as he has presented here, may be more than a technical survey of past psywar activity and history. The far-ranging, apparently loosely structured nature of the result of the author's efforts mirror, in the author's view, the far-ranging, quite unstructurable and undelineable nature of the topic under discussion.

PSYWAR
THEORY

Few things are harder to capture in the compass of a clear, comprehensive and undebatable definition than psychological war-

POLITICAL MILITARY FUNCTIONS

fare, or psywar as it now is often called (and at one point was called "sykewar" by some). In a very broad way, a definition could be quite simple: psywar is all that is brought to bear upon an enemy except physical force, for the purpose of contributing significantly to his defeat or influencing his behavior. As such, of course, psywar is quite ancient; in one form or another it has been practiced ever since the trumpet blew down the walls of Jericho or, more accurately, since men have battled individually or in groups, i.e., since our Neanderthalian days.

It can be said that psywar is the adjunct of all warfare, of all organized application of force. Of course, psywar can even be used without any application of force at all—in the form of deterrence or coercion or compellance, to forestall the need for the application of force. In our day, psywar finds itself more and more in that role in which, rather than being an adjunct to the exercise of force, it is meant to take its place; the entire Cold War is almost exclusively one gigantic round of psywar. But not altogether, of course: actual missiles are in place and operational, and reasonably invulnerable, and the other side has to be reasonably vulnerable, for psywar to be effective. Even here, psywar is only an adjunct. Theoretically, of course, one could conceive of a situation where psywar all by itself would yield a desired result, in the form of a pure bluff. But such situations, either in local tactical circumstances or on a global scale, are rare if not altogether unlikely.

Thus, our first clue as to psywar is that it is an adjunct to either cold or hot war, an effort to influence the other side either to refrain from certain forays of its own, to desist, or in the extreme case to surrender. Before an attempt can be made to perceive how that is done, a look must first be taken at the phenomenon that the admixture of psywar—in the total element mix of a situation—varies greatly with that situation. In the Cuban missile crisis, for example, an actual quarantine was set up and a number of ships were detained and boarded; but these acts were obviously not what motivated the Soviets to withdraw their missiles; they were only a tiny part of the total weight of imponderabilia let loose upon the Soviets. In fact, even the physical act of boarding the ships had psychological rather than physical impact.

Not all psywar designed to work on the enemy's mind need necessarily be expressed in words. The classic "show of the flag" near a potential enemy's coast, or the massing of troops in war (or peace) in a certain area, will set certain intellectual and emotional processes working on the other side. Even something much more remote—such as appropriation for some military equipment—can have the same effect, and be—deliberately or not—part and parcel of psywar campaigns.

However, in the majority of cases, psywar will be verbal or have at least a verbal element. This verbal element will generally be designed to create—or increase—fears that will contribute to motivating the other side to act in a manner less disadvantageous than they otherwise might. However, fear is only one basic emotion psywar seeks to arouse, and desisting from a certain course of action (the product of fear) is only one effect psywar aims at having. For example, it aims just as frequently at arousing hopes, to effect certain actions from which the enemy would otherwise desist. It may promise, reassure, and in various other ways try to dispel fears the enemy might have and which might be the mainstay for his resistance; and it may dispel them either by resorting to the truth or not, as the case may be.

In other words, psywar aims at making the enemy reassess his situation in such a way that his subsequent actions will be less unfavorable. To do this effectively, psywar will in most cases work on both sides of his collective personality. It will arouse his fear of certain punishments if he does such and such, and his hopes of gaining certain advantages if he does otherwise. Psywar, in other words, will (if competently conducted) orchestrate a variety of appeals. One of its many messages will be: "We have the power and resolve to crush you, but we will treat you well if you give up." This is a favorate message to troops in the field.

But psywar, to be effective, cannot just combine threats with blandishments. Though this combination is basic, we could hardly call it orchestration. Rather, psywar will take into account that most people determine their course of action by a myriad of considerations, both personal and impersonal, rational and irrational, material and nonmaterial. The soldier, in particular, is most often not just concerned about himself, but also about his country and—what may be regarded as in between—his family, friends, hometown. He fights for a cause with which he generally is in agreement. Psywar, aside from trying to exercise a direct influence on what he expects his immediate personal fate will be (death or captivity or triumph) will try to "unsell" him from his cause; that is axiomatic. It can do so in a variety of ways.

Essentially, there are two opposite poles here. Psywar can try to make the soldier believe that his cause is unattainable, or that it is not a good cause. In practice the two will usually be connected as most people tend to believe—in our highly ideological age—that really good causes cannot really be unattainable. Psywar may therefore say, in so many words: "You won't get what you try to get, and besides it's not worth getting (or even pernicious)," and usually spells out what one might call its counter-ideological efforts.

But an enemy's cause does not exist in a vacuum—it is to some extent the complement or supplement or the reverse side of one's own cause. In World War II, for example, the Soviet Union and the United States, as allies, invaded Germany from both east and west. Now, in both east and west, the Germans fought for the same cause, but they fought, or at least thought they fought, against quite different causes. The United States, in spite of all of Goebbels' efforts, was not really regarded by the Germans as fighting for the destruction of Germany, but the Soviet Union was seen that way. This illustrates, *inter alia,* that psywar should try to present one's own cause in such a way as to arouse in the enemy's mind, the question: "Is this war really necessary?" Facing the Russians, the Germans thought it really was; facing the Americans they finally thought it really was not. (Of course, that was not just the result of American psywar, but also of their preconceived notions.) In disabusing an enemy from regarding his war as really necessary, psywar can rarely operate at will. The reality and its projection are linked, and psywar, again, is mainly an adjunct: to reduce an enemy's fighting will by rearranging, in a positive direction, his thoughts and feelings about what we will do to him, will be easier the less frightful our cause actually is from his point of view.

In a way, that particular sequence takes place in a holdup: A aims his loaded pistol at B, in return for which B, to defend his life against A, might take any desperate act. But A tells B that there is nothing he wants less than to harm B; he only wants his money. His cause (if we can call it that for a moment) is not A's blood but his money, and B, if he believes it, will act differently than if he thought A's cause was his blood. Of course the analogy, as all analogies, is limping. Psywar will not way to the enemy: "We don't want your lives, we just want your country." This was done in past ages, though, and produced, more often than not, the accommodation on the part of those about to be vanquished. But in our day and age, and presumably in the future we are likely to proceed from the ideological basis (as does the enemy) that our (his) victory is not just good for us (him), but good for *everybody*; aside from whether this is in fact so or not, it is one of psywar's functions in what we might call our ideological age to credibly project this fact. We no longer promise mercy to those we are about to vanquish, as warriors did in another day and with the help of which promise they induced them to lay down their arms; we promise them the bliss of the institutions we believe in. One serious problem for strategic psywar at the time of this writing is that we have reached an almost unprecedented ideological escalation in our "rather dead than red" posture which is very hard, if not impossible, to "sell" to those who do not a priori share it.

Whether psywar can effectively aid the application of military violence by counter-ideological efforts will depend once again upon a whole range of things, but primarily upon our eloquence and manifest practices and the enemy's own eloquence and manifest practices. If we are strong supporters of our cause, we regard ourselves as men of firm convictions, but if the enemy firmly believes in his, we speak of him as "well indoctrinated."[1] But psywar cannot jump over its own shadow, though it often can come close to it. It cannot, for example, convince the majority of the North Vietnamese army that life in North Vietnam under what we (but not they, generally) call communism is miserable, poor, unjust, and worse than life would be under a different system. That is clearly proven by psywar intelligence (much more about psywar intelligence later), and it would do little good to run up against one of the enemy's most conspicuous strong points.

This does not mean, incidentally, that psywar must always shrink from attacking ideational strong points—on the contrary. Just as in physical war, *everything* is a potentially lucrative target, whether it is a weak point, a strong point, or something else. It just will require different strategies, tactics, and resources to attack at different points. Theoretically, and only seemingly paradoxically, an enemy's greatest vulnerability may well be his greatest strength, in the sense that if we can knock out the strongest pillar from under a bridge we will most likely succeed in bringing it down. There is, however, a limit to that, beyond which assults on enemy strong points, be they physical or psychological, are merely foolhardy or at best a waste of resources.

It is not too early in this essay to point out, in this connection, that one thing that distinguishes psywar from physical war is that it can be—and very often is—counter-productive if ineptly practiced. To the extent that psywar is direct or indirect, spoken or nonspoken communication—and all psywar is *communication* to such an extent that we will, for clarity's sake, stay away from that term altogether—it cannot but have some effect and leave some impression. Because psywar projects at all times more of ourselves than the actual message we mean to convey, it is an extremely sensitive instrument. It must be on target both in form and content, and for that reason good psychological warfare intelligence is of the utmost importance. This is one of the most difficult aspects of all of psywar, and the one most sinned against.

Of course, the actual situation in which psywar is being practiced will largely determine its form and content. We have, above, talked about the ideological warfare which is part of all contemporary psywar and likely to remain that in our lifetime. But we have also said that many other elements come into play, from the personal to the national, from the egotistical to the altruistic, from the general to the specific. Almost all psywar will have admixtures of all these elements, whether it is planned that way or not. But it is important that the right mixture be obtained, i.e., the one not just most relevant to a specific enemy, but also to a specific situation.

It follows that psywar, like all other wars, ranges from the strategic, in the broadest terms, to the tactical, in the most specific ones. The further away from the battle lines—or, in insurgency warfare, from actual operations—men are (on both sides), the more they tend to be concerned with the broad aims and aspects of the war, and ideological content, the chances of success for the enterprise as a whole, and so on. But the closer they are to action, the more directly involved in combat, the more they are concerned with life and limb and what will happen in the next hour rather than in the next year or decade. Combat and the nearness of death simplifies the picture dramatically and foreshortens all perspectives.

It would be foolish, therefore, to talk to a surrounded platoon in the middle of action, by leaflet or loudspeaker, about the fate of their country or the appeals of democracy. What is likely to have an impact on them is a new expectation as to whether they will be killed if they persist, or maltreated or even shot if they surrender. It thus is a law of psywar that it must, to be effective, gauge and try to exploit what the other side will be receptive to not only in the light of its own ideas and perceptions but also in the light of its actual situation. Whereas, in a lull, a particular man might be deeply influenced by some message of a political nature, or even by some music, he will, in extreme situations, not respond to such appeals at all, though very much to others. In brief, one might say that the closer to the action, the more the soldier is concerned with his *life*; the further away from it, the more with his *fate*. Psywar must gear itself to that.[2]

Nevertheless, we must come back to ideological warfare, with which, inevitably, all psywar in our days is so heavily permeated. In a certain way, psywar is forever engaged in political or ideological *conversion,* but with a very crucial difference that distinguishes it from most other conversion efforts. Psywar deals with groups rather than individuals, and to the extent that it succeeds, it brings the individual convert into a very severe, dangerous conflict with his fellows. Perhaps this is best illustrated with an analogy to the field of religion. The clergyman who tries to make a man accept, or profess anew, the Christian faith, is in a very different situation from the psywarrior. Aside from being face to face with his "prospect" and generally respected by him (most nonpracticing Christians have a residual respect for clergymen), he does not ask of his prospective convert anything that will bring him into conflict with society, his fellows, or his family; necessitate actions regarded as treasonous; or attach the stigma of disloyalty to him. Rather, the psywarrior faces a situation similar to the apostle who tried to make men accept a new point of view that brought them into conflict with their surroundings so severe as to make them eligible to be thrown to the lions if their "deviation" was discovered. Psywar faces these formidable obstacles and cannot succeed but in fact be only counter-productive if it does not remain very sensitive to these limitations—it asks at all times "an awful lot" of its targets.

It was found, for example, in World War II, that many members of the Nazi army had become disillusioned with Hitler, or were at least at the point of becoming so. But this did by no means suffice to make them lay down their arms and surrender to the Americans. It did not even, in many cases, reduce their fighting ardor, or, more precisely, their fighting effectiveness. Their manifest motivation for continuing the struggle was that they had no right to "let down their buddies" or their country in its obviously dire need, and so on. To counter this, psywar hit upon the rather ingenious device of handling the prospective enemy soldier, if it could not fully detach him intellectually from his own side, the rationalizations for not fighting on, or for no longer fighting at least with the old vigor. It told him, outright, that he had fought well and bravely for his country but that the game was now up, and that it was not only in his but in Germany's interest that he and his buddies quit fighting, as a quick end to the war would bring with it a cessation of the murderous bombing of the cities and the slaughter of his folks and the German people at large, that to desist was a positive, in fact patriotic, act on his part.

This line turned out to be very effective, and the psywarrior can learn from it. He must recognize its limitations, however, and understand that it cannot be duplicated at will. By almost any sane man's standards, what the psywarrior said there to the embattled German was the objective truth: the German and his family and Germany itself were indeed better off with rapid termination and American occupation—even under the unconditional surrender formula—than they all would have been in case of prolonged resistance. Such a situation does not exist as clearly in other situations at all, and certainly not in Vietnam which was one of many reasons psywar was so difficult to conduct there and remained conspicuously unsuccessful.

Of course, psywar does not always have to be either entirely or even partially "true." To what extent it has to be, or whether it has to be at all, will depend largely (but not entirely) upon whether it is tactical and immediate or strategic and geared for the long term. If we tell a surrounded platoon that there is an entire regiment encircling it and that, locked as they are in place, they will be destroyed if they do not surrender forthwith, we need not necessarily have the truth on our side to be effective; we merely need a sufficient appearance of the truth, or the eloquence to stimulate it. In a strategic situation, the matter is obviously reversed.[3]

One of the most important rules of strategic ideological warfare is that it will not merely, if effective, convince the other side of things it was not convinced of before, and thereby cause action (or nonaction) on a mass scale, but that it will, if at all successful, have a strong and paralyzing *divisive* effect on the other side. For example, it is often accepted (though with dubious justification) that political or ideological or other forms of psychological warfare cannot sway the "higher-ups," the knowledgeable, the articulate, the "decision maker," or even the "cadre." Thus the rank and file, perhaps because often by and large they have so much less to gain in case of victory and so much less to lose in case of defeat than their leaders, seem to be more easily swayed.

But to give the elite on the other side up for lost is to miss out on one of psywar's most lucrative targets. They are swayable, as past experience shows, not of course by simple slogans or broad promises of reconciliation (in which they do not consider themselves included) but by a truly incisive, doubt-arousing analysis of their own situation, designed to raise questions in their mind. Such corrosive doubts can best be raised by *questions* addressed to them by psywar (not of the rhetoric, stentorian kind, but real ones), rather than by brash assertions that merely reinforce their original posture. It would do no good, for example, to tell a Vietnamese leader: "Those treacherous Chinese will sell you down the river anytime." But it might have quite a corrosive effect on him if psywar were to ask gently: "Will the Chinese really come to your aid when you need them? You have often stated they would, but will they? Will they really run the risk of being bombed by the U.S.? We don't know. Do you?" The generally accepted belief that only strong assertion is effective psywar because it reflects strong, and therefore well-founded conviction, is quite erroneous, and psywar has often missed some of its best bets by insisting on using exclusively the generally serviceable, but not very sophisticated form of stern assertion.

PSYWAR PRACTICE

Since military psywar generally does not deal with enemy leaders, this essay deals primarily with mass psywar operations of armed forces during combat.

How is that influence to be exerted? It is always exerted in the way of some form of communication, but not always a verbal form. Sometimes it is nonverbal, sometimes partly verbal and partly nonverbal. Sometimes it will be a promise of something tangible (German soldiers in World War II were promised they would be evacuated to Canada or the U.S. where they could continue their studies), sometimes an assurance that certain things that are feared will not happen (the killing or ill treatment of prisoners). In the Vietnam War, for example, one strong impediment to defection has always been that the enemy soldiers expected to be killed or at the least brutally mistreated if—voluntarily or not—they would get into the hands of the government troops. These apprehensions, by and large, were only too justified. In such a case the psywarrior is faced with a dual problem, more often than not unsolvable: he must convince his "customers" that good treatment awaits them in case of surrender, but he also must see to it that such good treatment is actually forthcoming, as his line of communication between the two sides is not the only one, particularly not in a guerrilla war. In this connection, an important general lesson is to be learned: in insurgency wars, much more than in conventional wars, there are multiple communication lines crossing between the two sides (families, guerrillas, villagers) so that the psywarrior often will have to stick very closely to the truth if he wants to be, and remain, effective.

But what can he do if his side will not come around to giving defectors and surrenderers better treatment?" The answer is, very little. For his influence on his own side will generally be small, and he cannot really promise good treatment if the other side has ample information to the effect that they are not likely to get it. All he can do is continue to plead his case with his own authorities, and hope for the best. He will, in any event, then find himself in the position only too familiar to psywarriors who have actually practiced their craft—perceiving an issue that might be very profitable if only it could be resolved in the right way, but it often just is not. Such issues can become particularly important if in psywar, a third party is involved. In conventional war, only two forces were battling each other with the material and moral resources at their disposal. But in insurgency warfare, a third force is very much present: the local population. The psywarrior then finds himself in a tri-cornered situation and must adjust to it. The local population is his monitor, so to speak, with regard to much of what he conveys.

Of course, even in World War II, psywar—at least strategic psywar—had to take the noncombatant populations into account and often derived much benefit from a skillful inclusion of that population in its operations. For example, while tactical propaganda told the German soldiers that the war was lost, surrender no disgrace, and so on, strategic propaganda, through leaflets and radio, told the German home population that more bombing was to come and that the situation at the fighting fronts was not what Nazi papers told them it was. Such strategic propaganda, designed to make the home front crumble, also exhorted the German people to write to their soldiers about their suffering, which was in conflict with Hitler's orders that only "cheerful" news was to be dispatched to the soldiers fighting at the front. In this way, tactical and strategic, direct and indirect efforts were combined and quite successfully so. A vicious circle was created with many interlocking elements: doubt was aroused on the home front as to the happening at the fighting front; with it a credibility gap was opened which was further confirmed by soldiers writing back home or on furlough; the law was circumvented on whose unquestioning observance Hitler depended; defeatest collusion between home front and fighting front was encouraged; and so on.

Occasionally, the presence of a "third listener" can present complicated problems. It was found, for example, that the SS troops in Normandy were much more reluctant to surrender to the Allies than ordinary Wehrmacht soldiers and units, not necessarily because they were more faithful to Hitler and the war, but because they were under the impression Goebbels assiduously reinforced in the SS ranks. All SS soldiers would be executed, according to his line. The obvious thing to do, of course, would have been to promise the SS troops "pie in the sky" by radio and leaflet. However, such appeals might have greatly alienated the French population, on whose territory the actions were fought, whose hatred of the SS troops was, for good reasons, particularly intense, and whose full assistance we needed. An appeal was therefore designed which said that "contrary to certain rumors and official Nazi statements every single soldier falling into Allied captivity will, in accordance with the Geneva convention, receive precisely the same treatment, be he a soldier, a sailor, a marine, a Waffen-SS man or whatnot." This "played-down" message was not lost on the SS but acceptable to the French, and it was very effective on the SS soldiers.

Yet, in this connection, it should be pointed out—and we have touched on it above—that it is often hard to know whether (a) fear of mistreatment or (b) confidence in good treatment on the other side is of greater advantage. When held out, leniency is interpreted as weakness; it is, of course, possibly counter-productive, as it can encourage further fighting, with or without the commission of atrocities.[4] As a general rule, it would appear, all things considered, that the soldier who is frightened by the enemy fights harder. The Germans certainly fought much harder against the Soviets of whom they were afraid beyond what they in reality had to expect from them, than against the Western Allies.

Effects. Whatever the situation, the most important question the psywarrior must at all times ask himself—and he neglects it only too often—is what *effect* his communication is to have on his target in the best of cases. Unless psywar results in action (or nonaction such as refusing to fight) that is advantageous to his side, his efforts are not useful and often counter-productive. And, in order to result in action, the action suggested to the enemy soldier or soldiers must be within his capabilities. It therefore violates the tenets of sound psywar if, as was done in Vietnam for example, at one point, areas held by the enemy are showered with leaflets, shouting: "Stop this fratricidal war!" Aside from the fact that the recipient might ask: "Why don't *you* stop it if it's a fratricidal war?", individual soldiers—and we must always remember that our appeals reach individuals—are not exactly able to stop wars. Contrary to the layman, the professional radio or TV broadcaster, for example, knows that he does not, like the orator in a crowded forum, talk to multitudes, even though he talks to millions, but to individuals inside their own apartments. Similarly, the psywarrior communicates with individuals who are all the more set off from all the other individuals surrounding them by the very message the psywarrior tries to impart to them and which, if they were to heed it or even believe it, would make them subversive elements in his midst. It is one of the most common errors in military and political propaganda to demand from or even suggest to such individuals actions that even the crowd, if it were agreed, could hardly do. As action is always hard to suggest, psywar will, on occasion, be open-ended and designed merely to try to condition the enemy. It is perfectly legitimate on occasion for psywar to tell the other side its cause is not just or hopeless, and leave it at that for the time being, actions not always being called for. But there always should be a plan, a design as to what all this communication, at least theoretically, could optimally lead to, just as the efficient politician communicates for the sole, ultimate purpose of being elected if he is not yet in office, or getting continued support if he is. (In this connection, it will be generally better to suggest to the other side that *we* think its cause is bad rather than to communicate apodictically: "Your cause is bad . . ." as the latter approach is likely to create more resistance.)

PSYWAR
INTELLIGENCE

Of crucial importance to all psywar, be it tactical or strategic, or conducted by leaflet, radio or loudspeaker, is psywar intelligence. In the beginnings of formalized psywar operations in World War II, when the four so-called Mobile Radio Broadcasting companies (MBRs) were organized and used as organic parts of the U.S. Army, this was not recognized. Rather it was taken for granted that it was known what would have an effect, what kind of promises would tempt him, what kind of threats deter him, what kind of appeals move him. The G-2 organization in Normandy was indifferent, in fact hostile, to psywar intelligence needs, to the point of denying psywarriors, in the beginning, access to PW cages. G-2 took the position that, by making its routine G-2 reports available to the psywar elements of the 12th Army Group (which it grudgingly did in the beginning of the invasion of France) psywar was given all the knowledge it needed.

But psywar needs a very different kind of intelligence than what G-2 required for laying the plans for and executing its operations. Psywar must also know, it is true, what G-2 knows (though in less detail), but a greatly different type of knowledge is equally important for its operations. Perhaps the difference can best be defined in very general terms: G-2 needs to know the "what"— psywar needs to know the "why." G-2 needs to have facts on enemy strength, enemy planning, enemy capabilities, enemy equipment, weapons, roads, supplies. Psywar must know what the enemy thinks, feels, believes, doubts, hopes, wants. G-2 must know whether the *ratios* between, say, tanks and gas supplies are favorable for the enemy, or between men to be moved and transportation facilities; psywar must know whether the *relations* between, say, men and officers, or men and men, or soldiers and the home front are favorable or unfavorable for our side.

Naturally, this distinction delineates the difference between military and psywar intelligence requirements only roughly, and there is overlap. G-2, for example, in the course of a lengthening war, will want to know what the "quality" of the enemy replacements is—and this quality will be a ball of wax consisting of equipment, training, age, but also of "morale," the latter being of central importance to psywar. However, on balance, G-2 will want to know the physical, tangible situation and capabilities of the enemy, while psywar will want to know as much as possible about the intangible, nonphysical aspects of the enemy—the software, the invisible strands of his cohesion, the elements of incipient disintegration, the motivations—best elucidated by questions, the answers to which will show us why the enemy is fighting so tenaciously or surrendering occasionally, and what is holding his force together and what is working in the direction of its breaking up or becoming less effective in combat.

Psywar intelligence must remember, first of all, that people in general are poor judges of their own morale, motivations, states of mind, and so on, and poor observers of what goes on around them. For that reason, the problem of the captured enemy (both G-2's and psywar's most important source, though there are many others),[5] telling deliberate lies, or withholding information, which is such a great problem for G-2, is not psywar's problem. Psywar has other, much greater problems in that connection. It must dreg out of its source many of the things the source is often only dimly aware of, and which, above all, the source will inevitably express in such a fashion that *evaluation* is extremely difficult and risky.

This leads straight into the most calamitous error so often made by psywar intelligence—the overestimation of the negative factors in the captive's story. In war much more than in everyday life much is ambiguous where a man's morale and motivations are concerned. Many soldiers display high morale and excellent fighting spirit even though they have a very large catalogue of complaints when pressed. The point is that even under the most favorable of circumstances, "war is hell" for almost everybody in it; more precisely, war is *hardship, deprivation, danger, separation,* and so on, and no sane soldier is not plagued quite extensively and quite often by all of these. The psywar intelligence collector who places his focus on these elements will invariably emerge with the deceptive picture of an enemy force just about to dissolve in moans and tears which, generally, is far from the true situation.

Not only do all soldiers of all armies suffer a great deal during a war—they also like to complain about it to anybody who will listen, be he friend or enemy. This accounts for the famous "bitching" without which no army can possibly operate and which is not necessarily a sign of bad morale—though, to make matters still worse for the psywar intelligence man, it may be. The question will be whether there are counter-vailing powers at work, and how strongly. This indicates that a piece of psywar intelligence, unless it is part of a conglomerate of many, generally "soft" elements, is not likely to be worth anything, while a single piece of information (a weapons cache or machine gun emplacement at a certain point, a plan of attack on a certain date) may be of very great value to G-2. Psywar intelligence has to see everything in its place, in the proper proportion, in its context, if it wants to assess the state of an enemy force and detect its vulnerabilities to psywar operations.

A similarity between military and psywar intelligence, however, is that both are expected to provide (a) an overall assessment of the enemy and be (b) operationally useful guidance for all levels. In the field of psywar, the overall evaluation will be an assessment of the enemy's fighting strength in the nonhardware department. How can psywar best proceed here? The most successful method is to establish a number of *indicators* by which enemy morale and motivation can be evaluated. Past experience, not only in World War II and Korea, but also in the Vietnam War, has shown certain indicators to be more useful than others, and some of these—which are likely to be valid also in future wars—are enumerated below.

(1) How "necessary" does the enemy soldier consider the war that he is engaged in waging? Obviously morale does not always depend on how well creature comforts are provided for or even how visible progress may be in the pursuit of a certain enterprise. If I am

fully persuaded that a certain undertaking is absolutely vital, the point at which obstacles will deter me is not so easily reached, even if I, as an individual, am not particularly courageous or resolute. One of the great sources of strength of the Vietnamese soldiers in the Vietnam Wars—against the French and against the Americans—has always been that most of them considered that war is absolutely necessary for national and personal reasons. Most Americans were fully persuaded that from their point of view the war was by no means necessary, because our own intentions regarding their country always were, in our eyes, constructive and positive, and therefore, for them, with the possible exception of a handful of leaders, the war was not only not necessary but continued resistance on their part was foolish and pernicious. More will be said later about whether or not their *continued* belief that the war was absolutely necessary was a *psywar failure* on our part. Here we will merely point out that any strong belief on the part of an enemy that the war is really necessary is one of the principal indicators of high morale, no matter how depressed with his fate, his leadership, or even the course of events, the individual enemy soldier may be. For while such conviction may not always make him happy, it will make him about as effective as he can be.

(2) Another important indicator of the enemy's morale and resilience is his expectation of the war's outcome. Illogical though it may seem, in all wars both sides invariably expect to win, at least in the beginning; this not only goes for the leaders but by and large also for the men in the field. However, depending on the fortunes of war (and, of course, the effectiveness or lack thereof of psywar), this belief frequently undergoes changes. Naturally, uncertainty as to a war's outcome or even the expectation of defeat will corrode a force's valor, fighting spirit, and efficiency, so that "defeatism" is greatly feared by all leaders and commanders in war. It should be remembered that the expectation as to the outcome of a war may not only decline or increase or remain stable, it may also *vacillate,* and such vacillation often leads to gross misinterpretations by the psywarrior. If the Vietnamese War taught anything in that respect, it was that the enemy forces, by certain devices such as the "three-men cell," and the system of "criticism-selfcriticism" (*Kiem Teao*), had psychological devices at their disposal which made it possible for them to *resurrect* the belief in a favorable outcome in the minds of

men who had come to doubt it, and to do so *repeatedly*. In any event, expectations as to outcome are one of the cornerstones of high (or low) morale, and, as in the case of belief in the war's "necessity," they tend to transcend the individual's own attitudes and feelings: even the "bad" soldier will fight better when he thinks the war is going to be won (just as he will fight better when he thinks the war is an absolute necessity for himself and his country), than if he thinks it will not be.

(3) Do the men (and junior and even senior leaders) consider their own leadership to be responsible, qualified, and generally trustworthy? This question is intimately related to points (1) and (2) above: If a man who is asked to risk his life and undergo endless hardships is doubtful as to the war's justification or outcome, he will more easily question the quality and integrity of his leaders whom he is likely to expect will engage in war only as a last resort, and only if they can win it. A man's relationship with his leaders is of prime importance of psywar intelligence, partly to help it assess the overall as a specific situation, partly in order to produce materials that can be used in actual psywar operations to deepen the cleavage, intensify the antagonism, stimulate the suspicions between officers and men, or other groups (sometimes allies) in order to help corrode morale on the other side. If from PW interviews a state of harmony in the enemy camp seems to emerge, the psywarriors must be, and must warn others to be, very much on their guard—the enemy is then likely to be resilient and on the whole protected against psywar inroads. And if, as we have seen it in the war in Vietnam, even *defectors* whom we generally have reason to regard as disaffected elements, praise and approve of their former leaders both in military and human terms, we have reason to assume that morale on the other side, and the cohesion that goes with it, is very high indeed.

(4) How does the enemy soldier, and the force of which he is a part, get along with the population? It was Mao Tse-Tung who coined the phrase of the "fish and the water" when talking about the guerrilla soldier and the people in the countryside on whom he is so dependent not only for sustenance, a hiding place, and intelligence, but also for emotional reasons. One may assume that this element will always be of prime importance in insurgency and counter-insurgency. But even in conventional wars the relationship between the soldier and the popular environment in which he operates—and

the light in which he sees that relationship—is of crucial importance in the nonhardware end of the war. In World War II, for example, the German armies (and also the Italian and certainly the Japanese armies) fought most of their battles and spent most of their time in the "water" of foreign populations with whom they often did not get along very well. Of course, good relations were usually not the aim of their leaders who were bent not on "liberating" but on subjugating, and in certain cases even exterminating, the local people. But the leadership paid a price for that in soldiers' morale which became quite telling toward the end. It has also been a blow to North Vietnamese soldiers that they were not as much welcomed by those they had come to "liberate" in the South as they had been told and had believed they would be, and it has been a serious drain on their morale. Psywar intelligence will, therefore, always want to probe into the relationship between the soldiers and the people.[6]

(5) Consider now "their" view of "us." An enemy who sees us in very black colors will be more likely to consider the war absolutely necessary and not give in to us, while an enemy who does not really either fear or dislike us too much (as the Germans and Italians did not toward the end of World War II) will have rather poor fighting morale. Not only are considerations and calculations involved, but also more elementary feelings. For the soldier on the field of battle, hatred of the enemy is one of the strongest motivators of action and one of the greatest aids in overcoming fear and hardships. Thus, if he really hates his enemy, there is a strong indicator of high morale at work. For the psywarrior to probe effectively into this aspect of the enemy's makeup is particularly difficult. The reason is that (a) many Americans cannot imagine why anybody should hate us or even fear us, and (b) they do not tend to hate anybody themselves, often not even the enemy. One reason for this absence of active and passive hatred on our part is that we are very solidly convinced that our victory would not only be good for ourselves but also for the other side; perhaps not for some of their leaders, but for the "people." And as we do not intend to exploit the other side materially, i.e., in colonial fashion, we tend not to see why they should hate or even oppose us; we are likely to regard any hatred on his part for us as somewhat bizarre, and we are insensitive to it, dismissing it, if we perceived it at all, as "indoctrination." But he does often hate us and is likely to in future engagements, and psywar will always be well

advised to probe into this feeling toward us—to help gauge it on the one hand, and, where possible, to help change it through psywar operations on the other. (It must not be assumed, however, that psywar has the capability of transforming such feelings of hatred or strenuous disapproval or xenophobic rejection into positive feelings as a matter of routine. To view, as some have, U.S. failures in Vietnam as primarily psywar failures is very unrealistic both with regard to Vietnam and psywar.)

It goes without saying that the above five indicators do not exhaust the indicators of enemy morale. They appear to be the most general and important indicators of enemy morale. In addition to paying careful attention to these, psywar intelligence will in all given particular situations set up its own additional particular indicators of enemy morale and motivation.

As to the *method* or *methodology* of probing into the enemy's state of mind there is considerable controversy. It springs primarily from the current trend toward increasingly using quantitative methods of collection and analysis with the help of computers that permit us to establish correlations; refine the analysis; establish trends; and eliminate error, bias, and chance. The adherents of the quantitative school believe that in psywar intelligence, too, the latest survey techniques should be employed, and that simply "to conduct a lot" of interviews can only lead the psywar intelligence collector and analyst astray. Experience has shown, however, that modern survey and research methods have not been applied effectively to gauging enemy morale and motivation in war. Aside from the fact that in war there is, of course, no way of ever obtaining a representative sample of the crucial group, there are such great differences on the basis of past experience in combat and so on, among enemy soldiers, and such significant differences from unit to unit, region to region, and so on, that surveys are severely hampered. The psywar intelligence collector is not able to systematize his investigations beyond a certain point and cannot make them scientific in the strict sense of the word; war is too confused and confusing, too shifting and "messy" for that. Psywar intelligence therefore depends on its assessments and on the targets it reveals to the psywar operator (vulnerabilities) largely on "general knowledge" of an enemy and soldiers in war, and a good deal on "inspired" interpretation of the other. This may be unfortunate, but is not as crippling a limitation as it appears to be, if it is recognized.

The psywar interview has to be long and open-ended, and the heuristic element will always play a big part in it; therefore, the interviewer must be most alert at all times to the unexpected. What he will conduct, then, will be what has become, somewhat loosely, a *depth interview,* designed not only to cover a great deal of ground, but to help the interviewee recognize and verbalize aspects of his own feelings and reactions which he often was not ever fully aware of before. However, there must be, to preserve operational and general utility, a bottom to the depth of the interview, so to speak. To submit respondents to psychiatric interviews, i.e., to probe below the surface of the conscious, has not been useful for psywar in the past. If we find, as some psychologists believe to have found, that many Vietnamese hate the Americans because they unconsciously hated their fathers, there is—aside from the very dubious nature of the information and disproportionate cost in producing it—just nothing the psywarrior can do with it, precisely because it is dregged up from the unconscious. He cannot tell the Vietnamese: "Don't hate me, I'm not your father, your psyche has me mixed up with him." For, even if it were so, the Vietnamese would not be able to respond. Therefore, the psywarrior is best advised to restrict himself to learning what he can about the general cultural traits of those with whom he is dealing, through the work of cultural anthropologists.

In addition to interviewing, the psywarrior studies the opposition's words in his media, i.e., he must engage in *propaganda analysis.* He will study what the enemy says about himself, about us, and about the world in general, and, of course, particularly about the war in progress. Once he has established in his own mind a good grasp of the enemy's "line," he seeks to test, in interviews, just how well, or in what areas, those with whom he has a chance to communicate are "buying" their own official line, i.e., to find out how well indoctrinated they are. In these endeavors his mind must be open to the fact—so frequently brushed aside—that most of those exposed to a line covering a wide variety of aspects of life in general and the war in particular tend to "buy" some and reject other parts. The number of true believers who buy the full ideology is always rather small, but the number of those who buy some of what they are told is very large. Ideology and sentimentalism have convinced most of us, for example, that East Europeans behind the Iron Curtain are in the majority entirely "anti-communist." Studies have revealed, however, that they always did buy one or even quite a few of the communist tenets and probably still do, even after the invasion of Czechoslovakia. Similarly, in Vietnam, there is practically no Vietnamese, it seems, who is not in some agreement with one or the other *dicta* of the National Liberation Front or who does not have some glimmer of appreciation for Ho Chi Minh for having helped deliver him from the French.

EVALUATION OF PSYWAR INTELLIGENCE

An additional and crucial aspect of psywar intelligence is the evaluation function. Evaluation of psywar intelligence is, of course, a routine requirement, but evaluation of psywar needs special mention; it is one of the most important functions of psywar intelligence. It is an inordinately difficult task. In the first place, it must be realized that effect of psywar operations is to a considerable extent a matter of interpretation. In the second place, even a scrupulously honest and cooperative respondent cannot really trace what has affected him and how and what has not. A PW who had previously been exposed to a leaflet or loudspeaker appeal cannot reliably report what effect that had on him. Of course, the ultimate aim of psywar being behavior and action rather than mere intellectual or emotional response, the psywar evaluator could concentrate on action that was precipitated by his preceding psywar appeal and that might be more easily perceived. However, people are almost as unable to report reliably as to what elements precipitated in them certain actions. Finally, the evaluator of past psywar operations must guard against the pressures of his own establishment.

When psywar was practiced first in a concentrated and systematic fashion in World War II in France, the following situation arose rather frequently. The U.S. Army would face a certain Wehrmacht unit and ply it with leaflet and loudspeaker appeals. Nothing would happen. The psywar unit would tell the Germans that they were outnumbered, that they had no gas or other supplies to sustain operations, that we would soon attack them with tanks and aircraft in force, that at that moment the game would be up for them but that they should not worry too much about that, as we would treat them well. Yet nothing would happen. A few days later, the U.S.

Army would indeed launch an assault, and the German unit would offer practically no resistance, and surrender en masse. At that point, the U.S. combat officers, who at all times retained a certain disdain for psywar (though, at times, also had exaggerated expectations of it)—a disdain the effective psywarrior must harden himself to encounter in his military environment—would say to their psywar colleagues: "You see? Here you go talking to these people for days and nothing happens. But when we move in with our hardware, they just give up." To which the psywar man would, of course, reply: "If we hadn't softened them up for you, they would have stood and fought. Psywar's effects are not always visible, in the form of defectors who hold our leaflets over their heads, but often invisible, in weakening the fighting spirit. In fact, psywar's most frequent contribution is precisely that, and it is very hard to measure."

Yet, while this shows how difficult evaluation can be, evaluation of previously conducted psywar is one of the most important functions of psywar intelligence. It is particularly in connection with the evaluation of past psywar efforts that psywar intelligence finds itself on very difficult ground, methodologically, on the one hand, and under various unfortunate pressures on the other. There is, of course, no generally valid indicator as to what the moods, hopes, convictions, fears, and so forth, of a soldier are, and, similarly, no such indicators as to changes in these areas, no indicators for what, precisely, has brought such changes about. What a soldier's morale and motivation will be, and what fluctuations it will undergo, will at all times depend on the changing reality situation on the one hand and how it is perceived on the other; how he perceives it will be a result of what he is being told by his side, what he tells himself, and what he is being told by us. If the fortunes of war turn against him, it is, of course, next to impossible to determine whether and to what extent, if such deterioration of his situation is accompanied by a decline in his fighting effectiveness, this decline is the result of what he tells himself in the face of it, or what he is told, and if, as it is probable, the decline should be the result of a mix (of his own reactions to his deteriorating situation and our pointing this out to him and perhaps eloquently exaggerating it), it is very difficult to impossible to disentangle just what contribution psywar has made to his declining emotional fortunes.

This must not deter psywar intelligence from trying to get as many indications as possible of just how good and effective psywar's contribution to the impact mix on the enemy soldier has been. The intelligence officer can use the interview with captured soldiers and defectors, nevertheless, to receive some impressions. Naturally, the first element he must establish if he wants to evaluate an enemy soldier's response to psywar is *exposure*; a man cannot have been affected by psywar if he has not been exposed to it. He must generally have seen a leaflet or heard a broadcast in order to have reacted to it. However, to make matters still more intricate, even this is not absolutely necessary; the soldier can, as it happens not infrequently, be exposed to psywar indirectly, i.e., by conversation with his buddies before his capture or defection. But the interrogator who wishes to evaluate the effects of psywar must at first try to establish for himself as clearly as possible a picture of his respondent's type, timing, and duration of exposure. This can be quite difficult, partly because captured soldiers are prone to report on leaflets they have seen and broadcasts they have heard that never went their way. Moreover, the psywar intelligence officer often does not have a clear idea himself just what his side has launched. He must, of course, familiarize himself with its contents in great detail if he wants to gauge impact.

It is, of course, important for the psywar interrogator that he establish a good rapport with his respondent. Psywar intelligence must probe deeply into the mind of a man who must be reasonably relaxed and confident that what he says will not redound to his detriment (or to his advantage). In much of his questioning, the intelligence officer will stress the "why" behind a respondent's answers. Yet—and this is very important—the psywar interview must differ very considerably from the psychiatric interview (which our psywarrior would generally not be qualified to conduct anyway). The reason is that, as mentioned earlier, what can be dredged up out of an individual's subconscous is generally of no operational significance or utility.

In order to establish contact with his respondent the psywar interviewer need not necessarily be friendly or ingratiating. In fact, some rather aggressive interviewers who have argued with their respondents on ideological or other war-related matters have often produced some very valuable, and from the psywar point of view, eminently usable insights. For example, in the Vietnam War the interviewers—mostly Vietnamese working under loose American supervision—on quite a few occasions engaged in strenuous debates with their charges on the respective merits of the VC side. In the course of these debates it often became clear how very deeply ingrained the VC ideology was in many of the prisoners, particularly, of course, in the cadre, and how difficult it would be at best to make a dent in it with psywar devices. It was often quite clear, from the facility and articulateness with which the prisoners argued their case that they were more than merely indoctrinated. These findings were doubly significant as the respondents were, after all, in an exposed position and—one might have concluded from experience in other wars and other situations—inclined to curry favor with their captors. But they did not, nor did they show favorable responses to psywar efforts made against them.

As a result, some psywar agencies were able—long before anybody else—to state with relative certainty that the VC were a formidable, quite invulnerable, and much underestimated enemy. Psywar intelligence uncovered impressive information about the enemy which should have been but was not crucial since it was not taken seriously in judging just what lay ahead in Vietnam. In modern limited war in which there are so many more psychological and political elements than in other wars of the past, psywar intelligence is not just a means of garnering information about what appeals the enemy might be most susceptible to, and what the effect of launching such appeals by the various psywar media may have been, but how relevant a contribution psywar intelligence can make to a general assessment of the war as a whole.

In a parallel case to the discovery by psywar intelligence that the opponent in Vietnam was much stronger and more resilient than was generally supposed, psywar intelligence was able also to make some good predictions in World War II. During the fall of 1944, U.S. Army Intelligence generally regarded the Wehrmacht as licked, and the U.S. Army really postponed its final push to the spring of 1945 only because it had run out of certain logistical supplies and wanted to be certain of immediate success when it was ready to cross the Rhine. But psywar, on the basis of interrogations with only a few German noncoms, issued a warning it succeeded in annexing to a 12th U.S. Army G-2 report in November 1944, in which it stated that any army that had noncoms of such high fighting morale as the Wehrmacht was still a very dangerous enemy, capable of surprises.

The breakthrough in the Ardennes that led to the fierce battles in the Huertgen Forest and the encirclement of Bastogne, was a surprise to everyone except the psywarriors whose warnings had unfortunately not been taken too seriously.

Thus, psywar interviews can reveal much that is of importance even beyond psywar. One great difficulty is that with regard to psywar, *everything* a respondent reports is, or more precisely can be, of interest. While, ultimately, the psywar intelligence officer is concerned with the respondent's morale and motivation, i.e., his psychological processes, these tend to emerge only from an endless panorama of concerns. To complicate the picture still further, psywar intelligence does not at all restrict itself to dissecting the respondent, but also tries, through his answers, to dissect those of his buddies, superiors, or subordinates it never gets a chance to talk to, by trying to find how the respondent functioned inside his environment.

The psywar interview seeks to illuminate the respondent's background—social, educational, and life with regard to his entire experience—and his career in the army or the lack thereof, where and how he (and those around him) fought, fled, advanced, endured hardships, and were captured, so that a book length story could thus easily be written about a particular man, and not only the interviewer would bog down in what he would try to find, but the reader of his reports would not be able to peruse them. There is in fact an element at work in current psywar that is at work in all other aspects of military and nonmilitary existence: a proliferation of information. The psywar interrogator must therefore be able to select, condense, and judge at all times whether some information vein is worth exploring or not.

As the various services are, of course, interested in determining the psychological impact their particular type of warfare is having on the enemy, they not only tend to press the psywarrior for information, but often insist on comparative data; they want to know which weapons the other side was most afraid of, most demoralized by, and so on—a matter generally impossible to determine. And comparisons are requested that the psywarrior is really not able to make—unless it is of the negative kind: "Such and such caused us great difficulties, but with such and such we learned to cope early in the game."

A very thorough investigation of how the respondent fared in combat will, of course, be at all times of prime interest to the psywar intelligence officer. But he must remember that whether or not fighting morale is high or low is often discernible only from indirect evidence, not from direct statements made. If his description of a combat episode indicates that a soldier fought very well, then it may be inferred that his morale was very good—he need not state anything subjective to convince his interrogator of that.

VULNERABILITY
CONCEPT

While exploring a respondent's experiences and reactions in combat that is now over for him, the interrogator will search for what is called "vulnerabilities." Much confusion surrounds this concept. Contrary to the chain whose principal vulnerability is its weakest link, a soldier's vulnerability might be any of the links that hold his morale together. If, for example, a soldier's strongest propellant is his faith in his Fuehrer, he will obviously be most strongly affected if that faith can be shaken, for this is what holds him together. Thus, in psywar, a vulnerability is not just an obvious weak point, or a matter that is already a source of concern and irritation to a man, but can also be the lynch pin which, once detected, may yield a promising target of attack. In the case of the VC their own lynch pin—belief in their cause—turned out to be much less brittle than the Wehrmacht's belief in Hitler.

The psywar interrogator, further, will be concerned with a wide range of topics in the sense that he will want to know something about the broadest and most general aspects of his respondent's existence down to the lowliest trivia of his combat life. The latter are of particular importance in cases where troops are likely to be sufficiently long in one place to be the target of some psywar—say, some leaflet—actually based upon the findings of an interrogation. In such instances the discovery that a certain sergeant is disagreeable, or a certain officer a coward, or a certain cook somewhat less than an Escoffier, can be used to good advantage if, as an introduction to a further message, such information is "played back" to the soldiers in the line. Of course, it must be accurate, as it would otherwise arouse contempt. But if it is truly accurate, it is likely to have effects transcending its own trivial nature. It was found in World War II that the enemy, if he was made aware that we knew *something* about him, tended to conclude that we knew *everything* about him.

The contents of psywar must be accurate and the importance of striking precisely the right note cannot in psywar be overstressed; here, too, careful interrogation can help prevent mistakes or, once committed, rectify them later. To take an example in reverse: the VC, among many clumsy leaflets they unloosed upon the American G.I. in the Vietnam War, used one that began with the words, "Hey you chaps!" Now if they had been addressing British soldiers, the word "chaps" might have gone down easily, but with American troops it is likely to produce a jarring note that will interfere from the start with the consumption of the subsequent message (which, of course, may not have "gone over" anyway). German prisoners and deserters in World War II always pointed out what idiomatic mistakes had found their way into leaflets and loudspeaker appeals.

Psywar intelligence is under pressure—some of it self-generated—to establish *trends* in its findings. Are the enemy troops getting tired as compared to last year? Are they of poorer quality? Are they less well indoctrinated? In most cases the psywarrior will not be able to answer them, and transgress his limited capabilities if he tries. For he not only must operate with a haphazard collection of respondents who are not a scientific sample, he is, in addition, faced with so many variables in the respondent's history over the time that valid comparisons—the stuff of which trend studies consist after all—simply cannot be made, at least not on anything resembling a scientific basis. The psywarrior can, of course, perceive some gross changes in the responses he receives that may give him some indications. But unless a situation has radically changed on the other side, so that it manifests itself "obviously" in vastly changed behavior (unit desertions, mass routs), trends cannot with certainty be established, although with some experience and sensitivity they can often be perceived. The computer has so far been unable to provide help in this connection. This does not mean, of course, that in the hands of inspired psywarriors it will not be made to do so. Thus, the psywar interview if competently conducted will be anything but clear and simple, but diffuse and long. This makes it difficult to compare with other psywar interviews that are being collected, but it allows for penetrating insights. The uncertainties surrounding psywar intelligence need not inhibit the psywarrior, as he can construct a more appropriate message (specific and overall, direct and indirect) on the basis of it. Though a mistaken line can, like a false tactical or strategic move, be counter-productive, it is generally better for the psywarrior, just as for any other soldier, to do something rather than nothing, and his intelligence and empathy will be his guide.

The use of empathy will teach him, above all, not to forget that every recipient of a message tends to evaluate not just the message, but the sender. If A suggests a theoretically most enticing deal to B, but has in fact a record of several bankruptcies and a stretch in thy penitentiary the message will weigh less heavily in B's mind than A's record. In psywar, it is never enough to speak the "truth" and hope that it will do its work—it must also be anticipated just what the other side's response will be to the more basic fact that it is receiving a message from us. We tend to feel that when we call for peace or an end to some bloodshed, that others will be attracted to, and agree with, this noble aim, but we laugh if Kosygen or Mao calls for peace, regardless of how he words his message.

A distinction—among many others—must be made here between the use of threats and promises. A threat is more easily believed than a promise if we have no basic confidence in the other side; if a hold-up man says he is ready to kill me, I'll be inclined to take that for the absolute truth, no matter how distrustful I might be of him otherwise. Thus, credibility will on the whole, in war, be much harder to establish with positive than with negative messages. Psywar can, of course, use "black" propaganda, i.e., hide its own identity, or fake some more confident identity, to get certain messages across. But experience has shown that the range and effectiveness of black propaganda, contrary to its mysterious appeal, is limited.

SOME
PROPOSITIONS

In the layman's mind, the purpose of psywar is to produce defectors and deserters, to make men surrender individually or in units, to have men lay down their arms. Psywar's effectiveness tends to be judged by the same criteria. This is an erroneous approach. Even though defectors or deserters are objectives, wars are not won by generating deserters and defectors, not even insurgency or counter-insurgency wars. The fascination throughout the Vietnam encounter with defectors (whose rate, by some arbitrary standard, tended to be "high") was always an indication of ignorance on that basic point. Just as wars are not won by creating defectors, psywar is not primarily concerned with creating them, and its effectiveness cannot be judged by how many it produces. The purpose of psywar is to reduce the enemy's individual and collective psychological capability to carry on his mission; to stay his hand, if only the slightest bit; to reduce his enthusiasm and with it his valor; to slow him down by making him doubt or even by disaffecting him. Of those affected by the message, only a tiny fraction will actually defect, and those will generally have other reasons which psywar merely stimulated. The vast majority of the recipients of appeals will be affected differently in ways very hard to measure, and sophisticated psywar will always be much more concerned with having this general corroding, discouraging, daunting effect on the enemy's forces—either on all of his troops or on individual units, either at all times or on certain occasions—than on generating defectors which is a spectacular sideshow, but a sideshow nevertheless.

The following is an effort to present a number of propositions about psywar.

(1) Psywar must cover a very large range of appeals. Different men react to different appeals; different issues have appeal for different men. It is, as already pointed out, quite idle to try to determine precisely just what motivates the enemy soldier to fight, *if* we try to isolate out what specifically or primarily it is that keeps him fighting. He fights on the basis of a motivation mix, and that motivation mix is likely to consist of material and nonmaterial elements, and to vary from man to man, from officer to private, and so on. A certain controlled "buckshot" approach, is, therefore, logically the best way for psywar to proceed, and any vulnerability that has been detected, whether very clearly or not, and whether it seems to be very common or not, is a potentially lucrative target. The enemy's men, like our own, are all different in some ways, and all the same in others, and psywar must shape an image of their differences and similarities.

(2) Psywar seeks to resist the temptation, particularly in ideological, insurgency war, to see the enemy through its own

ideological spectacles, and thus as divided between "fanatics" and "stooges" on the one hand, and a mass of coerced "ants" on the other. Serious investigations of fascist or communist populations tend to show that only a very small percentage of the people, including the soldiers, fall actually into such categories. There were not too many Germans who accepted Hitler's program in its entirety, and there were very few who rejected it in its entirety. Similarly, there is practically not a single Vietnamese who does not buy some of the NLF's program, nor hardly any who has not some respect for Ho Chi Minh. Similarly, there are not too many who reject all of the Vietnamese struggle for what they call freedom and independence. The lesson here is that the man on the other side is three-dimensional, i.e., there are conflicts in his own make-up, and he is most likely to see his own system and the war it wages, not with either unlimited enthusiasm or disdain, but with *conflicting feelings*. This conflict is one of psywar's prime targets. It is not an easy target to exploit, but a profitable one if it can be exploited.

(3) Psywar does not demand, directly or indirectly, behavior from the man on the other side that, even if he agreed completely with the appeal addressed to him, he cannot do. It is senseless, and in fact counter-productive, as has been done in the Vietnamese War, to shower the jungle with millions of leaflets bearing the message: "Stop this fratricidal war!" The impotent, feeble recipient in the jungle might legitimately retort: "Why don't you stop it?" He can, if he agrees, do precisely nothing about it, and not even his opinions and feelings are changed. If he believes that it is a fratricidal war he will, without further effect, agree, and if not, he will, also without further effect, disagree. But to suggest to him, either directly or indirectly, but always delicately, what is in his own power to do or affect—not to report those who make adverse remarks, not to endanger himself unnecessarily when on patrol, not to worry too much about losing an engagement or falling into captivity—these are the goals of psywar.

(4) Psywar deals with very large issues, but it does not make *demands* on its targets when the large issues are under discussion. When psywar suggests to the other side that it cannot win its war, it is not demanding anything of the ordinary man with the rifle. It merely tries to dampen his enthusiasm, to reduce his fighting worth, by sowing doubt into his mind, to affect his action, indirectly. In

other words, limited objectives, within an individual's capability (these may be quite large—psywar can suggest to colonels to surrender their regiments when surrounded) can always be suggested, even demanded; unlimited things such as the righteousness of the other side's cause or one's own, the likely consequences of victory of one side or another, the very likelihood of victory itself, can only be discussed, in the hope that the effects will show up by themselves, often perhaps in unexpected ways.

(5) Psywar strives to be in harmony with the reality of the situation. It obviously makes no sense to tell a victoriously advancing enemy that he must lay down his arms, or to tell him daily that one will bomb him if one cannot muster any air strikes. Bluff has, of course, its place, but as it will rarely stand the test of time, it has limited application. But that should not discourage the psywarrior from suggesting, even when his own side is suffering reverses, to prepare the way for a changed situation. He can suggest to a victoriously advancing or otherwise temporarily successful enemy that his victory may well turn out to be of a Pyrrhic nature, and make him feel that there is no way for him to terminate the war on his terms. A leaflet was dropped on the Wehrmacht at the very height of its triumph after the fall of France, showing in red and black, with the help of a world map, just how little those in the euphoria of triumph had really gained, and how ominous the infinitely vaster unconquered areas were looming on the horizon.

(6) Psywar appeals must not only be in harmony with existing reality, they must also be in harmony with each other. This does not mean that a solid line must be hammered out and rigidly pursued. On the contrary, as said above, many appeals must be used simultaneously. But they must not contradict each other. Psywar cannot at the same time swear bloody revenge, for example, and the bliss of reconciliation, even though, if it is sophisticated, it will, of course, know how to evoke, simultaneously, certain hopes and certain fears.

(7) Psywar must not make use of slogans that have no real content, even though it is forever tempted to repeat them. There was no point in Vietnam to favor "land reform" when addressing VC forces. Because the land situation is a critical factor in the situation, and as a great deal of domestic efforts have centered on this subject, and as the Vietnamese soldiers are mostly men who live on the land and grow rice or manioc and pay taxes to a variety of "oppressors,"

they are great experts on the subject. What even a well meaning reader of the *New York Times* will accept as a serious war aim will reveal itself as an empty slogan to the simplest VC peasant. Thus, it must be very specific, if it can be, and profoundly knowledgeable on the subject it discusses.

(8) Psywar cannot effectively diverge from the policies it serves. Quite frequently, conflicts will arise in this connection. The psywar intelligence officer (or the area expert) will discern certain aspirations on the part of the adversary he thinks he might with good effect use as a lever; yet his hands are bound if the policies of his own side are in conflict with these aspirations. On the simplest, most physical level, the psywarrior cannot promise the VC soldier, for example, that in case he surrenders he will be well treated from the start, if in fact he is beaten and tortured more often than not by his GVN opponents; the psywarrior cannot promise the VC soldier that the GVN soldier committing such transgressions will be punished, when in fact he is not.

(9) Psywar can "soar freely" in handling selected strategic issues. When it comes to "unselling" the target soldier from his own system or from his own expectation of victory, the psywarrior's only limitation is his talent of dissuasion. He can add an effective element to that dissuasion if he uses "local talent" to support his point. It is an old practice—and happens to be a good one—to use prisoners and deserters as helpers in psywar; they can speak with much authority, and often considerable freedom, to their former comrades. The experienced psywar interrogator when he talks to prisoners will always keep an eye open for possible candidates to aid his psywar efforts.

(10) Psywar must try—and this is much easier said than done—to be *interesting*. The most devastating temptation for psywar is to formulate a self-righteous stentorian message that is demanding. Propaganda everywhere has, above all, the tendency to be boring for many reasons, not the least of which is that it generally is bare of information or thought or use to its recipient. Psywar has to have something to report, be it news that has so far been unavailable to the audience. It has to have elements which are both tempting and real, as well as acceptable. It has to shed at least some new light on old clichés. If it is, therefore, interesting, it even can, contrary to a common notion, be lengthy. The idea that brevity is essential is a

mistaken transfer from the advertising business with which psywar has virtually nothing in common. Advertising has to catch busy people unaware with matters of considerably less than vital concern to them. Psywar deals with very important matters for every individual in question. A slogan is, almost by definition, "empty," and, therefore, will rarely have the desired impact. It has been discovered that lengthy propaganda tracts and broadcasts found much response in World War II in situations where brief messages with "striking slogans" failed to score.

(11) Psywar must be geared in tone and level to its audience. This seems obvious, but is very hard indeed to accomplish. Here again the psywar interrogator, with his broad and far-ranging interview, is indispensable. In Vietnam, for example, interviews with PWs and defectors showed that the respondents, including simple "fighters" were—for the prejudiced Westerner—amazingly knowledgeable, eloquent, articulate, sophisticated. In fact, the ordinary Vietnamese prisoner revealed himself to be infinitely "smarter" and more sensible, if not sensitive, than his Nazi counterpart or even his Korean simile. To such people one can speak effectively only if one speaks to them on their own level. They may not know many of the things we know, but they know many others; some have, as in the case of the Vietnamese, an inherent respect for logic, coolness, directness, and each other. Anyone not aware of this will obviously be unable to communicate effectively to them even the most important information. Naturally, all these characteristics will change from situation to situation, and will have to be investigated in each case again by the psywar intelligence officer with the help of his interrogations.

Psywar must never talk down to the "other fellow" or be in any way haughty or imperious. It is important to remember on the basis of much evidence that it must not be ingratiating, with the help of jokes and other devices. It must not, as psywarriors have found out, be "chummy with the enemy." It must remember that it is an intruder, albeit—in its own mind—a constructive one, and, therefore, must be both modest and somewhat distant, like a stranger appearing on the scene who has what he considers to be an important function, in the midst of people very far from convinced, at the outset, that he has.

CONCLUSIONS

It is to be assumed on the basis of current indications that psywar will continue to be increasingly important, and move from the often marginal position it has occupied in the past into center stage. Wars nowadays tend to be fought far short of the capabilities of the adversaries; not only are nuclear weapons, strategic or tactical, not employed, but other obnoxious devices, such as CB, are not used, thus a greater margin is left for one's efforts. Another reason for likely increased emphasis on psywar is that new style wars tend to be proxy wars, with other, bigger forces looming in the background. A third reason is that wars are being fought less and less for conquest, or even counter-conquest, i.e., for obvious material reasons, but in order to spread, or prevent the spread of doctrines and methods of government. The result is a vast effort to force one's will upon the other side in ways other than by the employment of available violence; the aim is to conquer, in the clumsy phrase of the Vietnam War, "men's hearts and minds" rather than their territory or to destroy their armed forces. With the rapidly accelerating technological developments and the shrinking of distances, it might be surmised that the disproportion between the damage one has the capability of inflicting and the damage one is prepared to inflict will become increasingly large so that, on balance, violence—formerly the mainstay of war for thousands of years—may actually eventually occupy second rank. Psywar, in and by itself, but also, of course, in conjunction with usable or merely threatened or threatenable force, would then be called upon to bring forth the decision. All sides nowadays believe that the other side would actually be better off if it gave in—a posture rarely found among warriors in past history except for the time of the Crusades. In former "straight" wars it was taken for granted that the winner would gather considerable spoils while the loser would incur considerable losses. In the current posture in which both principal antagonists find themselves, they share the conviction that the people on the other side merely need to change their minds, and *everybody* will gain. And psywar, of course, is the logical instrument to bring about such mind changing.

It is not at all unlikely that psywar, cast into that role, will fail. People can be influenced only so far, and interrogations and other forms of exploring their minds and emotional make-up are severely limited, and likely to remain so. The extent to which we can influence people is, of course, a function, among other things, of how much we can first learn about them in order to manipulate them. Total manipulation, be it in the forms of "winning the hearts and minds" or "nation building," would require total information, and would have to fail on that ground alone—we cannot learn enough about people to make them do in every respect what we want them to do. In this author's view, the disastrous course of the Vietnam War (disastrous no matter how it ends) is to a large extent a psywar failure; we rely in that war much more heavily on psywar than in any previous war, what with pacification, hearts and minds, nation building, and so on, all of which have a most important psychological component. This psywar failure is in turn partly caused by the psywar intelligence failure: despite an unprecedented, staggering amount of research into the "nature" of the enemy, as an individual and a society, these endeavors are condemned to be unable to furnish adequate knowledge for a task that is beyond doing to begin with. Thus, psywar, from its inception has always been either grossly over-estimated or under-estimated as a capability. In this case psywar, in the broadest sense, was greatly over-estimated. It could not perform the necessary sorcery to make the VC fall away, or to stay the hand of the NVA, or make GVN and ARVN arise in glorious strength. Similarly, and most ominously, the psywar component of the bombing of the North—deterrence and coercion—was a resounding failure, and could not have been somewhat more uninspired. Especially inappropriate was the practice of throwing down for the population little gifts such as toys, food, or some other Woolworth type items to create the image that we were "bearing gifts," while at the same time discharging enormous bomb loads that killed many of them and their children, destroyed their land, and otherwise interfered with their lives as peasants or fishermen.

As everything else in our day, psywar is in flux; its limits and capabilities, though expanding, are uncertain, and the expectations vested in it excessive. It can be used to good advantage just as well as abused grossly and perniciously, perniciously, that is, not only for the targets but also for ourselves. Its most likely failure will come when we simply condemn it to ineffectiveness by using it for unattainable ends, or in conjunction with other efforts aimed at unattainable ends.

Psywar can do much to save lives and help one's cause prevail, to the extent that one's cause is in harmony with human aspirations on the other side, too. Whether it is or not is not in the hands of the psywarriors.

NOTES

1. If the reader should get the uneasy feeling at this point that we are getting here on treacherous ground or that, in fact, the author is being slightly subversive, he should remember that subversion is part of all psywar and that, to be effective in its application, the practitioner must be willing and able to face the situation (i.e., himself included) more sharply than anyone else. If he fails to do so, and merely pontificates either on his own side's merits or the other side's demerits—a mistake only too often committed in all forms of psywar—he does not earn his keep.

2. The element of time is also decisively affected by nearness to action or distance therefrom. For a man not just exposed to enemy fire, but merely to the extreme discomforts of war, time will seem much longer than to the harassed military bureaucrat somewhere in a field headquarters, or perhaps even in the zone of the interior who will readily think in terms of years, if only to get his paper work under control. Psywar should never be determined without the aid of those who have not soaked up the atmosphere of actual battle.

3. This is because, in a long-term situation, untruths tend to become revealed simply by the passage of time: if we threaten a large push we are unable to mount, and it never comes, the truth will be revealed. However, the lie, or to use a less painful word, the distortion, can be employed by psywar with impunity for the very long haul, particularly for postwar promises. Psywar can promise "pie in the sky" for *après guerre* and never be revealed as playing fast and loose with the truth, regardless of whether it is based on real policy intentions or not—at least not while the war is in progress.

4. In this connection, an enemy who commits atrocities can present a particularly thorny problem for psywar: if we promise him, explicitly and even implicitly, leniency as a device to desist, he may just go on doing what he does, at the expense of his victims and the good name of the cause; if we threaten him with dire punishment he may be inclined, at our expense, to fight "to the last man." Hitler tried to involve the entire German nation, including the Wehrmacht, in his genocidal crimes to create, for the purpose, *inter alia,* of

creating just such a dilemma for the allies and for allied psywar: to promise or even imply forgiveness while the atrocities were in progress could not but reflect allied moral and physical weakness, demean the allied cause, and so on; to threaten retribution was likely to create in the Germans, almost all of whom were implicated in one way or another and knew it only too well, the "desperate" resistance Hitler wanted. Roosevelt eventually found a partial solution to the problem in his much maligned—yet ingeniously correct—declaratory and actual policy of "unconditional surrender." Far from uniting the Germans and prolonging their resistance, it was—finally—clear evidence to them that "the game was up," and had very divisive and corrosive effects, while at the same time greatly strengthening and clarifying the allied cause. And as it did not speak of retribution, but merely of surrender, it did not create unifying terror among the Germans. Of course, it could only work to our advantage in this specific situation, with the Germans, at least on one level, very much and very uncomfortably aware of their very real collective guilt. To call for the unconditional surrender of a society strong and clear in its own righteousness would be a great mistake. In the case of Germany it was, for psywar and many other reasons, a stroke of genius.

5. For example, important other sources are captured enemy documents and enemy letters, either letters received from home or letters written by the soldiers but not yet mailed. In certain ways, information contained in such sources may be regarded as more reliable than information obtained by interrogations, as such information was not meant to be seen by enemy eyes. Yet, the enemy, like everyone else, suffers generally from either personal or institutional bias, and therefore distorts much of what he reports. It may be noted in this connection that sources, such as captured documents or letters, can in themselves be valuable and very convincing materials for actual psywar operations. A telling official report of casualties, or a pessimistic diary or letter, if "played back" to the enemy in a leaflet or broadcast, can be quite unsettling. More telling still were certain letters—in this case even more so the *optimistic* ones—that German soldiers in World War II had carried in their pockets and which, when taken off a dead enemy, were found to be drilled by a U.S. bullet (usually dramatically at four points as the letter was folded, German fashion, into four squares). The photograph of such a letter on a leaflet had quite an effect, when back in the hands of German Wehrmacht readers.

6. This is as good a place as any to point out that psywar intelligence, in most cases, is of dual utility: it tells us something about the other side, and can, often as not, be used in actual psywar operations. For example, if we hear that such and such causes the enemy some anxiety, we will not only take account of that in our assessment of him, but play it back to him usually with comment, in order to intensify the grievance, partly by exaggerating it, partly by irritating him with our knowledge of it.

REFERENCES

CARROLL, W. (1948) Persuade or Perish. Boston: Houghton-Mifflin.

LASSWELL, H. D. and D. BLUMENSTOCK (1939) World Revolutionary Propaganda. New York: Alfred A. Knopf.

LAZARSFELD, P. F. (1940) Radio and the Printed Page. New York: Duell, Sloane & Pearce.

LERNER, D. and G. W. STEWARD (1949) International Communication and Political Opinion: A Guide to the Literature. New York: Princeton University Press.

LINEBARGER, P. M. A. (1948) Psychological Warfare. Washington, D.C.: Infantry Journal Press.

SCHRAMM, W. (1954) The Process and Effects of Mass Communication. Urbana: University of Illinois Press.

THOMSON, C. A. H. (1948) Overseas Information Service of the U.S. Government. Washington, D.C.: Brookings Institution.

U.S. Department of the Army (n.d.) "Psychological warfare in combat operations." Field Manual 33-5.

Chapter 15

COVERT MILITARY OPERATIONS

PAUL W. BLACKSTOCK

Covert operations are only a part of the broad spectrum of foreign policy instruments. A considerably more comprehensive term—political or psychological warfare—has been loosely applied to the aggressive use of a wide range of essentially nonmilitary tools of foreign policy. These instruments range from overt political and economic pressure, aggressive action through international agencies such as the United Nations and its affiliated organizations, and the use of political parties, trade unions, and similar groups as "organizational weapons," for such clandestine activities as political assassination and the training, arming, and disposition of spies, saboteurs, and guerrillas to carry on subversive or revolutionary and counter-revolutionary movements.

POLITICAL WARFARE AND FOREIGN POLICY

In practice, the use of any of these methods of political warfare has been accompanied by propaganda activities ranging from straight news services and cultural relations programs to the most scurrilous forms of "black" or nonattributable propaganda and rumor-mongering. In time of war, military establishments enter the political warfare field with elaborate organizations to produce and deliver messages aimed at lowering morale, inducing desertion or defection, and, if possible, mutiny and revolution among both the enemy soldier and civilian populations.

A common denominator of all these methods is their purpose: they are used to extend the influence of one state over another by means short of a general or even a limited war. But limited military operations, such as border raids and demonstrations, guerrilla activities, and armed internal resistance or insurgency may also be an integral part of covert political warfare.

Theoretically, the wide range of activities loosely referred to as political warfare is actually aggressive but noncombatant intervention by one state in the internal affairs of another.

This is a comprehensive view, for many types of subversive or resistance operations may continue or even be intensified behind enemy lines after the outbreak of war, just as diplomatic contact between belligerents may also be continued. Moreover, it is frequently difficult to draw a line where open political warfare ends and clandestine activities begin. A coup d'état or revolution within a country may be carefully and secretly engineered from the outside, up to a certain point. The actual seizure of power, however, cannot possibly be concealed from the world, and the operation then becomes an open affair. But this does not mean that covert operations suddenly stop. Quite the contrary. Beneath the surface of events power is consolidated and counter-revolutionary elements are secretly eliminated—especially when the new regime is a police state—with little objective news leaking to the world at large. The same is true of covert operations in general: a foreign minister or a nationalist leader is murdered, a military attaché "falls off" a train, a "border incident" makes headlines. Such events are frequently only isolated, accidentally exposed incidents in the larger pattern of silent, clandestine warfare which goes on restlessly and unceasingly beneath the surface.

The common denominator underlying the aggressive use of nonmilitary instruments of foreign policy is their purpose: to extend the influence of one state over another. In the past, the ultimate extension of influence has been direct military intervention and conquest. Such aggression has been recognized as an instrument of policy, and an elaborate superstructure of international law dealing with the rules of war has been generally accepted. With the rise to power of Hitler and the rapid expansion of Nazi Germany, the

USSR, ironically enough, drew official attention to the need for a definition of *indirect aggression*. The Soviets introduced the term to describe Nazi political warfare and nonmilitary conquest. In fact, the alleged unwillingness of France and Great Britain to provide guarantees against such aggression was given by the Soviets as one reason for the breakdown of the tripartite conference with the French and British in mid-August 1939, when at the same time negotiations leading to the Nazi-Soviet Pact and World War II were already well under way.[1]

There is still no internationally accepted definition of indirect aggression, although there is a general recognition of the operational techniques involved. For example, in November 1950, a U.N. General Assembly resolution entitled "Peace Through Deeds" called upon all nations to refrain from "fomenting civil strife in the interest of a foreign power" and denounced such action as "the gravest of all crimes against peace and security throughout the world" (U.S. Department of State, 1950). The "pattern of conquest" involved was defined, in the official U.S. view, as "taking over a nation by means of indirect aggression; that is, under the cover of a fomented civil strife the purpose is to put into domestic control those whose real loyalty is to the aggressor" (U.S. Department of State, 1958b, 1958c). The late U.S. Secretary of State, John Foster Dulles, at the time of the crisis in Lebanon, denounced the political warfare activities of Nasser's regime as "indirect aggression," which he characterized as one of the most dangerous features of contemporary international life and one that required particular attention in the Middle East (Stebbins, 1959). Dulles stated, "We do not think that the words 'armed attack' [in Article 51 of the U.N. Charter] preclude treating as such an armed revolution which is fomented from abroad, aided and assisted from abroad" (U.S. Department of State, 1958a).

THE COLD WAR HERITAGE

In modern times, major threats to the established order in Western societies have arisen from two sources: dynamic forces working for social and political changes which have reached their culmination in such major upheavals as the French and Russian revolutions, and the traumatic heritage of two major world wars and their attendant "time of troubles" for millions.

There can be little question that in signing the Nazi-Soviet Pact in August 1939, and thus unleashing World War II, Stalin as a Communist, hoped that in the aftermath of political, economic, and social dislocation he would be able to intervene either directly by military occupation, or indirectly through the Communist parties in Western Europe, to further the ideals of World Revolution.

The bloc of Central European states from the Baltic to Bulgaria was lost to the West because of the way the war was fought. Under the policy loosely described as "containment," the Western European powers were saved from Communist domination by the Marshall Plan, as an economic response to Soviet aggression, and by the military shield of NATO and other Western alliances. The phenomenal political and economic recovery of Europe and the successful integration of the Federal Republic of Germany into the Western European system eliminated the immediate postwar threat that the USSR might gain control of the area through political warfare means.

From the beginning of the Cold War in 1947 throughout the 1950s, the U.S. was preoccupied with the "ideological struggle" against World Communism under the moralistic guidance of John Foster Dulles as Secretary of State and his brother Allen Dulles as head of the U.S. Central Intelligence Agency. The CIA was charged with responsibilities not only for collecting intelligence, but also with "overseas cloak and dagger and political action operations"—a euphemism for covert operations (Ransom, 1959).

In his preconfirmation testimony before the Senate Foreign Relations Committee on January 15, 1953, John Foster Dulles asserted his belief that the peoples suffering under Communist tyranny in Europe and Asia must and could be liberated:

> A policy which only aims at containing Russia where it now is, is, in itself, an unsound policy. . . . It is only by keeping alive the hope of liberation, by taking advantage of that wherever opportunity arises, that we will end this terrible peril which dominates the world . . . those who do not believe that results can be accomplished by moral pressure, by the weight of propaganda, just do not know what they are talking about [U.S. Congress, Senate, 1953: 5-6].

Thus pledged to seize the initiative in the East-West struggle, Dulles adopted essentially the same sort of "two-camp" image of the world which had characterized Soviet foreign policy as formulated in 1925 in Stalin's (1934) famous dictum, *Kto-Kogo (Who Defeats Whom)* and again in Andrei Zhdanov's speech, "The International Situation," at the founding of the Cominform in 1947 (*Pravda,* 1947). This image of two opposing camps locked in mortal combat, and the "either-or" attitude inspired by it reached its most extreme form in Dulles' Iowa State College speech of June 9, 1956, in which he declared that, "the principle of neutrality . . . has increasingly become an obsolete conception, and, except under very special circumstances, it is an immoral and shortsighted conception" (U.S. State Department, 1956). The "liberation" policy of the fledgling Eisenhower Administration was provided with intellectual elaboration in such works as James Burnham's, hopefully entitled *The Coming Defeat of Communism* (1950) or his *Containment or Liberation* (1953). It was severely denounced by an authoritative Soviet source as "the reckless policy designed to bring about the downfall of the socialist countries and the restoration of the colonial regimes in the East. Its features are intensified espionage and subversive activity and ideological sabotage against the countries of socialism, and interference in the internal affairs of independent and sovereign states" (Fedoseyev, 1957).

The Cold War turned the attention of Western observers to descriptive analyses of Soviet political warfare, "indirect aggression," or "subversion" as it is most frequently called. Until the United States became involved in the abortive invasion of Cuba in April 1961, the assumption had been implicit in most such literature that aggressive intervention in the internal affairs of other states was limited to totalitarian regimes such as Nazi Germany, Stalinist Russia, or Communist China. Thanks to the heritage of the Anglo-American legalistic-moralistic tradition in foreign affairs, any implication that the U.S. and its democratic allies might be seriously engaged in covert political operations had for the most part been studiously avoided. Even the most pragmatic literature dealing with political warfare, such as the monumental Daugherty-Janowitz *Psychological Warfare Casebook,* carefully avoided analysis of covert operations as such, although brief mention was made of "black propaganda."[2]

In his book, *The Craft of Intelligence,* Allen Dulles (1963b) lumps together "so-called wars of liberation, guerrilla wars, political penetration, subversion and 'popular fronts' " as "Communist methods for achieving piecemeal what they hesitate to attempt by direct military action." But he does not analyze the operative principles behind such communist subversive Cold War tactics. CIA's role in covert political warfare to counter such tactics is merely implied in the statement that the security and intelligence service of threatened countries

> need help which they can get only from a country like the U.S., which has the resources in funds, personnel, and techniques to aid them. . . . Both in the collection of information as to the peril that threatens and in the field of covert action, our intelligence services have an essential role to play—one that is new to this generation perhaps, but nonetheless vital[3] [Dulles, 1963a] .

There are excellent, time-honored reasons for official reticence with regard to covert political operations and the espionage on which they rely for intelligence support. Much of the indignation of the United States' allies over the handling of the U-2 spy-plane incident was due to the fact that President Eisenhower flouted accepted international conventions by accepting responsibility for the covert actions of a nonaccredited espionage agent. The traditional international code of behavior in such cases, in which an espionage or covert political agent is caught in the act, is firm disavowal of any knowledge or responsibility. Adherence to this polite fiction is a rule which, when reciprocally honored, permits all powers involved to minimize embarrassment and the tensions which result when secret agents are apprehended or their operations exposed. As previously noted, for more than forty years the Soviet Union has followed this principle religiously by officially denying any responsibility for the activities of its own espionage and political agents working through Communist parties abroad.

THE POST-COLD WAR PERIOD: REVOLUTION AND THE THIRD WORLD

The classical cold war period began with the founding of the Cominform in the fall of 1947 and ended with the death of Stalin in June 1953. But, as the Soviet poet Yevtushenko has observed,

"Stalin's Heirs" are still very much with us; not only Soviet but also U.S. policy is heavily burdened with the Stalinist heritage of the cold war period.

For the USSR the Geneva Summit Conference cleared the way for the 1956 Twentieth Party Congress and the new general line which recognized that in a world threatened with thermonuclear holocaust, coexistence is better than no existence, and that war—meaning general war—is no longer inevitable. Startled by the unexpected peaceful disintegration of the British and French colonial empires, Soviet leaders hailed the new states which emerged from this process as a "Third World," and ascribed to them the role of a "buffer zone" or "zone of peace" between the two camps. Henceforth, thanks to the emergence of the Third World, states with different political and economic systems could live together, so the general line runs, in a state of "peaceful coexistence."

At the same time, however, the Soviet leaders pledged themselves to a continuation of the "sharpest ideological struggle" against capitalism, and to the support of revolutionary movements against colonial or neocolonial regimes, including so-called "wars of national liberation." In contradiction to the main thrust of both Marxist and Leninist doctrine, the 1956 line no longer prescribed revolution as the only and inevitable road to power for Communist parties. For the last decade Soviet doctrine has recognized that parliamentary or democratic processes may provide a peaceful path to power, thus giving doctrinal sanction for Communist participation with bourgeois parties in united fronts for electoral purposes.

In the area of global military strategy the 1956 general line foreshadowed a consensus which has been slowly and painfully hammered out in the course of a continuing dialogue between U.S. and Soviet strategists and policy makers over the last decade. The 1955 Summit Conference resulted in basic agreement on a mutually recognized need for relaxing the acute tensions of the cold war period and paved the way for the uneasy detente which has characterized U.S.-Soviet relations during the last decade. This detente has been seriously jeopardized by notable excursions into brinkmanship on both sides such as the recurrent Berlin crises and the Cuban missile caper, and was threatened by the escalation of U.S. operations in Vietnam.

To Mao Tse-Tung and other Chinese Communists who hold tenaciously to the belief that political power grows out of the barrel of a gun, the Soviet Twentieth Party Congress line represents a betrayal of Leninist revolutionary principles, especially of Lenin's oft-quoted "two-camps" dictum that coexistence is unthinkable and war inevitable. Given their 1950 treaty of eternal friendship and alliance with the USSR, the Chinese have understandably had deep misgivings about the detente in American-Soviet relations. The Chinese have been particularly incensed at joint U.S.-Soviet efforts to limit membership in the nuclear club, as far as possible, to themselves. Diverging national interests as well as doctrinal differences thus led to a widening Sino-Soviet rift which by 1960 could no longer be concealed. Since then, the disintegration of the one-time "monolithic bloc" of the Communist world has accelerated. Even the Communist parties abroad are split into pro-Soviet and pro-Chinese factions or parties, some open, others concealed.

Developments of the post-Stalin era indicate that the USSR has reappraised its basic national interests and has radically reinterpreted Communist doctrine in order to bring it more into line with the political realities of the last decade and with strategic facts of life in the thermonuclear and space age. However, in contrast to Soviet flexibility, U.S. policy with respect to both communism and revolution remained largely immobilized in the rigid ideological framework of the cold war period. This is understandable, since the basic cold war policy of containment was highly successful in blocking Soviet expansion into Western Europe and the Middle East. This success led naturally to an uncritical attempt to extend the same formula to U.S. relations with the Third World especially in Southeast Asia which has emerged in the post-Stalinist decade. Although the two areas and their problems are vastly different, American foreign policy has simply substituted the Third World for Europe as the theater of the cold war struggle between what President Johnson has called "the forces of freedom" and the "forces of slavery." We have since been constrained to regard every internal convulsion in the newly emerging countries in terms of how it may affect the so-called "confrontation with communism."

Nothing could be more misleading. The revolutionary turbulence in the developing areas of the world is an inescapable adjunct to modernization and nationalism, the two major factors shaping both the internal and external politics of these areas. We should note to begin with that the Third World arose phoenix-like from the ashes of

World War II. Its complex revolutionary problems and movements today stem directly from forces and factors at work during the later stages of the second world war. Let us briefly review this wartime heritage.

The forces of native nationalism were unleashed during World War II, as indigenous resistance movements sought to overthrow either existing colonial regimes or alien occupying forces. Japanese forces, for example, overran much of China and Southeast Asia, including French Indo-China. The native nationalist movements received considerable stimulus from lofty Anglo-American declarations concerning the Four Freedoms, and the implicit promise of national self-determination which accompanied the presence of American fighting forces in several theaters. American wartime largesse continued after the war in the form of massive economic and military aid programs. The continuing American presence and programs had profoundly disturbing and ambivalent effects. They acted as both catalytic and corrosive forces, giving birth ultimately to what has since been dubbed "the revolution of rising expectations." These three factors—the traumatic heritage of wartime occupation and aspirations, native nationalism, and the revolution of rising expectations—have combined to dissolve the former empires of our European allies. However, in the immediate postwar period, our policy makers soon became preoccupied with containing the aggressive Soviet thrust against the Middle East and Central Europe which ushered in the classic cold war period. The developing areas were perforce forgotten as the Soviet menace to Europe required our policy planners to concentrate their attention on the Marshall Plan and its military shield, the NATO alliance. In turn NATO solidarity forced the U.S. to go along, however grudgingly, with the attempts of our allies to repress or contain indigenous nationalist movements which sought to bring an end to colonial rule. For example, the U.S. supported the French and contributed to their war against the Viet Minh in Indo-China until the fall of Dien Bien Phu in 1954. In fact the U.S. did not part company with the French and British until the Suez crisis of 1956.

Thus the classic cold war period cast our foreign policy and military programs into a rigidly anti-Communist mold. For years both Republican and Democratic administrations have sold foreign aid programs to both Congress and the American people as necessary sacrifices "to stem the tide of communism." This expedient has fixed in the public mind a highly exaggerated image of Communist capabilities and gains. Fear of Communist subversion within and without reached a hysterical pitch during the ascendancy of the late Senator Joseph McCarthy, and anticommunist propagandists still paint a picture of a world which will inevitably turn deepest Red unless the U.S. holds the line everywhere against communism and revolution.

A mirror image of the same process has been at work within the former Sino-Soviet bloc. As the Russians and Chinese contend for spiritual and temporal leadership of their own divided world, their leaders argue that although the historic British and French empires have disintegrated, nevertheless, there is an international civil war going on between the forces of nationalism and revolution. Both the USSR and Communist China claim the leadership of these latter forces. Thanks to American cold war support of its allies, Communist propaganda has successfully tarred the U.S. with the same colonial or neo-colonial brush as the British or French. Both the Soviet and Chinese Communists have been able to exploit "Yankee Go Home" appeals throughout the Third World, and these campaigns have in turn reinforced our own anti-Communist predilections. Thus the Cold War has been kept alive by ideologues and propagandists on both sides who reinforce each other's output with sets of essentially false but self-confirming hypotheses.

In the developing areas of the world nationalism and the drive for modernization have produced a series of recurrent political and social revolutions which have displaced traditional elites and various colonial and postcolonial ruling groups. As new ruling elites in the Third World consolidate their power and extend their privileges, the nepotism and corruption associated with traditional societies will almost certainly create burning political, economic, and social grievances. These in turn will lead to new revolutions. In spite of heroic if belated U.S. efforts to arrest the process, this is clearly what happened to the Diem regime in South Vietnam, and the pattern will repeat itself elsewhere. Naturally Soviet or Chinese Communist parties, or both, will seek to exploit such indigenous revolutionary movements, employing their separate strategies of subversion or political warfare. However, the traditional cold war assumption that Communists will automatically succeed in capturing and controlling such movements unless vigorously opposed by U.S. political warfare and counterinsurgency programs is patently false. The cycle of revolution in the developing areas is as open-ended as the process of modernization itself, from which it is inseparable. It bears little or no relationship to the frustrations and fears of political warriors on either side of the Bamboo and Iron Curtains, and even less relationship to their propaganda slogans about the struggle between the so-called forces of freedom (or national liberation) and forces of slavery (or neo-colonialism).

The Western states have naturally extolled the virtues of their democratic political systems and open societies as a framework for the modernization of the developing areas. For their part the USSR and Communist China hold up their authoritarian and socialist-based systems, not only as models, but as historical proof that backward, traditional societies can lift themselves by their own bootstraps. But by and large the nationalist leaders in the newly emerging states have shrewdly exploited their Third World position to obtain both Western and Communist aid without adhering strictly to the models advanced by either side. Outstanding examples of such leadership are Nasser, Bourghiba, and Ben Bella in North Africa; Tshombe, Sekou Toure, and recently deposed Kwame Nkrumah in Subsaharan Africa; in Asia and Southeast Asia, Norodom Sihanouk in Cambodia, and the recently reduced Sukarno in Indonesia. The outstanding feature of the developing areas is the "mixed" character of their social, economic, and political systems, although most of them are decidedly more authoritarian than democratic.

Thus Moscow, Peking, and the Western nations have all been somewhat disappointed at the meager results of their political warfare and foreign aid programs. For example, contrary to both Western fears and Soviet hopes, communism as an ideology has made little headway in the Middle East or in North and Subsaharan Africa, although the United Arab Republic, Ghana, and Guinea have accepted financial and/or military aid from the USSR or Communist China or both. From our own experience in Laos and Vietnam, the U.S. has also learned the hard way that massive military and foreign aid programs do not necessarily assure the cooperation of revolving political and ruling groups in the developing areas, much less control over them.

For all their combined efforts since World War II, the Soviet and Chinese Communists have established viable regimes only in North

Korea, North Vietnam, and possibly Cuba, which, since the Cuban missile crisis, has proved to be more of a liability than an asset. For its part, where the U.S. has most actively intervened—in South Korea, Laos, and South Vietnam—the resulting regimes have been something less than models of democracy and modernization. Nevertheless, in spite of the spectacular failures of the past on both sides, the developing areas of the world will continue to invite intervention. Nationalism and modernization have converted the Third World into a vast political warfare arena in which the Western powers, the USSR, and Communist China are engaged in a three-way struggle, both open and covert, to extend their power and influence.

COVERT OPERATIONS, ESCALATION AND DE-ESCALATION

Typically, in peacetime, covert military operations begin with the small-scale employment of "advisers" engaged in training local security police or military forces.

The American experience in Southeast Asia (especially Laos and Vietnam) indicates that covert political-military intervention tends to escalate beyond the covert threshold into open military or "counter-insurgency" operations which are outside the scope of this chapter. However, the point should be stressed that even after the open military intervention threshold has been passed there still remains an important area of covert operations which aims primarily at political, psychological, and sociological objectives which cannot be achieved by either the limited or massive use of direct military force. (These objectives will be discussed and illustrated in a later section of this chapter.)

While much has been written on the theoretical problems of escalation (Kahn, 1965), military de-escalation has been largely ignored and, so far as its political implications are concerned, is widely misunderstood. Military de-escalation, for which we have models in both the Congo and Laos, does not mean political withdrawal or abandonment of "the cause." After several years of covert military operations which at times crossed the threshold into open military intervention in Laos, the United States returned for the most part to the level of covert intervention from which it started; but this level was of considerable scope. The covert threshold was never really crossed in Africa, where both the Soviet and Chinese Communists have recently suffered major setbacks in Ghana, Guinea, and the Congo without the loss of American lives.

Covert political-military operations in times of either peace or war are difficult to manage and control and have many built-in limitations (Blackstock, 1964). During World War II, the U.S. Office of Strategic Services (OSS) and the British Special Operations Executive (SOE) were charged with the mission, in Churchill's words, "to set Europe ablaze." Both agencies ran into considerable opposition from the regular military establishments of their respective countries (Cookridge, 1967). Both British and American covert operations suffered from bureaucratic rivalries and from divided policy-making and operational responsibilities. Moreover, the political and psychological effects of such operations were dimly understood and often ignored.

More recently the political and social tasks of U.S. Special Forces teams have frequently been downgraded by regular military forces seeking to repress insurgency by the use of massive military force. Nevertheless, political-military operations, if they can be kept from escalating beyond the covert threshold, have many advantages over open counter-insurgency operations, which if at first they don't succeed, are an open invitation to an upward spiral of escalation.

In the first place, covert operations are unacknowledged and thus national prestige is not involved. If they misfire or if "strong men" such as Phoumi Nosovan in Laos or Ngo Dinh Nhu and Colonel Tung in Vietnam misuse their strength, the U.S. is not disgraced and can conveniently look the other way when the erstwhile protegé is replaced by another local coup d'état.

In the second place, clandestine operations offer a sophisticated escape from some of the rigidities of the cold war model. For example, in certain areas the U.S. can covertly cooperate with British, French, or even Soviet agencies to neutralize Communist Chinese influence without the risk of being labeled "soft on communism" by local "hardline" politicians and demagogues who use the cold war heritage to garner votes in elections. Such clandestine cooperation based on mutually supporting national interests may well have been a factor limiting the spread of Chinese Communist influence in the African theater. And, as previously noted, operational cover, protection from political interference, and a manipulative approach may make it easier for covert operations personnel to break through the vicious circle of cold war propaganda and operational models.

On the other hand, a former inspector general of CIA concludes after many years' study that "covert action" should be used "only in the most serious national emergency, and as a last resort before the use of military power. The use of covert action for the implementation of foreign policy may be even counter-productive when successful; when unsuccessful it can be catastrophic. The National Security Council should bear this in mind" (Kirkpatrick, 1968).

Following the failure of the Bay of Pigs operation, the Taylor Committee concluded that "in the future, CIA would continue to have responsibility for the kind of 'covert political action' that would, for example, head off a Communist attempt to gain control of a foreign labor union. But the responsibility for para-military operations would be assigned to a special warfare section of the Pentagon" (Hilsman, 1967). It appears that this rough principle of division of labor will continue in present and future crises which characterize the underdeveloped areas of the world. However, the relative merits or disadvantages of covert operations are viewed and the military establishment is thus charged with responsibility for plans and operations in this area.

OPERATIONAL TECHNIQUES

Whether in times of peace or open military hostilities, the principles on which covert political operations are based are best understood by assuming an oversimplified situation in which an aggressor state deliberately sets out to extend its control over another by intervening with nonmilitary techniques in its internal affairs.[4] With this model in mind, intervention by the aggressor state, whether carried out openly or secretly, may take several forms. These forms can be classed either as operational techniques or as stages in the extension of control by the aggressor. Three initial stages or processes may be distinguished and described: penetration or infiltration, forced disintegration or atomization (*Zersetzung*), and subversion and defection. Successful application of these techniques usually results in a period of covert control. In maximal cases, such as the Nazi or Communist takeover of certain Central European states, these initial stages have been followed by two others: seizure of power and open assimilation of the victimized state into the political system or power complex of the aggressor. Intensive persuasion is used in a variety of forms, ranging from propaganda to extreme violence, in order to catalyze each stage or process of intervention, and it is often an inseparable adjunct.

Infiltration-Penetration

Infiltration is the deliberate *planned* penetration of political and social groups within a given state by agents of an intervening power for manipulative purposes, i.e., to extend the influence and control of the aggressor state over its victim. To the extent that such penetration is deliberately manipulative, it is usually covert or secret. Here, as in all forms of such intervention, the motive or purpose is the distinctive criterion, and the term *penetration* is much more accurate in conveying this essential meaning than *infiltration,* which has been widely used in popular literature dealing with Communist political warfare activities. Purpose and the need for secrecy also distinguish penetration from mere presence or affiliation.

Most states exchange ambassadors or other envoys for purposes of representation abroad. Among major powers, typically large embassy staffs include military attaché, economic, and information offices whose members make a wide variety of political and social groups within the host state. Such contacts are perfectly open and indispensable for purposes of representation; their motive is not regarded as hostile, and there is no need for secrecy. However, many states maintain within their embassies abroad espionage or other agencies which attempt secretly to penetrate selected political and social groups in order to gather classified information which cannot be obtained through open sources. In some cases these agencies carry on covert political activities which, if disclosed, might be regarded as "unfriendly" or "aggressive" by the host country or by other countries similarly represented, and must, therefore, be kept secret. These offices and functions are thus usually given an innocuous "cover" to conceal both their existence—which is assumed by all concerned—and their extent.

In a time of mounting political tension between two states, relations may be broken. After official representation ceases, the

only controlled sources of information remaining will be through
agents who have previously been secretly recruited and who are left
behind. This is also the case with controlled political action within
the host country—which in case of war becomes enemy terrain. Thus,
after diplomatic relations are broken, political penetration is closely
analogous to military reconnaissance or commando-type operations,
in which patrols are sent out to penetrate or infiltrate territory
through enemy lines—terrain which is patently not their normal base
of operations.

Almost all genuinely international organizations with headquarters in the West, but especially those reaching politically
important masses, such as the International Labor and Youth
organizations, are useful for some degree of access for political
penetration. Within the Sino-Soviet bloc, however, only Soviet-
controlled counterparts of such organizations are permitted to
function. Here again, the distinction between penetration and mere
membership or affiliation lies only in the aggressive or manipulative
purpose involved.

In terms of a ready-made channel of intervention, the USSR is at
an obvious advantage in having at its disposal local Communist
parties abroad. Even where such parties have been declared illegal,
they may still serve as a means of penetration and exploitation of
underground resistance activity, as in Spain, to name only one
example. In such countries, peacetime operations are necessarily
conducted on the same basis as clandestine "stay-behind" operations
which follow a break in diplomatic relations or the outbreak of war.

Forced Disintegration—Atomization (Zersetzung)

Atomization or forced disintegration (Zerstzung) is the splitting
of the political and social structure of a victimized state until the
fabric of national morale disintegrates and the state is unable to resist
further intervention. Behind this operative principle is the assumption that political and social institutions are sound or viable only if
the political and social tensions normal to any society are held in
check, either through control mechanisms based on a democratic
consensus, or by more authoritarian techniques of control and
governance. Competition for power and status among political, class,
ethnic, religious, national minority, and other groups inevitably

creates tensions in any society. These tensions or vulnerabilities may be exploited by setting such groups against each other in hostile, uncompromising opposition. In this way, the fabric of national morale can be made to disintegrate and the internal political and social structure so weakened that the victimized state is unable to resist further intervention. This "softening up," or forced disintegration of political and social institutions, may serve other ends than intervention by one state in the internal affairs of another. For example, it may facilitate the seizure of power by a revolutionary conspiracy or by an aggressive political faction *within* the state, such as the Secret Army Organization (OAS) in Algeria.

The principle of divide and conquer, *divide et impera,* is, of course, as old as politics itself. But the modern use of the principle includes the deliberately planned manipulation of psychological and sociological factors by one state intervening in the affairs of another. Here the differences between nineteenth-century Czarist expansion and Nazi or Soviet intervention is most striking. When planning and executing all sorts of covert political actions in Bulgaria in the 1880s (including military insurrection and political assassination), Czarist agents and officials analyzed the structure and vulnerabilities of the target state in purely political terms, with little concern for any social or ideological tensions or forces which might be exploited. Although at times hopes ran high that Pan-Slavism as an ideological movement might be used as a springboard for expansion, it was not regarded as a corrosive force which could be used to weaken the political structure of the target states and thus facilitate Czarist intervention and control. By contrast, both the Nazi and Soviet states have extensively manipulated and exploited not only political but psychological and sociological tensions in those states in which they have intervened. There are many familiar examples. In Eastern Europe and the Balkans, basic social conflicts, the tensions between religious or racial minorities and their "persecution" by one another, have been systematically manipulated and exploited by both the Nazis and the Soviets. Czechoslovakia, as the victim first of Nazi and later of Soviet intervention and takeover, offers some of the most clearcut illustrations of the manipulation of racial or ethnic tensions. The *Volks-deutsche,* the minority of German descent, was successfully exploited by the Nazis, and the name of Konrad Henlein, leader of the Nazi Fifth Column, is synonymous with the word "traitor."

Both the Nazis and the Soviets have also made extensive use of tensions between the Czechs and the Slovaks to divide the country against itself and thus facilitate intervention and control.

Subversion

Subversion is the undermining or detachment of the loyalties of significant political and social groups within the victimized state, and their transference, under ideal conditions, to the symbols and institutions of the aggressor. The assumption behind the manipulative use of subversion is that public morale and the will to resist intervention are the products of combined political and social or class loyalties which are usually attached to national symbols, such as the flag, constitution, crown, or even the persons of the chief of state or other national leaders. Following penetration, and parallel with the forced disintegration of political and social institutions of the state, these loyalties may be detached and transferred to the political or ideological cause of the aggressor.

The ultimate goal of the intervening state may be maximal, i.e., seizure of power by a controlled internal faction within the victimized state, or liberation by invading forces trained and equipped outside the state. In either case, the goal can be achieved only with the passive acceptance of the masses and the active support of a counter-elite within the victimized state. Modern political and social theory emphasizes the importance of ruling political (including military) and social elites, both as targets of persuasion in general and, since they control the physical instruments of state power, as the logical targets of penetration and subversion in covert operations (Speier, 1952; Weber, 1947; Mosca, 1939). A contemporary descriptive sociology of Communist tactics has emphasized the skill and sophistication with which the "combat party" has manipulated psychological and sociological forces in a struggle for "total power" (Selznick, 1960). Operationally, however, the Russian statesmen of the less sociologically sophisticated nineteenth century fully understood the principles of using as instruments of policy abroad those military and political groups which have a chance of seizing power.

The social psychology of Communist subversion, especially the tendency of the moderate liberal to be pulled to the Left (the so-called "Stalinoid syndrome"), has been thoroughly analyzed in the enormous volume of current literature on the appeals of communism. The other side of the coin, the tendency of the political and social center to drift to the Right (which might be called "the authoritarian syndrome"), was equally important to the success of Nazi subversion in Western Europe.

As previously noted, since the Bolshevist seizure of power in November 1917, the world has been politically and ideologically bipolarized. This split in Western democratic societies along political, ideological, and social or "class" lines reached a peak in the period 1935-1940, the time of the Popular Front in France and the expansion of Nazi Germany. France was then probably more deeply divided "against herself" than at any time since (Luethy, 1955). This division greatly facilitated subversive operations by totalitarians of both the Left and the Right. In France, for example, the Nazis were highly successful in subverting high army, church, and social elite groups. As a result, prominent French Rightists in the years before the outbreak of World War II were openly declaring that they would rather see Reichschancellor Hitler on the Champs-Elysees than the Socialist Blum. At the same time the Communists successfully subverted not only many leaders within the French trade union movement but also broad masses of the laboring class in both France and Italy, especially the "toiling proletarians" of whom they are professed champions everywhere. The wartime desertion to Moscow of the French Communist leader, Maurice Thorez, in response to what he has called a "higher duty," symbolizes the end-point of subversion—open collaboration with the intervening power and ultimate treason.

Defection

Thus far we have noted the subversion of selected political and social groups capable of forming a counter-elite for purposes of seizing power and holding it, i.e., of establishing the legitimacy and permanency of a new regime. From the point of view of the planning, management, and regulation of covert operations aimed at achieving maximum influence and control in a target country, the formation of such a counter-elite is a prerequisite first step. But in the final analysis, all ruling elites are made up of private individuals. The subversion of a few key individuals in leadership positions may have important effects, especially in primitive, non-Western societies where individual religious, military, or ethnic group leaders frequently command personal followings which are relatively of much greater political importance than in the more pluralistic societies of the West.

In Western societies, particularly since the classic Cold War period (1947-1953), attention has centered on the subversion of private individuals, followed by their defection and flight or transfer to the "enemy" camp. Frequently, prior to actual flight abroad, the subverted individual engages in espionage activities, which, when later disclosed, result in sensational worldwide publicity turned to excellent advantage by the receiving power.

After the defector has been sponged dry for intelligence information, his "escape" from either the Eastern or Western camp is publicized for propaganda purposes, and, if qualified, the individual is then frequently employed in writing or screening propaganda materials. Exceptionally qualified individuals may even be used to provide high-level public relations guidance. The two British diplomats, Guy Burgess and Donald MacLean, who defected to Moscow in 1956, reportedly have provided such guidance to the Soviet regime, which at the time of the defection had embarked on a new course of relaxing tensions through widening cultural exchanges and, after the excesses of the Stalinist era, was badly in need of expert guidance in the creation of a better institutional image abroad.

For the most part, however, defectors, even the most intelligent and best educated ones, must be used with caution in political warfare planning and operations. In the first place, the individual who defects usually does so out of desperation, and he suffers not only from personal trauma but also from "culture shock" when placed in an alien environment. The ideological defector is a deviant from the norm of his own society. He is atypical, or he would not have been sufficiently repelled by the system in which he has been reared to leave it. And like emigrés generally, his usefulness decreases rapidly with the passage of time. A dissident himself, the defector tends to exaggerate greatly the depth and extent of dissidence in his old system. Ideological defection is an intensely personal experience, and the considerations or appeals which are effective in one case cannot be generalized for political warfare purposes. Defectors generally have proven to be an unstable lot. Few are able successfully to integrate themselves into their new surroundings and lead productive and useful lives in the alien world of political, social, and moral values in which they have elected to live. For this reason many re-defect and return to their homelands, in spite of the knowledge in some cases they they face almost certain death as traitors by so doing (as was probably the case with most re-defectors from the Stalinist regime).

For all these reasons, defection, which was once regarded as a major political warfar objective of both the U.S. and the USSR, has come to be regarded as a mixed blessing. High-level defectors from the diplomatic, intelligence, or security police services remain an important source of valuable information, especially when they bring with them codebooks, cipher systems, and important collections of secret documents.

From the point of view of building up a counter-elite within a target country, either for purposes of seizing power or for less ambitious political warfare operations, the subverted individual who remains in place and faithfully seres a foreign power is far more valuable than one who is forced to flee (when threatened by imminent exposure and arrest) or who defects for other more immediate personal reasons, such as escape from a nagging wife, mistress, or plant supervisor. "The defector in place" stays on the job but reports regularly to the controlling agency, usually through one of its agents who enjoys diplomatic immunity.

Intelligence agencies may boast of having "penetrated" enemy organizations by means of such individuals, and, technically speaking, the claim is true. But such penetrations through ideological defectors are lucky breaks (or natural disasters) and should not be confused with the operational task of penetration described in an earlier section of this chapter. It should also be emphasized that no intelligence agency is safe against the natural hazard of the true ideological defector, either one who stays in place (and is sooner or later exposed, or apprehended) or one who suddenly flees without warning. British intelligence was embarrassed when two career diplomats, Burgess and MacLean, defected to Moscow in 1956, and even more so by the sensational case of George Blake, a trusted British intelligence agent who was convicted in May 1961, after nine undetected years of espionage for the USSR. Even more embarrassing was the case of USSR as an espionage agent for over thirty years, at times in key intelligence positions involving joint U.S.–British Secret Intelligence Service operations. From his privileged position Philby was able to sabotage a joint CIA-SIS operation in 1950 during which armed bands which had been infiltrated into Albania were decimated with an estimated fifty percent casualties.[5]

For intelligence and espionage purposes, the occasional highly placed ideological defector will continue to be extremely useful. Paradoxically, however, the more sensitive the position a person occupies, the less useful he becomes as an agent for stirring up dissidence, subverting other individuals, and winning converts to serve the cause of an intervening power. Those who occupy sensitive, policy-making positions are (or should be) subject to recurrent security checks, and are thus in no position to contact, much less organize, disaffected or dissident elements in their own society. For this reason, even for routine low-level espionage purposes, the Soviet intelligence services have long since abandoned the use of local Communist parties as principal sources of recruits. As Allen Dulles has observed, "The Soviets know that the watchful eye which every government of necessity keeps trained on the local Communist party hardly recommends it for clandestine work" (Dulles, 1963a). On the other hand, Communist-infiltrated or -controlled "front organizations have been extremely useful for all kinds of subversive purposes" (Dulles, 1963b). Likewise in the political warfare operations of the U.S. and other Western powers, Western-oriented front or cover organizations have performed equally useful functions.

Covert Control

Penetration, forced disintegration, and subversion within the victimized state usually result in a period of covert control over politically significant actions by the intervening power. Such actions may be divided into three broad classes: (1) those which affect the relative power position of the target state *vis-à-vis* the intervening power, or (2) the vital foreign policy interests of the latter, and (3) actions which affect the relative power position *within* the target state of the political party, military group, or faction through which the intervening power seeks to extend its influence and control. These categories of politically significant action are useful for analysis and for political warfare planning purposes, but in practice they may be closely interrelated or overlapping.

Consider the typical case of intervention by a major power in the internal affairs (including civil war) of an underdeveloped country. In such a model the superior military force of the major power is taken for granted, as well as the fact that the real or alleged purpose of its intervention, whether open or covert, is to protect its foreign policy interests. Operations will thus be concentrated on strengthening the relative power position within the target state of a political party; faction (or coalition; or ethnic, religious, or military group through which the intervening power seeks to extend its influence and control. Here the term "military" must be extended to all local institutions such as the police, militia, or security police which in any significant way control the physical instruments of power, since in any "showdown" or series of physical confrontations, control over these instruments will be decisive.

This principle has been the rationale behind CIA operations over the last decade. In describing his concept of the cold war mission of the CIA, Allen Dulles (1963b) urges that our intelligence service must, wherever possible,

> help to build up the local defenses against (Communist) penetration by keeping target countries aware of the nature and extent of their peril and by assisting their internal security service wherever this can be done, or possibly only be done, on a covert basis.

> Many of the countries most seriously threatened do not have internal police or security services adequate to the task of obtaining timely warning of the peril of Communist subversion. For this they often need help and they can get it only from a country like the United States, which has the resources and techniques to aid them. Many regimes in the countries whose security is threatened welcome this help and over the years have profited greatly from it.

U.S. covert support of local military leaders such as Mobotu in the Congo or Phoumi Nosovan in Laos has also been based on this principle. Such covert support may secure the temporary domination of a given leader or faction against internal opposition. But such domination will be short-lived due either to the chronic political and social instability of new nations in the process of modernization or to the longer-term effects of native nationalism. Both of these factors constitute built-in limitations to the effectiveness of covert operations in underdeveloped areas, so that short-term pay-offs or gains are usually followed by later failures or losses. A local strong man can be covertly supported and controlled only so far until the foreign source of his power becomes an open secret and he is discredited in the eyes of his compatriots as a puppet of the intervening power. Once a local leader, through external help, has built up his military strength and authority to the point where he feels his internal position is secure, he may be expected to throw off external support and influence. This has been the dominant pattern throughout fifty years of Soviet experience beginning with Kemal Ataturk through Chiang Kai-shek and more recently Tito and Mao Tse-tung. Repeatedly Soviet-supported nationalist leaders have not only thrown off external controls but have exploited early Soviet support to increase their nuisance value before coming to terms with Western Powers.

The U.S. has also discovered to its dismay that this process can also work in the reverse direction. Nasser, who first rose to power with covert support from the CIA, has skillfully played both the U.S. and the USSR against each other to strengthen his internal position. Thus, although useful as a concept, covert control is never absolute or permanent, and at best can only be estimated, not accurately delimited or measured. Failure to grasp this principle may be one of the reasons why covert operations were consistently oversold to U.S. policy makers in the last two decades.

Turning from covert control of military dispositions as one class of politically significant actions, consider another broad category— that which affects the vital foreign policy interests of the intervening state. Here documentation is much more difficult to obtain, but operationally, the political end results can be equally decisive. There is nothing novel about the skillful use of subverted or "fellow-traveling" personnel at policy-making or executive levels, by an intervening power, to direct the formation and execution of policies favorable to its political interests, or negatively, to assure that at least no unfavorable action is taken. Thus, in prewar France, Pierre Laval effectively oriented French foreign policy in the interests of Nazi Germany.[6] In postwar France, another fellow-traveler, this time in the Communist entourage, was instrumental in shaping General de Gaulle's decision to sign the Franco-Soviet Treaty of Friendship and Alliance. Although the treaty itself was soon to become a dead letter, Pierre Cot continued his role of Communist fellow-traveler and won the Stalin peace prize in 1954.

Aggressive intervention through the use of covert operational techniques—penetration, disintegration, subversion, and the like—may end when the intervening power estimates that it has reached an adequate degree of control. If the control is sufficient to insure "benevolent nonbelligerency" in time of war, for example, it may adequately serve the immediate purposes of the aggressor, especially when actual seizure of power might involve prematurely the risk of war. Thus, Hitler apparently felt that the degree of covert control over Hungary in 1940 obviated the necessity of occupying that country. On the other hand, he felt that the presence of Nazi troops in both Rumania and Bulgaria "for training purposes" was essential to forestall rival Soviet penetration; both these moves were covertly prepared by staff officers appearing as "tourists" in civilian dress. It is ironic to note that when Soviet control, both open and covert, was obviously inadequate to handle the 1956 Hungarian revolt, massive Soviet forces were called in to suppress the uprising under the pretext that they were needed to defeat "counter-revolutionary forces" allegedly under the secret control of American and other "capitalist agents." The brutal Soviet suppression of the 1956 Hungarian uprising illustrates the principle that when covert operations end in such spectacular failure or are clearly inadequate, the two most likely alternatives open to the aggressor are to call them off or to intervene directly with military action.

Seizure of Power and Assimilation

Following penetration, disintegration, subversion, and a degree of covert control over the political and social institutions of the victimized state, the intervening power may openly seize power. The planning, timing, and support of the physical seizure of power are usually covert. The actual seizure itself cannot, of course, be concealed, and usually takes the form of a "spontaneous" coup-d'état or revolution, which, ideally, is timed to meet the requirements of the internal situation within the country, the international political situation, and the broad context of the foreign policy objectives of the aggressor. Theoretically, such seizure of power involves the careful correlation of a number of preliminary steps or procedures. The first of these is a preliminary estimate of the degree of success already obtained by atomization and subversion. Estimates are made, for example, of the amount of support or opposition to be expected from the political and social groups originally selected as targets—"progressive" intellectul elites, labor unions, racial or religious minorities, the church, the army, the police, para-military organizations, and so on. A second procedure is the selection and staging of an incident or pretext for the seizure of power. Next a survey is made of suitable forthcoming events, such as coming elections, the anniversary of a historic occasion, or possible decisive moves (such as a counter coup d'état) on the part of the opposition. As a result of such planning, a suitable incident—charges of election "fraud," assassination of key political figure, the burning of a Reichstag—is selected or staged, and the operation moves into its tactical stage. Under ideal conditions this phase also calls for careful planning and coordination of tactical operations, among te most important of which are the timing and types of support provided externally by the aggressor state.

Such support, in addition to intensified or diversionary propaganda and diplomatic maneuvers, frequently involves the use or threat of military force—the mobilization, movement, or massing of troops, conspicuous massing of airpower, and direct or indirect threat of war. On a local or internal level, planning along the following tactical lines is indicated: selection of key physical objectives to be seized, such as the seat of government, newspapers and radio stations, telephone and telegraph facilities, police, army, cabinet, and party headquarters; key individuals to be arrested, imprisoned, or assassinated; planning of preliminary terror in the form of kidnapping, murder, "treason" trials, and so forth.

Finally, just before actual tactical operations begin, the selection, briefing, and rehearsal of the forces to be used takes place. When all preliminary preparations are completed, preferably in the greatest secrecy, tactical operations begin according to plan with the seizure of the designated political and physical objectives, the arrest or assassination of key individuals selected.

Following actual physical takeover, the victimized state may be assimilated into the political system or power complex of the intervening power. Technically, this process may take a variety of forms, ranging from "benevolent" assimilation of the victim as an integral part of a unified, centralized state (for example, Nazi absorption of Austria), to toleration of formal independence (such as the postwar relationship of the USSR vis-à-vis Finland). In both these examples, most of the basic political and social institutions of the assimilated state were left relatively unaltered, since they could be effectively controlled politically, and in the case of Finland, the cost of forcing any closer assimilation might have been too great. On successive seizures of Poland, both the Nazi German and the Soviet regimes virtually destroyed previously existing political and social institutions. In order to prevent the formation of a counter-elite, they imposed the most rigid and ruthless forms of police-state controls, including the repression or physical liquidation of those elements from which it might be formed.

Propaganda, Manipulative Persuasion, and Terror

Propaganda in the context of political warfare, has been termed "the planned dissemination of news, information, special arguments, and appeals designed to influence the beliefs, thoughts, and actions of a specific group" (Daugherty and Janowitz, 1956: 2). The relationship of the rational use of force to persuasion is symbolized in the Latin motto which Louis XIV had inscribed on his cannons: *ultima ratio regum* (the *last* argument of kings). Soviet theory and practice subscribe to the same principle: "persuasion first, coercion afterward."[7] Persuasion has been defined as "the act of influencing the mind by arguments and reasons."

Persuasion is a broader term than propaganda, since in practice the "reasons" may be an admixture of threats and appeals which include a large element of spiritual or physical coercion and violence. For this reason, in political warfare, the more specific term is "manipulative persuasion." It includes the use of bribery, blackmail, and the threat or application of such physical acts of violence as kidnapping, torture, and the use of "controls" over selected targets or agents. A single, clear-cut example will serve to clarify the concept.

A half-frozen, half-starved prisoner of war is persuaded to collaborate with the enemy by a combination of threats of violence to his family (which is living in enemy-occupied territory) and promises of warm food and preferential treatment. His continued collaboration is then assured and controlled by a judicious combination of threats and rewards. This form of manipulative persuasion has been widely practiced in wartime and is standard practice in many covert operations in time of peace. The simplest and most familiar form of manipulative persuasion is bribery, in a variety of disguises ranging from unsolicited Christmas gifts to anonymous bank deposits in Switzerland. But manipulative persuasion frequently does spiritual and physical violence to its object and may have lasting traumatic effects.

In all stages of aggressive intervention, propaganda is used to inspire terror, and physical terror in turn is used for its propaganda effect. The use of assassination as a political weapon in the internal struggle for power, particularly in a revolutionary or counter-revolutionary conflict is familiar. In Czarist Russia, the conspiratorial terrorist organization Narodnaya Volya (The People's Will) after two years of intensive activity finally succeeded in assassinating Czar Alexander II in March 1881, an act which was followed by the brutal organized counter-terror of the Security Police, which quickly reduced the revolution "to a cottage industry" (Maynard, 1948). Sorel, the French apostle of "creative violence," laid the philosophic groundwork for the sporadic political terror and assassination, the so-called "propaganda of the deed," which characterized European revolutionary movements in the latter part of the nineteenth century. Political murder found its most devoted adherents prior to World War I in the Balkans, where the secret Macedonian terrorist society, IMRO, covered itself with infamy for years. Finally, a Serbian society achieved dubious immortality with the assassination of Archduke Francis Ferdinand at Sarajevo on June 28, 1914, an incident which escalated into World War I.

The Use and Abuse of Terror

Following the Russian Revolution, terrorism was frowned upon and fell into disrepute among orthodox Leninist revolutionaries, since in *What Is To Be Done* the master had condemned it as part of the superannuated tactical baggage of the Economists, a Right deviationist faction.[8] in January 1963, Soviet Premier Khruschev strongly reaffirmed Lenin's condemnation of assassination as an instrument of policy. Although his speech was delivered to a congress of the East German Socialist United (Communist) Party in Berlin, it was reportedly aimed as a warning to Cuban leader Fidel Castro and his followers not to employ terrorist tactics against Latin American politicians. Khruschev recalled that in the struggle for liberation against the Czarist regime there were people who "believed that one must take the axe in one's hands, commit terrorist acts against representatives of the regime, so as to secure the success of the revolution." Noting that Lenin's brother, Alexander Ulyanov, had been executed for an attempt on the life of the Czar, Khruschev quoted Lenin as saying on the day of his brother's execution, "We shall go another road. Only the road of struggle of the masses under the leadership of the party of the working class can secure victory. Lonely heroes can die beautifully, but they are not in a position to change the social-political order, nor to achieve victory in revolution" (Pravda, 1963; Washington Post, 1963).

In the late 1920s terror was used as a weapon against the USSR by the Russian emigres in Paris under the leadership of General Aleksander Pavlovich Kutyepov, who directed covert operations for the ROVS, the White Russian military forces. Beginning in June 1927, Kutyepov's Combat Organization launched a series of terrorist raids against the USSR. The terrorists hoped to duplicate the deeds of the Socialist Revolutionary Organization, the Narodnaya Volya, which had dramatized popular resistance to the Czarist regime. This time, at least in theory, a series of spectacular assassinations and bombings might spark general unrest and lead in turn to a renewed allied intervention and to the eventual overthrow of the Soviet regime. Ideologically such an intervention would take the form of an anti-Communist crusade to restore the traditional Russian Empire to its rightful place in the community of nations, and would hopefully return the emigré leaders to positions of power and influence in the new order.

Although armed and equipped for combat Kutyepov's special forces teams lacked the necessary intelligence base for extended underground operations. As a result, although engaged in covert military operations against a police state, his teams were no more than raiding parties in civilian clothes. Probably no more than fifteen agents divided into two- and three-man teams were directly involved, but Kutyepov's "vest pocket offensive" coincided with a number of external events on the international scene which produced genuine alarm among the Soviet leadership.

First, following a raid on Arcos Ltd., the Soviet trading company in London, on May 12, 1927, England broke off diplomatic relations with the USSR on May 27. Second, during the first week in June, Kutyepov's agents bombed the Leningrad Party club and murdered a minor OGPU official near Minsk in separate actions. At the same time the Soviet ambassador in Poland was assassinated by a young emigré terrorist not connected with Kutyepov's combat organization. By way of immediate reprisal the USSR executed twenty alleged spies and saboteurs. These dramatic events precipitated a Polish-Soviet diplomatic crisis and a full-blown war scare which Stalin skillfully exploited to expel Trotsky and other rivals. France, England, and Germany were soon drawn into the crisis which was not decompressed until the fall of 1927. Amidst a series of spectacular spy trails, the OGPU silently stepped up its counter-terror, arresting thousands in order to wipe the slate clean of internal opposition. The way was thus prepared for Stalin's brutal collectivization of agriculture and for the Five Year plans which laid the basis for the future industrial and military might of the USSR.

In spite of their bravery and determination, Kutyepov's terrorist agents were unable to assassinate any important political or OGPU leaders. Only a few isolated guards, security police, or Red Army soldiers were killed, and the one successful bombing of the Leningrad Party club resulted in merely random civilian casualties. For these meager returns eighty percent of the agents committed were killed in action or executed later by OGPU firing squads. It was a high price to pay, but the direct cost of terrorist operations is seldom low, and the indirect cost in the form of police reprisals and counter-terror has been frequently high. As to comparative direct costs, British SOE (Special Operations Executive) records show that of 480 agents who served in France during World War II, 106 were executed or killed in combat, 130 were captured of whom only twenty-six survived the German concentration camps (Cookridge, 1967).

The Kutyepov terror raids touched off the familiar cycle of terror, counter-terror and police repression which is characteristic of revolutionary or counter-revolutionary operations. In an ironic reversal of roles the monarchist emigrés abroad sought to duplicate the feats of Savinkov and other Socialist Revolutionary terrorists on the eve of the March Revolution which overturned the Czarist regime.

The theory behind the practice of such individual acts of terror is that they dramatize resistance to the *ancien regime,* and may produce an avalanche effect which will sweep it away. But in order to trigger an avalanche, with a small explosive charge, for example, the temperature and texture of the snow must be right. Similarly, in order for the terror raids to produce massive revolutionary effects, the political and social conditions must be such that they could probably be dispensed with anyway. Otherwise, according to Lenin's dictum, previously noted, "the individual hero can die a beautiful death, but he is unlikely to change the political and social order." General Kutyepov's vest pocket terror offensive is a classic example of this sound Leninist principle. On the other hand, given the political atmosphere and estimates at the time his combat organization went into action, a good case could be made for the offensive. Many people in high places at the time undoubtedly believed that a small spark might touch off a counter-revolutionary powder keg. This was certainly the hope and probably the conviction of the more conservative elements in the British establishment, including Churchill, Gregory—the civil service head of the Northern Division of the Foreign Office—and the King himself. In this regard, Kutyepov was traveling in the best of company.

One of the best analyses of why the Kutyepov terror raids were predestined to fail comes from the Soviets themselves. A lead editorial in *Izvestia* for July 8, 1927 discussed the failure of the combat team composed of Maria Zakharchenko, Staunitz-Opperput, and Voznesensky to achieve its object in terms which are generally applicable to similar covert operations. This analysis is one of the few examples of Soviet political theory in regard to covert operations and merits close attention. The article begins by noting that two days earlier (July 6) Deputy Chief Yagoda held a press conference in which he released the essential facts concerning the Zakharchenko-Opperput mission which the writer calls a "terroristic conspiracy." The article then continues:

> However, in this case we do not really have a *conspiracy* in the proper sense of the word. By definition the most important prerequisite for a conspiracy is large scale preparatory work inside the country against which it is directed. Although a few elements of the conspiratorial apparatus may be located abroad, the essential part, the broad base of the organization must be within the target country which the organization seeks to overthrow. Without such a base the conspiracy hangs in the air, and from the very beginning the conspirators must give careful thought to

coordinating their operations with the activity of the masses. Unless these conditions have been met it is hopeless to dream that a terroristic act may touch off events which will give history a shove and serve as the opening moments of a revolution.

Nothing of the sort took place so far as the Opperput group or other groups liquidated by the OGPU are concerned. . . . This was obviously not a conspiracy with roots in the USSR, but Intelligence and the Monarchists living abroad linked with it. These were not roots as it were but tentacles stretched toward the Soviet Union from without. . . . If the terroristic acts had originated in the USSR itself, if our internal conditions were such that (individual) terror could be converted into mass terror, then firing squads would be powerless to stop it.[9]

Ironically, since World War II, after having been formally abandoned by the political Left, terror and assassination have been adopted as a favorite instrument of right-wing extremist groups. For example, ultranationalists of the Secret Army Organization in Algeria and France have ecome foremost exponents of terrorist tactics.

In the context of political warfare, such as that which prevailed in Algeria for several years, physical terror, kidnapping, and assassination serve a double purpose. First, political opponents may be temporarily or permanently removed from the scene, and second, the violence itself is used to create fear and hatred and to discredit one political group in the eyes of another. Operationally, this is the essence of forced disintegration or atomization, by which the political and social structure of the state is split apart. The technique was effectively used by the Nazis in extending control and influence abroad and figured notably in their seizure of Czechoslovakia in 1938. More recently, such terror tactics have been incorporated into the doctrine of the dissident French officers and their Secret Army Organization, set forth in Colonel Lacheroy's "A Lesson in Revolutionary Warfare." A persistent campaign of bombings and assassinations resulted in over five hundred deaths and a thousand additional casualties in Algeria alone during 1961, and continued on a similar scale during the first quarter of 1962.

Although frowned upon as a matter of formal Leninist revolutionary doctrine, in practice the most brutal forms of coercion and violence have been employed by Communists. Communist terror has been used both as a technique of internal governance under the Stalinist regime in the USSR, and as a means of extending power and influence abroad to a point where covert control has been achieved. According to a recent U.S. Department of State (1961a) White Paper, *A Threat to the Peace, North Viet-Nam's Effort to Conquer South Viet-Nam,* terror has been effectively used by the Communist faction, the Viet Cong, in extending covert control over areas legally within the jurisdiction of the government of South Vietnam. The report states in part: "Assassination, often after the most brutal torture, is a favored Viet Cong tactic. Government officials, schoolteachers, even wives and children have been the victims. Literally hundreds of village chiefs have been murdered in order to assert Viet Cong power and to instill fear in the populace." The actual figures indicate a level of terrorist activity even higher than the ultranationalist reord in Algeria: "In 1960 the Government of the Republic of Viet-Nam claimed that about 1,400 local Government officials and civilians were assassinated by the Viet Cong. Approximately 700 persons were kidnapped during the year. In the first six months of 1961, more than 500 murders of officials and civilians were reported and about 1,000 persons were kidnapped" (U.S. Department of State, 1961a).

Political assassination and terror beget counter-terror, and before long both are subject to the law of diminishing returns. At one time, in response to Viet Cong terror tactics in Vietnam, "the CIA's 'Provincial Reconnaissance units' . . . acquired a fearsome reputation for their counter-terror and intelligence gathering operations" (Harwood, 1967).

Terrorist acts against key personnel and selected political, social, and economic institutions can create local socioeconomic chaos. But those institutions must be quickly replaced by other viable institutions or the people will turn against forces employing such terror. This is true of both local "insurgency" and general military operations: "An important element in the defeats of the Malayan, Philippine, and Greek Communist insurgencies was the fact that terrorist operations against the people backfired. Instead of insuring consolidated support through fear, terrorism engendered antipathy for the insurgents and thus alienated a significant portion of the masses" (Pustay, 1965).

Permanency, Legitimacy, and Mass Support

In connection with an analysis of the use of terror by General Kutyepov's combat organization (see above), it was observed that individual or small-scale acts of terror and violence make sense only when they are timed to trigger a revolutionary (or counter-revolutionary movement) which has been carefully prepared from within and which can quickly command mass support. This observation may be extended into the general principle that however successful in the short run, covert military operations which alienate mass support are almost certain to prove counter-productive. The principle merits brief amplification.

In the foregoing discussion of subversion we noted that social scientists have emphasized the importance of ruling political (including the military) and social elites as political warfare targets. These groups control the physical instruments of power—e.g., the army, police, militia—within the state. If the ultimate goal of the intervening state is seizure of power, the actual physical instruments of power must pass into the hands of either an internal faction or a "liberating" external force, or a combination of both. These forces must be able to maintain order and repel possible outside counter-forces until the new regime establishes its legitimacy and permanency. This last condition is one which has been almost entirely overlooked in the mass of Communist literature which deals extensively with the theory and technique of seizing power, but sadly neglects the dual problem of establishing legitimacy and permanency once power has been seized. Instead of facing up to this problem, Communist theory merely hides it under the vague formula "dictatorship of the proletariat," which in practice has meant the repressive paraphernalia of "socialist violence," including omnipresent fear of the secret police and, until recently, forced labor camps. But Western political theory has also overemphasized techniques of seizing power to the neglect of the principles underlying permanency and legitimacy once power has been seized.

Under the disturbed conditions created by World War I, a small group of professional revolutionaries in both Russia and Italy was able to seize power. This fact has led to a false belief that political history is made by resolute and compact minorities, and that almost any handful of dedicated men—the "counter-elite" in a typical political warfare situation—can both seize and hold power. As Ortega y Gasset pointed out as early as 1925, this notion is false. Once a minority has seized power, in order to hold it for any length of time, the minority must convert itself into a majority. In a tense political situation, a counter-elite must win at least passive acceptance by a majority of the population before it can hope to seize power in the first place. "In politics the social torso always decides and power is exercised by whoever succeeds in representing it." This principle accounts in part for the failure of the rash of abortive Communist-led or -inspired revolts after World War I in Berlin, Bavaria, Hungary, and elsewhere. By contrast, having once seized power in Germany, the Nazi minority, under the spell of Hitler's leadership, was able to win widespread popular support of a population subjected to the deprivations of mass strategic bombing attacks before the end of World War II. In a similar avalanche-like effect, the original tiny handful of Castro guerrillas, riding the wave of genuine social revolution which overthrew the Batista regime, was able to seize power in Cuba and then win majority support. The resulting regime not only has legitimacy within the traditional framework of Latin American political life, but also an element of permanency derived from public support both at home and elsewhere in Latin America, where the precept and example of *Fidelismo* have had wide popular appeal (Blackstock, 1964).

By contrast there seems to have been almost no consideration of the dual problem of legitimacy and permanency by those who planned the political warfare operations which ended in the abortive attempt to overthrow the Castro regime by external intervention in April 1961. Even if the landing at the Bay of Pigs had been a success and Castro had capitulated, there were so many discredited elements in the invading forces that the mass of Cubans would probably not have accepted them as a legitimate government which could command popular and relatively permanent support. Instead of the swift and bloodless seizure of power so confidently predicted, a protracted civil war would probably have resulted. The same observations apply to Che Guevara's spectacular failure to apply his own model of guerrilla warfare to Bolivia in October 1967. Even if his tactical operations had been crowned with local success instead of failure, it is extremely doubtful that his insurgents could have commanded enough popular support throughout the mass of the population to establish a legitimate and permanent regime.

NOTES

1. On the international legal aspects of indirect aggression, see the article by Gerhard Leibholz (1958).

2. For a review article dealing with *Casebook* and other recent contributions to the field, see Davison (1959).

3. The problems of national estimates and of congressional scrutiny are discussed at greater length in chapters twelve and seventeen of Dulles (1963b).

4. In modern academic jargon, a conceptual model of bilateral interstate relations is posited which excludes the unlimited use of military force but which maximizes nonmilitary aggression within the framework of what might be called the neo-Machiavellian syndrome, i.e., the marked tendency of the authoritarian elites controlling regimes such as those of Nazi Germany or of both Czarist and Stalinist Russia to employ covert operational techniques in a drive toward unlimited expansion wherever such expansion is not held in check by counter-forces.

5. See the authentic article by Geoffrey McDermott (1967), and Philby's memoirs (1968). For an earlier reference to the Albanian operation, see Christopher Felix (1963).

6. See Pertinax (1944: 375-390) and Namier (1950: 14, 35, 92-105 especially). For the case that Laval was not actually a Nazi agent, see Werth (1956: 93-119).

7. See Towster (1948: 20). On propaganda and violence as interrelated forms of persuasion, see Kris and Speier (1944: 3-22). On propaganda as "physical violence," see Chakoutine (1939: ch. 14). On the functional relationship of propaganda and terror, see Bramstedt (1945: 137-159). For a recent comparative analysis, see Kumata and Schramm (1955).

8. See Lenin (1952: 282-286). For a typical orthodox discussion of political assassination, see the chapter "Tirannicidio e terrorismo" in Lussu (1950: 145-155).

9. See *Izvestia* (1927). For a detailed exposition and situational analysis of the Kutyepov terror raids and the 1927 Soviet War Scare see Blackstock (1969: chs. 6-9).

REFERENCES

BLACKSTOCK, P. W. (1969) The Secret Road to War: Soviet vs. Western Intelligence, 1927-1939. Chicago: Quadrangle Books.

———(1964) The Strategy of Subversion: Manipulating the Politics of Other Nations. Chicago: Quadrangle Books.

BRAMSTEDT, E. K. (1945) Dictatorship and Political Police. London: Kegan Paul.

BURNHAM, J. (1953) Containment or Liberation. New York: J. Day.

———(1950) The Coming Defeat of Communism. New York: J. Day.

CHAKOUTINE, S. (1939) Le Viole des Foules par la Propagande Politique. Paris: Gallimard.

COOKRIDGE, E. H. (1967) Set Europe Ablaze. New York: Thomas Y. Crowell.

DAUGHERTY, W. E. and M. JANOWITZ (1956) A Psychological Warfare Casebook. Baltimore: Johns Hopkins Press.

DAVISON, W. P. (1959) "Pragmatic approaches to political communication." World Politics 12 (October): 120-131.

DULLES, A. (1963a) "The craft of intelligence." Harper's 226 (April): 128-174.

———(1963b) The Craft of Intelligence. New York: Harper & Row.

FEDOSEYEV, P. (1957) "Sociological theories and the foreign policy of imperialism." International Affairs (Moscow) 3: 10-22.

FELIX, C. (1963) A Short Course in the Secret War. New York: Dutton.

HARWOOD, R. (1967) "Viet pacification drags despite reorganizations." Washington Post (August 3).

HILSMAN, R. (1967) To Move a Nation. New York: Doubleday.

Izestia (1927) "Otkuda oni" (July 8).

KAHN, H. (1965) On Escalation, Metaphors and Scenarios. New York: Frederick A. Praeger.

KIRKPATRICK, L. (1968) The Real CIA. New York: Macmillan.

KRIS, E. and H. SPEIER (1944) German Radio Propaganda. New York: Oxford University Press.

KUMATA, H. and W. SCHRAMM (1955) Four Working Papers on Propaganda Theory. Urbana: University of Illinois Press.

LEIBHOLZ, G. (1958) "Aggression im volkerrecth und im bereich ideolo-gishcher auseinandersetzungen." Vierteljahreshefte fuer Zeitgeschichte 6: 165-171.

LENIN, V. I. (1952) Selected Works. Moscow: Foreign Language Publishing House.

LUETHY, H. (1955) France Against Herself. New York: Frederick A. Praeger.

LUSSU, E. (1950) Teoria dell 'Insurrezione. Rome: De Carlo.

MAYNARD, J. (1948) Russia in Flux. New York: Macmillan.

McDERMOTT, G. (1967) "James Bond might have learned from Philby." New York Times Magazine (November 12): 36-37.

MOSCA, G. (1939) The Ruling Class. New York: McGraw-Hill.

NAMIER, L. B. (1950) Europe in Decay. London: Macmillan.

PERTINAX [Andre Gerard] (1944) The Grave-diggers of France. New York: Doubleday.

PHILBY, K. (1968) My Silent War. New York: Grove Press.

Pravda (1963) January 17.
———(1947) October 22.
PUSTAY, J. S. (1965) Counterinsurgency Warfare. New York: Free Press.
RANSOM, H. H. (1959) Central Intelligence and National Security. Cambridge: Harvard University Press.
SELZNICK, P. (1960) The Organizational Weapon. New York: Free Press.
SPEIER, H. (1952) Social Order and the Risks of War. New York: George W. Stewart.
STALIN, J. V. (1934) Leninism. Moscow.
STEBBINS, R. P. (1959) The United States in World Affairs, 1958. New York: Oxford University Press.
TOWSTER, J. (1948) Political Power in the USSR, 1917-1947. New York: Oxford University Press.
U.S. Congress, Senate Committee on Foreign Relations (1953) Nomination of John Foster Dulles, Secretary of State-Designate: Hearings, 83rd Congress, 1st Session (January 15).
U.S. Department of State (1961a) A Threat to the Peace: North Viet-Nam's Effort to Conquer South Viet-Nam [White Paper].
———(1961b) Far Eastern Series 110, Publication 7308 (December).
———(1958a) Bulletin (July 21): 105.
———(1958b) Bulletin (August 4): 185, 188.
———(1958c) Bulletin (August 18): 266, 271.
———(1956) Bulletin (June 18): 999-1004.
———(1950) Bulletin (November): 767.
Washington Post (1963) November 29.
WEBER, M. (1947) Wirtschaft und Gesellschaft. Tuebingen: J. C. B. Mohr.
WERTH, A. (1956) France 1940-1955. London: R. Hale.

Chapter 16

ON THE FUNCTION OF THE MILITARY IN CIVIL DISORDERS

MARTIN BLUMENSON

*U*pon the outbreak of civil disorder, what is the function of the military troops called to help quell the violence? What have been the methods employed by armed forces to uphold the authority of government and the law and to restore order and civil peace? What has been the range of military response to civil disturbance in the United States?

In suppressing domestic violence, military forces have reacted on different levels of intensity.[1] How they have put down lawlessness and rioting suggests their place in American life.

Persistent opposition to the whiskey excises of 1791 and 1792 came to a climax in western Pennsylvania during the summer of 1794. Inflamed by backwoods dissidents calling for armed resistance to the tax, mobs rioted, burned the house of the district inspector of revenue, closed collectors' offices, and sent federal officials fleeing. When an associate justice of the Supreme Court advised that the laws of the United States were being resisted "by combinations too powerful to be suppressed by the ordinary course of judicial proceedings," President Washington conferred with Governor Thomas Mifflin of Pennsylvania (Coakley, 1969).

The Governor was reluctant to use military force against the large-scale disobedience, but the President decided to assert the authority of the United States. He issued a proclamation warning the insurgents and characterized their lawless activity as "open rebellion" (Weigley, 1967: 100). Because the President then lacked the authority to employ regular forces in such missions, he requisitioned the governors of Pennsylvania, New Jersey, Maryland, and Virginia for 12,950 militia troops, plus the necessary officers, to restore order and uphold the law.

He also dispatched three commissioners to the scene to observe the conditions, to negotiate with the insurgents, and to recommend a suitable course of action. Unable to gain assurance that the inhabitants would comply with the whiskey tax laws in the future, the commissioners reported "that we have still much reason to apprehend, that the authority of the laws will not be *universally* and perfectly restored, without military coercion" (Weigley, 1967; see also Rich, 1941: 2-20).

The militia members had so little desire to volunteer for action against their fellow citizens that drafts were imposed. These prompted rioting against enforced military service. Finally, by patriotic appeals and the widespread acceptance of hired substitutes, the quotas were met. Although all four of the states gathering militia forces had difficulties assembling and providing men with adequate arms and provisions, the troops from Pennsylvania and New Jersey made rendezvous at Carlisle late in September; those from Virginia and Maryland gathered at Fort Cumberland.

Early in October, the President rode to Carlisle, where he stayed for eight days, helping to organize, equip, and discipline the force. Many militiamen were ill-trained and stirred by a lust for plunder, and the President tried particularly to impress them with the need to act with a scrupulous regard for the rights of innocent citizens and with a strict conformance to the laws.

In mid-October, under the command of Governor Henry Lee of Virginia, the two forces set out for Pittsburgh, one traveling over Forbes' route across the mountains, the other following Braddock's road. Summer had given way to autumn, and winter was at hand. The march was hard on men fresh from civilian life. Bad weather, muddy roads, poor rations, and difficulties with horses and wagons delayed the movement.

When the troops reached the scene of the disorders at the end of the month, they found that the Whiskey Rebellion had evaporated.

Had the violence burned itself out? Or had the threat of force, together with the manifest intention of using it, been enough to dissipate the disorders? If a showdown, if physical confrontation, had become necessary, would the troops have been effective?

No one knows, of course. But by the time the military units reached the Pittsburgh area, most of the soldiers were incensed against the "Whiskey Boys," who had caused them such discomfort and privation.

Since that earliest experience in the history of the nation, regular, militia, and National Guard troops have been used on innumerable occasions to control domestic disorders. The Fries insurrection, slave revolts, nullification, Civil War draft riots, Reconstruction disturbances, strikes, the Coxeyite phenomenon, and violent racial conflicts prompted military intervention (National Advisory Commission on Civil Disorders, 1968: ch. 5, part 2).

The measures of control exerted by the military were somewhat varied. But the foremost impression of their utility in restoring order was their projection of disciplined strength. During the labor strikes of 1877, regular troops dissipated violence "by their presence alone"–without losing a single soldier or causing the death of a single civilian (Scheips, 1969a). During the Pullman and other railroad strikes in 1894, when small military forces were committed, they performed their duty "promptly and effectively" even though their small numbers taxed them "nearly to the limit" (Scheips, 1969a). Against the army of Jacob Coxey in the same year, uninformed forces quelled disorders because "mobs respected the military"; the "mere presence of the military caused the Coxeyites to turn away (Scheips, 1969b). Instructive in terms of the escalation of military force is the action against the Bonus Marchers in 1932. In May of that year, during the Great Depression, several thousand unemployed veterans of World War 1 from all over the country began to gather in Washington, D.C. They wished Congress to give them at once, rather than in thirteen years as promised, a bonus for their wartime service.

Congress suggested that the Army offer the Bonus Marchers surplus tents, cots, blankets, clothing, medical supplies, and mess facilities, but the War Department opposed encouraging these disaffected persons to remain in Washington, where they were a potential source of unrest and violence.[2]

What bothered the military was not only the general dissatisfaction in the country, the social and economic upheaval brought on by the depression, but also the prospect that the troops in the Washington area might be unresponsive to orders if called out for riot duty. There was a natural affinity between the marchers who were ex-soldiers and the members of the active forces, many of whom were also veterans of the "great war." An officer (see Blakeley, 1952: 27) stationed in Washington at the time later wrote, "Initially, the relations between the troops and the Marchers were so good as to cause some concern among War Department staff officers who . . . were somewhat doubtful about the reliability of the troops if their services were needed."

General Douglas MacArthur, the Army Chief of Staff, had already taken precautions. Early in June, he wired all the corps area commanders to ask whether any Communist elements were among the columns heading for Washington. The replies reflected an inability to appraise the social and political composition of the groups, and only one, from the commander in Baltimore, reported a "general feeling of unrest . . . some serious trouble is likely to arise at an early date" (see Killigrew, 1960).

The Chief of Staff also ordered two experimental vehicles—an armored car and a seventy-seven mm. self-propelled gun—moved from the Aberdeen Proving Grounds to Fort Myer, Virginia, on the outskirts of the capital, where they would be available in the event of trouble. The crews of these vehicles were instructed to reply, should anyone ask the reason for their transfer, that the equipment was being exhibited as the latest developments in Army mechanization.

MacArthur further directed Brigadier General Perry Miles, the senior unit commander in the capital, to prepare a new plan for civil emergency. Miles decided that, if disorder erupted, he would assemble his troops behind the White House, protect certain critical buildings, and be ready to employ his units in active operations according to the following concept:

> The greater part of the bonus marchers, General Miles wrote, have thus far resisted all attempts of the Communists to gain control of them but there are a number of well-known Communist leaders here and they are claiming credit for the instigation of the march. Any demonstration therefore will almost certainly contain ex-soldiers without a desire for Communist affiliations and Communists themselves who will try by overt acts,

possibly of violence to commit the veterans. Our operations, therefore, should contemplate giving an opportunity to the non-Communistic veterans to disperse, but of course the tactics employed must depend on the commander on the spot and the character of the emergency. For this reason, tear gas generators are provided which would be used in sufficient numbers to be effective if the character of one disorder did not require more drastic action at once.[3]

Early in June, when Congress appropriated funds to enable the veterans to return to their homes, more than five thousand of the estimated twelve thousand in Washington left the city. The House passed a Bonus Bill, but when Congress adjourned on July 16th without Senate action on it, other Bonus Marchers, probably two thousand more, drifted out of the capital.

Those who stayed inhabited—some with their wives and children—a shantytown, made of scrap lumber and tin, east of the capitol and across the Anacostia 'River. Others lived in several partially dismantled buildings below the capitol, buildings being demolished for a park.

On July 21st, the Washington police informed the Bonus Expeditionary Force leaders that the lack of sanitary facilities was creating a health hazard. Although the marchers had committed no overt act of violence, their presence constituted an annoyance in the city. They would have to go. Besides, the Treasury Department wished to repossess the partially dismantled buildings to continue their demolition (see National Advisory Commission, 1968: 293; see also Vance, 1967).

A week later, on the morning of July 28th, Washington policemen began to sweep the area below the capitol. After one building was cleared, a scuffle broke out. A panicky policeman fired his pistol wildly, killing a Bonus Marcher and wounding a passer-by.

As increasing numbers of people milled around, hurling invectives and an occasional shower of stones at the police, the district commissioners early that afternoon informed President Hoover that the situation was out of control. The President ordered the Secretary of War to disperse the Bonus Marchers, and close to 3 p.m., Secretary Patrick J. Hurley transmitted (see Killigrew, 1960; National Advisory Commission, 1967) the order to General MacArthur in these terms:

The President has just informed me that the civil government of the District of Columbia has reported to him that it is unable to maintain law and order in the District. You will have United States troops proceed immediately to the scene of disorder. Cooperate fully with the District of Columbia police force which is now in charge. Surround the affected area and clear it without delay. Turn over all prisoners to the civil authorities. In your orders insist that any women and children who may be in the affected area be accorded every consideration and kindness. Use all humanity consistent with due execution of this order.

About six hundred troops from the 3rd Cavalry, 1st Tank, and 12th Infantry Regiments were already assembling behind the White House. General Miles reported to General MacArthur, who showed him Hurley's order and who said that he, as chief of staff, would accompany the military units, "not with a view of commanding the troops but to be on hand as things progressed, so that he could issue necessary instructions on the ground" (see Killigrew, 1960: ch 7).

At 4:30, the troops started toward the affected area, infantry advancing with fixed bayonets, cavalry moving with drawn sabers to keep rioters from grabbing at bridles, tanks following to strengthen the show of force.

Below the capitol, an almost indiscriminate mixture of rioters, spectators, downtown shoppers, policemen in uniform, detectives in civilian clothes thronged the streets. Taking shelter in the partially demolished buildings was an unknown number of Bonus Marchers armed with stones, bricks, and pieces of concrete.

An infantry squad pushed into the building where resistance against the police had been fiercest, ignored the persons inside the edifice, and climbed the stairs to the roof. Their defensive position occupied, the Bonus Marchers evacuated the structure. Other troops were clearing the streets despite volleys of rocks thrown by disorderly individuals.

By about 6 p.m., the area was clear of rioters. The soldiers remained there and ate their supper. About 9 p.m., another order was issued, apparently originating with MacArthur. The troops were now to cross the river to the Anacostia Flats and evacuate all Bonus Marchers from their makeshift bivouac. Why drive them from their only place of shelter during the night? Apparently to prevent them from reorganizing and causing a more serious incident.

The troops marched the two miles or so to the Flats. After crossing the bridge at Eleventh Street, the infantry formed a line to exert what was termed "direct pressure" on the camp, while cavalry units guarded their left flank. An announcement informed the inhabitants that they had an hour, until 11:15 p.m., to remove their personal belongings and depart. While the troops waited for the deadline, several of them set fire to two isolated shacks to illuminate the area of operations. Whether these fires spread or whether Bonus Marchers fired their own tents is not clear. But soon most of the camp was in flames.

At the designated time, assisted by searchlights furnished by the fire and police departments, the infantry advanced through the burning camp. There was no resistance except from a few allegedly intoxicated individuals.

Having moved through the settlement, the infantrymen came under a barrage of rocks thrown from a group of perhaps one or two thousand people. To disperse them, the soldiers used tear gas. The mob fell back and scattered.

On the following morning the area was deserted, and at noon the troops were instructed to return to the city and evict a pocket of marchers that had formed in the southwest area. A steady exodus of Bonus Army veterans all day long from Washington indicated that the military units could return to their normal posts that evening.

What had ensured the reestablishment of order? On the one hand, there was a lack of leadership, organization, and cohesion—to say nothing of weapons—on the part of the Bonus Marchers. Conversely, there were discipline and response to orders, plus self-control and restraint, on the part of the troops.

The soldiers had encountered "a barrage of profanity, the throwing of missiles and the return of tear gas grenades." Many spectators had joined with the Bonus Marchers in using "insulting language toward the troops." Some ex-Army men tried to fraternize with the regulars and persuade them to disregard their orders (Killigrew, 1960: ch. 7).

In response, the infantry soldiers, according to a participant, met this duty with forbearance and restraint and throughout the operations remained calm and collected notwithstanding the resistance and insulting remarks of both Bonus Marchers and spectators. They used tactful force and were intent on accomplishing their mission effectively and satisfactorily (see Blakeley, 1952).

The cavalrymen also regarded their activities in a purely impersonal manner. "All took the attitude," their commander reported, "that the duty was just another job although a difficult one requiring unusual control. At no time was any sympathy shown to the Bonus Marchers" (see Killigrew, 1960).

Nor was there resentment displayed at the outset. Not until they became targets of volleys of rocks did the troops show hostility. They were soon "thoroughly angry but were easily restrained" by their officers (Blakeley, 1952).

> The punishment and casualties received were taken as a matter of course. On the second day the general attitude was more antagonistic and the men would undoubtedly have used their permitted weapons more severely if resistance had been encountered. . . .
>
> Undisciplined people on foot will not withstand the advance of the mounted man and they are universally afraid of being trampled by the horse. The saber was a great aid as a punishing power. The flat of the saber was used plentifully and the point some—mainly in threatening those showing an inclination to turn during retreat [in Killigrew, 1960].

Quickly realizing the serious intention of the regular troops to handle the situation, the marchers concluded that it would be hopeless to oppose them. Discipline and restraint, plus the capability of administering lethal power, together with a surprising use of nontoxic gas, permitted the troops to put down a disturbance. They exercised no unnecessary force, fired not a single shot, and inflicted no serious casualty. About a dozen soldiers were injured by rocks and bricks.

The meaning of the episode, as read by the military, was that the "mere presence" of military force was usually "sufficient to end many disorders" (see Killigrew, 1960). The fact is, the struggle, if the disturbance can be so dignified, was an unequal contest. Dispirited men who, if not on the verge of starvation, were suffering the effects of malnutrition, were easily dispersed by military force.

Far more serious were the racial disorders during World War II—in Mobile, Los Angeles, Beaumont (Texas), Harlem (New York City), and elsewhere. Of these, the most destructive was the outbreak of interracial violence in Detroit in 1943, which required the dispatch of regular forces, who used combat techniques, including gunfire, to bring the riot to a halt (see National Advisory Commission, 1968: 104).

Far different was the employment of troops in the late 1950s and early 1960s to uphold federal law. In September 1957, when mobs in Little Rock, Arkansas, prevented enforcement of a federal court order admitting nine Negro students to the Central High School, Governor Faubus called some National Guardsmen to active duty to prevent the spread of violence. These troops were on hand to sustain the Governor's conception of law and order, which was to deny the Negro students entrance into the school. President Eisenhower issued a "disperse and retire proclamation"; General Maxwell Taylor, the Army Chief of Staff, recommended federalizing and using National Guard forces; and the President "decided to dispatch regular troops." He was determined to employ a mixed force of Guardsmen and regulars to carry out the court order, and he authorized the Secretary of Defense to send the regular forces deemed necessary and to call into federal service "any or all" of the Arkansas National Guard (see Eisenhower, 1965: 170; Scheips, 1969b).

Approximately twelve hundred regular Army paratroopers flew to Little Rock, and the Secretary called all units and members of the Arkansas Air and Army National Guard, a total of about ten thousand men, to federal duty. Major General Edwin A. Walker, a regular officer commanding the Arkansas Military District, was placed in command of both forces.

While paratroop units established a cordon around the school during the night, about eighteen hundred Guardsmen assembled at Camp Robinson outside the city. The other members of the Guard were simply called to duty at their home stations.

After regulars dispersed a mob gathered around the school, National Guard units gradually replaced them. By the end of October, National Guard forces were the major elements preserving order at Little Rock. The last regular paratroopers were withdrawn late in November. From that date until the end of the school term in the following calendar year, the federalized Guard constituted the federal military presence.

One problem which had prompted nightmares before the fact failed to materialize. This was the prospect that some Guardsmen would refuse to serve in an assignment designed to enforce racial integration in the schools. For only several days earlier, the Governor had used the same troops for quite the opposite purpose. Yet no Guardsman legally obligated to report for active duty failed to do so because he opposed the mission for which the Guard was being called. Officers and men proved dutiful to the federal authority, and they carried out their assigned tasks faithfully, whatever their individual opinions of the issues involved and whether their military role was personally distasteful or not (Coakley, 1969).

Five years later, in September 1962, when James Meredith sought to enroll at the University of Mississippi, disturbances arose in Oxford. Because the Administration, in the words of Attorney General Robert F. Kennedy, "was plainly repelled by the idea of using American soldiers against American civilians," federal marshals at first tried, but unsuccessfully, by a show of massed strength and the use of tear gas, to disperse a mob that occasionally employed gunfire. The Mississippi National Guard having been federalized, the President's representative on the scene now telephoned Captain Murry C. Falkner at the Oxford Armory and instructed him to march his troop of Guard armored cavalry to the campus to help keep order The captain asked his squadron commander whether he should obey. Receiving an affirmative reply, the captain did so. Three hours later, a regular military police company, flying from Memphis, arrived and helped put down the riot. By October 6th, approximately twenty thousand regulars and ten thousand Guardsmen were helping local and state police keep the peace. A total of 166 federal marshals, forty-eight soldiers, thirty-six civilians, including three state troopers, were injured; two civilians died (see Scheips, 1969b).

In June 1963, when two Negro students tried to register at the University of Alabama in Tuscaloosa, Governor Wallace had 825 state troopers and deputized officers seal off access to the university. He then ordered six hundred Alabama National Guardsmen into Tuscaloosa to help the state police. When Deputy Attorney General Nicholas deB. Katzenbach, representing the federal authority, escorted the two Negro students to the university, he was met by wallace, who stood in the "schoolhouse door" to prevent desegregation of the state institution. Informed of Wallace's refusal to permit the entry of the Negro students in defiance of federal law, President Kennedy issued an executive order putting the Alabama National Guard into federal service. Several hours later, a few truckloads of federalized Guard Troops arrived on the campus. The commander, Brigadier General Henry V. Graham conferred with Katzenbach, then told Wallace that it was the General's "sad duty" to request the Governor to step aside. Obeying the authority of federal law as had

Graham, despite his personal preference, Wallace allowed the Negro students to register (Facts on File Yearbook, 1963).

Much the same occurred in March 1965, when President Johnson federalized selected units of the Alabama National Guard for active duty in conjunction with federal troops in order to protect the civil rights marchers walking from Selma to Montgomery (see Coakley, 1969).

What characterized the military force in these cases was the faithful response of troops to legally constitute orders. Whatever their personal preference in the controversial questions at stake, the discipline and cohesion of military organization proved stronger.

This period of military intervention of relatively low-level intensity gave way in the 1960s to a wave of violence involving Negroes and whites. Spontaneous explosions erupted without organized plan or conspiracy (National Advisory Commission, 1968: 89). They were marked by destruction and sometimes death. In 1963, serious disorders broke out in Birmingham, Savannah, Cambridge (Maryland), Chicago, and Philadelphia. In 1964, disturbances arose in Jacksonville, Cleveland, St. Augustine, Philadelphia (Mississippi), New York City, Rochester, northern New Jersey, and Philadelphia (Pennsylvania) (National Advisory Commission, 1968: 19-20).

A climax occurred in 1965 in Los Angeles, where, in the business district of Watts, the worst riot since the Detroit disorder of 1943 resulted in the deaths of thirty-four persons, the injury of hundreds, and property damage of approximately $35 million. Indecision, inaction, and confusion marked the early efforts of the police to control the disturbance. As the disorder spread, National Guard troops were called. But there were doubt and bewilderment on their proper deployment and role. Guardsmen and police used firearms extensively in response to reported sniper fire. Thirty-six hours after the appearance of the Guard troops, after four thousand persons had been arrested, "the main force of the riot had been blunted" (see National Advisory Commission, 1968: 20; Conot, 1967: 243).

One observer of the Watts disorder "concluded that he was now in the midst of a war." And in some respects, "It was a war, with all the latent hatred that war releases." The National Guard expended well over ten thousand rounds of ammunition, and all of it, for the Guardsmen had no other type, was armor-piercing, that is, designed to penetrate iron and steel and, consequently able to pass through brick, concrete, and stone (Conot, 1967: 219, 286, 353).

The troops overreacted in Watts. They failed to exercise self-restraint. A National Guard general officer, when conferring with the police, had said, "Well, we are not so much interested in doing this quick as in doing it right." But the Guardsmen had been swept up by emotion and only later was it being "discovered, in fact, that where there was a significant *show* of force, the utilization of force became unnecessary" (Conot, 1967: 243, 346; National Advisory Commission, 1968: 54).

This the Guard learned on the job. According to the Los Angeles chief of police, "The Guardsmen presented a professional talent to their job, never allowing their personal feelings to interfere with their assignment" (see U.S. Congress, House Committee on Armed Services, 1967: 5985). But this occurred only in the latter stages of their duty.

In 1966, a total of forty-three disorders and riots were reported in the nation. The worst occurred in Chicago, where 4,200 National Guardsmen restored order after more than five hundred persons were arrested and three persons were killed by stray bullets, and in the Hough section of Cleveland, where Guardsmen brought the rioting to an end after four nights of terror.[4]

But 1967 was even worse. Some forty thousand Guardsmen were called in twenty-nine outbreaks occurring in twenty states. Those in Newark, New Jersey and Detroit are most instructive for our purposes.

The riot in Newark was triggered on the evening of July 12th, and at 2:30 a.m., July 14th, Mayor Addonizio called Governor Hughes for assistance. According to the Governor's recollection, the Mayor "was quite upset and insisted on the deployment of State Police and National Guardsmen to the maximum extent possible. He told me that a riot was out of control" (see Governor's Select Commission on Civil Disorder, State of New Jersey, 1968; see also National Advisory Commission, 1968: 32-38). State police and National Guards were dispatched to assist the local police in Newark. Although the Governor took command of antiriot operations and decreed a "hard line," conferences on coordinating the various law-enforcement organizations lasted, it seemed, interminably, thereby delaying decision and the commitment of forces (National Advisory Commission, 1968: 35).

The Guard committed about four thousand men in Newark. Mixed state police and Guard patrols toured the riot area. Each patrol consisted of four vehicles; one carried two state policemen and one soldier, another carried two state policemen and a Newark policeman acting as guide, and each of the two other vehicles carried three Guardsmen. In addition, Guard soldiers picked up and transported persons under arrest, protected firemen, and guarded some strategic locations; they established blockades at 137 intersections around the riot area to seal it off—with at least three soldiers, sometimes more, at each post, and at least two soldiers and one Newark policeman at each check point, where vehicles were allowed to pass.

By the afternoon of July 14th, most of the looting had stopped, and the crowds were being contained and dispersed. By the following morning, the disorder had ended.

According to Major General James F. Cantwell, commander of the New Jersey National Guard and president of the National Guard Association, the dual mission of Guard forces impairs its efficiency in civil disturbance duty. Its first responsibility is toward the federal government; its second is to respond to the governor. But equipment is issued to the Guard on the basis of its primary mission—to be ready as a first-line federal reserve. "We do not have equipment," General Cantwell later said, "nor is it intended that the Guard would be equipped for this civil disorder operation." Furthermore, the training was hardly designed to make it possible for Guardsmen to cope with "sniper fire, guerrilla type activities within the cities and on the city streets and mixed into the civilian population, most of which are innocent bystanders" (Governor's Select Commission, 1968).

Each of the three law-enforcement agencies engaged—the Newark police, the state police, and the Guard—issued separate and independent instructions on the use of weapons. Cantwell ordered the Guardsmen to arm themselves, that is, to receive live ammunition. The subordinate commanders had no special instructions except to "control the fire," and senior officers at any given point were responsible for firing by the men under their command. In mixed patrols, Cantwell ordered the Guardsmen to return fire from snipers only on command of a military commander, regardless of the actions of the local or state police operating on the same patrol. "No one will command guardsmen except a guardsmen," the General explained. "No one will fire except on orders of his senior. All ammunition will be accounted for round by round from any individual's possession" (Governor's Select Commission, 1968).

The state police reported 152 sniping incidents; the Newark police reported seventy-nine. In response, Guardsmen expended 10,414 rounds of ammunition from rifles, carbines, and pistols—most of it from rifles.[5] There was little, if any, use of tear gas or fire hoses to control rioters.

"I think," the director of the Newark police later said, "a lot of the reports of snipers was due to the , I hate to use the word, 'trigger-happy' guardsmen, who were firing at noises and firing indiscriminately sometimes . . . the charges of widespread sniping were a lot of malarky used as justification to shoot the people and homes. . . . The amount of ammunition expended . . . was out of all proportion to the mission assigned" (Governor's Select Commission, 1968).

What it seemed like to the Newark police director was that "Guardsmen were firing upon police and police were firing back at them." There was, it appeared, a mutual "state of hysteria" (National Advisory Commission, 1968: 37). Twenty-three persons were killed, including six women and two children.

The head of the New Jersey National Guard later said,

> our job consisted primarily of sealing off the area . . . . Putting patrols and things of that sort on the streets to cut down the looting, all of which worked reasonably well. . . .
>
> We then encountered, as has been encountered elsewhere, a different type of action . . . the sniping, guerrilla-type action, warfare, whatever you might want to call it, in the congested, heavily congested areas. In our case we got considerable sniper fire from high-rise apartments. . . .
>
> . . . there was too much firing initially against snipers, because of the confusion . . . by no one quite knowing what to do, and probably thinking of a military action, and not understanding, possibly, initially, that we were in areas dealing with a sizeable number of people of varying degrees of being interested bystanders [U.S. Congress, House Committee on Armed Services, 1967: 5997-5998] .

The rioting in Newark, which spread to Plainfield and other parts of northern New Jersey, resembled "not an ordinary mob, this was an insurrection and guerrilla warfare." Probably the most effective control measure was the use of armored personnel carriers to move soldiers through dangerous streets. These vehicles looked like tanks. The automatic weapons—machine guns—mounted on the carriers were not loaded. But the appearance of the armored vehicles was "an effective weapon psychologically (U.S. Congress, House Committee on Armed Services, 1967: 6008).

Overreaction in Newark and the indiscriminate expenditure of ammunition had incited further disorder, whereas the mere presence and display of military force would probably have calmed it.

In the heart of the Negro ghetto in Detroit, an early morning police raid on an after-hours drinking establishment on July 23, 1967, triggered the appearance of a group of several hundred Negroes (for accounts of the Detroit riot, see National Advisory Commission, 1968: 47-61; Jordan, 1968; Lowinger and Huige, 1968; Wills, 1968). One person threw a bottle at a police cruiser, others shouted obscenities, and the mob surged down Twelfth Street breaking windows. Forty-five policemen on duty in the 19th Precinct rushed to the disturbed area and sealed off sixteen square blocks. In compliance with a policy formulated by Mayor Jerome Cavanagh and Police Commissioner Ray Girardin, the police followed a "walk soft" strategy. This policy had proved effective the previous summer when riots had flared in the city's East Side. Negro leaders had then cooled the situation, and the authorities expected that they would do so again. Feeling that police shooting their weapons into the air and making other displays of force would only inflame additional violence, the authorities ordered the police to make no attempt to enter the turbulent area, to place themselves in evidence on its fringes, to avoid using weapons or force to restrain crowds, and to guard public utility installations vulnerable to sabotage.

The relative inaction at the outset, it was later argued, permitted the riot to gain momentum, whereas prompt action might have stopped the violence.

The small band of demonstrators quickly multiplied, looting increased, fires broke out, and disorder and destruction fed upon themselves. The disorder spread over almost eleven square miles.

Although the director of the state police was informed that the incident was under control, he alerted forces for possible commitment. The Adjutant General of the National Guard was at Camp Grayling, two hundred miles away, conducting the annual summer encampment training for 4,300 Guardsmen; he alerted a brigade of the 46th Division for possible movement to the city. A battalion of three hundred troops at the Detroit Artillery Armory was available for quick commitment.

Optimism in Detroit that the violence would soon diminish began to dissipate during the afternoon as mobs continued to loot and to set fires. Around 2 p.m., the Mayor requested state police assistance, and half an hour later, 360 state policemen were on their way to the city. About that time, the Guard sent three helicopters to Detroit for aerial surveillance and four armored personnel carriers to transport law enforcement personnel through streets made dangerous by burning buildings.

Shortly after 4 p.m., Cavanagh asked Governor Romney to commit Guard units in support of civil authorities. Four hours later, state forces, both police and Guardsmen, began a sweeping movement through the riot quarters. They used twenty-man patrols, each consisting of fifteen soldiers and five policemen, plus a two and one-half ton truck to transport persons apprehended and arrested for lawless acts. As additional troops arrived that evening, they saturated the riot area. Nevertheless, around 10 p.m., after the Governor and Mayor toured the city in separate helicopters, they began to feel that the riot had assumed major proportions and that regular troops would be needed.

The riot area now covered fourteen square miles, and by 2 a.m., July 24th, citizens had reported a total of 5,839 lawless incidents—arson, looting, and disorder. A new element had also appeared: sniper fire aimed at firemen. Riflemen were then assigned to protect firefighters and their equipment. Major General Cecil Simmons, commander of the 46th Division involved in the city, after seeing the looting and hearing the sniping, said: "The laws of the State will be obeyed. We will use whatever force is necessary." Guardsmen received ammunition, together with instructions to shoot if they were fired upon (in Jordan, 1968: 24).

Indecision in Detroit whether regular troops would really be needed and hope that state forces alone could handle the situation finally gave way to the conviction, around 7 a.m., July 24th, that federal troops were required to prevent the rioting from reaching an uncontrollable stage. The guard commitment totaled 2,800, the fire department was taxed to its limits, and police were working virtually around the clock. Sniper activity hampered efforts to control fires or quell the disorder. Deaths numbered four or five, wounded eight hundred, arrested more than one thousand; more than three hundred fires were reported.

After a series of telephone conservations and telegrams, President Johnson, shortly after 11:30 a.m., agreed to dispatch regular troops. He sent Cyrus R. Vance as his personal representative, and Army Chief of Staff General Harold Johnson appointed Lieutenant General John C. Throckmorton to command the military forces and selected portions of the 82nd and 101st Airborne Divisions at Forts Bragg and Campbell for the mission.

Vance and Throckmorton met in Detroit with Romney and Cavanagh in the midafternoon of July 24th. They learned that a total of 483 fires had been reported, and that more then eighteen hundred arrests were straining detention facilities. In addition to the local and state police on duty, almost five thousand Michigan Guardsmen were on the streets and about three thousand more were in immediate reserve.

That evening, as contingents of regulars arrived at Selfridge Air Force Base near Detroit, the rioting seemed to calm down. At a meeting of Negro leaders, Congressman Charles Diggs said that the crisis called for an immediate deployment of federal troops, while Congressman John Conyers thought that this might provoke a flare-up. Vance and Throckmorton, who had made a two-hour auto tour of the worst areas, had seen no looting or sniping, and they judged the fires were coming under control. Their impression was that regular troops might not be necessary.

Then came a dramatic change. Suddenly, shortly after nightfall, the death toll soared to twelve. In large part it came from a more aggressive response to disorder by police and Guardsmen. The initial order to shoot to kill if under fire had been changed: they were now to shoot to kill in order to halt looters and fleeing felons. Five deaths from shooting rapidly occurred, and the number of reported incidents of arson and looting mounted drastically.

Around 11 p.m., Mr. Vance recommended to the President that regulars be deployed in Detroit and that the Michigan National Guard be federalized. The President agreed. After touring the city, General Throckmorton assigned responsibility for the area east of Woodward Avenue to the 82nd Airborne Division and the area west of Woodward to the Guard. His decision was rooted in two factors.

First, it appeared that the incident rate was increasing dangerously in the eastern part of the city. Second, Selfridge Air Force Base, where federal troops were arriving, was closer to that portion of the city, while the artillery armory used by the Guard was closer to the western part.

The western area of Detroit, which had been hardest hit on July 23rd and 24th, continued to be the scene of the most serious disorders, and the Guardsmen, poorly trained compared to the regulars, thus carried the heaviest burden of quelling the disorder. The area assigned to seasoned paratroopers quickly returned to normal and remained relatively quiet. Was this development merely coincidental? Or did it reflect a difference in the reactions of the two military forces?

The Governor's initial order to mobilize the Guard for riot duty carried the statement to "use what force you have to enforce all the laws of the State of Michigan. If this includes firing of weapons, you will fire weapons" (in Jordan, 1968: 33). This was the basis of the shoot to kill order to halt looting and arson.

Throckmorton reversed this order when he assumed command. He later explained why he took this action. First, his instructions from the Department of the Army—he was responsible directly to the Army Chief of Staff—emphasized the use of minimum force required by the mission. Army guidelines for dealing with riots, provided, in ascending order of priority, four possible levels of counter-violence: (1) soldiers carrying unloaded weapons with bayonets fixed and sheathed, (2) unloaded weapons with bayonets fixed, (3) riot control chemical agent CS, and (4) soldiers carrying loaded weapons and ready to use them.

Second, having toured the troubled areas between 5:15 and 7:15 on the evening of July 24th, he

saw nothing in that tour that to me would justify having soldiers on the streets with their weapons loaded. . . . I was confronted with a group of trigger-happy nervous soldiers in the National Guard. I had no intention of having any of those soldiers shoot innocent people, or small children. . . . It has been my experience that, regardless of how well trained they are, troops going into combat for the first time, where they are shot at, will be nervous and inclined to be trigger happy—that it takes two or three days for them to calm down and react more quietly and properly. This did not happen in the case of the airborne (Regular troops) because we have between 35 and 40 percent veterans from Vietnam in those units. . . . So they have had their baptism of fire, and they are in a position to tell the young, excited soldier to calm down and take it easy. This is not the case in the Guard. It was true, however, that after they had been on duty for a while and realized the conditions and the situation in which they were in, that they reacted the same as other troops do after their initial baptism [U.S. Congress, House Committee on Armed Services, 1967: 5877-5878].

Although he called for all soldiers to unload their weapons, to refrain from firing at looters, and to return sniper fire only on command of a commissioned officer, the Guard failed to comply. Five days after the order was issued, the Deputy Task Force Commander, Major General Charles P. Stone, found that a large majority of the Guardsmen—he estimated ninety percent of all he inspected—were still carrying loaded weapons (Stone, n.d.; U.S. Congress, House Committee on Armed Services, 1967: 5683-5690). In many cases, Guardsmen disobeyed because "the order was improperly disseminated and was never made clear to the men on the street. As a result the Guard was involved in a total of eleven deaths, in which nine innocent people died" (see Hersey, 1968: 290).

General Simmons, the National Guard commander of the Michigan troops employed in Detroit, wished to use more rather than less force. He argued that disorder would surely spread if the rioters learned that there would be no shooting of looters and that the Guardsmen "had their ammunition in their pockets" (see Jordan, 1968: 34; U.S. Congress, House Committee on Armed Services, 1967: 6061-6078).

But Throckmorton stood firm, and Simmons finally complied. Throckmorton, supported by Vance, was acting in the conviction that "force should be used with maximum restraint" (Vance, 1967).

Several months after the disorder was suppressed, officials of the Michigan National Guard still resented General Throckmorton's order to unload weapons. This state of mind was apparent when a member of Congress asked the State Adjutant General a leading question: "When you were denied all of the normal reactions that a law enforcement officer or a soldier would expect to put into effect, you became a bystander. How could you apprehend or stop looting under these conditions, General?"

"I don't know, sir," the General replied. "We disagreed with the policy entirely" (U.S. Congress, House Committee on Armed Forces,

"I don't know, sir," the General replied. "We disagreed with the policy entirely" (U.S. Congress, House Committee on Armed Forces, 1967: 5805).

The technique of self-restraint, nevertheless, seemed to work. After several days of a massive, yet controlled commitment of troops, together with police, in the streets, the riot died down and came to an end on July 27th. The withdrawal of regulars began on the following day and ended on August 2nd. The Guard remained in evidence for four more days.

A total of forty-three persons was killed during the riot; property damages amounted to approximately $50 million. According to a team of reporters who investigated the disorder, "A majority of the riot victims need not have died. Their deaths could have been—and should have been—prevented" (Hersey, 1968: 288). At least six were killed by the National Guard, "five of them innocent, the victims of what now seem to be tragic accidents." Five others were killed by bullets fired by the police or National Guard, four of them innocent of wrongdoing. Two looters were shot by store owners, three others by private citizens, two of whom were promptly charged with murder. Fire killed two looters, electric power lines killed a fireman and a civilian. One person was killed accidentally by a paratrooper, another was shot by an unknown gunman, and a third was murdered by unknown assailants (see Hersey, 1968; National Advisory Commission, 1968: 60-61).

To some observers, the riot resembled war. It "bordered on mass insurrection, more closely resembling guerrilla warfare than . . . the riots and disorders with which the Nation is more familiar" (see National Guardsman, 1967: 2). It looked like combat—with "Hit-and-run looters, elusive snipers; the task of operating with (and out of) patrol cars; the problem of being separated from one's officers for sentry duty or to 'ride shotgun' on a firetruck" (see Wills, 1968: 61).

And this the Guard was less able to cope with than regulars. There were "nearly" 5,000 Guardsmen in the city, but fatigue, lack of training, and the haste with which they had had to be deployed reduced their effectiveness" (see National Advisory Commission, 1968: 54). Their activities were marked by "slow response, tangled line of authority, uncertain deployment, insufficient training, disruption of the military units, isolation of individuals" (see Wills, 1968: 80). There were no mobs to disperse on darkened streets; there was rather the eerie quiet of a battlefield, shattered by an occasional round of fire. Regulars were accustomed to this sort of situation, and during the five days that 2,700 of them were stationed there, they expended 201 bullets (see National Advisory Commission, 1968: 56). In contrast, when a Guardsman's rifle went off accidentally, seventy-five nearby Guardsmen raised their weapons and started firing at residential buildings to defend themselves against unseen and in most instances nonexistent snipers (Lowinger and Huige, 1968).

The Guard troops were least effective in the early stages of the riot, when law enforcement was most badly needed. Far below active Army standards in appearance, bearing, courtesy, and general behavior, they showed inadequate discipline, primarily because of deficiencies in command and control (National Advisory Commission, 1968: 56; Jordan, 1968: 34). Some, perhaps many, of those in the Guard only to avoid being drafted for service in Vietnam, were suddenly taken from the safety and routine of training and placed on unknown and dangerous streets. This was more than they had bargained for. Yet they improved markedly as they gained experience and confidence. And this became "readily apparent to the citizens of the riot-affected sections of the city" (Vance, 1967; Jordan, 1968: 35; Stone, n.d.).

According to the Deputy Commander, General Stone:

> I believe that the improved command and control that existed in the (National Guard) division upon release from active Federal service (defederalization) was one of the major accomplishments of Task Force Detroit . . . you cannot expect a National Guard unit to function in a crisis situation without some period of shakedown and adjustment nor do they meet Regular Army standards initially [see Jordan, 1968: 35; U.S. Congress, House Committee on Armed Services, 1967: 5958, 5963; Stone, n.d.].

Another reason for the relatively poor performance of the Guard troops during their initial commitment was their almost exclusively white composition. A social club enjoying local prestige, it has in Michigan in its Army component a total authorized strength of 9,859 but only 127, a total of 1.3%, were Negroes; Negroes in the Air National Guard totaled only 0.9%.

Mr. Vance believed that more Negro Guardsmen would have overcome a barrier to communication with citizens on the streets. The racial nature of the conflict would have been less exaggerated (see Jordan, 1968: 35-36; National Advisory Commission, 1968: 274-278). He (1967) later reported:

Whether the substantially large percentage of Negro personnel in the airborne units from the Active Army was a major factor in their greater success in the maintenance of law and order cannot be precisely determined. However, a sampling of informed opinion throughout the riot-torn areas of Detroit revealed a strong conviction that a greater degree of integration of the police and National Guard would be of major importance in controlling future disorders.

General Throckmorton's command embraced regular Army and federalized Guard troops comprising Task Force Detroit, but he had no authority over the state and local police. The division of direction contributed to some confusion and poor coordination. On some occasions several units were unnecessarily dispatched to handle the same incident. The most emphatic condemnation of splintered control came from General Stone (n.d.) who wrote:

> There must be complete integration of the operations of the military both National Guard and Regular Army, with local and state police. The commander of the Task Force must have under his control all military and law enforcement personnel and possibly fire fighting personnel. Military and police headquarters must be collocated, each having communications to their respective headquarters and personnel. All elements down to and including patrols must contain both military and police members.

Governor Romney disagreed. Responsible for the public safety of the entire state, he felt that a unified command deprived state officers of the ability to redeploy state forces to other threatened areas. Once the Guard was federalized, he said, "A Governor has in effect sacrificed his authority over a substantial segment of his law enforcement personnel to that of the military" (see Jordan, 1968: 33). During the Detroit riot, when disorders erupted simultaneously in Grand Rapids, Flint, Pontiac, and other towns, Romney had few state police and no Guard units to dispatch there. But after a short interval, a Guard battalion was defederalized and sent to the worst of these outbreaks.

General Stone found "no apparent organization" on the part of the Detroit rioters, but rather "a wholesale assault on the law characterized by looting, arson and the destruction of property." The best way to stop the violence, he said, was to saturate the affected area as early as possible with the maximum number of law enforcement personnel, both police and military, and take quick action to arrest persons breaking the law. In order to impress the rioters, "the appearance, smartness, and military discipline must be exemplary. The image they portray has a very decided effect on the rioters and on the confidence they create among the (nonrioting) public" (see U.S. Congress, House Committee on Armed Services, 1967: 5683-5686; Stone, n.d.).

"If early in the game," General Stone (see U.S. Congress, House Committee on Armed Services, 1967: 5965) expanded,

> they (the National Guard troops) had looked like soldiers, and had created the image in the mind of the public, which is so essential in a situation like this—because if you look strong and if you look as if you can do the job, then the public is going to have confidence in you, and the looter or the rioter is going to be afraid to confront you.

Some "hard-line" advocate of counter-violence to suppress disorders persisted in characterizing the Detroit riot as warfare. "And were (you) in charge of the task force in the Detroit war, or whatever you want to call it?" one asked (U.S. Congress, House Committee on Armed Services, 1967: 5909). "I don't like that term, 'civil disturbance,'" another said, "Let's use the right term, 'guerrilla warfare'" (U.S. Congress, House Committee on Armed Services, 1967: 5950-5951).

Although General Stone inadvertently once used the term "combat in cities," the Army opposes this point of view (U.S. Congress, House Committee on Armed Services, 1967: 5685). "I hope this committee," the acting Chief of Staff, General Ralph E. Haines, said firmly, "does not reject the basic principle in the quelling of civil disturbances, which is to use minimum force consistent with mission accomplishment" (U.S. Congress, House Committee on Armed Services, 1967: 5977).

The experiences in 1967 led to a more effective reaction to disorders occurring in 1968. Federal troops were used in Baltimore, Chicago, and Washington, D.C., and although the disturbances were as explosive as any in the previous year, they were brought under control more expeditiously. All arose on the evening of April 4, 1968, out of the emotions stimulated by news of the shooting and death of Dr. Martin Luther King, Jr.

Department of the Army instructions to the three task force commanders were the same. There were to cooperate with and assist municipal law enforcement officers to assume their normal roles. They were to use the minimum force necessary to restore law and order. Weapons were to be fired only when authorized or when absolutely necessary to save life. Riot control chemical agents were to be used before live ammunition. Bullets fired against looters were to be aimed to wound rather than to kill. Weapons were to be carried unloaded, with bayonets sheathed, except upon order. Military forces were to work closely with the police. Troops were to make no unreasonable searches of persons, property, or automobiles. Civilian rather than military authorities were to take lawbreakers into custody.

In Chicago, disorders began to occur on the afternoon of April 5th, when groups of young persons roamed the West Side, looting, setting fires, and attacking motorists. Sniping was reported and twenty rounds were fired against the Fillmore police station. Lieutenant Governor Shapiro, after conferring with the Governor who was out of the state, called six thousand Illinois National Guard troops to state duty at 4 p.m. An hour later, the Department of the Army placed a predesignated civil disturbance brigade at Fort Hood, Texas, on a twelve-hour alert status and prepared a smaller force for movement upon a six-hour notice.

As violence continued into the night, Mayor Daley asked that part of the Guardsmen be deployed on the streets. At 10 p.m., half of the available troops were in support of the city's 10,500 policemen. Their orders were to shoot only in self-defense and only against clearly observed targets.

On April 6th, as the violence continued—125 fires were reported—eight hundred persons were arrested, and that afternoon, Shapiro requested regular troops. The President authorized the deployment of five thousand, and the Chief of Staff appointed Lieutenant General George R. Mather commanding general of Task Force Chicago. When Mather arrived in the city, he learned the 7,030 Guardsmen were on duty in state status—5,200 in their armories, 1,800 on the streets of Chicago.

Shortly after midnight, the Air and Army National Guard of Illinois was federalized, and selected units went under Mather's command. The disorder continued into the morning of April 7th, and violence increased during the early afternoon. But motorized and foot patrols of military forces asserted their presence throughout the troubled areas of the city and broke up mobs. By late afternoon, the situation was under at least loose control.

By midnight, the reported strength of Task Force Chicago was about eleven thousand troops—6,800 Guardsmen and four thousand regulars. Disorder flared momentarily during the early, dark hours of April 8th, but by daylight normal traffic and commercial patterns had been resumed. Although the city was still tense, reported incidents were at a low level. A slight increase occurred in the afternoon, then subsided.

On April 9th, Mather deployed troops to Grant Park to prevent disorder at a scheduled antiwar rally. There was no disturbance there, and incidents elsewhere in the city were few in number. On the following day, with the city calm for forty-eight hours, Mather discontinued dismounted patrolling in most areas. Early on April 11th, he took all his troops off the streets. That evening the Guard was restored to normal status and the regular troops began to withdraw.

The Chicago riot resulted in eleven deaths, all Negro civilians; 922 persons were injured, among them ninety-two police, forty-two firemen, and one soldier; there were at least 213 fires; 3,125 persons were arrested; property damage was estimated at $13 million. There was no verified case of sniping. The troops used neither bullets nor antiriot chemical agents.

Several days later, Mayor Daley announced at a press conference that he was instructing Chicago policemen to "shoot to kill" arsonists in the future and to "shoot to maim or cripple" looters. Attorney General Ramsay Clark publicly repudiated Daley's statement, pointing out that the best way to control riots was to use restraint and a minimum of gunfire. A few days later, Daley modified his original declaration but asserted that arsonists and looters should not be rewarded with what he called "permissive rights" (Facts on File Yearbook, 1968).

In Washington, D.C., the assassination of Dr. King brought crowds of shocked people into the streets. Mayor Walter E. Washington immediately alerted the police department to the potential danger of violence. About 8 p.m., a large group of persons, still peaceful, urged neighborhood stores to close their doors out of respect to Dr. King. An hour and a half later, the mood had become ugly and violence and looting rapidly spread up Fourteenth Street.

Because police patrols were too small to cope with the large number of rioters, they tried to seal off the area. By 4 a.m., April

5th, this manifestation of control had prompted the violence to subside But it flared in the afternoon and spread to other areas; large fires were burning in at least three sections of the city.

At 4 p.m., the Mayor submitted a formal request for military forces, and the President responded immediately. He issued a proclamation ordering rioters "to disperse and retire peaceably," and authorized the dispatch of troops. District of Columbia National Guardsmen, having been placed in a training status around noon, were on the streets at 5 p.m. An hour later they were under federal control. The first regulars—from units which had been preselected within a hundred-mile radius of the capital—began to arrive at Andrews Air Force Base.

General Haines commanded Task Force Washington, which consisted of about 11,500 regulars and eighteen hundred Guardsmen. He assigned the Guard to protect such vital buildings as the White House and the Capitol, detain looters, protect firemen, clear streets, and isolate trouble areas. He instructed regulars to patrol the streets actively, to apprehend instigators of violence, looters, arsonists, and the disorderly.

By late morning of April 6th, the military forces were fully deployed, and the incidence of reported crimes was declining rapidly. The only problem was some isolated looting and arson. Although the city remained quiet, the troops stayed on duty another nine days to be certain there would be no flare-up of violence.

Twelve persons died in the riot, none killed by soldiers; twelve hundred persons were injured, including seventy-five policemen and firemen, and sixteen military personnel. Property damage was estimated at $13 million. A total of 7,400 adults was arrested, most of them for violating the curfew. The troops fired fourteen rounds of ammunition; they discharged 5,250 grenades of CS riot-control chemical agent.

At the Mayor's request, the President had made Mr. Vance available to work with the city officials in controlling the disorder. Mr. Vance believed that the antiriot control techniques employed in Washington, D.C., showed great improvement over the way disorders had been handled in the preceding year.

Asked by a reporter whether there was "a great deal more restraint in the use of fire arms," Vance answered affirmatively. Soldiers, he said, had no bullets chambered in their weapons; they had ammunition "on them . . . in a pouch on the soldier" (District of Columbia Government, 1968; District of Columbia Committee, 1968).

On the evening of April 7th, a reporter said that he had heard that "no Federal troops had fired their weapons. Is this still true?"

Vance replied, "To the best of my knowledge that is still the case" (District of Columbia Government, 1968: 4).

Mr. Vance expanded his statement by saying, "We decided we would arrest everybody who was violating the law that we could apprehend and we would do that with the minimum force required to get the job done. And that has been done and I commend the police and the soldiers for the great job they have done on that" (District of Columbia Government, 1968: 5).

Among the techniques used more effectively were roving patrols superimposed on the static forces required to protect particular areas. These patrols were composed of military and police units working together, sometimes followed by patrol wagons so that looters apprehended by the military could be quickly turned over to the police for arrest (District of Columbia Government, 1968: 10-11).

A purely military response is not the official position of the U.S. Army, which has been stated many times. One of the most succinct statements was made by General Haines who said, late in 1967, that military forces "should be employed to quell civil disturbance only as a last resort. This is an unhappy duty which we do not relish" (U.S. Congress, House Committee on Armed Services, 1967: 5680-5681).

Whether the Army wishes it or not, it has received primary responsibility among the armed forces to assist the civil authorities quell disorder. Although the Army regards its first and foremost mission as the protection of the United States against external threat, it is prepared to take action against internal dangers that menace the welfare of the country. "Widespread civil disturbance" is in that category, for it "is a threat to the effective functioning of a government, lowers public morale, and destroys public relationships, confidence, and progress" (U.S. Department of the Army, 1968).

When troops are committed as an act of last resort to assist civil authorities restore order, the Army expects these soldiers to receive verbal abuse—obscene remarks, taunts, ridicule, jeers—and physical attacks on personnel and vehicles in order to anger and demoralize control forces and make them act in a brutal fashion. The Army anticipates troops to be subjected to missiles—vegetables, fruits, rocks, bricks, and bottles—even improvised bombs and demolitions, as well as gunfire.

Against these tactics, the Army says, "the well-disciplined execution of orders is the most effective force applied against rioters."

Regular Army or National Guard troops may detain or take into temporary custody civilians involved in a disturbance, but the Army prefers civil authorities to apprehend and arrest the disorderly and the lawless. "If force is required," the Army adds, "it must be reasonable and prudent to the circumstances" (U.S. Department of the Army, 1968).

The application of civil disturbance control is anything but simple. It is marked by a "multiplicity of missions . . . which creates the need for simultaneous commitment of forces in diversified operations." But it requires from troops, above all, the ability to retain their composure while operating under physical, mental, and emotional strain. They must be impartial, patient, and reveal no signs of fear while searching buildings, establishing and operating check-points and roadblocks, patrolling sensitive areas, guarding critical facilities, protecting firefighters, maintaining liaison with the police, and employing riot-control formations against massed mobs, snipers, and looters. Soldiers are not to harangue, dare, threaten, or try to bluff rioters. They must present an implacable appearance, treat all persons fairly, use no more force than necessary, and leave open to crowds an avenue of exit. This is a large order, and the Army recognizes that "The conduct of civil disturbance control operations taxes leadership skills just as fully as, and in some ways more uniquely than, combat operations" (U.S. Department of the Army, 1968).

According to the Army's official doctrine, "The commitment of military forces must be considered as a drastic last resort." The guiding principle is the utilization of minimum force consistent with mission. Troops are to avoid appearing as an invading alien force. Their purpose is to restore law and order with a minimum loss of life and property, together with due respect for the great number of citizens whose involvement in the disorder is purely accidental.

In general, whenever possible, control forces are to be visible rather than active. A well-equipped, highly disciplined control force coming into view may present a show of force that is enough to persuade rioters to disperse and retire. In other words, the military would rather deter than act.

The Army's most fundamental outlook comes from the belief that "The psychological impact on the civilian populace of being faced by an alert, well disciplined military force effectively deters some potential rioters and looters." Those who are not deterred from disorderly and unlawful conduct must be dealt with in other ways, but always with self-restraint.

But what if the show of force fails to deter? What is effective? According to Major General Geroge M. Gelston (see National Advisory Commission, 1967), adjutant general of the Maryland National Guard and a successful practitioner of the art of using military forces to control riots, "leadership and discipline is (sic) really more important than the tactics and techniques."

> even more than in combat, junior leadership by the junior officers and the noncommissioned officers out there on the corner, and discipline, is 95 percent of the whole business. Unlike combat, in this area you are fighting a restrained war, your whole effort is not to kill somebody. Rather, than to kill them, just try to control it by the Guards' presence, and the indication of what you could do if it were necessary to do it.

"Army training in its totality," the National Advisory Committee on Civil Disorders (1968: 280, 278) found, "produces the type of well-disciplined and self-supporting force essential for the control of a major disorder." The point is, "Controlling a civil disorder is not warfare. The fundamental objective . . . is to control the rioters, not to destroy them or any innocent bystanders."

Even chemical agents, which are generally regarded as the most effective antiriot weapon, should not be used indiscriminately. A great deal of tear gas was employed by police forces suppressing civil disorder in Kansas City, Missouri, in April 1968, and the effects were sometimes antithetical to the ones desired. According to the report later issued by the Mayor's Commission on Civil Disorder (1968),

> Although the use of tear gas is much more humane than the use of the baton or the gun . . . its psychological effect in rendering persons helpless who are responding from an underdog position, is to anger and frustrate

them, perhaps even more than would be true by the use of the baton or the gun. Tear gas is also less selective in that it subdues not only the person or persons creating a disturbance, but all other individuals who happen to be in the vicinity including, of course, those who may not be guilty of any wrongdoing.

In dispersing disorderly groups of people by the use of tear gas, the police unfortunately and inevitably are treating anti-rioters who are within the groups in the same manner that they are treating the offenders in the group. In short, no distinction between persons can be made. . . . This is most unfortunate because anti-rioters, who otherwise could possibly have considerable effect in preventing further trouble, cease assisting in the prevention of an escalation of the disturbance. Thus, it must remain a matter of judgment by the policeman on the spot, under all the circumstances, as to which method of subduing or dispersing people best fits the situation at hand.

The presence of guns on both sides makes it desirable to develop limited response weapons and to train men in their employment so that troops engaged in riot control cannot be panicked into a total response. They "must learn to live with danger, and limit it, and survive" (Wills, 1968: 167).

The Guard has performed well—in Watts, Milwaukee, Cambridge. But General Gelston, for instance, has never let the Maryland Guard load their weapons. He is very quick to use the lower steps of escalation—gas, bared bayonets. But he says, "These young men are not used to combat situations; and it is very easy for them to squeeze off a round by accident or in panic." It was difficult to make this rule work in Detroit, where everyone who had a gun seemed to be using it; where Guardsmen were scattered off to help policemen who carried (and used) loaded guns; where men were told to load their weapons only on the command of an officer, though many had not seen their own officer since they arrived in the city days before. They soon became convinced that one's life might depend, around the next corner, on having a clip in one's weapon—whatever that weapon might be [Wills, 1968: 53] .

Maintaining law and order in the United States is a civil—meaning nonmilitary—responsibility (see Engle in National Advisory Commission, 1967). The primacy of civil over military force and the primary responsibility of state rather than nation to put down domestic disorders have been traditional in American life. So is a prompt and energetic execution of the law (see Vance, 1967). Traditionally, law and order are upheld by using minimum force. But when local and state police or federal marshals are unable to enforce the laws, uphold the authority of government, and guarantee the lives and property of law-abiding citizens, a final resort is made to the military. They too are subordinate to civil authority, for the President as Commander in Chief or the governor as head of the state National Guard is a civilian rather than a military figure. Since civil power is deliberative, the military used in a civil context must operate under great restrictions.

Despite the subordination of military power to civil direction, the use of military forces to put down disorders gives the action a noncivil or military flavor. Troops are organized primarily to wage war against other organized groups in combat actions sometimes called the ordered or controlled employment of violence. Yet when civil authorities call for troops in a domestic crisis, the hope is always present that the mere threat of force will dissipate disorder and restore peaceful obedience to the laws.

For the fact is, military forces are, paradoxically, both ill-suited to put down civil disorders and very effective. They are inappropriate because they are formed and trained to destroy the organized military forces of foreign enemies. However, the characteristics of restraint (produced by self or military authority), cohesion (produced by organization and training), and responsiveness to orders (gained by practice that, at least theoretically, has become habit)—these guarantee success against disorderly civilian elements. For mobs are unorganized or, at best, organized in a rudimentary and primitive fashion that establishes a consolidation of human attachments for a temporary purpose only. They cannot oppose with any hope of success the steadfastness and manifest strength of a permanently organized force.

Yet if a situation develops beyond the state of simple confrontation, into combat, it is difficult to remain aloof and coldly self-contained. The Chicago police were unable or unwilling to do so during the violence in August 1968, and discipline broke down (see Walker, 1968; Life Magazine, 1968). Nor were the Michigan National Guardsmen in Detroit able to restrain themselves in 1967, when riot approached the intensity of combat. Regular troops, better trained and led, more experienced, have rarely lost their cool no matter how hot the excitement. Despite their training for war, which inculcates in soldiers an immediate reaction to hostile fire and an intense desire to destroy the enemy, the quality of obedience and response to orders has proved paramount.

Despite the Army's distaste for duty in suppressing civil disorder, the Department of the Army has primary responsibility for coordinating the planning for and assistance to civil authorities in domestic emergencies. To these ends, the Army continuously monitors civil disturbances in the United States. Headed by a lieutenant general, a Directorate for Civil Disturbance Planning and Operations in the Office of the Deputy of Chief of Staff for Military Operations keeps contingency plans up to date according to reports from an intelligence network and actual incidents emerging.

Active Army forces ready for deployment in the event of federal intervention to quell civil disorders vary from small "first units" selected for rapid movement, to a maximum force of fifteen thousand men, composed of seven brigade-size task forces drawn from the continental Army areas. Each Army headquarters also has detailed contingency plans for executing possible missions within its geographical area (see Jordan, 1968: 24-25; Hollis, 1967; National Advisory Commission, 1968: 79-81).

Exactly what missions the Army will have to undertake are unknown. According to David McCliffert, Under Secretary of the Army (before U.S. Congress, House Committee on Armed Services, 1967):

> The disorders which have plagued our cities this summer have not been riots, in the usual sense. They have not been marked by masses of people surging up and down the streets. Rather, the outbursts have taken the form of looting, arson, and sniping, and the form of our response to these outbreaks of crime cannot be quite the same as the responses which in the past have been designed to subdue and disperse a mob.

According to Brigadier General Harris Hollis (in National Advisory Commission, 1967):

> Yet the Army holds to its traditional reliance on—

> ... minimum application of force consistent with the necessity to accomplish the mission. . . .

> We in the Army believe that the historical definition of responsibility, which assigns to local authority the primary obligation for control over local disturbances, is a sound one, with the Federal Government coming to assist when that course is deemed necessary . . .

... the certainty of a quick response by military force is a deterrent to those who would bring about this disorder, particularly when this capability is evident to all those who would cause the disorder.

Thus the capabilities of the National Guard and the Active Army ought to provide for a quick, visible response when law and order breaks down and the resort to military force becomes necessary.

... the total spectrum of tactical training contributes to the effectiveness of units when coping with civil disorder. The most useful resource in a riot situation is a well-trained individual soldier.

From the beginning of the American state, the function of the military employed in civil disorder duty has been the same. The "purpose has been to quell violence—not to suppress people . . . to uphold law and order, to protect life and property, and to do so with firmness and fairness." U.S. troops are battle-trained, hardened, and tested; they are far better prepared to bring law and order to a troubled city than a National Guard unit sprinkled with raw recruits fresh from summer encampment. Furthermore, regular units, unlike the almost completely white National Guard units, are racially integrated, and they are less likely to invite racial retaliation.

Yet a new development arose in 1968. About forty Negro soldiers stationed at Fort Hood, Texas, demonstrated against being sent to Chicago in August 1968, for possible antiriot duty during the Democratic National Convention. Their reasons: "they thought that they might have to fight other Negroes there" (see Washington Post, 1968). Whether the incident is an aberration or portends widespread disobedience to orders, the greatest danger to any military force is that its internal cohesion will be destroyed. In 1931, during the Great Depression, when the Army was asked to help house unemployed and homeless men, the commanding general of the IX Corps Area, Malin Craig, in a letter of November 18, warned the Deputy Chief of Staff of the possible consequences of such action. "Very powerful reasons affecting morale," he wrote, "forbids (sic) in my opinion, that these floaters should be quartered in midst or in contact with our enlisted men" (see Killigrew, 1960: ch. 6).

Military leaders dislike to be called to curb domestic disorder. The most important reason is that they have no desire to be diverted from their primary mission: preparing to defend the nation against foreign enemies. In addition, they prefer to identify themselves with their fellow citizens; they have no wish to be alienated from the public; they fear harming innocents, they have no desire to wage war against Americans; they abhor being regarded as a conquering army at home. Fundamentally, the antiriot function is a police rather than a military function, and training for these dissimilar actions, despite their superficially similar conditions and situations, produces a schizophrenic state of mind.

NOTES

AUTHOR'S NOTE: I am indebted to Robert W. Coakley of the Army's Office of the Chief of Military History, to John B. Spore, Senior Editor of Army Magazine, and especially to Paul J. Scheips of the Army's Office of the Chief of Military History for fruitful discussions on the subject of this paper.

1. I have avoided inquiring into the causes of riots, the legal issues involved in using military force, and the role of the civil authorities, including police action, the imposition of curfews, and other riot-control measures.

2. The following is largely based on John W. Killigrew (1960: ch. 7). See also Arthur M. Schlesinger, Jr. (1957: 257-265, 267). I am indebted to Professor John W. Price of the University of Florida who made available to me the results of his research on the Bonus March incident.

3. Memo, Brigadier General Perry Miles for Chief of Staff, June 4, 1932, is cited in Killigrew (1960).

4. Various figures are given in different sources. The statistics used here are from the National Advisory Commission on Civil Disorders (1968: 21).

5. It has been suggested that the large expenditure of ammunition may be exaggerated because many individuals preferred to retain their bullets for future emergency rather than to turn them in after the riot. See Government Select Commission (1968).

REFERENCES

BINDER, L. J. (1969) "The hundred mile an hour war." Army 19 (March): 16-32.

BLAKELY, Maj. Gen. H. W. (1952) "When the Army was smeared." Combat Forces Journal 2 (February): 26-29.

Civil Disturbances and Disasters (1968) Department of the Army Field Manual 19-15. Washington, D.C.: U.S. Government Printing Office.

COAKLEY, R. W. (1969) "Federal use of militia and National Guard in civil disturbances: the Whiskey Rebellion to Little Rock," in R. Higham (ed.) Bayonets in the Streets: The Use of Troops in Civil Disturbances. Lawrence: University Press of Kansas.

CONOT, R. (1967) Rivers of Blood, Years of Darkness. New York: Bantam Books.

District of Columbia Government (1968) Report on Civil Disturbances in Washington, D.C., April, 1968. Washington, D.C. (April 30).

District of Columbia Committee on the Administration of Justice under Emergency Conditions (1968) Interim Report (May 25).

EISENHOWER, D. D. (1965) Waging Peace, 1956-1961. New York: Doubleday.

Facts on File Yearbook (1968).

———(1963).

Governor's Select Commission on Civil Disorder, State of New Jersey, (1968) Report for Action (February).

HERSEY, J. (1968) The Algiers Motel Incident. New York: Bantam Books.

HIGHAM, R. [ed.] (1969) Bayonets in the Streets: The Use of Troops in Civil Disturbances. Lawrence: University Press of Kansas.

JORDAN, D. (1968) "Civil disturbances: a case study of Task Force Detroit, 1967," in Perspectives in Defense Management. Washington, D.C.: Industrial College of the Armed Forces.

KILLIGREW, J. W. (1960) "The impact of the great depression on the Army, 1929-1936." Ph.D. dissertation. Indiana University.

Life Magazine (1968) December 6.

LOWINGER, P. and F. HUIGE (1968) "The National Guard in the 1967 Detroit Uprising." Detroit: Department of Psychiatry, Wayne State University School of Medicine and Lafayette Clinic. Unpublished.

MAILER, N. (1968) "The steps of the Pentagon." Harper's 237 (March): 47-80 ff.

Mayor's Commission on Civil Disorder (1968) Final Report. Kansas City, Mo. (August 15).

National Guardsman (1967) 21 (September).

NIHART, F. B. (1968) Letter to the Editor. Army 18 (March): 4-5.

RICH, M. B. (1941) The Presidents and Civil Disorder. Washington, D.C.: Brookings Institution.

RIGG, R. B. (1968) "Made in USA: urban guerrilla warfare." Army 18 (January): 24-31.

SCHEIPS, P. J. (1969a) "Darkness and light: the interwar years 1865-1898," in M. Matloff (ed.) American Military History. Washington, D.C.: Army Historical Series.

———(1969b) "Enforcement of federal judicial process by federal marshals: a comparison of Little Rock and Oxford," in R. Higham (ed.) Bayonets in the Streets: The Use of Troops in Civil Disturbances. Lawrence: University Press of Kansas.

SCHLESINGER, A. M., Jr. (1957) The Crisis of the Old Order. Boston: Houghton-Mifflin.

STONE, Maj. Gen. C. P. (n.d.) Report to Chief of Staff, U.S. Army.

U.S. National Advisory Commission on Civil Disorders (1968) Report. Washington, D.C. (March 1).

———(1967) Statements before the commission of Brigadier General Harris W. Hollis; Major General George M. Gelston, Adjutant General, State of Maryland; Byron Engle, director, Office of Public Safety, Agency for International Development; Major General R. L. Hill; Howard R. Leary, police commissioner, New York City; William M. Lombard, chief of police, Rochester, New York; and E. Wilson Purdy, Director of the Department of Public Safety of Dade County, Florida. Mimeographed release (September 20).

U.S. Congress, House Committee on Armed Services (1967) Hearings before the Special Subcommittee to Inquire into the Capability of the National Guard to Cope with Civil Disturbances, 90th Congress, 1st Session.

U.S. Department of the Army Field Manual 19-15 (1968) "Civil disturbances and disasters" (March).

VANCE, C. B. (1967) Final Report of Cyrus B. Vance, Special Assistant to the Secretary of Defense Concerning the Detroit Riots, July 23, through August 2, 1967. (Released September 12.)

WALKER, G. (1968) Rights in Conflict [The Walker Report]. New York: Bantam Books.

Washington Post (1968) August 29: 5.

———(1968) September 2: A4.

———(1968) September 8: A33.

———(1968) September 19: A3.

———(1968) September 20: A6.

General Bibliography

GENERAL BIBLIOGRAPHY

ABRAMS, Phillip (1962) "Democracy, technology and the retired British officer," pp. 150-189 in S. P. Huntington (ed.) Changing Patterns of Military Politics. New York: Free Press.

ADAMS, S. (1953) "Status congruency as a variable in small group performance." Social Forces 32: 16-22.

AFRIFA, Col. Akwasi A. (1966) The Ghana Coup, 24th February, 1966. New York: Humanities Press.

ALTMAN, I. (1966) "Aspects of the criterion problem in small groups research." Acta Psychologica 25: 101-131.

———and W. W. Haythorn (1967) "The ecology of isolated groups." Behavioral Science 12:169-182

ALTMAN, Stuart H. and Alan E. FECHTER (1967) "The supply of military personnel without a draft," in Papers and Proceedings of the Seventy-Ninth Annual Meeting of the American Economic Association. American Economic Review 57 (May): 19-31.

AMBLER, R. K., J. A. BERKSHIRE and W. F. O'CONNOR (1961) "The identification of potential astronauts." Research Report 33. Pensacola, Fla.: Naval School of Aviation Medicine (June).

ANDERSON, Edwin P. (1965) "An economic analysis of retired military officers in metropolitan Phoenix." Master's thesis. College of Business Administration, Arizona State University, Tempe, June 1965.

ANDRESKI, Stanislaw (1961) "Conservatism and radicalism of the military." Archives Europeennes de Sociologie 2 (Spring): 53-61.

———(1954) Military Organization and Society. London: Routledge & Kegan Paul.

APPEL, John W. (1966) "Preventive psychiatry," pp. 373-415 in Neuropsychiatry in World War II. Office of the Surgeon General, Department of the Army.

ARTHUR, R. A. (1966) "Psychiatric disorders in Naval personnel." Military Medicine (April): 354-361.

———(1965) "Stability in psychosis admission rates: three decades of Navy experience." Public Health Reports 80: 512-514.

Association of the Bar of the City of New York (1960) Conflict of Interest and Federal Service. Cambridge: Harvard University Press

BAEHR, M. E. and G. B. WILLIAMS (1967) "Underlying dimensions of personal background data and their relationship to occupational classification." Journal of Applied Psychology 51: 481-490.

BAIR, J. T. (1952) "The characteristics of the wanted and unwanted pilot in training and in combat." Memorandum Report No. 2. Pensacola, Fla.: Naval School of Aviation Medicine (February).

———and T. J. GALLAGHER (1958) "Volunteering for extra-hazardous duty." Naval Research Review (November): 12-19.

BARNETT, Corelli (1967) "The education of military elites." Journal of Contemporary History 2 (July).

BELL, G. B. and R. L. FRENCH (1950) "Consistency of individual leadership position in small groups of varying membership." Journal of Abnormal and Social Psychology 45: 764-767.

BEM, D. F. (1967) "Self-perception: the dependent variable of human performance." Journal of Organizational Behavior and Human Performance 2: 105-121.

BERKSHIRE, J. R. (1967) "Evaluation of several experimental aviator selection tests." Report No. 1003. Pensacola, Fla.: Naval Aerospace Medical Institute (March).

———and P. D. NELSON (1958) "Leadership peer ratings related to subsequent proficiency in the fleet." Special Report No. 58-20. Pensacola, Fla.: Naval School of Aviation Medicine.

BERRY, N. H. and P. D. NELSON (1966) "The fate of school drop-outs in the Marine Corps." Personnel and Guidance Journal 45: 20-23.

BEVILACQUA, Joseph J. (1967) "Civilization and health-welfare resource participation on an Army post." Ph.D. dissertation. University of Michigan.

BIDERMAN, Albert D. (1964) "Sequels to a military career," pp. 287-336 in M. Janowitz (ed.), The New Military: Changing Patterns of Organization. New York: Russell Sage Foundation.

———(1963) March to Calumny. New York: Macmillan.

———(1960) Needs for Knowledge Regarding the Military Retirement Problem: Summary Report of a Conference Held in Washington, D.C. Washington, D.C.: Bureau of Social Science Research, Inc.

———(1959) "The prospective impact of large scale military retirement." Social Problems 7 (Summer): 84-90.

———and Laure M. SHARP (1968) "The convergence of military and civilian occupational structures: evidence from studies of military retired employment." American Journal of Sociology 73 (July): 381-399.

———(1967) "Out of uniform: the employment experience of retired servicemen who seek a second career." Monthly Labor Review (January-February): 15-47.

BIENEN, Henry (1968) "Public order and the military in Africa: mutinies in Kenya, Uganda, and Tanganyika," pp. 35-70 in H. Bienen (ed.) The Military Intervenes. New York: Russell Sage Foundation.

BINDER, Edwin M. (1964) "The utilization of military retirees in teaching, administrative and service positions in education, 1965-1975." Master's thesis. Ohio State University.

BLACKSTOCK, Paul W. (1969) The Secret Road to War; Soviet vs. Western Intelligence, 1927-1939. Chicago: Quadrangle Books.

———(1964) The Strategy of Subversion: Manipulating the Politics of Other Nations. Chicago: Quadrangle Books.

BOBROW, Doris B. (1965) "Soldiers and the nation-state." Annals of American Academy of Political and Social Service (March): 66.

BOEGEL, T. J. (1961) "The potential resource for teachers from the ranks of retiring military personnel." Ph.D. dissertation. St. John's University, Jamaica, New York.

BOGART, Leo (1969) Social Research and the Desegregation of the U.S. Army. Chicago: Markham.

BOROFF, David (1963) "Annapolis: teaching young sea dogs old tricks." Harper's (January).

———(1963) "Air Force Academy: a slight gain in altitude." Harper's (February).

———(1963) "West Point: ancient incubator for a new deal." Harper's (December).

BRAMSTEDT, E. K. (1945) Dictatorship and Political Police. London: Kegan, Paul.

BRAY, C. W. (1962) "Towards a technology of human behavior for defense use." American Psychologist 17: 527-541.

BRILL, William H. (1967) Military Intervention in Bolivia: The Overthrow of Paz Estenssoro and the MNR. Washington, D.C.: Institute for the Study of Political Systems.

BROKAW, L. D. (1967) "Non-cognitive measures in selection of officers," pp. 35-47 in J. E. Uhlaner (ed.) Psychological Research in National Defense Today. Technical Report 5-1. Washington, D.C.: U.S. Army Behavioral Sciences Research Laboratory (June).

CALIFANO, J. A. (1957) "Limitations on the employment of retired Naval officers." JAG Journal (November): 2.

CALVERT, Peter A. R. (1967) "The 'typical Latin American revolution.'" International Affairs 43 (January): 85-95.

———(1967) "Revolution: the politics of violence." Political Studies 15 (February): 1-11.

CAUDILL, William (1955) "American soldiers in a Japanese community." Unpublished manuscript.

CAMPBELL, D. T. (1956) "Leadership and its effect upon the group." Monograph No. 83. Columbus: Ohio State University, Bureau of Business Research.

———and Thelma H. McCORMACK (1957) "Military experiences and attitudes toward authority." American Journal of Sociology 62 (March): 482-490.

CHAKOUTINE, Serge (1939) Le Viole des Foules par la propagande politique. Paris: Gallimard.

CHANG, Wen-lung, (1968) "A study of a Nationalist Chinese air police company: leadership and primary groups." Master's thesis. Department of Sociology and Anthropology, Kansas State University.

CHRISTIE, Richard (1962) "Changes in authoritarianism as related to situational factors." American Psychologist 7: 307-308.

———(1954) Transition from Civilian to Army Life. HumRRO Technical Report No. 13. Washington, D.C. (October).

CHRISTENSEN, J. M. et al. (1967) "Contributions of engineering psychology to military systems," pp. 208-227 in J. E. Uhlaner (ed.) Psychological Research in National Defense Today. Technical Report 5-1. Washington, D.C: U.S. Army Behavioral Sciences Research Laboratory (June).

Civilian Advisory Panel on Military Manpower Procurement (1967) "Report to the House Committee on Armed Services." Washington, D.C.: U.S. Government Printing Office.

CLAPHAM, Christopher (1968) "The December 1960 Ethiopian coup d'état." Journal of Modern African Studies 6 (December): 495-507.

CLARK, Harold and Harold SLOAN (1964) Classrooms in the Military. New York: Bureau of Publications, Teachers College, Columbia University.

CLEVELAND, Harlan et al. (1960) The Overseas American. New York: McGraw-Hill.

CLIFFORD-VAUGHAN, Michalina (1964) "Changing attitudes to the Army's role in French society." British Journal of Sociology 15 (December): 338-349.

CLINARD, D. M. and J. A. FOLTZ (1959) "Retirement and the law." JAG Journal (June-July): 3.

CLINE, Victor B. et al. (1955) "A survey of opinions regarding Operation Gyroscope in the First Division." Staff Memorandum. Washington, D.C.: Human Resources Research Office, George Washington University. (Springfield, Va.: CFSTI Document 173 200.)

COATES, Charles H. and Roland J. PELLEGRIN [eds.] (1965) Military Sociology. University Park, Md.: Social Science Press.

COHEN, Stephen P. (1969) "The untouchable soldier: caste, politics and the Indian Army." Journal of Asian Studies 28: 453-468.

COLLINGS, K. T. (1963) "Employment of retired military officers in the West Coast area: a pilot study." Master's thesis. University of Washington.

Committee of Retired Army, Navy and Air Force Officers (1958) Retirement from the Armed Forces. 2nd ed. Harrisburg, Penn.: Military Service Publishing.

CONDIT, D. M. and B. H. COOPER et al. (1968) Challenge and Response in Internal Conflict, Vols. I, II, III. Washington, D.C.: American University, Center for Research in Social Systems.

CONOT, Robert (1967) Rivers of Blood, Years of Darkness. New York: Bantam Books.

CRAWFORD, Elizabeth (1965) "Education for policy roles: an analysis of lecturers and reading materials at selected colleges." CFSTI Document No. AD 669-840. Springfield, Virginia.

CROKER, George W. (1969) "Some principles regarding the utilization of social science research within the military," pp. 185-194 in E. T. Crawford and A. Biderman (eds.) Social Scientists and International Affairs. New York: John Wiley.

CUTRIGHT, Philip (1964) A Pilot Study of Factors in Economic Success or Failure: Based on Selective Service and Social Security Records. Washington, D.C.: U.S. Department of Health, Education and Welfare, Social Security Administration, Division of Research and Statistics (June).

DAUGHERTY, W. E. and Morris JANOWITZ (1956) A Psychological Warfare Casebook. Baltimore: Johns Hopkins Press.

DAVENPORT, Roy K. (1947) "The Negro in the Army: a subject of research." Journal of Social Issues 3: 32-39.

DAVIS, Arthur K. (1948) "Bureaucratic patterns in the Navy officer corps." Social Forces 27 (December): 143-153.

DEMETER, Karl (1965) The German Officer-Corps in Society and State. New York: Frederick A. Praeger.

DEUTSCH, Karl W. (1964) "External involvement in internal war," pp. 100-110 in H. Eckstein (ed.) Internal War. New York: Macmillan.

DICKS, H. V. (1952) "Observations on contemporary Russian behavior." Human Relations 5.

———(1944) The Psychological Foundations of the Wehrmacht. London: Directorate of Army Psychiatry, War Office, D.A.R. (February).

———, Edward A. SHILS, and Herbert S. DINERSTEIN (1951) Service Conditions and Morale in the Soviet Armed Forces. Santa Monica, Calif.: RAND Corporation.

DOLLARD, John (1943) Fear in Battle. New Haven: Institute of Human Relations, Yale University.

DuBOIS, P. H., Jane LOEVINGER, and G. C. GLESER (1952) "The construction of homogeneous keys for a biographical inventory." Research Bulletin 52-18. Lackland AFB, Tex.: Human Resources Research Center, Air Training Command (May).

DUFF, Donald F. and Ransom J. ARTHUR (1967) "Between two worlds: Filipinos in the U.S. Navy." American Journal of Psychiatry 123, 7: 836-843.

DULLES, Allen (1963) The Craft of Intelligence. New York: Harper & Row.

DUNCAN, Otis Dudley and Robert W. HODGE (1964) "Educational and occupational mobility: a regression analysis." American Journal of Sociology (May): 642.

DUNNETTE, M. D., J. P. CAMPBELL, and M. D. HAKEL (1967) "Factors contributing to job satisfaction and job dissatisfaction in six occupational groups." Journal of Organizational Behavior and Human Performance 2: 143-174.

du PICQ, Ardant (1958) Battle Studies: Ancient and Modern. Translated by Col. J. N. Greeley and Maj. R. C. Cotton from the 8th French ed. Harrisburg, Pa.: Military Service Publishing. [Original edition 1880.]

EDINGER, Lewis J. (1963) "Military leaders and foreign policy-making." American Political Science Review 57 (June): 392-405.

EGBERT, R. L. et al. (1957) "Fighter I: an analysis of combat fighters and non-fighters." Technical Report No. 44. Alexandria, Va.: Human Resources Research Office, George Washington University (December).

EILBERT, L. R. and R. GLASER (1959) "Differences between well and poorly adjusted groups in an isolated enviornment." Journal of Applied Psychology 43: 271-274.

ELSON, JoAnn [ed.] (1965) Abstracts of Personnel Research Reports: VI. 1954-1965. Technical Report No. 65-23. Lackland AFB, Tex.: Personnel Research Laboratory, Aerospace Medical Division, Air Force Systems Command (December).

EVANS, James C. and David A. LANE, Jr. (1956) "Integration in the armed services." Annals of the American Academy of Political and Social Science 304: 7-85.

FECHTER, Alan E. (1967) The Supply of First Term Military Officers. Study S-290. Arlington, Va.: Institute for Defense Analyses (March).

———and Bette S. MAHONEY (1967) "The economics of military retirement." Research Paper P-414. Arlington, Va.: Institute for Defense Analyses, Program Analysis Division (July).

FEDOSEYEV, P. (1957) "Sociological theories and the foreign policy of imperialism." International Affairs (Moscow): 10-22.

FEIT, Ewald (1968) "Military coups and political development: some lessons from Ghana and Nigeria." World Politics 20 (January): 179-193.

FELIX, Christopher (1963) A Short Course in the Secret War. New York: Dutton.

FIEDLER, F. E. (1967) A theory of Leadership Effectiveness. New York: McGraw-Hill.

FISHER, Sydney N. [ed.] (1963) The Military in the Middle East. Columbus: Ohio State University Press.

FLANAGAN, J. C. [ed.] (1948) The Aviation Psychology Program in the Army Air Forces. Army Air Forces Aviation Psychology Research Reports. Washington, D.C.: U.S. Government Printing Office.

FLYER, E. S. (1963) "Prediction of unsuitability among first-term airmen from aptitude indexes, high school reference data, and basic training evaluations." Technical Report No. 63-17. Lackland AFB, Tex.: Personnel Research Laboratory, Aerospace Medical Division, Air Force Systems Command.

———and N. R. POTTER (1959) "Characteristics of basic airmen willing to volunteer for a six-year tour in missile squadrons." Technical Note 59-35. Lackland AFB, Tex.: Personnel Laboratory, Wright Air Development Division, Air Research and Development Command.

FRENCH, R. L. (1951) "Sociometric status and individual adjustment among Naval recruits." Journal of Abnormal and Social Psychology 46: 64-72.

FRIEDMAN, Robert P. and Charles LEISTNER [eds.] (1968) "Compulsory service systems—how can the United States best maintain manpower for an effective defense system." The Forensic Quarterly 42 (May, August).

FUCHS, E. F. (1967) "Screening potential enlisted men," pp. 10-18 in J. E. Uhlaner (ed.) Psychological Research in National Defense Today. Technical Report 5-1. Washington, D.C.: U.S. Army Behavioral Sciences Research Laboratory (June).

GAGNE, R. W. [ed.] (1962) Psychological Principles in Systems Development. New York: Holt, Rinehart & Winston.

GARRETT, D. G. (1961) "Retirement experiences and employment status of United States Air Force retired enlisted personnel." Master's thesis. University of New Mexico.

GEORGE, Alexander L. (1967) The Chinese Communist Army in Action: The Korean War and Its Aftermath. New York: Columbia University Press.

GEORGE, C. E. (1962) "Some determinants of small group effectiveness." Research Memorandum No. 26. Fort Benning, Ga.: U.S. Army Infantry Human Research Unit (October).

GINZBERG, Eli et al. (1959) The Ineffective Soldier: The Lost Divisions. New York: Columbia University Press.

———and Douglas W. BRAY (1953) The Uneducated. New York: Columbia University Press.

GLASER, Daniel (1946) "The sentiments of American soldiers abroad toward Europeans." American Journal of Sociology 51: 433-438.

GLASS, Albert J. (1966) "Army Psychiatry before World War II," pp. 3-23 in Neuropsychiatry in World War II. Washington, D.C.: Office of the Surgeon General, Department of the Army.

———et al. (1961) "The current status of army psychiatry." American Journal of Psychiatry 117 (February): 673-683.

———(1956) "Psychiatric prediction and military effectiveness." U.S. Armed Forces Medical Journal 12: 1427-1443.

GOLDWERT, Marvin (1968) "Rise of modern militarism in Argentina." Hispanic American Historical Review 48 (May): 189-205.

GOODACRE, D. M. (1951) "The use of sociometric tests as a predictor of combat effectiveness." Sociometry 14: 148-153.

GORDON, M. A. and R. A. BOTTENBERG (1962) "Prediction of unfavorable discharge by separate educational levels." Technical Report No. 62-5. Lackland AFB, Tex.: Personnel Research Laboratory, Aerospace Medical Division, Air Force Systems Command.

GRAHAM, Hugh D. and Ted R. GURR (1969) Violence in America: Historical and Comparative Perspectives. New York: Bantam Books.

GREER, F. C., W. O. PEARSON and M. D. HAVRON (1957) "Evasion and survival problems and the prediction of crew performance." Technical Report No. 57-14. Lackland AFB, Tex.: Air Force Personnel and Training Research Center, Air Research and Development Command (December).

GRINKER, Roy E. and John SPIEGEL (1945) Men Under Stress. Philadelphia: Blakiston.

GROPPE, L. B., R. W. ALVORD, and J. V. POLAND (1967) "Air Force officer performance evaluation: rating trends and relationships from 1954 through 1965." Technical Report No. 67-12. Lackland AFB, Tex.: Personnel Research Laboratory, Aerospace Medical Division, Air Force Systems Command (October).

GRUNDY, Kenneth W. (1968) "Negative image of Africa's military." Review of Politics 30 (Spring): 28-35.

GRUSKY, O. (1964) "The effects of succession: a comparative study of military and business organization," in M. Janowitz, (ed.) The New Military. New York: Russell Sage Foundation.

GUNDERSON, E. K. E. (1966) "Adaptation to extreme environments." Report 66-17. San Diego, Calif.: Navy Medical Neuropsychiatric Research Unit.

———(1964) "Performance evaluations of Antarctic volunteers." Report 64-19. San Diego, Calif.: Navy Medical Neuropsychiatric Research Unit.

———and E. C. KEPGER (1966) "The predictive validity of clinical ratings for an extreme environment." British Journal of Psychiatry 112: 405-412.

———and P. D. NELSON, (1966) "Personality differences among Navy occupational groups." Personnel Guidance Journal 45: 956-961.

———(1966) "Criterion measures for extremely isolated groups." Personnel Psychology 19: 67-80.

———(1965) "Biographical predictors of performance in an extreme environment." Journal of Psychology 61: 59-67.

———(1965) "Socioeconomic status and Navy occupations." Personnel Guidance Journal 44: 263-266.

———(1962) "Clinical agreement in assessment for an unknown environment." Report 62-4. San Diego, Calif.: Navy Medical Neuropsychiatric Research Unit (April).

GUTTERIDGE, William F. (1965) Military Institutions and Power in the New States. New York: Ferderick A. Praeger.

HAGGIS, Maj. Arthur (1961) "An appraisal of the administration, scope, concept, and function of the U.S. Army troop information program." Ph.D. dissertation. Wayne State University.

HALL, Edward T., Jr. (1947) "Race prejudice and Negro-white relations in the Army." American Journal of Sociology 52: 401-409.

HARE, A. P., E. F. BORGATTA, and R. F. BALES [eds.] (1955) Small Groups. New York: Alfred A. Knopf.

HAUSMAN, William and David M. RIOCH (1967) "Military Psychiatry." Archives of General Psychiatry 16: 727-739.

HAVRON, M.D., R. J. FAY, and J. E. McGRATH (1952) "The effectiveness of small military units." Report No. 980. Washington, D.C.: Personnel Research Section, AGO, Department of the Army.

HAVRON, M.D., F. C. GREER, and E. H. GALANTER (1952) "An interview study of human relationships in an effective infantry rifle squad." Report No. 983. Washington, D.C.: Personnel Research Section, AGO, Department of the Army.

HAYTHORN, W. W. (1968) "The composition of groups: a review of the literature." Acta Psychologica 28: 97-128.

———(1957) "A review of research on group assembly." Technical Note 57-62. Lackland AFB, Tex.: Air Force Personnel and Training Research Center, Air Research and Development Command (May).

HELME, W. H. and A. A. ANDERSON (1964) "Job performance of EM scoring low on AFQT." Technical Report No. 146. Washington, D.C.: U.S. Army Personnel Research Office, Department of the Army.

HEMPHILL, J. K. (1949, 1950) Situational Factors in Leadership. Columbus: Ohio State Personnel Research Board.

HIATT, R. S. (1963) "Consultant or staff officer: a critical analysis of a mental hygiene consultation service innovation." Proceedings, Thirteenth Annual Army Social Work Conference. Social Service Consultant, Office of the Surgeon General, Department of the Army (May) Mimeographed.

HIGGINSON, Thomas W. (1962) Army Life in a Black Regiment. New York: Collier Books.

HIGHAM, R. [ed.] (1969) Bayonets in the Streets: The Use of Troops in Civil Disturbances. Lawrence: University Press of Kansas.

HILL, William G. (1964) "An examination of two approaches for analyzing family group interaction." Proceedings, Fourteenth Annual Military Social Work Conference. Social Service Consultant, Office of the Surgeon General, Department of the Army (May).

HILSMAN, Roger (1967) To Move a Nation. New York: Doubleday.

HOMANS, George C. (1946) "The small warship." American Sociological Review 11: 294-300.

HOPKINS, J. J. (1959) "Behavior trait ratings by peers and references." Technical Report 59-360. Lackland AFB, Tex.: Personnel Laboratory, Wright Air Development Center, Air Force Research and Development Command (December).

HOROWITZ, Irving L. (1967) "The military elites," pp. 146-189 in S. M. Lipset and A. Solari (eds.) Elites in Latin America. New York: Oxford University Press.

———[ed.] (1967) The Rise and Fall of Project Camelot. Cambridge: Massachusetts Institute of Technology.

———(1966) Three Worlds of Development: The Theory and Practice of International Stratification. New York: Oxford University Press.

Human Behavior in Military Society (1946) Special Issue of the American Journal of Sociology 51 (March): 359-508.

HumRRO (1968) Bibliography of Publications as of 30 June 1968. Alexandria, Va.: Human Resources Research Office, George Washington University (September).

HUNT, W. A. (1955) "A rationale for psychiatric selection." American Psychologist 10: 199-204.

———, R. S. HERRMANN, and H. NOBLE, (1957) "The specificity of the psychiatric interview." Journal of Clinical Psychology 13: 49-53.

———, C. L. WITTSON, and H. I. HARRIS (1944) "The screen test in military selection." Psychological Review 11: 37-46.

HUNTER, Floyd A. (1952) Host Community and Air Force Base. Chapel Hill: Institute for Research in Social Science, University of North Carolina. (Springfield, Va.: CFSTI Document 491 624.)

HUNTINGTON, Samuel (1963) "Power expertise and the military profession." Daedalus 92 (Fall).

———(1957) The Soldier and the State. Cambridge: Harvard University Press.

HUREWITZ, J. C. (1969) Middle East Politics: The Military Dimension. New York: Frederick A. Praeger.

HYMAN, H. H. (1953) "The value systems of different classes: a social psychological contribution to the analysis of stratification," in R. Bendix and S. Lipset (eds.) Class, Status, and Power. New York: Free Press.

JANOWITZ, Morris [ed.] (1969) The New Military: Changing Patterns of Organization. New York: W. W. Norton.

———(1968) "Armed forces and society: a world perspective," pp. 15-38 in J. A. A. van Doorn (ed.) Armed Forces and Society: Sociological Essays. The Hague: Mouton.

———(1964) The Role of the Military in Political Developmnt of New Nations. Chicago: University of Chicago Press.

———(1960) The Professional Soldier: A Social and Political Portrait. New York: Free Press.

———(1959) "Changing patterns of organizational authority: the military establishment." Administrative Science Quarterly 3 (March): 473-493.

———(1959) Sociology and the Military Establishment. New York: Russell Sage Foundation.

———(1957) "Military elites and the study of war." Journal of Conflict Resolution 1 (March): 9-18.

———and Roger LITTLE (1965) Sociology and the Military Establishment. New York: Russell Sage Foundation.

JENKINS, J. G. (1948) "Nominating technique as a method of evaluating air groups morale." Journal of Aviation Medicine 19: 12-19.

———, E. S. EWART, and J. B. CARROLL (1950) "The combat criterion in Naval aviation." Report No. 6. Washington, D.C.: National Research Council Committee on Aviation Psychology (January).

JOFFEE, Ellis (1965) Party and Army: Professionalism and Political Control in the Chinese Officer Corps, 1949-1964. Cambridge: Harvard East Asian Monograph No. 19.

JOHNSON, Chalmers (1967) Revolutionary Change. Boston: Little, Brown.

———(1964) Revolution and the Social System. Stanford, Calif.: Hoover Institute Studies.

JOHNSON, John J. (1964) The Military and Society in Latin America. Stanford, Calif.: Stanford University Press.

JOHNSON, L. C. (1967) "Sleep and sleep loss—their effect on performance." Naval Research Review 20: 16-22.

JORDAN, A. (1968) "Army service schools." Encyclopedia Americana.

JORDAN, David (1968) "Civil disturbances: a case study of Task Force Detroit, 1967," in Perspectives in Defense Management. Washington, D.C.: Industrial College of the Armed Forces (August).

KAHN, Herman (1965) On Escalation, Metaphors and Scenarios. New York: Frederick A. Praeger.

KARDINER, Abraham (1941) The Traumatic War Neuroses. Cambridge: Paul B. Hoeber.

KARPINOS, Bernard D. (1968) "Results of the examination of youths for military service, 1967," in Supplement to Health of the Army. Washington, D.C.: U.S. Department of the Army, Office of the Surgeon General, Medical Statistics Agency (December).

———(1967) "Mental test failures," pp. 35-53 in Sol Tax (ed.) The Draft. Chicago: University of Chicago Press.

KATZ, A. and L. K. BURKE (1955) "Prediction of combat effectiveness of officer candidate school graduates." Technical Research Note 50. Washington, D.C.: Personnel Research Branch, AGO, Departmof the Army (November).

KATZENBACH, E. L. (1965) "The demotion of professionalism at the war colleges." Naval Institute Proceedings (March).

KENWORTHY, E. G. (1951) "The case against Army segregation." Annals of the Academy of Political and Social Science 275: 27-33.

KILLIGREW, John W. (1960) "The impact of the great depression on the Army, 1929-1936." Ph.D. dissertation. Indiana University.

KINKEAD, Eugene (1959) In Every War But One. New York: W. W. Norton.

KIRKPATRICK, Lyman (1968) The Real CIA. New York: Macmillan.

KISEL, J. G. (1963) "A conceptual framework for case consultation in the military systems." Proceedings, Thirteenth Annual Army Social Work Conference. Social Service Consultant, Office of the Surgeon General, Department of the Army (May). Mimeographed.

KLASSEN, Albert D., Jr. (1966) Military Service in American Life since World War II: An Overview. Report 117. Chicago: National Opinion Research Center, University of Chicago (September).

KLIEGER, W. A., A. V. DUBUISSON, and J. E. DEJUNG (1961) "Predictions of unacceptable performance in the Army." Technical Research Note 113. Washington, D.C.: Human Factors Research Branch, TAG, Research and Development Command (June).

KOLKOWICZ, Roman (1967) The Soviet Military and the Communist Party. Princeton: Princeton University Press.

KRIS, Ernst and Hans SPEIER (1944) German Radio Propaganda. New York: Oxford University Press.

KUMATA, Hideya and Wilbur SCHRAMM (1955) Four Working Papers on Propaganda Theory. Urbana: University of Illinois Press.

LAMMERS, Cornelius Jacobus (1963) Het Koninklijk Instituut voor de Marine. [In Dutch with English summary; translated title: The Royal Institute of the Navy: A Sociological Analysis of the Socialization of Candidate Officer Groups in the Royal Netherlands Navy.] Amsterdam: Van Gorcum.

LAMPOS, Lt. Col. Nicholas T. (1962) "The retired military executive: his problems in making the transition from a military to a civilian career." Master's thesis. Boston University College of Business Administration.

LANG, Kurt (1969) The Sociology of War: A Selected and Annotated Bibliography. Inter-University Seminar on Armed Forces and Society. Chicago: University of Chicago.

———(1965) "Military organizations," pp. 838-878 in J. G. March (ed.) Handbook of Organizations. Chicago: Rand McNally.

LANIER, D., Jr. (1963) "Mental health education at an Army basic training center—concepts of an operation model." Proceedings, Thirteenth Annual Army Social Work Conference. Social Service Consultant, Office of the Surgeon General, Department of the Army (May). Mimeographed.

LASSWELL, Harold (1951) Politics: Who Gets What, When, How. New York: Free Press.

———(1941) "The garrison state." American Journal of Sociology 46 (January): 455-468.

———and Dorothy BLUMENSTOCK (1939) World Revolutionary Propaganda. New York: Alfred A. Knopf.

LEE, Ulysses G. (1966) The Employment of Negro Troops in World War II. Washington, D.C.: Office of the Chief of Military History, Department of the Army.

LEIBHOLZ, Gerhard (1958) "Aggression im volkerrecth und im bereich ideologischer auseinandersetzungen." Vierteljahreshefte fuer Zeitgeschichte 6: 165-171.

LEIDEN, Carl and Karl M. SCHMITT [eds.] (1968) The Politics of Violence: Revolution in the Modern World. Englewood Cliffs, N.J.: Prentice-Hall.

LEIGHTON, Alexander (1949) Human Relations in a Changing World. New York: Dutton.

LEJINS, Peter B. (1957) "Juvenile delinquency and the armed forces," in Juvenile Delinquency. Report No. 130. U.S. Senate Report, 85th Congress, 1st Session.

LENZ, Allen J. (1967) "Military retirement and income maximization: an examination of the economic incentives to extended military service." Ph.D. dissertation. Stanford University.

LERNER, Daniel and George W. STEWARD (1949) International Communication and Political Opinion: A Guide to the Literature. New York: Princeton University Press.

LEWIS, Noland and Bernice ENGLE (1954) Wartime Psychiatry. New York: Oxford University Press.

LEWIS, Michael A. (1939) England's Sea-Officers: The Story of the Naval Profession. London: Allen & Unwin.

LIEUWIN, Edwin (1964) Generals vs. Presidents. New York: Frederick A. Praeger.

LINDQUIST, Ruth (1952) The Family Life of Officers and Airmen in a Bomb Wing. Chapel Hill: Institute for Research in Social Science, University of North Carolina. (Springfield, Va.: CFSTI Document AD 491 621.)

LINEBARGER, Paul M. A. (1948) Psychological Warfare. Washington, D.C.: Infantry Journal Press.

LISSAK, Moshe (1964) "Modernization and role expansion of the military in developing countries: a comparative analysis." Comparative Studies in Society and History 9 (April): 233-255.

LITTLE, R. W. (1970) "Field Research in Military Organization," in R. W. Habenstein (ed.) Pathways To Data. Chicago: Aldine.

———(1969) "The Dossiers in military organization," in S. Wheeler (ed.) On Record: Files and Dossiers in American Life. New York: Russell Sage Foundation.

———(1968) Selective Service and American Society. New York: Russell Sage Foundation.

———(1964) "Buddy relations and combat performance," pp. 195-224 in M. Janowitz (ed.) The New Military: Changing Patterns of Organization. New York: Russell Sage Foundation.

———(1955) "Solidarity in the mass Army." Combat Forces Journal 5 (February): 26-31.

———(1955) "A study of the relationship between collective solidarity and combat role performance." Ph.D. dissertation. Michigan State University.

LOTT, A. J. and B. E. LOTT (1965) "Group cohesiveness as interpersonal attraction: a review of relationships with antecedent and consequent variables." Psychological Bulletin 64: 259-309. ·

LOWINGER, Paul and Frida HUIGE (1968) "The National Guard in the 1967 Detroit uprising." Detroit: Department of Psychiatry, Wayne State University School of Medicine and Lafayette Clinic. Unpublished.

LOWRY, R. P. (1965) "Changing military roles: neglected challenge to rural sociologists." Rural Sociology 30: 219-225.

LYONS, Gene and John MASLAND (1959) Education and Military Leadership. Princeton: Princeton University Press.

MAAS, Henry [ed.] (1951) Adventure in Mental Health. New York: Columbia University Press.

MAILER, Norman (1968) "The steps of the Pentagon." Harper's 237 (March) 47-80 ff.

MANDELBAUM, David G. (1952) Soldier Groups and Negro Soldiers. Berkeley: University of California Press.

MARLOWE, David H. (1959) "The basic training process," pp. 75-98 in K. L. Artiss (ed.) The Symptom as Communication in Schizophrenia. New York: Grune & Stratton.

MARSHALL, S. L. A. (1947) Men Against Fire. New York: William Morrow.

MASLAND, John and Laurence RADWAY (1957) Soldiers and Scholars. Princeton: Princeton University Press.

MASSEY, R. J. (1963) "A survey study of the integration of retired Naval Academy graduates into the national economy." Unpublished report. Armed Forces Management Association.

MATHEWS, J. (1951) "Research on the development of valid situational tests of leadership." Report No. 912. Washington, D.C.: Personnel Research Section, AGO, Department of the Army.

MAZRUI, Ali A. (1968) "Anti-militarism and political militancy in Tanzania." Journal of Conflict Resolution 12 (September): 269-284.

———and D. S. ROTHCHILD (1967) "Soldier and the state in East Africa: some theoretical conclusions on the Army mutinies of 1964." Western Political Quarterly 20 (March): 82-96.

McCRARY, John W. (1967) "Human factors in the operation of U.S. military units augmented with indigenous troops." Professional Paper 48-67. Alexandria, Va.: George Washington University, Human Resources Research Office (November).

McNEIL, Maj. John S. and Col. Martin B. GIFFEN (1967) "Military retirement: the retirement syndrome." American Journal of Psychiatry 123 (January): 848-854.

MEDLAND F. F. and J. L. OLANS, (1964) "Peer rating stability in changing groups." Research Note 142. Washington, D.C.: U.S. Army Personnel Research Office.

MERTON, Robert K. and Paul F. LAZARSFELD [eds.] (1950) Studies in the Scope and Method of "The American Soldier." New York: Free Press.

MEYERS, Samuel M. and Albert D. BIDERMAN [eds.] (1968) Mass Behavior in Battle and Captivity: The Communist Soldier in the Korean War. Chicago: University of Chicago Press.

MILLIS, Walter and James REAL (1963) The Abolition of War. New York: Macmillan.

MILLS, C. Wright (1956) The Power Elite. New York: Oxford University Press.

MIRA, Emilio (1943) Psychiatry in War. New York: W. W. Norton.

MONTALVO, Frank F. (1964) "Homeostasis in functional and dysfunctional family systems." Proceeding s, Fourteenth Annual Military Social Work Conference, Social Service Consultant, Office of the Surgeon General, Department of the Army (May).

MORGAN, R. (1961) "Clinical social work in the U.S. Army, 1947-1959." Ph.D. dissertation. Washington, D.C.: Catholic University of America.

———(1953) "Psychiatric social work in a combat area." U.S. Armed Forces Medical Journal 4 (June): 847-856.

MORSH, J. R., Job Analysis Bibliography. Technical Report 62-2. Lackland AFB, Tex.: Personnel Research Laboratory, Aerospace Medical Division, Air Force Systems Command (March).

MOSKOS, Charles C., Jr. (1969) "Racial relations in the armed forces," in C. C. Moskos, Jr. (ed.) The American Enlisted Man. New York: Russell Sage Foundation.

———(1968) "Personal remarks on sociological research in the third world." Behavioral Scientist 12: 26-30.

———(1967) The Sociology of Political Independence. Cambridge: Schenkman.

———(1967) "A sociologist appraises the G.I." New York Times Magazine (September 24).

———(1966) "Racial integration in the armed forces." American Journal of Sociology 72: 132-148.

———(1957) "Has the Army killed Jim Crow?" Negro History Bulletin (November): 27-29.

MUELLER, William R. (1945) "The Negro in the Navy." Social Forces 24: 110-115.

National Analysts, Inc. (1968) "A study of military attitudes among Negro males—16 to 25 years of age, nationally and in Camden, New Jersey." Philadelphia: (February) Mimeographed.

NELSON, Dennis D. (1956) The Integration of the Negro into the U.S. Navy. New York: Farrar, Straus, & Young.

NELSON, Paul D. (1965) "Psychological aspects of Antarctic living." Military Medicine 130: 485-489.

———and Newell H. BERRY (1966) "Dimensions of peer and supervisor ratings in a military setting." Report 66-1. San Diego, Calif.: Navy Medical Neuropsychiatric Research Unit.

———(1968) "Cohesion in Marine recruit platoons." Journal of Psychology 68: 63-71.

———(1965) "The relationship between an individual's sociometric status in different groups over a two-year period." Journal of Psychology 60: 31-37.

NEY, V. (1961) Notes on Guerrilla Warfare. Washington, D.C.: Command Publications.

NICHOLS, Lee (1954) Breakthrough on the Color Front. New York: Random House.

NORTH, Liisa (1966) Civil-Military Relations in Argentina, Chile, and Peru. Berkeley, Calif.: Institute of International Studies, University of California.

OI, Walter Y. (1967) "The economic cost of the draft," in Papers and Proceedings of the Seventy-Ninth Annual Meeting of the American Economic Association. American Economic Review 57 (May): 19-31.

O'KEEFE, Daniel E. (1966) "Psychiatric social work," pp. 605-630 in Neuropsychiatry in World War II. Office of the Surgeon General, Department of the Army.

Operations Research Office (1955) Project Clear: The Utilization of Negro Manpower in the Army. Chevy Chase, Md.: Johns Hopkins University (April).

ORLOV, A. (1963) Handbook of Intelligence and Guerrilla Warfare. Ann Arbor: University of Michigan Press.

OSANKA, Franklin M. (1962) "Internal warfare: guerrilla warfare." International Encyclopedia of the Social Sciences 7: 503-507.

——— [ed.] (1962) Modern Guerrilla Warfare. New York: Free Press.

O.S.S. Assessment Staff (1948) Assessment of Men. New York: Rinehart.

PAGE, Charles H. (1946) "Bureaucracy's other face." Social Forces 25 (October): 88-94.

PARET, Peter (1968) French Revolutionary Warfare from Indo-China to Algeria. New York: Frederick A. Praeger.

PARKS, David (1968) G.I. Diary. New York: Harper & Row.

Personal Response Project (1967) Assessment of Attitudes Between USMC Personnel and Civilian Workers Employed on U.S. Bases in Japan, Okinawa, and Vietnam. Fleet Marine Force, Pacific (Forward), mimeographed (July).

PIKE, Dolas (1966) Viet Cong. Cambridge: MIT Press.

PIPPING, K. (1947) "The social life of a machine gun company." Acta Academiae Aboensis Humaniora 17. [English summary.]

PLAG, J. A. (1964) "The practical value of a psychiatric screening interview in predicting military effectiveness." Report No. 64-7. San Diego, Calif.: Navy Medical Neuropsychiatric Research Unit.

———and R. J. ARTHUR (1965) "Psychiatric re-examination of unsuitable Naval recruits: a two-year follow-up." American Journal of Psychiatry 122: 534-541.

———and J. M. GOFFMAN (1967) "The armed forces qualification test: its validity in predicting military effectiveness." Personnel Psychology 20: 323-340.

———(1967) "Dimensions of psychiatric illness among first-term Naval enlistees." Report No. 67-27. San Diego, Calif.: Navy Medical Neuropsychiatric Research Unit.

———(1966) "A formula for predicting effectiveness in the Navy from characteristics of high school students." Psychology in the Schools 3: 216-221.

———(1966) "The prediction of four-year effectiveness among Naval recruits." Military Medicine 131: 729-735.

POOL, Ithiel de Sola et al. (1955) The Satellite Generals: A Study of Military Elites in the Soviet Sphere. Stanford: Stanford University Press.

PROXMIRE, William B. (1969) "Over 2,000 retired high ranking military officers now employed by 100 largest military contractors." Congressional Record S3072-3081 (March 24).

PUSTAY, John S. (1965) Counterinsurgency Warfare. New York: Free Press.

PYE, Lucian W. (1956) Guerrilla Communism in Malaya. Princeton: Princeton University Press.

RADLOFF, R. and R. HELMREICH (1968) Groups Under Stress. New York: Appleton-Century-Crofts.

RAHE, R. H., J. D. McKEAN, and R. J. ARTHUR (1967) "A longitudinal study of life-change and illness patterns." Report No. 67-1. San Diego, Calif.: Navy Medical Neuropsychiatric Research Unit.

RAINES, G. N. et al. (1954) "Psychiatric selection for military service." Journal of the American Medical Association 156: 817-821.

RANSOM, Harry H. (1959) Central Intelligence and National Security. Cambridge: Harvard University Press.

RICH, Milton B. (1941) The Presidents and Civil Disorder. Washington, D.C.: Brookings Institution.

RIESSMAN, Leonard (1956) "Life careers, power, and the Professions: the retired Army general." American Sociological Review 21 (April): 215-221.

ROBY, T. B. (1954) "An empirical evaluation of work partner choices after limited contact." Technical Report 54-69. Lackland AFB, Tex.: Air Force Personnel and Training Research Center, Air Research and Development Command (December).

ROSE, Arnold M. (1956) "Psychoneurotic breakdown among Negro soldiers." Phylon 17: 61-73.

———(1947) "Army policies toward Negro soldiers—a report on a success and a failure." Journal of Social Issues 3: 26-31.

ROUCEK, J. (1962) "Sociological elements of a theory of terror and violence." American Journal of Economics and Sociology 21: 165-172.

SCHEIPS, Paul J. (1969) "Darkness and light: the interwar years 1865-1898," in M. Matloffle, American Military History. Washington, D.C.: Army Historical Series.

———(1969) "Enforcement of federal judicial process by federal marshals: a comparison of Little Rock and Oxford," in R. Higham (ed.) Bayonets in the Streets: The Use of Troops in Civil Disturbances. Lawrence: University Press of Kansas.

SCHELLING, Thomas C. (1962) "A special surveillance force," pp. 87-105 in I. Wright, W. M. Evan, and D. Morton (eds.) Preventing World War III. New York: Simon & Schuster.

SELLS, S. B. [ed.] (1961) Proceedings: Tri-Service Conference on Research Relevant to Problems of Small Military Groups under Isolation and Stress. Air Force Contract 41(657)-323. Fort Worth: Texas Christian University (March).

———and D. J. MACE (1963) "Prediction of Air Force adaptability of basic airmen referred for psychiatric evaluation." Technical Report 63-23. Lackland AFB, Tex.: Personnel Research Laboratory, Aerospace Medical Division, Air Force Systems Command (September).

SELZNICK, Philip (1960) The Organizational Weapon. New York: Free Press.

SHARP, Laure and Albert D. BIDERMAN (1966) The Employment of Retired Military Personnel. Washington, D.C.: Bureau of Social Science Research, Inc.

SHARTLE, C. L. and R. M. STOGDILL (1952) Studies in Naval Leadership. Columbus: Ohio State University Research Foundation.

SHELBURNE, James and Kenneth GROVES (1965) Education in the Armed Forces. New York: Center for Applied Research in Education.

———and L. BROKAW (1967) "Military education," in Encyclopedia of Educational Research, American Educational Research Association.

SHELLASE, Leslie (n.d.) "Bibliography of social work," in The First Twenty Years, 1942-1962, Social Service Consultant, Office of the Surgeon General, Department of the Army.

SHILS, Edward A. (1950) "Primary groups in the American Army," pp. 16-39 in R. K. Merton and P. F. Lazarsfeld (eds.) Studies in the Scope and Method of "The American Soldier." New York: Free Press.

———and M. JANOWITZ (1948) "Cohesion and disintegration in the Wehrmacht in World War II." Public Opinion Quarterly 12 (Summer): 280-315.

SHOENBERGER, R. W., R. J. WHERRY, Jr., and J. R. BERKSHIRE (1963) "Predicting success in aviation training." Research Report No. 7. Pensacola, Fla.: Naval School of Aviation Medicine, Naval Aviation Medical Center (September).

SIMONS, William E. (1965) Liberal Education in the Service Academies. New York: Bureau of Publications, Teachers College, Columbia University.

SLADEN, F. S. [ed.] (1943) Psychiatry and the War. Springfield, Ill.: Charles C. Thomas.

SMITH, T. H., C. D. GOTT, and R. A. BOTTENBERG (1967) "Predicting the potential for active duty success of rehabilitated Air Force prisoners." Technical Report 67-16. Lackland AFB, Tex.: Personnel Research Laboratory, Aerospace Medical Division, Air Force Systems Command (October).

SPEIER, Hans (1952) Social Order and the Risks of War. New York: George W. Stewart.

STARKS, Leslie E. (1952) "Development of the social service program," in Symposium on Military Social Work. Social Services Branch, Office of the Surgeon General, Department of the Army (May). Mimeographed.

STILLMAN, Richard J., III (1968) Integration of the Negro in the U.S. Armed Forces. New York: Frederick A. Praeger.

STOCKSTILL, Louis and James HESSMAN (1968) "Modernizing military pay." Journal of the Armed Forces 105 (May): 2 ff.

STOLZ, L. M. (1954) et al. Father Relations of War-Born Children. Stanford: Stanford University Press.

STOUFFER, Samuel A. et al. (1949) The American Soldier. 4 vols. Princeton: Princeton University Press.

TANTER, Raymond (1966) "Dimensions of conflict behavior within and between nations, 1958-1960." Journal of Conflict Resolution 10 (March): 41-65.

TAX, Sol [ed.] (1967) The Draft—A Handbook of Facts and Alternatives. Chicago: University of Chicago Press.

THOMPSON, James D. (1956) "Authority and power in 'identical' organizations." American Journal of Sociology 62 (November): 290-301.

THOMSON, Charles A. H. (1948) Overseas Information Service of the U.S. Government. Washington, D.C.: Brookings Institution.

TORGERSON, F. G. (1962) "Annual report of the Social Service Consultant." Proceedings, Twenty Years of Army Social Work. Social Service Consultant, Office of the Surgeon General, Department of the Army. Mimeographed.

———(1960) Collected Papers from a Short Course on Current Trends in Army Social Work. Washington, D.C.: Walter Reed Army Institute of Research, Walter Reed Army Medical Center (November).

———(1956) "A historical study of the beginnings of individualized social services in the United States Army." Ph.D. dissertation. School of Social Work, University of Minnesota.

TORRANCE, E. P. (1957) "What happens to the sociometric structure of small groups in emergencies and extreme conditions?" Group Psychotherapy 10 (September): 212-220.

———(1954) "The development of a preliminary life experience inventory for the study of fighter interceptor pilot combat effectiveness." Technical Report 54-89. Lackland AFB, Tex.: Air Force Personnel and Training Research Center, Air Research and Development Command (December).

TUPES, E. C. (1969) "Attitude research in the U.S. Air Force," in Manpower Research in the Defense Context (NATO Conference Proceedings). London: English Universities Press.

———and R. C. CHRISTAL (1968) "Stability of personality trait rating factors obtained under diverse conditions." Technical Note 58-61. Lackland AFB, Tex.: Personnel Laboratory, Wright Air Development Center, Air Research and Development Command (May).

TURNER, Ralph H. (1947) "The Naval disbursing officer as a bureaucrat." American Sociological Review 12 (June): 342-348.

UHLANER, J. E. [ed.] (1967) Psychological Research in National Defense Today. Washington, D.C.: U.S. Army Behavioral Sciences Research Laboratory (June).

———(1968) "The research psychologist in the Army—1917-1967." Technical Research Report No. 13. Pensacola, Fla.: Naval School of Aviation Medicine, Naval Aviation Medical Center (November).

U.S. Advisory Committee on Non-Military Instruction [Karl R. Benetsen, chairman] (1962) Report. Washington, D.C.: Secretary of Defense (July 20).

———(1962) Staff papers. Washington, D.C.: Secretary of Defense (July 20).

U.S. Arms Control and Disarmament Agency, Economics Bureau (1968) World Military Expenditures and Related Data. Research Report 68-52. Washington, D.C.: U.S. Government Printing Office.

U.S. Bureau of the Census (1960) Historical Statistics of the United States, Colonial Times to 1957. Washington, D.C.: U.S. Government Printing Office.

U.S. Chamberlin Board (1950) Report of Board of Officers on Utilization of Negro Manpower in the Army (February 9).

U.S. Civil Service Commission (1966) "Report on the survey of retired members of uniformed services, June-July, 1966." United States Senate Committee on Post Office and Civil Service, November.

———(1965) Report on the Operations of the Executive Branch Under Title II of the Dual Compensation Act.

U.S. Commission on Civil Rights [Hannah Commission] (1963) "The Negro in the armed forces," pp. 169-224 in Civil Rights '63. Washington, D.C.: U.S. Government Priting Office.

U.S. Congress, House Committee on Armed Services (1967) Special Subcommittee on Service Academies, Report and Hearings, 90th Congress, 1st and 2nd Sessions.

———(1960) Subcommittee for Special Investigations of the Committee on Armed Services, Employment of Retired Commissioned Officers by Defense Department Contractors. 86th Congress, 1st Session. Washington, D.C.: U.S. Government Printing Office.

———(1959) Hearings Before thy Subcommittee for Special Investigations of the Committee on Armed Services, Retired Military and Civilian Personnel by Defense Industries. 86th Congress, 1st Session. Washington, D.C.: U.S. Government Printing Office.

U.S. Congress, Senate (1967) Federal Staff Retirement Systems. Senate Document No. 14, 90th Congress., 1st Session. Washington, D.C.: U.S. Government Printing Office.

———(1962) Committee on Armed Services, Cold War Education and Speech Review Policies. Hearings before the Special Preparedness Committee of the Committee on Armed Services, 87th Congress, 2nd Session.

———(1961) Committee on Armed Services, A Study of the Military Retired Pay System and Certain Related Subjects. 87th Congress, 1st Session. Washington, D.C.: U.S. Government Printing Office.

———(1961) Hearings Before the Subcommittee of the Committee on Appropriations, H.R. 7851, Making Appropriations for the DepartmenDeense for the Fiscal Year Ending June 30, 1962. 87th Congress, 1st Session. Washington, D.C.: U.S. Government Printing Office.

———(1961) Senator William Fulbright Memorandum on "Propaganda activities of military personnel directed at the public." Congressional Record (August 2).

U.S. Department of the Air Force (1957) Air Force Guide for Retirement. AFP 34-4-3 (January 31).

U.S. Department of the Army (1965) Retired Army Personnel Handbook. Pamphlet No. 600-5. Washington, D.C.: Headquarters, Department of the Army (March).

U.S. Department of the Army, Office of the Chief of Research and Development (1965) Marginal Man and Military Service. Washington, D.C.: U.S. Government Printing Office (December).

U.S. Department of the Army, Social Service Consultant (1955-1960) Proceedings, Annual MilitarySocial Work Conferences.

U.S. Department of Defense, Office of the Assistant Secretary of Defense, Manpower and Reserve Affairs (1969) "Modernizing military pay." Report prepared by the Retirement Study Group, Compensation and Career Development Directorate.

———(1964) "Medical care for retired military personnel and their dependents." Unpublished report to the Secretary of Defense by the Defense Study Group on Health Care for Retired Personnel and Their Dependents.

U.S. Department of Defense (1961) Teaching as a Second Career. DOD PAM 7-10. Washington, D.C.: Office of Armed Forces Information and Education (May 3).

U.S. Department of Defense, Office of the Secretary of Defense (1966) Officer Education Study, Vols. I, II, III. OSD/Manpower.

———(1955) POW ... The Fight Continues After the Battle. Washington, D.C.: Advisory Committee on Prisoners of War.

———(1951) Report of the Working Group on Human Behavior Under Conditions of Military Service. A Joint Project of the Research and Development Board and the Personnel Policy Board in the Office of the Secretary of Defense, Washington, D.C.

U.S. Department of Labor and the Air Force Association (1963) Proceedings: The First National Conference on the Utilization of Retired Military Personnel. Washington, D.C.: Air Force Association.

U.S. Department of the Navy Bureau of Naval Personnel (1963) BUPERS Abstracts of Research Reports. Bureau of Naval Personnel Technical Bulletin 63-8. Washington, D.C.: Department of the Navy (August).

U.S. Department of the Navy, Office of Naval Research (1961) "Occupational analysis: one route to improved selection procedures and better utilization of available talent" (by R. E. Christal), pp. 49-55 in Proceedings: Tri-Service Conference on Selection Research. Washington, D.C.: Department of the Navy (October).

———(1961) "Theoretical considerations in the development and use of a non-cognitive battery" (by A. S. Glickman and D. Kipnis), pp. 9-34 in Proceedings: Tri-Service Conference on Selection Research. Washington, D.C.: Department of the Navy (October).

U.S. National Advisory Commission on Civil Disorders (1968) Report. Washington, D.C. (March 1).

U.S. National Advisory Commission on Selective Service (1967) In Pursuit of Equity: Who Serves When Not All Serve? Washington, D.C.: U.S. Government Printing Office.

U.S. President's Commission on an All-Volunteer Armed Force (1970) Report. Washington, D.C.: U.S. Government Printing Office.

U.S. President's Committee on Equal Opportunity in the Armed Forces [Gesell Committee] (1963) Initial Report: Equality of Treatment and Opportunity for Negro Personnel Stationed within the United States. (June). Mimeographed.

———(1964) Final Report: Military Personnel Stationed Overseas and Membership and Participation in the National Guard. (November). Mimeographed.

U.S. President's Committee on Equality of Treatment and Opportunity in the Armed Forces [Fahy Committee] (1950) Freedom to Serve: Equality of Treatment and Opportunity in the Armed Forces. Washington, D.C.: U.S. Government Printing Office.

U.S. President's Committee on Religion and Welfare in the Armed Forces [Frank L. Weil, chairman] (1949) Report of Committee on Information and Education in the Armed Forces. Washington, D.C. (December 1).

VAGTS, Alfred (1937) A History of Militarism. New York: W. W. Norton.

VAN DOORN, Jacques A. A. (1969) Military Professionalism and Military Regimes. The Hague: Mouton.

———[ed.] (1968) Armed Forces and Society: Sociological Essays. The Hague: Mouton.

———(1956) Sociologie van de organisatie: beschouwingen over organiseren in het bijzonder gebaseerd op een onderzoek van het militaire system. Leiden: H. E. Stenfert Kroese.

VATIKIOTIS, Panayiotis J. (1967) Politics and the Military in Jordan: The Arab Legion, 1921-1957. New York: Frederick A. Praeger.

WATSON, J. H. (1963) "A study of social and occupational adjustment in relation to civilian and military identification of United States Air Force retired officers." Ph.D. dissertation. State College, Mississippi.

WEIL, Frank E. G. (1947) "The Negro in the armed forces." Social Forces 26: 95-98.

WHERRY, R. J., Jr., N. E. STANDU, and E. C. TUPES (1957) "Relationship between behavior trait ratings by peers and later officer performance of USAF OCS graduates." Technical Note 57-125. Lackland AFB, Tex.: Air Force Personnel and Training Research Center, Air Research and Development Command (October).

WICKENDEN, Elizabeth (1955) Military Defense and Social Welfare. New York: National Association of Social Workers (November).

WILKINS, W. F. (1969) "Attitudes and values as predictors of military performance," in Manpower Research in the Defense Context (NATO Conference Proceedings). London: English Universities Press.

———(1954) "The selection of Marine Corps platoon leaders." United States Armed Forces Medical Journal 5: 1184-1191.

WILLIAMS, Richard H. (1954) Human Factors in Military Operations: Some Applications of the Social Sciences to Operations Research. Technical Memorandum ORO-T-259. Chevy Chase, Md.: Operations Research Office.

WOOL, Harold (1968) The Military Specialist: Skilled Manpower for the Armed Forces. Baltimore: Johns Hopkins Press.

WRIGHT, G. (1962) "Reflections on the French resistance." Political Science Quarterly 77: 336-349.

YERKES, R. M. [ed.] (1921) Psychological Examining in the United States Army. Vol. XV. (Memoirs of the National Academy of Sciences). Washington, D.C.: U.S. Government Printing Office.

ZASLOFF, J. J. (1968) Political Motivation of the Viet Cong: The Vietminh Regroupees. Memorandum RM-4703/2-ISA/ARPA. Santa Monica, Calif.: RAND Corporation (May). [Original edition August 1966.]

ZAWODNY, J. K. [ed.] (1962) "Unconventional warfare." Annals of the American Academy of Political and Social Sciences 341: 1-107.

———(1960) "Unexplored realms of underground strife." American Behavioral Scientist 4: 3-5.

APPENDIXES

Department of Defense

PERSONNEL SUMMARY

ACTIVE DUTY MILITARY PERSONNEL 31 December 1969

	Total Dept of Defense	Army	Navy	Marine Corps	Air Force
TOTAL	3,297,888	1,431,839	721,707	301,675	842,667
Officer	407,952	167,556	81,183	25,217	133,996
Enlisted	2,876,679	1,260,528	634,772	276,458	704,921
Officer Candidates	13,257	3,755	5,752	–	3,750

CIVILIAN PERSONNEL 31 December 1969

	Total Dept of Defense	OSD-JCS	Army	Navy (Incl. Marine Corps)	Air Force	Other Defense Agencies
TOTAL	1,371,317	2,391	541,450	415,183	345,124	67,169
Direct Hire	1,262,801	2,391	469,297	402,108	321,849	67,156
Indirect Hire	108,516	–	72,153	13,075	23,275	13

NATIONAL GUARD AND RESERVES 31 December 1969

	Total Dept of Defense	Army	Navy	Marine Corps	Air Force
TOTAL	3,414,239	2,080,721	554,641	217,586	561,291
In Paid Status	(1,007,686)	(700,328)	(126,569	(48,946)	(131,843)
National Guard	479,627	394,776	–	–	84,851
In Paid Status	(478,310)	(393,459)	–	–	(84,851)
Reserves	2,934,612	1,685,945	554,641	217,586	476,440
In Paid Status	(529,376)	(306,869)	(126,569)	(48,946)	(46,992)

OFFICER TRAINING IN COLLEGES October 1969

	Total Dept Def	Army	Navy	Air Force
Reserve Officers' Training Corps	161,507[a]	115,266	8,876	37,365

a. Excludes 137,594 in Junior Division, Military Schools and National Defense Cadets Corps.

565

Department of Defense

TOTAL ACTIVE DUTY MILITARY PERSONNEL 1916-1969[a]

	Total Dept of Defense	Total War Dept.	Army and Air Force		Navy (Excluding Coast Guard)	Marine Corps
			Army[b]	Air Force[b c]		
30 Jun 1916	179,376	108,339	Reliable		60,376	10,601
30 Jun 1917	643,833	421,467	data not		194,617	27,749
30 Jun 1918	2,897,167	2,395,742	available		448,606	52,819
11 Nov 1918	4,315,239f	3,711,504f	(3,516,481)	(195,023)g	530,338f	73,397
30 Jun 1920	343,302	204,292	(195,242)	(9,050)g	121,845	17,165
30 Jun 1923	247,011	133,243g	(123,802)	(9,441)	94,094	19,674
30 Jun 1932	244,902	134,957	(119,929)g	(15,028)	93,384	16,561
30 Jun 1933	243,845g	136,547	(121,448)	(15,099)	91,230g	16,068g
30 Jun 1935	251,799	139,486	(123,239)	(16,247)	95,053	17,260
30 Jun 1936	291,356	167,816	(150,583)	(17,233)	106,292	17,248
30 Jun 1937	311,808	179,968	(160,821)	(19,147)	113,617	18,223
30 Jun 1938	322,932	185,488	(164,399)	(21,089)	119,088	18,356
30 Jun 1939	334,473	189,839	(166,384)	(23,455)	125,202	19,432
30 Jun 1940	458,365	269,023	(217,858)	(51,165)	160,997	28,345
30 Jun 1941	1,801,101	1,462,315	(1,310,190)	(152,125)	284,427	54,359
31 Dec 1941	2,149,157	1,688,271	(1,334,110)	(354,161)	383,150	77,736
30 Jun 1942	3,858,791	3,075,608	(2,311,193)	(764,415)	640,570	142,613
30 Jun 1943	9,044,745	6,994,472	(4,797,358)	(2,197,114)	1,741,750	308,523
31 Mar 1944	10,868,226	7,759,995	(5,348,701)	(2,411,294)h	2,668,754	439,477
30 Jun 1944	11,451,719	7,994,750	(5,622,458)	(2,372,292)	2,981,365	475,604
31 May 1945	12,124,418h	8,293,766h	(5,983,330)	(2,310,436)	3,359,283	471,369
30 Jun 1945	12,123,455	8,267,958	(5,985,699)h	(2,282,259)	3,380,817	474,680
31 Jul 1945	12,076,047	8,188,924	(5,926,832)	(2,262,092)	3,405,525h	481,598
31 Aug 1945	11,913,639	8,025,726	(5,772,544)	(2,253,182)	3,402,800	485,113h
30 Jun 1946	3,030,088	1,891,011	(1,435,496)	(455,515)	983,398	155,679
31 May 1947	1,626,130	1,022,807	(719,193)	(303,614)i	509,098	94,225
30 Jun 1947	1,582,999	991,285	(685,458)	(305,827)	498,661	93,053
31 Mar 1948	1,398,726i	d	539,998i	368,348	409,966	80,414
30 Jun 1948	1,445,910	d	554,030	387,730	419,162	84,988
30 Jun 1949	1,615,360	d	660,473	419,347	449,575	85,965

Date	Total					
31 May 1950	1,459,395	d	595,905	408,844	379,930i	74,716
30 Jun 1950	1,460,261	d	593,167	411,277	381,538	74,279i
30 Jun 1951	3,249,455	d	1,531,774	788,381	736,680	192,620
31 Mar 1952	3,674,874	d	1,668,579j	952,706	810,153	243,436
30 Apr 1952	3,685,054j	d	1,658,084	971,017e	813,936	242,017
30 Jun 1952	3,635,912	d	1,596,419	983,261ej	824,265j	231,967
31 Jan 1953	3,512,949	d	1,508,058	958,709	808,604	237,578
30 Jun 1953	3,555,067	d	1,533,815	977,593	794,440	249,219j
30 Jun 1954	3,302,104	d	1,404,598	947,918	725,720	223,868
30 Jun 1955	2,935,107	d	1,109,296	959,946	660,695	205,170
30 Jun 1956	2,806,441	d	1,025,778	909,958	669,925	200,780
30 Jun 1957	2,795,798	d	997,994	919,835	677,108	200,861
30 Jun 1958	2,600,581	d	898,925	871,156	641,005	189,495
30 Jun 1959	2,504,310	d	861,964	840,435	626,340	175,571
31 Dec 1959	2,487,096	d	876,258	829,422	610,644k	170,772
31 May 1960	2,465,065k	d	868,116	814,153	611,500	171,296
30 Jun 1960	2,476,435	d	873,078	814,752	617,984	170,621k
31 Dec 1960	2,494,136	d	876,662	810,823k	630,311	176,340
31 May 1961	2,473,350	d	856,233k	819,410	621,135	176,572
30 Jun 1961	2,483,771	d	858,622	821,151	627,089	176,909
30 Jun 1962	2,807,819	d	1,066,404	884,025	666,428	190,962
30 Jun 1963	2,699,677	d	975,916	869,431	664,647	189,683
30 Jun 1964	2,687,409	d	973,238	856,798	667,596	189,777
30 Jun 1965	2,655,389	d	969,066	824,662	671,448	190,213
30 Jun 1966	3,094,058	d	1,199,784	887,353	745,205	261,716
30 Jun 1967	3,376,880	d	1,442,498	497,494	751,619	285,269
30 Jun 1968	3,547,902	d	1,570,343	904,850	765,457	307,252
30 Jun 1969	3,460,162	d	1,512,169	862,353	775,869	309,771

a. All military personnel on extended or continuous active duty. Data include special categories of such personnel, as follows: Nurses, retired personnel, Navy and Marine Corps Reservists associated with Reserve Activities, and officer candidates. Excludes Reserves on Active Duty for Training.

b. Represents "Command Strength" prior to 30 June 1956.

c. Army Air Forces and its predecessors for period prior to 18 Sept. 1947.

d. War Department abolished effective 18 Sept. 1947.

e. Includes Army personnel in training for SCARWAF duty.

f. Approximately WW-I peak.

g. Approximately low point between WW-I and WW-II.

h. WW-II peak.

i. Post WW-II low.

j. Korean War peak.

k. Post Korean War low.

Department of Defense

MILITARY PERSONNEL ON ACTIVE DUTY BY GRADE IN WHICH SERVING

31 December 1969

	Total Dept Def	Army	Navy	Marine Corps	Air Force
TOTAL	3,297,888	1,431,839	721,707	301,675*	842,667
Officers – Total	407,952	167,556	81,183	25,217	133,996
Gen of Army – Fleet Adm	1	1	–	–	–
General – Admiral	40	17	8	2	13
Lt. General – Vice Adm	142	47	42	9	44
Maj Gen ⎱ – Rear Adm	1,156	195 ⎱ 261		28	156
Brig Gen ⎰		253 ⎰		39	224
Colonel – Captain	18,181	6,319	4,455	717	6,690
Lt. Colonel – Commander	43,993	16,469	9,098	2,008	16,418
Major – Lt. Cmdr	69,987	24,220	13,740	3,873	28,154
Captain – Lieut	116,859	42,669	22,232	6,645	45,313
1st Lieut – Lieut (JG)	67,917	22,589	17,875	6,469	20,984
2nd Lieut – Ensign	58,893	30,637	8,889	4,174	15,193
Chief Warrant Officer W-4	3,182	1,755	531	91	805
Chief Warrant Officer W-3	3,428	3,236	50	140	2
Chief Warrant Officer W-2	14,626	11,674	2,196	756	–
Warrant Officer W-1	9,547	7,475	1,806	266	–
Enlisted – Total	2,876,679	1,260,528	634,772	276,458	704,921
E-9	16,687	5,195	3,511	1,174	6,807
E-8	44,909	17,685	9,377	4,117	13,730
E-7	157,906	59,567	42,335	9,047	46,957
E-6	291,695	105,387	81,020	16,076	89,212
E-5	495,548	204,472	103,498	34,891	152,687
E-4	710,815	343,235	139,888	50,109	177,583
E-3	521,793	170,727	141,675	54,893	154,498
E-2	371,815	171,066	93,588	54,518	52,643
E-1	265,511	183,194	19,880	51,633	10,804
Officer Candidates – Total	13,257	3,755	5,752	–	3,750
Cadets USMA	3,755	3,755	–	–	–
Midshipmen USNA	4,148	–	4,148	–	–
Cadets USAFA	3,750	–	–	–	3,750
Naval Enlisted Off. Cand.	1,604	–	1,604	–	–

*Revised

568

Department of Defense

GRADE TITLES OF ENLISTED PERSONNEL

Pay Grade	Army NCOs	Army Specialists[a]	Navy[b]	Marine Corps	Air Force
E-9	Sergeant Major		Master Chief Petty Officer	Sergeant Major; Master Gunnery Sergeant	Chief Master Sergeant
E-8	Master Sergeant; First Sergeant		Senior Chief Petty Officer	First Sergeant; Master Sergeant	Senior Master Sergeant
E-7	Platoon Sergeant; Sergeant First Class	Specialist 7	Chief Petty Officer	Gunnery Sergeant	Master Sergeant
E-6	Staff Sergeant	Specialist 6	Petty Officer, 1st Class	Staff Sergeant	Technical Sergeant
E-5	Sergeant	Specialist 5	Petty Officer, 2nd Class	Sergeant	Staff Sergeant
E-4	Corporal	Specialist 4	Petty Officer, 3rd Class	Corporal	Sergeant
E-3	Private First Class		Seaman[c]	Lance Corporal	Airman First Class
E-2	Private		Seaman Apprentice[d]	Private First Class	Airman
E-1	Private E-1		Seaman Recruit[d]	Private	Airman Basic

a. For rank and precedence, within the Army, specialist grades fall between Corporal and Private First Class. Among the Services, however, rank and precedence are determined by pay grade.

b. In general, titles for Petty Officers are according to "Rating" (Naval Skill) such as Boatswain, Gunner's Mate, Yeoman, Storekeeper, etc. Personnel in pay grades E-3, E-2 and E-1 are not considered as possessing Ratings. The titles listed denote the "Rate" or pay grade.

c. E-3 pay grade also includes Airman, Construction Man, Dental Man, Fireman, Hospital Man and Stewardsman.

d. E-1 and E-2 pay grades also include Recruits and Apprentices in 6 Rates listed in footnote c.

DOD ACTIVE DUTY MILITARY PERSONNEL BY GEOGRAPHIC LOCATION

A. Shore-based[a]

	United States				Outlying U.S. Areas[b]	Foreign Countries and Areas	Total Shore-based
	Continental U.S.	Alaska	Hawaii	Total United States			
30 Jun 1968	2,029,079	31,157	42,560	2,102,796	41,054	1,083,168	3,227,018
30 Sep	1,985,977	30,270	42,332	2,058,579	41,742	1,074,942	3,175,263
31 Dec	1,925,276	30,500	39,352	1,995,128	42,060	1,068,083	3,105,271
31 Mar 1969	1,958,279	31,348	40,178	2,029,805	41,203	1,060,335	3,131,343
30 Jun	1,919,208	30,869	39,139	1,989,216	40,556	1,060,682	3,090,454
30 Sep 1969	1,978,981	30,889	43,018	2,052,888	38,784	1,041,094	3,132,766
31 Dec	1,900,955	31,281	39,237	1,971,473	40,635	996,028	3,008,136

B. Afloat (Navy and Marine Corps)

	United States and Outlying Areas	Foreign Countries and Areas	Total Afloat
30 Jun 1968	204,296	116,588	320,884
30 Sep	183,613	130,712	314,325
31 Dec	199,607	103,352	302,959
31 Mar 1969	191,997	128,559	320,556
30 Jun	275,475	94,233	369,708
30 Sep 1969	185,706	130,799	316,505
31 Dec	197,342	92,410	289,752

C. Total Shore-based and Afloat

	United States and Outlying Areas	Foreign Countries and Areas	Total Shore-based and Afloat
30 Jun 1968	2,348,146	1,199,756	3,547,902
30 Sep	2,283,934	1,205,654	3,489,588
31 Dec	2,236,795	1,171,435	3,408,230
31 Mar 1969	2,263,005	1,188,894	3,451,899
30 Jun	2,305,247	1,154,915	3,460,162
30 Sep 1969	2,277,378	1,171,893	3,449,271
31 Dec	2,209,450	1,088,438	3,297,888

a. Includes Navy personnel temporarily shore-based.
b. Consists primarily of Guam, Panama Canal Zone and Puerto Rico.

Department of Defense

ESTIMATED AGE DISTRIBUTION OF MALE MILITARY PERSONNEL ON ACTIVE DUTY
30 June 1948 through 30 June 1969

(Thousands)

Attained Age	30 Jun 1948	30 Jun 1950	30 Jun 1951	30 Jun 1952	30 Jun 1953	30 Jun 1954	30 Jun 1955	30 Jun 1956	30 Jun 1957	30 Jun 1958	30 Jun 1959	30 Jun 1960	30 Jun 1961	30 Jun 1962	30 Jun 1963	30 Jun 1964	30 Jun 1965	30 Jun 1966	30 Jun 1967	30 Jun 1968	30 Jun 1969
TOTAL	1,431	1,438	3,210	3,590	3,510	3,264	2,900	2,773	2,764	2,573	2,472	2,445	2,452	2,776	2,669	2,658	2,625	3,061	3,342	3,510	3,421
17	53	40	35	60	41	63	80	83	65	51	47	62	54	46	48	49	42	38	29	27	38
18	130	87	145	141	131	148	185	194	181	140	136	140	160	155	135	121	136	152	135	123	131
19	164	147	276	271	276	237	273	278	280	234	208	215	237	263	235	208	188	348	316	266	291
20	159	175	376	407	559	361	302	304	298	259	228	227	234	268	285	260	237	392	558	567	482
21	111	140	462	480	503	514	343	277	261	218	198	188	187	226	234	282	279	333	455	574	509
22	68	91	429	473	454	417	285	253	256	191	172	153	139	186	175	221	249	267	286	297	389
23	63	62	270	427	333	308	230	195	229	233	203	160	137	201	173	186	199	206	216	225	233
24	61	53	152	260	224	220	177	145	135	179	177	168	152	182	188	165	149	146	167	176	172
25	58	53	123	138	140	154	139	120	113	95	99	101	106	130	136	121	106	111	131	147	139
26	64	53	108	106	89	99	110	106	95	85	81	81	82	102	88	87	82	85	100	110	108
27	61	51	93	89	70	68	82	85	86	80	76	73	74	87	76	75	72	72	72	79	76
28	55	54	85	78	61	58	60	72	76	78	76	72	68	70	70	68	67	69	62	63	63
29	51	56	84	73	63	55	53	53	60	70	76	73	67	67	65	66	66	66	62	60	54
30	46	52	78	74	60	54	53	51	48	56	68	72	73	67	63	60	59	65	61	61	56
31	39	48	73	72	62	53	52	49	46	48	52	62	70	73	62	59	59	61	59	62	55
32	35	42	64	65	59	56	51	49	48	46	46	51	62	72	69	63	59	61	58	61	57
33	31	36	59	56	56	57	53	49	49	47	47	46	54	63	67	63	60	60	56	63	55
34	27	31	46	53	51	53	52	52	47	47	48	43	44	52	56	64	64	60	56	61	56
35	23	27	41	42	46	47	49	54	50	45	45	46	43	44	52	57	65	65	58	59	56
36	19	22	34	36	37	41	43	47	50	49	47	45	45	43	42	48	58	63	59	64	56
37	17	19	28	28	33	34	41	43	48	49	50	45	44	45	40	40	47	54	59	62	53
38	15	16	24	26	27	29	34	38	41	47	49	47	42	43	39	36	37	39	48	57	50
39	13	13	21	22	23	23	28	32	39	40	44	46	44	39	36	35	31	31	37	45	46
40 and Over	68	70	104	113	112	115	125	144	163	186	201	229	234	252	235	224	214	217	202	201	196
40-44												152	156	162	145	134	121	121	106	103	112
45-49	a	a	a	a	a	a	a	a	a	a	a	55	55	64	65	66	68	69	68	68	54
50 and Over												22	23	26	25	24	25	27	28	30	30
Median Age in Years	23.5	23.6	22.7	22.9	22.5	22.7	22.9	23.0	23.2	23.8	24.2	24.5	24.5	24.2	24.3	24.0	23.9	23.0	22.6	22.7	22.7

a. Source data incomplete for ages 40 and over.

Note: Estimated from Army and Air Force sample survey data (or tabulations when available), and from Navy and Marine Corps tabulations, for dates available nearest the "as of" dates, supplemented by gain and loss data where necessary, and adjusted from "year birth" to "attained age" where required.

Department of Defense

ESTIMATED EDUCATIONAL LEVEL OF MILITARY PERSONNEL ON ACTIVE DUTY
31 DECEMBER 1969[a]

(Cumulative Percent)

	Total DoD	Army	Navy	Marine Corps	Air Force
COMMISSIONED OFFICERS					
Graduated from College	76.3%	70.5%	82.3%	64.3%	81.3%
Completed 2 or more years College	86.3	84.0	88.9	73.2	89.6
Completed some College	92.4	92.8	94.4	82.0	92.9
Graduated from High School	99.9	100.0	99.8	99.3	100.0
Total Commissioned Officers	100.0	100.0	100.0	100.0	100.0
WARRANT OFFICERS					
Graduated from College	2.2%	2.4%	0.6%	1.9%	8.8%
Completed 2 or more years College	18.4	21.2	5.5	6.5	25.2
Completed some College	46.8	50.2	37.0	22.1	37.2
Graduated from High School	99.0	99.5	97.9	94.4	99.9
Total Warrant Officers	100.0	100.0	100.0	100.0	100.0
ENLISTED					
Graduated from College	4.9%	8.8%	1.7%	0.7%	2.6%
Completed 2 or more years College	13.4	21.7	7.7	4.4	7.1
Completed some College	21.3	30.8	15.7	10.6	13.4
Graduated from High School	82.0	79.8	78.1	65.9	95.5
Compl. 2 or more years High School	94.1	92.6	92.8	89.0	99.8
Completed some High School	97.3	96.4	97.0	95.9	99.9
Graduated from Grade School	99.1	98.6	99.3	99.0	100.0
Total Enlisted	100.0	100.0	100.0	100.0	100.0

a. Approximation from available service reports dated variously 6-30-1969 through 1-1-1970, weighted by 31 December 1969 strengths to arrive at DoD totals. Sources: Army officer data from report "Civilian Education Level Army Department Officers as of Mid-month November 1969" adjusted to include estimate for general officers. Army enlisted data from sample survey as of 30 November 1969. Navy officer data from tabulation for 1-1-1970, and enlisted data from tabulation for 6-30-1969. Marine Corps and Air Force data from tabulations as of 31 December 1969.

Department of Defense

ACTIVE DUTY MILITARY PERSONNEL AND THEIR DEPENDENTS

Worldwide – 30 September 1969

| Military Service | Military Personnel (Excluding Officer Candidates) | | Dependents | | | | | |
| | | | All Types | | Wives | | | |
	Total Number	Number of Males	Total Number	No. Per Military Person	Total Number	Percent of Male Military Personnel	Children	Other
TOTAL, DEPT. OF DEFENSE	3,434,915	3,408,664	4,359,652	1.28	1,566,589	46.0	2,474,145	318,918
Officers	415,568	402,314	900,194	2.24	310,844	77.3	571,496	17,854
Enlisted	3,019,347	3,006,350	3,459,458	1.15	1,255,745	41.8	1,902,649	301,064
ARMY	1,510,397	1,498,023	1,860,223	1.24	661,370	44.1	953,793	245,060
Officers	169,983	164,697	371,311	2.25	128,260	77.9	231,934	11,117
Enlisted	1,340,414	1,333,326	1,488,912	1.12	533,110	40.0	721,859	233,943
NAVY	758,178	756,148	792,150	1.05	315,234	41.7	471,488	5,428
Officers	86,006	83,086	176,070	2.12	62,871	75.7	111,713	1,486
Enlisted	672,172	673,062	616,080	0.92	252,363	37.5	359,775	3,942
MARINE CORPS	311,627	308,878	176,662	0.57	73,261	23.7	102,510	891
Officers	25,233	24,936	45,970	1.84	14,754	59.2	31,066	150
Enlisted	286,394	283,942	130,692	0.46	58,507	20.6	71,444	741
AIR FORCE	854,713	845,615	1,530,617	1.81	516,724	61.1	946,354	67,539
Officers	134,346	129,595	306,843	2.37	104,959	81.0	196,783	5,101
Enlisted	720,367	716,020	1,223,774	1.71	411,765	57.5	749,571	62,438

Department of Defense

WOMEN MILITARY PERSONNEL ON ACTIVE DUTY, OFFICERS AND ENLISTED BY SERVICE
31 May 1945 to Date

	TOTAL DOD			ARMY			NAVY				MARINE CORPS			AIR FORCE		
	Total	Officers	Enlisted and Off. Cand.	Total	Officers	Enlisted	Total	Officers	Enlisted	Officer Candidates	Total	Officers	Enlisted	Total	Officers	Enlisted
31 May 1945	266,256a	82,772	183,484	155,870a	62,775	93,095	92,021	19,188	72,808	25	18,365	809	17,556	Included with Army		
30 Jun 1948	14,458	7,982	6,476	8,095	4,829	3,266	4,030	2,412	1,618	—	167	8	159	2,166	733	1,433
30 Jun 1950	22,069	8,455	13,614	10,982	4,431	6,551	5,193	2,447	2,746	—	580	45	535	5,314	1,532	3,782
30 Sep 1951	41,848	14,582	27,266	18,283b	7,207	11,076	10,081	4,149	5,932	—	2,227	99	2,128	11,257	3,127	8,130
31 Oct 1952	48,675b	15,165	33,510	17,118	7,154	9,964	12,414b	3,968	8,446	—	2,559	150	2,409	16,584	3,893	12,691
30 Jun 1953	45,485	14,436	31,049	15,261	6,501	8,760	11,644	3,636	8,008	—	2,662	160	2,502	15,918	4,139	11,779
30 Jun 1954	38,600	12,801	25,799	12,594	5,807	6,787	10,218	3,273	6,945	—	2,502	163	2,339	13,286	3,558	9,728
30 Jun 1956	33,646	11,175	22,471	12,646	4,876	7,770	8,066	2,852	5,214	—	1,747	113	1,634	11,187	3,334c	7,853
30 Jun 1958	31,176	10,809	20,367	11,464	4,390	7,074	7,247	2,696	4,551	—	1,645	115	1,530	10,820	3,608c	7,212
30 Jun 1960	31,550	10,772	20,778	12,542	4,263	8,279	8,071	2,711	5,360	—	1,611	123	1,488	9,326	3,675	5,651
30 Jun 1962	32,213	11,168	21,045	13,074	4,353	8,721	8,666	2,740	5,847	79	1,697	121	1,576	8,776	3,954	4,822
30 Jun 1964	29,795	10,609	19,186	11,730	3,772	7,958	7,741	2,678	4,863	200	1,448	128	1,320	8,876	4,031	4,845
31 Dec 1965	32,244	10,787	21,457	13,075	3,865	9,210	8,327	2,692	5,327	308	1,755	145	1,610	9,087	4,085	5,002
31 Dec 1966	34,046	12,151	21,895	13,869	4,589	9,280	8,416	2,902	5,156	358	2,119	193	1,926	9,642	4,467	5,175
31 Dec 1967	37,232	13,202	24,030	15,692	5,143	10,549	8,466	3,038	5,157	271	2,651	229	2,422	10,423	4,792	5,631
31 Jul 1968	38,694	13,290	25,404	16,000	5,067	10,933	8,625	3,029	5,290	306	2,785	225	2,560	11,284	4,969	6,315
30 Sep	39,088	13,338	25,750	15,994	5,021	10,973	8,609	3,052	5,228	329	2,849	252	2,597	11,636	5,013	6,623
30 Nov	39,573	13,392	26,181	16,181	5,098	11,083	8,659	2,986	5,307	366	2,934	290	2,644	11,799	5,018	6,781
31 Jan 1969	39,587	13,639	25,948	16,261	5,357	10,904	8,626	3,053	5,366	207	2,903	290	2,613	11,797	4,939	6,858
31 Mar	39,550	13,492	26,058	16,138	5,264	10,874	8,555	3,010	5,320	225	2,875	287	2,588	11,982	4,931	7,051
31 May	39,019	13,321	25,698	15,590	5,175	10,415	8,587	2,959	5,409	219	2,805	285	2,520	12,037	4,902	7,135
31 Jul	39,832	13,179	26,653	15,952	5,184	10,768	8,668	2,917	5,405	346	2,749	281	2,468	12,463	4,797	7,666
30 Sep	40,607	13,254	27,353	16,200	5,286	10,914	8,719	2,920	5,330	469	2,749	297	2,452	12,939	4,751	8,188
30 Nov	41,787	13,213	28,574	17,108	5,315	11,793	8,782	2,847	5,428	507	2,608	290	2,318	13,289	4,761	8,528

a. World War II peak women strength.
b. Korean War period peak women strength.
c. Includes male nurses and medical specialists.

Department of Defense

PRINCIPAL WARS IN WHICH THE UNITED STATES PARTICIPATED:
U.S. MILITARY PERSONNEL SERVING AND CASUALTIES[a]

Wars	Branch Of Service	Number Serving	Casualties		
			Battle Deaths	Other Deaths	Wounds not Mortal[i]
Revolutionary War	Total	j	4,435	–	6,188
1775-1783	Army	–	4,044	–	6,004
	Navy	–	342	–	114
	Marines	–	49	–	70
War of 1812	Total	286,730k	2,260	–	4,505
1812-1815	Army	–	1,950	–	4,000
	Navy	–	265	–	439
	Marines	–	45	–	66
Mexican War	Total	78,718k	1,733	–	4,152
1846-1848	Army	–	1,721	11,550	4,102
	Navy	–	1	–	3
	Marines	–	11	–	47
Civil War (Union	Total	2,213,363k	140,414	224,097	281,881
Forces only)[b]	Army	2,128,948	138,154	221,374	280,040
1861-1865	Navy }	84,415	2,112	2,411	1,710
	Marines }		148	312	131
Spanish-American War	Total	306,760	385	2,061	1,662
1898	Army[g]	280,564	369	2,061	1,594
	Navy	22,875	10	0	47
	Marines	3,321	6	0	21
World War I	Total	4,734,991	53,402	63,114	204,002
(6 April 1917-	Army[f]	4,057,101	50,510	55,868	193,663
11 November 1918)	Navy	599,051	431	6,856	819
	Marines	78,839	2,461	390	9,520
World War II	Total	16,112,566	291,557	113,842	670,846
(7 December 1941-	Army[g]	11,260,000	234,874	83,400	565,861
31 December 1946)[c]	Navy[h]	4,183,466	36,950	25,664	37,778
	Marines	669,100	19,733	4,778	67,207
Korean War	Total	5,720,000	33,629	20,617	103,284
(25 June 1950-	Army	2,834,000	27,704	9,429	77,596
27 July 1953)[d]	Navy	1,177,000	458	4,043	1,576
	Marines	424,000	4,267	1,261	23,744
	Air Force	1,285,000	1,200	5,884	368

a. Data prior to World War I are based upon incomplete records in many cases. Casualty data are confined to dead and wounded personnel and therefore exclude personnel captured or missing in action who were subsequently returned to military control. U.S. Coast Guard data are excluded.

b. Authoritative statistics for the Confederate Forces are not available. Estimates of the number who served range from 600,000 to 1,500,000. The Final Report of the Provost Marshal General, 1863-1866, indicated 133,821 Confederate deaths (74,524 battle and 59,297 other) based upon incomplete returns. In addition, an estimated 26,000-31,000 Confederate personnel died in Union prisons.

c. Data are for the period 1 December 1941 through 31 December 1946 when hostilities were officially terminated by Presidential Proclamation, but few battle deaths or wounds not mortal were incurred after the Japanese acceptance of Allied peace terms on 14 August 1945. Numbers serving from 1 December 1941-31 August 1945 were: Total, 14,903,213; Army, 10,420,000; Navy, 3,883,520; and Marine Corps, 599,693.

d. Tentative final data based upon information available as of 30 September 1954, at which time 24 persons were still carried as missing in action.

e. Number serving covers the period 21 April-13 August 1898, while dead and wounded data are for the period 1 May-31 August 1898. Active hostilities ceased on 13 August 1898, but ratifications of the treaty of peace were not exchanged between the United States and Spain until 11 April 1899.

f. Includes Air Service. Battle deaths and wounds not mortal include casualties suffered by American forces in Northern Russia to 25 August 1919 and in Siberia to 1 April 1920. Other deaths cover the period 1 April 1917-31 December 1918.

g. Includes Army Air Forces.

h. Battle deaths and wounds not mortal include casualties incurred in October 1941 due to hostile action.

i. Marine Corps data for World War II, the Spanish-American War and prior wars represent the number of individuals wounded, whereas all other data in this column represent the total number (incidence) of wounds.

j. Not known, but estimates range from 184,000 to 250,000.

k. As reported by the Commissioner of Pensions in his Annual Report for Fiscal Year 1903.

Dashes (–) indicate that information is not available.

Department of Defense

SELECTIVE SERVICE CALLS, INDUCTIONS, AND INDUCTEES ON ACTIVE DUTY

Fiscal Years 1963-1968

	Calls				Inductions					Inductees on Active Duty End of Month				
	Total	Army	Navy	Marine Corps	Total	Army[a]	Navy	Marine Corps[a]	Air Force[a]	Total	Army	Navy	Marine Corps	Air Force
FY 1963														
Jul 1962	5,000	5,000	—	—	4,827	4,821	—	5	1		185,449	—	108	NA
Aug	5,000	5,000	—	—	5,406	5,400	—	6	—		180,985	—	106	NA
Sep	5,000	5,000	—	—	5,360	5,360	—	-	—		178,349	—	99	NA
Oct	4,000	4,000	—	—	5,299	5,295	—	3	1		175,084	—	90	NA
Nov	4,000	4,000	—	—	5,099	5,095	—	4	—		171,575	—	89	NA
Dec	6,000	6,000	—	—	5,758	5,754	—	4	—		171,215	—	85	NA
Jan 1963	4,000	4,000	—	—	5,069	5,068	—	1	—		171,356	—	83	NA
Feb	4,000	4,000	—	—	4,558	4,552	—	5	1		173,866	—	106	NA
Mar	9,000	9,000	—	—	9,199	9,189	—	10	—		181,183	—	107	NA
Apr	10,000	10,000	—	—	9,938	9,937	—	1	—		189,414	—	98	NA
May	10,000	10,000	—	—	9,620	9,616	—	4	—		197,266	—	97	NA
Jun	4,000	4,000	—	—	4,305	4,300	—	5	—		198,172	—	97	NA
Total FY 1963	70,000	70,000	—	—	74,438	74,387	—	48	3			—		NA
FY 1964														
Jul 1963	7,000	7,000	—	—	6,664	6,662	—	2	—		195,193	—	95	NA
Aug	12,000	12,000	—	—	11,330	11,326	—	4	—		193,708	—	94	NA
Sep	12,000	12,000	—	—	10,804	10,802	—	2	—		183,329	—	92	NA
Oct	17,000	17,000	—	—	16,453	16,452	—	1	—		182,471	—	87	NA
Nov	17,000	17,000	—	—	19,417	19,415	—	2	—		184,956	—	85	NA
Dec	13,000	13,000	—	—	13,005	13,003	—	2	—		180,598	—	80	NA
Jan 1964	16,000	16,000	—	—	17,619	17,612	—	7	—		186,866	—	82	NA
Feb	12,000	12,000	—	—	13,953	13,950	—	3	—		192,507	—	78	NA
Mar	14,000	14,000	—	—	14,957	14,953	—	4	—		199,517	—	78	NA
Apr	12,000	12,000	—	—	13,038	13,034	—	4	—		206,002	—	81	NA
May	7,000	7,000	—	—	7,919	7,916	—	3	—		208,599	—	80	NA
Jun	6,000	6,000	—	—	5,564	5,563	—	1	—		205,188	—	77	NA
Total FY 1964	145,000	145,000	—	—	150,723	150,688	—	35	—			—		NA
FY 1965														
Jul 1964	8,000	8,000	—	—	7,801	7,798	—	3	—		210,585	—	74	NA
Aug	3,300	3,300	—	—	3,856	3,849	—	7	—		209,084	—	77	NA
Sep	6,200	6,200	—	—	4,799	4,792	—	7	—		206,975	—	82	NA
Oct	6,600	6,600	—	—	6,207	6,205	—	2	—		208,687	—	81	NA
Nov	8,600	8,600	—	—	7,906	7,903	—	3	—		211,071	—	82	NA
Dec	7,800	7,800	—	—	7,793	7,789	—	4	—		213,478	—	81	NA
Jan 1965	5,400	5,400	—	—	5,858	5,854	—	4	—		214,587	—	81	NA
Feb	3,000	3,000	—	—	3,705	3,699	—	6	—		211,338	—	80	NA
Mar	7,900	7,900	—	—	8,250	8,247	—	3	—		210,626	—	80	NA
Apr	13,700	13,700	—	—	13,761	13,756	—	5	—		215,940	—	85	NA

Month	1	2	3	4	5	6	7	8	9	10	11	12
May	15,100	15,100	—	—	14,707	14,702	—	5	222,405	—	90	NA
Jun	17,000	17,000	—	—	17,912	17,903	—	9	233,883	—	90	NA
Total FY 1965	102,600	102,600	—	—	102,555	102,497	—	58	—	—	—	—
FY 1966												
Jul 1965	17,100	17,100	—	—	18,861	18,852	—	9	245,010	—	93	NA
Aug	16,500	16,500	—	—	17,863	17,858	—	5	251,109	—	97	NA
Sep	27,400	27,400	—	—	24,772	24,769	—	3	265,477	—	97	NA
Oct	31,600	29,000	2,600	—	29,302	26,718	2,582	2	278,494	2,582	95	NA
Nov	38,350	34,300	—	4,050	35,216	31,732	3	3,481	291,211	2,570	3,559	NA
Dec	40,200	40,200	—	—	36,482	36,446	—	36	317,579	2,535	3,464	NA
Jan 1966	37,280	29,300	—	7,980	35,269	27,630	—	7,639	331,903	2,524	10,884	NA
Feb	25,400	22,400	—	3,000	33,307	29,816	—	3,491	345,411	2,520	14,114	NA
Mar	22,400	18,400	—	4,000	27,476	23,226	—	4,250	353,146	2,509	17,657	NA
Apr	19,200	19,200	—	—	23,021	22,505	—	516	358,924	2,507	17,483	NA
May	40,600	40,600	—	—	37,909	37,749	—	160	387,356	2,504	17,194	NA
Jun	18,500	18,500	—	—	20,252	20,208	—	44	395,292	2,501	17,129	NA
Total FY 1966	334,530	312,900	2,600	19,030	339,730	317,509	2,585	19,636	—	—	—	—
FY 1967												
Jul 1966	28,500	28,500	—	—	29,351	29,331	—	20	414,152	2,494	16,975	NA
Aug	36,600	36,600	—	—	37,051	37,037	—	14	443,534	2,490	16,822	NA
Sep	37,300	37,300	—	—	39,361	39,353	—	8	472,892	2,491	16,705	NA
Oct	49,200	49,200	—	—	50,576	50,573	—	3	512,223	2,489	16,575	NA
Nov	37,600	37,600	—	—	36,662	36,654	—	8	536,088	2,487	16,485	NA
Dec	12,100	12,100	—	—	13,391	13,381	—	10	539,463	2,480	16,379	NA
Jan 1967	15,600	15,600	—	—	17,965	17,959	—	6	549,041	2,476	16,258	NA
Feb	10,900	10,900	—	—	12,736	12,731	—	5	552,738	2,474	16,172	NA
Mar	11,900	11,900	—	—	12,690	12,664	—	26	552,280	2,475	16,102	NA
Apr	11,400	11,400	—	—	11,675	11,661	—	14	548,753	2,478	16,000	NA
May	18,000	18,000	—	—	17,196	17,187	—	9	546,555	2,472	15,899	NA
Jun	19,800	19,800	—	—	20,546	20,538	—	8	546,264	2,470	15,743	NA
Total FY 1967	288,900	288,900	—	—	299,200	299,069	—	131	—	—	—	—
FY 1968												
Jul 1967	19,900	19,900	—	—	20,662	20,653	—	9	541,803	2,453	15,645	NA
Aug	29,000	29,000	—	—	30,093	30,077	—	16	546,369	2,390	15,514	NA
Sep	25,000	25,000	—	—	27,523	27,508	—	15	543,585	2,228	15,336	NA
Oct	17,000	17,000	—	—	18,193	18,181	—	12	535,417	312	15,168	NA
Nov	22,000	22,000	—	—	21,939	21,925	—	14	523,977	155	13,188	NA
Dec	18,200	18,200	—	—	17,838	17,827	—	11	513,240	94	11,708	NA
Jan 1968	34,000	34,000	—	—	30,946	30,933	—	13	516,657	64	6,745	NA
Feb	23,300	23,300	—	—	26,412	26,397	—	15	515,515	56	4,349	NA
Mar	41,000	41,000	—	—	37,393	37,370	—	23	530,308	47	1,295	NA
Apr	48,000	44,000	—	4,000	41,611	38,650	—	2,961	541,485	40	3,884	NA
May	45,900	44,000	—	1,900	36,210	34,868	—	1,342	545,431	38	5,014	NA
Jun	20,000	20,000	—	—	30,776	29,833	—	943	549,603	38	5,617	NA
Total FY 1968	343,300	337,400	—	5,900	339,596	334,222	—	5,374	—	—	—	—

a. Includes former members of reserve components who failed to meet prescribed training obligations and were inducted into their parent services for 2-year active duty tours.

Department of Defense

"UNADJUSTED" REENLISTMENT RATES FOR TOTAL REGULARS AND INDUCTEES
FY 1950 TO DATE

	Total Regulars					Inductees
	Total Dept Def	Army	Navy	Marine Corps	Air Force	Army
FY 1950	59.3%	61.8%	65.6%	35.1%	54.7%	n.a.
FY 1951-1953	54.6	50.9	61.0	50.0	56.1	n.a.
FY 1954	23.7	22.0	23.7	18.1	31.2	n.a.
FY 1955	27.2	59.0	14.2	20.6	23.5	3.0
FY 1956	43.6	59.0	32.6	37.8	44.2	3.5
FY 1957	45.9	49.6	44.9	29.1	49.4	2.7
FY 1958	48.6	48.1	43.7	39.8	54.8	4.7
FY 1959	48.6	52.4	34.3	31.9	61.5	5.1
FY 1960	40.9	52.1	34.4	20.3	44.0	9.1
FY 1961	53.1	57.8	44.3	36.3	57.4	11.6
FY 1962	57.5	52.8	50.5	41.8	71.1	20.1
FY 1963	53.1	51.5	47.4	35.4	66.3	11.2
FY 1964	50.4	52.0	41.5	30.3	61.4	3.6
FY 1965[a]	49.8	47.9	39.1	31.8	61.5	8.4
FY 1965[b]	50.2	47.9	40.7	32.9	61.5	8.4
FY 1966	49.6	49.5	44.0	33.9	55.6	10.2
FY 1967	42.2	44.1	37.9	22.0	50.1	20.8
FY 1968	43.5	45.5	35.8	23.0	54.5	11.5
FY 1969	34.2	29.9	34.2	14.3	46.0	9.4
FY 1970						
Jul 1969	37.0	28.4	37.6	16.4	69.3	10.3
Aug	34.6	28.9	26.3	18.2	56.9	12.9
Sep	29.7	28.3	19.5	10.1	60.2	14.0
Oct	25.9	27.8	13.1	13.3	57.7	6.7
Nov	30.9	27.3	23.5	11.1	54.1	5.0
Dec	30.3	32.7	29.0	10.7	35.2	3.5
Total 6 Mos	30.9	28.8	22.7	13.0	53.5	8.5

"UNADJUSTED" REENLISTMENT RATES FOR "FIRST-TERM" AND "CAREER" REGULARS
FY 1955 TO DATE

	First-Term Regulars					Career Regulars				
	Total Dept Def	Army	Navy	Marine Corps	Air Force	Total Dept Def	Army	Navy	Marine Corps	Air Force
FY 1955	15.8%	38.9%	9.0%	16.5%	14.4%	73.6%	82.4%	73.2%	33.7%	70.2%
FY 1956	22.8	28.2	11.5	23.7	29.3	89.7	88.8	94.9	82.1	87.9
FY 1957	24.7	18.9	15.6	17.0	36.5	85.8	83.2	85.8	83.1	91.4
FY 1958	27.6	17.2	22.6	24.2	39.8	85.2	80.4	89.0	82.5	91.8
FY 1959	30.0	21.5	23.4	20.2	45.7	87.4	83.9	90.1	76.5	92.9
FY 1960	21.2	23.5	21.3	11.1	24.1	84.6	83.2	90.9	67.4	86.2
FY 1961	25.3	26.0	27.8	18.3	23.5	88.2	87.3	91.0	78.7	88.8
FY 1962	27.4	23.8	28.3	20.0	35.3	88.8	86.8	92.2	83.1	89.5
FY 1963	24.9	22.2	25.1	15.5	35.1	88.3	89.2	93.3	84.6	85.4
FY 1964	25.2	27.9	22.5	14.4	29.5	87.5	84.4	90.1	85.7	89.9
FY 1965[a]	24.0	25.7	21.4	15.2	27.3	87.0	84.1	86.7	84.0	89.2
FY 1965[b]	24.0	25.7	22.8	16.3	25.5	87.2	84.1	87.3	84.5	89.3
FY 1966	23.2	28.0	23.7	16.3	18.9	87.7	83.4	89.6	88.6	89.7
FY 1967	18.8	23.7	18.9	10.6	16.8	81.1	74.2	80.9	77.9	88.0
FY 1968	19.6	28.0	16.8	11.9	18.1	78.8	67.6	79.4	76.0	87.7
FY 1969	14.9	17.4	16.3	7.4	15.2	77.9	64.5	78.4	74.5	86.0
FY 1970										
Jul 1969	18.2	16.0	17.8	8.7	40.1	79.9	65.1	82.1	76.7	93.6
Aug	16.3	16.1	11.2	9.2	29.6	79.1	68.3	81.1	87.4	84.9
Sep	12.8	16.0	7.6	5.0	28.8	78.5	68.1	77.7	77.9	86.3
Oct	10.9	16.3	4.6	6.0	25.9	72.9	59.5	68.3	78.5	87.5
Nov	14.0	16.7	9.3	5.0	22.9	69.8	50.0	82.8	74.4	85.4
Dec	12.6	18.6	11.8	4.7	10.4	81.8	71.6	89.0	69.1	87.6
Total 6 Mos	13.7	16.5	9.0	6.3	23.2	76.7	62.7	79.6	77.6	87.2

a. Old Definition.
b. New Definition.

Department of Defense

"UNADJUSTED" REENLISTMENT RATES FOR TOTAL REGULARS BY MAJOR OCCUPATIONAL GROUP AND SERVICE, FY 1965 TO DATE

	Total All Groups		Infantry, Gun Crews & Allied Specialists		Electronics Equipment Repairmen		Communications & Intelligence Specialists		Medical and Dental Specialists		Other Technical and Allied Specialists		Administrative Specialists and Clerks		Elec/Mechanical Equip Repairmen		Craftsmen		Service and Supply Handlers		Miscellaneous	
	Eligibles	Reenl Rate	Eligibles	Reenl Rate	Eligibles	Reenl Rate	Eligibles	Reenl Rate	Eligibles	Reenl Rate	Eligibles	Reenl Rate	Eligibles	Reenl Rate	Eligibles	Reenl Rate	Eligibles	Reenl Rate	Eligibles	Reenl Rate	Eligibles	Reenl Rate
TOTAL DoD																						
FY 1965	461,635	50.2	46,157	50.2	53,773	51.5	39,126	44.1	18,551	50.9	10,125	50.5	88,863	57.7	102,288	49.1	26,081	49.5	51,977	60.0	24,694	13.2
FY 1966	399,698	49.6	37,009	50.7	47,876	48.1	34,083	43.3	15,836	51.5	8,427	49.8	75,337	55.9	90,735	46.7	23,556	48.2	47,351	57.6	19,488	31.6
FY 1967	408,967	42.2	44,139	41.4	47,477	44.6	35,134	40.6	16,303	44.9	8,711	42.9	74,793	47.8	91,949	40.8	26,500	39.0	48,402	45.1	15,559	14.9
FY 1968	385,918	43.5	44,274	43.6	47,248	47.1	33,893	37.8	14,539	45.4	8,775	44.8	67,405	49.1	91,479	39.2	27,370	37.8	44,268	44.1	6,667	60.0
FY 1969	528,859	34.2	72,389	33.8	64,021	37.8	40,303	30.9	17,497	37.3	12,118	33.9	101,502	36.5	116,841	32.0	33,814	29.8	59,342	34.9	11,032	36.3
Army																						
FY 1965	158,433	47.9	31,969	54.6	15,482	45.4	16,114	38.4	8,658	52.0	3,655	42.2	24,466	45.0	24,708	42.6	5,212	44.7	17,958	58.8	211	100.0
FY 1966	134,050	49.5	26,188	53.0	11,366	45.1	12,752	40.4	6,850	55.5	2,736	46.4	26,703	48.8	21,037	42.7	4,104	39.5	14,778	59.1	5,541	67.3
FY 1967	132,145	44.1	27,119	49.8	11,707	40.9	10,534	46.2	7,310	48.2	2,569	39.5	26,372	44.1	22,741	36.2	4,837	36.0	15,234	51.3	3,722	31.8
FY 1968	116,465	45.5	26,351	53.7	9,827	39.8	10,204	33.6	5,924	44.0	2,319	38.5	22,117	40.9	19,156	38.6	4,116	45.9	12,676	49.9	3,775	88.2
FY 1969	175,134	29.9	32,944	41.8	17,480	24.0	13,361	25.0	7,715	31.0	4,209	20.2	39,024	25.0	32,097	23.9	7,630	22.3	17,783	35.6	2,891	76.8
Navy																						
FY 1965	104,683	40.7	2,401	54.7	11,431	40.6	10,822	36.6	5,491	40.6	2,133	46.3	10,025	52.3	30,769	42.1	9,320	46.3	7,328	66.8	14,963	14.0
FY 1966	94,167	44.0	2,598	58.6	11,366	45.1	10,010	40.6	4,937	41.1	1,913	47.2	9,291	56.2	28,419	42.2	8,418	51.4	6,624	69.1	10,591	16.0
FY 1967	114,981	37.9	2,419	44.0	14,785	41.9	12,438	36.8	5,338	35.0	2,289	42.6	11,637	47.4	35,133	36.8	11,265	42.7	8,137	57.6	11,540	8.6
FY 1968	108,571	35.8	2,674	42.0	15,554	40.8	12,007	33.4	4,599	41.5	2,279	37.0	11,557	39.1	33,530	32.3	15,479	30.4	8,271	50.5	2,621	13.5
FY 1969	108,041	34.2	2,393	33.1	15,206	40.5	11,034	30.3	4,435	41.1	2,147	38.9	12,394	34.3	32,766	33.2	11,734	27.8	8,095	49.7	7,837	20.1
Marine Corps																						
FY 1965	31,490	32.9	10,000	27.2	1,736	32.5	2,575	28.8	—	—	668	42.1	5,595	43.9	6,150	31.7	1,179	32.4	3,583	35.2	4	100.0
FY 1966	22,754	33.9	6,756	28.7	1,397	31.3	1,855	30.5	1	100.0	475	38.1	4,157	45.3	4,173	34.9	992	30.2	3,012	31.8	6	100.0
FY 1967	37,126	22.0	12,886	16.6	3,103	19.7	3,523	15.6	44	59.1	682	24.9	5,738	33.3	5,761	25.3	1,084	23.7	4,301	24.0	4	50.0
FY 1968	37,299	23.0	13,094	16.1	1,746	27.3	2,973	21.6	4	100.0	733	28.1	6,073	32.3	5,532	28.4	1,602	23.0	5,539	19.4	3	100.0
FY 1969	66,523	14.3	29,659	9.5	2,375	17.5	4,778	14.4	2	100.0	883	21.4	8,650	22.9	10,136	17.4	2,304	14.8	7,728	14.7	8	100.0
Air Force																						
FY 1965	167,029	61.5	1,787	95.9	25,124	61.4	9,615	66.2	4,402	61.5	3,669	62.9	38,777	72.3	40,661	61.1	10,370	56.7	23,108	62.7	9,516	9.8
FY 1966	148,727	55.6	1,467	96.5	21,752	52.3	9,466	52.6	4,048	57.5	3,303	55.9	35,186	62.3	37,106	53.7	10,112	50.8	22,937	56.6	3,350	21.2
FY 1967	124,715	50.1	1,715	91.0	17,882	53.6	8,639	49.4	3,611	52.9	3,171	49.6	31,046	53.7	28,314	52.7	9,314	37.9	20,730	40.0	293	50.2
FY 1968	123,583	54.5	2,155	90.0	20,121	55.3	8,709	54.4	4,012	51.8	3,444	57.7	27,658	63.4	33,261	48.1	6,173	55.1	17,782	44.6	268	52.6
FY 1969	179,161	46.0	7,393	95.9	28,960	46.5	11,130	45.5	5,345	43.3	4,879	45.8	41,434	50.9	41,842	40.9	12,146	39.4	25,736	35.9	296	16.2

Department of Defense

RESERVE COMPONENT PERSONNEL NOT ON ACTIVE DUTY BY COMPONENT[a]

30 June 1946 to Date

	Total Dept. Defense	Army National Guard b c	Army Reserve	Naval Reserve	Marine Corps Reserve	Air National Guard[b]	Air Force Reserve
1946 30 Jun	d	–	d	222,130	22,807	d	d
1947 30 Jun	2,026,537	78,241	710,094	763,385	45,536	10,087	419,194
1948 30 Jun	2,597,251	289,531	752,271	987,319	111,122	29,048	427,960
1949 30 Jun	2,485,779	313,805	588,972	1,027,595	123,817	41,418	390,172
1950 30 Jun	2,630,564	352,883	613,526	1,115,285	128,839	45,084	374,947
31 Dec	2,172,467	274,212	480,372	963,591	53,116	44,554	356,622
1951 30 Jun	2,002,480	241,547	465,484	919,726	40,367	20,114	315,242
31 Dec	1,951,892	241,123	497,723	840,679	52,577	11,807	307,983
1952 30 Jun	1,938,710	234,206	520,376	770,837	81,435	15,006	316,850
31 Dec	1,987,270	250,724	572,145	735,716	75,931	27,164	325,590
1953 1 Jan[e]	1,951,661	250,724	572,145	701,202	74,836	27,164	325,590
30 Jun	2,096,398	278,164	798,026	665,571	78,455	35,556	240,626
31 Dec	2,251,564	296,654	945,603	637,943	92,164	40,311	238,889
1954 30 Jun	2,487,360	338,669	1,108,967	595,359	138,846	49,845	255,674
31 Dec	2,664,449	357,185	1,344,245	491,795	157,214	56,490	257,520
1955 30 Jun	2,985,296	378,046	1,648,626	466,067	185,677	61,306	245,574
31 Dec	3,243,941	390,241	1,796,578	502,972	202,752	64,115	287,283
1956 30 Jun	3,581,173	420,535	1,975,559	547,640	229,641	63,534	344,264
31 Dec	3,585,868	418,790	1,887,928	574,879	249,574	64,880	389,817
1957 30 Jun	3,631,671	441,798	1,839,474	583,733	270,300	67,950	428,416
31 Dec	3,799,715	434,203	1,929,752	643,515	283,188	69,029	440,028
1958 30 Jun	4,022,061	442,369	2,034,598	674,763	301,376	69,995	498,960
31 Dec	4,184,494	431,946	2,139,611	706,326	310,147	70,252	526,212
1959 30 Jun	4,354,005	404,036	2,282,550	727,727	315,930	70,994	552,768
31 Dec	4,290,678	401,881	2,286,937	719,025	297,836	71,020	513,979
1960 30 Jun	4,147,294	407,549	2,217,472	672,227	258,477	70,820	520,749
31 Dec	3,971,287	413,699	2,075,694	654,137	253,244	69,887	504,626
1961 30 Jun	3,756,246	400,455	1,893,747	648,446	242,691	70,895	500,012
31 Dec	3,340,072	356,118	1,648,254	602,893	211,350	51,317	470,140
1962 30 Jun	2,994,633	366,517	1,445,901	539,185	177,581	50,319	415,130
31 Dec	2,693,808	379,572	1,243,595	494,481	144,560	67,177	364,423
1963 30 Jun	2,435,532	368,017	1,092,834	466,712	134,336	74,325	319,308
31 Dec	2,508,416	382,042	1,134,004	460,637	129,389	74,931	327,413
1964 30 Jun	2,550,716	389,067	1,131,782	471,451	136,001	73,217	349,198
31 Dec	2,537,243	382,915	1,110,537	475,599	130,615	73,231	364,346
1965 30 Jun	2,576,405	385,981	1,128,566	467,681	134,002	76,410	383,765
31 Dec	2,671,445	423,452	1,146,452	485,504	137,081	79,639	399,317
1966 30 Jun	2,768,628	426,258	1,222,165	479,830	148,977	79,883	411,515
31 Dec	2,731,832	422,934	1,190,452	487,367	138,107	82,455	410,517
1967 30 Jun	2,757,614	420,465	1,217,984	479,213	144,288	83,758	411,806
31 Dec	2,770,818	419,336	1,235,674	469,371	145,056	85,837	415,544
1968 30 Jun	2,844,734	390,798	1,335,230	458,249	167,910	75,261	417,286
31 Jul	2,862,600	391,017	1,353,513	457,928	164,719	75,460	419,963
31 Aug	2,890,956	391,837	1,370,213	465,136	168,989	75,707	419,074
30 Sep	2,926,838	392,275	1,399,631	470,864	167,884	75,726	420,458
31 Oct	2,987,216	391,469	1,436,750	481,213	169,774	75,862	432,148
30 Nov	3,045,354	391,048	1,480,793	491,324	172,239	75,900	434,050
31 Dec	3,072,244	390,111	1,492,659	498,901	172,651	77,889	440,033
1969 31 Jan	3,095,235	389,801	1,513,106	501,353	175,976	78,510	436,489
28 Feb	3,119,731	388,363	1,532,905	501,643	178,287	78,712	439,821
31 Mar	3,159,064	387,868	1,556,137	499,593	180,201	78,415	456,850
30 Apr	3,193,441	388,579	1,574,793	501,914	188,829	78,553	460,773
31 May	3,217,958	389,709	1,585,234	503,734	195,493	78,768	465,020
30 Jun	3,259,467	389,862	1,605,906	509,222	202,578	83,414	468,485
31 Jul	3,279,205	388,888	1,618,942	507,559	209,793	83,261	470,762
31 Aug	3,291,677	389,154	1,631,594	509,191	209,306	83,810	468,622
30 Sep	3,328,289	390,463	1,657,349	518,694	209,718	84,641	467,424
31 Oct	3,356,276	389,340	1,667,329	536,897	208,826	85,163	468,721
30 Nov	3,392,193	389,824	1,687,508	547,064	212,589	85,307	469,901
31 Dec	3,414,239	394,776	1,685,945	554,641	217,586	84,851	476,440

a. Includes Reserves on active duty for reserve training purposes.

b. Includes "Inactive" National Guard. Army for 30 June 1950 to date. Air Force for 30 June 1951 through 31 March 1953.

c. Represents strength of Federally Recognized units less non-recognized officers for 1947 and 1948, and strength of Federally Recognized units for 30 June 1949 and thereafter.

d. Not available.

e. 31 December 1952 strength revised to reflect change in definition of components in accordance with the Armed Forces Reserve Act of 1962.

Department of Defense

RESERVE COMPONENT PERSONNEL BY RESERVE CATEGORY
31 March 1954 to Date[a]

	TOTAL						OFFICERS						ENLISTED (Incl. Officer Candidates)					
			Ready						Ready						Ready			
	Total	Total Ready	On Active Duty	Not on Active Duty	Standby	Retired	Total	Total Ready	On Active Duty	Not on Active Duty	Standby	Retired	Total	Total Ready	On Active Duty	Not on Active Duty	Standby	Retired
1954 31 Mar	2,747,387	2,470,902	329,750	2,141,152	216,674	59,811	914,015	671,157	234,998	436,159	192,630	50,228	1,833,372	1,799,745	94,752	1,704,993	24,044	9,583
30 Jun	2,821,436	2,546,258	334,076	2,212,182	207,176	68,002	916,429	672,905	236,489	436,416	184,818	58,706	1,905,007	1,873,353	97,587	1,775,766	22,358	9,296
31 Dec	2,994,108	2,758,084	329,659	2,428,425	160,111	75,913	882,195	675,899	236,924	438,975	140,210	66,086	2,111,913	2,082,185	92,735	1,989,450	19,901	9,827
1955 30 Jun	3,305,888	3,026,650	320,592	2,706,058	198,592	80,646	866,139	617,282	238,186	379,096	178,054	70,803	2,439,749	2,409,368	82,406	2,326,962	20,538	9,843
31 Dec	3,567,106	3,317,152	323,165	2,993,987	163,859	86,095	857,476	636,690	243,171	393,519	144,594	76,192	2,709,630	2,680,462	79,994	2,600,468	19,265	9,903
1956 30 Jun	3,916,117	3,662,628	334,944	3,327,684	161,899	91,590	850,504	623,961	233,938	390,023	145,241	81,302	3,065,613	3,038,667	101,006	2,937,661	16,658	10,288
31 Dec	3,948,195	3,679,443	362,327	3,317,116	171,729	97,023	845,689	622,786	232,567	390,219	136,423	86,480	3,102,506	3,056,657	129,760	2,926,897	35,306	10,543
1957 30 Jun	4,010,870	2,818,317	379,199	2,439,118	1,091,399	101,154	840,604	563,221	225,499	337,722	187,411	89,972	3,170,266	2,255,096	153,700	2,101,396	903,988	11,182
31 Dec	4,157,942	2,864,691	358,227	2,506,464	1,186,497	106,754	828,215	556,440	210,665	345,775	176,944	94,831	3,329,727	2,308,251	147,562	2,160,689	1,009,553	11,923
1958 30 Jun	4,335,515	2,742,278	313,454	2,428,824	1,478,678	114,559	808,645	553,873	186,278	347,595	172,947	101,825	3,526,870	2,208,405	127,176	2,081,229	1,305,731	12,734
31 Dec	4,463,277	2,740,991	278,783	2,462,208	1,600,641	121,645	809,206	526,996	177,901	349,095	174,506	107,704	3,654,071	2,213,995	100,882	2,113,113	1,426,135	13,941
1959 30 Jun	4,600,633	2,702,226	246,628	2,455,598	1,770,362	128,045	804,860	525,094	171,734	353,360	166,443	113,323	3,795,773	2,177,132	74,894	2,102,238	1,603,919	14,722
31 Dec	4,519,462	2,675,519	228,784	2,446,735	1,706,195	137,748	802,226	522,364	168,274	354,090	154,969	121,893	3,717,236	2,153,155	60,510	2,092,645	1,548,226	15,855
1960 30 Jun	4,367,059	2,637,454	219,765	2,417,689	1,585,208	144,397	803,518	517,549	163,757	353,792	158,574	127,395	3,563,541	2,119,905	56,008	2,063,897	1,426,634	17,002
31 Dec	4,188,407	2,628,049	217,120	2,410,929	1,400,587	159,771	808,212	508,544	161,488	347,056	159,017	140,651	3,380,195	2,119,505	55,632	2,063,873	1,241,570	19,120
1961 30 Jun	3,965,507	2,606,900	209,261	2,397,639	1,187,474	171,133	804,778	498,626	159,375	339,251	157,365	148,787	3,160,729	2,108,274	49,886	2,058,388	1,030,109	22,346
31 Dec	3,708,987	2,471,682	368,915	2,102,767	1,052,357	184,948	804,193	497,551	178,404	319,147	146,958	159,684	2,904,794	1,974,131	190,511	1,783,620	905,399	25,264
1962 30 Jun	3,359,548	2,364,999	364,915	2,000,084	796,398	198,151	796,140	480,740	182,052	298,688	145,939	169,461	2,563,408	1,884,259	182,863	1,701,396	650,459	28,690
31 Dec	2,926,149	2,155,530	232,341	1,923,189	556,537	214,082	786,019	470,201	172,358	297,843	136,636	179,182	2,140,130	1,685,329	59,983	1,625,346	419,901	34,900
1963 30 Jun	2,669,144	1,925,784	233,612	1,692,172	508,216	235,144	799,374	460,375	173,036	287,339	145,174	193,825	1,869,770	1,465,409	60,576	1,404,833	363,042	41,319
31 Dec	2,738,220	1,960,329	229,804	1,730,525	522,937	254,954	804,380	446,839	171,463	275,376	150,918	206,623	1,933,840	1,513,490	58,341	1,455,149	372,019	48,331

Date																		
1964 30 Jun	2,781,067	2,029,493	230,351	1,799,142	482,476	269,098	798,797	435,431	172,388	263,043	147,549	215,817	1,982,270	1,594,062	57,963	1,536,099	334,927	53,281
31 Dec	2,770,112	2,025,665	232,869	1,792,796	456,409	288,038	805,996	433,806	174,680	259,126	144,354	227,836	1,964,116	1,591,859	58,189	1,533,670	312,055	60,202
1965 30 Jun	2,808,250	2,033,352	231,845	1,801,507	471,873	303,025	809,977	425,158	169,591	255,567	147,420	237,399	1,998,273	1,608,194	62,254	1,545,940	323,453	65,626
31 Dec	2,916,643	2,131,408	245,198	1,886,210	464,872	320,363	808,911	414,122	170,317	243,805	143,169	251,620	2,107,732	1,717,286	74,881	1,642,405	321,703	68,743
1966 30 Jun	3,026,042	2,223,040	257,414	1,965,626	467,650	335,352	822,638	420,761	175,641	245,120	141,097	260,780	2,203,404	2,802,279	81,773	1,720,506	326,553	74,572
31 Dec	3,013,157	2,159,415	281,325	1,878,090	502,579	351,163	839,598	422,020	188,004	234,016	144,231	273,347	2,173,559	1,737,395	93,321	1,644,074	358,348	77,816
1967 30 Jun	3,061,055	2,166,337	303,441	1,862,896	535,491	359,227	865,026	439,208	209,215	229,993	144,711	281,107	2,196,029	1,727,129	94,226	1,632,903	390,780	78,120
31 Dec	3,088,024	2,267,665	317,206	1,950,459	409,285	411,074	875,292	452,207	227,012	225,195	130,884	292,201	2,212,732	1,815,458	90,194	1,725,264	278,401	118,873
1968 30 Jun	3,194,731	2,340,601	349,997	1,990,604	395,154	458,976	879,107	449,082	236,828	212,254	128,647	301,378	2,315,624	1,891,519	113,169	1,778,350	266,507	157,598
31 Jul	3,211,872	2,346,342	349,272	1,997,070	393,910	471,620	884,229	452,126	237,016	215,110	127,472	304,631	2,327,643	1,894,216	112,256	1,781,960	266,438	166,989
31 Aug	3,237,934	2,365,257	346,978	2,018,279	397,549	475,128	888,617	454,273	236,974	217,299	127,567	306,777	2,349,317	1,910,984	110,004	1,800,980	269,982	168,351
30 Sep	3,272,406	2,389,527	345,568	2,043,959	404,532	478,347	891,082	456,020	237,933	218,087	127,184	307,878	2,381,324	1,933,507	107,635	1,825,872	277,348	170,469
31 Oct	3,323,249	2,427,520	336,033	2,091,487	413,935	481,794	891,219	456,468	237,925	218,543	125,160	309,591	2,432,030	1,971,052	98,108	1,872,944	288,775	172,203
30 Nov	3,376,934	2,471,054	331,580	2,139,474	421,787	484,093	894,376	456,873	239,302	217,571	126,691	310,812	2,482,558	2,014,181	92,278	1,921,903	295,096	173,281
31 Dec	3,392,779	2,480,796	320,535	2,160,261	425,772	486,211	887,449	454,406	238,901	215,505	121,353	311,690	2,505,330	2,026,390	81,634	1,944,756	304,419	174,521
1969 31 Jan	3,415,341	2,485,867	320,106	2,165,761	431,663	479,811	889,327	456,830	239,612	217,218	118,344	314,153	2,526,014	2,029,037	80,494	1,948,543	313,319	183,658
28 Feb	3,439,149	2,500,336	319,418	2,180,918	434,575	504,238	889,184	457,324	239,624	217,700	114,406	317,454	2,549,965	2,043,012	79,794	1,963,218	320,169	186,784
31 Mar	3,480,359	2,530,310	321,295	2,209,015	436,350	513,699	891,171	460,256	241,238	219,018	112,077	318,838	2,589,188	2,070,054	80,057	1,989,997	324,273	194,861
30 Apr	3,515,340	2,560,298	321,899	2,238,399	435,238	519,804	892,399	459,416	241,100	218,316	112,770	320,213	2,622,941	2,100,882	80,799	2,020,083	322,468	199,591
31 May	3,536,061	2,583,049	318,103	2,264,946	427,839	525,173	888,052	460,205	242,326	217,879	106,311	321,536	2,648,009	2,122,844	75,777	2,047,067	321,528	203,637
30 Jun	3,570,393	2,615,622	310,926	2,304,696	425,924	528,847	889,615	462,114	239,787	222,327	103,682	323,819	2,680,778	2,153,508	71,139	2,082,369	322,242	205,028
31 Jul	3,589,884	2,639,990	310,679	2,329,311	419,335	530,559	890,987	464,277	239,626	224,651	102,194	324,516	2,698,897	2,175,713	71,053	2,104,660	317,141	206,043
31 Aug	3,601,165	2,652,761	309,488	2,343,273	412,269	536,135	893,690	465,537	239,202	226,335	102,405	325,748	2,707,475	2,187,224	70,286	2,116,938	309,864	210,387
30 Sep	3,635,574	2,689,241	307,285	2,381,956	403,883	542,450	899,190	468,131	238,997	229,134	103,576	327,483	2,736,384	2,221,110	68,288	2,152,822	300,307	214,967
31 Oct	3,659,312	2,714,225	303,036	2,411,189	398,426	546,661	901,139	465,590	238,115	227,475	106,783	328,756	2,758,183	2,248,635	64,921	2,183,714	291,643	217,905
30 Nov	3,688,017	2,742,110	295,824	2,446,286	394,967	550,940	901,826	464,767	235,410	229,357	107,426	329,633	2,786,191	2,277,343	60,414	2,216,929	287,541	221,307
31 Dec	3,699,543	2,764,483	285,304	2,479,179	380,759	554,301	902,662	463,709	231,497	232,212	107,686	331,267	2,796,881	2,300,774	53,807	2,246,967	273,073	223,034

a. Marine Corps Reserve detail by reserve category not available prior to 31 March 1954.
This tabulation shows the trends in numbers of personnel assigned to the reserve categories established by the Armed Forces Reserve Act of 1952.
Although these categories became effective on 1 January 1953, complete reports by reserve category were unavailable prior to 31 March 1954.
Screening of the Ready Reserve is continuous to assure current availability of all members.
Following legislation establishing a ceiling on the number of Ready Reserves, effective 30 June 1957, the number of Ready Reserves not on active duty was maintained at slightly in excess of 2,400,000 until the
spring of 1961, then dropped below 1,700,000 in 1963, and increased to 2,479,000 at the end of 1969.

Department of Defense

RESERVE COMPONENT STRENGTH SUMMARY AS OF 31 DECEMBER 1969

RESERVES BY TYPE OF DUTY

	Total	Officer	Enlisted[a]
TOTAL	3,699,543	902,662	2,796,881
On Active Duty	285,304	231,497	53,807
Not on Active Duty	3,414,239	671,165	2,743,074

a. Includes officer candidates.

RESERVES BY RESERVE CATEGORY

	Total	Officer	Enlisted[a]
TOTAL	3,699,543	902,662	2,796,881
Ready Reserve	2,764,483	463,709	2,300,774
On Active Duty	285,304	231,497	53,807
Not on Active Duty	2,479,179	232,212	2,246,967
Active Status	2,477,862	231,905	2,245,957
Inactive Status[b]	1,317	307	1,010
Standby Reserve	380,759	107,686	273,073
On Active Status	276,000	27,745	248,255
Inactive Status	104,759	79,941	24,818
Retired–Retired Status	554,301	331,267	223,034

a. Includes officer candidates.
b. Inactive National Guard.

RESERVES IN "PAID STATUS"

	Pay Group	Total	Officer	Enlisted
TOTAL IN PAID STATUS	All	1,007,686	121,909	885,777
Paid Drill Training	A,B,C,F	952,895	105,442	847,453
Drill Pay Status	A,B,C	892,454	105,442	787,012
Undergoing Active Duty Basic Trg.	F	60,441	–	60,441
Paid Active Duty Training Only[a]	D,E	54,791	16,467	38,324

a. Revised FY 1970 plan as listed in FY 1971 Budget. To be revised at end of year when actual numbers of participants during FY 1970 are known.

This table summarizes the current status of our Reservists–members of Department of Defense reserve components.

Members of the Ready Reserve are subject to active duty in time of national emergency proclaimed by the President, as well as in time of war or national emergency declared by Congress. The Ready Reserve includes Reservists on active duty who were counted as part of active military strength in preceding tables. Ready Reservists not on active duty participate, to the extent required and subject to the availability of funds, in drills or training periods regularly scheduled throughout the year, in two weeks annual active duty training, and/or in various school and special active duty training programs.

Members of the Standby Reserve can be ordered involuntarily to active duty only as the result of Congressional action, and after the Director of Selective Service has determined their availability for active duty. They are not required to actively participate in reserve training.

The Retired Reserve consists of members of the reserve components who qualify for retirement through length of service, disability, etc., and who are formally placed on reserve retired lists.

584

RESERVE COMPONENT PERSONNEL IN "PAID STATUS"

30 JUNE 1947 TO DATE

Pay Group	TOTAL IN PAID STATUS	Paid Drill Training			Paid Active Duty Training Only[b]
		Total	Drill Pay Status	Undergoing Active Duty Basic Trg[a]	
	All	A,B,C,F	A,B,C	F	D,E
30 Jun 1947		230,996	230,996	–	n.a.
30 Jun 1948		534,372	534,372	–	n.a.
30 Jun 1949		796,861	796,861	–	n.a.
30 Jun 1950		839,170	839,170	–	n.a.
30 Jun 1951		557,444	557,444	–	n.a.
30 Jun 1952		506,102	506,102	–	n.a.
30 Jun 1953		578,254	578,254	–	n.a.
30 Jun 1954		696,837	696,837	–	n.a.
30 Jun 1955		826,196	826,196	–	n.a.
30 Jun 1956	949,859	925,688	905,877	19,811	24,171
30 Jun 1957	1,069,312	1,046,982	973,485	73,497	22,330
30 Jun 1958	1,025,041	985,030	930,869	54,161	40,011
30 Jun 1959	1,061,578	1,006,588	954,066	52,522	54,990
30 Jun 1960	1,078,589	997,162	931,072	66,090	81,427
30 Jun 1961	1,085,665	1,004,760	936,916	67,844	80,905
30 Jun 1962	958,013	889,117	825,716	63,401	68,896
30 Jun 1963	964,361	896,499	843,060	53,439	67,862
30 Jun 1964	1,047,542	953,256	871,384	81,872	94,286
30 Jun 1965	1,002,493	932,469	890,581	41,888	70,024
30 Jun 1966	1,054,095	969,188	929,204	39,984	84,907
30 Jun 1967	1,065,564	982,670	887,877	94,793	82,894
30 Jun 1968	1,000,941	922,318	909,261	13,057	78,623
30 Jun 1969	1,013,067	960,404	921,830	38,574	52,663
31 Jul 1969	1,009,940	955,149	907,062	48,087	54,791
31 Aug	1,007,807	953,016	895,742	57,274	54,791
30 Sep	1,010,373	955,582	902,147	53,435	54,791
31 Oct	1,006,074	951,283	897,734	53,549	54,791
30 Nov	1,004,321	949,530	886,988	62,542	54,791
31 Dec	1,007,686	952,895	892,454	60,441	54,791

a. Formerly designated "3-6 Month Active Duty Training."

b. Number of participants in no paid drills and 15-30 days paid active duty training during the fiscal year. Budget plan estimates listed for FY 1970 as shown in FY 1971 Budget; to be revised at end of year when actual data are available.

Department of Defense

RESERVE OFFICERS' TRAINING CORPS ENROLLMENT AT BEGINNING AND END OF SCHOOL YEAR, OCTOBER 1965 TO DATE

SENIOR RESERVE OFFICERS' TRAINING CORPS

School Year	Total DoD	Army Total	Army Scholarship[a]	Army Non-scholarship	Navy Total	Navy Regular[a]	Navy Contract	Air Force Total	Air Force Scholarship[a]	Air Force Non-scholarship
1965-66: Oct 1965	254,922	168,034	987	167,047	8,197	5,350	2,847	78,691	970	77,721
May 1966	221,923	148,688	969	147,719	7,733	4,885	2,848	65,502	996	64,506
1966-67: Oct 1966	264,208	182,605	1,954	180,651	9,346	5,437	3,909	72,257	1,887	70,370
May 1967	216,124	151,679	1,909	149,770	8,941	4,953	3,988	55,504	1,756	53,748
1967-68: Oct 1967	237,050	169,689	3,082	166,607	9,661	5,310	4,351	57,700	2,476	55,224
May 1968	195,925	141,495	2,908	138,587	9,443	4,911	4,532	44,987	2,038	42,949
1968-69: Oct 1968	218,466	157,031	4,056	152,975	10,162	5,446	4,716	51,273	3,976	47,297
May 1969	174,722	125,126	3,800	121,326	9,063	4,604	4,459	40,533	3,866	36,667
1969-70: Oct 1969	161,507	115,266	4,846	110,420	8,876	5,050	3,826	37,365	4,445	32,920

a. Financial Assistance programs under Sec. 2107, Title 10.

JUNIOR RESERVE OFFICERS' TRAINING CORPS, AND NATIONAL DEFENSE CADET CORPS

School Year	Total Jr. ROTC & NDCC No. of Schools	Total Jr. ROTC & NDCC Enrollment	Junior ROTC Total No. of Schools	Junior ROTC Total Enrollment	Army	Navy	Marine Corps	Air Force	N.D.C.C. Army No. of Schools	N.D.C.C. Army Enrollment
1965-66: Oct 1965	414	91,212	287	62,913	62,913	–	–	–	127	28,299
May 1966	413	85,131	287	58,722	58,722	–	–	–	126	26,409
1966-67: Oct 1966	458	102,253	419	89,996	87,338	–	–	2,658	39	12,257
May 1967	461	94,875	422	84,061	80,151	542	710	2,658*	39	10,814
1967-68: Oct 1967	628	123,444	591	114,095	97,339	6,550	1,654	8,552	37	9,349
May 1968	631	111,493	594	103,259	87,672	5,359	1,676	8,552	37	8,234
1968-69: Oct 1968	735	133,041	701	126,233	102,003	8,455	2,469	13,306*	34	6,808
May 1969	758	121,660	725	115,520	91,655	8,445	2,114	13,306*	33	6,140
1969-70: Oct 1969	836	137,594	805	133,615	105,497	9,100	2,441	16,577	31	3,979

*Estimated.

Department of Defense

DOD RETIRED MILITARY ANNUITANTS

| | Non-disability | Disability | | Fleet Reserve | Survivor Benefits (No. of Families) | Total |
| | | Temporary | Permanent | | | |
			Year-End Number			
Actual						
30 Jun 1950	58,752	150	54,302	18,725	–	131,929
30 Jun 1953	66,918	9,438	64,493	13,466	–	154,315
30 Jun 1955	80,062	14,681	66,081	18,209	499	179,532
30 Jun 1957	97,352	12,146	66,653	22,595	1,128	199,874
30 Jun 1959	118,950	13,150	69,629	26,660	1,881	230,270
30 Jun 1960	133,254	14,064	71,233	35,144	2,312	256,007
30 Jun 1961	158,385	15,094	72,749	43,566	2,807	292,601
30 Jun 1962	180,591	15,287	76,740	52,863	3,271	328,752
30 Jun 1963	219,587	15,047	80,783	63,092	3,713	382,222
30 Jun 1964	256,158	14,247	85,243	72,072	4,187	431,907
30 Jun 1965	293,606	13,283	89,719	79,783	4,643	481,034
30 Jun 1966	333,826	11,940	96,210	82,723	5,149	529,848
30 Jun 1967	376,482	13,453	101,908	92,545	5,746	590,134
30 Jun 1968	419,168	15,331	107,299	103,057	6,476	651,331
30 Jun 1969	463,334	19,470	114,651	109,299	7,202	713,956
			Average Number			
Actual						
FY 1950	56,162	33	54,073	18,429	–	128,697
FY 1953	63,790	7,320	63,925	12,181	–	147,216
FY 1955	77,219	14,100	65,298	17,046	349	174,012
FY 1957	91,819	12,115	65,743	21,583	949	192,209
FY 1959	113,570	12,716	68,753	25,841	1,665	222,545
FY 1960	126,489	13,532	70,442	30,343	2,098	242,904
FY 1961	146,445	14,765	71,992	40,154	2,558	275,914
FY 1962	172,508	15,335	73,949	48,601	3,043	313,436
FY 1963	202,967	15,448	78,548	58,392	3,475	358,830
FY 1964	241,190	14,625	82,840	68,266	3,932	410,853
FY 1965	281,350	13,774	87,197	75,734	4,408	462,463
FY 1966	316,835	12,457	92,857	81,521	4,896	508,566
FY 1967	358,623	12,363	99,441	88,414	5,439	564,280
FY 1968	400,713	14,380	104,533	98,754	6,116	624,496
FY 1969	447,740	17,472	111,897	107,746	6,833	691,688

INTER-UNIVERSITY SEMINAR
ON ARMED FORCES AND SOCIETY

In 1960, the Inter-University Seminar on Armed Forces and Society was established under an initial grant from the Russell Sage Foundation. During the first years of its existence, this seminar permitted a small group of university social scientists interested in the study of military institutions to hold regular meetings and undertake selected research. The purpose was to supply a focal point for communication and criticism for the members who were carrying on their research independently and at widely scattered universities. All the members of the seminar were concerned with scholarly and professional publication of their work.

Progressively, the number of individuals involved and the scope of the interest of the Inter-University Seminar have grown. The initial focus on the internal structure of the American military establishment has broadened to include the impact of the military on American society.

The interest of the seminar has also come to encompass a comparative approach to the military in both industrialized and developing nations, and research issues connected with revolution and internal rebellion. These endeavors have been related to the Research Group on Armed Forces and Society of the International Sociological Association which has conducted international seminars in London (1967 and 1965) and in Evian, France (1966). Members of the seminar were present at the Seventh World Congress of Sociology (Varna, Bulgaria, 1970). Throughout this period members have been engaged in writing on arms control and disarmament and U.N. peacekeeping.

The Inter-University Seminar has emphasized individual and independent research and scholarship. Group efforts are designed for data collection which cannot be undertaken by single individuals. The Inter-University Seminar does not engage in what has come to be called "policy oriented" research for specific public and private agencies. The seminar has operated since its founding under the chairmanship of Morris Janowitz, University of Chicago. Roger Little, University of Illinois at Chicago Circle, served for a number of years as executive secretary and has been succeeded by Sam Sarkesian, Loyola University. Charles Moskos, Northwestern University, became associate chairman in 1968.

The Inter-University Seminar places a strong emphasis on maintaining and strengthening intellectual collaboration among its members. In this field vigorous criticism is of fundamental importance. There is no university in the United States which has a strong concentration in the social science analysis of military institutions. Therefore, exchange of ideas and viewpoints across university lines are essential for intellectual development. The seminar has pressed for an interdisciplinary approach. Initially, it included only sociologists, but in time the scope has broadened to involve social psychologists, political scientists, and historians. The members of the seminar differ widely in their strategic views, but they all hold the common view that an intellectual and objective analysis of military institutions is a goal worth striving for. They believe that such research and analysis, conducted along scholarly lines, constitutes a responsible and worthwhile contribution to public policy and a world without war.

On the basis of these terms, the members of the seminar, as individuals, maintain intellectual and research contacts with civilian and military officials in the United States and abroad. Without these field work contacts, there can be no valid scholarship on contemporary development. The members of the seminar are constantly exploring the complex professional problems involved in research on the military (see Janowitz, 1968).

In the decade ahead, the Inter-University Seminar will seek to develop an emphasis on the impact of the military on U.S. society, particularly the consequences of the Vietnam conflict, and the emerging trend toward a volunteer armed force. Studies are under way on the role of black personnel in the armed forces and their adjustment to civilian society as veterans. Comparative studies will include not only those of military institutions in the new nations, but also those in the nations of Western Europe where the decline in traditional roles is producing drastic transformations. The seminar members believe that greater collaboration with historians in the study of social recruitment and professionalism and civil-military relations will be fruitful. The interest on the sociopolitical aspects of arms control and peacekeeping activities, and the adaptation of the military to these requirements will continue to be central concerns.

In addition to a variety of specialized meetings, the Inter-University Seminar conducts annually a general seminar on research in progress. It also established an archive of documents and unpublished materials which is managed by Charles Moskos at Northwestern University. In addition to making available small grants for research, the seminar has an active fellowship program to enable students to pursue graduate training in political science, sociology, social psychology, and history as related to the issues of armed forces and society.

BIBLIOGRAPHY OF PUBLICATIONS

BIENEN, H. (1968) "Military assistance and political development in tropical Africa," in R. Butwell (ed.) Foreign Policy and National Development. University of Kentucky Press.

———[ed.] (1968) The Military Intervenes. New York: Russell Sage Foundation.

BOPEGAMAGE, A. (1969) "The military as a modernizing agent in India." (June).

COLAS, J. (1970) "The social and career correlates of military intervention in Nigeria" (February).

JANOWITZ, M. (1968) "International perspectives on militarism." American Sociologist 3 (February): 12-16.

———[ed.] (1964) The New Military. New York: Russell Sage Foundation.

———(1964) The Military in the Political Development of New Nations. Chicago: University of Chicago Press.

———(1960) The Professional Soldier: A Social and Political Portrait. New York: Free Press.

———(1959) "Changing patterns of organizational authority: the case of the military." Administrative Science Quarterly (March).

———(1959) Sociology and the Military Establishment. New York: Russell Sage Foundation.

———with R. LITTLE (1965) Sociology and the Military Establishment. New York: Russell Sage Foundation.

KIM, C. I. E. (1969) "The role of the military in South Korean politics" (December).

KROES, R. (1969) "Military intervention in domestic politics: a framework for analysis" (May).

LANG, K. (1969) Sociology of the Military: A Selected and Annotated Bibliography. Inter-University Seminar on Armed Forces (January 1).

———(1965) "Military sociology: a trend report and bibliography." Current Sociology 13, 1: 1-55.

LaTOUCHE, D. (1969) "The military in Africa: a research design" (December).

LITTLE, R. W. [ed.] (1969) Selective Service in American Society. New York: Russell Sage Foundation.

———(1968) "Basic education and youth socialization in the armed forces." American Journal of Orthopsychiatry 38 (October): 869-876.

LOVELL, J. P. (1970) "Recruitment in the military establishment of the Republic of Korea." Journal of Comparative Administration (January).

———(1969) "Professional orientation and policy perspectives of military professionals in the Republic of Korea." Midwest Journal of Political Science (August): 415-438.

LUCKHAM, R. (1969) The Nigerian Military: A Case Study of International Breakdown. Inter-University Seminar on Armed Forces and Society.

MEYERS, S. M. and A. D. BIDERMAN [eds.] (1968) Mass Behavior in Battle and Captivity: The Communist Soldier in the Korean War. Chicago: University of Chicago Press.

MOSKOS, C. C., Jr. (1970) The American Enlisted Man. New York: Russell Sage Foundation.

———(1966) "Racial integration in the armed forces." American Journal of Sociology 72 (September): 132-148.

PALM, J. (1970) "The education of the senior military-decision maker" (February).

ROGHMANN, K. (1970) "Leadership style: the case of the new West German armed forces" (February).

SEGAL, D. R. (1967) "Selective promotion in officer cohorts." Sociological Quarterly 8 (Spring): 199-206.

VAN DOORN, J. [ed.] (1969) Military Professions and Military Regimes. The Hague: Mouton.

———[ed.] (1968) Armed Forces and Society. The Hague: Mouton.

WAMSLEY, G. L. (1969) Selective Service and a Changing America. Charles E. Merrill.

ABOUT THE CONTRIBUTORS

Albert D. Biderman, research sociologist, is associated with the Bureau of Social Science Research, Washington, D.C. His research has included a continuing concern with the behavior of prisoners of war and the social and economic position of retired military personnel. His investigations into American prisoners of war in Korea have been published under the title, March to Calumny (1963).

Paul W. Blackstock is a member of the Department of Political Science of the University of South Carolina. He is the author of numerous studies of intelligence operations, subversion, and covert operations, including The Strategy of Subversion, Manipulating the Politics of Other Nations (1964) and The Secret Road to War: Soviet vs. Western Intelligence, 1927-1939 (1969).

Martin Blumenson, who served as a military historian in the Department of the Army, is professor of history at Acadia University, Newfoundland. Among his numerous historical writings is Kasserine Pass (1967).

Donald A. Devis has had extensive experience in the field of social work in both civilian and military settings. Presently an assistant professor of psychiatry (social work) at Emory University in Atlanta, Georgia, his publications include "Social Work in the Military Child Guidance Clinic" (1962).

Alexander L. George is a member of the Political Science faculty of Stanford University. In addition to his work on the application of content analysis to the study of international mass communication, he is an authority on the organization, behavior, political indoctrination, and performance of the Chinese Communist military force. This work has appeared in a volume entitled, The Chinese Communist Army in Action: The Korean War and its Aftermath (1967).

Morris Janowitz, professor of sociology at the University of Chicago, is the author of The Professional Soldier: A Social and Political Portrait (1960). He has served as chairman of the Inter-University Seminar on Armed Forces and Society since its inception in 1961 and is also chairman of the Research Group on Armed Forces and Society of the International Sociological Association. He is a member of the Social Science Advisory Board, U.S. Arms and Disarmament Agency.

Amos A. Jordan, political scientist, is chairman of the Department of Political Science, United States Military Academy. He has done extensive research on military education and troop information programs.

Konrad Kellen is a mass communications and morale analyst of many years in governmental service. His long experience includes service during World War II as a member of the Second Mobile Radio Broadcasting Company in the European Theater of Operations, Chief Information Department, Free Radio Europe, and, subsequently, a member óf the RAND Corporation.

William Kornhauser is the author of The Politics of Mass Society (1959). He is presently a member of the faculty of the Department of Sociology, University of California.

Roger Little, Professor of Sociology, University of Illinois at Chicago Circle, formerly taught at the United States Military Academy. He has conducted research on primary groups, manpower, and casualties in military organization. He edited Selective Service and American Society (1969).

Charles C. Moskos, Jr., sociologist at Northwestern University, is the associate director of the Inter-University Seminar on Armed Forces and Society. He has published various articles on political change in the developing nations and on racial integration in the armed services; he has published a sociological study, The American Enlisted Man (1970).

Paul D. Nelson, a lieutenant commander in the Medical Service Corps of the United States Navy, is the head of the Human Effectiveness Branch, Research Division, Bureau of Medicine and Surgery, Department of the Navy.

Franklin Mark Osanka, a sociologist at North Central College, has conducted many studies on guerrilla warfare. He is the editor of Modern Guerrilla Warfare (1962).

Bernard J. Wiest is the director, Social Service Division, Department of Psychiatry, Medical School, Emory University. His research activities, based on his experiences as a social work officer and research social worker (U.S. Army), include "Social Work Research in an Army Medical Service Program" (1966).

Harold Wool, manpower economist, has had many years of government service. He is now director for procurement policy, Office of the Secretary of Defense. He is the author of The Military Specialist: Skilled Manpower for the Armed Forces (1968).

INDEX

INDEX

NAME INDEX

SUBJECT INDEX

Proxmire Investigation, see Retired,
  military
Psychiatry, combat, 322-324
  social, 326-327, 331-333
  screening, psychiatric, 97
  see also Social Work
Psychological Warfare, aims of, 419,
  420
  defined, 418
  effects of, 428-429, 450-451
  German army, use against, 423-424,
    427, 440-441
  ideological conversion, 423
  Intelligence information, 429-431,
    437-442
  in Vietnam, 421-451 passim
  morale, effects on, 431-435
  methodology, 435
  strategic, 422, 424, 427
  tactical, 422, 424, 425, 427
  techniques, suggested, 445-449
  see also Motivation; Propaganda

Race, see Civil Disorders; Minority
  Groups
Recruitment, enlistment programs,
  57-58
  history, U.S., 55-57
  mental standards, 58-62
  minority groups, 276-277
  officer procurement programs,
    62-67
  Project 100,000, 61-62
  psychiatric screening, 97
  social, 26-28
  see also Guerrilla Warfare; Minority
    Group; Personnel; Schools; Vol-
    unteer Army
Retired, military, expenditures for,
  131-133
  Hebert Committee, 154-155, 157-
    158

income, 133-134, 194
"Michigan survey," 159n. 1
Proxmire investigation, 155-156,
  158-159
recomputation, of salary, 133-134
residence of, 135
two-step annuity plan, 134
see also Second Career
Revolution, and conflict, 377-378
  and mass mobilization, 379
  and polarization, 378
  defined, 381
  types of, 375-376, 383-391
Reserve Officers Training Corps, curricula, 223-224
  history of, 220-221
  opposition to, on campuses,
    224-225
  purpose of, 222-223
  see also Recruitment; Schools

Schools, civilian, use of, 237
  Command and Staff colleges,
    228-230
  Officer Candidate School, 63, 64
  service academies, 65, 200, 215-219
  see also Recruitment; Reserve Offi-
    cers Training Corps
Second Careers Programs, 127, 134-135
  earnings, 137-139, 141-142
  in defense programs, 153
  in government, 148-151
  in teaching, 151
  occupational distribution, 143-146
  skill utilization, 140-143
  see also Retired, military
Selective Service, Act, 56-57, 87-88n.
  eligibility 71-72
  see also Recruitment; Volunteer
    Army
Service Academies, see Recruitment,
  military; Schools

DATE DUE   (DA Pam 28-30)